DISCOURSE :
AN
ILLUSTRATIVE
READER

DISCOURSE: AN ILLUSTRATIVE READER

DANIEL KNAPP
San Francisco State College

McGRAW-HILL BOOK COMPANY
New York   St. Louis   San Francisco   London   Sydney   Toronto   Mexico   Panama

DISCOURSE:
AN
ILLUSTRATIVE
READER

Library of Congress Catalog Card Number 69-17455

35076

1 2 3 4 5 6 7 8 9 0 MAMM 7 6 5 4 3 2 1 0 6 9

ACKNOWLEDGMENTS

HENRY ADAMS, "The Court of the Queen of Heaven" from *Mont St. Michel and Chartres*. Copyright 1933 by Charles F. Adams. Reprinted by permission of Houghton Mifflin Company.

JAMES BALDWIN, "Notes of a Native Son" from *Notes of a Native Son* by James Baldwin. Reprinted by permission of the Beacon Press. Copyright © 1955 by James Baldwin.

MAX BEERBOHM, "Some Words on Royalty" from *The Incomparable Max* by Max Beerbohm. Reprinted by permission of Dodd, Mead and Company.

BERNARD BERELSON, "Voting Behaviour" and "Death (Biological)." Both appeared in the *Encyclopaedia Britannica* and are reprinted by permission of the *Encyclopaedia Britannica*.

JOHN CIARDI, "The Resonance of the Civilizing Tongue" from *Dialogue with an Audience* by John Ciardi. Copyright © 1959 by John Ciardi. Published by J. B. Lippincott Company.

R. G. COLLINGWOOD, "Progress as Created by Historical Thinking" from *The Idea of History* by R. G. Collingwood. Oxford University Press, 1946. Reprinted by permission.

CHARLES GALTON DARWIN, "The Pursuit of Happiness" from *The Next Million Years* by Charles Galton Darwin. Copyright 1952 by Charles Galton Darwin. Reprinted by permission of Doubleday and Company, Inc.

JOHN DOS PASSOS, "Art and Isadora" from *The Big Money* by John Dos Passos. Copyright 1938 by John Dos Passos, renewed 1964. Published by Houghton Mifflin Company.

HAVELOCK ELLIS, "The Philosophy of Dancing" from *The Dance of Life* by Havelock Ellis. Copyright 1951 by F. Cyon. Reprinted by permission of the Houghton Mifflin Company.

E. M. FORSTER, "The Return from Siwa" from *Pharos and Pharillon* by E. M. Forster. Reprinted by permission of Alfred A. Knopf, Inc. Copyright 1923 by E. M. Forster.

EDWARD GIBBON, "The Slavery of the Romans" from *The Decline and Fall of the Roman Empire*.

ROBERT GRAVES, "The Devil Is a Protestant" from *Five Pens in Hand* (Catacrok) by Robert Graves. Copyright © 1958 by International Authors N.V. Reprinted by permission of Willis Kingsley Wing, A. P. Watt and Sons, and Cassell and Company, Ltd.

J. R. GREEN, "The Norman Conquest" from *A Short History of the English People*. Published by E. P. Dutton and Everyman's Library.

GRAHAM GREENE, "The Revolver in the Corner Cupboard" from *The Lost Childhood and Other Essays* by Graham Greene. Copyright 1951 by Graham Greene. Published by Bodley Head Ltd. Reprinted by permission of The Viking Press, Inc., and Laurence Pollinger Ltd.

J. B. S. HALDANE, "What Is Life?" from *What Is Life?* by J. B. S. Haldane. Reprinted by permission of George Allen and Unwin Ltd.

ROBERT HENDERSON, "The Enameled Wishbone." Reprinted by permission of the author and The Macmillan Company from *The Enameled Wishbone and Other Touchstones* by Robert Henderson. Copyright © 1961 by Robert Henderson. Originally published in *The New Yorker*.

THOMAS HOBBES, "Of the Natural Condition of Mankind" from *Leviathan* by Thomas Hobbes.

ALDOUS HUXLEY, "Usually Destroyed" from *Collected Essays* by Aldous Huxley. Copyright 1955 by Aldous Huxley. Reprinted by permission of Harper and Row, Publishers, Mrs. Laura Huxley, and Chatto and Windus, Ltd.

RANDALL JARRELL, "A Sad Heart at the Supermarket." First appeared in *Daedalus*. Reprinted by permission of *Daedalus* and published by the American Academy of Arts and Sciences.

D. H. LAWRENCE, "Flowery Tuscany" from *Phoenix: The Posthumous Papers of D. H. Lawrence*, edited by Edward D. McDonald. All rights reserved. Reprinted by permission of The Viking Press, Inc., Laurence Pollinger Limited, and the estate of the late Mrs. Frieda Lawrence.

ALEXANDER H. LEIGHTON, "Hiroshima Aftermath" from *Human Relations in a Changing World* by Alexander H. Leighton. Copyright © 1949 by Alexander H. Leighton. Published by E. P. Dutton and Co., Inc. Reprinted by permission of Russell and Volkening and *The Atlantic Monthly*.

WILLIAM LETWIN, "Four Fallacies about Economic Development," *Daedalus*,

Summer, 1963. Reprinted by permission of *Daedalus.* Published by the American Academy of Arts and Sciences, Boston, Massachusetts, Vol. 92, No. 3, *Themes in Transition.*

ROBERT LOWIE, "The World View of the Crow Indian" from *The Crow Indians* by Robert H. Lowie. Copyright 1935 by Robert H. Lowie; 1963 by Luella Cole Lowie. Used by permission of Holt, Rinehart and Winston, Inc. All rights reserved.

THOMAS MALTHUS, "Population and Depopulation" from *An Essay on the Principle of Population,* 1st edition.

H. L. MENCKEN, "The Cult of Hope" from *Prejudices,* second series, by H. L. Mencken. Copyright 1920 by Alfred A. Knopf, Inc. Renewed 1948 by H. L. Mencken. Reprinted by permission of the publisher.

A. A. MILNE, "An Immortal Name" from *By Way of Introduction* by A. A. Milne. Copyright 1929 by E. P. Dutton and Company, Inc. Renewal © 1957 by Mrs. Daphne Milne. Reprinted by permission of the publisher.

E. E. MORISON, "A Case Study of Innovation." Reprinted from *Engineering and Science,* April, 1950. Published at the California Institute of Technology. Reprinted by permission of the author and *Engineering and Science.*

HERBERT J. MULLER, "St. Sophia and the Uses of the Past." First appeared in *The Virginia Quarterly Review,* Winter, 1949. Reprinted by permission of *The Virginia Quarterly Review.*

VLADIMIR NABOKOV, "My Russian Education" from *Speak, Memory (Conclusive Evidence)* by Vladimir Nabokov. Appeared originally in *The New Yorker,* September 18, 1948. Copyright © 1947, 1948, 1949, 1950, 1951, 1960, 1967 by Vladimir Nabokov. Reprinted by permission of Vladimir Nabokov, Harper and Row, Publishers, and *The New Yorker.*

GEORGE ORWELL, "Marrakech" from *Such, Such Were the Joys* by George Orwell. Copyright 1945, 1952, 1953 by Sonia Brownell Orwell. Reprinted by permission of Harcourt, Brace and World, Inc., and Martin Secker and Warburg Ltd.

C. S. PEIRCE, "The Concept of God" from *The Philosophy of Pierce* by C. S. Peirce, edited by Justus Buchler. Published by Barnes and Noble, 1940.

JOHN RUSKIN, "On War" from *Crown of Wild Olive* by John Ruskin.

SACHEVERELL SITWELL, "Cupid and the Jacaranda" from *Cupid and the Jacaranda* by Sacheverell Sitwell. Published by The Macmillan Company and reprinted by permission of David Higham Associates Ltd.

WILLIAM STYRON, "This Quiet Dust." First appeared in *Harper's Magazine.* Copyright 1968 by William Styron. Reprinted by permission of Harold Matson Company, Inc.

JOHN M. SYNGE, "An Autumn Night in the Hills." Reprinted from *The Complete Works of John M. Synge,* courtesy of Random House, Inc.

THUCYDIDES, "The Melian Debate," translated by Rex Warner from *The Peloponnesian War*. Reprinted by permission of Penguin Books and the translator's agents, Bodley Head Ltd.

JAMES THURBER, "Doc Marlowe." Copyright © 1937 by James Thurber. Copyright © 1965 Helen W. Thurber and Rosemary Thurber Sauers. From *Let Your Mind Alone*. Published by Harper and Row, Publishers. Originally printed in *The New Yorker*.

H. M. TOMLINSON, "A Lost Wood" from *A Mingled Yarn* by H. M. Tomlinson. Permission granted by The Society of Authors as the literary representative of the Estate of the late H. M. Tomlinson.

M. C. TYLER, "The Literary Record of Seventeenth-century Virginia" from *A History of American Literature, 1607–1765* by M. C. Tyler.

GEORGE WALD, "The Origin of Life" from *Scientific American*, August, 1954. Reprinted with permission. Copyright © 1954 by Scientific American, Inc. All rights reserved.

EDMUND WILSON, "Origins of Socialism: Babeuf's Defense" from *To the Finland Station*. Reprinted by permission of the author.

VIRGINIA WOOLF, "Two Parsons" from *The Second Common Reader* by Virginia Woolf. Copyright 1932 by Harcourt, Brace and World, Inc. Renewed 1960 by Leonard Woolf. Reprinted by permission of the publishers, Leonard Woolf, and Hogarth Press Ltd.

PREFACE

Readers for college composition courses usually are organized by one of three general principles: Some are thematically oriented, others are linguistically oriented, still others are rhetorically oriented. This reader, although unusual in several respects, is rhetorically oriented; and I should like to explain how and why.

Intelligent thought is fundamental to intelligent writing, and students write best about what they find relevant to their own concerns: Every English teacher will assent to these truisms, and will work to bring them to life in his class. Accordingly, I have tried to include here essays on a reasonably large and significant spectrum of subjects; tried hard to include essays that deal with the immediate or the ultimate issues of our civilization—even pairing essays on occasion; and tried also, in the apparatus provided for each essay, to suggest my own view of its relevance to modern life.

But I have not constructed a thematic reader, for four reasons. First, what is relevant to the concerns of one student will not necessarily be relevant to those of another, and any given subject can be relevant in many different ways. Second, a thematic structure too easily can push even the most dedicated teacher of writing into the role of an authority on subjects in which he is no expert.   Third, the matter most obviously relevant to a student studying writing is writing itself—not as an ancilla to the social sciences, nor as a kind of ritual observance peculiar to educated man, but as an art of discovery.   Last, though the immediate relevance of a student's reading to his experience is certainly important, in a composition course, the immediate relevance of his writing to that experience is more important still: His reading should prompt him to write about his own experience, and should provide him with compositional models, but should not preempt the field in which, finally, he must make his own discoveries.   I have been more concerned to hit the nerve of an essential issue, therefore, than to find its immediate and popular thematic expression; and more concerned to suggest, in my apparatus, lines by which a student can understand the rhetorical model offered by the reading, and lines by which he can approach his own parallel experience, than to ask the obvious questions about meaning and content—questions that every good teacher will bring up in any case.   Because a counterpoint between rhetorical and thematic organization is often very useful, however, I have grouped appropriate selections by theme under boldface heads in the Index.

For quite different reasons I have avoided an overtly linguistic orientation.   To the art of composition, a fairly large vocabulary and an ability to handle (if not to analyze) grammatical forms are evident prerequisites.   But to devote the only course in composition that most college students ever take to vocabulary building and grammatical analysis is surely to stultify the excitement of writing—and, indeed, to make the course redundant for any student already able to write a decent paragraph.   Training in composition simply is not the same as training in standard English, however valuable and indeed necessary the latter may be.   Culturally disadvantaged students, to be sure, have special needs; but most of our entering freshmen have spent years with standard grammar and vocabulary building, and they look to a college course for something more.

If the bed of standard English is too short for the average college student, the bed of linguistic philosophy is surely too long.   I myself find the study of language fascinating; but I have seen no convincing evidence that a knowledge of linguistic theory makes anybody write better, no evidence that students find that theory preeminently relevant—no evidence, indeed, that their difficulties as writers are directly related to misapprehensions about the nature of language.

Those difficulties seem to me to lie elsewhere and to be much more obvious. First, students are often inexperienced as people. And second, they generally do not know how to pull together the facts and ideas they do command. Most of their college education will be concerned with the systematic transmission of experience; this is not uniquely the job of a class in composition, however liberal its plan, however essential its matter, however tingling its issues. A course in composition should be designed to help students with the second difficulty: to show them how to compose facts and ideas into adequate forms, adequate discourses. That only—but that is quite enough. To attempt it is to attempt one of the hardest and most necessary parts of a liberal education.

Originality is no special virtue in a textbook, and I have not tried to startle. Nonetheless, the table of contents does reveal that in several substantial respects the organization of this text is somewhat unusual. First, I have grouped the traditional forms of discourse—description, narration, exposition, argument—in a way that emphasizes the close kinship between description and narration as *mimetically* ordered forms, and between exposition and argument, as *logically* ordered forms. The important consequences of this system of classification are suggested in the introductions to Parts I and II. Second, illustration is given a great deal more attention here than in the usual rhetoric reader: thus the text's subtitle, *An Illustrative Reader*. It has always seemed strange to me that the question of illustration receives such scanty treatment in textbooks, for the questions springing from any systematic look at this topic strike me as absolutely crucial. Third, an entire section is devoted to point of view as a universally functioning element in composition. Discussions of point of view are common, certainly; but such discussions often merely contrast writers of differing opinions or make a false equation between point of view in general and the personal point of view in particular. The discussion here attempts to show how the writer's voice within nonfictional discourse and the angle from which he asks us to view his subject are related to that subject, to his purposes, his audience, his role in actual life. Fourth, the introduction on tone discusses not only how tone is created but also why it is important—what kind of meaning it communicates, what its value is to reader and writer.   Last, these introductions are rather unusual for a book of this kind: their method is inductive and analytic, and they are unusually detailed.   These are fairly large differences between this text and the usual one of its kind.   Some relatively minor differences, such as the treatment of comparison and contrast as a technique of illustration, need no singling out here.   Even a casual skimming of the introductions will show at what points I have diverged from the common rhetoric—and, I hope, why.

Daniel Knapp
San Francisco State College
January, 1969

CONTENTS

INTRODUCTION

This anthology is made up almost entirely of complete essays. The essay is difficult to define. The word *essai* means literally a trial or an attempt—in this case, at delineation of a problem, a meaning, a process, or whatever; it suggests a certain experimentalism or tentativeness, an admitted lack of finality. As the selections illustrate, an essay can look like anything from autobiography ("My Russian Education") to philosophy ("Progress as a Result of Historical Thinking"); it can run five hundred words or ten thousand; it can sound almost like poetry or fantasy. But all essays have three things in common: they are relatively brief; they are in prose; and they are not fictional. After a little experience, we do not mistake an essay for a short story or a treatise.

Most of the writing we do falls roughly within the range of the essay. That is, our problems in composing our ideas and the techniques available to us are the problems and techniques of the essayist. He faces the job of sorting out his ideas, of discriminating the relevant from the irrelevant, and so do we. He must consider closely his purposes and his readers so that nothing in his essay detracts from its effectiveness. He must cast his relevant ideas into some reasonably coherent order.

He must find a way of introducing his subject, of keeping it in focus, of closing it off, that will place his attitude toward it in a clear, appropriate light. He must try to give his essay a certain roundness or completeness, so that the expectations created by his first sentences are met before his last, and the drama of discourse is properly concluded. He must link up the parts of his composition so that each part leads clearly and apparently inevitably to the next. He must persuade the reader that the subject is a part of, and bears on, the real world and that it is worth a certain kind of judgment, emotional response, or action. He must do all these things within the limits of factual statement, limited space, and the resources of prose. These are usually our problems as writers also, whether we call our compositions essays, essay-type exams, term reports, studies, white papers, or manifestos. Essays, then, can offer us useful models for our own writing—though only our private experience and thought can tell us what to write about.

Essays are usually classed as falling within one or more of four major rhetorical styles: description, narrative, exposition, and argument. *Description* is the most slippery of the four terms. San Francisco, the Battle of Hastings, the atom, surfing, the causes of the American Revolution—all can be "described." But as a form of discourse, description lays claim to a more precise meaning, in terms of the order or sequence in which it relates things. Description suggests a development largely within space: The things it talks about are characteristically things that we think of as linked up in space—connected, as it were, by the movement of the eye. In this sense, an essay on the causes of the American Revolution is not a description, although an essay that tries to render the look of a small town, almost as a photograph or a painting might, is a description.

Narrative, like description, is very close to our sense of the concrete world. We can define narrative as a form of discourse linked by the order of time. In this sense, the subject of narrative is event connected not by eye but by memory. Thus, we might call an essay presenting the events of the American Revolution a narrative, while we would call an essay on the look of Valley Forge in winter a description. Both description and narrative create linguistic imitations of the real world.

Such a distinction between description and narrative has some value; but in actual writing the two styles combine constantly, because the real world does not appear to us either in time or in space exclusively, but in both at once. A narrative without description, and so without a spatial appearance, seems incomplete, dead—in short, unreal. And a description without narrative seems waxen. For these reasons, I discuss narrative and description together in this text.

Obviously, not all the senses of "description" have been exhausted thus far. We still have surfing, the atom, and the causes of the American Revolution—what do we call descriptions of these? In fact, such subjects are not subjects located in time and space in the same sense that one can talk of an atomic pile as located there. If we describe an atom, our purpose is to show how it is constructed, how it behaves—not how it "looks."

The difference between a description of structure and a description of objects in space is more salient if we think of an essay on the causes of the American Revolution. We may wish to enumerate those causes, to show how they are connected to one another, to rank them by greater and less, and so on. But whatever we do, we certainly are not going to worry about the physical look of those causes. Descriptions of atoms or of causes are not concerned with appearance.

These last subjects fall, in fact, in a different dimension from that of space-time: the dimension of logic. This dimension is the province of the two other major styles of discourse, *exposition* and *argument*. We know roughly what we mean by these terms: An exposition is a kind of explanation of something, and an argument is an effort to convince somebody of something. But what kind of something? If we want to understand how the two styles are related, why explaining differs from convincing and why exposition and argument are carried forward as they are, we have to look closer.

Let us take the word "dance." This word represents a kind of physical action in the real world, an action made up of various connected gestures, noises, and so on. But it also represents an idea connected with other ideas. For example, the dance is a kind of human activity —often a sport, frequently an art, sometimes a ceremony. As sport, different dances exercise different muscles. As art, different dances have different styles. As ceremony, different dances have different powers and purposes. We can even speak of a philosophy of dance, and suggest that life itself is a kind of dance or that thought is a dance of ideas.

Such observations move far away from the world of appearances in time and space. We are still talking about that world, of course, for the dance is really performed in time and space, however much abstracted ("drawn out") from that world our words may be. But we are really concerned with definition, classification, cause and effect, and the like; and our aim is the linking up of abstract terms within a logically coherent and suggestive system of ideas. We can distinguish two general approaches to writing about a given set of abstract terms. One approach confines itself to describing that set. This approach is expository: Its aim is to give a clear, systematic explanation of a structure already well worked out and accepted. "The American Revolution is generally ascribed to five major causes. . . ."

A group of ideas may be dealt with in another way, however. We may try to change an idea, either in whole or in part, or we may try to persuade a skeptical audience to accept it. This approach to ideas is argumentative; its aim is to create a different system from the one generally accepted. "In actual fact, the American Revolution began not because the colonists loved liberty but because—like all men— they loved power. The official explanations always mask this motive, because they are afraid of it. . . ."

Exposition and argument differ, then, in angle of attack. The order of argument is finally a new order, something that needs to be fought for because it is not yet accepted. The order of exposition is finally an old order, beyond likelihood of contest, needing no defense.

But it should also be evident that within every exposition there is a concealed argument, originally responsible for the set of ideas being explained, while within any argument there is an explanation of a previous set of ideas which is presently being modifie￼ or rejected. Each style forms the skeleton of the other. Indeed, though a theoretical distinction between exposition and argument is useful, in actual writing it breaks down more often than not. For these reasons, the two styles are dealt with together in Part II.

The last parts of this text take up the problem of composition from slightly different angles. Part III is on illustration, Part IV on point of view, Part V on tone.

Illustration is dealt with here as a kind of middle ground between writing that renders the real world in time and space and writing that composes ideas into logical order. When we ask of description or narrative, "What is the point?" or, more crudely, "What is the moral?" we recognize that an effective description or narrative is built around a few central ideas, and illustrates them. Similarly, if we ask of exposition and argument, "What are the facts, what do these ideas actually have behind them?" we acknowledge that an exposition or argument needs to be confirmed by reference to the real world—by illustration. Part III is concerned with the characteristics of this middle ground.

Point of view, as spoken of here, is not "the writer's opinion"; it is first, an angle of approach, and second, a technique for grouping ideas or achieving a distinct tone by use of a particular compositional "voice." Any essay has a point of view, more or less personal or impersonal, more or less important to its style and sequence. Part IV illustrates the nature of point of view in its relations to subject, focus, tone, audience, and context.

Tone is both the first and the last major element in writing: First because it hits us in the first sentences and even in the title of an essay; last because our emotional response to a composition is in many respects the most durable of our responses. In part, tone is the product of all the other choices of the writer: his form of discourse, his use of illustration, his "voice." In part, and more immediately, it is the consequence of specific words, rhythms, sound patterns, openings and closings. The importance of tone to the writer is immense, for it is the chief means by which he can communicate to his audience a living sense of the value of his subject, as distinct from its logical or apparent shape. Part V takes up the methods by which tone is established and the relation of tone to the other elements of composition.

The forms of discourse, illustration, point of view, and tone have been presented here as if separable. They must be separated, in order to be discussed; but the final point is that compositions are units. The successful essay fuses all aspects of composition into a single structure, unique and not easily reducible to formula. The discussions in this text are inevitably schematic; yet in the long run, good writing is a private enterprise, guided by intuition much sharpened through study and practice. A book like this cannot hope to prescribe how that intuition should work; it can do no more than offer models and suggestions that may become useful from time to time.

DISCOURSE IN MIMETIC ORDER: DESCRIPTION AND NARRATIVE

Description suggests the rendering of a scene, a cluster of things arranged in space, as if in a fraction of a moment. A descriptive passage is a map of sense impressions rendered in language:

1 From the mound of Telham the Normans saw the host of the English gathered thickly behind a rough trench and a stockade on the height of Senlac. Marshy ground covered their right; on the left, the most exposed part of the position, the hus-carles or body-guard of Harold, men in full armor and wielding huge axes, were grouped round the Golden Dragon of Wessex and the Standard of the King. The rest of the ground was covered by thick masses of half-armed rustics who had flocked at Harold's summons to the fight with the stranger. . . .
   (J. R. Green, "The Norman Conquest," pp. 15–16.)

2 The bridge, when we reached it, was a narrow wooden structure fastened up on iron bars which pierced large boulders in the bed of the river. An immense grey flood was struggling among the stones, looking dangerous and desolate in the half-light of the evening, while the wind was so great that the bridge wailed and quivered and whistled under our feet. . . .
   (J. M. Synge, "An Autumn Night in the Hills," p. 35.)

3 In the bazaar huge families of Jews, all dressed in the long black robe and little black skull cap, are working in dark fly-infested booths that look like caves. A carpenter sits cross-legged at the prehistoric lathe, turning chair-legs at lightning speed. He works the lathe with a bow in his right hand and guides the chisel with his left foot, and thanks to a lifetime of sitting in this position, his left leg is warped out of shape. At his side, his grandson, aged six, is already starting on the simpler parts of the job.

(G. Orwell, "Marrakech," p. 24.)

These scenes are all fixed in a kind of present to which the reader becomes a witness. The layout of facts in the first passage is obviously spatial: From the mound, behind a trench, on the height, on the left, grouped round the Golden Dragon of Wessex—our eye follows the eye of the Norman. The layout of the second passage is more complex, but again follows the eye through space: The superstructure of the bridge leads to a view of its supports, which lead in their turn to the boulders, and thence to the river; from the flood of the river we pass to the flood of the wind, and so return to the bridge. The whole description renders the scene as it stands in the moment between the writer's reaching the bridge and his stepping on it—the beginning and end of the same event frame the picture. In the third passage, our eye shifts swiftly from the bazaar as a whole to a group of booths, to a single booth's interior, to a carpenter within that booth, to his grandson. The sense of a moment in space is emphasized by the specifically spatial linking of fact: in the bazaar, at a lathe, right, left, at his side. And the sense of timelessness is emphasized by the use of the continuous present: Huge families are working, a carpenter sits, his grandson is already starting, and so on.

The internal connections within each of the three passages, then, are essentially spatial; time is frozen, in order to render the moment. Nonetheless, we have the strongest impression of movement: The Normans are about to attack ("A general charge of the Norman foot opened the battle; in front rode the minstrel Taillefer tossing his sword in the air. . . ."); the traveler is about to cross the bridge ("a few paces further on we came to a cottage. . . ."); the Jews of the bazaar are in violent motion (a carpenter turns chair legs, a bow works a lathe, a foot guides a chisel)—and very soon something will happen ("I was just passing the coppersmith's booths when somebody noticed

I was lighting a cigarette.")   It is in part this sense of movement that makes these descriptions vivid.

But the language of each section conveys a great deal more than merely the physical scene, and a foreshadowing of action.   Let us strip the first passage to a relatively bare factual expression:

> The English army was placed on the hill of Senlac. Marshy ground lay to its right; Harold's household troops were stationed on the left.   Many badly armed peasants made up the main force.

We lose the whole "feel" of the scene.   The Normans still see the English, but we do not see them doing it.   The loftiness and vague importance of "height" has been dissipated by its transformation into "hill"; the change of "the host of the English" to "the English army," and of "the hus-carles or body-guard of Harold, men in full armor and wielding huge axes," into "Harold's household troops" has destroyed the personality of the English warriors.   Similar changes in the other two passages would affect them in parallel ways—would diminish their value as pieces of description.

At least tentatively, let us conclude:

1 A descriptive passage generally connects its materials in a way that leads the reader's attention through space as if naturally, by a series of sensory clues—words that tell us which way to look, which direction a noise comes from, etc.   The easiest way to do this is to use such linking words and phrases as "beyond," "on the right," "to the side."   The linking of facts in a sequence that clearly connects one fact to another in a pattern of sensory awareness, of spatial continuity, need not be so obvious, however: In the second excerpt, we pass from bridge to supports, from supports to boulders, from boulders to river, from river to wind, from wind to bridge again— a clear pattern that nonetheless makes no use of explicit spatial links.   Such links are implicit: The bridge rests on iron bars that pierce boulders that lie in the river, etc.

2 Description attempts to show a scene, to make it present, and not merely to tell about it.   The peculiar value of description is most intense when the scene is most fully rendered in image—when the picture it produces in our minds is so vivid and significant as to make comment almost unnecessary.   Were we merely told that the Jews of Marrakech are poor, miserable, industrious, and without hope,

we would be saddened but not much concerned.   Our emotions are roused by this passage because we see them so.

3 Our ability to "see" the ghetto or the battle in turn depends greatly on words that appeal powerfully to the senses—especially to the eye —that produce images as well as ideas.   Thus "host gathered" instead of "army was placed," "immense grey flood" instead of "a large amount of water," "dark fly-infested booths that look like caves" instead of "shops."   The more specific or concrete a detail can be made without blurring the focus of description, the more vivid the effect usually is: "the Golden Dragon of Wessex" instead of "the Dragon of Wessex" or "the flag."   A choice between two such phrases as "the host of the English" and "the English army" at first seems to have nothing to do with concreteness; yet "host" suggests a crowd of individuals, of specific bodies—an impression reinforced by the plural "the English."   "The English army" is far less vivid precisely because it fails to produce as concrete an image of masses of men.

A second element in the vividness of the descriptive image is the presence in it of actual or incipient movement.   This sense of movement in turn is conveyed largely by the use of verbs, and verbs which appeal especially to vision: "saw," "gathered," "wielding," "grouped," etc.

4 The detail of a description and the exact language used to convey it are in no sense accidental; they are determined by the effort to produce a certain "feel" or effect.   Detail enhancing that effect is carefully disposed and rendered within the pattern (note the effect of "men in full armor and wielding huge axes") while detail not necessary to the effect is omitted.   (How big were the rival armies? How were the Normans armed? How high is "height"?)

5 Not only the detail of a descriptive passage but also its sequence, the order in which its individual elements are arranged, result from a particular thematic design: The Norman eye ranges over the English host from the impossible to the possible point of attack, from the edge of the English position to the banner of the King, from the territory to be conquered to the man who represents it—and then shows us that there is little to fear once Harold is killed: "The rest of the ground was covered by thick masses of half-armed rustics. . . ." Harold becomes England.   Similarly the static, material bridge leads to the vaguely menacing and animated water, thence to the more spiritual threat of the wind; and the ghetto in Marrakech moves

from group to individual ("huge families of Jews. . . . A carpenter"), from grandfather to grandson, from the fate of all to the fate of each, from the fate of the past to the fate of the future. In each case, a rearrangement of the sequence would result in a strikingly different effect. Behind each set of details lies a controlling idea, an effort to "say" one thing rather than another, create one impression rather than another.

A comparison of the following sentences can add one further—and obvious—principle:

In the bazaar huge families of Jews, all dressed in the long black robe and little black skull cap, are working in dark fly-infested booths that look like caves.

In the bazaar there were many Jewish families. Some of these families were huge. All the Jews were dressed in the long black robe and little black skull cap, are working in dark fly-infested people. They were working in dark fly-infested booths that looked like caves.

There is no detail in the first sentence that is not in the second; the sequence of detail is the same in both; even the language is very close. Yet the vividness of the scene has been much diminished by an unnecessary larding in of colorless words and consequent sentence breaks. The principle is:

6 The more a description avoids words and phrases that do not produce images or that impede their continuity ("there were," "some of these," "and so on," "characteristic of that people"), the more vivid it will be.

Description, then, makes an effort to re-create the real world as it appears in space at a particular time. In a sense, description is *mimetic:* It *imitates* the real world by trying to find an adequate linguistic version or translation of it, a rendering in words of its form, texture, color, movement.

But the word "imitation" should not mislead us: These imitations are not at all slavish, and are certainly not random. The choice of detail, the choice of language, the choice of sequence, all compound into a significant pattern of thought, aiming at a significant effect. Behind all successful description is both an idea of what the rendered scene actually *means,* and an estimate of the importance that meaning should have: The Jews of Marrakech mean *this,* we should feel about them *so.* Effective description is metaphorical and symbolic: It presents us with images that stand for ideas.   (For further discussion of this point see the preface on Illustration, Part III.)

The final, yet in some ways the most important, factor in the planning of a descriptive passage is implied in the last paragraph: Description must aim at an effect on somebody.   But what affects one kind of reader in one way will not necessarily so affect another kind of reader. Green writes for the ordinary educated man, who will understand a spectacular and dramatic image better than a statistical table.   Were Green's audience made up of military men, he would have to choose different details—comparative armament, organization and tactics, and so forth.   A student of early feudalism, or of law, or of mass psychology, would wish for still another set of details, another pattern of emphasis—in short, another *idea.*   Green's concern for his audience does not determine entirely what he is trying to say about the Conquest, but it does determine in large part the manner in which he tries to say it.

Narrative suggests the rendering of an event or a string of events arranged in some sequence of time.   Much of the effect of description depends on its ability to suggest incipient movement; in fact, description is most frequently met with as part of narrative.   Exactly because narrative resorts continually to description in order to give a surface or texture to the events it renders, it develops more slowly—the pause to describe the scene slows down the plunge through event; therefore only a complete narrative can illustrate the full resources of the style. But even a very slight shift from the order of space to that of time reveals many of the characteristics of narrative:

> A general charge of the Norman foot opened the battle; in front rode the minstrel Taillefer, tossing his sword in the air and catching it again while he chanted the song of Roland.   He was the first of the host who struck a blow, and he was the first to fall. The charge broke vainly on the stout stockade behind which the English warriors plied axe and javelin with fierce cries of "Out, out!" and the repulse of the Norman faction was followed by a repulse of the Norman horse.   Again and again the Duke rallied and led them to the fatal stockade. . . .   His Breton troops, entangled in the marshy ground on his left, broke in disorder, and as panic spread through the army a cry arose that the Duke was slain.   William tore off his helmet. . . .

Time dominates the passage, and words indicating shifts in time hold its sentences together: a charge *opened,* he was the *first,* the repulse *was followed, again and again, as* panic spread. With no loss to the sequence—though with considerable loss to everything else—we could write: "*Then* they charged, *then* Taillefer was killed, *then* the footmen were thrown back, *then* the horse were thrown back, *then* the Duke led them forward," etc.

At first, such a sequence may seem inevitable, a necessary aspect of the event being dealt with.   But we can think of other ways of dealing with the Battle of Hastings:

1 A decisive defeat at Hastings left the English momentarily incapable of further resistance, and the Normans marched on London. . . .

2 Few versions of the decisive battle near Hastings are left to us; nevertheless its broad outlines remain clear. The fatigue of the English, the superior armament of the Norman horse, and one lucky Norman arrow combined to destroy Anglo-Saxon England. . . .

3 Standing behind a hasty stockade thrown up by Harold's orders, the weary English waited for the Norman attack.   As the onslaught of the foreign infantry broke against them, the English levies—mere farmers for the most part, summoned from their plows with what weapons they could find—hacked and thrust with grim determination, crying, "Out! Out!"   Driven from the fatal stockade, the Normans streamed away across the slope; the Norman cavalry, riding through them against the English host, were hurled back in turn. From where he stood in the center of a stern ring of hus-carles, beneath the Golden Dragon of Wessex, Harold had earlier marked a body of the enemy working through the marsh on his right; now he ordered a sudden attack.   The Norman detachment, caught in the soggy ground, panicked and fled wildly; Harold saw the whole enemy host infected with the panic, breaking in disorder. . . .

Green's first major decision was to talk about the battle itself, and not merely about its result—he could have passed it over as easily as our first version does.   Why he decided to write about the battle as battle, and not merely as political turning point, becomes clear when we note that in all three of our versions *Duke William disappears,* while in

Green's original Duke William dominates the entire action. In our first and second versions William's personality is irrelevant—in the first, because all personalities are irrelevant, in the second, because William is not among the factors important in the Norman success. In the last version, by contrast, Harold is important and William is in the remote background.

The structure of Green's narrative, then, is determined not by anything intrinsic to the event but by Green's own wish to place Duke William at its center: William the Conqueror of England. This choice of the Duke as narrative center is contingent, in turn, on a larger decision about what is significant in the event. The heroic personality of the Duke is made the most significant element in the conquest of England; the battle gives Green a chance to present an image of that personality. The order of events would not be altered if we were to write:

> A general charge of the Norman foot opened the battle. The charge broke vainly on the English stockade, and the repulse of the Norman footmen was followed by a repulse of the Norman horse. Again and again the Normans charged. The Breton troops, entangled in the marshy ground to the left, broke in disorder; after a momentary general panic, the Normans re-formed and again advanced to the attack. . . .

But the focus of Green's account would be lost.

Green's effort to place the character of William at the center of events can account for the otherwise strange treatment of Taillefer. Militarily and politically both, the minstrel is totally insignificant; had he been left out of the account completely, we would have lost nothing—except a sense of the temper, the character of the Conquest, as Green wishes us to see it. As Taillefer appears, he is a precursor of the Duke himself, a kind of lesser symbol of the Norman spirit. He leads the first charge, in a spirit of chivalric bravado; his heroic failure anticipates and thus magnifies the heroic success of the Duke himself. He is the only other specific Norman mentioned; if we strike him out, the Duke himself seems less, and if we move him to the end of the sequence—to a list of casualties, for example, he becomes irrelevant. He stands in both comparison and contrast to the Norman duke, and thus illuminates him. (For further discussion of comparison and contrast as compositional technique, see the introduction to Part III, *The Middle Ground: Illustration.*)

The appearance of Taillefer at the beginning of the battle rather than at the end in a casualty list is justifiable, then, because that is where the minstrel must appear if he is to act as foil for the Duke. His appearance is paralleled, in a sense, by the absence in the opening sentences of any mention of the Breton troops whose panic nearly costs William control of his army. Presumably the Bretons were there at the beginning; certainly they must have marched forward before being driven into retreat; yet we first hear of them when they fly. The reason is obvious: They were not important before. Like Taillefer, they enter the narrative only when they become significant in terms of the total action.

The relative scale, or size, of the various elements in the battle is also determined by Green's thematic intention. As we have seen, Taillefer is insignificant—only one man, in one charge, and soon dead. Yet he is given two sentences, while the major part of the battle is summarized in one: "Again and again the Duke rallied them. . . ." Similarly, the fact that William tore off his helmet in the middle of the battle has little or no military or political importance; its value is its function as an image of William's character. Green could have written, "The Normans, again certain that the Duke lived. . . ." He chose to focus on the Duke directly, instead.

Even so brief a fragment of narrative, then, can suggest some principles of effective writing:

1 Narrative is tied together by time, and its facts are most naturally and clearly linked by words or phrases suggesting transitions in time: "then," "afterward," "while," "first," "as," and so forth. The linking of facts in a temporal sequence need be no more obvious than the linking of facts in a spatial sequence, however: "a general charge *opened* the battle," "he was the *first* to fall." Indeed, we assume that the events of a narrative follow each other in the order in which they are mentioned—that the sequence of composition is the sequence of event. Such explicit linking terms as "meanwhile," are used chiefly to signal departures from this simple sequence.

2 In a more indirect but easily visible way the sequence of narrative is not only a sequence of time but also a sequence of cause and effect. A narrative, after all, is a composition, not a natural fact, and its parts are arranged according to a theory of congruence: Taillefer is the first to strike and *therefore* the first to fall; the Breton troops panic and *therefore* a rumor that William is dead sweeps the army.

In ordinary life we generally assume that if one event follows another event, the first must be the cause of the second. The assumption is natural and, *when there are only two events,* entirely proper. (When there are more than two events, as there usually are except in scientifically controlled circumstances, this habit of thinking can trap us into gross errors—see the discussion of fallacious reasoning in the Glossary.) In effective narrative, the writer usually sorts out these causal connections and composes events so as to make the sequence in which we hear about them also the sequence of cause and effect—unless, for special reasons, he tries to surprise us. In this sense, carefully constructed narrative is in fact a form of historical explanation.

Relations of cause and effect explain also what may strike us at first as almost irrelevant descriptive detail. Taillefer charges first, chanting the *Song of Roland* and tossing his sword in the air. We can suggest at least one set of causal connections among the three acts: because Taillefer is a minstrel, he is a dramatic performer and knows the *Song of Roland* by heart; because he knows it by heart, he is steeped in its ethic; because he is steeped in its ethic, and is a dramatic performer, he charges first, chanting and tossing his sword in the air.

3 Like description, then, narrative presents a pattern, not simply an accidental or unshaped cluster of things; and the composition of events in a specific narrative will depend on the meaning the writer in fact perceived and tries to present through a narrative image. Events not significant in that pattern are properly omitted, however significant they might be in another pattern, and events significant in that pattern are reported in a causal structure, at the time and on the scale of their significance: Taillefer's death, the English battle cry, the Breton advance into the marsh are noted precisely where they are most relevant to the narrative image that Green is working to create, and are given a scale appropriate to that image.

4 The writer of narrative generally makes use of a specific point of view or focal center within the sequence of event. Green makes use of Duke William, arranging and judging the importance of events around the Duke as center; another writer might use King Harold; a third, Taillefer; a fourth, someone not present at the battle; a fifth, himself. Each of these choices would have a distinct compositional result, in detail, sequence, tone, and theme. Green chooses William because the relationship between the personality of the Duke and the Conquest is his central concern. (For further discussion of point of view as a factor in composition see the introduction to **Part IV.**)

In the beginning of this brief discussion of narrative we noted that description is met with most frequently in conjunction with narrative. Thus, the principles that make for effective description also make for effective narrative: The two forms of discourse can no more be separated than time and space can. As the life of description depends finally on the presence of incipient or continuous movement, i.e., of latent narrative, so the life of narrative depends finally on the presence of the significant descriptive image: The charge of the Normans becomes real not only because it moves but also because it presents itself to us in the image of Taillefer tossing his sword in the air and chanting the *Song of Roland.*

Like description, narrative presents us with no slavish copy of un-arranged facts. Instead, it shows us a chain of images that, when successful, form a clear, vivid, economically phrased imitation of events, shaped by the writer's vision of what those events mean and of how they can be composed so as to render their meaning. Like description, too, narrative is written for an audience as well as with an intention; in its choice of detail, sequence, point of view, and tone, it must take account of the background and expectations of its probable readers.

The excerpts we have been discussing are descriptions and narratives of specific events or scenes in the real world; but order within space and time can be used to link quite different kinds of material as well. Suppose we wish to describe the workings of an atomic pile or the game of golf. We may wish to follow the process that converts it into energy and radioactive slag in order to show clearly how each stage of the pile works, how it is designed, and why; we may wish to follow the stages of a typical game of golf for similar reasons. In such explanations, the order of time and space can provide a useful linking system. Such a composition is usually called expository narrative; it is discussed in this text as a special kind of exposition, in Part II.

Some of the essays that follow are almost pure narrative and descrip-tion: Their mode is mimetic; their links, the links of time and space. A good many, however, are mixed: Although predominantly concerned with scene or event, they organize fact in logical ways, explicitly in sequences of cause and effect, inclusion and exclusion. The order of time and space and the order of logic are inseparable in actual thought.

Description and narrative take their patterns from the writer's estimate of what is important and meaningful, and that estimate results from a perception of design in appearance and event. The reader's estimate of importance and meaning results from a perception of the writer's design in selecting and shaping appearance and event. In this sense, description and narrative underlie every exposition and argument, while exposition and argument underlie every description and narrative.

J. R. GREENE

 ## THE NORMAN
CONQUEST

From the moment of their settlement on the Frankish coast, the Normans had been jealously watched by the English kings; and the anxiety of Æthelred for their friendship set a Norman woman on the English throne. The marriage of Emma with Æthelred brought about a close political connexion between the two countries. It was in Normandy that the King found a refuge from Swegen's invasion, and his younger boys grew up in exile at the Norman court. Their presence there drew the eyes of every Norman to the rich land which offered so tempting a prey across the Channel. The energy which they had shown in winning their land from the Franks, in absorbing the French civilization and the French religion, was now showing itself in adventures on far-off shores, in crusades against the Moslem of Spain or the Arabs of Sicily. It was this spirit of adventure that roused the Norman Duke Robert to sail against England in Cnut's day under pretext of setting Æthelred's children on its throne, but the wreck of his fleet in a storm put an end to a project which might have anticipated the work of his son. It was that son, William the Great, as men of his own day styled him, William the Conqueror as he was to stamp himself by one event on English history, who was now Duke of Normandy. The full grandeur of his indomitable will, his large and patient statesmanship, the loftiness of aim which lifts him out of the petty incidents of his age, were as yet only partly disclosed.   But there never had been a moment from his boyhood when he was not among the greatest of men.   His life from the very first was one long mastering of difficulty after difficulty.   The shame of his birth remained in his name of "the Bastard."   His father Robert had seen Arlotta, a tanner's daughter of the town, as she washed her linen in a little brook by Falaise; and loving her he had made her the mother of his boy.   The departure of Robert on a pilgrimage from which he never returned left William a child-ruler among the most turbulent baronage in Christendom; treason and anarchy surrounded him as he grew to manhood; and disorder broke at last into open revolt.   But in 1047 a fierce combat of horse on the slopes of Val-es-dunes beside Caen left the young Duke master of his duchy and he soon made his mastery felt.   "Normans" said a Norman poet "must be trodden down and kept under foot, for he only that bridles them may use them at his need."   In the stern order he forced on the land Normandy from this hour felt the bridle of its Duke.

William and France   Secure at home, William seized the moment of Godwine's exile to visit England, and received from his cousin, King Eadward, as he afterwards asserted, a promise of succession to his throne.   Such a promise however, unconfirmed by the Witenagemote, was valueless; and the return of Godwine must have at once cut short the young Duke's hopes.   He found in fact work enough to do in his own duchy, for the discontent of his baronage at the stern justice of his rule found support in the jealousy which his power raised in the states around him, and it was only after two great victories at Mortemer and Varaville and six years of hard fighting that outer and inner foes were alike trodden under foot.   In 1060 William stood first among the princes of France.   Maine submitted to his rule.   Britanny was reduced to obedience by a single march.   While some of the rebel barons rotted in the Duke's dungeons and some were driven into exile, the land settled down into a peace which gave room for a quick up-growth of wealth and culture.   Learning and education found their centre in the school of Bec, which the teaching of a Lombard scholar, Lanfranc, raised in a few years into the most famous school of Christendom.   Lanfranc's first contact with William, if it showed the Duke's imperious temper, showed too his marvellous insight into men. In a strife with the Papacy which William provoked by his marriage with Matilda, a daughter of the Count of Flanders, Lanfranc took the side of Rome.   His opposition was met by a sentence of banishment, and the Prior had hardly set out on a lame horse, the only one his house could afford, when he was overtaken by the Duke, impatient that he should quit Normandy. "Give me a better horse and I shall go the quicker," replied the imperturbable Lombard, and William's wrath passed into laughter and good will. From that hour Lanfranc became his minister and counsellor, whether for affairs in the duchy itself or for the more daring schemes of ambition which opened up across the Channel.

William and England William's hopes of the English crown are said to have been revived by a storm which threw Harold, while cruising in the Channel, on the coast of Ponthieu. Its count sold him to the Duke; and as the price of return to England William forced him to swear on the relics of saints to support his claim to its throne. But, true or no, the oath told little on Harold's course. As the childless King drew to his grave one obstacle after another was cleared from the Earl's path. His brother Tostig had become his most dangerous rival; but a revolt of the Northumbrians drove Tostig to Flanders, and the Earl was able to win over the Mercian house of Leofric to his cause by owning Morkere, the brother of the Mercian Earl Eadwine, as his brother's successor. His aim was in fact attained without a struggle. In the opening of 1066 the nobles and bishops who gathered round the death-bed of the Confessor passed quietly from it to the election and coronation of Harold. But at Rouen the news was welcomed with a burst of furious passion, and the Duke of Normandy at once prepared to enforce his claim by arms. William did not claim the Crown. He claimed simply the right which he afterwards used when his sword had won it of presenting himself for election by the nation, and he believed himself entitled so to present himself by the direct commendation of the Confessor. The actual election of Harold which stood in his way, hurried as it was, he did not recognize as valid. But with this constitutional claim was inextricably mingled resentment at the private wrong which Harold had done him, and a resolve to exact vengeance on the man whom he regarded as untrue to his oath. The difficulties in the way of his enterprize were indeed enormous. He could reckon on no support within England itself. At home he had to extort the consent of his own reluctant baronage; to gather a motley host from every quarter of France and to keep it together for months; to create a fleet, to cut down the very trees, to build, to launch, to man the vessels; and to find time amidst all this for the common business of government, for negotiations with Denmark and the Empire, with France, Britanny, and Anjou, with Flanders and with Rome which had been estranged from England by Archbishop Stigand's acceptance of his pallium from one who was not owned as a canonical Pope.

Stamford Bridge   But his rival's difficulties were hardly less than his own. Harold was threatened with invasion not only by William but by his brother Tostig, who had taken refuge in Norway and secured the aid of its King, Harald Hardrada. The fleet and army he had gathered lay watching for months along the coast. His one standing force was his body of hus-carles, but their numbers only enabled them to act as the nucleus of an army. On the other hand the Land-fyrd or general levy of fighting-men was a body easy to raise for any single encounter but hard to keep together. To assemble such a force was to bring labour to a standstill. The men gathered under the King's standard were the farmers and ploughmen of their fields. The ships were the fishing-vessels of the coast. In September the task of holding them together became impossible, but their dispersion had hardly taken place when the two clouds which had so long been gathering burst at once upon the realm. A change of wind released the landlocked armament of William; but before changing, the wind which prisoned the Duke brought the host of Tostig and Harald Hardrada to the coast of Yorkshire. The King hastened with his household troops to the north and repulsed the Norwegians in a decisive overthrow at Stamford Bridge, but ere he could hurry back to London the Norman host had crossed the sea and William, who had anchored on the twenty-eighth of September off Pevensey, was ravaging the coast to bring his rival to an engagement. His merciless ravages succeeded in drawing Harold from London to the south; but the King wisely refused to attack with the troops he had hastily summoned to his banner. If he was forced to give battle, he resolved to give it on ground he had himself chosen, and advancing near enough to the coast to check William's ravages he entrenched himself on a hill known afterwards as that of Senlac a low spur of the Sussex downs near Hastings. His position covered London and drove William to concentrate his forces. With a host subsisting by pillage, to concentrate is to starve; and no alternative was left to the Duke but a decisive victory or ruin.

Battle of Hastings   On the fourteenth of October William led his men at dawn along the higher ground that leads from Hastings to the battle-field which Harold had chosen. From the mound of Telham the Normans saw the host of the English gathered thickly behind a rough trench and a stockade on the height of Senlac. Marshy ground covered their right; on the left, the most exposed part of the position, the hus-carles or body-guard of Harold, men in full armour and wielding huge axes, were grouped round the Golden Dragon of Wessex and the Standard of the King.   The rest of the ground was covered by thick masses of half-armed rustics who had flocked at Harold's summons to the fight with the stranger.   It was against the centre of this formidable position that William arrayed his Norman knighthood, while the mercenary forces he had gathered in France and Britanny were ordered to attack its flanks.   A general charge of the Norman foot opened the battle; in front rode the minstrel Taillefer, tossing his sword in the air and catching it again while he chaunted the song of Roland.   He was the first of the host who struck a blow, and he was the first to fall. The charge broke vainly on the stout stockade behind which the English warriors plied axe and javelin with fierce cries of "Out, out," and the repulse of the Norman footmen was followed by a repulse of the Norman horse.   Again and again the Duke rallied and led them to the fatal stockade.   All the fury of fight that glowed in his Norseman's blood, all the headlong valour that spurred him over the slopes of Val-ès-dunes, mingled that day with the coolness of head, the dogged perseverance, the inexhaustible faculty of resource which shone at Mortemer and Varaville.   His Breton troops, entangled in the marshy ground on his left, broke in disorder, and as panic spread through the army a cry arose that the Duke was slain.   William tore off his helmet; "I live," he shouted, "and by God's help I will conquer yet."   Maddened by a fresh repulse, the Duke spurred right at the Standard; unhorsed, his terrible mace struck down Gyrth, the King's brother; again dismounted, a blow from his hand hurled to the ground an unmannerly rider who would not lend him his steed. Amidst the roar and tumult of the battle he turned the flight he had arrested into the means of victory.   Broken as the stockade was by his desperate onset, the shield-wall of the warriors behind it still held the Normans at bay till William by a feint of flight drew a part of the English force from their post of vantage.   Turning on his disorderly pursuers, the Duke cut them to pieces, broke through the abandoned line, and made himself master of the central ground.   Meanwhile the French and Bretons made good their ascent on either flank.   At three the hill seemed won, at six the fight still raged around the Standard where Harold's hus-carles stood stubbornly at bay on a spot marked afterwards by the high altar of Battle Abbey.   An order from the Duke at last brought his archers to the front.   Their arrow-flight told heavily on the dense masses crowded around the King and as the sun went down a shaft pierced

Harold's right eye. He fell between the royal ensigns, and the battle closed with a desperate melly over his corpse.

Night covered the flight of the English army: but William was quick to reap the advantage of his victory. Securing Romney and Dover, he marched by Canterbury upon London. Faction and intrigue were doing his work for him as he advanced; for Harold's brothers had fallen with the King on the field of Senlac, and there was none of the house of Godwine to contest the crown. Of the old royal line there remained but a single boy, Eadgar the Ætheling. He was chosen King; but the choice gave little strength to the national cause. The window of the Confessor surrendered Winchester to the Duke. The bishops gathered at London inclined to submission. The citizens themselves faltered as William, passing by their walls, gave Southwark to the flames. The throne of the boy-king really rested for support on the Earls of Mercia and Northumbria, Eadwine and Morkere; and William, crossing the Thames at Wallingford and marching into Hertfordshire, threatened to cut them off from their earldoms. The masterly movement forced the Earls to hurry home, and London gave way at once. Eadgar himself was at the head of the deputation who came to offer the crown to the Norman Duke. "They bowed to him," says the English annalist, pathetically, "for need." They bowed to the Norman as they had bowed to the Dane, and William accepted the crown in the spirit of Cnut. London indeed was secured by the erection of a fortress which afterwards grew into the Tower, but William desired to reign not as a conqueror but as a lawful king. At Christmas he received the crown at Westminster from the hands of Archbishop Ealdred amid shouts of "Yea, Yea," from his new English subjects. Fines from the greater landowners atoned for a resistance which now counted as rebellion; but with this exception every measure of the new sovereign showed his desire of ruling as a successor of Eadward or Ælfred. As yet indeed the greater part of England remained quietly aloof from him, and he can hardly be said to have been recognized as king by Northumberland or the greater part of Mercia. But to the east of a line which stretched from Norwich to Dorsetshire his rule was unquestioned, and over this portion he ruled as an English king. His soldiers were kept in strict order. No change was made in law or custom. The privileges of London were recognized by a royal writ which still remains, the most venerable of its muniments, among the city's archives. Peace and order were restored. William even attempted, though in vain, to learn the English tongue that he might personally administer justice to the suitors in his court. The kingdom seemed so tranquil that only a few months had passed after the battle of Senlac when leaving England in charge of his brother, Odo Bishop of Bayeux, and his minister, William Fitz-Osbern, the King returned in 1067 for a while to Normandy. The peace he left was soon indeed disturbed. Bishop Odo's tyranny forced the Kentishmen to seek aid from Count Eustace of Boulogne; while the Welsh princes supported a similar rising against Norman oppression in the west. But as yet the bulk of the land held fairly to the new king. Dover was saved from Eustace; and the discontented fled over sea to seek refuge in lands as far off as Constantinople, where Englishmen from this time formed great part of the body-guard or Varangians of the Eastern Emperors. William returned to take his place again as an English King. It was with an English force that he subdued a rising in the south-west with Exeter at its head, and it was at the head of an English army that he completed his work by marching to the North. His march brought Eadwine and Morkere again to submission; a fresh rising ended in the occupation of York, and England as far as the Tees lay quietly at William's feet.

The Norman Conquest   It was in fact only the national revolt of 1068 that transformed the King into a conqueror. The signal for this revolt came from Swegen, King of Denmark, who had for two years past been preparing to dispute England with the Norman, but on the appearance of his fleet in the Humber all northern, all western and south-western England rose as one man. Eadgar the Ætheling with a band of exiles who had found refuge in Scotland took the head of the Northumbrian revolt; in the south-west the men of Devon, Somerset, and Dorset gathered to the sieges of Exeter and Montacute; while a new Norman castle at Shrewsbury alone bridled a rising in the West. So ably had the revolt been planned that even William was taken by surprize. The outbreak was heralded by a storm of York and the slaughter of three thousand Normans who formed its garrison. The news of this slaughter reached William as he was hunting in the forest of Dean; and in a wild outburst of wrath he swore "by the splendour of God" to avenge himself on the North. But wrath went hand in hand with the coolest statesmanship. The centre of resistance lay in the Danish fleet, and pushing rapidly to the Humber with a handful of horsemen William bought at a heavy price its inactivity and withdrawal. Then turning westward with the troops that gathered round him he swept the Welsh border and relieved Shrewsbury while William Fitz-Osbern broke the rising around Exeter. His success set the King free to fulfil his oath of vengeance on the North. After a long delay before the flooded waters of the Aire he entered York and ravaged the whole country as far as the Tees. Town and village were harried and burned, their inhabitants were slain or driven over the Scottish border. The coast was especially wasted that no hold might remain for future landings of the Danes. Crops, cattle, the very implements of husbandry were so mercilessly destroyed that a famine which followed is said to have swept off more than a hundred thousand victims. Half a century later indeed the land still lay bare of culture and deserted of men for sixty miles northward of York. The work of vengeance once over, William led his army back from the Tees to York, and thence to Chester and the West. Never had he shown the grandeur of his character so memorably as in this terrible march. The winter was hard, the roads choked with snowdrifts or broken by torrents, provisions failed; and his army, storm-beaten and forced to devour its horses for food, broke out into mutiny at the order to cross the bleak moorlands that part Yorkshire from the West. The mercenaries from Anjou and Britanny demanded their release from service. William granted their prayer with scorn. On foot, at the head of the troops which still clung to him, he forced his way by paths inaccessible to horses, often helping the men with his own hands to clear the road, and as the army descended upon Chester the resistance of the English died away.

For two years William was able to busy himself in castle-building and in measures for holding down the conquered land. How effective these were was seen when the last act of the conquest was reached. All hope of Danish aid was now gone, but Englishmen still looked for help to Scotland where Eadgar the Ætheling had again found refuge and where his sister Margaret had become wife of King Malcolm. It was probably some assurance of Malcolm's aid which roused the Mercian Earls, Eadwine and Morkere, to a fresh rising in 1071. But the revolt was at once foiled by the vigilance of the Conqueror. Eadwine fell in an obscure skirmish, while Morkere found shelter for a while in the fen country where a desperate band of patriots gathered round an outlawed leader, Hereward. Nowhere had William found so stubborn a resistance: but a causeway two miles long was at last driven across the marshes, and the last hopes of English freedom died in the surrender of Ely. It was as the unquestioned master of England that

William marched to the North, crossed the Lowlands and the Forth, and saw Malcolm appear in his camp upon the Tay to swear fealty at his feet.

Lines of Inquiry

1 The center of Green's narrative of the conquest of England by the Normans is Duke William himself.

   a Is Green trying to record the events of the conquest or to explain them?

   b How might his choice of the Duke as narrative center be explained in terms of his purpose? What advantages does he gain by grouping the events of the conquest about the personality of the Duke?

   c Could he have ordered the sequence of events without using any single person as narrative center?

   d What would have been the probable effects on the sequence of the narrative, on the scale of its various parts, and on the "meaning" or significance of the entire event, had Green chosen Harold as its narrative center? (It may be helpful to think of the effect of such changes on specific parts of the narrative, e.g., the account of William's character, of the uprising of 1068.)

2 The first part of Green's account is given over to a description of William's personality.

   a What are the elements in his character with which Green is concerned? Why is there so little about his marriage?

   b Could the anecdote about Lanfranc have been placed earlier in the account? Why is it given virtually the same scale as the crushing of treason and anarchy in Normandy?

   c What use does Green make of the Duke's early history, in the succeeding account of the conquest?

   d What is the effect on us of Green's anticipatory "It was that son, William the Great, as men of his own day styled him, William the Conqueror as he was to stamp himself by one event in English history. . . ."? Why did Green describe the Duke's character before describing the conquest—why not afterward?

   e Why is there, by contrast, so little about Harold? If Green had undertaken a description of Harold, where in the sequence of events should he have placed it?

3 The Battle of Hastings takes up exactly as much space in Green's narrative as the entire rebellion of 1068—why? On

what day was the battle fought? On what day did the uprising begin? Why is there a difference in this respect, in
Green's treatment of the two sequences?

4 *a* Look at the openings of the first three paragraphs. What
do they have in common? Why?

  b Look at the end of paragraph 1 and the beginning of paragraph 2; the end of paragraph 2 and the beginning of 3; the
end of 3 and the beginning of 4; and so on. How are the
paragraphs bound one to another? What principle seems
to determine the break from one paragraph to another?

  c Is that same principle followed through the rest of the
narrative?

5 Green concludes his narrative with an account of the surrender
of Malcolm.

  a What is the effect of the last sentence of the account? How
is it related to the total action of the narrative? (Consider,
" 'They bowed to him,' the English annalist says pathetically,
'for need.' ")

  b Is there anything approaching a common vocabulary or a
common set of images in the descriptions of the submission
of William's enemies?

  c In what way is the epithet "the Conqueror" reflected in the
language Green chooses to describe William's acts?

Lines of Experiment

1 Try to rewrite Green's account from an English point of view
—say, Harold's, or Hereward's. What difficulties do you run
into immediately? What do you conclude concerning the relationship of point of view to information?

2 As Green has interpreted it, the history of William's conquest of England is in essence simply the history of a single
man's successful effort to dominate his immediate world. For
this success everybody can find parallels in his own experience. Take a similar circumstance that is known to you in
some detail and block out the important stages in the central
action. You may use the frame of Green's account as a model,
if you wish; obviously, the specific events will be of no use.
Your subject may be a swimmer's pursuit of a title, a boy's
pursuit of a girl, a student's pursuit of a scholarship or a job,
an embryonic musician's effort to master the guitar or the trumpet, etc. Decide what the relative importance of each stage of
the action is, in what sequence the stages should be presented,

what relationship each stage has to the ones that precede it and that follow it. Now you are in a position to write a serious narrative.

3 Go to the library and read about the early years of an historical figure well known to you and to your friends—Lincoln, Booth, Hemingway, Franklin Roosevelt, etc. You are about to write a twenty-page narrative essay on your subject's life, and you have two pages at most that you can spend on the early years. Write those two pages. Be careful to select the most important details and to frame them so that their importance is clear.

4 Give an account, in narrative form, of a crucial historical event —battle, siege, surrender, invention, experiment, marriage, birth, death. Before you begin to write, review the discussion of description and narrative in the introduction to this part; try to make your account as vivid, as meaningful, as "shaped" as you can. What kind of audience are you writing for? Can you begin to write without deciding whom you are writing for?

GEORGE ORWELL

 MARRAKECH

As the corpse went past the flies left the restaurant table in a cloud and rushed after it, but they came back a few minutes later.

The little crowd of mourners—all men and boys, no women—threaded their way across the market-place between the piles of pomegranates and the taxis and the camels, wailing a short chant over and over again. What really appeals to the flies is that the corpses here are never put into coffins, they are merely wrapped in a piece of rag and carried on a rough wooden bier on the shoulders of four friends. When the friends get to the burying-ground they hack an oblong hole a foot or two deep, dump the body in it and fling over it a little of the dried-up, lumpy earth, which is like broken brick. No gravestone, no name, no identifying mark of any kind. The burying-ground is merely a huge waste of hummocky earth, like a derelict building-lot. After a month or two no one can even be certain where his own relatives are buried.

When you walk through a town like this—two hundred thousand inhabitants, of whom at least twenty thousand own literally nothing except the rags they stand up in—when you see how the people live, and still more how easily they die, it is always difficult to believe that you are walking among human beings. All colonial empires are in reality founded upon that fact. The people have brown faces—besides, there are so many of them! Are they really the same flesh as yourself? Do they even have names? Or are they merely a kind of undifferentiated brown stuff, about as individual as bees or coral insects? They rise out of the earth, they sweat and starve for a few years, and then they sink back into the nameless mounds of the graveyard and nobody notices that they are gone. And even the graves themselves soon fade back into the soil. Sometimes, out for a walk, as you break your way through the prickly pear, you notice that it is rather bumpy underfoot, and only a certain regularity in the bumps tells you that you are walking over skeletons.

I was feeding one of the gazelles in the public gardens.

Gazelles are almost the only animals that look good to eat when they are still alive, in fact, one can hardly look at their hindquarters without thinking of mint sauce. The gazelle I was feeding seemed to know that this thought was in my mind, for though it took the piece of bread I was holding out it obviously did not like me. It nibbled rapidly at the bread, then lowered its head and tried to butt me, then took another nibble and then butted again. Probably its idea was that if it could drive me away the bread would somehow remain hanging in mid-air.

An Arab navvy working on the path nearby lowered his heavy hoe and sidled slowly towards us. He looked from the gazelle to the bread and from the bread to the gazelle, with a sort of quiet amazement, as though he had never seen anything quite like this before. Finally he said shyly in French:

"*I* could eat some of that bread."

I tore off a piece and he stowed it gratefully in some secret place under his rags. This man is an employee of the Municipality.

When you go through the Jewish quarters you gather some idea of what the medieval ghettoes were probably like.   Under their Moorish rulers the Jews were only allowed to own land in certain restricted areas, and after centuries of this kind of treatment they have ceased to bother about overcrowding.   Many of the streets are a good deal less than six feet wide, the houses are completely windowless, and sore-eyed children cluster everywhere in unbelievable numbers, like clouds of flies.   Down the centre of the street there is generally running a little river of urine.

In the bazaar huge families of Jews, all dressed in the long black robe and little black skull-cap, are working in dark fly-infested booths that look like caves.   A carpenter sits crosslegged at a prehistoric lathe, turning chair-legs at lightning speed.   He works the lathe with a bow in his right hand and guides the chisel with his left foot, and thanks to a lifetime of sitting in this position his left leg is warped out of shape. At his side his grandson, aged six, is already starting on the simpler parts of the job.

I was just passing the coppersmiths' booths when somebody noticed that I was lighting a cigarette.   Instantly, from the dark holes all round, there was a frenzied rush of Jews, many of them old grandfathers with flowing grey beards, all clamouring for a cigarette.   Even a blind man somewhere at the back of one of the booths heard a rumour of cigarettes and came crawling out, groping in the air with his hand.   In about a minute I had used up the whole packet.   None of these people, I suppose, works less than twelve hours a day, and every one of them looks on a cigarette as a more or less impossible luxury.

As the Jews live in self-contained communities they follow the same trades as the Arabs, except for agriculture.   Fruit-sellers, potters, silversmiths, blacksmiths, butchers, leatherworkers, tailors, water-carriers, beggars, porters—whichever way you look you see nothing but Jews.   As a matter of fact there are thirteen thousand of them, all living in the space of a few acres.   A good job Hitler wasn't here.   Perhaps he was on his way, however.   You hear the usual dark rumours about the Jews, not only from the Arabs but from the poorer Europeans.

"Yes, mon vieux, they took my job away from me and gave it to a Jew.   The Jews! They're the real rulers of this country, you know. They've got all the money.   They control the banks, finance—everything."

"But," I said, "isn't it a fact that the average Jew is a labourer working for about a penny an hour?"

"Ah, that's only for show! They're all moneylenders really. They're cunning, the Jews."

In just the same way, a couple of hundred years ago, poor old women used to be burned for witchcraft when they could not even work enough magic to get themselves a square meal.

All people who work with their hands are partly invisible, and the more important the work they do, the less visible they are. Still, a white skin is always fairly conspicuous. In northern Europe, when you see a labourer ploughing a field, you probably give him a second glance. In a hot country, anywhere south of Gibraltar or east of Suez, the chances are that you don't even see him. I have noticed this again and again. In a tropical landscape one's eye takes in everything except the human beings. It takes in the dried-up soil, the prickly pear, the palm tree and the distant mountain, but it always misses the peasant hoeing at his patch. He is the same colour as the earth, and a great deal less interesting to look at.

It is only because of this that the starved countries of Asia and Africa are accepted as tourist resorts. No one would think of running cheap trips to the Distressed Areas. But where the human beings have brown skins their poverty is simply not noticed. What does Morocco mean to a Frenchman? An orange-grove or a job in Government service. Or to an Englishman? Camels, castles, palm trees, Foreign Legionnaires, brass trays, and bandits. One could probably live there for years without noticing that for nine-tenths of the people the reality of life is an endless, back-breaking struggle to wring a little food out of an eroded soil.

Most of Morocco is so desolate that no wild animal bigger than a hare can live on it. Huge areas which were once covered with forest have turned into a treeless waste where the soil is exactly like broken-up brick. Nevertheless a good deal of it is cultivated, with frightful labour. Everything is done by hand. Long lines of women, bent double like inverted capital L's, work their way slowly across the fields, tearing up the prickly weeds with their hands, and the peasant gathering lucerne for fodder pulls it up stalk by stalk instead of reaping it, thus saving an inch or two on each stalk. The plough is a wretched wooden thing, so frail that one can easily carry it on one's shoulder, and fitted underneath with a rough iron spike which stirs the soil to a depth of about four inches. This is as much as the strength of the animals is equal to.   It is usual to plough with a cow and a donkey yoked together.   Two donkeys would not be quite strong enough, but on the other hand two cows would cost a little more to feed.   The peasants possess no harrows, they merely plough the soil several times over in different directions, finally leaving it in rough furrows, after which the whole field has to be shaped with hoes into small oblong patches to conserve water.   Except for a day or two after the rare rainstorms there is never enough water.   Along the edges of the fields channels are hacked out to a depth of thirty or forty feet to get at the tiny trickles which run through the subsoil.

Every afternoon a file of very old women passes down the road outside my house, each carrying a load of firewood.   All of them are mummified with age and the sun, and all of them are tiny.   It seems to be generally the case in primitive communities that the women, when they get beyond a certain age, shrink to the size of children.   One day a poor old creature who could not have been more than four feet tall crept past me under a vast load of wood.   I stopped her and put a five-sou piece (a little more than a farthing) into her hand.   She answered with a shrill wail, almost a scream, which was partly gratitude but mainly surprise.   I suppose that from her point of view, by taking any notice of her, I seemed almost to be violating a law of nature.   She accepted her status as an old woman, that is to say as a beast of burden.   When a family is travelling it is quite usual to see a father and a grown-up son riding ahead on donkeys, and an old woman following on foot, carrying the baggage.

But what is strange about these people is their invisibility.   For several weeks, always at about the same time of day, the file of old women had hobbled past the house with their firewood, and though they had registered themselves on my eyeballs I cannot truly say that I had seen them.   Firewood was passing—that was how I saw it.   It was only that one day I happened to be walking behind them, and the curious up-and-down motion of a load of wood drew my attention to the human being beneath it.   Then for the first time I noticed the poor old earth-coloured bodies, bodies reduced to bones and leathery skin, bent double under the crushing weight.   Yet I suppose I had not been five minutes on Moroccan soil before I noticed the overloading of the donkeys and was infuriated by it.   There is no question that the donkeys are damnably treated.   The Moroccan donkey is hardly bigger than a St. Bernard dog, it carries a load which in the British Army would be considered too much for a fifteen-hands mule, and very often its pack-saddle is not taken off its back for weeks together. But what is peculiarly pitiful is that it is the most willing creature on earth, it follows its master like a dog and does not need either bridle or halter. After a dozen years of devoted work it suddenly drops dead, whereupon its master tips it into the ditch and the village dogs have torn its guts out before it is cold.

This kind of thing makes one's blood boil, whereas—on the whole—the plight of the human beings does not. I am not commenting, merely pointing to a fact. People with brown skins are next door to invisible. Anyone can be sorry for the donkey with its galled back, but it is generally owing to some kind of accident if one even notices the old woman under her load of sticks.

As the storks flew northward the Negroes were marching southward— a long, dusty column, infantry, screw-gun batteries, and then more infantry, four or five thousand men in all, winding up the road with a clumping of boots and a clatter of iron wheels.

They were Senegalese, the blackest Negroes in Africa, so black that sometimes it is difficult to see whereabouts on their necks the hair begins. Their splendid bodies were hidden in reach-me-down khaki uniforms, their feet squashed into boots that looked like blocks of wood, and every tin hat seemed to be a couple of sizes too small. It was very hot and the men had marched a long way. They slumped under the weight of their packs and the curiously sensitive black faces were glistening with sweat.

As they went past a tall, very young Negro turned and caught my eye. But the look he gave me was not in the least the kind of look you might expect. Not hostile, not contemptuous, not sullen, not even inquisitive. It was the shy, wide-eyed Negro look, which actually is a look of profound respect. I saw how it was. This wretched boy, who is a French citizen and has therefore been dragged from the forest to scrub floors and catch syphilis in garrison towns, actually has feelings of reverence before a white skin. He has been taught that the white race are his masters, and he still believes it.

But there is one thought which every white man (and in this connection it doesn't matter twopence if he calls himself a socialist) thinks when he sees a black army marching past. "How much longer can we go on kidding these people? How long before they turn their guns in the other direction?"

It was curious, really.   Every white man there had this thought stowed somewhere or other in his mind.   I had it, so had the other onlookers, so had the officers on their sweating chargers and the white N.C.O.'s marching in the ranks.   It was a kind of secret which we all knew and were too clever to tell; only the Negroes didn't know it.   And really it was like watching a flock of cattle to see the long column, a mile or two miles of armed men, flowing peacefully up the road, while the great white birds drifted over them in the opposite direction, glittering like scraps of paper.

Lines of Inquiry

1 This essay is a composite of scenes; in that sense, it is a descriptive essay.   It was noted earlier that all description has a design, and is an effort to render a meaningful picture.   Marking off the scenes, take one—for example, the scene beginning "I was feeding one of the gazelles . . ."—and note how it develops from picture to significance.

  a Are the other scenes developed in a similar pattern?   How do you account for the differences that do exist in the pattern of development?

  b What happens if we move the scenes about—put the last first, the scene in the gardens last?   What do you conclude about the sequence of scenes in this essay?

2 Orwell does not mention the public buildings of Marrakech, nor the hotel he stayed in, nor a host of other possible and available details.   One principle behind his choice of details is suggested by his comment on the first scene: In Marrakech, it is difficult to believe you are walking among human beings.

  a Does the choice and treatment of the later scenes carry this general idea further?

  b Take one scene and draw up a list of the kinds of details Orwell gives: what is the principle behind his choice?   (You may find it useful to imagine details that Orwell must have seen and yet did not employ.)

3 Examine the boundaries of each scene.

  a How are the scenes linked to one another?   Can you substitute a different or more explicit system of linking for the one that Orwell uses?

  b Take the boundary between the first and second scenes. Eliminating Orwell's linking passage, think of two other ways by which these two scenes could be linked.   What effect would each alternative have on the meaning of the two scenes?   Why do you think Orwell chose the specific kind of linking passage here that he did? Omit the linking passage entirely. Is the essay strengthened or weakened? Is Orwell's point clearer or more obscure?

   c The scenes are highly concrete, particular, and vivid; by contrast, the transitions are much more abstract, general, and invisible. Which—scene or transitional passage—makes it easier "to believe that you are walking among human beings"?

4 Orwell's essay begins, "As the corpse went past the flies left the restaurant table in a cloud and rushed after it, but they came back a few minutes later." Does this opening have any relationship to the kind of detail Orwell employs in his later scenes, or to the theme of the essay? What does it suggest about the point of view from which we will follow the scenes?

5 Look at the last scene in the essay. What is the point of the storks? Do you see any relationship between the first sentence of the essay and the last?

6 Orwell provides interpretations for most of his scenes. Is it possible to interpret any of them differently? Try to recast one scene, according to a different interpretation; what elements of the scene do you have to change if you change the interpretation?

Lines of Experiment

1 Taking a city, town, or district with which you are closely familiar, or one that you are prepared to visit with a critical eye, choose from its life a single typical scene. The scene may be actual or merely probable. Before you try to describe it, arrange the specific elements of the scene in several different sequences, and choose the most effective sequence—the one that makes your meaning most visible. In writing, be brief and try to keep adjectives and adverbs *out* of your first draft: you can add them later with a surer hand. Make the meaning of the scene depend largely from movement, from something happening within it.

2 Choose several other scenes that echo, modify, or expand the meaning of your first choice. These scenes are the raw material of an essay. Try arranging them in several different sequences before you begin to write; choose the sequence that seems to express your interpretation of their meaning best. Find a way of linking the scenes so that this sequence seems both natural and in itself important—so that meaning rises from the sequence of scenes as well as from the individual scenes themselves. Scenes may be linked by shifts in time (with place a constant), by shifts in place (with time a constant), by shifts in both time and place within a narrow geography, by shifts in internal point of view, by shifts from specific to general statement and back again, and in a wide variety of other ways. Consider more than one option before you choose.

JOHN MILLINGTON SYNGE

AN AUTUMN NIGHT IN THE HILLS

A few years ago a pointer dog of my acquaintance was wounded by accident in a wild glen on the western slope of County Wicklow. He was left at the cottage of an under-keeper, or bailiff—the last cottage on the edge of two ranges of mountains that stretch on the north and west to the plain of Kildare—and a few weeks later I made my way there to bring him down to his master.

It was an afternoon of September, and some heavy rain of the night before had made the road which led up to the cottage through the middle of the glen as smooth as a fine beach, while the clearness of the air gave the granite that ran up on either side of the way a peculiar tinge that was nearly luminous against the shadow of the hills. Every cottage that I passed had a group of rowan trees beside it covered with scarlet berries that gave brilliant points of colour of curious effect.

Just as I came to the cottage the road turned across a swollen river which I had to cross on a range of slippery stones. Then, when I had gone a few yards further, I heard a bark of welcome, and the dog ran down to meet me. The noise he made brought two women to the door of the cottage, one a finely made girl, with an exquisitely open and graceful manner, the other a very old woman. A sudden shower had come up without any warning over the rim of the valley, so I went into the cottage and sat down on a sort of bench in the chimney-corner, at the end of a long low room with open rafters.

"You've come on a bad day," said the old woman, "for you won't see any of the lads or men about the place."

"I suppose they went out to cut their oats," I said, "this morning while the weather was fine."

"They did not," she answered, "but they're after going down to Aughrim for the body of Mary Kinsella, that is to be brought this night from the station.   There will be a wake then at the last cottage you're after passing, where you saw all them trees with the red berries on them."

She stopped for a moment while the girl gave me a drink of milk.

"I'm afraid it's a lot of trouble I'm giving you," I said as I took it, "and you busy, with no men in the place."

"No trouble at all in the world," said the girl, "and if it was itself, wouldn't any one be glad of it in the lonesome place we're in?"

The old woman began talking again:

"You saw no sign or trace on the road of the people coming with the body?"

"No sign," I said, "and who was she at all?"

"She was a fine young woman with two children," she went on, "and a year and a half ago she went wrong in her head, and they had to send her away.   And then up there in the Richmond asylum maybe they thought the sooner they were shut of her the better, for she died two days ago this morning, and now they're bringing her up to have a wake, and they'll bury her beyond at the churches, far as it is, for it's there are all the people of the two families."

While we talked I had been examining a wound in the dog's side near the end of his lung.

"He'll do rightly now," said the girl who had come in again and was putting tea-things on the table.   "He'll do rightly now.   You wouldn't know he'd been hurted at all only for a kind of a cough he'll give now and again.   Did they ever tell you the way he was hit?" she added, going down on her knees in the chimney-corner with some dry twigs in her hand and making a little fire on the flag-stone a few inches from the turf.

I told her I had heard nothing but the fact of his wound.

"Well," she said, "a great darkness and storm came down that night and they all out on the hill. The rivers rose, and they were there groping along by the turf track not minding the dogs. Then an old rabbit got up and run before them, and a man put up his gun and shot across it. When he fired that dog run out from behind a rock, and one grain of the shot cut the scruff off his nose, and another went in there where you were looking, at the butt of his ribs. He dropped down bleeding and howling, and they thought he was killed. The night was falling and they had no way they could carry him, so they made a kind of a shelter for him with sticks and turf, and they left him while they would be going for a sack."

She stopped for a moment to knead some dough and put down a dozen hot cakes—cut out with the mouth of a tumbler—in a frying pan on the little fire she had made with the twigs. While she was doing so the old woman took up the talk.

"Ah," she said, "there do be queer things them nights out on the mountains and in the lakes among them. I was reared beyond in the valley where the mines used to be, in the valley of the Lough Nahanagan, and it's many a queer story I've heard of the spirit does be in that lake."

"I have sometimes been there fishing till it was dark," I said when she paused, "and heard strange noises in the cliff."

"There was an uncle of mine," she continued, "and he was there the same way as yourself, fishing with a big fly in the darkness of the night, and the spirit came down out of the clouds and rifted the waters asunder. He was afeared then and he run down to the houses trembling and shaking. "There was another time," she went on, "a man came round to this country who was after swimming through the water of every lake in Ireland. He went up to swim in that lake, and a brother of my own went up along with him. The gentleman had heard tell of the spirit but not a bit would he believe in it. He went down on the bank, and he had a big black dog with him, and he took off his clothes.

" 'For the love of God,' said my brother, 'put that dog in before you go in yourself, the way you'll see if he ever comes out of it.' The gentleman said he would do that and they threw in a stick or a stone and the dog leapt in and swam out to it. Then he turned round again and he swam and he swam, and not a bit nearer did he come.

" 'He's a long time swimming back,' said the gentleman.

" 'I'm thinking your honour'll have a grey beard before he comes back,' said my brother, and before the word was out of his mouth the dog went out of their sight, and the inside out of him came up on the top of the water."

By this time the cakes were ready and the girl put them on a plate for me at the table, and poured out a cup of tea from the tea-pot, putting the milk and sugar herself into my cup as is the custom with the cottage people of Wicklow.   Then she put the tea-pot down in the embers of the turf and sat down in the place I had left.

"Well," she said, "I was telling you the story of that night.   When they got back here they sent up two lads for the dog, with a sack to carry him on if he was alive and a spade to bury him if he was dead.   When they came to the turf where they left him they saw him near twenty yards down the path.   The crathur thought they were after leaving him there to die, and he got that lonesome he dragged himself along like a Christian till he got too weak with the bleeding.   James, the big lad, walked up again him first with the spade in his hand.   When he seen the spade he let a kind of a groan out of him.

"That dog's as wise as a child, and he knew right well it was to bury him they brought the spade.   Then Mike went up and laid down the sack on the ground, and the minute he seen it he jumped up and tumbled in on it himself.   Then they carried him down, and the crathur getting his death with the cold and the great rain was falling.   When they brought him in here you'd have thought he was dead.   We put up a settle bed before the fire, and we put him into it.   The heat roused him a bit, and he stretched out his legs and gave two groans out of him like an old man.   Mike thought he'd drink some milk so we heated a cup of it over the fire.   When he put down his tongue into it he began to cough and bleed, then he turned himself over in the settle bed and looked up at me like an old man.   I sat up with him that night and it raining and blowing.   At four in the morning I gave him a sup more of the milk and he was able to drink it.

"The next day he was stronger, and we gave him a little new milk every now and again.   We couldn't keep him near the fire.   So we put him in the little room beyond by the door and an armful of hay in along with him.   In the afternoon the boys were out on the mountain and the old woman was gone somewhere else, and I was chopping sticks in the lane.   I heard a sort of a noise and there he was with his head out through the window looking out on me in the lane.   I was afraid he was lonesome in there all by himself, so I put in one of our old dogs to keep him company.   Then I stuffed an old hat into the window and I thought they'd be quiet together.

"But what did they do but begin to fight in there all in the dark as they were.   I opened the door and out runs that lad before I could stop him. Not a bit would he go in again, so I had to leave him running about beside me. He's that loyal to me now you wouldn't believe it.   When I go for the cow he comes along with me, and when I go to make up a bit of hay on the hill he'll come and make a sort of bed for himself under a haycock, and not a bit of him will look at Mike or the boys."

"Ah," said the old woman, as the girl got up to pour me out another cup from the tea-pot, "it's herself will be lonesome when that dog is gone, he's never out of her sight, and you'd do right to send her down a little dog all for herself."

"You would so," said the girl, "but maybe he wouldn't be loyal to me, and I wouldn't give a thraneen for a dog as wasn't loyal."

"Would you believe it," said the old woman again, "when the gentleman wrote down about that dog Mike went out to where she was in the haggard, and says 'They're after sending me the prescription for that dog,' say he, 'to put on his tombstone.'   And she went down quite simple, and told the boys below in the bog, and it wasn't till they began making game of her that she seen the way she'd been humbugged."

"That's the truth," said the girl, "I went down quite simple, and indeed it's a small wonder, that dog's as fit for a decent burial as many that gets it."

Meanwhile the shower had turned to a dense torrent of mountain rain, and although the evening was hardly coming on, it was so dark that the girl lighted a lamp and hung it at the corner of the chimney.   The kitchen was longer than most that I have met with and had a skeleton staircase at the far end that looked vague and shadowy in the dim light. The old woman wore one of the old-fashioned caps with a white frill round the face, and entered with great fitness into the general scheme of the kitchen.   I did not like leaving them to go into the raw night for a long walk on the mountains, and I sat down and talked to them for a long time, till the old woman thought I would be benighted.

"Go out now," she said at last to the girl, "go out now and see what water is coming over the fall above, for with this rain the water'll rise fast, and maybe he'll have to walk down to the bridge, a rough walk when the night is coming on."

The girl came back in a moment.

"It's riz already," she said. "He'll want to go down to the bridge." Then turning to me: "If you'll come now I'll show you the way you have to go, and I'll wait below for the boys; it won't be long now till they come with the body of Mary Kinsella."

We went out at once and she walked quickly before me through a maze of small fields and pieces of bog, where I would have soon lost the track if I had been alone.

The bridge, when we reached it, was a narrow wooden structure fastened up on iron bars which pierced large boulders in the bed of the river. An immense grey flood was struggling among the stones, looking dangerous and desolate in the half-light of the evening, while the wind was so great that the bridge wailed and quivered and whistled under our feet. A few paces further on we came to a cottage where the girl wished me a good journey and went in to wait for her brothers.

The daylight still lingered but the heavy rain and a thick white cloud that had come down made everything unreal and dismal to an extraordinary degree. I went up a road where on one side I could see the trunks of beech trees reaching up wet and motionless—with odd sighs and movements when a gust caught the valley—into a greyness overhead, where nothing could be distinguished. Between them there were masses of shadow, and masses of half-luminous fog with black branches across them. On the other side of the road flocks of sheep I could not see coughed and choked with sad guttural noises in the shelter of the hedge, or rushed away through a gap when they felt the dog was near them. Above everything my ears were haunted by the dead heavy swish of the rain. When I came near the first village I heard a loud noise and commotion. Many cars and gigs were collected at the door of the public-house, and the bar was filled with men who were drinking and making a noise. Everything was dark and confused yet on one car I was able to make out the shadow of a coffin, strapped in the rain, with the body of Mary Kinsella.

Lines of Inquiry

1 At first glance, this personal narrative seems singularly pointless: A man goes into the country to get a dog, is told a couple of anecdotes, and walks back. If we divide the narrative into

parts, we find that far the largest part is made up of the anecdotes told by the girl and her mother. The narrator's trip is
a kind of frame for these anecdotes.

  a What is the relation between the frame and its contents?
  Where do the two meet in the narration?

  b Could Synge have told the anecdotes and let the rest drop
  with no loss of meaning?

  c What do the anecdotes have in common? How do they
  bear on the narrator's mood at the end?

2 Let us call the anecdotes: *A*, the anecdote of Mary Kinsella; *B*,
the anecdote of the accidentally wounded dog; *C*, the anecdote
of the drowned or murdered dog. *C* is enclosed in *B*, which in
turn is enclosed in *A*. The anecdotes could have been made
to succeed each other simply—first *A*, then *B*, then *C*, each
from beginning to end; or first *B*, then *C*, then *A;* or first *C*,
then *B*, then *A*.

  a What is the effect of their actual order—that is, what is the
  relationship of *C* to *B*, and of both *C* and *B* to *A?* Could *C*
  be omitted? Could *A?*

  b Which of the three is the real center of the narrative?
  Where is the wounded dog at the end?

  c Could Synge have used a few more anecdotes profitably, or
  are these three enough to make the point he was after?

3 How is the transition between one anecdote and another managed, and with what effect?

4 Look at the openings of the first four paragraphs.

  a What do they have in common? What pattern of development do they show?

  b Imagine the opening with the second paragraph left out:
  What, if anything, does the scene lose?

  c What function does the description in the second and third
  paragraphs have in the total essay?

5 Could a full-scale narrative be written around *C*, the anecdote
of the drowned or murdered dog? If so, what element of that
story probably would become the center of the narrative—that
is, go through a pattern of development?

6 Much of the effect of this essay comes from relatively small
details. What seem to be the purposes of the following?

  a The scarlet berries on the rowan trees

  b The change in the weather

  c The color and size of the drowned dog

d The flood and the wind and fog

e The sheep

f The public house, with a bar full of "men who were drinking and making a noise"

Lines of Experiment

1 Take a series of anecdotes linked in subject or in theme, but not in historical fact. (The following list may suggest a suitable subject or theme: cats, horses, teachers; the drama, factory life, farming; funeral, weddings, baptisms, initiations.) Weighing the meaning of each anecdote, eliminate all but three or four that seem closely related to theme *but that do not duplicate one another*. These anecdotes are the raw material of your composition. Arrange them in several trial sequences, and choose the sequence that seems most meaningful and dramatic.

Your next job is to find a way of linking these scenes. You may simply list them; you may link them by passage of *time* or change of *place;* you may link them by interpretations of their meaning. You may choose one as a frame for the others, as Synge does. Or you may follow some quite different system. Your final narrative need not be literally true in all respects. Consider what at least two different systems have to offer you, in reinforcing or defining your theme, before you begin to write.

2 Doubtless you have been a member of a group of people swapping stories in a bull session. Write an essay in which no more than three people tell one another stories on the same general topic—poverty, prejudice, love, the army, the war, education, hunting, or something similar. (Three people will give you a chance to contrast different kinds of stories; two might limit you too closely; and four might become confusing.) Use no more than four stories in all, unless you are absolutely sure you can keep your essay from flying apart. Four will give one story to each participant, which is appropriate if you have three people present, and two stories to one participant, which will provide you with structural variety and a chance to show some development between his first story and his second.) You probably must *(a)* find a narrative way into your bull session, in order to make it appear natural that people should sit around telling stories to one another; *(b)* fit the characters of each story to the character of its teller, in order to preserve psychological probability; *(c)* arrange the stories in a sequence that makes the point you want to make in a dramatically effective way. Again, your essay need not be literally true in every detail—

and all of the above advice should be disregarded if it gets in the way of a good composition.   If everything else fails, start a bull session yourself, and take notes.

GRAHAME GREENE

 ## THE REVOLVER
IN THE
CORNER CUPBOARD

I can remember very clearly the afternoon I found the revolver in the brown deal corner cupboard in the bedroom which I shared with my elder brother.   It was the early autumn of 1922.   I was seventeen and terribly bored and in love with my sister's governess—one of those miserable, hopeless, romantic loves of adolescence that set in many minds the idea that love and despair are inextricable and that successful love hardly deserves the name.   At that age one may fall irrevocably in love with failure, and success of any kind loses half its savour before it is experienced.   Such a love is surrendered once and for all to the singer at the pavement's edge, the bankrupt, the old school friend who wants to touch you for a dollar.   Perhaps in many so conditioned it is the love for God that mainly survives, because in his eyes they can imagine themselves remaining always drab, seedy, unsuccessful, and therefore worthy of notice.

The revolver was a small genteel object with six chambers like a tiny egg stand, and there was a cardboard box of bullets.   It has only recently occurred to me that they may have been blanks; I always assumed them to be live ammunition, and I never mentioned the discovery to my brother because I had realized the moment I saw the revolver the use I intended to make of it.   (I don't to this day know why he possessed it; certainly he had no license, and he was only three years older than myself.   A large family is as departmental as a Ministry.)

My brother was away—probably climbing in the Lake District—and until he returned the revolver was to all intents mine.   I knew what to do with it because I had been reading a book (the name Ossendowski comes to mind as the possible author) describing how the White Russian officers, condemned to inaction in South Russia at the tail-end of the counter-revolutionary war, used to invent hazards with which to escape boredom.   One man would slip a charge into a revolver and turn the chambers at random, and his companion would put the revolver to his head and pull the trigger.   The chance, of course, was six to one in favour of life.

How easily one forgets emotions.   If I were dealing now with an imaginary character, I would feel it necessary for verisimilitude to make him hesitate, put the revolver back into the cupboard, return to it again after an interval, reluctantly and fearfully, when the burden of boredom became too great.   But in fact I think there was no hesitation at all, for the next I can remember is crossing Berkhamsted Common, gashed here and there between the gorse bushes with the stray trenches of the first Great War, towards the Ashridge beeches.   Perhaps before I had made the discovery, boredom had already reached an intolerable depth.

I think the boredom was far deeper than the love.   It had always been a feature of childhood: it would set in on the second day of the school holidays.   The first day was all happiness, and, after the horrible confinement and publicity of school, seemed to consist of light, space and silence.   But a prison conditions its inhabitants.   I never wanted to return to it (and finally expressed my rebellion by the simple act of running away), but yet I was so conditioned that freedom bored me unutterably.

The psycho-analysis that followed my act of rebellion had fixed the boredom as hypo fixes the image on the negative.   I emerged from those delightful months in London spent at my analyst's house—perhaps the happiest months of my life—correctly orientated, able to take a proper extrovert interest in my fellows (the jargon rises to the lips), but wrung dry.   For years, it seems to me, I could take no aesthetic interest in any visual thing at all: staring at a sight that others assured me was beautiful, I would feel nothing.   I was fixed in my boredom. (Writing this I come on a remark of Rilke: "Psycho-analysis is too fundamental a help for me, it helps you once and for all, it clears you up, and to find myself finally cleared up one day might be even more helpless than this chaos.")

Now with the revolver in my pocket I was beginning to emerge.   I had stumbled on the perfect cure.   I was going to escape in one way or another, and because escape was inseparably connected with the Common in my mind, it was there that I went.

The wilderness of gorse, old trenches, abandoned butts was the unchanging backcloth of most of the adventures of childhood. It was to the Common I had decamped for my act of rebellion some years before, with the intention, expressed in a letter left after breakfast on the heavy black sideboard, that there I would stay, day and night, until either I had starved or my parents had given in; when I pictured war it was always in terms of this Common, and myself leading a guerilla campaign in the ragged waste, for no one, I was persuaded, knew its paths so intimately (how humiliating that in my own domestic campaign I was ambushed by my elder sister after a few hours).

Beyond the Common lay a wide grass ride known for some reason as Cold Harbour to which I would occasionally with some fear take a horse, and beyond this again stretched Ashridge Park, the smooth olive skin of beech trees and the thick last year's quagmire of leaves, dark like old pennies. Deliberately I chose my ground, I believe without any real fear—perhaps because I was uncertain myself whether I was play-acting; perhaps because so many acts which my elders would have regarded as neurotic, but which I still consider to have been under the circumstances highly reasonable, lay in the background of this more dangerous venture.

There had been, for example, perhaps five or six years before, the disappointing morning in the dark room by the linen cupboard on the eve of term when I had patiently drunk a quantity of hypo under the impression that it was poisonous: on another occasion the blue glass bottle of hay fever lotion which as it contained a small quantity of cocaine had probably been good for my mood: the bunch of deadly nightshade that I had eaten with only a slight narcotic effect: the twenty aspirins I had taken before swimming in the empty out-of-term school baths (I can still remember the curious sensation of swimming through wool): these acts may have removed all sense of strangeness as I slipped a bullet into a chamber and, holding the revolver behind my back, spun the chambers round.

Had I romantic thoughts about the governess? Undoubtedly I must have had, but I think that at the most they simply eased the medicine down. Boredom, aridity, those were the main emotions. Unhappy love has, I suppose, sometimes driven boys to suicide, but this was not suicide, whatever a coroner's jury might have said of it: it was a gamble with six chances to one against an inquest. The romantic flavour—the autumn scene, the small heavy compact shape lying in the fingers—that perhaps was a tribute to adolescent love, but the discovery that it was possible to enjoy again the visible world by risking its total loss was one I was bound to make sooner or later.

I put the muzzle of the revolver in my right ear and pulled the trigger. There was a minute click, and looking down at the chamber I could see that the charge had moved into place. I was out by one. I remember an extraordinary sense of jubilation. It was as if a light had been turned on. My heart was knocking in its cage, and I felt that life contained an infinite number of possibilities. It was like a young man's first successful experience of sex—as if in that Ashridge glade one had passed a test of manhood. I went home and put the revolver back in the corner cupboard.

The odd thing about this experience was that it was repeated several times. At fairly long intervals I found myself craving for the drug. I took the revolver with me when I went up to Oxford and I would walk out from Headington towards Elsfield down what is now a wide arterial road, smooth and shiny like the walls of a public lavatory. Then it was a sodden unfrequented country lane. The revolver would be whipped behind my back, the chambers twisted, the muzzle quickly and surreptitiously inserted beneath the black and ugly winter tree, the trigger pulled.

Slowly the effect of the drug wore off—I lost the sense of jubilation, I began to gain from the experience only the crude kick of excitement. It was like the difference between love and lust. And as the quality of the experience deteriorated so my sense of responsibility grew and worried me. I wrote a very bad piece of free verse (free because it was easier in that way to express my meaning without literary equivocation) describing how, in order to give a fictitious sense of danger, I would "press the trigger of a revolver I already know to be empty." This piece of verse I would leave permanently on my desk, so that if I lost my gamble, there would be incontrovertible evidence of an accident, and my parents, I thought, would be less troubled than by an apparent suicide—or than by the rather bizarre truth.

But it was back at Berkhamsted that I paid a permanent farewell to the drug. As I took my fifth dose it occurred to me that I wasn't even excited: I was beginning to pull the trigger about as casually as I might take an aspirin tablet. I decided to give the revolver—which was six-chambered—a sixth and last chance.   Twirling the chambers round, I put the muzzle to my ear for the last time and heard the familiar empty click as the chambers revolved.   I was through with the drug, and walking back over the Common, down the new road by the ruined castle, past the private entrance to the gritty old railway station—reserved for the use of Lord Brownlow—my mind was already busy on other plans.   One campaign was over, but the war against boredom had got to go on.

I put the revolver back in the corner cupboard, and going downstairs I lied gently and convincingly to my parents that a friend had invited me to join him in Paris.

Lines of Inquiry

1 In a sense, this essay is about "the war against boredom."   The essay's incident is frightening, but in a peculiar, distant way.

   a What has the focus of the essay (on the revolver) to do with its theme?

   b What relationship do you see between "the war against boredom" and the manner in which the objects and events of this essay are described?

   c What establishes Greene's essential narrative sequence? (Consider the first and last paragraphs.)   How is the structure of the *essay* related to the structure of the *revolver?*

   d How would you describe the essay's tone?

2 Greene's essay is written, of course, in a personal voice, for he is speaking of an event in his own life.   Julius Caesar and Henry Adams also wrote about events in their own lives; yet *The Gallic War* and *The Education of Henry Adams* are both written in the third person—as if the writer and main character of the books were different people.   Could Greene have referred to himself, in this essay, in the third person?   What would happen to our distance from his subject if he had?   What changes would you expect to see in the essay's focus?   In its tone?   In its convincingness?

3 Here is the opening sentence (slightly revised) of each of the first five paragraphs.   Compare them to their originals.   In each case, what does the original offer, *in context,* that the revision does not?   How are the sentences related, as a sequence?

   a "I remember very clearly the afternoon I found the revolver."

   b "The revolver was small."

   c "My brother was away."

   d "I did not hesitate."

   e "I was thoroughly bored."

4 Greene offers us many details we do not need to know in order
to understand what he did. Here are several. What is the
effect of each on us? Is this effect part of or separate from
the meaning of the essay as a whole?
   a The corner cupboard is of "brown deal."
   b His absent brother was "probably climbing in the Lake Dis-
     trict."
   c The Common was "gashed . . . with the stray trenches of
     the first Great War."
   d Greene put the muzzle of the revolver in his right ear.
   e While at Oxford, Greene performed his ritual challenge to
     death "beneath the black and ugly winter tree."
   f The gritty old railway station (see the last paragraph) was
     "reserved for the use of Lord Brownlow."

5 What is the significance in context of
   a The fact that Greene is always by himself, without friends or
     public moments
   b The transformation of the "sodden, unfrequented country
     lane" to a "wide arterial road, smooth and shiny like the
     walls of a public lavatory"
   c Greene's remark that "as the quality of the experience de-
     teriorated so my sense of responsibility grew and worried
     me"
   d The lie with which the essay concludes

6 Greene says that had he died it would have been neither accident nor suicide.
   a What is "the rather bizarre truth" of the matter?
   b How is this bizarre truth related to his earlier attempts to
     poison and to drown himself?

7 a Why did Greene not take as the focus of his essay one of
     these earlier incidents—why did he choose the incident of the
     revolver instead?
   b What distinction is Greene making when he says that the
     difference between his first and last game of Russian roulette
     was "like the difference between love and lust"?

8 Greene makes the point that if he were dealing with an imaginary character he would feel it necessary to make the character hesitate, and so forth, before taking the gun from the corner
cupboard. Why, if in real life he himself did not hesitate?
What do you conclude concerning the relationship between
fictional and historical accounts? Between imagination and
reality?

9 If one were to view Greene's essay as illustrative, what might it be said to illustrate? Merely the trouble children can get into in "the war against boredom"? Or something larger? What does Greene's attitude toward psychoanalysis have to do with all of this? What is it, finally, that Greene is suggesting about the defeat of boredom? What is he suggesting about its genesis?

Lines of Experiment

1 Not all of us either dream of or attempt the game of Russian roulette, but the boredom of which Greene speaks is not unusual, nor are attempts to escape from it—in adolescence, middle life, and old age. Greene's essay is valuable because it illustrates both the problem of boredom and its personal importance and points toward an explanation of its source. Write your own essay on boredom. You may take as a compositional center a personal narrative, as here, or you may use a method of logical development—definition or classification of boredom, and so forth—as a way of ordering and focusing your ideas. There are two things you must be concerned with in your essay, at least by implication. First, why do people become bored? And second, how can their boredom be relieved—and how not? Greene's essay offers one set of answers, one set of images; you must find your own.

2 Boredom is an emotion, and personal narrative is probably the most effective way of revealing or communicating an emotional set; for however widely shared, an emotion is peculiarly private in its nature. I may *tell* someone else that I am happy, but I alone can *know* how I feel.

Boredom is a peculiarly final emotion, however, almost an absence of emotion. Drawing on your own experience or on that of a friend, write a personal narrative designed to communicate intelligently an understanding of one of these emotions—and to communicate as well something of how it feels—through the careful creation of tone. The main point in writing such an essay is to consider nothing in the field of meaning accidental; each grain of an incident is held there by a magnetic core of significant thought, even though its significance may not be clear until it is examined.

Nonetheless, in shaping your material, you will find it useful to focus on one subject or event of central significance, placing other illustrative objects or events in a subordinate position, and to select for your illustrative center something that will enable

you to establish exactly the tone you are after. Again, however, do not allow yourself to be trapped into trying to plan
everything in advance; work out the main structure in very
simple terms, and then feel your way from sentence to sentence.

ROBERT HENDERSON

 ## THE ENAMELED
WISHBONE

Come what may, I change my razor blade each Saturday morning,
and as I did so on a hot one not long ago in mid-July, I found
myself worrying about the Civil War. The trouble had to do with
continuity—connection. I buy my blades in metal clips of ten or
twenty, and I prefer twenties, as a rule. You can look twice as far
ahead with them; they promise more. A set that is new in the
middle of summer will span a whole other season. It will take you
past the end of the heat and almost into winter, and there is no telling
what is going to happen while it lasts. Then when it is done, you can
glance backward if you want to. I play this game a good deal, as a
matter of fact. Equipment of some kind is always handy. It can
be played with a new shirt or an old calendar. I like to feel the
connections between here and there. I am for continuity first, last,
and always. Then, what, I wondered (starting a new set of blades,
peering ahead and reflecting that they would help get me ready for
Thanksgiving dinner)—what did I have against the celebration of
the centennial of the Civil War? *There* was continuity with a vengeance.

I have always thought that I more or less owned that war, perhaps
because one of my grandfathers was in it and I knew him. Over the
years, I may have read a dozen books about it, and always the articles
in Sunday supplements on Lincoln's birthday. As a small boy, I
fought in it every chance I got. Trapped by a girl, I would refuse
to play regular house. I was not to be a commuting father; I belonged

to the Ninth Ohio, or no game. "Got a lot of slaves to free today," I would tell her, hustling off to work. Once in a while, in the interval since, I have run into someone who also owned the war, and we have talked about it, regarding each other as rare and fine. Now Civil War buffs—as the papers call them—are a dime a dozen. (A buff is an enthusiast about going to fires, according to Webster, and I guess the definition fits, though the fire has been out for a while.) Reenactments more precise than mine bang away as the dates roll around. There are more new books on the war in a week than I have read all told. Documentation is on the loose. Facsimiles are rampant. And I am in no position to make light of reenactments, eschew books, deplore facts. Besides, if I already have some connection with the war, surely the more I know about it, the more connected I will be.

Well, continuity is peculiar. Later that day, in the afternoon, running Saturday errands, I went to return a borrowed raincoat to a friend whose name is Edward. He is bulky, abstracted, and as bitten with sequence as I am. For instance, he keeps a green enameled wishbone in his kitchen. It has gone along with him and his wife through several changes of dwelling, but he has no idea why it was saved to begin with, or who saved it after what feast. He bought an old house years ago and found the wishbone hanging there unpainted. When he enameled the kitchen green, he enameled the bone, making it his. When he had to leave the house, which he loved, he took the wishbone with him, and he seems to feel (when he thinks of it at all) that in a small way it is a talisman, and holds things together for him.

His wife let me in that Saturday, out of the heat, and steered me to Edward's study—a place that just encases him and a small concentration of litter. I squeezed in, said hello to Edward, and at once believed that he had a Christmas tree there, for the smell of evergreen was unmistakable. Then it was gone; it was only a whiff. But for an astonished moment I had caught a glimpse of the tree I helped put up last December—the lights in the tinsel, the slope of the branches, the angel askew on top—and (by natural resonance, or osmosis, or echo) glimpses of other Christmases. Back and back. Wreaths and candles. Fires in the grate. Carols and frost. Then I saw, in a vase on a shelf beside me, a couple of dusty sprays of red eucalyptus. "*That's* what smells like Christmas," I said to Edward.

He looked apologetic. "Funny stuff," he said. "It lasts forever. Dottie's been trying to throw it out for six months, but I won't let her. I sort of like to sniff it when I come in here. It takes me back."

I said it had just taken me back, too, and he looked surprised.   Then
he looked abstracted again.   "It's been a long time since Australia,"
he said, and I remembered that he had once lived, with *his* grandfather, down there, where the eucalyptus comes from to start with.
Apparently, continuity could run away from the vase on the shelf in
diverse directions and still be continuity for each of us.

I stayed a few minutes, gave Edward his coat, and went on to my
other errands, the Civil War still plucking at my sleeve.   I was wondering what there was about it that I cherished, and just exactly what
the nature of my connection with it was.   I could hop a season into
the cherished future with a package of razor blades, or fade back to
Christmases past (while Edward took off for Australia) on a whiff
of dried evergreen leaves.   And yet all the vouched-for reminders
of the war—the facsimiles, the reenactments—couldn't budge me.

Edward lives uptown, on the West Side; I live a good distance down
from him, on the East.   I was supposed to meet my wife at an outdoor
market to buy plants for window boxes.   I was late.   The sky was
dark.   Thunder came over the river.   So I took a cab, and the cab
went hurrying through Central Park.   Most people had already run
for shelter.   The cab went around a shoulder of rock and along past
a small wooded ridge where the wind was shaking the trees.   And
there, sure enough, they were, as they have been all my life in half
the landscapes that I see.   Imagined horsemen.   Shadowy cavalry slipping along the ridge, in and out of the edge of the woods.   They ride
chiefly in storms and at sunset.   They are in gray or butternut—
Mosby's men, doubtless; the Armies of the Union are on my side.
And I thought how, from trains, I notice pickets in the spotted shade of
a creek bank as I go by—how skirmishers will lurk behind a country
church or slip through a cornfield.

The source—one source—of these apparitions seemed simple, when I
considered it.   (I have seldom given much thought to the apparitions
themselves; they are just there.)   They come from songs, and from a
Miss Evelyn Whitby, who taught fifth grade.   She lived in a big house
she had inherited, along with a barn and a clover meadow full of bees.
She always led the school assembly in singing, both arms punishing the
air—a dark woman with sombre eyes that grew bright as she gave
herself a couple of preliminary twirls.   She liked both rousing songs
and sad ones, and believed that the most rousing and the saddest in
the world were those of the Civil War.   She would work her class up

to a song before she taught it to them, and if she thought the story it told was skimpy she filled it out. Extra cavalry charges. Extra dolor. By the time she got around to singing a sad one—"We shall meet but we shall miss him, there will be one vacant chair"—there wouldn't be a dry feminine eye in the room, and even the boys would look woebegone. On the other hand, everyone loved to shout the battle cry of freedom for her. And when we rose in the assembly and rallied round the flag, we knew just what we were singing about. We were singing about men who kept tenting at night on a little slope back of the school, which Miss Whitby had indicated mournfully as she sang about them. We were singing about marching through the little woods beyond the slope, and charging across Miss Whitby's clover meadow, as she let us do, bringing the jubilee. We were singing about grapes of wrath being trampled out on the floor of Miss Whitby's own barn, where, somehow, they were stored.

So the Civil War to me is rousing, grievous, and local, as only its songs in combination with Miss Whitby could have made it. It took place in homelike surroundings—in back yards and orchards and corn-fields—and in fact it often really did, big as it was. But (out of the Park now, going south on Seventh, the squall diminishing) I couldn't say that what I cherished, what I was connected to by the songs and apparitions, was the war itself as much as it was Miss Whitby and her meadow and her barn.

My wife was waiting for me at the market. The rain was over, but the air still smelled of it, and the leaves of the plants lined in racks were wet and glinting. The hot day was gone, a fresh one was break-ing, and we were grateful. We browsed for a while, cool and pleased, and then bought a few plants, mostly begonias. And as we started home with them I thought that they might hook me up for quite a while with the green, washed half hour just past, and then I realized that *it* had, a while before, lightly hooked itself up with Mosby's raiders. "I was wondering about the Civil War," I told my wife, and she nodded, unsurprised. "I mean, how I am connected with it," I said, and she said that would be through my grandfather, most likely.

Yes, to an extent. For one thing, I suspect that he, too, felt, looking back, that it had been a war of wood lots, though also an affair of flags. I guess that for him a real war was one hammered out between neighbors looking for the right. He never paid much attention to World War I, which he regarded as an expedition to straighten out people he didn't know. He had a permanent bruise, made by his musket, on the heel of his right hand; bullets tearing his tent had wakened him at Shiloh; he had caught a fever and lain out with it in mud and rain; he had been a prisoner in a bad camp; and I did understand from him and from these things that the war was real. But he had a little of Miss Whitby about him, too, when he looked back, and (turning that way myself, as we reached home) it dawned on me that I really hadn't known him very well. I knew that he was tall, stooped, kind, and sententious, and that he gave me cinnamon candy and took me to see Charlie Chaplin. I partly recalled a browned photograph of him as a youth in a forage cap, and—better—the worn red plush of the case the photograph was kept in. I remembered the bruise. But what mainly came back was a kind of roll call he had of the Civil War that skipped the fever and the prison camp and was long on bugles and honor. He liked to say major words and phrases— the War of the Rebellion, the Rock of Chickamauga, the Army of the Cumberland, Old Glory. He gave all his generals their full names. He must have put such things into sentences, but to me the words and names were without syntax, and (getting out the trowel, lining up the begonias by the window boxes) it occurred to me that the roll call, or litany, and the little I did know of my grandfather were what I was truly connected to. The war itself was on the far side of him and it.

So the mournful, personal, musical war also had warlike reverberations and glory, and was real, if only by definition. I tucked the begonias in among the other plants in our boxes, and found myself wondering in what way I was attached to the Civil War by potted violets, which somehow, themselves, seemed appropriate. And when I figured the answer out, I saw that the link wasn't the violets—they were just a link with the begonias. It was a man who once gave some violets to an aunt of mine.

Like Miss Whitby, she had a house, and, in addition, a mulberry tree in her front yard. I visited her one summer about the time I quit freeing the slaves and took to more specialized exploits. When I was at war, I was very fond of sniping; it was restful—except for tree climbing, which I enjoyed—and attractively furtive. The mulberry tree was ideal for it, and I was in huge luck, for I had an authentic enemy—a small, straight man with a round white beard who went by on his way to the grocer's and back every morning. He was in town to visit his daughter and her family. He had been a captain under Braxton Bragg, my grandfather's opponent at Shiloh, and I picked him off daily from the branches of the tree, shivering as I fired. I was hypnotized by him, and deeply unsettled by his presence in the North. At night, I thought about him and his dangerous nearness, and I tried never to let him see me, even off duty. But once, carried away by bravery, I let out a series of derisive Rebel yells at him, and he stopped and stared at the tree, his beard jutting. He looked more puzzled than angry, as I think back; he may not have recognized the derision, let alone the war cry. At any rate, he went on, but I shinnied down the tree and ran into the house in terror.

That night, after dark, he came to my aunt's door. I went with her to answer his knock, and when I saw him there against the darkness I was too frightened to back away. But then, though I don't think I heard much of what he said, I saw that he was shaking. He had been left with his six-year-old grandson, and the boy had disappeared. Now the old man was going from door to door at night, searching among strangers. He spoke quietly and courteously, but he shook and he was hatless. I had never before seen him without a hat. I knew that he was terrified, and I was shocked. I almost cried in front of him. My aunt reached out suddenly and touched his hand when she had to tell him that the boy wasn't there. He thanked her and turned away into the dark, and for the first time I guessed that they, too—the Johnnies, the Rebs, Bragg's men—could be frightened, need help, and grow old.

Of course, in war one's enemies are always ordinary men (I thought, smoothing the topsoil in the final window box, wondering where the earth had come from, out of whose meadow). That goes without saying. But though I have heard and read about Confederates and looked at pictures of them, thinking such ancient thoughts, the old man at the door is my real connection to the enemy. He always shows up and stands between me and it. My aunt telephoned a few neighbors after he had gone, and located what she called "that little fiend," and then she caught up with the old man, again by phone. He brought her the pot of violets the next day.

I do have other lines of continuity to the war, naturally—odd little zigzag ones that appear from time to time—but none of them ever takes me the whole way to it, which is what the reenacters want to do. Antietam has borrowed the snow of a winter weekend when I read about Piper's cornfield and Poffenberger's wood and the Dunker church, sitting beside the picture window of a friend's split-level in Connecticut. I visited Lincoln's house in Springfield once, and perhaps it linked me to him and the war, but I wouldn't swear that it didn't first take me to lilacs in Walt Whitman's dooryard, and even to the spring night when I read about them, in college. (The girl I was going with at the time, a neat blonde, may still not know she is part of the Civil War.) So I have to say that I am connected to the war by a chain of uneven, unlikely links, and that they are what I cherish about it. They *are* it.

One more thing. Edward's wishbone. It gives him his own link with that house and its rooms, but it must have meant something else to the person who hung it there: an occasion. Well, one is attached to an occasion by the things one can recall about it, the small things— the smell of lilacs or violets that may have attended it, the way an elderly relative talked, the songs an old friend sang—and any minor talismans one can save. So I guess I feel as if the reenacters are for all the world like Edward, except that what he does is his affair and what they do is mine. They are enameling my war, so to speak, my particular war, which they don't know anything about. They are keeping it green, all right, but they are trying to take it away with them, and I wish they would let it alone. I like it right in the house where it always was.

Lines of Inquiry

1 One idea tends to create another—an answer, as it were, to a question implicit in the first. Viewed in this way, writing of any kind—even narrative—is a kind of continuous dialogue of the writer with himself. What is prompted in any given person by an idea or an anecdote, however, depends not only on the idea or anecdote itself but also on the stock of values, attitudes, and experiences in the mind it encounters.

a This essay was written during the centennial of the Civil War. In what way might the essay be said to be a response to that centennial?

b What is the relevance of the opening paragraph, about razor blades, to the point of the essay? Is the comic incongruity here thematically destructive or useful? Could Henderson have used an old calendar (he mentions it as an alternative) in the way that he used a package of razor blades? *Why* razor blades?

c At first, the contents of this essay—the images and ideas generated in Henderson's mind by the centennial—seem very miscellaneous, and their sequence haphazard. How do you account for this apparently illogical and inconsequential structure?

d Choose three of your current or immediate past teachers. What responses would the centennial of the Civil War be likely to create in each of them, and why?

2 What function does each of the following details have in the structure of Henderson's essay?

a The dried eucalyptus in Edward's study

b The begonias in the market

c The mulberry tree in Henderson's aunt's front yard

d The potted violets

e The lilacs in Walt Whitman's dooryard

How do you account for these recurrent references to flowers? Why flowers in particular?

3 There are four extended anecdotes in this essay. The central figures are Edward, Mrs. Whitby, Henderson's grandfather, and the old Confederate captain, who appear in that order. How do you account for the order? What would happen to the tone of the essay if it began with the captain and ended with Miss Whitby? Are the anecdotes different in kind, or merely parallel and incremental?

4 Much of this essay's effect is the result of a careful choice of detail. Take the last of Henderson's anecdotes, the one concerning the old Confederate captain:

a What is the effect of the captain's "round white beard" on Henderson? On us?

b Why does the aunt call the missing boy "that little fiend"? What does her reaction tell us about the captain?

c Why is the captain not wearing his hat when we last see him?

d Why does Henderson, remembering the incident, pause to wonder where the earth in his windowbox comes from, "out of whose meadow"?

e What does Henderson mean when he says, "The old man at the door is my real connection with the enemy. He always shows up and stands between me and it"?

5 In a sense, Henderson is distinguishing between two kinds of narrative continuity; his illustrations are evidence of his point.

a How would you characterize these two kinds?

b How is the anecdote concerning Henderson's grandfather related to this distinction? Are the other anecdotes so closely related? What detail in this anecdote best makes the distinction between the two kinds of continuity?

c Why is Henderson making the distinction at all?   Which of the two kinds of continuity does he find the more valuable? What connection does his attitude here have to the tone he establishes in the essay?

6 What do the italic phrases in the following passages refer to, and what significance do they point to?

"On the other hand, everyone loved to shout the *battle cry of freedom* for her.   And when we rose in the assembly and *rallied round the flag,* we knew just what we were singing about.   We were singing about men who kept *tenting at night* on a little slope back of the school, which Miss Whitby had indicated mournfully as she sang about them.   We were singing about marching through the little woods beyond the slope, and charging across Miss Whitby's clover meadow, as she let us do, *bringing the jubilee.*   We were singing about *grapes of wrath* being trampled out on the floor of Miss Whitby's own barn, where, somehow, they were stored."

7 Here are five sentences, slightly revised; their originals follow in parentheses.   In each case, what has been lost between original and revision?

   a As a small boy, I often pretended to fight the Civil War. ("As a small boy, I fought in it every chance I got.")

   b Once in a while since childhood, I have run into someone who was also interested in the war and we have talked about it, much pleased with one another.   ("Once in a while, in the interval since, I have run into someone who also owned the war, and we have talked about it, regarding each other as rare and fine.")

   c Documentation is frequent, and many facsimiles have been published.   ("Documentation is on the loose.   Facsimiles are rampant.")

   d There was a slight wind as the cab went through Central Park.   ("The cab went around a shoulder of rock and along past a small wooded ridge where the wind was shaking the trees.")

   e It had been a local war, though also a national one.   "(It had been a war of wood lots, though also an affair of flags.")

Lines of Experiment

1 Henderson's structure is made up of four illustrative anecdotes grouped by his memory around a particular historical subject, the Civil War.   The meaning of that subject for the narrator is thus defined.   Choosing a subject of your own, use a similar technique, a piling up of illustrative anecdotes, to define its meaning for you. The subject may be highly specific (a race riot, a fire, a student demonstration, a book, a poem, a bird), highly general (patriotism, virtue, education, happiness), or even highly symbolic (Independence Day, Sunday, the Egyptian Room at the museum, the airport, the college union, 12:01 A.M. on January 1). The important thing is to choose illustrative anecdotes that develop your meaning, that move it along from one point to another. Give yourself a choice among anecdotes; think of more than you can use, and cast the ones that seem most significant into several alternate sequences before you write your final version. Do not be afraid to find out what you think by writing a draft: You can always cut it into segments, and through rearrangement, try the effect of different sequences. Almost all effective writing involves a good deal of trial and error.

2 Henderson clearly does not think much of the usual centennial history; it enamels his war for him and he would rather it did not. Every year is the centennial of something, usually of many things. Write a centennial essay of your own. (See E. O. Emerson, *A History of the Nineteenth Century, Year by Year*.) Do not forget that the past justifies itself in terms of the present; you must find an introduction that will account for your choice and a conclusion that will justify it in terms of your reader's concerns. (Who, by the way, is your reader?) If you do not care for centennials, try anniversaries.

3 Examined as we have examined it here, Henderson's essay seems worked out from the top down: first an idea, then a set of illustrative narratives, finally pen in hand. The process of writing is hardly ever precisely like this, however. Often, a writer will be disturbed by a vague feeling that something happening around him—the rain, the planting of begonias, the enameled wishbone—has a significance that he has not quite grasped, a relevance to something else he is thinking of; and his essay will spring from that vague impression—from the bottom up, so to speak.

Work at an essay from the bottom up. Let something you see, you remember, you read, prompt a chain of illustrative narrative. Follow that chain to an idea, thence to actual paragraphs and sentences. After you have finished with your first draft, check over what you have done. This kind of essay often requires more revision than one in which the writer is exactly certain from the beginning what it is he wants to say, how all

the stories add up.   Probably you will have to cut and transpose
in order to get exactly the effect you are after.   Not only the
general shape and sequence of your illustrative narratives will
be important here, but also and especially their concrete, specific, and vivid details.

VLADIMIR NABOKOV

 MY RUSSIAN
EDUCATION

1

I was eleven years old when my father decided that the tutoring I
had had, and was still having, at home, might be profitably supplemented by my attending Tenishev School.   This school, one of the
most remarkable in St. Petersburg, was a comparatively young institution of a much more progressive type than the ordinary *Gymnasium,* to
which general category it belonged.   Its course of study, consisting
of sixteen "semesters" (eight *Gymnasium* classes), would be roughly
equivalent in this country to the last six years of school plus the first
two years of college.   Upon my admittance, in January, 1911, I found
myself in the third "semester," or in the beginning of the eighth grade
according to the American system.

School was taught from the fifteenth of September to the twenty-fifth
of May, with a couple of interruptions: a two-week inter-semestral
gap—to make place, as it were, for the huge Christmas tree that
touched with its star the pale-green ceiling of our prettiest drawing
room—and a one-week Easter vacation, during which painted eggs
enlivened the breakfast table.   Since snow and frost lasted from
October well into April, no wonder the mean of my school memories
is definitely hiemal.

When Ivan the first (who vanished one day) or Ivan the second (who
was to see the time when I would send him forth on romantic errands)

came to wake me around 8 A.M., the outside world was still cowled in brown hyperborean gloom. The electric light in the bedroom had a sullen, harsh, jaundiced tinge that made my eyes smart. Invariably I was confronted by some chunk of unfinished homework. Mornings were botched, and such things as the lessons in boxing and fencing that a wonderful rubbery Frenchman, Monsieur Loustalot, used to give me had to be discontinued.

He still came, almost daily, however, to spar or fence with my father. After gulping down a cup of tepid cocoa in the dining room downstairs, I would dash, with my fur coat half on, through the green drawing room (where an odor of fir, hot wax and tangerines would linger long after Christmas had gone), toward the library, from which came a medley of stamping and scraping sounds. There I would find my father, a big, robust man, looking still bigger in his white training suit, thrusting and parrying, while his agile instructor added brisk exclamations (*"Battez!"*, *"Rompez!"*) to the click-clink of the foils.

Panting a little, my father would remove the convex fencing-mask from his perspiring pink face to kiss me good morning. The place combined pleasantly the scholarly and the athletic, the leather of books and the leather of boxing gloves. Fat armchairs stood along the book-lined walls. An elaborate "punching ball" affair purchased in England—four steel posts supporting the board from which the pear-shaped striking bag hung—gleamed at the end of the spacious room. The purpose of this apparatus, especially in connection with the machine-gun-like ra-ta-ta of its bag, was questioned and the butler's explanation of it reluctantly accepted as true, by some heavily armed street fighters who came in through the window in 1917. When the increasing savagery of Lenin's regime made it imperative for us to leave St. Petersburg, that library disintegrated, but queer little remnants of it kept cropping up abroad. Some twelve years later, in Berlin, I picked up from a bookstall one such waif, bearing my father's *ex libris*. Very fittingly, it turned out to be *The War of the Worlds* by Wells. And after another decade had elapsed, I discovered one day in the New York Public Library, indexed under my father's name, a copy of the neat catalogue he had had privately printed when the phantom books listed therein still stood, ruddy and sleek, on his shelves.

2

He would replace his mask and go on with his stamping and lunging while I hurried back the way I had come. After the warmth in the entrance hall, where logs were crackling in the large fire-place, the out-door air gave an icy shock to one's lungs. I would ascertain which of our two cars, the Benz or the Wolseley, was there to take me to school. The first, a mouse-grey landaulet, manned by a gentle, pale-faced chauffeur, was the older one.   Its lines had seemed positively dynamic in comparison with those of the insipid, noseless and noiseless, electric coupé that had preceded it; but, in its turn, it acquired an old-fashioned, topheavy look, with a sadly shrunken bonnet, as soon as the long, black English limousine came to share its garage.

To get the newer car was to start the day zestfully.   Pirogov, the second chauffeur, was a very short, pudgy fellow with a russet complexion that matched well the shade of the furs he wore over his corduroy suit and the orange-brown of his leggings.   When some hitch in the traffic forced him to apply the brakes (which he did by suddenly distending himself in a peculiar springy manner), or when I bothered him by trying to communicate with him through the squeaky and not very efficient speaking tube, the back of his thick neck seen through the glass partition would turn crimson.   He frankly preferred to drive the hardy con-vertible Opel we used in the country during three or four seasons, and would do so at sixty miles per hour: indeed, the very essence of summer freedom—schoolless untownishness—remains connected in my mind with the motor's extravagant roar that the opened muffler would release on the long, lone highway.   When in the second year of World War One Pirogov was mobilized, he was replaced by dark, wild-eyed Tsiganov, a former racing ace, who had participated in various contests both in Russia and abroad and had had several ribs broken in a bad smash in Belgium.   (Later, sometime in 1917, soon after my father resigned from Kerenski's cabinet, Tsiganov decided—notwithstanding my father's energetic protests—to save the powerful Wolseley car from possible confiscation by dismantling it and distributing its parts over hiding places known only to him.)

Although heavy snowfalls were much more usual in St. Petersburg than, say, around Boston, the several automobiles that circulated among the numerous sleighs of the town before World War One, somehow never seemed to get into the kind of hideous trouble that modern cars get into on a good New England white Christmas.   Many strange forces had been involved in the building of the city.   One is led to suppose that the arrangement of its snows—tidy drifts along the sidewalks and a smooth solid spread on the octangular wood blocks of the pavement—was arrived at by some unholy co-operation between the geometry of the streets and the physics of the snow clouds.   Anyway, driving to

school never took more than a quarter of an hour. Our house was
No. 47 in Morskaia Street. Then came Prince Oginski's (No. 45),
then the Italian Embassy (No. 43), then the German Embassy (No.
41), and then the vast Marie Square, after which the house numbers
continued to dwindle. There was a small public park on the left side
of the square. In one of its linden trees an ear and a finger had been
found one day—remnants of a terrorist whose hand had slipped while
he was arranging a lethal parcel in his room on the other side of the
square. Those same trees (a pattern of silver filigree in a mother-of-
pearl mist out of which the bronze dome of St. Isaac's arose in the
background) had also seen children shot down at random from the
branches into which they had climbed in a vain attempt to escape the
mounted gendarmes who were quelling the First Revolution (1905–06).
Quite a few little stories like these were attached to squares and streets
in St. Petersburg.

Upon reaching Nevski Avenue, one followed it for a long stretch,
during which it was a pleasure to overtake with no effort some cloaked
guardsman in his light sleigh drawn by a pair of black stallions snorting
and speeding along under the bright-blue netting that prevented lumps
of hard snow from flying into the passenger's face. A street on the
left side with a lovely name—Karavannaia [the Street of Caravans]—
took one past an unforgettable toyshop. Next came the Cinizelli Circus
(famous for its wrestling tournaments). Finally, after crossing an
ice-bound canal, one drove up to the gates of Tenishev School in
Mokhovaia Street [the Street of Mosses].

3

In becoming one of the leaders of the Constitutionalist Democratic
Party (later renamed "party of the People's Freedom"), my father
had contemptuously forfeited his court title. After refusing to drink the
Czar's health at a certain banquet, he had coolly advertised his court
uniform for sale in the newspapers. His speeches in the First Duma
[Parliament] and his articles in the periodicals of his party had won
him national fame. He was a learned jurist. Belonging, as he did by
choice to the great classless intelligentsia of Russia, he thought it right
to have me attend a school that was distinguished by its democratic
principles, its policy of nondiscrimination in matters of rank, race and
creed, and its up-to-date educational methods.

Apart from that, the Tenishev School differed in nothing from any
other school in time or space. As in all schools, the boys tolerated

some teachers and loathed others, and, as in all schools, there was a constant interchange of obscene quips and erotic information. Being good at games, I would not have found the whole business too dismal if only my teachers had been less intent in trying to save my soul.

They accused me of not conforming to my surroundings; of "showing off" (mainly by peppering my Russian papers with English and French terms, which came naturally to me); of refusing to touch the filthy wet towels in the washroom; of fighting with my knuckles instead of using the slaplike swing with the underside of the fist adopted by Russian scrappers. The headmaster who knew little about games, though greatly approving of their consociative virtues, was suspicious of my always keeping goal in soccer "instead of running about with the other players." Another thing that provoked resentment was my driving to and from school in an automobile and not traveling by street-car or horse-cab as the other boys, good little democrats, did. With his face all screwed up in a grimace of disgust, one teacher suggested to me that the least I could do was to have the automobile stop two or three blocks away, so that my schoolmates might be spared the sight of a liveried chauffeur doffing his cap. It was as if the school were allowing me to carry about a dead rat by the tail with the understanding that I would not dangle it under people's noses.

The worst situation, however, arose from the fact that even then I was intensely averse to joining movements or associations of any kind. I enraged the kindest and most well-meaning among my teachers by declining to participate in extra-curricular group work—debating societies with the solemn election of officers and the reading of reports on historical questions, and, in the higher grades, more ambitious gatherings for the discussion of current political events. The constant pressure upon me to belong to some group or other never broke my resistance but led to a state of tension that was hardly alleviated by everybody harping upon the example set by my father.

My father was, indeed, a very active man, but I viewed his activities through a prism of my own, which split into many enchanting colors the rather austere light my teachers glimpsed. In connection with his varied interests—criminological, legislative, political, editorial, philanthropic—he had to attend many committee meetings, and these were often held at our house. That such a meeting was forthcoming might be always deduced from a peculiar sound in the far end of our large and resonant entrance hall. There, in a recess under the marble staircase, our *shveitsar* [doorman] would be busy sharpening pencils when I came home from school. For that purpose he used a bulky old-fashioned machine, with a whirring wheel, the handle of which he rapidly rotated. For years he had been the tritest type of faithful old servant imaginable, full of wisdom and wit and quaint sayings; but that pencil-sharpening chore must have considerably embittered the poor fellow, for it later turned out that he had got into touch with the Czar's secret police—tyros, of course, in comparison to Dserzhinski's or Iagoda's men, but still fairly bothersome.

Around eight in the evening, the hall would house an accumulation of greatcoats and galoshes. In a committee room, next to the library, at a long baize-covered table (where those beautifully pointed pencils had been laid out), my father and his colleagues would gather to discuss some phase of their opposition to the Czar. Above the hubbub of voices, a tall clock in a dark corner would break into Westminster chimes; and beyond the committee room were mysterious depths—storerooms, a winding staircase, a pantry of sorts—where one night the Czar's police placed a fat, blear-eyed spy who went laboriously down on his knees when discovered. But how on earth could I discuss all this with schoolteachers?

4

The reactionary press never ceased to attack my father's party, and I had got quite used to the more or less vulgar cartoons which appeared from time to time—my father and Miliukov handing over Saint Russia on a plate to World Jewry and that sort of thing. But one day, in the winter of 1911 I believe, the most powerful of the Rightist newspapers employed a shady journalist to concoct a scurrilous piece containing insinuations that my father could not let pass. Since the well-known rascality of the actual author of the article made him "non-duelable" (*neduelesposobnyj,* as the Russian dueling code had it), my father called out—"called upon" is really the correct term—the somewhat less disreputable editor of the paper in which the article had appeared.

A Russian duel was a much more serious affair than the conventional Parisian variety. It took the editor several days to make up his mind whether or not to accept the challenge. On the last of these days, a Monday, I went, as usual, to school. In consequence of my not reading the newspapers, I was absolutely ignorant of the whole thing. Sometime during the day I became aware that a magazine opened at a certain page was passing from hand to hand and causing titters. A well-timed pounce put me in possession of what proved to be the latest copy of a cheap weekly containing a lurid account of my father's challenge, with idiotic comments on the choice of weapons he had offered his foe.   Sly digs were taken at his having reverted to a feudal custom that he had condemned in his own writings.   There was also a good deal about the number of his servants and the number of his suits.   I found out that he had chosen for second his brother-in-law, Admiral Kolomeitsev, a hero of the Japanese war.   During the battle of Tsushima, this uncle of mine, then holding the rank of captain, had managed to bring his destroyer alongside the burning flagship and save the naval commander-in-chief.

After classes, I ascertained that the magazine belonged to one of my best friends.   I charged him with betrayal and mockery.   In the ensuing fight, he crashed backward into a desk, catching his foot in a joint and breaking his ankle.   He was laid up for a month, but gallantly concealed from his family and from our teachers my share in the matter.

The pang of seeing him carried downstairs was lost in my general misery.   For some reason or other, no car came to fetch me that day, and during the cold, dreary, incredibly slow drive home in a hired sleigh I had ample time to think matters over.   Now I understood why, the day before, my mother had been so little with me and had not come down to dinner.   I also understood what special coaching Thernant, a still finer *maître d'armes* than Loustalot, had of late been giving my father.   What would his adversary choose, I kept asking myself—the blade or the bullet? Or had the choice already been made? Carefully, I took the beloved, the familiar, the richly alive image of my father at fencing and tried to transfer that image, minus the mask and the padding, to the dueling ground, in some barn or riding school. I visualized him and his adversary, both bare-chested, black-trousered, in furious battle, their energetic movements marked by that strange awkwardness which even the most elegant swordsmen cannot avoid in a real encounter.   The picture was so repulsive, so vividly did I feel the ripeness and nakedness of a madly pulsating heart about to be pierced, that I found myself hoping for what seemed momentarily a more abstract weapon.   But soon I was in even deeper distress.

As the sleigh crept along Nevski Avenue, where blurry lights swam in the gathering dusk, I thought of the heavy black Browning my father kept in the upper right-hand drawer of his desk.   I knew that pistol as well as I knew all the other, more salient, things in his study; the *objets d'art* of crystal or veined stone, fashionable in those days; the glinting family photographs; the huge, mellowly illumined Perugino; the small, honey-bright Dutch oils; and, right over the desk, the rose-and-haze pastel portrait of my mother by Bakst: the artist had drawn her face in three-quarter view, wonderfully bringing out its delicate features—the upward sweep of the ash-colored hair (it had greyed a dozen years before, when she was in her twenties), the pure curve of the forehead, the dove-blue eyes, the graceful line of the neck.

When I urged the old, rag-doll-like driver to go faster, he would merely lean to one side with a special half-circular movement of his arm, so as to make his horse believe he was about to produce the short whip he kept in the leg of his right felt boot; and that would be sufficient for the shaggy little hack to make as vague a show of speeding up as the driver had made of getting out his *knutishko*. In the almost hallucinatory state that our snow-muffled ride engendered, I refought all the famous duels a Russian boy knew so well. I saw Pushkin, mortally wounded at the first fire, grimly sit up to discharge his pistol at d'Anthès. I saw Lermontov smile as he faced Martynov. No Russian writer of any repute had failed to describe *une rencontre,* a hostile meeting, always of course of the classical *duel à volonté* type (not the ludicrous back-to-back-march-face-about-bangbang performance of movie and cartoon fame). Among several prominent families, there had been tragic deaths on the dueling ground in more or less recent years. Slowly my dreamy sleigh drove up Morskaia Street, and slowly dim silhouettes of duelists advanced upon each other and leveled their pistols and fired—at the crack of dawn, in damp glades of old country estates, on bleak military training grounds, or in the driving snow between two rows of fir trees.

And behind it all there was yet a very special emotional abyss that I was desperately trying to skirt, lest I burst into a tempest of tears, and this was the tender friendship underlying my respect for my father; the charm of our perfect accord; the bicycle rides we took together in summer; the Wimbledon matches we followed in the London papers; the butterflies we discussed; the chess problems we solved; the Pushkin iambics that rolled off his tongue so triumphantly whenever I mentioned some minor poet of the day; and, especially, that habitual exchange of homespun nonsense and private jokes which is the secret code of happy families.

At last I was home, and immediately upon entering the vestibule I became aware of loud, cheerful voices. With the patness of dream arrangements, my uncle the Admiral was coming downstairs. From the red-carpeted landing above, where a Greek statue presided over a malachite bowl for visiting cards, my parents were still speaking to him, and as he came down the steps, he looked up with a laugh and slapped the balustrade with the gloves he had in his hand. I knew at once that there would be no duel, that the challenge had been met by an apology, that all was right. I brushed past my uncle and reached the landing. I saw my mother's serene everyday face, but I could not look at my father. And then it happened: my heart welled in me like that wave on which the *Buiny* rose when her captain brought her alongside the burning *Suvorov,* and I had no handkerchief.

All this was a long time ago, and several years were to pass before a certain night in 1922, at a public lecture in Berlin, when my father shielded the lecturer (his old friend Miliukov) from the bullets of two Russian Fascists and, while vigorously knocking down one of the assassins, was fatally shot by the other. But no shadow was cast by that future event upon the bright stairs of our St. Petersburg house, and the large, cool hand resting on my head did not quaver, and several lines of play in a difficult chess composition were not blended yet on the board.

Lines of Inquiry

1 The title of this essay announces its subject as Nabokov's Russian education; the first sentence tells us the name of his school.

  a How much of the essay is devoted to his actual schooling— how much of his school life is really presented?

  b What is the time span of the essay?

  c What kinds of facts are given us about the Tenishev school? Do you see any pattern, any common denominator, as it were, in these facts? What do you conclude about Nabokov's reasons for writing about his school?

2 Much of the essay revolves about Nabokov's life at home.

  a Is Nabokov himself the center of that account? What relationship do you see between Nabokov's life at school and his life at home?

  b What is the central incident of the essay?

  c Why should there be a central incident at all in an essay on education?

3 What is the meaning of the title? And what does Nabokov learn?

4 The essay is divided into four sections.

  a How are those sections linked?

  b Nabokov writes of several topics in the essay. Go through the essay, one part at a time, and list the topics in the order in which they are composed. Now compare the list of topics within each part, one to another. What topics recur in all parts?

c Take "street war" as a theme or topic: Where, in each of the first three parts, does this topic appear? How do you account for its place in the sequence of each of these three parts?

d Now take the list of topics and re-sort them not by section but by topic: all the references to street war together, etc. Suppose a composition written from such an outline of topics —would the result be stronger, weaker, or simply different from the result obtained by Nabokov?

e Follow the references to fencing all the way through the essay. What do you discover about its development? How is this development related to the essay's handling of *time*— specifically, to the fact that Nabokov's account covers a certain span?

5 *a* What seems to be the purpose, in the second part, of the long description of the family automobiles, chauffeurs, etc.?

b Would a simple description of the neighborhood have served Nabokov as well as his description of the drive to the Tenishev school does? Imagine the essay with this part omitted; would anything be lost? (Consider the structure of the fourth part.)

6 Much of the success of this essay depends on Nabokov's use of small and apparently irrelevant details. What importance do you find in such details as the following?

a The Christmas tree and the Easter eggs

b The punching bag in the library

c The name of the book that Nabokov found, "very fittingly," in Berlin

d The identity of the three houses next to the Nabokovs'

e The toy shop in the Street of the Caravans

f The doorman's pencil sharpener

g The Russian word for "nonduelable"

h The portrait of Nabokov's mother, by Bakst

i Chess

j The battle of Tsushima

7 What does the last paragraph have to do with Nabokov's education? What happens, in this paragraph, to the natural sequence of time? Could this paragraph be omitted from the essay without loss to its description of Nabokov's education?

Lines of Experiment

1 Each person's education—using the word in Nabokov's sense
—is different; as a subject, the topic is perennial and important.
Write an essay on your own education. If you try to summarize your studies in school, kindergarten through twelfth
grade, you probably will write a very dull and mechanical
essay—you will be better off choosing a narrative focus, or
center, for the essential part of your education. This focus
may be on a single school subject, such as history—or, better,
on a part of that subject, such as the American Civil War; it
may be on an important incident in your own private world—
a birth, a death, a moment of failure or of success, an accident,
another person's triumph or despair; it may be on a place, or
an object—a building, a farm, a hot dog stand, a forgotten
diary, a school yearbook, a phonograph record; it may be on
something of a quite different order still. The essential thing
is that it offer you a *narrative* or *descriptive image* that can
summarize the really important part of your education. In
writing, be careful to present the details of your subject so that
the reader will sense its significance in your education. Do not
be afraid to throw details out of their natural sequence; the
order you are concerned with is the order of your education,
and only secondarily the order of time; and though you may
focus your composition on a single past event, all past events
are available as they are relevant. Do not worry unduly because your education is incomplete; it always will be.

2 Essentially, Nabokov's essay has two poles, or basic elements:
his school and his home; the one is used to set off the meaning
of the other. Write a personal narrative that employs the same
structural device. Note that, though Nabokov's school and
his home were different in many ways, they do not defeat each
other's meaning in this essay, because their points of contrast
illuminate one another. (What is the essential point of contrast between them?) Note also that these elements are not
equally treated: One is dominant, and the other really serves
as its foil. You must choose your own dominant narrative element first, and then choose its foil; and obviously, the central
incident must be within the dominant narrative.

3 In his revision of *Speak, Memory* (the book from whose
original version "My Russian Education" is taken) Nabokov
makes some substantial changes in this essay. Compare the
revised and the original versions carefully and minutely, with
special attention to (*a*) use of details, (*b*) narrative sequence,

(*c*) focus.   Write a brief essay enumerating and illustrating the
kinds of changes Nabokov made.   You will not be able to discuss all the changes; therefore, you must focus on the most
important and the most representative ones.   Your ultimate
interest, of course—an interest that should be reflected in your
conclusions—is in the significance of these changes.

E. M. FORSTER

 ## THE RETURN
FROM SIWA

Alexander the great founded Alexandria.   He came with Dinocrates,
his architect, and ordered him to build, between the sea and the lake,
a magnificent Greek town.   Alexander still conceived of civilization
as an extended Greece, and of himself as a Hellene.   He had taken
over Hellenism with the ardour that only a proselyte knows.   A Balkan
barbarian by birth, he had pushed himself into the enchanted but
enfeebled circle of little city states.   He had flattered Athens and
spared Thebes, and preached a crusade against Persia, which should
repeat upon a vaster scale the victories of Marathon and Salamis.   He
would even repeat the Trojan war.   At the Dardanelles his archæologi-
cal zeal was such that he ran naked round the tomb of Achilles.   He
cut the knot of Gordius.   He appeased the soul of Priam.

Having annexed Asia Minor, Syria, Palestine, and Egypt from the
Persians, and having given his orders to Dinocrates, he left the city
he was building, and rode with a few friends into the western desert.
It was summer.   The waters of Lake Mariout, more copious then than
now, spread fertility for a space.   Leaving their zone, he struck south,
over the limestone hills, and lost sight of civilization whether of the
Hellenic or non-Hellenic type.   Around him little flat pebbles shim-
mered and danced in the heat, gazelles stared, and pieces of sky slopped
into the sand.   Over him was the pale blue dome of heaven, darkened,
if we are to believe his historian, by flocks of obsequious birds, who

sheltered the King with their shadows and screamed when he rode the wrong way.   Alexander went on till he saw below him, in the fall of the ground, the canals and hot springs and olives and palms of the Oasis of Siwa.

Sekhet-Amit the Egyptians called it, and worshipped their god Amen there, whom the Greeks call Ammon, worshipped him in the form of an emerald that lay in a sacred boat, worshipped him as a ram also. Instead of the twin mud-cities of Siwa and Aghurmi, Alexander saw pylons and colonnades, and descending into the steamy heat of the Oasis approached a lonely and mysterious shrine.   For what was it mysterious?   Perhaps merely for its loneliness.   The distance, the solitude of the desert, touch travellers even to-day, and sharpen the imaginations of men who have crossed in armoured cars, and whom no god awaits, only a tract of green.   Alexander rode, remembering how, two hundred years before him, the Persians had ridden to loot the temple, and how on them as they were eating in the desert a sandstorm had descended, burying diners and dinner in company. Herein lay the magic of Siwa.   It was difficult to reach.   He, being the greatest man of his epoch, had of course succeeded.   He, the Philhellene, had come.   His age was twenty-five.   Then took place that celebrated and extraordinary episode.   According to the official account the Priest came out of the temple and saluted the young tourist as Son of God.   Alexander acquiesced and asked whether he would become King of this World.   The reply was in the affirmative. Then his friends asked whether they should worship him.   They were told that they should, and the episode closed.   Some say that it is to be explained by the Priest's bad Greek.   He meant to say Paidion ("my child") and said Paidios ("O Son of God") instead.   Others say that it never took place, and Walter Savage Landor has imagined a conversation in the course of which the Priest scares the King by a snake.   A scare he did get—a fright, a psychic experience, a vision, a "turn."   His development proves it.   After his return from Siwa his aspirations alter.   Never again does he regard Greece as the centre of the world.

The building of Alexandria proceeded, and copied or magnified forms from the perishing peninsula overseas.   Dinocrates planned Greek temples and market-places, and they were constructed not slavishly but with intelligence, for the Greek spirit still lived.   But it lived consciously, not unconsciously as in the past.   It had a mission, and no missionary shall ever create.   And Alexander, the heroic chaos of whose heart surged with desire for all that can and can not be, turned away from his Hellenic town-planning and his narrow little antiquarian crusade, and flung himself again, but in a new spirit, against the might of Persia.   He fought her as a lover now.   He wanted not to convert but to harmonize, and conceived himself as the divine and impartial ruler beneath whom harmony shall proceed.   That way lies madness. Persia fell.   Then it was the turn of India.   Then the turn of Rome would have come and then he could have sailed westward (such was his expressed intention) until he had conquered the Night and eastward until he had conquered the Day.   He was never—despite the tuition of Aristotle—a balanced young man, and his old friends complained that in this latter period he sometimes killed them.   But to us, who cannot have the perilous honour of his acquaintance, he grows more lovable now than before.   He had caught, by the unintellectual way, a glimpse of something great, if dangerous, and that glimpse came to him first in the recesses of the Siwan Oasis.   When at the age of thirty-three he died, when the expedition that he did not seek stole towards him in the summer-house at Babylon, did it seem to him as after all but the crown of his smaller quests? He had tried to lead Greece, then he had tried to lead mankind.   He had succeeded in both.   But was the universe also friendly, was it also in trouble, was it calling on him, on him, for his help and his love? The priest of Amen had addressed him as "Son of God."   What exactly did the compliment mean?   Was it explicable this side of the grave?

Lines of Inquiry

1 Forster's essay is a chapter in *Pharos and Pharallon,* a book centering on the history of Alexandria.   How does the city itself enter into the composition?   (Look at the opening sentences in the first, second, and fourth paragraphs.)

2 Obviously, the essay's real subject is a good deal larger than the actual founding of the city.
  a What is that larger subject?
  b How does the anecdote of Alexander's visit to Siwa function in relation to the real subject?
  c Why does Forster not begin with the ride to Siwa—leaving Alexandria out of it?
  d What focus is implied by the essay's title?
  e How do you explain the fact that though the ride *out* to Siwa is presented vividly, the ride *back* is not even hinted at —despite the title?

3 a What is the essential point of the first paragraph?

b How is that point reflected in the sequence of its sentences?

c How is it reflected in the use of the word "Greek"?

d Underline each occurrence of this word, or of its near-synonym "Hellene," in the essay. What seems to be its function—identification or emphasis? Where is it used the last time? How does the pattern of its use reflect the theme of the essay?

4 Whose point of view within the essay do we follow? How does that point of view account for the sequence of events? How does Forster use that point of view to furnish linkage between one element and another of that sequence? (Note how the temple of Siwa first becomes visible to us.)

5 *a* How would you describe Forster's attitude toward Alexander? Where do you find evidences of this attitude?

b A careful reader will note a change in Forster's tone between the first three paragraphs and the last. What is the evidence for this change? What does it mean?

6 Mark in the essay each time that Forster refers to the modern world.

a Are these references necessary? (Strike them out and see what happens to the essay.)

b Do they have anything in common?

c How do these references bear on the subject and theme of the essay?

7 Why does Forster conclude his essay in a series of questions? Stop the essay with "that glimpse came to him first in the recesses of the Siwan oasis"—what happens to the meaning of the essay?

8 Here are four brief excerpts from Forster's prose, each somewhat revised but with its essential informational content intact. The original of each excerpt is given in parentheses immediately afterward. What is the effect of each change? How is Forster's choice of words in each instance related to the point he is trying to make? If we can preserve the informational content of a sentence intact and yet lose its point, what is the nature of that point?

a Alexander the Great built Alexandria on the model of a magnificent Greek town. ("Alexander the Great founded Alexandria. He came with Dinocrates, his architect, and ordered him to build, between the sea and the lake, a magnificent Greek town.")

b The fascination of Siwa was that it was difficult to reach. Naturally, he reached it, when he was twenty-five. ("Herein lay the magic of Siwa. It was difficult to reach. He, being the greatest man of his epoch, had of course succeeded. He, the Philhellene, had come. His age was twenty-five.")

c Alexander, whose desires were limitless, left the planning of Alexandria and attacked Persia, but in a new spirit. ("And Alexander, the heroic chaos of whose heart surged with desire for all that can and can not be, turned away from his Hellenic town-planning and his narrow little antiquarian crusade and flung himself again, but in a new spirit, against the might of Persia.")

d When he died, in Babylon, he was thirty-three. ("When at the age of thirty-three he died, when the expedition that he did not seek stole toward him in the summer-house at Babylon, did it seem to him as after all but the crown of his smaller quests?")

Lines of Experiment

1 Forster's essay unites around a single episode at a single place a summary of Alexander's entire career as a conqueror and a judgment of its meaning. At first, many familiar events in history seem to have a parallel, condensed importance: Hannibal's crossing of the Alps, Caesar's passage of the Rubicon River, John Brown's attack on Harper's Ferry Arsenal, the shelling of Fort Sumter, the dropping of an atomic bomb on Hiroshima. The ride to Siwa is somewhat different from such events, however, in that in itself it is not especially dramatic (note Forster's handling of the actual dialogue at the temple). It represents not the *climax* of Alexander's career, its most emotionally powerful moment, but its *crisis* or turning point, the moment when the full meaning of that career is suddenly evident and fixed.

History is full of such moments as this also, but they are harder to find and to write about. Yet the decision to shell Fort Sumter is historically more important than the shelling itself; and the decision to drop the atomic bomb, not the bombing itself, is the turning point in modern warfare.

Essays that focus on the moment of crisis can be significant, powerful, and brief. Choose an historical series of events well known to you—one close to home—and look for its moment of crisis. An essay focused on this moment may seem simple, but you probably will have to do some serious thinking before you will be able to finish your composition (a first draft may help you, however, to see what you really have to find out before you can finish). *First,* you must identify the person (or persons) whose decision was fatal for that series of events. *Second,* you must find out why the decision took the shape that it did—and this will involve you, unavoidably, in finding out something about the history and character of the person (or persons) you have identified, if you do not know that history and character well. *Last,* you must judge the significance of the moment, against a larger perspective of ideas, in which it becomes of concern to us: you must view your historical subject as *illustrative.* (Thus Forster: "He had caught, by the unintellectual way, a glimpse of something great, if dangerous. . . .") If you wish to attempt a famous career—Napoleon's, Washington's, Lenin's—and shudder at the effort, bear in mind that *The Return from Siwa* is only three pages long.

2 List a brief, connected series of events fairly well known to you. (Examples: a basketball team's effort to win the championship; the closing of the corner candy store; a campaign for student body president; a love affair; the mental breakdown of a friend; a boy's estrangement from his parents.) Choose from the series one episode that seems to establish the significant shape of the final pattern—its crisis, in effect. Eliminate from your list all the elements that seem to have no relationship to the point of your central episode, and from the remainder single out the dramatic climax—the most poignant moment. Your essay probably will take the pattern of an introductory summary of events before the crucial episode (see Forster's first paragraph), a central description and narration of that episode, and a concluding, brief dramatic scene that can illustrate the central idea with maximum emotional force. Imagine several alternate arrangements of content and sequence before you begin to write, and choose the one that seems to capture best the significance of the whole and to transfer most fully to your probable reader your own feelings about it.

JOHN DOS PASSOS

 ART AND ISADORA

In San Francisco in eighteen seventyeight Mrs. Isadora O'Gorman Duncan, a highspirited lady with a taste for the piano, set about divorcing her husband, the prominent Mr. Duncan, whose behavior we are led to believe had been grossly indelicate; the whole thing made her so nervous that she declared to her children that she couldn't keep anything on her stomach but a little champagne and oysters; in the middle of the bitterness and recriminations of the family row,

into a world of gaslit boardinghouses kept by ruined southern belles and railroadmagnates and swinging doors and whiskery men nibbling cloves to hide the whiskey on their breaths and brass spittoons and fourwheel cabs and basques and bustles and long ruffled trailing skirts (in which lecturehall and concertroom, under the domination of ladies of culture, were the centers of aspiring life)

she bore a daughter whom she named after herself Isadora.

The break with Mr. Duncan and the discovery of his duplicity turned Mrs. Duncan into a bigoted feminist and an atheist, a passionate follower of Bob Ingersoll's lectures and writings; for God read Nature; for duty beauty, *and only man is vile.*

Mrs. Duncan had a hard struggle to raise her children in the love of beauty and the hatred of corsets and conventions and manmade laws. She gave pianolessons, she did embroidery and knitted scarves and mittens.

The Duncans were always in debt.

The rent was always due.

Isadora's earliest memories were of wheedling grocers and butchers and landlords and selling little things her mother had made from door to door,

helping hand valises out of back windows when they had to jump their bills at one shabbygenteel boardinghouse after another in the outskirts of Oakland and San Francisco.

The little Duncans and their mother were a clan; it was the Duncans against a rude and sordid world. The Duncans weren't Catholics any more or Presbyterians or Quakers or Baptists; they were Artists.

When the children were quite young they managed to stir up interest among their neighbors by giving theatrical performances in a barn; the older girl Elizabeth gave lessons in society dancing; they were westerners, the world was a goldrush; they weren't ashamed of being in the public eye. Isadora had green eyes and reddish hair and a beautiful neck and arms. She couldn't afford lessons in conventional dancing, so she made up dances of her own.

They moved to Chicago. Isadora got a job dancing to *The Washington Post* at the Masonic Temple Roof Garden for fifty a week. She danced at clubs. She went to see Augustin Daly and told him she'd discovered

the Dance

and went on in New York as a fairy in cheesecloth in a production of *Midsummer Night's Dream* with Ada Rehan.

The family followed her to New York. They rented a big room in Carnegie Hall, put mattresses in the corners, hung drapes on the wall and invented the first Greenwich Village studio.

They were never more than one jump ahead of the sheriff, they were always wheedling the tradespeople out of bills, standing the landlady up for the rent, coaxing handouts out of rich philistines.

Isadora arranged recitals with Ethelbert Nevin

danced to readings of Omar Khayyám for society women at Newport. When the Hotel Windsor burned they lost all their trunks and the very long bill they owed and sailed for London on a cattleboat

to escape the materialism of their native America.

In London at the British Museum

they discovered the Greeks;

the Dance was Greek.

Under the smoky chimneypots of London, in the sootcoated squares they danced in muslin tunics, they copied poses from Greek vases, went to lectures, artgalleries, concerts, plays, sopped up in a winter fifty years of Victorian culture.

Back to the Greeks.

Whenever they were put out of their lodgings for nonpayment of rent Isadora led them to the best hotel and engaged a suite and sent the waiters scurrying for lobster and champagne and fruits outofseason; nothing was too good for Artists, Duncans, Greeks;

and the nineties London liked her gall.

In Kensington and even in Mayfair she danced at parties in private houses,

the Britishers, Prince Edward down,

were carried away by her preraphaelite beauty

her lusty American innocence

her California accent.

After London, Paris during the great exposition of nineteen hundred. She danced with Loïe Fuller. She was still a virgin too shy to return the advances of Rodin the great master, completely baffled by the extraordinary behavior of Loïe Fuller's circle of crack-brained invert beauties. The Duncans were vegetarians, suspicious of vulgarity and men and materialism. Raymond made them all sandals.

Isadora and her mother and her brother Raymond went about Europe in sandals and fillets and Greek tunics.

staying at the best hotels leading the Greek life of nature in a flutter of unpaid bills.

Isadora's first solo recital was at a theater in Budapest;

after that she was the diva, had a loveaffair with a leading actor; in Munich the students took the horses out of her carriage. Everything was flowers and handclapping and champagne suppers. In Berlin she was the rage.

With the money she made on her German tour she took the Duncans

all to Greece.   They arrived on a fishingboat from Ithaca.   They posed
in the Parthenon for photographs and danced in the Theater of Dionysus
and trained a crowd of urchins to sing the ancient chorus from the
Suppliants and built a temple to live in on a hill overlooking the ruins
of ancient Athens, but there was no water on the hill and their money
ran out before the temple was finished.

so they had to stay at the Hôtel d'Angleterre and run up a bill there.
When credit gave out they took their chorus back to Berlin and put
on the *Suppliants* in ancient Greek.   Meeting Isadora in her peplum
marching through the Tiergarten at the head of her Greek boys marching in order all in Greek tunics, the kaiserin's horse shied,

and her highness was thrown.

Isadora was the vogue.

She arrived in St. Petersburg in time to see the night funeral of the
marchers shot down in front of the Winter Palace in 1905.   It hurt
her.   She was an American like Walt Whitman; the murdering rulers
of the world were not her people; the marchers were her people; artists
were not on the side of the machineguns; she was an American in a
Greek tunic; she was for the people.

In St. Petersburg, still under the spell of the eighteenthcentury ballet
of the court of the Sunking,

her dancing was considered dangerous by the authorities.

In Germany she founded a school with the help of her sister Elizabeth
who did the organizing, and she had a baby by Gordon Craig.

She went to America in triumph as she'd always planned and harried
the home philistines with a tour; her followers were all the time getting
pinched for wearing Greek tunics; she found no freedom for Art in
America.

Back in Paris it was the top of the world; Art meant Isadora.   At the
funeral of the Prince de Polignac she met the mythical millionaire
(sewingmachine king) who was to be her backer and to finance her
school.   She went off with him in his yacht (whatever Isadora did was
Art)

to dance in the Temple at Paestum

only for him,

but it rained and the musicians all got drenched.   So they all got drunk instead.

Art was the millionaire life.   Art was whatever Isadora did.   She was carrying the millionaire's child to the great scandal of the oldlady club-women and spinster artlovers when she danced on her second American tour;

she took to drinking too much and stepping to the footlights and bawling out the boxholders.

Isadora was at the height of glory and scandal and power and wealth, her school going, her millionaire was about to build her a theater in Paris, the Duncans were the priests of a cult, (Art was whatever Isadora did),

when the car that was bringing her two children home from the other side of Paris stalled on a bridge across the Seine.   Forgetting that he'd left the car in gear the chauffeur got out to crank the motor.   The car started, knocked down the chauffeur, plunged off the bridge into the Seine.

The children and their nurse were drowned.

The rest of her life moved desperately on

in the clatter of scandalized tongues, among the kidding faces of re-porters, the threatening of bailiffs, the expostulations of hotelmanagers bringing overdue bills.

Isadora drank too much, she couldn't keep her hands off goodlooking young men, she dyed her hair various shades of brightred, she never took the trouble to make up her face properly, was careless about her dress, couldn't bother to keep her figure in shape, never could keep track of her money

but a great sense of health

filled the hall

when the pearshaped figure with the beautiful great arms tramped forward slowly from the back of the stage.

She was afraid of nothing; she was a great dancer.

In her own city of San Francisco the politicians wouldn't let her dance in the Greek Theater they'd built under her influence.   Wherever she went she gave offense to the philistines.   When the war broke out she danced the *Marseillaise,* but it didn't seem quite respectable and she gave offense by refusing to give up Wagner or to show the proper respectable feelings

of satisfaction at the butchery.

On her South American tour

she picked up men everywhere,

a Spanish painter, a couple of prizefighters, a stoker on the boat, a Brazilian poet,

brawled in tangohalls, bawled out the Argentines for niggers from the footlights, lushly triumphed in Montevideo and Brazil; but if she had money she couldn't help scandalously spending it on tangodancers, handouts, afterthetheater suppers, the generous gesture, no, all on my bill. The managers gypped her. She was afraid of nothing, never ashamed in the public eye of the clatter of scandalized tongues, the headlines in the afternoon papers.

When October split the husk off the old world she remembered St. Petersburg, the coffins lurching through the silent streets, the white faces, the clenched fists that night in St. Petersburg, and danced the *Marche Slave*

and waved red cheesecloth under the noses of the Boston old ladies in Symphony Hall,

but when she went to Russia full of hope of a school and work and a new life in freedom, it was too enormous, it was too difficult: cold, vodka, lice, no service in the hotels, new and old still piled pellmell together, seedbed and scrapheap, she hadn't the patience, her life had been too easy;

she picked up a yellowhaired poet

and brought him back

to Europe and the grand hotels.

Yessenin smashed up a whole floor of the Adlon in Berlin in one drunken party, he ruined a suite at the Continental in Paris. When he went back to Russia he killed himself. It was too enormous, it was too difficult.

When it was impossible to raise any more money for Art, for the crowds eating and drinking in the hotel suites and the rent of Rolls-Royces and the board of her pupils and disciples,

Isadora went down to the Riviera to write her memoirs to scrape up some cash out of the American public that had awakened after the war to the crassness of materialism and the Greeks and scandal and Art, and still had dollars to spend.

She hired a studio in Nice, but she could never pay the rent.   She'd quarreled with her millionaire.   Her jewels, the famous emerald, the ermine cloak, the works of art presented by the artists had all gone into the pawnshops or been seized by hotelkeepers.   All she had was the old blue drapes that had seen her great triumphs, a redleather handbag, and an old furcoat that was split down the back.

She couldn't stop drinking or putting her arms round the neck of the nearest young man, if she got any cash she threw a party or gave it away.

She tried to drown herself but an English naval officer pulled her out of the moonlit Mediterranean.

One day at a little restaurant at Golfe Juan she picked up a goodlooking young wop who kept a garage and drove a little Bugatti racer.

Saying that she might want to buy the car, she made him go to her studio to take her out for a ride;

her friends didn't want her to go, said he was nothing but a mechanic, she insisted, she'd had a few drinks (there was nothing left she cared for in the world but a few drinks and a goodlooking young man);

she got in beside him and

she threw her heavilyfringed scarf round her neck with a big sweep she had and

turned back and said,

with the strong California accent her French never lost:

Adieu, mes amis, je vais à la gloire.

The mechanic put his car in gear and started.

The heavy trailing scarf caught in a wheel, wound tight.   Her head was wrenched against the side of the car.   The car stopped instantly; her neck was broken, her nose crushed, Isadora was dead.

Lines of Inquiry

1 This brief biographical essay is broken into unnumbered sections.

    a What technique does Dos Passos use to distinguish sections from paragraphs?

    b Examine the first sentences of each section; what linking device does Dos Passos use?

    c Read the linking phrases only, one after another; what is their effect? Do you see any line of development among them?

2 Underline the words "dance" and "dancing" whenever they appear in the essay.

    a In which section do they appear most frequently? On the average, how many times per section do they appear? Which sections leave them out?

    b Would Dos Passos have done better or worse by using synonyms—"Isadora performed," or "Isadora appeared," etc.?

    c Can you connect your answers to *a* and *b* to Dos Passos's development of his subject?

    d Trace through the essay the words "art," "materialism," "scandal," "the Greeks." What purpose seems to lie behind the pattern in which these words are used?

    e Might one infer from these repetitions a useful principle of composition?

3 How would you group the sections themselves so as to reflect the underlying dramatic movement of this biography?

    a Where does the crisis of Isadora's life occur?

    b Read the sections on either side of the crisis: What significance do you see in Dos Passos's handling of events at this point? In his handling of prose?

    c Reread the first two sections. Could Dos Passos have begun with the third section, slightly altered?

    d Now read the last two sections. Is there any relationship between introduction and conclusion?

4 Look at the first and second sentences of the essay.

    a Where does the first sentence end? Why does it end there? Is there anything odd about the word order of its concluding phrase?

    b Consider the second sentence in the same way. Does this highly irregular sentence structure serve any purpose? Rephrase these two sentences in standard English syntax; what, if anything, do they lose?

    c Do you see any general distinction between the kind of information conveyed by the highly irregular sentence forms and the kind conveyed by the more or less standard ones?

    d With this in mind, look at the sentence construction of the last section. Where does the emphasis fall? Why?

5 Dos Passos begins with the divorce of Isadora's parents.

    a Would the effect be the same if he had begun with their marriage? Or with Isadora's birth? What is Dos Passos's point in beginning where he does?

    b Mark the stages of his shift of narrative focus from Isadora's mother to Isadora herself. What happens to Isadora's mother thereafter?

6 Look through the essay for echoes of the title phrase.

    a Where do you find them, and why there?

    b What seems to be Dos Passos's attitude toward (*1*) Isadora, and (*2*) art?

    c Why does he spend so much time on the St. Petersburg massacre and so little on Isadora's relationship to Gordon Craig?

    d What seems to be the function of Dos Passos's references to Prince Edward, the Prince de Polignac, the kaiserin, the Winter Palace, etc.?

    e Why does he tell us that Yessenin smashed up a suite at the Adlon, another at the Continental, and then killed himself after his return to Russia—what has this to do with "Art and Isadora"?

7 In the following sentences, specific words or phrases are italicized. All the italicized passages could have been omitted; they add no essential facts to the historical record. Why did Dos Passos use them?

    a ". . . the whole thing made her so nervous that she declared to her children that she couldn't keep anything on her stomach *but a little champagne and oysters.* . . ."

    b "and went on in New York as a fairy *in cheesecloth* in a production of Midsummer Night's Dream with Ada Rehan."

    c "At the funeral of the Prince de Polignac she met the *mythical* millionaire (sewingmachine king) who was to be her backer. . . ."

    d "but a great sense of health
filled the hall
when *the pearshaped figure with the beautiful great arms tramped forward slowly from the back of the stage.*"

    e "She tried to drown herself but an English naval officer pulled her out of the *moonlit* Mediterranean."

    f "One day at a little restaurant at Golfe Juan she picked up a goodlooking young *wop* who kept a garage. . . ."

g "The car stopped instantly; her neck was broken, *her nose crushed,* Isadora was dead."

Lines of Experiment

1 A biography is not the entire record of a life—such a record is impossible—but the record of its significance from the author's point of view. To write a very brief biography, like "Art and Isadora," requires the ruthless elimination of thousands of details in the life of the subject; the writer's conception of the meaning of that life must be clear and steady enough to make possible a bold surgical hand with mere fact. Because Dos Passos has a firm conception, he can record Isadora's life in simple outlines. But in part he succeeds because Isadora's life had a marked pattern—because Isadora had already defined herself, in a sense, and deliberately gave to her life a dramatic shape.

Take someone you know a good deal about—relative, friend, ancestor; doctor, surfer, soldier—whose life also appears in a striking dramatic contour, and cast that life into a brief biography. The questions you will have to answer are all interrelated; for some of them you will not find the answers except by writing a first draft. The life you have chosen will seem dramatic exactly because it is meaningful, because it expresses in a narrative image an important cluster of ideas and emotions. What is that meaning? (You probably will be unable to *say* exactly what that meaning is, for it may well be too complex to be expressed except in the narrative image itself.) Looked at in this way, what incidents are central, what incidents are peripheral? What parts of the actual life can be omitted from your composition—or, better, what parts *must* be included? Where does the crisis occur? What is the dramatic climax? At what point does the significant pattern begin? When does it end? What moves it from one stage to another?

Such a biography is in effect a series of vignettes. Distance from the subject is tremendously valuable in preserving the clarity of its outline. As an aid in keeping sufficiently distant from the person you have chosen as your subject, you may wish to submerge entirely his relationship to you, and even to change his name. The moment you start discussing yourself, you will be partly engaged in *autobiography.*

2 Choose as your subject a well-known and fairly recent historical figure whose career is over, and write his biography in brief. Look deliberately for one whose life falls into a strong dramatic (but not necessarily violent) pattern, e.g., Winston Churchill, Harry S. Truman, Douglas MacArthur, John F. Kennedy, Malcolm X, Marilyn Monroe. *These familiar names are given only as examples;* probably you will be better off choosing a subject whose life falls in a less general sector of activity, one well known to you—space exploration, for instance, or baseball, or singing, or music. "Art and Isadora" is less than 2,000 words long. Your essay probably will not be so detailed. Aim for 1,000 words.

ALEXANDER H. LEIGHTON

 ## HIROSHIMA AFTERMATH

I

We approached Hiroshima a little after daybreak on a winter day, driving in a jeep below a leaden sky and in the face of a cold wet wind. On either side of the road black flat fields were turning green under winter wheat. Here and there peasants worked, swinging spades or grubbing in mud and water with blue hands. To the north, looming close over the level land, mountains thrust heavy summits of pine darkly against the overcast. To the south and far away, the bay lay in dull brightness under fitful rain.

"Hiroshima," said the driver, a GI from a Kansas farm who had been through the city many times, "don't look no different from any other bombed town. You soon get used to it. You'll see little old mud walls right in the middle of the town that wasn't knocked down. They been exaggerating about this bomb."

Within a few miles the fields along the road were replaced by houses and shops that looked worn and dull, but intact. On the road itself people straggled to work, some on bicycles, most of them on foot; tattered and bandy-legged old men, girls with red cheeks and bright eyes, ancient women under towering bundles, middle-aged men looking stiff in Western business suits.   At a bus stop a crowd stood waiting in a line almost long enough to fill a train.   Half a mile farther on we passed the bus, small, battered and gray, standing obliterated by the cloud of smoke that came from the charcoal burner at the back, while the driver stood working at its machinery.

Children of all ages waved, laughed and shouted at us as had children in other parts of Japan.

"Hallo-goodabye! Hallo-goodabye!" "Jeepu! Jeeeepu!"

Like the children of Hamelin to the piper, they came rushing at the sound of our approach from doorways and alleyways and from behind houses to line up by the road and cheer.   One fellow of about six threw himself into the air, his little body twisting and feet kicking in a fit of glee.

The adults gazed at us with solemn eyes or looked straight ahead.

Presently a two-story trade school appeared, with boards instead of window glass, and then a factory in the same condition.   Soon there were shops and houses all along the way with windows missing.   A house came into view with its roof pressed down, tiles scattered and walls bulged outward.   A shop with no front, like an open mouth, showed its contents public and private clear to the rear window.

The road turned to the Ota River where the tide was running out and boats lay heaved over on the beach.   The air came still cooler from the water and with it a damp, dirty smell of shore.   Down stream figures small in the distance dug for shellfish and were reflected in pools.   A bridge started out and stopped suddenly like a headless neck.

Now every house and shop was damaged and lay with only one end or a corner standing—a disorderly herd of animals with backs broken struggling to rise.

Then all the buildings ended and we came as if from a forest out on to a plain, as if from tumult into silence.

Imagine a city dump with its smells of wet ashes, mold and things rotting, but one that runs from your feet out almost to the limits of vision. As is often the case with level and desolate places on the earth, the sky seemed close above it.   The predominant colors were red and yellow, crumbles of stone, bricks, red earth and rust.   Low walls made rectangles that marked where houses had been, like sites of prehistoric villages.   Here and there in the middle distance, a few large buildings stood about, buttes in the rubble of the plain.

"You see them?" said the driver, as if it were a triumph for his side. "The bomb didn't knock them down."

Running like ruler lines through the waste were black roads surprisingly dotted with people, some on foot and some in carts of all sizes, drawn by man, woman, horse or cow.   Clothing was old and tattered, suitable for the denizens of a dump, and of every combination from full European to full Japanese.   People looked as if they had grabbed what they could from a rummage sale to cover their bodies.

We slowed down to go around a piece of cornice that lay partly across the road like a glacial boulder and from somewhere in a band of children came the gift of a tangerine that landed on the floor of the jeep. Wondering at them, I picked it up and put it in my pocket.

When crossing a bridge we could see down through the swiftly running water to the stones and shells on the bottom.   Their clearness gave an odd contrast to the disorder of the land.

We passed a number of trees turned black, but still holding up leafless branches in perpetual winter.

The drive ended at one of the large buildings that was still standing, a former bank, now a police headquarters, where I had an appointment with the chief, to arrange for office space and other necessities.

The driver said, as he got out, "This is it."

II

The bank building which housed the police headquarters was a well-made structure of stone, three stories high.   Through an imposing entrance my interpreter and I went past tall and solid metal doors that were bent inward like cardboard and no longer usable.   The lobby was large and high, but dark, because it had no window glass and the openings were boarded to keep out the wind.   Through poor light there loomed the white face of a clock up on one wall, its hands pointing to 8:10, the time it had stopped on August 6.

Behind the counters were the tables and desks where the police officers and clerks worked.   At the time we entered, they were in two groups, each around a charcoal brazier, talking together in low voices, their hands held out to the coals.

The chief ushered us into his office, a small square room with a green baize cover on a table and a window in which the pane had been replaced. On the wall was a notice board that had been cut by fragments of glass, some of which were still sticking in it like small daggers.

The police chief was a small man, lean, with a little mustache and gold on his teeth. His hair was gray and his face long. Tea was served as we talked, but though he spoke pleasantly, it was to the point and he did not seem interested in general conversation.

Our business over, I asked to have a look from the roof and was conducted to a parapet from where we could search Hiroshima from all sides.

From warm tea we came back to silence, cold, and the stretches of destruction. Real silence, as Thomas Hood has said, is not under the ocean nor in the uninhabited deserts, but among the ruins where men have been. From the height more miles of rubble were visible than could be seen lower down, and the people on the roads were stragglers who gave scale to the emptiness. The city seemed to have been stripped naked of everything but its cemeteries which stood out in small granite clumps of orderly stones, gray and narrow like teeth in a comb, the hard remaining bones of the city after the flesh had dissolved.

As I looked, I felt angry at the police chief, his men, and even the people I could see walking down below. I felt an impulse to agree with the jeep driver's words, "They been exaggerating about this bomb." Somebody was making too much of all this. That is the way it must be—

Then there came, like a huge round fish swimming out of vague green into sharp focus, the image of the white-faced clock in the gloom with its hands at 8:10. In the years when that clock had been going, Hiroshima had been a city, at first unknown to Europe and America, then a friendly source of emigrants to the United States, and finally an enemy port. It lay on a delta between the mouths of the Ota and was traversed by canals and an ancient highway that connected Kyoto in the east with Shimonoseki in the west. Close around the city stood mountains covered with red pine, while before it stretched the bay, indented with headlands and spread with islands, in places narrow and deep like a fjord. In shallows near shore rows of poles stood as if in a bean patch, set in the sea to anchor oysters and to catch edible seaweed passing in the tide. In deeper water fishing boats with hawkish prows and planked with red pine tended nets. A few fishermen used cormorants to make their catch.

Since Hiroshima had been a chief source of emigrants to California and there had been much traveling back and forth of relatives, the influence of the United States was marked. On main streets there were movies and restaurants with façades that would have fitted into shopping districts of Bakersfield or San Diego.

But Hiroshima was also ancient. Its feudal castle raised a five-story keep that could be seen a long distance over the level land of the delta. There were three large temples and many smaller ones and the tombs of the Asano family and of the wife and son of the leader of the Forty-Seven Ronin, Oishi Yoshio. There were also Christian churches whose bells mingled with the temple gongs and the honking of auto horns and the rattling of trolleys.

The people of the city made their living by buying and selling farm produce and fish, by making mountain pines into boats for the fishing fleet of the Inland Sea, by meat packing, rubber processing and oil refining, by making textiles from the cocoons of wild silkworms, by brewing rice and grape wine, by manufacturing paper umbrellas, needles, *tabi* socks, small arms, metal castings, and by utilities and services such as electricity, transportation, schools and hospitals.

During the war there was an increase of industrialization, and plants grew up, chiefly on the outskirts.

There was a famous gay district with little streets along which a person walking in the night could hear laughter and the twang of the *samisen* and geishas singing.

Although not a fortified town Hiroshima was a major military command station, supply depot and staging area because of its protected position and because of Ujina Harbor with access to the Pacific, the Sea of Japan and the China Sea. More than a third of the city's land was taken up with military installations and from the harbor troopships left for Korea, Manchuria, China and the southern regions.

However, toward the end of hostilities, most of the shipping had ceased because of sinkings in the Inland Sea.

The population of Hiroshima was given as over 340,000 before the war, but this was reduced by evacuation prior to the atomic bomb, probably to about 250,000.

A movement on the part of the police officer at the parapet broke the reverie and brought me back to Hiroshima of the present and the view from the roof of the bank.

It is not really certain how many the bomb killed, but it was probably between 70,000 and 80,000.

III

In the two weeks of our stay we made our headquarters on the third floor of the bank.   Using random selection, some members of the team gathered in a small sample of the population from the ruins of the city, from the damaged suburbs and from untouched outlying towns and villages in mountain valleys and even from an island down the bay. Other members sat all day long interviewing these men and women— shopkeepers, factory workers, laborers, housewives, cooks, teachers, farmers, fishermen and many more.   Some of the respondents were frightened and wordless and others were overtalkative, but for the most part they were quiet and willing.

In addition to the work with the selected sample, there were interviews with the police chief, the officials in the city hall, the mayors of near-by towns and with the governor of the prefecture and his assistants.   Members of the team struck up conversations with people on bridges, by way-side stalls where cuttlefish were sold, or in the shacks amid the debris. One member of the team developed a friendship with a newspaperman and I spent many hours talking informally with a doctor.

Bit by bit the things we learned fitted together to make a picture of how the atomic bomb had seemed to the people of Hiroshima.   Some of the details did not emerge until the total results were in and the findings of other investigators were analyzed and compared.   The result has been reported elsewhere together with figures and technical details.[1]   A general descriptive picture will be given here.

[1] (1) *The Effects of Atomic Bombs on Hiroshima and Nagasaki:* The U.S. Strategic Bombing Survey, 30 June 1946, Government Printing Office, Washington, D.C.
(2) *Summary Report (Pacific War):* U.S. Strategic Bombing Survey, 1 July 1946, Government Printing Office, Washington, D.C.
(3) *The Effects of Strategic Bombing on Japanese Morale:* June 1947. Government Printing Office, Washington, D.C. [Author's note.]

IV

The morning of August 6, 1945, was warm with fleeting clouds—not different from a thousand other summer mornings that had come and gone without incident, the kind of weather that gives confidence in the even tenor of unfolding time.   People stirred themselves to get breakfasts, soldiers moved in the barracks and walked across the drill grounds, children prepared for school, housewives pushed back sliding doors to air their homes.

About seven o'clock there was an air-raid warning and three planes were reported in the vicinity.   No one was much disturbed.   For a long time B-29's flying over in small numbers had been a common sight.

By eight o'clock, the all clear was sounded and people were thinking again of the day's plans, looking forward to their affairs and engagements of the morning and afternoon.   The castle keep stood in the sun.   Children bathed in the river.   Farmers labored in the fields and fishermen on the water.   City stores and factories got under way with their businesses.   In a mountain town, before its hall, the mayor and his staff were making their regular morning bows to the Emperor.

In the heart of the city near the buildings of the prefectural government and at the intersection of the busiest streets, almost everybody had stopped and stood in a crowd gazing up at "three parachutes" floating down through the blue air.

The bomb exploded several hundred feet above their heads.

"I heaved a sigh of relief," the weaponeer of the plane is reported to have said, "because I knew the bomb was a success.   A few fires were visible around the edges of the smoke, but we could see nothing of the city except the dock area where buildings were falling down."

The people around Hiroshima in the fields, in the mountains and on the bay saw a light, brilliant even in the sun, and felt heat.

A small-town official was crossing a bridge on his bicycle about ten miles from the heart of the city when he felt the right side of his face seared and, thinking that he had sunstroke, he jumped to the ground.

A woman who was washing dishes noticed that she felt "very warm on the side of my face next the wall.   I looked out the window toward the city and saw something like a sun in bright color."

At a slower pace after the flash came the sound of the explosion, which some people have no recollection of hearing, while others described it as an earth-shaking roar, like thunder or a big wind.

A black smoky mass, lit up with color, ascended into the sky and impressed beholders with its beauty.   Red, gold, blue, orange and many other shades mingled with the black.   One man, who looked on from the mountains, thought it like a globe of the world spinning.   Nearer to the city almost everyone thought that an ordinary bomb had landed very close to him, and only realized the extent of the damage later.

A man who was oiling the machinery in a factory saw the lights go out and thought that something must be wrong with the electricity.   "But when the roof started crumbling down, I was in a daze, wondering what was happening.   Then I noticed my hands and feet were bleeding."

Another who was putting points on needles was knocked unconscious and when he came to, found "all my surroundings burned to the ground and flames raging here and there.   I ran home for my family without knowing I was burned around my head.   When I arrived home, our house was devastated and destroyed by flames.   I ran to the neighbors and inquired about my family and learned that they had all been taken to safety across the river."

An invalid who was drinking tea said, "The iron roof sidings came swirling into my room and everything was black.   Rubble and glass and everything you can think of was blasted into my house."

A businessman in his office figuring on his advice slip had the roof come down on his head and a body was blown into the next room.

Said a woman, "I was in the back of the house doing the washing.   All of a sudden, the bomb exploded.   My clothes were burned off and I received burns on my legs, arms and back.   The skin was just hanging loose.   The first thing I did was run into the air-raid shelter and lie there exhausted.   Then I thought of my baby in the house and ran back to it.   The whole house was knocked down and was burning.   My mother and father came crawling out of the debris, their faces and arms just black.   I heard the baby crying, and crawled in and dug it out from under the burning embers.   It was pretty badly burned.   My mother carried it back to the shelter."

It was in the heart of the city that death prevailed and few who were there are left to tell us about it.   In part the picture has to be reconstructed, as in archeology, from the remains.

The crowd that stood gazing upward at the "parachutes," went down withered and black, like a burned-out patch of weeds.   Flames shot out of the castle keep. Trolleys bulging with passengers stopped, and all died at once leaving burned figures still standing, supporting each other, and "fingers fused to the straps." The military at their barracks and offices were wiped out. So, too, were factories full of workers, including students from schools, volunteers from neighboring towns working on the firebreaks, children scavenging for wood, the mayor's staff, the units for air-raid precaution, fire, welfare and relief. The large war industries, since they were on the fringe of the city, were for the most part not seriously damaged. Most of the personnel in the prefectural government offices were killed, though the governor himself happened to be in Tokyo. In hospitals and clinics, patients, doctors and nurses all died together, as did the priests and pastors of the temples and the churches. Of 1,780 nurses, 1,654 were killed, and 90 per cent of the doctors were casualties.

People who were in buildings that sheltered them from the instantaneous effects that accompanied the flash were moments later decapitated or cut to ribbons by flying glass. Others were crushed as walls and floors gave way even in buildings that maintained their outer shells erect.

In the thousands of houses that fell, people were pinned below the wreckage, not killed in many cases, but held there till the fire that swept the city caught up with them and put an end to their screams.

The police chief said that he was in his back yard near a chicken coop when the bomb went off. He was knocked down and a concrete wall fell over him, but he was able to extricate himself and go at once toward the police station in the bank. "Houses were all caved in by the road as I went along. Many people were pinned under them, wounded. The sight was pitiful. Many people were running toward safety. When I arrived at the office, I found ten policemen; some were severely wounded. These were evacuated to a place of safety where they could get aid. We tried to clean up the glass from the windows, but fire was spreading and a hot southerly wind was blowing. We used a hose with water from a hydrant and also formed a bucket brigade.

"About 1 P.M. we began to apply first aid to the people outside, since the fire seemed under control as far as this building was concerned. A doctor came to help. He himself was wounded in one leg. By night this place was covered by a mass of people. One doctor applied all the first aid."

Another doctor who was at a military hospital outside Hiroshima said that about an hour after the bomb went off, "many, many people came rushing to my clinic. They were rushing in all directions of the compass from the city. Many were stretcher cases. Some had their hair burned off, were injured in the back, had broken legs, arms and thighs. The majority of the cases were those injured from glass, many had glass imbedded in the body. Next to the glass injuries, the most frequent were those who had their faces and hands burned, and also the chest and back. Most of the people arrived barefooted, many had their clothes burned off. Women were wearing men's clothes and men were wearing women's. They had put on anything they could pick up along the way.

"On the first day about two hundred and fifty came who were so injured they had to stay in the hospital and we also attended about five hundred others. Of all of these about one hundred died."

A talkative man in a newspaper office said that the most severely burned people looked like red shrimps. Some had skin which still burned sagging from the face and body, with a "reddish-white skin underneath showing."

A reporter who was outside the city at the time of the explosion, but who came in immediately afterward, noticed among the dead a mother with a baby held tightly in her arms. He saw several women running around nude, red from burns, and without hair. Many people climbed into water tanks kept for putting out fires, and died there. "The most pathetic cases were the small children looking for their parents. There was one child of about eleven with a four-year-old on his back, looking for his mother in vain.

"I was unhurt and I felt ashamed to walk around among so many tragic persons."

Shortly after the bomb fell there was a high wind or "fire storm" engendered by the heat that tore up trees, and whirling over the river made waterspouts. In some areas rain fell.

Although the fire burned for days, major destruction did not take very long. A fisherman who had been out on the bay said, "I saw suddenly a flash of light. I thought something burned my face. I hid in the boat face down. When I looked up later, Hiroshima was completely burned."

V

Hiroshima, of course, never had been prepared for a disaster of the magnitude which overtook it, but in addition the organized sources of aid that did exist were wiped out along with everything else. As a result, rescue had to come from surrounding areas and soon trucks and trains were picking up the wounded while hospitals, schools, temples, assembly halls and tents were prepared to receive them. However, the suburbs and surrounding areas were overwhelmed by the rush of immediate survivors out of the bombed region, and so for about a day help did not penetrate far into the city. This, together with the fact that survivors who were physically able were stunned and bewildered, resulted in great numbers of the wounded dying from lack of aid.

The vice-mayor of a neighboring town that began receiving the wounded about 11:30 in the morning said: "Everybody looked alike. The eyes appeared to be a mass of melted flesh. The lips were split up and also looked like a mass of molten flesh. Only the nose appeared the same as before. The death scene was awful. The color of the patient would turn to blue and when we touched the body the skin would stick to our hands."

Those who ventured into Hiroshima were greeted by sights they were reluctant to describe. A businessman reported that "the bodies of half-dead people lay on the roadside, on the bridges, in the water, in the gardens and everywhere. It was a sight no one wants to see. Practically all of these people were nude and their color was brownish-blackish and some of their bodies were dripping. There was a fellow whose head was half burned so that I thought he was wearing a hat."

In the public parks great numbers of both wounded and dead were congregated, the former adding constantly to the ranks of the latter. There were cries for aid and cries for water and there were places where nameless shapes merely stirred.

In the late afternoon aid began to come farther into the city from the outer edges. Rice balls and other food were brought. From their mission up the valley a number of Jesuits came, and one of them, Father Siemes, gave a vivid and careful description of what he had seen, when he was later interviewed by members of the Bombing Survey in Tokyo. He said, "Beneath the wreckage of the houses along the way, many have been trapped and they scream to be rescued from the oncoming flames. They must be left to their fate."

On the bridge, he encountered a procession of soldiers, dragging "themselves along with the help of staves or carried by their less severely injured comrades. . . . Abandoned on the bridge there stand, with sunken heads, a number of horses with large burns on their flanks.

"Fukai, the secretary of the mission, is completely out of his mind. He does not want to leave the house as the fires are burning closer, and explains that he does not want to survive the destruction of his fatherland." He had to be carried away by force.

After dark, the priests helped pull from the river two children who suffered chills and then died. There was a sandspit in the river covered with wounded who cried for help and who were afraid that the rising tide would drown them.

After midnight, "only occasionally do we hear calls for help."

Many of the injured were brought to an open field right behind Hiroshima station and tents were set up for them. Doctors came in from the neighboring prefectures and from near-by towns such as Yamaguchi, Okayama and Shimane.

One of the newspapermen reported that when he came into the city ashes were everywhere. "They got into my ears and nose; and for a month it was difficult to clear out the damage because of the hot ashes."

A fisherman who came to Hiroshima to see what had happened said: "I cannot describe the situation in words, it was so pitiful. To see so many people dead was a terrible sight. Their clothes were shredded and their bodies puffed up, some with tongues hanging out. They were dead in all shapes."

As late as the second day the priests noted that among the cadavers there were many wounded who were still alive. "Frightfully injured forms beckoned to us and then collapsed."

They carried some to the hospitals, but "we cannot move everybody who lies exposed to the sun." It did not make much difference anyway, for in the hospitals there was little that could be done. They just lay in the corridors, row on row, and died.

A businessman came into Hiroshima on the third day. "The guards," he said, "told us that we would have to wait before we could come looking for missing persons. They said that maybe in a week there would be lists from which you could find if your relatives were in a hospital, school, or killed. There were trucks busy with rescue work.

"I went to my brother's house in the suburbs and found that all were wounded but none killed. They were stunned and could hardly speak. The next day, one of the four children died. She got black and blue in the face, just as if you had mashed your finger, and died fifteen minutes after that.   In another half hour, her sister did the same thing, and she died also."

People were very nervous when American planes flew over, fearing that more bombs would be dropped.   The doctor reported that whenever a plane was seen, people would rush into shelters.   "They went in and out so much that they did not have time to eat.   They were so nervous that they could not work."

The businessman said: "Before the bomb fell, people were so used to American planes that they would not go to a shelter.   Afterward, they were so nervous that any kind of spark would scare them, any kind of spark they saw.   That was because of the flash of the atomic bomb."

The destroyed heart of Hiroshima consisted of 4.4 square miles.   The police chief told how the dead were collected and burned.   "Many could not be identified.   In cases where it was possible, the corpses or the ashes were given to the immediate family.   Mostly, the cremation was done by the police or the soldiers, and the identified ashes given to the family.   The ashes of those not identified were turned over to the City Hall. There still are boxes in the city hall.   Occasionally even now one is identified, or is supposed to be identified, and is claimed."

For many days funeral processions moved along the roads and through the towns and villages all around Hiroshima.   The winds were pervaded by the smell of death and cremation.   At night the skies were lit with the flames of funeral pyres.

VI

Very few if any of the people we interviewed at Hiroshima attempted to make a play for sympathy or to make us feel guilty.   The general manner was one which might be interpreted as due either to apathy and absence of feeling consequent on shock, or to reserve that masked hate.   It was probably a mixture of both, in varying degrees in different people.   However, overlying this with almost everyone, there appeared to be a determination to co-operate and oblige.

When asked for their views regarding the atomic bomb, many spoke with apparent frankness and gave a variety of opinions.   An official of a small town outside of Hiroshima that was untouched said, "Everyone was resigned to the fact that it was part of the war."

The vice-mayor of another town felt that "if America had such a weapon, there was no use to go on. Many high-school students in Hiroshima who were wounded in the raid spoke incoherently on their deathbed saying, 'Please avenge that raid for us somehow.' However, most of the people felt that since it was war, it was just *shikata ga nai,* could not be helped. But we were united in the idea that we had to win the war."

The newspaper reporter said that after the bomb some felt that this was the end, while others wanted to go on regardless. "Those who had actually experienced the bomb were the ones who wanted to quit, while those who had not wanted to go on."

The doctor reported that people said: "If the enemy has this kind of bomb, everyone is going to die, and we wish the war would hurry up and finish. We cannot fight against a bomb like that."

A woman whose soldier husband was killed in the blast said: "When I first saw the destruction I wondered if mankind could make such a bomb. I felt sharply the difference in advancement between the American and Japanese scholars. Personally, though many are resentful against America, I feel no animosity. It was an understood war and the use of weapons was fair. I only wonder why they didn't let the people know of this bomb and give us a chance before bombing us to give up."

The police chief believed that the general reaction among the people was one of surprise and a feeling that "we have taken the worst beating, we have been the goats." He said: "They felt that America had done a terrible thing and were very bitter, but after the surrender they turned on the Japanese military. They felt they had been fooled and wondered if the military knew that the bomb was coming and why they did not take steps.

"The bomb made no difference in the fighting spirit of the people, it drew them together and made them more co-operative.

"My eldest son was killed, but I felt that it was destiny that ruled. When I see people who got away without any injury, I feel a little pang of envy naturally, but I don't feel bitter toward them."

A businessman thought "It was cruel to drop the bomb where ordinary people are living. I don't see why they didn't drop it in some army camp or something."

A housewife wondered, "Is there any use in such a bomb? I saw so many burned people streaming past our home, I saw so many of them."

A woman who escaped with her family, but whose house was burned, said: "After the atomic bomb exploded, I felt that now I must go to work in an ammunition plant.   After seeing all the injured people, it seems that only one out of a hundred people escaped with no bad effects.   My sons told me that they would not forget the atomic bomb even when they grew up."

Another wife and mother said: "When I reached where my husband worked, I saw the building crumbled.   I went almost crazy.   I searched for him but could not find him.   I found my only son dead, crushed under a stone.   I carried my son back home and cremated his body, but my husband's body was not found.   There were so many dead who could not be recognized.   I felt bitter against the enemy and the war."

There was one woman who said, "If there is such a thing as ghosts, why don't they haunt the Americans?"

Perhaps they do.

For one thing, pity has persistent and haunting qualities, and is the more terrible for being fruitless.   There are of course semi-automatic devices of mind for warding off its full poignancy.   Preoccupation with work, jokes with teammates, playing with the responsive children, giving away candies and similar actions can overlay perceptions with a temporary padding.   Even feelings of anger at the victims for threatening your composure by existing can for a time displace other thoughts.   Reasoning can seem to make the present tragedy less by showing that it is not so bad as things that others have done or would have done.   Arguments of justification can be conjured up on grounds of necessity, and one can try to prove that lives have been saved and that the future as a result is really brighter for everybody.

But, in spite of all, a consciousness creeps in that all this is irrelevant and does not make the tragedy less.   Then moments come when the recollection of a tangerine given by a child, a stopped clock, or an old woman picking about in the rubble of what had been her life, causes the protecting mists to vanish and leaves one alone with an unbearable realization of human suffering.

One afternoon an elderly schoolteacher spent several hours telling me in careful English about life in Hiroshima as it used to be and how the city had become "transformed from Paradise to Hades."   He was a gray-haired man with a quiet manner and his tone was not one of bitterness, but rather of wonder.   When we parted he was standing on the steps of the shattered city hall within which were the stacks of white boxes full of the ashes of the unidentified dead.   His farewell word was, "Godspeed."

EPILOGUE

Poking in the ruins of Hiroshima one day and thinking about the clock in the bank with its hands at 8:10, I came on the stone figure of a dog, one of that grinning type derived from China which commonly guards the entrances to temples.   It was tilted on its pedestal, but undamaged, and the grin gleamed out as if it were hailing me.   Its rakish air and its look of fiendish satisfaction with all that lay around drew me on to inspect it more closely.

It was then apparent that the look was not directed at me, but out somewhere beyond, in a way that brought home my littleness and insignificance. It was, of course, only a piece of stone, and it displayed no particular artistic merit, yet in looking at it I felt that I was the clod, while it had a higher, sentient wisdom locked up within.

The look and the feeling it inspired were familiar, and I tried to remember where I had seen it before.   The eyes were creased in a fashion that did not exactly connote mirth and the lips were drawn far back in a smile that seemed to blend bitterness, glee and compassion.   The word "sardonic" came to mind, and this led to recognition and a realization of terrible appropriateness.

All who have had acquaintance with the dead know the curious smile that can creep over the face as *rigor mortis* sets in, a smile of special quality known in medical language as *risus sardonicus*.   The dog had this look and it seemed to me probable that some ancient Oriental sculptor in seeking an expression for temple guardians that would drive off evil spirits had taken this death grin as his model, and thus it had come down through hundreds of years to this beast looking out on Hiroshima.

Many a soldier has seen this face looking up at him from the field of battle, before he himself wore it, and many a priest and doctor has found himself alone with it in a darkened room.   As with the dog, at first the look seems to be directed at you, and then beyond you, as if there lay behind it knowledge of the huge joke of life which the rest of us feel vaguely but cannot comprehend. And there is that tinge of compassion that is as dreadful as it is unknowable.

As I continued to study this stone face it seemed to me that the grin was not directed at the waste and the destruction around, at the red and yellow and the smells, any more than it was directed at me. It was not so much a face looking at Hiroshima as it was the face of Hiroshima. The carved eyes gazed beyond the rubble, beyond the gardens of radishes and fields of winter wheat, beyond the toiling adults and the rippling children with their tangerines and shouts of "Hallo-goodaby!" surging up with new life like flowers and weeds spreading over devastation, beyond the mountains with red pines in the blue sky, beyond all these, over the whole broad shoulder of the world, to where in cities and towns clocks on wrists and public towers still ticked and moved. The face seemed to be smiling and waiting for the harvest of the wind that had been sown.

Lines of Inquiry

1 Leighton's essay is broken into seven sections, including the Epilogue.

  a On what basis are these divisions adopted?

  b Assign to each section a characterizing phrase, so as to have a simple outline consisting of seven phrases. Could the sequence of phrases be changed? How many different sequences seem possible to build into a complete essay?

  c Choosing two of these alternative sequences, determine what effect the use of each would have on the meaning of the essay.

  d In your judgment, why did Leighton choose the sequence he did? Could the essay have begun with the fourth section?

2 *a* Look at the break between the first and second sections. How are the two sections linked? How is the second section linked to the third? The third to the fourth? The fourth to the fifth?

  b Are the linking elements always verbal—repetitions of key words or phrases, for example? Can you make a rudimentary classification of types of linkage, based on Leighton's practice?

  c Which of these links seem to you most successful, and which least so?

  d Of the six section breaks, which seems the most abrupt? Why? What is the effect of that abruptness?

3 Leighton himself is thoroughly present within his essay: He is its internal point of view.   How does his explicit presence help to hold the sequence together?   If Leighton had kept his presence out of the essay, what else would change?

4 Part of Leighton's purpose obviously is to communicate something of the horror of his subject.
  a What proportion of his account is given over to the numbers of dead, the buildings destroyed, etc.?
  b Where are exact figures given, and why there?   How does Leighton communicate not the fact but the meaning of this kind of destruction?
  c Why does he keep quoting the Japanese?
  d The bombing itself is described in the fourth section: How is that section constructed?   What is the sequence of examples within that section—in what pattern is the damage reported?   Why?

5 Much of Leighton's account turns on relatively small details.   How do the following function, in relation to the point of his narrative?
  a The driver from Kansas   d The elderly schoolteacher
  b The children   e "Hallo-goodabye!"
  c The clock

6 At many points Leighton's prose communicates a good deal more than a simple factual statement—it conveys an attitude, almost a judgment, as well.   In each of the following phrases, what meaning is contributed by the italicized words?
  a "Here and there peasants worked, swinging spades or grubbing in mud and water *with blue hands*."
  b "The driver said, as he got out, '*This is it*.'"
  c "A bridge started out and stopped suddenly *like a headless neck*."
  d "'*I heaved a sigh of relief*,' the weaponeer of the plane is reported to have said, '*because I knew the bomb was a success*.'"
  e "In part the picture has to be reconstructed, *as in archeology*, from the remains."
  f In hospitals and clinics, patients, doctors and nurses all died *together*."
  g "The police chief said that he was in his back yard *near a chicken coop* when the bomb went off."
  h "A *talkative young man in a newspaper office* said that the most severely burned people looked like red shrimps."

7 a What is the function of the Epilogue?
  b Of the thousands of details available to him, why did

Leighton choose as the center of this section a sculpture of a dog?

c Why does the essay end in description instead of in narration? Would the essay have been better if he had ended with the schoolteacher's "Godspeed"?

8 In one way, Leighton's essay can be viewed as a condemnation of the United States for its use of the bomb. Yet he reports, and even emphasizes, not only the "reserve that masked hate" of the Japanese, but also their willingness to cooperate, and their wonder. Why? How is the Japanese reaction related to the point of the Epilogue?

9 Leighton gives several references to government publications dealing with the atomic bomb. Look them up in your library. What kinds of facts are they concerned with? How do you account for the differences between this essay and the official reports? Can you come to any general conclusions about composition?

Lines of Experiment

1 From the writer's point of view, Leighton's essay is interesting as a solution to a difficult problem: the problem of how to describe a single event of absolute horror in terms that can convey its human significance as well as its brutality. Most of the formal features of the essay are part of his attempt to make Hiroshima not only visible but also comprehensible: not merely so horrible as to be numbing, nor so schematic as to be meaningless.

Choose a single event that you know a good deal about already or are willing to study in detail. Avoid events that are *purely* accidental; the significance of accidents is fairly simple, unless they are the results of human failures. Consider the meaning —the human significance—of the event you single out; that meaning, not the event itself, is the real center of your composition. Decide what details contribute to that meaning and, putting all other details aside, arrange your essential material in several trial sequences. While you are working out the sequence, also work out the linking system that can bind it together in a plausible and congruent way. Will you enter the essay yourself, to "manage" the sequence—as Leighton does? Or are the transitions in time and space so clear and appropriate themselves that you can stay out of it? Work for a tight sequence: If in doubt about a fact, leave it out.

2 Gather all the information you can on the effects of fission and

fusion bombs, and write an essay whose subject rises naturally out of your reading. *The following titles are intended to be merely suggestive:*

a If an H-bomb Had Fallen on Hiroshima
b The Bombing of Nagasaki
c The Atom Bomb as a Military Weapon
d Why Hiroshima Was Bombed
e Civil Defense
f Nuclear Warfare and the American Conscience
g Childhood in the Nuclear Age
h Why I Am Sick of the A-bomb

DISCOURSE IN LOGICAL ORDER: EXPOSITION AND ARGUMENT

Exposition and argument are related in that both deal with the ordering of facts and ideas into systems.   But whereas pure exposition attempts to present systems that are not contested, pure argument attempts to create new or modified systems, and anticipates some degree of contest. The one attempts merely to inform; the other attempts both to inform and to convince.

METHOD
IN EXPOSITION

Definition   Perhaps the most basic process in logically ordered discourse, after identification of its subject, is *definition:*

What is Life?   I am not going to answer this question.   In fact, I doubt if it will ever be possible to give a full answer, because we know what it feels like to be alive, just as we know what redness or pain or effort are.   So we cannot describe them in terms of anything else.   But it is not a foolish question to ask, because we often want to know whether a man is alive or not, and when we are dealing with the microscopic agents of disease, it is clear enough that bacteria are alive, but far from clear whether viruses, such as those which cause measles and smallpox, are so.

So we have to try to describe life in terms of something else, even if the description is quite incomplete. We might try some such expression as "the influence of spirit on matter." But this would be of little use for several reasons. For one thing, even if you are sure that man, and even dogs, have spirits, it needs a lot of faith to find a spirit in an oyster or a potato. For another thing, such a definition would certainly cover great works of art, or books which clearly show their author's mind, and go on influencing readers long after he is dead. Similarly, it is no good trying to define life in terms of a life force. . . .

(J. B. S. Haldane, "What Is Life?" pp. 122–123.)

This excerpt is evidently neither narrative nor description. Time and space have not disappeared, exactly; they are still there, behind "man" and "virus" and "potato." But man, virus, and potato are not images, nor even names of specific things: They are the names of classes of things, and the writer is defining, setting limits to, an idea. To render "life" mimetically would be to show somebody living, a series of living acts—somehow to embody "life" in a kind of image. To render life logically is to describe it in terms of "something else."

The difference between this kind of thinking and the kind discussed in Part I is reflected in the difference in linking words. The world of time and space is linked imitatively by such words as "now," "then," "near," "far," "to the right," and so forth. The Haldane passage, by contrast, uses "if," "because," "so," "but," "for one thing," "for another," "therefore"—words that name relationships not among things in time and space but among ideas within systems of ideas. The linking words suggest contingency (if . . . then), cause-effect (because . . . therefore), qualification (but, in addition to), proof (for one thing . . . for another), and so on. Such linking words function differently in different contexts, but we can easily see that they resemble very little the links used in description and narrative. What we have here is a passage held together in logical, not in temporal or spatial, relations.

What are the marks of this rendering of an idea in terms of "something else"? In his first sentence, Haldane justifies the need for a definition: The job is difficult but necessary, because "we often want to know whether a man is alive or not." Two preliminary points about definition emerge here. First, definitions do not try to give a full picture of the thing defined: They are concerned with its distinguishing marks, its *boundaries*. Second, definitions must be worth something, they must be important. There is no point in defining something if nothing is gained by doing so. The need for a good definition can usually be shown in the consequences of a bad one: The live man may be pronounced dead.

The simplest kind of definition involves saying the word and pointing to the thing the word is agreed to mean: *That* is a *cow*. But definition by pointing or showing ("ostensive definition") is not always useful or possible: "Life is what I feel like," though an authentic and defensible statement, does not help us to know whether a man is alive or dead, or whether a book is: It does not discriminate between life and death. In order to do so, we need a definition in terms of "something else." The question is, what kind of something else? Haldane is trying to draw a boundary line between two physical states. But when we say, "That's really living!" we suggest a totally different kind of boundary line; when we say "That painting has a lot of life in it," we suggest still another. The differences are those of context and purpose. *Definition is focused;* it does not deal with words by themselves, as signs of ideas by themselves, but with words in a context, as signs of ideas within that context.

Therefore, the kind of boundary line we need in any particular context must be determined by the kind of distinction we are after. The trouble with "life is the influence of spirit on matter" is that it will not make the physical distinction that Haldane needs: As a boundary line, it takes in some things that obviously are not physically alive (books) and leaves outside some things that obviously are physically alive (oysters and potatoes). An adequate definition includes nothing that *is not* meant in the context of discussion and excludes nothing that *is* meant. We say that the things defined and the defining phrase cover exactly the same ground: They are *convertible.* For example, to say that an oyster is a mollusk is to place an oyster in a class, but not to define it, for there are other kinds of mollusks: A mollusk is not necessarily an oyster. So the defining phrase must be made more precise in order to be convertible.

Arriving at a definition frequently involves a sequence of successively more precise distinctions—almost a process of trial and error. Thus, pointing to life will not give us a usable boundary, so we must define it in terms of something else. "We might try . . . 'the influence of spirit on matter.'" But the boundary will not work: It includes books and excludes oysters. So let us try another, a definition in terms of a life force. The method is partly a negative one, by necessity: In order to show that our boundaries are the only ones that will work,

we have to show that other boundaries will not. The "other boundaries" Haldane puts before us are the customary ones: By showing
that they are untenable, he shows the need for a new definition.

The first element in the sequence of definition, then, is a justification
of the need for one. The second element ordinarily is the demonstration of the failure of customary definitions to make the distinction aimed
at. The third element is to show what a true definition *must* include
(oysters, men, bacteria) and what it *cannot* include (books, rivers).
The fourth, of course, is to find the proper defining phrase. Once we
have found a phrase that converts exactly with the things defined, we
have done the job.

This process of narrowing down also means making some clear assumptions about the probable reader of the definition. He is presumed
not only to know what a potato is but also to lack the faith necessary to find spirit residing in one. In this sense, then, definitions must
be drwan with some awareness of the knowledge and belief of the
audience: "Life" does not include books; "things with spirit" do not
include potatoes or oysters. If the necessary basis in common belief
for a specific kind of definition does not already exist, it must be
created before that definition can become useful.

Classification   Classification is closely related to definition:

> Dancing and architecture are the two primary and essential arts.
> The art of dancing stands at the source of all the arts that express
> themselves first in the human person. The art of architecture is
> the beginning of all the arts that lie outside the person. Music,
> acting, poetry, proceed in the one mighty stream; sculpture, paint-
> ing, all the arts of design in the other. There is no primary art,
> outside these two arts, for their origin is far earlier than man him-
> self; and dancing comes first.
> (H. Ellis, "The Philosophy of Dancing," pp. 128–129.)

This passage suggests a somewhat different way of saying what an idea
means. Let us change the passage to read:

> Dancing is a primary and essential art, whose origin is earlier than
> man.

What the revision loses reveals what Ellis gained by using classification
as a compositional method. Classification establishes the importance

of a thing by showing where it stands in a field of similar things (dancing is a primary and essential art); by establishing an inventory of subordinate topics, almost an outline of leading ideas (the age-old importance of dancing; its relations to other arts; its history as a form of expression; its final significance); and by suggesting a kind of solidity and definiteness of idea, an "edge" of reality—the frame of ideas around the subject. All this is lost in the second version.

Classification involves the setting of limits to an idea, and thus involves a kind of definition. However, in this selection the limits and significance of the idea are not established by means of a direct, convertible equation (dancing $= X$), but by means of something like a chart that fixes dancing in the field of ideas surrounding it. This chart is drawn in a specific sequence. First, we are told the general title of the chart, the basic category to which the ideas belong: Dancing is an *art*. Second, we are told the "rank" of dancing in particular in that chart: Dancing is a *primary and essential art*. Third, dancing is differentiated from the single other art of equal rank: Dancing begins *within* the human person, architecture begins *outside* it. Fourth, the arts subsidiary to dancing—music, acting, poetry—and the parallel subsidiary arts of architecture—painting, sculpture—are enumerated. Fifth, the justification for this system of classification is given: Dancing and architecture have an origin earlier than man himself. Last, a justification is given for a specific concern with dancing: "Dancing comes first."

Two processes are going on simultaneously. One tells us what dancing *is* by locating it within a particular boundary system or class, i.e., the class of primary art forms. The other process tells us what dancing is *worth* relative to the other members of that class. A simple definition could accomplish the first. Classification adds the second.

Yet the entire passage provides not a single clue to the concrete differences that would enable us to tell a dance from a sculpture; it is assumed, evidently, that we already have that information. In this respect, classification and definition have clearly distinguishable ends. But in nearly every other respect the two methods of composition show considerable similarities:

1 The specific system of classification established here is far from inevitable; it is arbitrary, the sole decision of the writer. Dancing is not only an art, but also a recreation, a form of exercise, a method of courtship, and many other things; and it would be as legitimate to map its place among other recreations (golf, tennis, hunting, reading, and so forth) as among other arts. Like definition, then, classification is purposive; it has an end in view. And this purpose shows in a special principle of division, a special set of boundaries. If dancing were to be classified as a recreation, the principle by which it is classified separately here (an expression within the human person) would hardly apply; nor could it be called a primary recreation (hunting might be that). We would have to find the principles of division appropriate for the things we are attempting to classify—private recreation and public recreation, perhaps, or physical and mental, or destructive and constructive.

2 A system of classification pretends to describe the boundaries and interior structure of a class, and therefore must be *complete*: It must be able to account for all instances that clearly belong within it. If we classify the arts, the system we adopt must be capable of classifying *all* the arts: dancing, architecture, music, poetry, "all the arts of design," and so forth. Further, the system must be *consistent*: If we say that dancing and architecture are the two primary arts, we cannot call poetry a primary art, or dancing a secondary art, and if we say that "all the arts of design" are descended from architecture, we cannot then say that sculpture is descended from dancing. If our system of classification is not consistent and complete, *as a system,* it will be of little value, because we will always feel that conclusions based on a shaky classification are likely themselves to be shaky. In a sense, one might say that, like definition, a system of classification and the things classified must be *convertible*. Merely to say, "Dancing is an art and a recreation" is *not* to classify dancing nor to define it, but to identify it, rather vaguely. Fishing too is an art, in a sense, and a recreation. Such an identification will help to identify what is being talked about, but will not offer the special compositional clues of a full system of classification.

3 A system of classification is not only purposive, it is *focused*. Dancing, not architecture, is Ellis's interest, and though we may hear more about poetry or music, we probably will hear little about sculpture or industrial design—and discussions of poetry and music will focus on these arts as forms of dancing. A system of classification exists in order to establish a field of ideas related to a central subject and important to the discussion of that subject.

4 A method of classification identifies not only what is included within

the boundaries of its true subject (dancing contains poetry, drama, and so forth) but what is excluded, however close by: Like definition, classification uses negatives in order to distinguish its real subject, to clear away misleading ideas or lines of inquiry. But there must be some justification for this process. The subjects cleared away must be potentially misleading. There is no point in saying that dancing is not boilermaking, but there is some point, for the purposes of Ellis's argument, in saying that dancing is not architecture.

5 A system of classification, like a definition, makes some assumptions about the audience. The reader must have a general sense of what is being classified, and some general principles of classification, in order to find one system of classification preferable to another: He must have some idea of what a dance is, and some willingness to make a distinction between what is inside and what is outside the human person—indeed, he must be able to see that distinction as a fairly radical one (some cultures do not). For a reader who felt such a distinction to be unimportant or meaningless, a classification of the arts based on that distinction would seem unimportant or meaningless also.

Analysis   One step beyond classification in turn is analysis:

According to the traditional view of voting as presented in classical texts of democratic theory, inspired by the political views of the 18th century enlightenment, the voter is supposed to be interested in politics and to express that interest by broad, continuous and critical attention to the flow of electoral news and talks in the communication medium. He is supposed to be well informed on campaign issues, events and personalities; to give impartial, rational consideration to the issues at hand; to judge political proposals in the light of general principles dictated by the public interest; and to discuss political matters with his fellow voters so that a wide popular debate on the issues will be held, led by the candidates themselves. The key words used to describe the voter in political theory are such terms as informed, interested, rational, principled. That is what the voter is supposed to be like; what is he really like?

(Bernard Berelson, "Voting Behaviour," p. 146.)

In a sense, the excerpt presents a classification; but its point is to separate for study not things distinct in themselves (e.g., dancing and architecture) but things so closely connected that they must be studied in relation to one another.   *The focus of an analysis is on the relations among all the parts—or at least the significant parts—of a single whole.*

The Berelson passage suggests two ways in which the parts of its particular subject—the voter—can be analyzed. First, those parts function in a particular way and in a particular sequence: The voter seeks information about political issues; then he considers that information; then he arrives at a rational judgment on the basis of principle. An expansion of this analytic scheme would show how the voter becomes informed—through newspapers, and so forth; how he considers his information—through debates, conversations, and the like; and how he arrives at a rational judgment in accordance with principle— by checking one claim against another and all claims against his experience, or the Constitution, or the Sermon on the Mount. Such an analysis would show as how the voter behaved, according to the traditional view. In the same spirit we might show how a steam engine worked, or how the first moonship will work.

One might also analyze the classical idea of the voter by studying the causal relationships among his activities. *Because* the voter is interested, he becomes informed; because he is informed, he arrives at rational political principles; because he has rational political principles, he is capable of voting rationally. If we call the first kind of analysis *functional,* we can call the second *causal.* The difference is essentially one of emphasis, as the example itself makes clear: It is often difficult to show how something works without to some extent also showing why it works as it does. But this difference in emphasis can be important: An analysis of voting behavior that tells us how people vote but not why they vote as they do is likely to be trivial, whereas an analysis of the automobile engine that tells us why it came to be invented but not how it works is likely to have limited practical value.

In some important respects a successful analysis resembles a successful definition or classification. First, like definition and classification, analysis exists within a context of discussion, and its structure is determined by its purpose: It is definite and limited in focus. The excerpt, for example, tells us the classical theory of voting behavior: The voter does this, then this, then that. But it does not tell us who was qualified to vote, according to this theory, nor how many such voters there were, nor how they got to be qualified, nor what their typical political options or opinions were, nor even if one man's vote could be worth more than another's. Such questions might interest us—in another context.

Second, analysis assumes a particular audience. The excerpt assumes that its reader will not be interested solely in the technical, or the historical, or the psychological, or even the political aspects of voting behavior. It assumes also that we know what a "communication medium" is, and have some vague notion of what is meant by "classical texts of democratic theory." But, if such an analysis were to be directed to a convention of public relations men, for example, it would clearly have to consider the special interests and experience of such a group. Where clear assumptions cannot be made, a common vocabulary and frame of reference must be established before further progress can be made. In fact, the discussion above, of the classical view of voting behavior, is merely an effort to establish a common background for the discussion of what voting behavior "is really like"—the real subject of the complete essay.

This last point can suggest one further resemblance between analysis and definition. Analysis too can best justify itself by showing that traditional analyses are inadequate. In this sense, analysis often proceeds by negatives: "That is what the voter is supposed to be like; but what is he really like?"

Expository narrative One further and highly important difference exists between analysis and the other methods of exposition. In a sense, Berelson defines and classifies the voter and his behavior. Both definition and classification are based on a static, convertible equation (the voter $= X$, the parts of voting behavior $= x, y,$ and z); analysis, on the other hand, is based on something approaching a description of characteristic action: The voter is a man who does this, then that, then that. In other words, once an analysis has classified the parts of its subject, it tends to take a narrative form. The reason is obvious: Processes and causal sequences are things that exist in the continuity of time and space, and an explanation of processes and causal sequences pretty well has to make use of that continuity.

Expanded versions of this kind of analysis are frequently called *expository narrative*. The characteristics of expository narrative are easier to see if we imagine a clearly outlined process—for example, the building of a house: first the survey of the ground, then the drawing up of plans, then the excavation, and so on. The sequence of time and space allows the writer to order such a process clearly and economically, especially if he adopts a specific point of view within the narrative from which to follow that sequence—e.g., the foreman's, or the contractor's. (For further discussion of point of view as a linking device in expository narrative, see the introduction to Part IV.)   But the time-space linking within such a narrative is superficial, only a way of connecting and thus explaining the stages of the process.   Underlying these stages, determining their pattern, is a strict causal sequence: If you want to build a house, then you must survey the ground; in order to support the house, you must have a foundation; in order to make a foundation, you must excavate.   Expository narrative in fact has an explicitly logical structure, in which the causes behind any given event are certain and determine the focus and sequence of discussion.

Ordinary narrative generally has a logical substructure also, as we saw in Part I, but that structure is concerned with particular events, not general processes, and its causal structure is far less precise.   As the writer injects into expository narrative actions logically irrelevant to the process—an accident to a particular workman, the smell of raw wood, the whine of the table saw, the collapse of the roof—he tends to move into narrative proper and away from strictly functional or causal analysis.   Such illustrative narratives have their own value, of course, as ways of giving humanity to processes otherwise disagreeably impersonal.   But they assume that human involvement in the process, and not the process itself, is the real subject.

Illustration   It is obvious that an expository narrative is a form of illustration—the most convenient way, in fact, to illustrate the functional or causal patterns.   Illustration is a chief element in all forms of expository discourse.   Potatoes, oysters, books are used to illustrate the inadequacy of traditional metaphysical definitions of "life."   Music, acting, poetry are used to illustrate the arts that express themselves within the human person.   The voter is used as illustration of the way classical theory viewed voting behavior.

In every case illustration is a primary way of connecting ideas and facts; it makes up, therefore, a kind of middle ground between logic and image.   Partly for this reason and partly because a given illustration can be and often is so extended as to dominate every aspect of an essay's structure, illustration is discussed separately in the following part of this text.   Here we need point out only that definition, classification, and analysis cannot proceed far without the aid of illustration, which connects the word to the thing.   *That* is what I mean by a cow.   A potato, a man, an oyster is what I mean by alive.   A book, an idea, an influence is what I do not mean by alive.   As a practical matter, the writer finally must point to the kind of thing he is actually talking about, if he wishes to be understood and taken to be handling the actual world.

METHOD
IN ARGUMENT

Argument often lies concealed in explanation.   Haldane uses definition as a way of arguing for a particular view of "life."   Ellis uses classification as a way of arguing for a particular view of dancing.   Berelson uses analysis to begin an argument for a particular theory of voting behavior. If an explanation does not organize and present, at least in summary form, an underlying structure of argument, its system can seem merely a miscellaneous collection of ideas, with no necessary shape.   Similarly, though an argument is an attempt to create a new or modified system of ideas, no argument is totally new: All begin with and base themselves on what is already known—that is, on arguments already decided and so subjects for exposition.   Both forms of discourse are concerned with truth.

Consistency   In the absence of clear celestial guides, when a human being says that a statement is true, he probably means that it is consistent with the observable facts and with his other ideas about the meaning of those facts.   Rational thought involves a kind of sorting out of the elements of a given situation and an effort to group them in as consistent a pattern as possible.   Ordinarily we are hardly conscious of the process.   Someone points to an orange and says, "That is an orange."   We accept the statement as true because we see the orange and agree on the meaning of the word: There is no observable inconsistency.   If he says, "An orange is good to eat," we accept the statement as true because it is consistent with our own experience and with general opinion: We already think an orange is good to eat.   But if he points to a rotten orange, and says, "Oranges are good to eat, and that is an orange, so that must be good to eat," we disagree: His statements look consistent but are contradicted by the orange—*not all* oranges are good to eat.   If he says, "Oranges are good to eat, and oranges are fruits, so fruits must be good to eat," we disagree again: Some fruits are poisonous.   If he says, "Oranges are good, oranges are fruits, apples are fruits, so apples are good too," we agree and disagree both: His facts are right but his reasoning is poor—he has arrived at the right conclusion for the wrong reasons.

Behind such a dialogue is the demand for consistency in statement and fact—that is, men want their ideas to be expressed in credible and recognizable patterns. This demand appears to be the starting point for most of our rational thought. Indeed, it is largely when we become aware of some inconsistency in our ideas that we discover things to reconsider and to sort out more precisely: "That is what the voter is supposed to be like; what is he really like?"

The kinds of consistency involved in exposition and argument can be broken arbitrarily into two classes: consistency among statements and consistency of statement with fact. Do not confuse the two, for as the examples concerning oranges have shown, statements may be consistent with one another but not with fact (the case of the rotten orange), and statements may be inconsistent with one another and still be true (the case of the apple). It is useful, therefore, to distinguish between *validity,* or consistency among statements, and *truth,* or consistency of statements with fact.

Consistency of statements with fact must be judged separately in every actual instance. In some general respects, this kind of consistency is discussed in Part III, for illustration is a primary means of demonstrating consistency of statement with fact. Consistency among statements, in turn, has been studied for many centuries, and made the subject of a variety of formal rules which are properly a subject for special study, under trained logicians. For our purposes here, we shall focus on consistency as a principle, and not on formal logical rules.

Logical process   Haldane's attempt, quoted earlier, to formulate a good definition of life, provides some illustrative examples of logical processes. Essentially, the excerpt makes three main statements: (1) A full description of life is impossible; (2) some definition of life is nonetheless necessary; (3) life cannot be defined as "the influence of spirit on matter." If we view each of these main ideas as itself composed of a series of statements and attempt an expanded paraphrase that can bring out an internally consistent development of idea, we might get patterns such as these:

1 a Because we agree that life is a thing we feel directly,
   b And because we agree that all things that we feel directly cannot be fully described,
   c It follows that life is a thing that cannot be fully described.

2 But:
   a Because we agree that definition is the method by which we distinguish among like but separate things,

  b And because we agree that living and nonliving matter frequently are like but separate things,

  c And because we agree that a method for distinguishing between living and nonliving matter is necessary.

  d It follows that a definition of life is necessary.

3 *Now:*

  a Because we agree that potatoes and oysters are alive,

  b If we suppose that life is "the influence of spirit on matter,"

  c Then we must agree that the life of potatoes and oysters is "the influence of spirit on matter."

  d But this conclusion cannot be believed.

  e It follows that life is not "the influence of spirit on matter."

4 *And also*

  a Because we agree that *either* life is not the influence of spirit on matter, *or* books are alive,

  b And because we also agree that books are not alive,

  c It follows that life is not the influence of spirit on matter.

Were we to push these paraphrases further in the direction of formal logic, we could find other and more elegant ways of phrasing these idea sequences.   But the paraphrases here serve the purpose.   What can they tell about logical process and about its relation to composition— aside from the fact that no composition has ever been written or ever should be written in such a form?

Probably the most obvious thing about them is that although the conclusion of each series ("It follows that. . . .") is really present in Haldane's composition, many of the preliminary statements of the paraphrases are not—they are merely implied, and we have to spell them out ourselves.   Haldane does not say that "all things that we feel directly cannot be fully described."   He says, "We know what it feels like to be alive, just as we know what redness or pain or effort are.   So we cannot describe them in terms of anything else."   He does not say that "definition is the method by which we distinguish among like but separate things"; he talks of "whether a man is alive or not" and of viruses and bacteria.   He does not point out that potatoes and oysters are alive.   He does not once use a phrase like "Because we agree that . . . ," yet we know he certainly expects that we *do* agree.   One may conclude that in an ordinary composition, many of the steps necessary to get us consistently to our conclusions can be skipped.

But why?   Why can some steps be skipped and not others?   Look at the preliminary statements in each of the paraphrases.   Though they vary in subject and kind, they have one thing in common: it is assumed that we are going to agree to them.   ("Because we agree that. . . .") Thus: "Life is a thing we feel directly"; "Potatoes and oysters are alive"; "A definition is a standard way of distinguishing among like but separate things"; "Books are not alive."   Haldane does not need to make such statements explicitly because he knows that they are part of our *common beliefs.*

In logical processes, such preliminary statements are called the *premises of argument.*   The premises of an argument are simply the ideas the audience is willing to accept without contest.   This body of ideas is frequently also called the *common ground,* an area of fundamental agreement from which it is possible to reason consistently to a conclusion. The establishment of a common ground is necessary in any argument, for the obvious reason that, if we cannot agree about the facts and standards by which we judge, we cannot agree about anything else either.   In any argument, much of the common ground is simply assumed, implied, never mentioned directly; the only premises which must be mentioned are those likely to be invisible to the reader—those which he will consent to, but must be reminded of.   For example, a clergyman will not need to be reminded that he believes in God; but he may need to be reminded that a belief in God implies a belief that life is not a total accident.   Ordinarily, when the ground of an argument is so familiar to its audience as to be self-evident, there is little point in presenting it.   So there is no point in saying, "Potatoes and oysters are alive," "Books are not alive."

On the other hand, the group of premises Haldane actually had to write out are not self-evident.   "We know what it feels like to be alive, just as we know what redness or pain or effort are.   So we cannot describe them in terms of anything else."   In effect, redness, pain, and effort help us to locate what is being talked about.   They also support the statement they illustrate by reminding us of the trouble we have in describing redness, and so forth—those things we feel directly.   Premises have varying degrees of certainty or obviousness, and therefore require varying degrees of explanation or support: The common ground is not equally solid everywhere, and where it is not solid it must be made so.

The search for consistency in these patterns takes several forms.   In one form—the most common—we can agree to the premises without reservation, but we must see what conclusion follows consistently from them.   In another, we agree only tentatively to one premise ("If we suppose that . . . .") in order to see where it will lead us; finding that it leads us to an inconsistent or incredible conclusion, we reject the premise as false. In still a third, we establish two alternatives, only one of which can be true; discovering one to be false, we declare the other true.

The use of "not" in paraphrases 3 and 4 suggests a further point: the value of the negative approach. The elimination of alternatives is even more useful in argument than it is in exposition. If from a wide range of apparent possibilities we can eliminate all but one, we have arrived at the only probable conclusion. Negative argument not only increases the certainty of a conclusion, but also frequently makes arriving at a conclusion easier, because saying what a thing is *not* is often easier than saying what it *is*.

Logical process, then, is a way of linking statements so that if two or more statements are agreed to be true, a further statement must be agreed to be true; and if that further statement cannot be agreed to be true, then one of its premises must be false. In a sense, all logical thought is contingent: *If* we agree with the premises, and *if* the process itself is linked properly, *then* we must agree with the conclusion, because the conclusion simply combines the terms of the premises in a consistent pattern. When we accept a logical chain as adequate, we say in effect that the premises are consistent with the facts and with our interpretation of what such facts mean, that the conclusion follows consistently from the premises, and that no vital matters have been left out of account.

Induction and deduction One can look at these logical chains as reflecting two different but complementary ways of thinking. One is *deductive:* From certain general statements taken as true, certain specific conclusions follow. This form of reasoning is based on a prior agreement about a class of things—about "all things that we feel directly," for example, or "all things that are alive." If redness is in the class of "all things that we feel directly," then what is true of all such things will be true of redness. The classic example of this kind of deductive process runs: All men are mortal; Socrates is a man; therefore Socrates is mortal. What is true of the class will be true of each of its members. (But see the section on fallacious reasoning in the Glossary for a necessary caution about deductive thought.)

Deduction, then, assumes the existence of general truths, and reasons from them to the truth about particulars. *Induction* reverses the process.   Instead of reasoning from the general to the particular, it reasons from the particular to the general: Effort, pain, redness are all things we feel directly; we cannot describe them fully, nor can we describe fully anything else in the class of things we feel directly; therefore, all things that we feel directly we cannot describe fully.

Deduction and induction are not, of course, separate from each other in a full argument; the one flows into the other.   To the practicing writer, the distinction between inductive and deductive thinking is important for two reasons.   First, it suggests that general statements depend for their truth on accurate observation of specific facts and that specific facts become meaningful as they can be grouped into classes about which general statements can profitably be made; it reminds him that particular facts lead to general truths, and general truths support themselves by particular facts.   Second, it suggests two principles or kinds of sequence in argument.   The first kind begins with a list of facts, and concludes with the general assertions those facts justify.   The second kind of sequence begins with a general assertion and documents that assertion with the facts that justify it.   Any full argument will reflect both kinds of thought.

Completeness   Several other aspects of Haldane's discussion are worth noting.   First, a given single point is argued more than once, *and from different angles each time.*   Thus the argument for the impossibility of describing fully what we feel directly is made to rest not on redness alone, nor on redness and blueness and greenness, but on redness, pain, and effort—three entirely different aspects of "feeling."   Similarly, we are asked to consider not potatoes alone, nor potatoes and oats, but potatoes and oysters—the "lowest" of two quite different classes of life.   What we have are different directions of argument, in fact, despite a similarity in form.   The introduction of the argument about books changes even the form, from a clearly "if-then" argument to an "either-or" argument.   One may conclude that even when a given conclusion follows consistently from agreed premises, one kind of argument seldom —perhaps never—is enough: Arguments need at least an illustrative *completeness,* as well as an internal consistency, in order to be satisfying.

This need for completeness appears to be as instinctive as the need for consistency, and is perhaps the same thing.   If we see an incomplete circle, we tend to try to finish it off not in a straight line but in a consistent curve; a triangle with 2½ sides strikes us not as a new figure but as an incomplete triangle.   In argument, the more different lines we can follow to the same conclusion the firmer that conclusion is. If we can show that the dropping of two atomic bombs on Japan was not only ethically questionable but also militarily unnecessary and politically stupid, we shall have strengthened the conclusion that those bombs should not have been dropped. In many questions, especially those involving ideas by their nature uncertain or indefinite—for example, moral or political ideas—an absolutely airtight argument is virtually impossible to arrive at. Should a citizen of a democracy disobey laws that he feels to be unjust, though approved by a majority vote? If all wars are evil, should a good man consent to participate even in the most justifiable of all wars? Is socialism more effective than capitalism as a form of economic organization—and what do we mean by "effective"? Such questions submit to no single line of argument. Men must be content with the most nearly convincing and complete set of arguments they can find—the one that takes the most into account and leaves the fewest unresolved inconsistencies.

Pivot terms In some respects the most notable feature of the para- phrases (pp. 114–115) is their dependence on such terms as "all," "some," "if-then," "either- or," "but," "therefore," "because." Words of this kind are sometimes called "pivot terms," in that they tell the readers which way to turn from one statement to another—how to link them up. They are the boundary posts of logical process: They say "Here you come to a second premise (and, but), or to a second argument (for one thing, for another), or to a conclusion (then, therefore, it follows that); here you come to a set of mutually exclusive alternatives (either- or) or to a premise accepted only temporarily (if we suppose that)." And so on. Without such pivot terms to show how one idea is con- nected to another, argument is crippled. Part of the problem with the rotten orange—the apparent consistency in statement, the inconsistency in fact—came from the omission of the pivot term "all." Had I written "If all oranges are good to eat, and if that is an orange, then that orange is good to eat," the problem would immediately be visible: The first premise is unacceptable. Haldane is able to leave out some of those pivot terms because they are obvious. Others, he must include—for example, the terms connecting one series with another. The pivot term between 1 and 2 tells us that 2 is a qualification of 1: "*But* we often want to know. . . ."; the link between 2 and 3 tells us that we are beginning a new logical chain: "*We might try* some such expres- sion. . . ."; the link between 3 and 4 tells us that we have two alternate logical routes to the same conclusion ("For one thing . . . for another. . . .").   These larger logical links are seldom self-evident—the author, in this case Haldane, simply cannot afford to leave them out or trust the reader to supply them.

Exposition and focus in argument   It is extremely important to note that the best part of the paraphrases is not argument but exposition, constructed by the methods of exposition.   Behind the assertion "Potatoes and oysters are alive" lie definitions of the potato and the oyster and a classification of certain phenomena as alive and others as not; behind both definition and classification are processes of analysis, of the habits of the potato, the functioning of the oyster.   The point made earlier about the common ground is important here: If the processes of definition, classification, analysis, and illustration that underlie a premise are not sound, the premise will not be sound and the argument must fail, for a conclusion can have no greater logical value than its premises. For this reason, argument frequently turns on the examination of premises.   If it is not true that the voter makes rational judgments on sound information and in accordance with principle, then political theory about the meaning of democratic elections must change accordingly.

The chief focus of argument, then, is on the acceptability of the premises. In pursuing an argument, we explain the less obvious premises with great care in order to lead the audience to our conclusion.   In attacking an argument, we examine the premises for flaws.

But an argument has also a pattern by which the premises are linked up—a pattern outlined by pivot terms—and it has a conclusion.   In a successful argument, the pattern must be consistent, the "hookup" must bring us unavoidably to a specific conclusion; and the conclusion arrived at must itself be consistent enough with a larger field of ideas to be acceptable.

Here again a negative instance will clarify the nature of successful argument.   Suppose that we accept the expository elements of an argument angles can we attack the pattern by which the premises are given us, and thus the conclusion's validity?   First, we can point out that the or the validity of the conclusion?   First, we can point out that the pivot terms are used incorrectly or imprecisely—that "some" does not mean "all," that "either-or" may present us with a false alternative, that "if we agree that" does not mean "because we agree that," and so on.

We might also find that the conclusion does not follow inevitably from the premises, or outruns their warrant—that the premises are linked up improperly.   "If all oranges are fruits and if apples are fruits, it follows that all apples are oranges" uses a mistaken process of inference. The popular rule of thumb that runs "If all communist countries are socialist then all socialist countries are communist" shows a similarly mistaken inference. "She is lovely, she uses Slotion" reflects a classic fallacy that needs no comment.

Or we might accept or even disregard the premises for the moment and attack the conclusion directly—the thing we are actually being asked to accept—as obviously inconsistent, within a wider and directly provable frame of facts and ideas: Sweden is a socialist but not a communist country; rotten oranges are not good to eat. We can attack a conclusion directly even more forcibly by extending it until it results in some obvious absurdity: Potatoes and oysters do not show the influence of spirit on matter.

A successful argument, then, strives not only to base itself on the most solid common ground it can find—frequently rejecting one set of ideas or line of support exactly because the ground there is not solid enough —but also to link its ideas in the most careful and lucid way, to keep its conclusions within the warrant of the premises, and to test those conclusions for their consistency with a larger field of ideas. It anticipates contest, and thus is careful to leave no unnecessary flank unguarded and open to attack.

Persuasion Though the final aim of a good argument is to arrive at the truth, its immediate aim is to convince: If it is aimed at a barbershop audience—or at a philosophers' club—it must find terms of arguments that will be understood there. To repeat, the choice of audience seriously affects the choice of a common ground: An argument on behalf of birth control will have to shift the bases for its conclusions as it is addressed to the Roman Catholic College of Cardinals, the United States Senate, the American college student, the housewife, the American Psychiatric Association, or a contraception clinic in the Eastern Ghats. But this is not the only way in which audience affects the strategy and structure of argument. For example, when an audience does not know the basic facts or does not share a clear common ground, the inductive sequence may be far more effective than the deductive, for induction permits us to put the facts first—in effect, to create a common ground at the opening of discussion.

Further, with any given audience some kinds or directions of argument will be more effective than others. A rigorous, abstract logical process, making much careful use of pivot terms, will attract people used to systematic logic, but may repel or simply puzzle others. A composition tumbling from one concrete illustration to another will fetch one audience and seem overdone to another. Too many lines of argument can have for some readers the effect of too many excuses. A sharp satirical attack on the conclusion of a line of argument, showing its inconsistency or final absurdity, may be far easier to follow, far more dramatic, and so, far more persuasive for some audiences than a slow demolition of its premises would be. The dramatic impact of an argument is important to its convincingness; thus its sequence is in part dramatic as well as logical; and it is common practice for the most striking and powerful parts of an argument to be reserved for the end.

But too much can be sacrificed to the wish to persuade. Arguments can be simplified to such a degree that they become valueless; they can be aimed so blatantly at the grandstand that they antagonize otherwise friendly readers; they can also become dishonest, sacrificing the means —logical argument—to the end—persuasion. Any argument that deliberately bases itself on false premises, suppresses or distorts fact, or conceals a shuffling of terms under smooth talk, irrelevant emotional appeals, and the like, does its audience and finally itself no good. (This, at least, has been one premise of our intellectual culture; you may wish to consider its truth, or at least its pragmatic value.)

But within the limits of ethical responsibility, any argument has the right and indeed the obligation to make the best case it can, and thus the right to use the point of attack, the pattern of illustration, the dramatic sequence, and the actual phrasing most likely to be effective with a given audience in a given circumstance.

J. B. S. HALDANE

 WHAT IS LIFE?

I am not going to answer this question. In fact, I doubt if it will ever be possible to give a full answer, because we know what it feels like to be alive, just as we know what redness or pain or effort are. So we cannot describe them in terms of anything else.   But it is not a foolish question to ask, because we often want to know whether a man is alive or not, and when we are dealing with the microscopic agents of disease, it is clear enough that bacteria are alive, but far from clear whether viruses, such as those which cause measles and smallpox, are so.

So we have to try to describe life in terms of something else, even if the description is quite incomplete.   We might try some such expression as "the influence of spirit on matter."   But this would be little use for several reasons.   For one thing, even if you are sure that man, and even dogs, have spirits, it needs a lot of faith to find a spirit in an oyster or a potato.   For another thing, such a definition would certainly cover great works of art, or books which clearly show their author's mind, and go on influencing readers long after he is dead.   Similarly it is no good trying to define life in terms of a life force.   George Bernard Shaw and Professor C. E. M. Joad think there is a life force in living things.   But if this has any meaning, which I doubt, you can only detect the life force in an animal or plant by its effects on matter.   So we should have to define life in terms of matter.   In ordinary life we recognize living things partly by their shape and texture.   But these do not change for some hours after death.   In the case of mammals and birds we are sure they are dead if they are cold.

This test will not work on a frog or a snail.   We take it that they are dead if they will not move when touched.   But in the case of a plant the only obvious test is whether it will grow, and this may take months to find out.   All these tests agree in using some kind of motion or change as the criterion of life, for heat is only irregular motion of atoms. They also agree in being physical rather than chemical tests.   There is no doubt, I think, that we can learn a lot more about life from a chemical than from a physical approach.   This does not mean that life has been fully explained in terms of chemistry.   It does mean that it is a pattern of chemical rather than physical events.   Perhaps I can make this clear by an example.

Suppose a blind man and a deaf man both go to performances of *Macbeth* and of *Alexander Nevksy*.   The deaf man will understand little of the play.   He will not know Duncan was murdered, let alone who did it.   The blind man will miss far less.   The essential part of Shakespeare's plays are the words.   But with the film it will be the other way round.

What is common to all life is the chemical events.   And these are extraordinarily similar in very different organisms.   We may say that life is essentially a pattern of chemical happenings, and that in addition there is some building of a characteristic shape in almost all living things, characteristic motion in most animals, and feeling and purpose in some of them.   The chemical make-up of different living things is very different.   A tree consists largely of wood, which is not very like any of the constituents of a man, though rather like a stuff called glycogen which is part of most, if not all, of our organs.   But the chemical changes which go on in the leaves, bark, and roots of a tree, particularly the roots, are surprisingly like those which go on in human organs.   The roots need oxygen just as a man does, and you can see whether a root is alive, just as you can see whether a dog is alive, by measuring the amount of oxygen which it consumes per minute.   And the oxygen is used in the same kinds of chemical processes, which may roughly be described as controlled burning of foodstuffs at a low temperature.   Under ordinary circumstances oxygen does not combine with sugar unless both are heated.   It does so in almost all living things through the agency of what are called enzymes.   Most of the oxygen which we use has first to unite with an enzyme consisting mainly of protein, but containing a little iron.   Warburg discovered this in yeast in 1924.   In 1926 I did some rather rough experiments which showed the same, or very nearly the same, enzyme in green plants, moths, and rats.   Since then it has been found in a great variety of living things.

Just the same is true for other processes.   A potato makes sugar into starch and your liver makes it into glycogen by substantially the same process.   Most of the steps by which sugar is broken down in alcoholic fermentation and muscular contraction are the same.   And so on.   The end results of these processes are of course very different.   A factory may switch over from making bren guns to making sewing machines or bicycles without very great changes.   Similarly the chemical processes by which an insect makes its skin and a snail its slime are very similar, though the products differ greatly.

In fact, all life is characterized by a fundamentally similar set of chemical processes arranged in very different patterns.   Thus, animals use up foodstuffs, while most plants make them.   But in both plants and animals the building up and breaking down are both going on all the time.   The balance is different.

Engels said that life was the mode of existence of proteins (the word which he used is often translated as "albuminous substances").   This is true in so far as all enzymes seem to be proteins.   And it is true in so far as the fundamental similarity of all living things is a chemical one.

But enzymes and other proteins can be purified and will carry on their characteristic activities in glass bottles. And no biochemist would say they were alive.

In the same way Shakespeare's plays consist of words, whereas words are a very small part of Eisenstein's films. It is important to know this, as it is important to know that life consists of chemical processes. But the arrangement of the words is even more important than the words themselves. And in the same way life is a pattern of chemical processes.

This pattern has special properties. It begets a similar pattern, as a flame does, but it regulates itself as a flame does not except to a slight extent. And of course it has many other peculiarities. So when we have said that life is a pattern of chemical processes, we have said something true and important. It is practically important because we are at last learning how to control some of them, and the first fruits of this knowledge are practical inventions like the use of sulphonamides, penicillin, and streptomycin.

But to suppose that one can describe life fully on these lines is to attempt to reduce it to mechanism, which I believe to be impossible. On the other hand, to say that life does not consist of chemical processes is to my mind as futile and untrue as to say that poetry does not consist of words.

Lines of Inquiry

1 A good definition must be convertible: The thing defined and the defining phrase must cover exactly the same ground. Do you find a convertible definition of life in Haldane's essay?

   a If you do, draw a circle on a sheet of paper. The edge of the circle is the definition you have found; all things you are willing to call alive should be within the circle; and all things you are not willing to call alive should be outside it. Are the boundaries of the definition precise and accurate enough to make this separation possible? Obviously, you will not be able to inventory all things within the circle or outside it: How, then, must you proceed to find out if the definition works?

   b If you do not find a convertible definition in Haldane's essay, how do you account for its absence? (You must consider here how far Haldane pushes his search for an adequate definition, and why he stops where he does.) Now construct what you think to be an adequate definition of life. Test it by the method of *a* above.

2 *a* Make a brief list of the essential points of Haldane's essay—
the stages of his argument—first to last. You will have to
find your own phrasing sometimes. Do you see any general
line of development? Are you able to rearrange the sequence in which the points are made, without changing the
argument?

b Consider the passages of the essay that you have omitted
from your list of essential points: What is their relationship
to that list? What made you decide that these passages
were not essential?

c Is the order of your list, as you have abstracted it, inductive
or deductive? Can you call the entire essay either inductive
or deductive? How do you explain your answer? Can you
shift the order of ideas and illustrations within the essay so as
to make it even more clearly either an inductive or a deductive order? What do you conclude about induction and
deduction?

3 Consider carefully the title and the first and last two paragraphs.
Do you see any relationship between the essay's introduction
(its title is part of its introduction) and its conclusion? Imagine the last two paragraphs omitted: Would the logical conclusion of the essay—its thesis—be damaged? If so, in what
way? If not, how would you justify the inclusion of the last
two paragraphs? What can you decide about the relationship
and uses of introductions and conclusions?

4 Haldane was an eminent biologist. This essay is a chapter in
a survey of modern scientific thought on the processes, meaning, and conditions of biological life: the survey is addressed
to a mass audience. How does the choice of audience appear
to affect Haldane's style—his vocabulary, sentence structure,
connectives, choice of illustrations, and so on? Suppose the
essay was directed to (*a*) an audience of English teachers; (*b*)
an audience of physicists; (*c*) the audience of a sophisticated
intellectual magazine, like *The New Yorker* or *Harpers*. What
changes would you expect Haldane to make, in directing his
essay to each of these in turn?

5 Haldane was not only an eminent biologist; he was also an
eminent political radical. If one were to argue that in its
materialism, its citing of Engels, its quiet contempt for faith,
this essay shows a communist bias and therefore is clearly
propaganda, how might you reply? What do you conclude
about the relations between the motives of a writer and the
truth of what he says?

6 Look at the last paragraph in the essay.

    a Does there seem to be a contradiction between Haldane's saying that life consists of chemical processes and his saying that he believes life can never be explained as mechanism? What definition of mechanism seems implied?

    b How would you reply to the argument that: (*1*) if life is a pattern of chemical processes, and (*2*) if life is not a mechanism, then (*3*) something more than chemical processes must enter into life?

7 *a* Does Haldane convince you that a definition of life is necessary? Why do we need to know if viruses are alive?

    b Could it be argued that Haldane's own definition of life is as useless as any of those he dismisses? Could it be argued that *all* definitions of life are useless?

8 *a* Try to arrange the following in order of abstraction—the most concrete and specific first, the least concrete and specific last: man, law, race, truth, Thomas Jefferson, capital, viruses, justice, potato, money, rain, beauty, poem, love. How do you account for the trouble you run into?

    b Take one of these words, and try to construct for it as sturdy a ladder of abstractions as you can, rising from the most specific thing below it, in the direction of the concrete, to the most general thing above it, in the direction of the abstract. As you consider your list, what seems to account for the number of steps on the ladder?

    c Take four of your terms, and try to define each one (you may use a dictionary). Which terms are the hardest to define?

Lines of Experiment

1 Write an evaluation of Haldane's "What Is Life?" You are free to take any position from total praise to total condemnation, but you may find it strategically wise to stop short of either. In planning your essay, remember that you cannot deal with all the possible arguments for or against Haldane's conclusions; you must focus your discussion. You might concentrate on a specific group of Haldane's premises, or on the process of reasoning by which he reaches his conclusions, or on those conclusions themselves.

If you are arguing *against* Haldane's essay, you will want to think about: (*a*) the consistency of the premises with fact; (*b*) the consistency of one statement with another; (*c*) the consistency of the conclusions with a wider field of ideas. But it is unlikely that you will want to argue on all these lines; an argument of this kind generally must be focused not only on a specific subject but also on a specific aspect of the logical process, in order to be effective and persuasive.

If you are arguing *in favor of* Haldane's essay, you will want to think about the same things—but you will be concerned to find a way to defend them against possible attack. You might decide, for example, what is the most vulnerable part of Haldane's argument, and, by defending that, show that even here his argument holds. You might demonstrate the absurdity of believing anything else. (This, of course, is what Haldane himself tries to do.) You might even dramatize and condense the arguments both for and against, by staging a debate.

2 Write an essay to be called "What Is Pain?" or "What Is Emotion?" or "What Is Effort?"—something of the sort. (To understand what "the sort" is, reread the first paragraph of Haldane's essay.) You may copy Haldane's approach as freely as you wish, although his approach probably will have limited value in your composition—unless you take a purely physical or chemical view of your subject.

If you find yourself writing a long essay, it is your own fault. "What Is Life" is around 1,500 words long—no more than seven typewritten pages. And the subject is rather large, in the abstract. *Focus* brings it to a manageable size.

HAVELOCK ELLIS

THE PHILOSOPHY
OF DANCING

I

Dancing and architecture are the two primary and essential arts. The art of dancing stands as the source of all the arts that express themselves first in the human person. The art of architecture is the beginning of all the arts that lie outside the person. Music, acting, poetry, proceed in the one mighty stream; sculpture, painting, all the arts of design, in the other. There is no primary art outside these two arts, for their origin is far earlier than man himself; and dancing came first.

That is one reason why dancing, however it may at times be scorned by passing fashions, has a profound and eternal attraction even for those one might suppose furthest from its influence. The philosopher and the child are here at one. The joyous beat of the feet of children, the cosmic play of philosophers' thoughts, rise and fall to the same rhythm. If we are indifferent to the art of dancing we have failed to understand, not merely the supreme manifestation of physical life, but also the supreme symbol of spiritual life.

The significance of dancing, in the wide sense, thus lies in the fact that it is simply an intimate concrete appeal of that general rhythm which marks all the physical and spiritual manifestations of life. Dancing is the primitive expression alike of religion and of love,—of religion from the earliest human times we know of, and of love from a period long anterior to the coming of man. The art of dancing, moreover, is intimately entwined with all human traditions of war, of labor, of pleasure, of education, while some of the wisest philosophers and the most ancient civilizations have regarded the dance as the pattern in accordance with which the moral life of man must be woven. To realize, therefore, what dancing means for mankind,—the poignancy and the many-sidedness of its appeal,—we must survey the whole sweep of human life, both at its highest and at its deepest moments.

II

"What do you dance?" When a man belonging to one branch of the great Bantu division of mankind met a member of another, said Livingstone, that was the question he asked. What a man danced, that was his tribe, his social customs, his religion; for, as an anthropologist has recently put it, "a savage does not preach his religion, he dances it." There are peoples in the world who have no secular dances, only religious dances, and some investigators believe that every dance was of religious origin. That view seems too extreme, even if we admit that some even of our modern dances, like the waltz, may have been originally religious. It is more reasonable to suppose, with Wundt, that the dance was, in the beginning, the expression of the whole man.

Yet among primitive peoples religion is so large a part of life that the dance inevitably becomes of supreme religious importance. To dance was at once both to worship and to pray. Just as we still find in our Prayer Books that there are divine services for all the great fundamental acts of life, for birth, for marriage, for death, as well as for the cosmic procession of the world as marked by ecclesiastical festivals, and for the great catastrophes of nature, such as droughts, so also it has ever been among primitive peoples. For all the solemn occasions of life, for bridals and for funerals, for seed-time and for harvest, for war and for peace, for all these things, there were fitting dances.

To-day we find religious people who in church pray for rain or for the restoration of their friends to health. Their forefathers also desired these things but, instead of praying for them, they danced for them the fitting dance which tradition had handed down, and which the chief or the medicine-man solemnly conducted. The gods themselves danced, as the stars dance in the sky,—so at least the Mexicans, and we may be sure many other peoples, have held,—and to dance is therefore to imitate the gods, to work with them, perhaps to persuade them to work in the direction of our own desires. "Work for us!" is the song-refrain, expressed or implied, of every religious dance. In the worship of solar deities in various countries it was customary to dance around the altar, as the stars dance around the sun. Even in Europe the popular belief that the sun dances on Easter Sunday has perhaps scarcely yet died out. To dance is to take part in the cosmic control of the world. Every sacred dionysian dance is an imitation of the divine dance.

All religions, and not merely those of primitive character, have been at the outset, and sometimes throughout, in some measure saltatory. This is the case all over the world. It is not more pronounced in early Christianity and among the ancient Hebrews who danced before the ark, than among the Australian aborigines whose great *corroborees* are religious dances conducted by the medicine-men with their sacred staves in their hands. Every American Indian tribe seems to have had its own religious dances, varied and elaborate, often with a richness of meaning which the patient study of modern investigators has but slowly revealed. The Shamans in the remote steppes of Northern Siberia have their ecstatic religious dances, and in modern Europe the Turkish dervishes—perhaps of related stock—still dance in their cloisters similar ecstatic dances, combined with song and prayer, as a regular part of devotional service.

These religious dances, it may be realized, are sometimes ecstatic, sometimes pantomimic. It is natural that this should be so. By each road it is possible to penetrate toward the divine mystery of the world. The auto-intoxication of rapturous movement brings the devotee, for a while at least, into that self-forgetful union with the not-self which the mystic ever seeks. Pantomimic dances, on the other hand, with their effort to heighten natural expression and to imitate natural processes, bring the dances into the divine sphere of creation and enable them to assist vicariously in the energy of the gods. The dance thus becomes the presentation of a divine drama, the vital reënactment of a sacred history in which the worshiper is enabled to play a real part. In this way ritual arises.

It is in this sphere—highly primitive as it is—of pantomimic dancing crystallized in ritual, rather than in the sphere of ecstatic dancing that we may to-day in civilization witness the survivals of dance in religion. The Divine Services of the American Indian, said Lewis Morgan, took the form of "set dances, each with its own name, songs, steps, and costume." At this point the early Christian worshiping the Divine Body was able to enter into spiritual communion with the ancient Egyptian or the American Indian. They are all alike privileged to enter, each in his own way, a sacred mystery, and to participate in the sacrifice of a heavenly Mass.

What by some is considered to be the earliest known Christian ritual —the "Hymn of Jesus," assigned to the second century—is nothing but a sacred dance. Eusebius in the third century stated that Philo's description of the worship of the Therapeuts agreed at all points with Christian custom, and that meant the prominence of dancing, to which indeed Eusebius often refers in connection with Christian worship. It has been supposed by some writers that the Christian Church was originally a theatre, the choir being the raised stage,—even the word *choir,* it is argued, meaning an enclosed space for dancing. It is certain that at the Eucharist the faithful gesticulated with their hands, danced with their feet, flung their bodies about. Chrysostom, who referred to this behavior round the Holy Table at Antioch, only objected to drunken excesses in connection with it; the custom itself he evidently regarded as traditional and right.

While the central function of Christian worship is a sacred drama, a divine Pantomime, the associations of Christianity and dancing are by no means confined to the ritual of the Mass and its later more attenuated transformations. The very idea of dancing had a sacred and mystic meaning to the early Christians, who had meditated profoundly on the text, "We have piped unto you and ye have not danced." Origen prayed that above all things there may be made operative in us the mystery "of the stars dancing in Heaven for the salvation of the Universe." St. Basil, who was enamored of natural things, described the angels dancing in Heaven, and later the author of the *Dieta Salutis* (said to have been St. Bonaventura), which is supposed to have influenced Dante in assigning so large a place to dancing in the *Paradiso,* described dancing as the occupation of the inmates of Heaven, and Christ as the leader of the dance. Even in more modern times an ancient Cornish carol sang of the life of Jesus as of a dance, and represented him as declaring that he died in order that man "may come unto the general dance."

This attitude could not fail to be reflected in practice. Genuine and not merely formalized and unrecognizable dancing, such as the traditionalized Mass, must have been frequently introduced into Christian worship in early times. Until a few centuries ago it remained not uncommon, and it still persists in remote corners of the Christian world. In English cathedrals dancing went on until the fourteenth century. At Paris, Limoges, and elsewhere in France, the priests danced in the choir at Easter up to the seventeenth century; in Roussillon up to the eighteenth century. Roussillon is a province with Spanish traditions, and it was in Spain that religious dancing took deepest root and flourished longest. In the cathedrals of Seville, Toledo, Valencia, and Xeres there was formerly dancing, although it now survives only at a few special festivals in the first. At Alaro in Majorca, also, at the present day, a dancing company called Els Cosiers, on the festival of St. Roch, the patron saint of the place, dance in the church, in fanciful costumes, with tambourines, up to the steps of the high altar, immediately after Mass, and then dance out of the church. In another part of the Christian world, in the Abyssinian Church,—an offshoot of the Eastern Church, —dancing is said still to form a part of the worship.

Dancing, we may see throughout the world, has been so essential, so fundamental a part of all vital and undegenerate religion, that whenever a new religion appears, a religion of the spirit and not merely an anæmic religion of the intellect, we should still have to ask of it the question of the Bantu: What do you dance?

III

Dancing is not only intimately associated with religion, it has an equally intimate association with love. Here indeed the relationship is even more primitive, for it is far older than man. Dancing, said Lucian, is as old as love. Among insects and among birds, for instance, it may be said that dancing is often an essential part of courtship. The male dances, sometimes in rivalry with other males, in order to charm the female; then, after a short or long interval, the female is aroused to share his ardor and join in the dance; the final climax of the dance is in the union of the lovers. This primitive love-dance of insects and birds reappears among savages in various parts of the world, notably in Africa, and in a conventionalized and symbolized form it is still danced in civilization to-day. It is indeed in this aspect that dancing has so often aroused reprobation, from the days of early Christianity until the present, among those for whom the dance has merely been, in the words of a seventeenth-century writer, a series of "immodest and dissolute movements by which the cupidity of the flesh is aroused."

But in Nature and among primitive peoples it has its value precisely on this account. It is a process of courtship and, even more than that, it is a novitiate for love, and a novitiate which was found to be an admirable training for love. Among some peoples, indeed, as the Omahas, the same word meant both to dance and to love. Here we are in the sphere of sexual selection. By his beauty, his energy, his skill, the male must win the female, so impressing the image of himself on her imagination that finally her desire is aroused to overcome her reticence. That is the task of the male throughout nature, and in innumerable species besides man it has been found that the school in which the task may best be learned is the dancing school. The moths and the butterflies, the African ostrich, and the Sumatran Argus pheasant, with their fellows innumerable, have been the precursors of man in the strenuous school of erotic dancing, fitting themselves for selection by the females of their choice as the most splendid progenitors of the future race.

From this point of view, it is clear, the dance performed a double function. On the one hand, the tendency to dance, arising under the obscure stress of this impulse, brought out the best possibilities the individual held the promise of; on the other hand, at the moment of courtship, the display of the activities thus acquired developed, on the sensory side, all the latest possibilities of beauty which at last became conscious in man. That this came about we cannot easily escape concluding. How it came about, how it happens that some of the least intelligent of creatures thus developed a beauty and a grace that are enchanting even to our human eyes, is a miracle effected by the mystery of sex, which we cannot yet comprehend.

When we survey the human world, the erotic dance of the animal world is seen not to have lost but rather to have gained influence. It is no longer the males alone who are thus competing for the love of the females.   It comes about by a modification in the method of sexual selection that often not only the men dance for the women, but the women for the men, each striving in a storm of rivalry to arouse and attract the desire of the other.   In innumerable parts of the world the season of love is a time which the nubile of each sex devote to dancing in each other's presence,—sometimes one sex, sometimes the other, sometimes both, in the frantic effort to display all the force and energy, the skill and endurance, the beauty and grace, which at this moment are yearning within them to be poured into the vital stream of the race's life.

From this point of view of sexual selection we may better understand the immense ardor with which every part of the wonderful human body has been brought into the play of the dance.   The men and women of races spread all over the world have shown a marvelous skill and patience in imparting rhythm and music to the most unlikely, the most rebellious regions of the body, all wrought by desire into potent and dazzling images.   To the vigorous races of Northern Europe in their cold damp climate, dancing comes naturally to be dancing of the legs, so naturally that the English poet, as a matter of course, assumes that the dance of Salome was a "twinkling of the feet."   But on the opposite side of the world, in Japan and notably in Java and Madagascar, dancing may be exclusively dancing of the arms and hands, in some of the South Sea islands even of the hands and fingers alone.   Dancing may even be carried on in the seated posture, as occurs at Fiji in a dance connected with the preparation of the sacred drink, *ava*.   In some districts of Southern Tunisia dancing, again, is dancing of the hair, and all night long, till they perhaps fall exhausted, the marriageable girls will move their heads to the rhythm of a song, maintaining their hair in perpetual balance and sway.   Elsewhere, notably in Africa, but also sometimes in Polynesia, as well as in the dances that had established themselves in ancient Rome, dancing is dancing of the body, with vibratory or rotatory movements of breasts or flanks.

The complete dance along these lines is, however, that in which all the play of all the chief muscle-groups of the body is harmoniously interwoven.   When both sexes take part in such an exercise, developed into an idealized yet passionate pantomime of love, we have the complete erotic dance.   In Spain the dance of this kind has sometimes attained its noblest and most harmoniously beautiful expression.   It is in the relation of these dances to the primitive mystery of sexual selection that their fascination lies.   From the narratives of travelers, it would appear that it was especially in the eighteenth century that among all classes in

Spain dancing of this kind was immensely popular. The Church tacitly encouraged it, as an Aragonese canon told Baretti in 1770, in spite of its occasional indecorum, as a useful safety-valve for the emotions. It was not less seductive to the foreign spectator than to the people themselves. The grave traveler Peyron, toward the end of the century, growing eloquent over the languorous and flexible movements of the dance, the bewitching attitudes, the voluptuous curves of the arms, declares that when one sees a beautiful Spanish woman dance one is inclined to fling all philosophy to the winds. And even that highly respectable Anglican clergyman, the Reverend Joseph Townsend, was constrained to state that he could "almost persuade myself" that if the fandango were suddenly played in church the gravest worshipers would start up to join in that "lascivious pantomime."

There we have the rock against which the primitive dance of sexual selection suffers shipwreck as civilization advances. And that prejudice of civilization becomes so ingrained that it is brought to bear even on the primitive dance. The Pygmies of Africa are described by Sir H. H. Johnston as a very decorous and highly moral people, but their dances, he adds, are not so. Yet these dances, though in Johnston's eyes, blinded by European civilization, "grossly indecent," he honestly, and inconsistently, adds are "danced reverently."

IV

From the vital function of dancing in love, and its sacred function in religion, to dancing as an art, a profession, an amusement, may seem, at the first glance, a sudden leap. In reality the transition is gradual, and it began to be made at a very early period in diverse parts of the globe. All the matters that enter into courtship tend to fall under the sway of art; their æsthetic pleasure is a secondary reflection of their primary vital joy. Dancing could not fail to be first in manifesting this tendency. But even religious dancing swiftly exhibited the same transformation; dancing, like priesthood, became a profession, and dancers, like priests, formed a caste. This, for instance, took place in old Hawaii. The *hula* dance was a religious dance; it required a special education and an arduous training; moreover, it involved the observance of important taboos and the exercise of sacred rites; therefore it was carried out by paid performers, a professional caste.

In India, again, the Devadasis, or sacred dancing girls, are at once both religious and professional dancers. They are married to gods, they are taught dancing by the Brahmins, they figure in religious ceremonies, and their dances represent the life of the god they are married to, as well as the emotions of love they experience for him. Yet at the same time, they also give professional performances in the houses of rich private persons who pay for them. It thus comes about that to the foreigner the Devadasis scarcely seem very unlike the Ramedjenis, the dancers of the street, who are of very different origin, and mimic in their performances the play of merely human passions. The Portuguese conquerors of India called both kinds of dancers indiscriminately Balheideras (or dancers) which we have corrupted in Bayaderes.

In our modern world professional dancing as an art has become altogether divorced from religion, and even, in any vital sense, from love; it is scarcely even possible, so far as western civilization is concerned, to trace back the tradition to either source. If we survey the development of dancing as an art in Europe, it seems to me that we have to recognize two streams of tradition which have sometimes merged, but yet remain in their ideals and their tendencies essentially distinct. I would call these traditions the Classical, which is much the more ancient and fundamental, and may be said to be of Egyptian origin, and the Romantic, which is of Italian origin, chiefly known to us as the ballet. The first is, in its pure form, solo dancing, and is based on the rhythmic beauty and expressiveness of the simple human personality when its energy is concentrated in passionate movement. The second is concerted dancing, mimetic and picturesque, wherein the individual is subordinated to the wider and variegated rhythm of the group. It may be easy to devise another classification, but this is simple and instructive enough for our purpose.

There can scarcely be a doubt that Egypt has been for many thousands of years, as indeed it still remains, a great dancing centre, the most influential dancing-school the world has ever seen, radiating its influence south and east and north. We may perhaps even agree with the historian of the dance, who terms it "the mother-country of all civilized dancing." We are not entirely dependent on the ancient wall-pictures of Egypt for our knowledge of Egyptian skill in the art. Sacred mysteries, it is known, were danced in the temples, and queens and princesses took part in the orchestras that accompanied them. It is significant that the musical instruments still peculiarly associated with the dance were originated or developed in Egypt; the guitar is an Egyptian instrument, and its name was a hieroglyphic already used when the Pyramids were being built; the cymbal, the tambourine, triangles, and castanets, in one form or another, were all familiar to the ancient Egyptians, and with the Egyptian art of dancing they must have spread all round the shores of the Mediterranean, the great focus of our civilization, at a very early date.   Even beyond the Mediterranean, at Cadiz, dancing that was essentially Egyptian in character was established, and Cadiz became the dancing-school of Spain.   The Nile and Cadiz were thus the two great centres of ancient dancing, and Martial mentions them both together, for each supplied its dancers to Rome.   This dancing, alike whether Egyptian or Gaditanian, was the expression of the individual dancer's body and art; the garments played but a small part in it, they were frequently transparent, and sometimes discarded altogether.   It was, and it remains, simple, personal, passionate dancing; classic, therefore, in the same sense as, on the side of literature, the poetry of Catullus is classic.

Ancient Greek dancing was essentially classic dancing as here understood.   On the Greek vases, as reproduced in Emmanuel's attractive book on Greek dancing and elsewhere, we find the same play of the arms, the same sideward turn, the same extreme backward extension of the body, which had long before been represented in Egyptian monuments.   Many supposedly modern movements in dancing were certainly already common both to Egyptian and Greek dancing, as well as the clapping of hands to keep time, which is still an accompaniment of Spanish dancing.

It seems clear, however, that, on this general classic and Mediterranean basis, Greek dancing had a development so refined and so special that it exercised no influence outside Greece.   Dancing became indeed the more characteristic and the most generally cultivated of Greek arts.   It may well be that the Greek drama arose out of dance and song, and that the dance throughout was an essential and plastic element in it.   It is said that Æschylus developed the technique of dancing, and that Sophocles danced in his own dramas.   In these developments, no doubt, Greek dancing tended to overpass the fundamental limits of classic dancing and fore-shadowed the ballet.

The real germ of the ballet, however, is to be found in Rome, where the pantomime with its concerted and picturesque method of expressive action was developed; and Italy is the home of Romantic dancing.   The same impulse which produced the pantomime, produced more than a thousand years later, in the same Italian region, the modern ballet.   In both cases, one is inclined to think, we may trace the influence of the same Etruscan and Tuscan race which so long has had its seat here, a

race with a genius for expressive, dramatic, picturesque art.   We see
it on the walls of Etruscan tombs and again in pictures of Botticelli and
his fellow Tuscans.   The modern ballet, it is generally believed, had its
origin in the spectacular pageants at the marriage of Galeazzo Visconti,
Duke of Milan, in 1489.

The popularity of such performances spread to the other Italian courts,
including Florence; and Catherine de Medici, when she became Queen
of France, brought the Italian ballet to Paris.   Here it speedily became
fashionable.   Kings and queens were its admirers, and even took part
in it; great statesmen were its patrons.   Before long it became an established institution with a vital life and growth of its own, maintained
by distinguished musicians, artists, and dancers.

Romantic dancing, to a much greater extent than what I have called
classic dancing, which depends so largely on simple personal qualities,
tends to be vitalized by transplantation and the absorption of new influences, provided that the essential basis of technique and tradition
is preserved in the new development.   Lulli in the seventeenth century
brought women into the ballet; Camargo discarded the fashionable un-
wieldy costumes, so rendering possible all the freedom and airy grace
of later dancing; Noverre elaborated plot unraveled by gesture and
dance alone, and so made the ballet a complete art-form.

In the French ballet of the eighteenth century a very high degree of
perfection seems thus to have been reached, while in Italy where the
ballet had originated it decayed, and Milan which had been its source
became the nursery of a tradition of devitalized technique carried to
the finest point of delicate perfection.

The influence of the French school was maintained as a living force
into the nineteenth century, overspreading the world, by the genius of a
few individual dancers.   When they had gone the ballet slowly and
steadily declined.   As it declined as an art, so also it declined in credit
and in popularity; it became scarcely respectable even to admire dancing.   Thirty years ago, the few who still appreciated the art of dancing
—and how few they were!—had to seek for it painfully and sometimes
in strange surroundings.   A recent historian of dancing, in a book published so lately as 1906, declared that "the ballet is now a thing of the
past, and, with the modern change of ideas, a thing that is never likely
to be resuscitated."   That historian never mentioned Russian ballet, yet
his book was scarcely published before the Russian ballet arrived, to
scatter ridicule over his rash prophecy by raising the ballet to a pitch

of perfection it can rarely have surpassed, as an expressive, emotional, even passionate form of living art.

The Russian ballet was an offshoot from the French ballet, and illustrates once more the vivifying effect of transplantation on the art of romantic dancing.   The Empress Anna introduced it toward the middle of the eighteenth century, and appointed a French ballet master and a Neapolitan composer to carry it on; it reached a high degree of technical perfection during the following hundred years, on the traditional lines, and the principal dancers were all imported from Italy.   It was not until recent years that this firm discipline and these ancient traditions were vitalized into an art-form of exquisite and vivid beauty by the influence of the soil in which they had slowly taken root.   This contact, when at last it was effected, involved a kind of revolution; for its outcome, while genuine ballet, has yet all the effect of delicious novelty.   The tradition by itself was in Russia an exotic without real life, and had nothing to give to the world; on the other hand a Russian ballet apart from that tradition, if we can conceive such a thing, would have been formless, extravagant, bizarre, not subdued to any fine æsthetic ends.

What we see here, in the Russian ballet as we know it to-day, is a splendid and arduous technical tradition, brought at last—by the combined genius of designers, composers, and dancers—into real fusion with an environment from which during more than a century it had been held apart: Russian genius for music, Russian feeling for rhythm, Russian skill in the use of bright color, and, perhaps, above all, the Russian orgiastic temperament and the general Slav passion for folk-dancing, shown in all branches of the race, Polish, Bohemian, Bulgarian and Servian.   The result has been that our age sees one of the most splendid movements in the whole history of romantic dancing.

V

Dancing as an art, we may be sure, cannot die out but will always be undergoing a re-birth.   Not merely as an art but also as a social custom, it perpetually emerges afresh from the soul of the people.   Less than a century ago the polka thus arose, extemporized by the Bohemian servant girl, Anna Slezakova, out of her own head for the joy of her own heart, and only rendered a permanent form, apt for world-wide popularity, by the accident that it was observed and noted down by an artist.   Dancing had forever been in existence as a spontaneous custom, a social discipline.   Thus it is, finally, that dancing meets us, not only as love, as religion, as art, but also as morals.

All human work, under natural conditions, is a kind of dance.   In a large and learned work, supported by an immense amount of evidence, Karl Bücher has argued that work differs from the dance not in kind but only in degree, since they are both essentially rhythmic.   In the memory of those who have ever lived on a sailing ship—that loveliest of human creations now disappearing from the world—there will always linger the echo of the chanties which sailors sang as they hoisted the topsail yard or wound the capstan or worked the pumps.   That is the type of primitive combined work, and it is indeed difficult to see how such work can be effectively accomplished without such a device for regulating the rhythmic energy of the muscles.

The dance-rhythm of work has thus acted socializingly in a parallel line with the dance-rhythms of the arts, and indeed in part as their inspirer.   Thus, as Bücher points out, poetic metre may be conceived as arising out of work; metre is the rhythmic stamping of feet, as in the technique of verse it is still metaphorically so called; iambics and trochees, spondees and anapæsts and dactyls may still be heard among blacksmiths smiting the anvil or navvies wielding their hammers in the streets.   In so far as they arose out of work, music and singing and dancing are naturally a single art.   Herein the ancient ballad of Europe is a significant type.   It is, as the name indicates, a dance as much as a song, performed by a singer who sang the story and a chorus who danced and shouted the apparently meaningless refrain; it is absolutely the chanty of the sailors, and is equally apt for the purposes of con-certed work.   And yet our most complicated musical forms are evolved from similar dances.   The symphony is but a development of a dance-suite,—in the first place folk-dances,—such as Bach and Händel com-posed.   Indeed a dance still lingers always at the heart of music, and even at the heart of the composer.   Mozart used often to say, so his wife stated, that it was dancing, not music, that he really cared for. Wagner believed that Beethoven's seventh symphony—to some of us the most fascinating of all of them, and the most purely musical—was an apotheosis of the dance, and even if that belief throws no light on the intention of Beethoven it is at least a revelation of Wagner's own feeling for the dance.

It is, however, the dance itself, apart from work and apart from the other arts, which, in the opinion of many to-day, has had a decisive influence in socializing, that is to say in moralizing, the human species. Work showed the necessity of harmonious rhythmic coöperation, but the dance developed that rhythmic coöperation and imparted a beneficent impetus to all human activities. It was Grosse, in his *Beginnings of Art,* who first clearly set forth the high social significance of the dance in the creation of human civilization. The participants in a dance, as all observers of savages have noted, exhibit a wonderful unison; they are, as it were, fused into a single being stirred by a single impulse. Social unification is thus accomplished. Apart from war, this is the chief factor making for social solidarity in primitive life; it was indeed the best training for war, as for all the other coöperative arts of life. All our most advanced civilization, Grosse insisted, is based on dancing. It is the dance that socialized man.

Thus, in the large sense, dancing has possessed peculiar value as a method of national education. As civilization grew self-conscious this was realized. "One may judge of a King," according to an ancient Chinese maxim, "by the state of dancing during his reign." So also among the Greeks: it has been said that dancing and music lay at the foundation of the whole political and military as well as the religious organization of the Dorian states.

In the narrow sense, in individual education, the great importance of dancing came to be realized, even at an early stage of human development, and still more in the ancient civilizations. "A good education," Plato declared in the *Laws,* the final work of his old age, "consists in knowing how to sing well and dance well." And in our own day one of the keenest and most enlightened of educators has lamented the decay of dancing. The revival of dancing, Stanley Hall declares, is imperatively needed to give poise to the nerves, schooling to the emotions, strength to the will, and to harmonize the feelings and the intellect with the body which supports them.

It can scarcely be said that these functions of dancing are yet generally realized and embodied afresh in education. For if it is true that dancing engendered morality, it is also true that in the end, by the irony of fate, morality, grown insolent, sought to crush its own parent, and for a time succeeded only too well. Four centuries ago dancing was attacked by that spirit, in England called Puritanism, which at that time spread over the greater part of Europe, just as active in Bohemia as in England, and which has indeed been described as a general onset of developing Urbanism against the old Ruralism. It made no distinction between good and bad, nor paused to consider what would come when dancing went. So it was that, as Rémy de Gourmont remarks, the drinking-shop conquered the dance, and alcohol replaced the violin.

But when we look at the function of dancing in life from a higher and wider standpoint, this episode in its history ceases to occupy so large a place. The conquest of dancing has never proved in the end a matter for rejoicing, even to morality, while an art which has been so intimately mixed with all the finest and deepest springs of life has always asserted itself afresh. For dancing is the loftiest, the most moving, the most beautiful of the arts, because it is no mere translation or abstraction from life; it is life itself. It is the only art, as Rahel Varnhagen said, of which we ourselves are the stuff.

It thus comes about that, beyond its manifold practical significance, dancing has always been felt to possess also a symbolic significance. Marcus Aurelius was accustomed to regard the art of life as like the dancer's art, though that Imperial Stoic could not resist adding that in some respects it was more like the wrestler's art. In our own time, Nietzsche, from first to last, showed himself possessed by the conception of the art of life as a dance, in which the dancer achieves the rhythmic freedom and harmony of his soul beneath the shadow of a hundred Damoclean swords. The dance lies at the beginning of art, and we find it also at the end. The first creators of civilization were making the dance, and the philosopher of to-day, hovering over the dark abyss of insanity, with bleeding feet and muscles strained to the breaking-point, still seems to himself to be weaving the maze of the dance.

Lines of Inquiry

1 This essay is divided into five sections.

    a Assign to each section a characterizing phrase, so as to have a topic outline reflecting these divisions. What accounts for the sequence of topics?

    b Consider alternative sequences; choosing one of these alternatives, consider the consequences for the essay were it to be followed instead of the original sequence.

    c How are the sections linked? Eliminate the section break between the first and second sections, i.e., read through it. What is the result? Would a simple transitional phrase be a better way of moving from the matter of section I to that of section II?

    d Compare the opening paragraphs of these two sections: Are they related in any way?

e Now look at the closing paragraph of the second section: How is it related to the first paragraph of that section? Are the other sections constructed in a similar fashion?

f Look at the introductory paragraphs and then read the last section, entire: How is introduction related to conclusion? What is the emotional effect of that relationship?

2 Construct a graph or chart of the system of classification employed by Ellis in the first section of this essay. Obviously, you will start with "the two primary and essential arts." Your chart will begin like this:

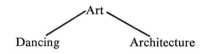

$$\text{Art}$$
$$\text{Dancing} \qquad \text{Architecture}$$

Ellis himself gives you examples of the arts classifiable as secondary to each.

a How many of these secondary arts will you include in your chart? On what basis will you include them? What will determine when you stop?

b Your next job is to decide how the author's remarks about dancing in relation to religion and love may be incorporated. Religion is not treated precisely as a subclass of the dance, nor the dance precisely as a subclass of religion: What is their relationship to one another?

c Read the third paragraph carefully. Is Ellis trying to suggest in this paragraph that war, labor, pleasure, education, and morality are all aspects—subclasses—of the dance? What does your reply suggest to you about systems of classification?

d In section IV, Ellis classifies dancing as either Classical or Romantic. Can you incorporate this classification in your chart? If not, why not?

e Consider your answers to *a* and *b* above. Why does Ellis begin his essay with a classification? What does classification as a rhetorical method offer the writer?

3 The sequence of illustrations in the second section falls into a marked pattern: What is Ellis's intention in following that pattern? If he were writing in Bantu, might he choose a different pattern? What general principle of composition seems to be reflected here, in his practice?

4 Why does Ellis give what is virtually a capsule history of the dance, in the fourth section? Why not give it in the very beginning, instead?

5 *a* Here are five sentences, all taken from the first section of the essay. What do they have in common?

    (*1*) "Dancing and architecture are the two primary and essential arts."

    (*2*) "The philosopher and the child are here at one."

    (*3*) "If we are indifferent to the art of dancing, we have failed to understand, not merely the supreme manifestation of physical life but also the supreme symbol of spiritual life."

    (*4*) "Dancing is the primitive expression alike of religion and of love."

    (*5*) "To realize, therefore, what dancing means for mankind . . . we must survey the whole sweep of human life, both at its highest and at its deepest moments."

  b Read the first three paragraphs in the second section, and underline each instance in which Ellis uses the same basic rhetorical technique. This technique is employed in the essay on a much larger and more complex scale as well— where, and why?

  c How is this aspect of Ellis's technique related to what he has to say about dancing?

6 Much of the effect of this essay derives from small stylistic details. What is the force of each of the following, within its context? Can you begin to devise a system for classifying these elements—a way of distinguishing them from one another, by a word or a phrase?

  a "Even in Europe, the popular belief that *the sun dances on Easter Sunday* has perhaps scarcely yet died out."

  b "For all the solemn occasions of life, *for bridals and for funerals, for seed time and for harvest, for war and for peace,* for all these things, there were fitting dances."

  c "In the memory of those who have ever lived on a sailing ship—*that loveliest of human creations, now disappearing from the world*—there will always linger the echo of the chanties which sailors sang. . . ."

  d "For if it is true that dancing *engendered* morality, it is also true that in the end, by the irony of fate, morality, *grown insolent, sought to crush its own parent.* . . ."

  e "Marcus Aurelius was accustomed to regard the art of life as like the dancer's art, though *that Imperial Stoic* could not resist adding that in some respects it was more like the wrestler's art."

7 *a* Could one argue that music is the art "at the source of all the arts that express themselves first in the human person"?

b If one were to set out to destroy Ellis's argument (is it an argument?), how could one proceed? Haldane's method in "What Is Life?" may suggest one line; a close consideration of the classification used by Ellis in his opening paragraph may suggest other lines of attack.

8 a Could Ellis's essay itself be called a kind of dance? How would you describe its sequence, as a pattern of expression analogous to that of the dance?

b If you were to try to dance it, what might you be able to communicate—and what would you necessarily lose?

Lines of Experiment

1 Ellis's discussion of dancing turns on a classification. Choose a congenial subject—a sport, a study, a war, a building, a vacation, a school, a human type—and approach it through a system of classification. You need not present your subject in a flattering light: The most dismal sport can be brought into focus by means of classification as readily as the most exciting one can. Use your first paragraph to establish the lines of your classification. The system of classification you adopt should lead directly to the point you want to make. Ellis's system makes it possible to place dancing at the center of human activity and to treat it with high seriousness; a different system could easily be made to lead to a satirical analysis of one style of dancing: "Some dances are serious, others are comic—a few are idiotic. The folk-fling is clearly idiotic."

2 Write a narrative or descriptive essay on dancing. You need not adopt Ellis's attitude, and if dancing seems uncongenial, choose another specific subject.

"The Philosophy of Dancing" is neither narrative nor descriptive, of course: Ellis purposes to establish the significance of an idea by relating it logically to other ideas—to religion, love, etc. "Art and Isadora" by John Dos Passos (see p. 72) forms an interesting point of comparison between the mimetic and the logical, and may provide you with a more immediate model. Dos Passos does not define, or classify: He *shows*. Art—and dancing—is what Isadora did. In your own essay, focus on the image. Nonetheless, before you begin to write you may find it useful to consider what class your specific image falls into—what like things lie around it, and what its rank is in relation to those like things. Such a system of classification, by placing a subject firmly within the field of its peers, can suggest not merely points of contrast and comparison but even insights into its meaning and value. Both are useful in composition: the points of contrast and comparison as a way of placing a subject in perspective, of setting it off, and so defining its shape; the insights into its meaning and value as a way of controlling the sequence of detail and the tonal effects for which every sentence should strive.

BERNARD BERELSON

 VOTING BEHAVIOUR

This term deals with the people's choice—why do people vote as they do?   In most of the democratic countries of the west, large numbers of citizens eligible for the ballot do not vote at all, and the decision to support one candidate rather than another is by no means based simply and directly on individual consideration of the political issues involved. Most research on the topic centres on the social and psychological factors underlying voting decisions.   Although it mainly reflects U.S. practice in presidential elections, such research does perhaps provide some insight into voting behaviour generally.

According to the traditional view of voting as presented in classical texts of democratic theory, inspired by the political views of the 18th-century Enlightenment, the voter is supposed to be interested in politics and to express that interest by broad, continuous and critical attention to the flow of electoral news and talks in the communication mediums. He is supposed to be well informed on campaign issues, events and personalities; to give impartial, rational consideration to the issues at hand; to judge political proposals in the light of general principles dictated by the public interest; and to discuss political matters with his fellow voters so that a wide popular debate on the issues will be held, led by the candidates themselves.   The key words used to describe the voter in political theory are such terms as informed, interested, rational, principled.   That is what the voter is supposed to be like; what is he really like?

Influence of Social Status   First, as to the basis of voting: people's votes are closely tied to their social position.   In this way, the vote serves as the political projection and expression of a country's social fabric.   In the United States in the second half of the 20th century, there were three major factors of a sociological character that affected the vote decision:

1 Ecological, *i.e.,* environmental differences in viewpoint, reflecting the distinctive regional outlooks of, for instance, the south or New England or such residential differences as the suburb against the metropolis.

2 Socioeconomic status, under which are included such characteristics as class, occupation, income level and class identification (*i.e.,* the voter's feeling as to what class he belongs to, regardless of where "objective" criteria place him).   There is, however, substantial deviation between the class-predicted vote and actual vote.   Substantial numbers do not vote with their class—and there are probably more deviants from the "labour vote" than from the corresponding "business vote."

3 Ethnic or "minority" characteristics such as race, nationality and, importantly, religion.   This factor receives less overt attention, possibly because of its greater social sensitivity.   The plain fact is that the two-party vote in the U.S., at least in national elections, can be closely tied to the ethnic identification of the voters.   This is true not only of Negro-white differences but also differences in voting behaviour between native born and foreign born, between groups of diverse national origin and finally between Protestants on the one hand and Catholics and Jews on the other.   Indeed, there is a good reason to believe that the influence of religion on vote—simply in the sense of religious membership or identification—is stronger than the class or socioeconomic difference.   If there is a "class vote" in the U.S. there is a "religious vote" as well.

But that is not the whole story.   In part, such political differences by strata, whatever their historical origins, are sustained by the day-to-day personal relations in the family, in the work place and among friends. First, there is a hereditary vote—the child following the politics of the parents—and there is near unanimity on political questions inside the family, within as well as between generations.   Similarly, there is high political agreement among friends and among co-workers.   In short, the typical voter is encapsulated in a congenial and harmonious atmosphere in which political preferences are communicated to him informally and indirectly in a socially reinforcing manner.

In addition, there is the continuity provided by the "party habit," *i.e.,* the tendency to go along with the same selection made earlier, partly as a way of justifying one's preceding vote decisions.

Small wonder, then, that voting preferences are usually quite stable. Most voters do not change their minds during a presidential campaign, and large numbers do not change from one election to the next. It typically requires a substantial change in one's social position, either relatively or absolutely, to effect a major change in vote—for example, for the society, a depression that stirs up the political situation enough to challenge the preferences of many; for the group, a politically tinged event such as regional unemployment or the threat of racial desegregation; for the individual, an upward movement in occupational mobility that involves shifts in residence, friendships, standards of living and social judgment.

Shifts in Party Allegiance   But some people do change their votes; who are they?   Evidence suggests that they are the less partisan-minded voters who are relatively indifferent to the above considerations, or are subject to conflicting group claims on their loyalty.   Certainly only a minority in the United States are highly interested, by any reasonable definition, in the political scene in normal times, and the most partisan individuals are precisely the people who change their votes least frequently and with greatest difficulty.   The less interested are the less partisan, and as such they are less likely to have their vote based solidly on the types of characteristics noted above; they may be subject to social cross pressures on their vote, having a foot in each camp, so that the outcome of the election means less to them.   For example, wealthy members of an ethnic group may be under such cross pressures: their wealth may incline them in one direction and their ethnic status in the other.   Their personal associations tend to be in the same situation, and so reinforce the conflict.   There are always a number of people so situated that the election results are seen by them to be of little personal consequence.   They are the people who tend not to follow the progress of the campaign in newspapers and on television or radio; who are most influenced by their personal contacts with friends and party workers; who are least concerned about the issues of the campaign; and who settle their vote late in the campaign.

Thus voting behaviour creates a striking spectacle in which the most interested and most knowledgeable are the least open to persuasion, most of them knowing well ahead of the campaign, long before either candidates or platforms are selected, how they will vote.

On the other hand, those most subject to change are the least involved and the most likely to shift their preference on frivolous grounds.

Issues   As to the content of politics, the important issues appear to be of two kinds—what have been called "position" issues and "style" issues.   The former are typically of an economic sort, having to do with taxation, farm prices, labour-management relations and similar matters; that is, they are tied quite clearly to the socioeconomic position of the voter and they appeal to him, and have consequences for him, in that connection.   Style issues deal more with matters of political taste, *e.g.*, civil liberties, prohibition, immigration, intergroup relations or government corruption; they are more likely to be tied to ethnic and regional considerations.   Style issues are probably more likely to be crucial when position issues are quiescent, and the great historical issues, like slavery, contain elements of both.

At any given time, only a few issues are really in contention insofar as public attitudes are concerned.   The adherents of opposing sides actually agree on a large number of matters of political importance—what the issues are, what is likely to happen, what criteria to judge by, what the rules of the political game are.   The partisans differ on those issues that happen to be in the "political gateway" at the moment, for example, the rich man-poor man issues of the New Deal era.   But neither the electorate, nor probably the system, can handle more than a few issues at any given time in a large and heterogeneous country.

U.S. Presidential Campaigns.   Now how does a brief presidential campaign in the U.S. reflect this view of the basis of voting, the stability of political preferences, and the content of the political program?

The campaign defines which issues shall be prominent, and even dominant, and each side seeks to get its definition accepted rather than its opponent's.   One effect of this effort is that partisans increasingly agree with their own candidate by resolving "inconsistent" opinions in favour of the central party opinion, and even by misperceiving the candidates' positions on subsidiary issues in order to bring them into harmony with one's own preferences.   Thus over-all, the campaign organizes many small disagreements into one big disagreement, namely, which party shall hold power. What starts as a mass of diverse opinions, with cleavages running every which way in the electorate, is organized by the campaign into a single basic difference of opinion between the two sets of party supporters.

The campaign reinforces the faithful: it recharges the interest of the already convinced and provides them with the political rationale currently active. The partisan tends to select his own side's material from that provided by communications mediums. Thus, the campaign not only reguarantees his basic vote but also transforms many partisans into effective personal campaigners within their own circles. The campaign brings into action the latent votes of those predisposed to one or the other side through their social identifications and associations; it thus "brings out" the vote, but only in a particular direction. It converts the doubtful, who, though few, often carry the balance of power in close elections.

The campaign has the polarizing effect of promoting consensus within social groups and cleavage between them. Under its impact, people come to agree more with people like themselves, in socioeconomic or ethnic terms, and to disagree more with people on the other side.

Thus, it is seen, the foundations of American political parties are in social groups with inter- and intragenerational solidarity, and political interests and social traditions reinforce one another by means of the campaign.

In summary, as it has been said,

> The usual analogy between the voting "decision" and the more or less carefully calculated decisions of consumers or business men or courts may be quite incorrect. For many voters political preferences may better be considered analogous to cultural tastes—in music, literature, recreational activities, dress, ethics, speech, social behavior. Consider the parallels between political preferences and general cultural tastes. Both have their origin in ethnic, sectional, class, and family traditions. Both exhibit stability and resistance to change for individuals, but flexibility and adjustment over generations for the society as a whole. Both seem to be matters of sentiment and disposition rather than "reasoned preferences." While both are responsive to changed conditions and unusual stimuli, they are relatively invulnerable to direct argumentation and vulnerable to indirect social influences. Both are characterized more by faith than by conviction and by wishful

expectation rather than careful prediction of consequences. . . . (Bernard Berelson *et al., Voting, a Study of Opinion Formation in a Presidential Campaign,* pp. 310–311, Chicago: University of Chicago Press, 1954.)

Implications for Democratic Theory   Finally, what are the implications of this description of voting behaviour for the political theory of democracy?   Some of the "requirements" for the democratic citizens were noted above, yet we find that taken by and large the citizens do not fulfill the standards.   Substantial proportions of the electorate are not particularly interested in political matters, or well informed on them.   They vote their class or regional or even religious interests rather than "the public interest."   There is often little that is specifically political in the considerations that lead to their vote; the decision often arises out of a pervasive group understanding rather than a process of ratiocination.   Indeed, it can be said that for many citizens the decision as to how to vote is not really an individual matter at all but a kind of collective decision in which a whole group of people, from the family to the social stratum, work their way to a final position without much conscious and deliberative thought.

This image of voting violates traditional ideals of democratic participation, yet the system works.   What can be said about this seeming discrepancy?

The political philosophy we have inherited has given more consideration to the virtues of the typical citizen of the democracy than to the working of the system as a whole . . . Liberal democracy is more than a political system in which individual voters and political institutions operate.   For political democracy to survive, other features are required: The intensity of conflict must be limited, the rate of change must be restrained, stability in the social and economic structure must be maintained, a pluralistic social organization must exist, and a basic consensus must bind together the contending parties.   (Berelson *et al., ibid.*)

The classical tradition, in this view, demanded political virtue of the citizen in too extreme, too doctrinal and too general a form.   What is required is a voting population that is not homogeneous but heterogeneous in its political quality.   For example, as the system requires conciliation of opposing interests, it is facilitated by the people who are indifferent to political matters and thus provide a cushion between the partisans.   As the system requires stability, it is furnished by the voters with strong party loyalties.   As the system requires flexibility, it is facilitated again by the low-interest changers.

> The need for heterogeneity arises from the contradictory functions we expect our voting system to serve. We expect the political system to adjust itself and our affairs to changing conditions; yet we demand too that it display a high degree of stability. We expect the contending interests and parties to pursue their ends vigorously and the voters to care; yet, after the election is over, we expect reconciliation. We expect the voting outcome to serve what is best for the community; yet we do not want disinterested voting unattached to the purposes and interests of different segments of that community. We want voters to express their own free and self-determined choices; yet, for the good of the community, we would like voters to avail themselves of the best information and guidance available from the groups and leaders around them. We expect a high degree of rationality to prevail in the decision; but were all irrationality and mythology absent, and all ends pursued by the most coldly rational selection of political means, it is doubtful if this system would hold together.

> In short, our electoral system calls for apparently incompatible properties—which, although they cannot all reside in each individual voter, can (and do) reside in a heterogeneous electorate. What seems to be required of the electorate as a whole is a distribution of qualities . . . (Berelson *et al., ibid.*)

In this way the countless acts of voting behaviour performed by millions of individual voters add up to a working political system.

Bibliography   Paul F. Lazarsfeld, Bernard Berelson, and Hazel Gaudet, *The People's Choice,* 2nd ed. (1948); V. O. Key, *Southern Politics in State and Nation* (1949); Samuel Lubell, *The Future of American Politics* (1952); Angus Campbell *et al., The Voter Decides* (1954); Bernard Berelson *et al., Voting: a Study of Opinion Formation in a Presidential Campaign* (1954); S. M. Lipset *et al.,* "The Psychology of Voting: An Analysis of Political Behavior," in Gardner Lindzey (ed.), *Handbook of Social Psychology* (1954); R. S. Milne and H. C. Mackenzie, *Straight Fight: a Study of Voting Behaviour in the Constituency of Bristol North-East at the General Election of 1951* (1954); Arthur Kornhauser *et al., When Labor Votes: a Study of Auto Workers* (1956); Mark Benney, A. P. Gray, and R. H. Pear, *How People Vote* (1956); Anthony Downs, *An Economic Theory of Democracy* (1957).

Lines of Inquiry

1 This essay is taken from the *Encyclopaedia Britannica.*

a What is the audience of such an essay?

b How does the essay's origin help to account for its form? For its opening paragraph? For its use of subtitles?

c Note the outline suggested at the beginning of the section headed "U.S. Presidential Campaigns." Why was this outline not used to provide section titles? What method of exposition is the basis of the outline?

d Consider the subtitles as a topic outline: How does their sequence reflect the purposes and assumptions of an essay in the *Encyclopaedia Britannica?*

2 Look at the transitions between sections. In every case but one, the author appears to follow a standard method of moving from one topic to another. How is this method of transition connected to the purpose of the article? Would the one exceptional transition be more effective or less so, if cast in the pattern of the others?

3 Read the first sentence in each paragraph in the first three sections.

a How many of these sentences contain pivot terms? What general pattern of terms recurs in each section?

b What paragraphs are not introduced by such terms? Why?

4 a Does this essay go further than a simple analysis of voting behavior?

b What is the function of the last section—in what way does it differ from the others? How is this last section related to the introduction?

c Omit the second paragraph of the essay, and skim through to the conclusion. Does the second section suffer? Does the conclusion?

5 Go through the essay and mark in the margin each time the structure of idea turns on the technique of classification.

a What is the function of classification in these instances? What do you conclude concerning the relation between classification and analysis?

b In the section titled "Issues," political issues are classified as either issues of position or issues of style. Could political issues also be classified as major and minor? As moral, technical, and psychological? As real or unreal? As perennial and temporary?

c "Style issues deal more with matters of political taste, e.g.,

civil liberties, prohibition, immigration . . ."—what effect
do the words "style" and "taste" have in this context?

d What categories might a politician use to classify political
issues? What point of view does the classification employed
in this essay represent?

6 "Voting Behaviour" seems unconcerned with the moral aspects
of political life—is it?

a What definition of democracy seems to underlie the concluding section?

b What are the functions of a government that "works," as this
essay uses the term?

c Can you conceive of a different definition of democracy? Of
a government that works?

7 Earlier, it was pointed out that an argument may be tested at
several points: for the truth of its premises; for the validity of
its inferences from these premises; and for the consistency of
its conclusions with a wider field of ideas. Consider each
aspect of this argument.

a How could one test its premises? Which of the premises
seems the weakest?

b Which of the conclusions seems the weakest? Why?

c Can you construct a classification that distinguishes the kinds
of statements that are inherently weak from the kinds that
are inherently strong?

Lines of Experiment

1 The debate is an ancient technique by which contending arguments can be tested for their validity and truth. It is, in fact,
the father of written argument, and an unexpressed debate lies
beneath the structure of most argumentative essays. The
debate in this instance is between "the traditional view" of
voting behavior, based on the assumption that man is a rational animal capable of discerning and choosing the good, and
"the modern view," based on research that presents man as a
social animal whose decisions are largely the reflex of group
identification, custom, and self-interest. Other views are possible, of course. One common competing view suggests that
change in behavior patterns is possible: Some early Americans
thought that only as men become politically free and educated
do they become capable of rational decision; some late Marxists
think that only as men become economically free can they
become politically and intellectually so, and thus capable of
rational decision.

Write an essay in the form of a debate on the general subject taken up in the essay on voting behavior. Your participants may be students, voters, members of a bridge club, politicians, businessmen, persons of different race or economic class or religion. You are free to throw political philosophers into debate, too, but such an essay will demand much knowledge of political theory: A writer often succeeds better by using subjects that fall within his immediate experience than by going afield. You should choose proponents of different views—where complete agreement exists in advance, debate is unnecessary—and the character of each participant should match the character of his argument. Probably you should restrict yourself to three speakers; more than three can create confusion, unless the focus is carefully maintained. Try to find a narrative frame that will facilitate the movement of the debate, without overshadowing it. The frame need not be "natural"—debates have been staged in heaven, in cemeteries, in marketplaces, in beer halls, in beds, in computers, and elsewhere. One choice of a frame will facilitate a relatively abstract discourse; another will facilitate a satire. But be wary: The temptations of the narrative frame are strong, and it can only too easily become itself the real focus of discussion.

2 Write an essay on *one aspect* of the political behavior of a group well known to you: your neighbors; the people of your home town; your parents' friends—or your own; your teachers; the people you work with. Keep the group fairly small, and select from it a few people to use as specific reference points and illustrations—as representatives of the whole. Stay away from your own family, unless you have a strong impulse to write about it: An objective view of a subject so close is very difficult to achieve.

You have essentially five questions—though not all of them have to be answered, necessarily, in your essay. What is political behavior? What specific aspect of this group's political behavior would be most possible and fruitful to discuss? How does this group behave politically? Why do they behave as they do? What is the larger significance of their behavior?

Your definition will entail the classifying of some kinds of acts as political and of others as nonpolitical—as economic, religious, recreational, etc. The definition you will come to probably will be arbitrary, cut to your actual purposes: "When I speak of political behavior I mean any form of behavior intended to influence the constitution and the acts of government," or "All forms of behavior that are not biological are political."

One of these definitions is far broader than the other; but both are far too broad as subjects to be useful. Thus your next problem: to choose a specific aspect of political behavior—one that you can hope to write about in a brief essay dealing not only with abstractions but also with specific people. Your definition may frame your subject, in this instance, but cannot identify it.

The three remaining questions also require some effort at classsification—first, of acts; second, of motives; third, of conclusions. But remember that a system of classification will not provide you with a compositional sequence, nor tell you automatically what you must focus on; you must decide.

C. S. PEIRCE

 # THE CONCEPT OF GOD

"Do you believe in the existence of a Supreme Being?" Hume, in his *Dialogues Concerning Natural Religion,* justly points out that the phrase "Supreme Being" is not an equivalent of "God," since it neither implies infinity nor any of the other attributes of God, excepting only Being and Supremacy. This is important; and another distinction between the two designations is still more so. Namely, "God" is a vernacular word and, like all such words, but more than almost any, is *vague.* No words are so well understood as vernacular words, in one way; yet they are invariably vague; and of many of them it is true that, let the logician do his best to substitute precise equivalents in their places, still the vernacular words alone, for all their vagueness, answer the principal purposes. This is emphatically the case with the very vague word "God," which is not made less vague by saying that it imports "infinity," etc., since those attributes are at least as vague. I shall, therefore, if you please, substitute "God," for "Supreme Being" in the question.

I will also take the liberty of substituting "reality" for "existence." This is perhaps overscrupulosity; but I myself always use *exist* in its strict philosophical sense of "react with the other like things in the environment." Of course, in that sense, it would be fetichism to say that God "exists." The word "reality," on the contrary, is used in ordinary parlance in its correct philosophical sense. . . . So, then, the question being whether I believe in the reality of God, I answer, Yes. I further opine that pretty nearly everybody more or less believes this, including many of the scientific men of my generation who are accustomed to think the belief is entirely unfounded. The reason they fall into this extraordinary error about their own belief is that they precide (or render precise) the conception, and, in doing so, inevitably change it; and such precise conception is easily shown not to be warranted, even if it cannot be quite refuted. Every concept that is vague is liable to be self-contradictory in those respects in which it is vague. *No* concept, not even those of mathematics, is absolutely precise; and some of the most important for everyday use are extremely vague. Nevertheless, our instinctive beliefs involving such concepts are far more trustworthy than the best established results of science, if these be precisely understood. For instance, we all think that there is an element of order in the universe. Could any laboratory experiments render that proposition more certain than instinct or common sense leaves it? It is ridiculous to broach such a question. But when anybody undertakes to say *precisely* what that order consists in, he will quickly find he outruns all logical warrant. Men who are given to defining too much inevitably run themselves into confusion in dealing with the vague concepts of common sense.

If a pragmaticist is asked what he means by the word "God," he can only say that just as long acquaintance with a man of great character may deeply influence one's whole manner of conduct, so that a glance at his portrait may make a difference, just as almost living with Dr. Johnson enabled poor Boswell to write an immortal book and a really sublime book, just as long study of the works of Aristotle may make him an acquaintance, so if contemplation and study of the physico-psychical universe can imbue a man with principles of conduct analogous to the influence of a great man's works or conversation, then that analogue of a mind—for it is impossible to say that *any* human attribute is *literally* applicable—is what he means by "God." Of course, various great theologians explain that one cannot attribute *reason* to God, nor perception (which always involves an element of surprise and of learning what one did not know), and, in short, that his "mind" is necessarily so unlike ours, that some—though wrongly—high in the church say that it is only negatively, as being entirely different from everything else, that we can attach any meaning to the Name. This is not so; because the discoveries of science, their enabling us to *predict* what will be the course of nature, is proof conclusive that, though we cannot think any thought of God's, we can catch a fragment of His Thought, as it were.

Now such being the pragmaticist's answer to the question what he means by the word "God," the question whether there really *is* such a being is the question whether all physical science is merely the figment—the arbitrary figment—of the students of nature, and further whether the *one* lesson of Gautama Buddha, Confucius, Socrates, and all who from any point of view have had their ways of conduct determined by meditation upon the physico-psychical universe, be only their arbitrary notion or be the Truth behind the appearances which the frivolous man does not think of; and whether the superhuman courage which such contemplation has conferred upon priests who go to pass their lives with lepers and refuse all offers of rescue is mere silly fanaticism, the passion of a baby, or whether it is strength derived from the power of the truth. Now the only guide to the answer to this question lies in the power of the passion of love which more or less overmasters every agnostic scientist and everybody who seriously and deeply considers the universe. But whatever there may be of *argument* in all this is as nothing, the merest nothing, in comparison to its force as an appeal to one's own instinct, which is to argument what substance is to shadow, what bed-rock is to the built foundations of a cathedral.

By experience must be understood the entire mental product. Some psychologists whom I hold in respect will stop me here to say that, while they admit that experience is more than mere sensation, they cannot extend it to the whole mental product, since that would include hallucinations, delusions, superstitious imaginations and fallacies of all kinds; and that they would limit experience to sense-perceptions. But I reply that my statement is the logical one. Hallucinations, delusions, superstitious imaginations, and fallacies of all kinds are experiences, but experiences misunderstood; while to say that all our knowledge relates merely to sense-perception is to say that we can know nothing—not even mistakenly—about higher matters, as honour, aspirations, and love.

Where would such an idea, say as that of God, come from, if not from direct experience?   Would you make it a result of some kind of reasoning, good or bad?   Why, reasoning can supply the mind with nothing in the world except an estimate of the value of a statistical ratio, that is, how often certain kinds of things are found in certain combinations in the ordinary course of experience.   And scepticism, in the sense of doubt of the validity of elementary ideas—which is really a proposal to turn an idea out of court and permit no inquiry into its applicability— is doubly condemned by the fundamental principle of scientific method —condemned first as obstructing inquiry, and condemned second because it is treating something other than a statistical ratio as a thing to be argued about.   No: as to God, open your eyes—and your heart, which is also a perceptive organ—and you see him.   But you may ask, Don't you admit there are any delusions?   Yes: I may think a thing is black, and on close examination it may turn out to be bottle-green.   But I cannot think a thing is black if there is no such thing to be seen as black.   Neither can I think that a certain action is self-sacrificing, if no such thing as self-sacrifice exists, although it may be very rare.   It is the nominalists, and the nominalists alone, who indulge in such scepticism, which the scientific method utterly condemns.

Lines of Inquiry

1 Much of this essay is difficult to follow without close attention to the terms of discussion.   Some terms Peirce defines; others he expects us to recognize.

   a Look up the following terms.   Can they be defined precisely?

   (*1*) Fetishism   (*3*) Skepticism
   (*2*) Pragmatism   (*4*) Nominalism

   b What difference do you see between the terms Peirce defines and the ones he does not define?

   c What accounts for his defining the one kind of term and his not defining the other?

2 Earlier, it was suggested that a clash of opinion—a debate—is implicit in most argumentative essays.   The subject up for debate here is "the existence of God"—a very common subject.

   a How is this underlying debate reflected in the form of Peirce's essay?

b He chooses his adversaries deliberately, in a sense: Who are they?   Why does he choose this particular set of adversaries?

c In what way do they influence the structure of his essay?

d What is the development of idea from one section to another —what accounts for the sequence of questions?   (Try changing it.)

3 With what point of view does Peirce approach his subject? How does this point of view account for the style of his discussion?

4 The essay begins with a distinction between "Supreme Being" and "God."

a What rhetorical function does definition perform in the opening paragraphs?

b What logical function does it perform?   Are the two functions different?

c Follow the words "precise" and "vague" through the first two paragraphs of this essay.   What is the effect of their constant recurrence?   Could the words "indefinite" and "definite" be used equally well?

5 *a* What theory about the relationship between words and the concepts they represent is implied in Peirce's insistence that "in many cases vernacular words alone, for all their vagueness, answer the principal purposes"—that some words cannot be precisely defined without ceasing to represent the concepts they in fact represent?

b What does he mean by "the principal purposes"?

c If vague words answer the principal purposes, why bother with definitions?

6 Peirce says that *all* vernacular words are vague.

a Test this statement by finding the most precise vernacular word you can.   In what sense, if at all, could it be said to be vague?

b Peirce goes further: He says that no concept—"not even those of mathematics"—is absolutely precise.

(*1*) Is "one" a precise concept?

(*2*) Is "two"?

(*3*) Is "1 + 1 = 2"?

7 Peirce takes the position, in his second paragraph, that "our instinctive beliefs [about our most important everyday concepts] are far more trustworthy than the best established results of science, if these be precisely understood."

a What does he mean by "precisely understood"?

b Can you find a way of testing this assertion?

c What attitude does Peirce seem to have toward logical inquiry? Would one be justified logically in concluding from this essay that Peirce disdained logic as a useless exercise?

d How would you reply to the argument that Peirce is being inconsistent—i.e., illogical—in that he attempts by logical means to define the limits of logical process?

8 The essay concludes in the following way: "I cannot think a thing is black if there is no such thing to be seen as black. Neither can I think that a certain action is self-sacrificing, if no such thing as self-sacrifice exists. . . ."

a Why does Peirce use two examples here?

b Present in extended form the entire argument implied in these phrases. How would you describe the technique of argument Peirce employs here? Can you test the validity of the argument?

c Could such an argument be made to lead to the conclusion that dragons exist?

9 Peirce remarks that "reasoning can supply the mind with nothing in the world except an estimate of the value of a statistical ratio, that is, how often certain kinds of things are found in certain combinations, in the ordinary course of experience. Test this assertion against the following statements:

a All men are mortal; Socrates is a man; therefore, Socrates is mortal.

b 2 + 2 = 4.

c Honesty is the best policy.

d Voting behavior is largely conditioned by the socioeconomic status of the voter, and not by his "reasoned preferences."

Lines of Experiment

1 Peirce remarks at one point that "to say that all our knowledge relates to sense-perception is to say that we can know nothing—not even mistakenly—about higher matters, as honour, aspirations, and love." Take one of these "higher matters," or another from the same category, and write an essay on it as a concept.

In developing your subject, you need not follow Peirce's line of reasoning nor adopt the point of view of the philosopher. (The premise that instinct is the foundation of argument will help you here.) You may show that the concept is empty, that the word is no longer understood, that it is part of the general mumbo jumbo by which cultures are held together; or you may insist that the concept is central to a decent society, that all human behavior assumes its reality, etc.

Many different avenues can lead you to the heart of your subject; nonetheless, you may wish to keep in mind several governing considerations. *First,* is the question you are trying to answer phrased properly, in its essential terms? Some questions are difficult to answer largely because of the way they are put. Try several methods of phrasing the question, and use the one that seems clearest. *Second,* who are your important adversaries—what arguments do you have to combat? No argument can hope to meet all possible lines of opposition; therefore, the most powerful adversaries are the ones most important to refute. *Third,* what kind of argument is likely to prove most convincing, given your intention and your audience? *Last,* what questions will each stage of your argument prompt in a reader, and which of these questions is it essential that you answer? A written argument requires the writer to stand ready to become his own adversary—a kind of devil's advocate, ready to question his own reasoning, in the interest of an argument finally proof against criticism.

2 Doubtless some of your beliefs—about religion, race, politics, sex, sport, education, art—are under attack from one quarter or another—time makes such attacks inevitable. Choose one such belief (it need not be your own) and write an essay defending it. You need not adopt a fashionable view; the challenge to your argumentative power will be greater if you adopt an unpopular one. The considerations mentioned in *1* above, may be useful to you in developing your subject. As an exercise, examine the apparently most damaging argument against that belief (in Peirce's case, the apparently most damaging argument is that the concept of God is too vague to be meaningful) and try to show that when rightly understood even that argument is in your favor. After all, the most damaging argument is the one that you really have to beat if you wish to prove your point.

JOHN CIARDI

THE RESONANCE
OF THE
CIVILIZING TONGUE

Ours must be a literary age, because the instant a person mentions literature everyone in sight begins to defend it. Helen of Troy had fewer heroes between her and the Greeks than literature has between it and whatever besiegers are at the gates.

It may be that some sort of attacking force does, in fact, exist. If it does, I am not worried by it. It is the defenders I am wary of, and foremost among them are those apologists who begin by asserting that "Literature Is Useful," and who thereupon proceed to praise the study of literature in the name of communication skills. Reduced to its basic absurdity, their argument is that the study of literature is important because it prepares a man to write a better business letter and thus to become more employable within the corporate structure of American society. One may as well argue that surgical training is important because it prepares a man to do a better job of carving his Christmas goose. It does, but who cares?

It is a debasement to make the study of literature a substitute for the minimum course in literacy. The fact that a certain amount of what goes on in educational theory argues for just such a substitution is no justification, but a cause for concern. The study of literature is self-justifying. No apology is required. None is in order.

Literature is one of the central continuing experiences of the race. It is no cultural ornament. It is as discrete a method of knowledge as is science, and the kind of knowledge literature makes available is not approachable by scientific method. Through literature, the voices of mankind's most searching imaginations remain alive to all time. No man is half-civilized until those voices have sounded within him. A savage, after all, is simply a human organism that has not received enough news from the human race. Literature is one most fundamental part of that news. One needs to hear Job lift his question into the wind; it is, after all, every man's question at some time. One needs to stand by Oedipus and to hold the knife of his own most terrible resolution. One needs to come out of his own Hell with Dante and to hear that voice of joy hailing the sight of his own stars returned to. One needs to run with Falstaff, roaring in his own appetites and weeping into his own pathos. What one learns from those voices is his own humanity. He learns what it is to carry about within mortal meat a bulb of brain wired to a bush of dendrites. Until he has heard those voices deeply within himself, what man can have any sizable idea of himself?

Literature, however, is never about ideas, but always and only about *the experience of ideas.* Scientists and philosophers discuss ideas. The reader of a good poem does not discuss ideas with the poet; he *becomes* the poet and relives the experience of the poet's imagination.

That experience is a subtle and far-reaching thing. In the act of a good poem or of a play or novel or short story, the good reader lives a life, or a part of a life, which otherwise could not have occurred to him. And he is detached from that experience at the same time that he knows his own life is very much involved. That experience, moreover, is heightened by being shaped into form; the accidental is eliminated. If the form is good, everything works toward perception. There are no distractions. And because form is indestructible, the experience is always there to be returned to. Should life distract him, the reader can always return to the purity of experience within form, to find once more, and ever green, the center of value uncluttered by peripheral confusions.

The experience of great literature, above all, is inseparable from the experience of great language, and language is forever one of the profoundest activities of the human race. Language greatly used has all the sanction of a sacrament; the race is as incapable of forgetting a great poem as it is of losing its last wish under the stars. The resonance of great language taking place within the forms of great imagination is the civilizing force. To dismiss that resonance as merely useful is to strip society of its culture and to offer it only a technology in return. That resonance is to the life of man what breath is to his body. Art is the way the mind breathes.

As a practicing pessimist, I can locate most of my fears for the future of the United States in the disappearance of that fundamental resonance from the language of official pronouncement. Certainly a nation so lacking in resonance that it can accept federal prose as a language capable of legislating human destinies is a nation part way to the door of darkness. Does any man seriously believe he can hope to discover who we are by reading the day's prose from Washington?

Let him try it, and then let him return to the Declaration of Independence to hear again the resonance of what we were in the beginning. "We hold these truths to be self evident, that all men are created equal, that they are endowed by their Creator with certain unalienable Rights, that among these are Life, Liberty and the pursuit of Happiness."

Who can imagine a statement of such force and resonance except as the product of minds shaped and informed by a life-giving contact with all that continuity of experience we call the humanities? There is no education and there is no civilization except as it keeps alive and transmits that resonance. There is no society worth preserving except as that resonance echoes in the voices of its laws, its legislators, and its citizens. There is no question of defending literature. It defends us. Without its voices in us, we are all indefensible.

Lines of Inquiry

1 Ciardi announces in his first paragraph that his purpose is not to defend literature from its attackers, if any. Yet he is defending literature nonetheless.

  a From whom?

  b Why does he say he is not defending it?

  c How is the introduction related to the conclusion?

  d Read the conclusion without its last three sentences: What does the essay lose?

2 a Underline the words "literature" and "experience" each time they occur in the essay. Do you see any pattern in the use of these terms?

  b What are Ciardi's essential points? Look for a single sentence in the essay that summarizes his point—that serves as nucleus, so to speak. Where in the essay does it fall? Suppose it led off the essay; what would be lost? What is the relationship of this sentence to the title?

3 It was said in Part I of this text that narration follows a dramatic structure, in a sense: Every sequence of events has a crisis, or turning point, where its meaning becomes clear, and a climax, or peak of action, where its emotional impact is strongest.

   a Can you find analogous points of crisis and climax in this
   essay?   Could its structure be said to be dramatic?

   b Does your answer here illuminate any of the purely stylistic
   elements in the essay—its syntax, for example, or its choice
   of illustrations?

   c Consider the other expository or argumentative essays you
   have read thus far—do some of those also appear to be
   dramatically as well as logically shaped?

   d On the basis of your answers, can you arrive at any tentative
   conclusions about the essay as a form?

4 In argument, it was suggested earlier, one very effective strategy
is to focus unexpectedly on the strongest points to be made
against one's own position; by showing that even the strongest
contrary arguments, when properly understood, do not hold
water, it is possible to suggest that no contrary arguments do.
(What would you judge to be the validity of such an inference?)
Thus Peirce (see "The Concept of God," p. 156) attacks the
argument that the word "God" is too vague to mean anything
by saying that the most meaningful and useful words are
invariably vague.

   a Ciardi does not openly use such a line of argument.   Why,
   however, does he turn on his apparent allies, "those apologists
   who begin by asserting that 'Literature Is Useful' "?   To
   understand this tactic, we need to ask a further question:
   What is the strongest argument *against* the importance of
   literature?   Considering this, what is Ciardi's actual argument?

   b After demolishing the notion that literature is useful "because
   it prepares us to write a better business letter," Ciardi calls
   literature "as discrete a method of knowledge as is science."
   What kind of use does this literary method of knowledge
   have?   What happens, in this essay, to the definition of
   "useful"?

   c What has Ciardi done to the strongest opposing argument?

5 The precise meaning of each of the following sentences is extremely hard to render.   Why?

"A savage, after all, is simply a human organism that has not
received enough news from the human race."

"Language greatly used has all the sanction of a sacrament; the
race is as incapable of forgetting a great poem as it is of losing
its last wish under the stars."

"There is no education and there is no civilization except as it
keeps alive and transmits that resonance."

"Art is the way the mind breathes."

a Are the statements true?   Does it matter whether or not they are true?

b Would you conclude that the sentences are incantatory—part of a verbal ritual, as it were—rather than meaningful? What is the purpose of incantation—what meaning, if any, does it communicate?   What are the purposes of these statements?

6 Much of the effect of this essay comes from small details of phrasing.   Here are three rephrased sentences; Ciardi's original follows in each case in parentheses.   What kind of meaning is lost in the revisions?   In each case, how is that kind of meaning conveyed?

a The study of literature is a good in itself, needing no apologies.   ("The study of literature is self-justifying.   No apology is required.   None is in order.")

b He learns what it is to have a brain in his body.   ("He learns what it is to carry about within mortal meat a bulb of brain wired to a bush of dendrites.")

c Literature preserves great writing for us.   ("Through literature, the voices of mankind's most searching imaginations remain alive to all time.")

Lines of Experiment

1 Ciardi's essay is part of a long line of defenses of the poetic imagination.   Attacks on that imagination are equally frequent; Plato, for example, opposed poets on the ground that poetry lied about the gods and consistently misrepresented reality.

Ciardi's essay presents either directly or by implication many of the general arguments on behalf of poetry; from those arguments, you should be able to infer the arguments of the opposition.   Write your own attack on or defense of literature. Do not be deterred by the size of the subject: How long is Ciardi's essay?

Before you begin, however, you may find it useful to consider your problem from several sides.   *First,* what kind of subject is appropriate?   Unless you know a great deal about literature in general, you probably will do well to focus on a subject with which you are thoroughly familiar even if it is not formally literary—e.g., science fiction, the spy story, the western, the political manifesto, the limerick.   *Second,* how does one discover what to attack or defend?   Here a brief classification may be useful, not only in isolating virtues and separating virtues from defects but also in providing a clue to the sequence in which these virtues and defects can be discussed. Probably, too, a concentration on the main points, even on one or two main points only, would be useful as a way of giving to your composition a thematic center, even a dramatic line of development. *Third,* who are your adversaries? You must consider the possibility that you will have friends you do not want, as well as enemies you must acknowledge. *Last,* who is your audience? What relevant ideas can you assume to be common ground? What relevant ideas do you know not to be common ground? The former need no discussion, the latter demand it.

2 It is a truism, no doubt thoroughly demonstrated in your own experience, that friends are sometimes just as dangerous as enemies. At one time or another, the drama, democratic institutions, higher education, patriotism, birds, primitive societies, temperance, the poor, and the aged have all suffered from their friends. Select a notable instance in which something you care about—a sport, a school, a club, an art, a neighborhood, a park, a building—suffered from its friends. In constructing your essay, consider that friends of this kind frequently miscarry by not understanding the thing they have befriended—by taking its accidental elements for its essential ones. Your job as a writer is to define that error and to use it as a way of showing what those essential elements are and what they are worth.

C. G. DARWIN

THE PURSUIT
OF HAPPINESS

. . . Happiness has been the subject of a great deal of magnificent literature, but it has also been the subject of more trite aphorisms and of more bad philosophy than almost any other in the world. In venturing to discuss it I am acutely conscious that I shall probably be joining the ranks of the bad philosophers, but it has seemed to me that since happiness is of such principal importance to man, I could hardly be justified in evading the subject. My main theme is to be the *pursuit* of happiness, and this is different from happiness itself. A great part of human conduct is dictated by the motive, "I am going to do so and so, because I think it will make me happier," though the prescription is all too often faulty. However that may be, the result is some course of action, and this will affect the external world, so that it becomes relevant to history. It is this that justifies its consideration here.

Before coming to this side of the question, however, it will be well to begin by considering happiness itself. Much happiness comes quite unsought, and in examining their memories for the chief happy or unhappy incidents of their life, most people will find that the really important ones were concerned with entirely intimate matters of a personal kind, which had little relation to the conditions of the external world. Such occasions of happiness or unhappiness will presumably always be among the most important things in life, and since they are independent of the outer world they will continue much the same in the future as in the past. There is undoubtedly a great difference among individuals, in that some are naturally cheerful and others naturally melancholy, and as these are inherent characteristics there is nothing to be done about them, but it is relevant to the present inquiry to ask which type has the greater survival value. To put the matter in its crudest form, is a naturally cheerful person likely to have a larger family than a melancholy one, for if so, then there would be a prospect of a slow increase of cheerfulness throughout the human race. I cannot answer this question at all, but I can see no reason to believe that cheerfulness should triumph, rather than melancholy. There is also the very greatest difference among individuals in the pitch of their emotions, in that some are alternately intensely happy or miserable, while others take both emotions much more placidly. Here again the question arises whether there is survival value in intense emotions, and again it is not easy to answer, though it may be noted that such emotions tend to go with an instability of character which may often lead to forming bad judgments in the other activities of life, and these bad judgments can hardly help in survival.

Among the inherent tendencies of people towards happiness or unhappiness, there is one characteristic, and a very sinister one, which cannot be overlooked. In any boys' school where discipline gets at all slack it is practically universal for there to be bullying. This means that there are many of mankind who positively enjoy making their fellows miserable; it is by no means a majority, but it is certainly not a negligible minority.   It is no use arguing that this is only a boyish failing and that in later life the bully will become a virtuous citizen.   Conditions in this country give little scope for the exercise of brutality by adults, but this has not always been so, and it is not so in many parts of the world even now: it is the strong arm of the law, and not a change in his nature, that has restrained the bully.   It is not easy to see anything that will tend to eliminate him, because his selfishness is a positive help to his survival in all conditions but those of the highest and most stable civilization, and even these conditions only check the expression of his propensities without destroying them.   In thinking of the future happiness of mankind, it is a sobering thought that there will be quite a perceptible fraction of humanity that definitely gets satisfaction, and so presumably happiness, from making its fellows unhappy.

Among the more external conditions of human life a great deal of misery is directly due to physical pain, and if these sufferings can be removed either by cure or by means of harmless opiates, it will clearly increase the sum of human happiness.   Medical science has already accomplished much in this direction, and it holds promise of a great deal more, so that in this obvious sense man may confidently expect to be happier in the future.   But there is another side of physical suffering that it is not so easy to judge about, and that is hunger.   If population pressure is to be a main feature of human history, there will usually be a marginal fraction of humanity living on the verge of starvation, which cannot be reckoned as a happy state.   However, it is hard to be sure even about this, for the starvation is not usually continuous, but comes in periodically recurring famines, and there is room for happiness in the intervals. To those of us who have never experienced real hunger this may seem unlikely, but it is reported by those who know the Eskimos well, that they are the most cheerful people on earth, and this though they are certainly the race living most continually on the verge of starvation.

In so far as happiness is regarded as an object of pursuit, there is the implication that it is at least partly within the control of the pursuer. Such happiness is a less deep emotion than those I have been considering, and its antithesis can hardly be described as melancholy or misery, but rather as discontent.   Much discontent arises from noble motives, but it has regretfully to be admitted that the motive lying behind the widest range of discontent is mere envy, that most unamiable of human characteristics.   But whatever the motive, it certainly produces great unhappiness, and it is the kind that stimulates the sufferer into seeking a cure.   Man is a very poor prescriber for his own troubles, and he usually sees his grievance, whether real or imaginary, as the only thing in the world that stands between him and a permanent state of perfect bliss.   Of course as soon as he has succeeded in removing the grievance, he at once finds another, and this again becomes the most important thing in the world, with eternal happiness once again just round the corner.   The target of the pursuit will always evade the pursuer.

It is not recognized by most people that happiness does not come from a state, but from a change of state.   That it is so is illustrated by the total failure of every writer to describe a satisfactory paradise, whether in heaven or on earth.   The tedium of eternity has almost become a joke, and the descriptions of the earthly utopias are no better.   Most of them fail to recognize that the human mind cannot hold any emotion for long at an even intensity, but that it always soon degenerates into something much more tepid.   A few authors of course have recognized this.   Thus Samuel Butler describes the criticism of the Christian heaven by an Erewhonian, who points out how much better it would be if one always thought that one's wishes were going to be thwarted, and then at the last moment they were fulfilled.   Then there is the (almost certainly mythical) American preacher, who told his congregation that heaven would not consist in the playing of harps, but would, like earth, be a centre of busy activity; we can be fairly sure that no "bears" would have been allowed on the celestial stock exchange, but the preacher did recognize that it is a change of state, and not a state, that makes for happiness.

But it is not simply a change of state that makes for happiness; there must be something unexpected about it.   Butler's Erewhonian would very soon have got bored by knowing that he was certain not to be really disappointed.   Again, in some professions there is an automatic annual increase of salary, but this change is apt to be mentally discounted long in advance; contrast it with the real joy at receiving an unexpected promotion.   A great proportion of mankind enjoy gambling.   If their conditions are bad, this is easily understandable, because the remote chance of betterment is worth taking; but very many people in secure and prosperous conditions also find it almost necessary to gamble, and this is because it provides just the element of uncertainty, otherwise missing in their lives, that is essential for their happiness.

The external conditions then that are most likely to produce happiness are benefits received at uncertain intervals, and to make the individual continuously conscious of his happiness there must obviously be several such benefits during the course of his life.   In the present economic conditions the prescription for a great many people would all too often be ten per cent more pay for ten per cent less work, with the dose necessarily repeated at not infrequent intervals.   This is to put the matter very crudely, but it does subscribe to the general human view on the antithesis between work and pleasure.   The prescription is of course fantastically impossible of achievement over the course of the ages. Even in a single lifetime the cumulative effect of compound interest would defeat it, and though the son could not expect to start where his father left off, yet he would expect to start above where his father had started, so that the law of compound interest—it is true that it would be at a lower rate—would again come in for the succeeding generations. There is no chance of this sort of thing continuing over a thousand years, let alone a million years, unless there are intervening periods of disaster, to give occasion for a new start.   The really wonderful thing about the last century has been that exciting improvements of condition have been happening at frequent intervals for about six generations. And even so, it is not very evident that those living in the present conditions of enhanced prosperity are any *happier* than the people described by Dickens.

A chief question, from the point of view of this essay, is whether there is any survival value in happiness.   Are the naturally happy people more likely to be the ancestors of future generations, than are the rest, for if they are, then a greater number of the future race will tend to inherit this happy disposition.   The answer is very doubtful, and it may well be negative.   The reason lies in the fact that contentment is not a stimulus to action like discontent.   It must of course be recognized that there is a good deal of what I may call stimulated discontent, for many political leaders find it useful to stir up discontent among their adherents, even though these may really be of the contented type.   Leaving aside this stimulated discontent, a man who has the spur of his own genuine discontent to drive him will struggle harder to achieve success than will the contented type.   On the average, he will be more successful, but the success will not content him, so that he will always be spurred on to further efforts.   If this success is, as in the long run it will be, associated with his making a greater contribution to later generations, it follows that the discontented type will increase in numbers at the expense of the contented type.   This argument leads to the disappointing conclusion that future man will be more discontented than man of the present day.   I do not want to press it strongly but in the light of it, no matter what the future conditions of life may be, there seems absolutely no reason to expect any notable increase in the sum of human happiness.

In connection with the matter of human happiness it is a very pertinent question to ask whether man really enjoys being civilized, for on the answer to some extent depends the stability of future civilization.   In the past there have been so many cases of the decay of civilizations, that it is rather tempting to believe that the majority really find a state of barbarism more congenial.   Thus the civilization of the Mayas had already seriously decayed under the rule of the Aztecs, long before it was destroyed by the Spaniards.   Again the Roman Empire was destroyed by the onslaught of the Germans, in spite of the fact that it had been steadily, and on the whole successfully, civilizing many of them for two or three centuries before the collapse; they found the barbaric life more satisfying.   To take a modern example, the Republic of Liberia was re-peopled by negroes returned to it from America.   These had seen civilization, even if they may not themselves have gained much profit from it, but anyhow they showed little wish to avoid the relapse.

There are no doubt many causes that have led to such relapses into barbarism, but a chief one is the existence of the class of men I have called bullies.   Such men are apt to be brave and self-confident, but selfish and concerned only with their personal interests, and above all indifferent to the sufferings of those around them.   Such men, always ready to assume leadership, only interested in their own advantage, and indifferent to the fate of their fellows, are perfectly adapted instruments for destroying the delicate balance of civilization.

Now though it is indisputable that many civilizations have relapsed into barbarism, each of them must after all have grown out of barbarism before it could relapse, so that instead of arguing that man has relapsed into barbarism on account of his dislike of civilization, one might argue with almost equal force that he has become civilized because he does not like barbarism.   The best answer to the question which of the two he prefers can be given by examining the parallel of another human taste. Originally man was a hunter, and very many people still retain the trace of it in that they find a spontaneous, almost instinctive, joy in the chase, which they can get in no other way.   About ten thousand years ago there came the agricultural revolution.   This was a totally new thing for man—and indeed for the whole animal kingdom, except for the independent discovery of it by a few insects.   At first it can have had no emotional appeal at all, but rather the reverse; the discoverers must have felt they were doing a disagreeable and tedious job and they only did it because it was so clearly advantageous. For a long time the great majority would retain the emotions of the hunter, and would only cultivate the soil under the impulsion of stark necessity.

The practice of agriculture was an *acquired character,* and so it had to be acquired anew in each generation, and many must have revolted against the tedium and gone back to the more congenial practice of hunting. But there would be some whose nature was more tolerant of farming who would stay farmers, and those of their sons who inherited the taste would continue on the farm, while their brothers would drift back to hunting, so that there would be an "unconscious selection" towards agriculture. The new habit of life would gradually establish itself in some men's heredity, carrying with it an emotional appeal which might ultimately become as strong as had always been the appeal of hunting to the rest of the race. I do not know if biological principles could tell how long the creation of such an instinct would take, but there is no need to ask the question, because we have the answer before us. There are a great many people now existing—that is, certainly after less than ten thousand years—who undoubtedly have the instinct for agriculture; these are the people who derive deep emotional satisfaction from gardening, even when they are in no way driven to it by economic necessity. Though Voltaire might be claimed as a typical product of the age of civilization, he really belongs to the age of agriculture, for he represents Candide, in his disgust at the world round him, as finding his ultimate satisfaction in the cultivation of his garden.

The same sort of thing must be happening with the urban revolution. In China and the Levant this goes back for several thousand years, and already the promotion of the taste for civilization from an acquired to an inherent human character must have begun, but for most of the world this can hardly be so yet. After all, in western Europe and America, it is hardly more than thirty generations since most of the ancestors of the present city dwellers were completely barbarous, and it is therefore not surprising that many of their descendants should regard civilization as a disagreeable necessity without emotional appeal. This explains why so many civilizations have been rather short-lived, but it also answers the question whether man really likes being civilized. There can be no doubt whatever of the advantage of being civilized, in that it permits of larger populations, and these will prevail by their numbers against the smaller populations of barbarism. Some of the citizens may not like being civilized at the present time, but that does not matter, for in due course their descendants will grow to like it emotionally and instinctively, by the same process of "unconscious selection" from among them, as has happened with agriculture. The process has begun already, and in the course of a few thousand years at most, a great fraction of mankind will feel spontaneously the emotional appeal of civilization.

Let me follow this train of thought to its conclusion. If the agricultural revolution has followed hunting into our instincts, and if the urban revolution is going the same way, what about the scientific revolution, which has only just begun? The majority of mankind certainly have no taste for science; they regard the subject as a disagreeable necessity only practised for its obvious material advantages, and they relapse from it with enthusiasm towards the more instinctive tastes of the earlier revolutions. Nevertheless, the advantages of the new acquired character are evident, and there can be little doubt that it will follow the same course as the previous ones by the gradual selection of those who find the new system naturally congenial. In this way I shall expect that before the end of ten thousand years, science will make an emotional appeal to the instincts of a majority of the human race, of the same intensity as the emotions they now derive from the arts of the city, from the garden and from the chase.

Lines of Inquiry

1 This essay is part of a book attempting to predict in general terms what the world will be like for the next million years.
  a In what ways does this intention influence the essay's form and focus?
  b One obvious consequence of this intention is that Darwin seldom employs specific illustrations; can you think of any other reasons why the specific illustration of "happiness" might be difficult? Can you think of any way Darwin might have got around the difficulty of illustration? What kind of appeal to experience does he make?

2 The author of this essay is the grandson of the eminent biologist, Charles Darwin, author of the theory of evolution that bears his name.
  a How does the Darwinian idea that the fittest survive enter into this essay?
  b Could one argue that the ability to be happy is itself a kind of fitness? What might C. G. Darwin say to that?
  c How would you reply to the statement that C. G. Darwin

thinks as he does because his grandfather took the same line, and therefore his argument is inconsiderable?

3 a How does Darwin introduce his topic? How is that introduction related to the sequence of his argument?

    b Darwin never defines happiness in this essay; why not? Can you connect this refusal to define the essay's central concept with Peirce's remarks about the meaning of vernacular words? (See C. S. Peirce, "The Concept of God," p. 156.)

    c What is the real question of the essay, if it is not "What is happiness?"

4 Underline in the first sentence of each paragraph the word "happiness" whenever it occurs.

    a In which opening sentences does it occur? In which does it not occur?

    b What function does its reiteration serve? Or—to put the question differently—why does it disappear where it does?

5 Make a brief outline of the essay. You will find it difficult to understand the essay's structure from a mere inventory of topics: You must find a way to classify these topics so as to reflect Darwin's effort to answer his question. What was Darwin classifying, in order to arrive at a systematic structure of argument?

6 a Darwin changes his angle of approach to his subject very frequently; why? Would the essay be stronger if it concentrated on a single approach to the subject, rather than shifting from one to another as it does?

    b What principle of argument does this shift in angle of approach reflect?

    c Do any of the arguments repeat themselves? (Consider especially the two versions of his argument concerning naturally cheerful people, and note the differences in their context. Is he answering the same question each time?)

    d Which of his arguments appear to be inconclusive? Would he have done better to have left inconclusive arguments out?

    e Are these arguments, inconclusive for his arguments about happiness in general, also inconclusive for us, his readers?

    f What is your reaction to the following: "It is reported by those who know the Eskimos well, that they are the most cheerful people on earth, and this though they are certainly the race living most continually on the verge of starvation"?

    g What is the effect on the reader of Darwin's last argument, concerning whether or not man really enjoys being civilized? What is his answer to the question?

h At first his analysis seems optimistic at this point—but what point is he really making about human happiness? Why does he not make that point explicitly?

i Taking the entire essay into consideration, how would you sum up the emotional state of future man, as Darwin sees him?

Lines of Experiment

1 Write an essay predicting the future with respect to a single topic. The following are merely categories from which you may perhaps quarry a suitable subject:

Population	Poetry
Cities	Individual freedom
Agriculture	Food
War	Women's rights
Love and sex	Taxes

In working out your composition, you will find the careful, limited stating of the question essential. "What about poetry?" or "What about love?" can only prompt the counterquestion, "Well, what about it?" You may find classification the most useful key to structure in such an essay: "The Future of Individual Freedom" can only be dealt with by means of a classification of the kinds of freedom implicated in the topic. Such a subject also will demand to be considered from two points of view: necessarily from your own, as an inhabitant of the twentieth century; but also from that of the persons to come after. What is slavery to one may be freedom to the other.

2 Write an essay attacking either prophetic arguments in general or Darwin's argument in particular—or both at once. In constructing your argument, consider both the premises and the conclusions of the contrary view: You can demolish an argument by showing that its premises outrun the warrant of the facts, that its conclusions do not follow from its premises, that its conclusions are contradicted by experience or by other ideas accepted generally as true.

Will you take up the opposing arguments one by one, attacking each in its weakest point? Or will you search for a common premise or a common flaw in all the arguments and attack that? Which would be the more effective strategy, from the logical point of view? Which would be the more effective strategy from the rhetorical point of view?

GEORGE WALD

 THE ORIGIN
OF LIFE

About a century ago the question, How did life begin?, which has
interested men throughout their history, reached an impasse. Up to
that time two answers had been offered: one that life had been created
supernaturally, the other that it arises continually from the nonliving.
The first explanation lay outside science; the second was now shown to
be untenable. For a time scientists felt some discomfort in having no
answer at all. Then they stopped asking the question.

Recently ways have been found again to consider the origin of life as a
scientific problem—as an event within the order of nature. In part
this is the result of new information. But a theory never rises of itself,
however rich and secure the facts. It is an act of creation. Our
present ideas of this realm were first brought together in a clear and
defensible argument by the Russian biochemist A. I. Oparin in a book
called *The Origin of Life,* published in 1936. Much can be added now
to Oparin's discussion, yet it provides the foundation upon which all
of us who are interested in this subject have built.

The attempt to understand how life originated raises a wide variety of
scientific questions, which lead in many and diverse directions and
should end by casting light into many obscure corners. At the center
of the enterprise lies the hope not only of explaining a great past event—
important as that should be—but of showing that the explanation is
workable. If we can indeed come to understand how a living organism
arises from the nonliving, we should be able to construct one—only of
the simplest description, to be sure, but still recognizably alive. This is
so remote a possibility now that one scarcely dares to acknowledge it;
but it is there nevertheless.

One answer to the problem of how life originated is that it was created.

This is an understandable confusion of nature with technology. Men are used to making things; it is a ready thought that those things not made by men were made by a superhuman being. Most of the cultures we know contain mythical accounts of a supernatural creation of life. Our own tradition provides such an account in the opening chapters of *Genesis*. There we are told that beginning on the third day of the Creation, God brought forth living creatures—first plants, then fishes and birds, then land animals and finally man.

SPONTANEOUS GENERATION

The more rational elements of society, however, tended to take a more naturalistic view of the matter. One had only to accept the evidence of one's senses to know that life arises regularly from the nonliving: worms from mud, maggots from decaying meat, mice from refuse of various kinds. This is the view that came to be called spontaneous generation. Few scientists doubted it. Aristotle, Newton, William Harvey, Descartes, van Helmont, all accepted spontaneous generation without serious question. Indeed, even the theologians—witness the English Jesuit John Turberville Needham—could subscribe to this view, for *Genesis* tells us, not that God created plants and most animals directly, but that He bade the earth and waters to bring them forth; since this directive was never rescinded, there is nothing heretical in believing that the process has continued.

But step by step, in a great controversy that spread over two centuries, this belief was whittled away until nothing remained of it. First the Italian Francesco Redi showed in the 17th century that meat placed under a screen, so that flies cannot lay their eggs on it, never develops maggots. Then in the following century the Italian abbé Lazzaro Spallanzani showed that a nutritive broth, sealed off from the air while boiling, never develops microorganisms, and hence never rots. Needham objected that by too much boiling Spallanzani had rendered the broth, and still more the air above it, incompatible with life. Spallanzani could defend his broth; when he broke the seal of his flasks, allowing new air to rush in, the broth promptly began to rot. He could find no way, however, to show that the air in the sealed flask had not been vitiated. This problem finally was solved by Louis Pasteur in 1860, with a simple modification of Spallanzani's experiment. Pasteur too used a flask containing boiling broth, but instead of sealing off the neck he drew it out in a long, S-shaped curve with its end open to the air. While molecules of air could pass back and forth freely, the heavier particles of dust, bacteria and molds in the atmosphere were trapped on the walls of the curved neck and only rarely reached the broth. In such a flask the broth seldom was contaminated; usually it remained clear and sterile indefinitely.

This was only one of Pasteur's experiments. It is no easy matter to deal with so deeply ingrained and common-sense a belief as that in spontaneous generation. One can ask for nothing better in such a pass than a noisy and stubborn opponent, and this Pasteur had in the naturalist Félix Pouchet, whose arguments before the French Academy of Sciences drove Pasteur to more and more rigorous experiments. When he had finished, nothing remained of the belief in spontaneous generation.

We tell this story to beginning students of biology as though it represents a triumph of reason over mysticism. In fact it is very nearly the opposite. The reasonable view was to believe in spontaneous generation; the only alternative, to believe in a single, primary act of supernatural creation. There is no third position. For this reason many scientists a century ago chose to regard the belief in spontaneous generation as a "philosophical necessity." It is a symptom of the philosophical poverty of our time that this necessity is no longer appreciated. Most modern biologists, having reviewed with satisfaction the downfall of the spontaneous generation hypothesis, yet unwilling to accept the alternative belief in special creation, are left with nothing.

I think a scientist has no choice but to approach the origin of life through a hypothesis of spontaneous generation. What the controversy reviewed above showed to be untenable is only the belief that living organisms arise spontaneously under present conditions. We have now to face a somewhat different problem: how organisms may have arisen spontaneously under different conditions in some former period, granted that they do so no longer.

THE TASK

To make an organism demands the right substances in the right proportions and in the right arrangement. We do not think that anything more is needed—but that is problem enough.

The substances are water, certain salts—as it happens, those found in the ocean—and carbon compounds. The latter are called *organic* compounds because they scarcely occur except as products of living organisms.

Organic compounds consist for the most part of four types of atoms: carbon, oxygen, nitrogen and hydrogen. These four atoms together constitute about 99 per cent of living material, for hydrogen and oxygen also form water. The organic compounds found in organisms fall mainly into four great classes: carbohydrates, fats, proteins and nucleic acids. The fats are simplest, each consisting of three fatty acids joined to glycerol. The starches and glycogens are made of sugar units strung together to form long straight and branched chains. In general only one type of sugar appears in a single starch or glycogen; these molecules are large, but still relatively simple. The principal function of carbohydrates and fats in the organism is to serve as fuel—as a source of energy.

The nucleic acids introduce a further level of complexity. They are very large structures, composed of aggregates of at least four types of unit—the nucleotides—brought together in a great variety of proportions and sequences. An almost endless variety of different nucleic acids is possible, and specific differences among them are believed to be of the highest importance. Indeed, these structures are thought by many to be the main constituents of the genes, the bearers of hereditary constitution.

Variety and specificity, however, are most characteristic of the proteins, which include the largest and most complex molecules known. The units of which their structure is built are about 25 different amino acids. These are strung together in chains hundreds to thousands of units long, in different proportions, in all types of sequence, and with the greatest variety of branching and folding. A virtually infinite number of different proteins is possible. Organisms seem to exploit this potentiality, for no two species of living organism, animal or plant, possess the same proteins.

Organic molecules therefore form a large and formidable array, endless in variety and of the most bewildering complexity. One cannot think of having organisms without them. This is precisely the trouble, for to understand how organisms originated we must first of all explain how such complicated molecules could come into being. And that is only the beginning. To make an organism requires not only a tremendous variety of these substances, in adequate amounts and proper proportions, but also just the right arrangement of them. Structure here is as important as composition—and what a complication of structure! The most complex machine man has devised—say an electronic brain—is child's play compared with the simplest of living organisms. The especially trying thing is that complexity here involves such small dimensions. It is on the molecular level; it consists of a detailed fitting of molecule to molecule such as no chemist can attempt.

THE POSSIBLE
AND IMPOSSIBLE

One has only to contemplate the magnitude of this task to concede that the spontaneous generation of a living organism is impossible. Yet here we are—as a result, I believe, of spontaneous generation. It will help to digress for a moment to ask what one means by "impossible."

With every event one can associate a probability—the chance that it will occur. This is always a fraction, the proportion of times the event occurs in a large number of trials. Sometimes the probability is apparent even without trial. A coin has two faces; the probability of tossing a head is therefore $1/2$. A die has six faces; the probability of throwing a deuce is $1/6$. When one has no means of estimating the probability beforehand, it must be determined by counting the fraction of successes in a large number of trials.

Our everyday concept of what is impossible, possible or certain derives from our experience: the number of trials that may be encompassed within the space of a human lifetime, or at most within recorded human history. In this colloquial, practical sense I concede the spontaneous origin of life to be "impossible." It is impossible as we judge events in the scale of human experience.

We shall see that this is not a very meaningful concession. For one thing, the time with which our problem is concerned is geological time, and the whole extent of human history is trivial in the balance. We shall have more to say of this later.

But even within the bounds of our own time there is a serious flaw in our judgment of what is possible. It sounds impressive to say that an event has never been observed in the whole of human history. We should tend to regard such an event as at least "practically" impossible, whatever probability is assigned to it on abstract grounds. When we look a little further into such a statement, however, it proves to be almost meaningless. For men are apt to reject reports of very improbable occurrences. Persons of good judgment think it safer to distrust the alleged observer of such an event than to believe him. The result is that events which are merely very extraordinary acquire the reputation of never having occurred at all.   Thus the highly improbable is made to appear impossible.

To give an example: Every physicist knows that there is a very small probability, which is easily computed, that the table upon which I am writing will suddenly and spontaneously rise into the air.   The event requires no more than that the molecules of which the table is composed, ordinarily in random motion in all directions, should happen by chance to move in the same direction.   Every physicist concedes this possibility; but try telling one that you have seen it happen.   Recently I asked a friend, a Nobel laureate in physics, what he would say if I told him that.   He laughed and said that he would regard it as more probable that I was mistaken than that the event had actually occurred.

We see therefore that it does not mean much to say that a very improbable event has never been observed.   There is a conspiracy to suppress such observations, not among scientists alone, but among all judicious persons, who have learned to be skeptical even of what they see, let alone of what they are told.   If one group is more skeptical than others, it is perhaps lawyers, who have the harshest experience of the unreliability of human evidence.   Least skeptical of all are the scientists, who, cautious as they are, know very well what strange things are possible.

A final aspect of our problem is very important.   When we consider the spontaneous origin of a living organism, this is not an event that need happen again and again.   It is perhaps enough for it to happen once.   The probability with which we are concerned is of a special kind; it is the probability that an event occur *at least once*.   To this type of probability a fundamentally important thing happens as one increases the number of trials.   However improbable the event in a single trial, it becomes increasingly probable as the trials are multiplied.   Eventually the event becomes virtually inevitable.   For instance, the chance that a coin will not fall head up in a single toss is $1/2$.   The chance that no head will appear in a series of tosses is $1/2 \times 1/2 \times 1/2$ . . . as many times over as the number of tosses.   In 10 tosses the chance that no head will appear is therefore $1/2$ multiplied by itself 10 times, or $1/1,000$.   Consequently the chance that a head will appear at least once in 10 tosses is $999/1,000$.   Ten trials have converted what started as a modest probability to a near certainty.

The same effect can be achieved with any probability, however small, by multiplying sufficiently the number of trials. Consider a reasonably improbable event, the chance of which is 1/1,000. The chance that this will not occur in one trial is 999/1,000. The chance that it won't occur in 1,000 trials is 999/1,000 multiplied together 1,000 times. This fraction comes out to be 37/100. The chance that it will happen at least once in 1,000 trials is therefore one minus this number— 63/100—a little better than three chances out of five. One thousand trials have transformed this from a highly improbable to a highly probable event. In 10,000 trials the chance that this event will occur at least once comes out to be 19,999/20,000. It is now almost inevitable.

It makes no important change in the argument if we assess the probability that an event occur at least two, three, four or some other small number of times rather than at least once. It simply means that more trials are needed to achieve any degree of certainty we wish. Otherwise everything is the same.

In such a problem as the spontaneous origin of life we have no way of assessing probabilities beforehand, or even of deciding what we mean by a trial. The origin of a living organism is undoubtedly a stepwise phenomenon, each step with its own probability and its own conditions of trial. Of one thing we can be sure, however: whatever constitutes a trial, more such trials occur the longer the interval of time.

The important point is that since the origin of life belongs in the category of at-least-once phenomena, time is on its side. However improbable we regard this event, or any of the steps which it involves, given enough time it will almost certainly happen at least once. And for life as we know it, with its capacity for growth and reproduction, once may be enough.

Time is in fact the hero of the plot. The time with which we have to deal is of the order of two billion years. What we regard as impossible on the basis of human experience is meaningless here. Given so much time, the "impossible" becomes possible, the possible probable, and the probable virtually certain. One has only to wait: time itself performs the miracles.

ORGANIC MOLECULES

This brings the argument back to its first stage: the origin of organic compounds. Until a century and a quarter ago the only known source of these substances was the stuff of living organisms. Students of chemistry are usually told that when, in 1828, Friedrich Wöhler synthesized the first organic compound, urea, he proved that organic compounds do not require living organisms to make them. Of course it showed nothing of the kind. Organic chemists are alive; Wöhler merely showed that they can make organic compounds externally as well as internally. It is still true that with almost negligible exceptions all the organic matter we know is the product of living organisms.

The almost negligible exceptions, however, are very important for our argument. It is now recognized that a constant, slow production of organic molecules occurs without the agency of living things. Certain geological phenomena yield simple organic compounds. So, for example, volcanic eruptions bring metal carbides to the surface of the earth, where they react with water vapor to yield simple compounds of carbon and hydrogen. The familiar type of such a reaction is the process used in old-style bicycle lamps in which acetylene is made by mixing iron carbide with water.

Recently Harold Urey, Nobel laureate in chemistry, has become interested in the degree to which electrical discharges in the upper atmosphere may promote the formation of organic compounds. One of his students, S. L. Miller, performed the simple experiment of circulating a mixture of water vapor, methane (CH_4), ammonia (NH_3) and hydrogen—all gases believed to have been present in the early atmosphere of the earth—continuously for a week over an electric spark. The circulation was maintained by boiling the water in one limb of the apparatus and condensing it in the other. At the end of the week the water was analyzed by the delicate method of paper chromatography. It was found to have acquired a mixture of amino acids! Glycine and alanine, the simplest amino acids and the most prevalent in proteins, were definitely identified in the solution, and there were indications it contained aspartic acid and two others. The yield was surprisingly high. This amazing result changes at a stroke our ideas of the probability of the spontaneous formation of amino acids.

A final consideration, however, seems to me more important than all the special processes to which one might appeal for organic syntheses in inanimate nature.

It has already been said that to have organic molecules one ordinarily needs organisms. The synthesis of organic substances, like almost everything else that happens in organisms, is governed by the special class of proteins called enzymes—the organic catalysts which greatly accelerate chemical reactions in the body.   Since an enzyme is not used up but is returned at the end of the process, a small amount of enzyme can promote an enormous transformation of material.

Enzymes play such a dominant role in the chemistry of life that it is exceedingly difficult to imagine the synthesis of living material without their help.   This poses a dilemma, for enzymes themselves are proteins, and hence among the most complex organic components of the cell. One is asking, in effect, for an apparatus which is the unique property of cells in order to form the first cell.

This is not, however, an insuperable difficulty.   An enzyme, after all, is only a catalyst; it can do no more than change the *rate* of a chemical reaction.   It cannot make anything happen that would not have happened, though more slowly, in its absence.   Every process that is catalyzed by an enzyme, and every product of such a process, would occur without the enzyme.   The only difference is one of rate.

Once again the essence of the argument is time.   What takes only a few moments in the presence of an enzyme or other catalyst may take days, months or years in its absence; but given time, the end result is the same.

Indeed, this great difficulty in conceiving of the spontaneous generation of organic compounds has its positive side.   In a sense, organisms demonstrate to us what organic reactions and products are *possible*. We can be certain that, given time, all these things must occur.   Every substance that has ever been found in an organism displays thereby the finite probability of its occurrence.   Hence, given time, it should arise spontaneously.   One has only to wait.

It will be objected at once that this is just what one cannot do.   Everyone knows that these substances are highly perishable.   Granted that, within long spaces of time, now a sugar molecule, now a fat, now even a protein might form spontaneously, each of these molecules should have only a transitory existence.   How are they ever to accumulate; and, unless they do so, how form an organism?

We must turn the question around.   What, in our experience, is known to destroy organic compounds?   Primarily two agencies: decay and the attack of oxygen.   But decay is the work of living organisms, and we are talking of a time before life existed.   As for oxygen, this introduces a further and fundamental section of our argument.

It is generally conceded at present that the early atmosphere of our planet contained virtually no free oxygen. Almost all the earth's oxygen was bound in the form of water and metal oxides. If this were not so, it would be very difficult to imagine how organic matter could accumulate over the long stretches of time that alone might make possible the spontaneous origin of life. This is a crucial point, therefore, and the statement that the early atmosphere of the planet was virtually oxygen-free comes forward so opportunely as to raise a suspicion of special pleading. I have for this reason taken care to consult a number of geologists and astronomers on this point, and am relieved to find that it is well defended. I gather that there is a widespread though not universal consensus that this condition did exist. Apparently something similar was true also for another common component of our atmosphere—carbon dioxide. It is believed that most of the carbon on the earth during its early geological history existed as the element or in metal carbides and hydrocarbons; very little was combined with oxygen.

This situation is not without its irony. We tend usually to think that the environment plays the tune to which the organism must dance. The environment is given; the organism's problem is to adapt to it or die. It has become apparent lately, however, that some of the most important features of the physical environment are themselves the work of living organisms. Two such features have just been named. The atmosphere of our planet seems to have contained no oxygen until organisms placed it there by the process of plant photosynthesis. It is estimated that at present all the oxygen of our atmosphere is renewed by photosynthesis once in every 2,000 years, and that all the carbon dioxide passes through the process of photosynthesis once in every 300 years. In the scale of geological time, these intervals are very small indeed. We are left with the realization that all the oxygen and carbon dioxide of our planet are the products of living organisms, and have passed through living organisms over and over again.

FORCES
OF DISSOLUTION

In the early history of our planet, when there were no organisms or any free oxygen, organic compounds should have been stable over very long periods. This is the crucial difference between the period before life existed and our own. If one were to specify a single reason why the spontaneous generation of living organisms was possible once and is so no longer, this is the reason.

We must still reckon, however, with another destructive force which is disposed of less easily.   This can be called spontaneous dissolution— the counterpart of spontaneous generation.   We have noted that any process catalyzed by an enzyme can occur in time without the enzyme. The trouble is that the processes which synthesize an organic substance are reversible: any chemical reaction which an enzyme may catalyze will go backward as well as forward.   We have spoken as though one has only to wait to achieve syntheses of all kinds; it is truer to say that what one achieves by waiting is *equilibria* of all kinds—equilibria in which the synthesis and dissolution of substances come into balance.

In the vast majority of the processes in which we are interested the point of equilibrium lies far over toward the side of dissolution.   That is to say, spontaneous dissolution is much more probable, and hence proceeds much more rapidly, than spontaneous synthesis.   For example, the spontaneous union, step by step, of amino acid units to form a protein has a certain small probability, and hence might occur over a long stretch of time.   But the dissolution of the protein or of an intermediate product into its component amino acids is much more probable, and hence will go ever so much more rapidly.   The situation we must face is that of patient Penelope waiting for Odysseus, yet much worse: each night she undid the weaving of the preceding day, but here a night could readily undo the work of a year or a century.

How do present-day organisms manage to synthesize organic compounds against the forces of dissolution?   They do so by a continuous expenditure of energy.   Indeed, living organisms commonly do better than oppose the forces of dissolution; they grow in spite of them.   They do so, however, only at enormous expense to their surroundings.   They need a constant supply of material and energy merely to maintain themselves, and much more of both to grow and reproduce.   A living organism is an intricate machine for performing exactly this function. When, for want of fuel or through some internal failure in its mechanism, an organism stops actively synthesizing itself in opposition to the processes which continuously decompose it, it dies and rapidly disintegrates.

What we ask here is to synthesize organic molecules without such a machine.   I believe this to be the most stubborn problem that confronts us—the weakest link at present in our argument.   I do not think it by any means disastrous, but it calls for phenomena and forces some of which are as yet only partly understood and some probably still to be discovered.

FORCES
OF INTEGRATION

At present we can make only a beginning with this problem.   We know that it is possible on occasion to protect molecules from dissolution by precipitation or by attachment to other molecules.   A wide variety of such precipitation and "trapping" reactions is used in modern chemistry and biochemistry to promote syntheses.   Some molecules appear to acquire a degree of resistance to disintegration simply through their size.   So, for example, the larger molecules composed of amino acids —polypeptides and proteins—seem to display much less tendency to disintegrate into their units than do smaller compounds of two or three amino acids.

Again, many organic molecules display still another type of integrating force—a spontaneous impulse toward structure formation.   Certain types of fatty molecules—lecithins and cephalins—spin themselves out in water to form highly oriented and well-shaped structures—the so-called myelin figures.   Proteins sometimes orient even in solution, and also may aggregate in the solid state in highly organized formations. Such spontaneous achitectonic tendencies are still largely unexplored, particularly as they may occur in complex mixtures of substances, and they involve forces the strength of which has not yet been estimated.

What we are saying is that possibilities exist for opposing *intra*molecular dissolution by *inter*molecular aggregations of various kinds.   The equilibrium between union and disunion of the amino acids that make up a protein is all to the advantage of disunion, but the aggregation of the protein with itself or other molecules might swing the equilibrium in the opposite direction: perhaps by removing the protein from access to the water which would be required to disintegrate it or by providing some particularly stable type of molecular association.

In such a scheme the protein appears only as a transient intermediate, an unstable way-station, which can either fall back to a mixture of its constituent amino acids or enter into the formation of a complex structural aggregate: amino acids $\rightleftharpoons$ proteain $\rightarrow$ aggregate.

Such molecular aggregates, of various degrees of material and architectural complexity, are indispensable intermediates between molecules and organisms.   We have no need to try to imagine the spontaneous formation of an organism by one grand collision of its component molecules.   The whole process must be gradual.   The molecules form aggregates, small and large.   The aggregates add further molecules, thus growing in size and complexity.   Aggregates of various kinds interact with one another to form still larger and more complex structures. In this way we imagine the ascent, not by jumps or master strokes, but gradually, piecemeal, to the first living organisms.

FIRST ORGANISMS

Where may this have happened?   It is easiest to suppose that life first arose in the sea.   Here were the necessary salts and the water.   The latter is not only the principal component of organisms, but prior to their formation provided a medium which could dissolve molecules of the widest variety and ceaselessly mix and circulate them.   It is this constant mixture and collision of organic molecules of every sort that constituted in large part the "trials" of our earlier discussion of probabilities.

The sea in fact gradually turned into a dilute broth, sterile and oxygen-free.   In this broth molecules came together in increasing number and variety, sometimes merely to collide and separate, sometimes to react with one another to produce new combinations, sometimes to aggregate into multimolecular formations of increasing size and complexity.

What brought order into such complexes?   For order is as essential here as composition.   To form an organism, molecules must enter into intricate designs and connections; they must eventually form a self-repairing, self-constructing dynamic machine.   For a time this problem of molecular arrangement seemed to present an almost insuperable obstacle in the way of imagining a spontaneous origin of life, or indeed the laboratory synthesis of a living organism.   It is still a large and mysterious problem, but it no longer seems insuperable.   The change in view has come about because we now realize that it is not altogether necessary to *bring* order into this situation; a great deal of order is implicit in the molecules themselves.

The epitome of molecular order is a crystal.   In a perfect crystal the molecules display complete regularity of position and orientation in all planes of space.   At the other extreme are fluids—liquids or gases—in which the molecules are in ceaseless motion and in wholly random orientations and positions.

Lately it has become clear that very little of a living cell is truly fluid.

Most of it consists of molecules which have taken up various degrees of orientation with regard to one another. That is, most of the cell represents various degrees of approach to crystallinity—often, however, with very important differences from the crystals most familiar to us. Much of the cell's crystallinity involves molecules which are still in solution—so-called liquid crystals—and much of the dynamic, plastic quality of cellular structure, the capacity for constant change of shape and interchange of material, derives from this condition. Our familiar crystals, furthermore, involve only one or a very few types of molecule, while in the cell a great variety of different molecules come together in some degree of regular spacing and orientation—*i.e.,* some degree of crystallinity. We are dealing in the cell with highly mixed crystals and near-crystals, solid and liquid. The laboratory study of this type of formation has scarcely begun. Its further exploration is of the highest importance for our problem.

In a fluid such as water the molecules are in very rapid motion. Any molecules dissolved in such a medium are under a constant barrage of collisions with water molecules. This keeps small and moderately sized molecules in a constant turmoil; they are knocked about at random, colliding again and again, never holding any position or orientation for more than an instant. The larger a molecule is relative to water, the less it is disturbed by such collisions. Many protein and nucleic acid molecules are so large that even in solution their motions are very sluggish, and since they carry large numbers of electric charges distributed about their surfaces, they tend even in solution to align with respect to one another. It is so that they tend to form liquid crystals.

We have spoken above of architectonic tendencies even among some of the relatively small molecules: the lecithins and cephalins. Such molecules are insoluble in water yet possess special groups which have a high affinity for water. As a result they tend to form surface layers, in which their water-seeking groups project into the water phase, while their water-repelling portions project into the air, or into an oil phase, or unite to form an oil phase. The result is that quite spontaneously such molecules, when exposed to water, take up highly oriented positions to form surface membranes, myelin figures and other quasi-crystalline structures.

Recently several particularly striking examples have been reported of the spontaneous production of familiar types of biological structure by protein molecules. Cartilage and muscle offer some of the most intricate and regular patterns of structure to be found in organisms. A fiber from either type of tissue presents under the electron microscope a beautiful pattern of cross striations of various widths and densities, very regularly spaced. The proteins that form these structures can be coaxed into free solution and stirred into completely random orientation. Yet on precipitating, under proper conditions, the molecules realign with regard to one another to regenerate with extraordinary fidelity the original patterns of the tissues.

We have therefore a genuine basis for the view that the molecules of our oceanic broth will not only come together spontaneously to form aggregates but in doing so will spontaneously achieve various types and degrees of order. This greatly simplifies our problem. What it means is that, given the right molecules, one does not have to do everything for them; they do a great deal for themselves.

Oparin has made the ingenious suggestion that natural selection, which Darwin proposed to be the driving force of organic evolution, begins to operate at this level. He suggests that as the molecules come together to form colloidal aggregates, the latter begin to compete with one another for material. Some aggregates, by virtue of especially favorable composition or internal arrangement, acquire new molecules more rapidly than others. They eventually emerge as the dominant types. Oparin suggests further that considerations of optimal size enter at this level. A growing colloidal particle may reach a point at which it becomes unstable and breaks down into smaller particles, each of which grows and redivides. All these phenomena lie within the bounds of known processes in nonliving systems.

THE SOURCES OF ENERGY

We suppose that all these forces and factors, and others perhaps yet to be revealed, together give us eventually the first living organism. That achieved, how does the organism continue to live?

We have already noted that a living organism is a dynamic structure. It is the site of a continuous influx and outflow of matter and energy. This is the very sign of life, its cessation the best evidence of death. What is the primal organism to use as food, and how derive the energy it needs to maintain itself and grow?

For the primal organism, generated under the conditions we have described, only one answer is possible. Having arisen in an oceanic broth of organic molecules, its only recourse is to live upon them. There is only one way of doing that in the absence of oxygen. It is called fermentation: the process by which organisms derive energy by breaking organic molecules and rearranging their parts. The most familiar example of such a process is the fermentation of sugar by yeast, which yields alcohol as one of the products. Animal cells also ferment sugar, not to alcohol but to lactic acid. These are two examples from a host of known fermentations.

The yeast fermentation has the following over-all equation: $C_6H_{12}O_6$ $\rightarrow 2\ CO_2 + 2\ C_2H_5OH +$ energy. The result of fragmenting 180 grams of sugar into 88 grams of carbon dioxide and 92 grams of alcohol is to make available about 20,000 calories of energy for the use of the cell. The energy is all that the cell derives by this transaction; the carbon dioxide and alcohol are waste products which must be got rid of somehow if the cell is to survive.

The cell, having arisen in a broth of organic compounds accumulated over the ages, must consume these molecules by fermentation in order to acquire the energy it needs to live, grow and reproduce. In doing so, it and its descendants are living on borrowed time. They are consuming their heritage, just as we in our time have nearly consumed our heritage of coal and oil. Eventually such a process must come to an end, and with that life also should have ended. It would have been necessary to start the entire development again.

Fortunately, however, the waste product carbon dioxide saved this situation. This gas entered the ocean and the atmosphere in ever-increasing quantity. Some time before the cell exhausted the supply of organic molecules, it succeeded in inventing the process of photosynthesis. This enabled it, with the energy of sunlight, to make its own organic molecules: first sugar from carbon dioxide and water, then, with ammonia and nitrates as sources of nitrogen, the entire array of organic compounds which it requires. The sugar synthesis equation is: $6\ CO_2 + 6\ H_2O +$ sunlight $\rightarrow C_6H_{12}O_6 + 6\ O_2$. Here 264 grams of carbon dioxide plus 108 grams of water plus about 700,000 calories of sunlight yield 180 grams of sugar and 192 grams of oxygen.

This is an enormous step forward. Living organisms no longer needed to depend upon the accumulation of organic matter from past ages; they could make their own. With the energy of sunlight they could accomplish the fundamental organic syntheses that provide their substance, and by fermentation they could produce what energy they needed.

Fermentation, however, is an extraordinarily inefficient source of energy. It leaves most of the energy potential of organic compounds unexploited; consequently huge amounts of organic material must be fermented to provide a modicum of energy. It produces also various poisonous waste products—alcohol, lactic acid, acetic acid, formic acid and so on. In the sea such products are readily washed away, but if organisms were ever to penetrate to the air and land, these products must prove a serious embarrassment.

One of the by-products of photosynthesis, however, is oxygen. Once this was available, organisms could invent a new way to acquire energy, many times as efficient as fermentation. This is the process of cold combustion called respiration: $C_6H_{12}O_6 + 6\ O_2 \rightarrow 6\ CO_2 + 6\ H_2O$ + energy. The burning of 180 grams of sugar in cellular respiration yields about 700,000 calories, as compared with the approximately 20,000 calories produced by fermentation of the same quantity of sugar. This process of combustion extracts all the energy that can possibly be derived from the molecules which it consumes. With this process at its disposal, the cell can meet its energy requirements with a minimum expenditure of substance. It is a further advantage that the products of respiration—water and carbon dioxide—are innocuous and easily disposed of in any environment.

LIFE'S CAPITAL

It is difficult to overestimate the degree to which the invention of cellular respiration released the forces of living organisms. No organism that relies wholly upon fermentation has ever amounted to much. Even after the advent of photosynthesis, organisms could have led only a marginal existence. They could indeed produce their own organic materials, but only in quantities sufficient to survive. Fermentation is so profligate a way of life that photosynthesis could do little more than keep up with it. Respiration used the material of organisms with such enormously greater efficiency as for the first time to leave something over. Coupled with fermentation, photosynthesis made organisms self-sustaining; coupled with respiration, it provided a surplus. To use an economic analogy, photosynthesis brought organisms to the subsistence level; respiration provided them with capital. It is mainly this capital that they invested in the great enterprise of organic evolution.

The entry of oxygen into the atmosphere also liberated organisms in another sense. The sun's radiation contains ultraviolet components which no living cell can tolerate. We are sometimes told that if this radiation were to reach the earth's surface, life must cease. That is not quite true. Water absorbs ultraviolet radiation very effectively, and one must conclude that as long as these rays penetrated in quantity to the surface of the earth, life had to remain under water. With the appearance of oxygen, however, a layer of ozone formed high in the atmosphere and absorbed this radiation. Now organisms could for the first time emerge from the water and begin to populate the earth and air. Oxygen provided not only the means of obtaining adequate energy for evolution but the protective blanket of ozone which alone made possible terrestrial life.

This is really the end of our story. Yet not quite the end. Our entire concern in this argument has been to bring the origin of life within the compass of natural phenomena. It is of the essence of such phenomena to be repetitive, and hence, given time, to be inevitable.

This is by far our most significant conclusion—that life, as an orderly natural event on such a planet as ours, was inevitable. The same can be said of the whole of organic evolution. All of it lies within the order of nature, and apart from details all of it was inevitable.

Astronomers have reason to believe that a planet such as ours—of about the earth's size and temperature, and about as well-lighted—is a rare event in the universe. Indeed, filled as our story is with improbable phenomena, one of the least probable is to have had such a body as the earth to begin with. Yet though this probability is small, the universe is so large that it is conservatively estimated at least 100,000 planets like the earth exist in our galaxy alone. Some 100 million galaxies lie within the range of our most powerful telescopes, so that throughout observable space we can count apparently on the existence of at least 10 million million planets like our own.

What it means to bring the origin of life within the realm of natural phenomena is to imply that in all these places life probably exists—life as we know it. Indeed, I am convinced that there can be no way of composing and constructing living organisms which is fundamentally different from the one we know—though this is another argument, and must await another occasion. Wherever life is possible, given time, it should arise. It should then ramify into a wide array of forms, differing in detail from those we now observe (as did earlier organisms on the earth) yet including many which should look familiar to us— perhaps even men.

We are not alone in the universe, and do not bear alone the whole burden of life and what comes of it.   Life is a cosmic event—so far as we know the most complex state of organization that matter has achieved in our cosmos.   It has come many times, in many places— places closed off from us by impenetrable distances, probably never to be crossed even with a signal.   As men we can attempt to understand it, and even somewhat to control and guide its local manifestations. On this planet that is our home, we have every reason to wish it well. Yet should we fail, all is not lost.   Our kind will try again elsewhere.

Lines of Inquiry

1 Make a brief list of the questions dealt with in this essay.   Use the essay's subtitles where you can.

    a What accounts for the sequence in which Wald composes his ideas?

    b Try putting the last question first and the first last; why is the result unsatisfactory?

    c What do you conclude concerning the essential character of expository introductions and conclusions?

2 The body of this essay is an effort to explain how life came into being.   In his analysis, Wald employs both temporal and logical sequence.

    a How do the two sequences interlock?

    b Which is dominant?

    c Could Wald have written this analysis without employing the sequence of time?

3 Some astronomers recently have cast doubt on the assumption that the universe contains a large number of planets like our own.

    a What portions of Wald's argument would the discovery that the earth is unique invalidate?   Imagine the essay without those portions.   Does the composition "feel" finished?

    b What portion of the section you have struck out is essential to our feeling that the essay is complete?   What do you conclude about completeness in exposition?

4 Mark in the essay each occasion on which Wald concedes that his line of argument has brought him up against an impossibility—only to show that the impossibility is not impossible at all.

    a Where do these reversals occur?

    b Which reversal is central to Wald's argument?   On what method of dealing with ideas does it depend?

    c Point to the parallel reversals of opinion in the essay: Are they necessary, logically speaking, to Wald's argument? Why emphasize these reversals at all?

d In this connection, why does Wald give a "blow by blow" account of the past controversy over life's origin? Why not simply sum up the two sides and let it drop?

e "Reversal" is an old principle of the drama, first described in Aristotle's *Poetics*. Could it be said that in Wald's essay too, a dramatic as well as a logical principle influences the shape of composition?

5 How many times in Wald's essay does the successful pursuit of his argument depend on the rephrasing of a question, or of a statement, in order to bring out a distinction that was masked in the original and familiar form of the question? What do you conclude from your answer concerning (a) familiar questions and (b) the relationship between logical process and the making of distinctions?

6 a Does Wald take an explicit position on the truth of the opening chapters of Genesis? What appears to be his attitude toward religious explanations of the origin of life?

b Where in his essay does he mention such explanations, and why there particularly?

c What evidence of his attitude toward religion do you find? What is his treatment of the Christian tradition in this essay?

d Which of the following conclusions seem to follow logically from Wald's argument?

(1) God did not create man.

(2) There is no God.

(3) God did not create life.

(4) The story of Genesis is factually mistaken.

(5) The belief that God created life is not rational.

7 Wald's point of view is that of the scientist, and he writes for the audience of *Scientific American*—a literate, educated audience interested in the natural sciences but not necessarily scientifically trained. Make a brief list of the ways in which these two considerations influence the character of Wald's analysis—for example, in emphasis, choice of subject, tone, focus, sequence, and illustration. Considering your list, what changes would you expect to see under each category if Wald were to revise the essay with each of the following audiences in mind: (a) biologists, (b) clergymen, (c) mathematicians, (d) a science fiction fan club. Can you think of any audiences for which such an essay would be entirely inappropriate?

8 A. I. Oparin was a Russian scientist; *The Origin of Life* was

published under Josef Stalin. If one were to argue that the modern case for spontaneous generation was first argued by a Russian scientist because the Russians are Marxists, and Marxists, like all materialists, are anxious to discredit the idea of a supernatural world, what would you reply?

9 What is the function in Wald's essay of the following italicized words or phrases?

a "It is no easy matter to deal with so deeply ingrained and common-sense a belief as that in spontaneous generation. *One can ask for nothing better in such a pass than a noisy and stubborn opponent, and this Pasteur had. . . .*"

b "Genesis tells us, not that God created plants and most animals directly, but that He bade the earth and waters to bring them forth; *since this directive was never rescinded, there is nothing heretical in believing that* the process has continued."

c "Most modern biologists, having reviewed *with satisfaction* the downfall of the spontaneous generation hypothesis. . . ."

d "The situation we must face is *that of patient Penelope waiting for Odysseus, yet much worse: each night she undid the weaving of the preceding day, but here a night could readily undo the work of a year or a century.*"

Lines of Experiment

1 Analyze a technical problem or process in which you have special interest.   You may find an appropriate subject among such areas of study as the following: space exploration, cybernetics, automobile design, city planning, architecture, genetics, medicine, horticulture, civil defense, guerilla warfare.

These areas are too broad to be analyzed in themselves; an analysis explains why or how a certain thing comes about—its focus is on a specific process or a pattern of cause and effect, not on an area of study.   Your *first* job, then, is to focus your composition on a reasonable subject for analysis.   "Space exploration" will not do, for it can embrace political, economic, medical, psychological, and even moral considerations, as well as physical ones.   The building of a vehicle strong enough to use in the exploration of space, on the other hand, would be a topic suitable for analysis.

Your *second* job is to consider the questions within the problem and to arrange them in a sequence that makes the answer to each reveal the next question.   That sequence will not always be obvious, and may depend on the pattern of emphasis you strive for: Whether one begins with the hull, the engine, or the crew of a spaceship may depend on dramatic as well as on logical factors.

Third, you must frame an introduction that not only will announce your subject but also will focus the reader's attention on the aspect you intend to make central.

Fourth, you must bear in mind as you conclude that the larger implications of an analysis are the real measure of its importance.

2 Write an analytic account of a phenomenon within your own experience. Your subject may be an election, a riot, a mass panic, the persecution of an eccentric neighbor, a passion for model boats, the failure of a business, a friend's dropping out of school, etc. (Probably you will be wise not to focus such an essay on your own life, or to choose an incident in which you are a central figure; why?) The suggestions given in *1* above may be useful to you in framing your composition.

THOMAS MALTHUS

 ## POPULATION AND SUBSISTENCE

In New Jersey, the proportion of births to deaths on an average of seven years, ending in 1743, was as 300 to 100. In France and England, taking the highest proportion, it is as 117 to 100. Great and astonishing as this difference is, we ought not to be so wonderstruck at it as to attribute it to the miraculous interposition of heaven. The causes of it are not remote, latent and mysterious, but near us, round about us, and open to the investigation of every inquiring mind. It accords with the most liberal spirit of philosophy to suppose that not a stone can fall or a plant rise without the immediate agency of divine power. But we know from experience that these operations of what we call nature have been conducted almost invariably according to fixed laws. And since the world began, the causes of population and depopulation have probably been as constant as any of the laws of nature with which we are acquainted.

The passion between the sexes has appeared in every age to be so nearly the same that it may always be considered, in algebraic language, as a given quantity. The great law of necessity which prevents population from increasing in any country beyond the food which it can either produce or acquire, is a law so open to our view, so obvious and evident to our understandings, and so completely confirmed by the experience of every age, that we cannot for a moment doubt it. The different modes which nature takes to prevent or repress a redundant population do not appear, indeed, to us so certain and regular; but though we cannot always predict the mode we may with certainty predict the fact. If the proportion of births to deaths for a few years indicate an increase of numbers much beyond the proportional increased or acquired produce of the country, we may be perfectly certain that unless an emigration takes place the deaths will shortly exceed the births, and that the increase that had taken place for a few years cannot be the real average increase of the population of the country. Were there no other depopulating causes, every country would, without doubt, be subject to periodical pestilences or famines.

The only true criterion of a real and permanent increase in the population of any country, is the increase of the means of subsistence. But even this criterion is subject to some slight variations, which are, however, completely open to our view and observations. In some countries population appears to have been forced; that is, the people have been habituated by degrees to live almost upon the smallest possible quantity of food. There must have been periods in such countries when population increased permanently, without an increase in the means of subsistence. China seems to answer to this description. If the accounts we have of it are to be trusted, the lower classes of people are in the habit of living almost upon the smallest possible quantity of food and are glad to get any putrid offals that European labourers would rather starve than eat. The law in China which permits parents to expose their children has tended principally thus to force the population. A nation in this state must necessarily be subject to famines. Where a country is so populous in proportion to the means of subsistence that the average produce of it is but barely sufficient to support the lives of the inhabitants, any deficiency from the badness of seasons must be fatal. It is probable that the very frugal manner in which the Gentoos are in the habit of living contributes in some degree to the famines of Indostan.

In America, where the reward of labour is at present so liberal, the lower classes might retrench very considerably in a year of scarcity without materially distressing themselves. A famine therefore seems to be almost impossible. It may be expected that in the progress of the population of America the labourers will in time be much less liberally rewarded. The numbers will in this case permanently increase, without a proportional increase in the means of subsistence.

In the different States of Europe there must be some variations in the proportion between the number of inhabitants and the quantity of food consumed, arising from the different habits of living that prevail in each State. The labourers of the South of England are so accustomed to eat fine wheaten bread that they will suffer themselves to be half starved before they will submit to live like the Scotch peasants. They might perhaps in time, by the constant operation of the hard law of necessity, be reduced to live even like the lower Chinese: and the country would then, with the same quantity of food, support a greater population. But to effect this must always be a most difficult, and every friend to humanity will hope, an abortive attempt. Nothing is so common as to hear of encouragements that ought to be given to population. If the tendency of mankind to increase be so great as I have represented it to be, it may appear strange that this increase does not come when it is thus repeatedly called for. The true reason is that the demand for a greater population is made without preparing the funds necessary to support it. Increase the demand for agricultural labour by promoting cultivation, and with it consequently increase the produce of the country, and ameliorate the condition of the labourer, and no apprehensions whatever need be entertained of the proportional increase of population. An attempt to effect this purpose in any other way is vicious, cruel, and tyrannical, and in any state of tolerable freedom cannot therefore succeed. It may appear to be the interest of the rulers and the rich of a State to force population, and thereby lower the price of labour and consequently the expence of fleets and armies, and the cost of manufactures for foreign sale: but every attempt of the kind should be carefully watched and strenuously resisted by the friends of the poor, particularly when it comes under the deceitful garb of benevolence, and is likely on that account to be cheerfully and cordially received by the common people. . . .

I have mentioned some cases where population may permanently increase without a proportional increase in the means of subsistence. But it is evident that the variation in different States between the food and the numbers supported by it is restricted to a limit beyond which it cannot pass. In every country the population of which is not absolutely decreasing, the food must be necessarily sufficient to support and to continue the race of labourers.

Other circumstances being the same, it may be affirmed, that countries are populous according to the quantity of human food which they produce, and happy according to the liberality with which that food is divided, or the quantity which a day's labour will purchase. Corn countries are more populous than pasture countries, and rice countries more populous than corn countries. The lands in England are not suited to rice, but they would all bear potatoes: and Dr. Adam Smith observes that if potatoes were to become the favourite vegetable food of the common people, and if the same quantity of land was employed in their culture as is now employed in the culture of corn, the country would be able to support a much greater population; and would consequently in a very short time have it.

The happiness of a country does not depend, absolutely, upon its poverty or its riches, upon its youth or its age, upon its being thinly or fully inhabited, but upon the rapidity with which it is increasing, upon the degree in which the yearly increase of food approaches to the yearly increase of an unrestricted population. This approximation is always the nearest in new colonies, where the knowledge and industry of an old State operate on the fertile unappropriated land of a new one. In other cases, the youth or the age of a State is not in this respect of very great importance. It is probable that the food of Great Britain is divided in as great plenty to the inhabitants, at the present period, as it was two thousand, three thousand, or four thousand years ago. And there is reason to believe that the poor and thinly inhabited tracts of the Scotch Highlands are as much distressed by an overcharged population as the rich and populous province of Flanders.

Were a country never to be over-run by a people more advanced in arts but left to its own natural progress in civilization, from the time that its produce might be considered as an unit to the time that it might be considered as a million, during the lapse of many hundred years, there would not be a single period when the mass of the people could be said to be free from distress, either directly or indirectly, for want of food. In every State in Europe, since we have first had accounts of it, millions and millions of human existences have been repressed from this simple cause, though perhaps in some of these States, an absolute famine has never been known.

Famine seems to be the last, the most dreadful resource of nature. The power of population is so superior to the power in the earth to produce subsistence for man that premature death must in some shape or other visit the human race. The vices of mankind are active and able ministers of depopulation. They are the precursors in the great army of destruction; and often finish the dreadful work themselves. But should they fail in this war of extermination, sickly seasons, epidemics, pestilence, and plague, advance in terrific array and sweep off their thousands and ten thousands. Should success be still incomplete, gigantic inevitable famine stalks in the rear, and with one mighty blow levels the population with the food of the world.

Must it not then be acknowledged by an attentive examiner of the histories of mankind, that in every age and in every State in which man has existed or does now exist,

That the increase of population is necessarily limited by the means of subsistence.

That population does invariably increase when the means of subsistence increase. And,

That the superior power of population is repressed, and the actual population kept equal to the means of subsistence by misery and vice.

Lines of Inquiry
1 Malthus's analysis of the relationship between the number of people a country can support and the amount of food it can produce expressed a long-known and obvious truth; the conclusions he drew from that analysis, however, were sufficiently forceful and original that ever since his formulation has been called "the Malthusian law of population." Malthus's essential reasoning is summarized at the end of this selection.

a Of the three statements made there, which are premises and which are conclusions?

b Does the sequence by which the selection itself is developed echo the sequence of these last statements?

c How do you account for the elements in this selection that resemble neither premises nor conclusions?

d Could the structure of this argument be said to reflect a debate with a silent adversary? If so, at what points do you see evidence of this debate?

e What are the essential elements in Malthus's argument, i.e., the elements on whose truth or falsity the entire argument depends? Are there any elements in it that might be termed accidental, i.e., nonessential?

2 It has frequently been suggested that Malthus's argument, now 200 years old, was proved wrong by events: As an obvious instance, the level of subsistence in America has not declined, though Malthus predicted it would.

a Can you think of other parts of Malthus's argument that no longer hold?

b Does his argument depend on the truth of his prediction concerning America?

c Can you think of any reason why Malthus's law might have failed to demonstrate itself in famines, epidemics, etc., over the past two centuries?

d The current population of the world is expected to double by A.D. 2000 and, without artificial restraints, to double again every twenty-five years thereafter. Does such a prediction in itself confirm or refute Malthus?

e What evidence would be conclusive proof that Malthus's law is false?

3 *a* What does Malthus's discussion suggest to be the future of happiness? Does he define happiness? Why does he introduce the question of happiness at all? (If he had omitted it, what would have been the effect on this discussion?)

b If one were to follow Malthus's line of reasoning with respect to happiness, what ought to be the political condition of the happiest countries?

c Does Malthus's reasoning here conflict with C. G. Darwin's discussion of happiness (see "The Pursuit of Happiness," p. 168)?

4 Malthus was a clergyman. After the publication of his book, he was called various unflattering names: It was even suggested that he was impious.

a From what premises might this last accusation have been launched?

b Are those premises defensible?

c How might Malthus be defended from such a charge?

5 a As Malthus develops his argument here, what happens to his tone? Can you see any stylistic changes in the essay, as it aproaches the conclusion?

b What accounts for the order in which Malthus enumerates the natural checks on population in his conclusion?

c By "vice" Malthus meant, among other more obvious things, the use of contraceptive devices. Since the eighteenth century, most of the world has changed its judgment in this respect. If one accepts this change in judgment, if only for the sake of argument, could it be claimed that the Malthusian law is invalid, on the ground that Malthus misclassified efforts at birth control?

Lines of Experiment

1 Presumably when you finished this essay you felt one of three things: (*a*) Malthus was right, or (*b*) he was wrong, or (*c*) he was right in some respects and wrong in others. Write an argument reflecting your conviction. You need not focus specifically on Malthus or on the Malthusian controversy.

As you shape your essay, you will probably do well to test every one of your arguments against an invisible adversary: The argument that you cannot demolish yourself *may* withstand hostile criticism, but the argument that you can demolish yourself is virtually certain to be demolished by others as well. In every discussion of the value of an argument, several questions arise. *First,* are the premises of the argument sound or unsound? *Second,* if they are true in some respects but not in others, to what extent should the conclusions of the argument be modified accordingly? *Third,* If they seem generally true yet the specific consequences that should accompany their truth do not accompany them (as starvation in America should accompany the Malthusian law), are these specific failures caused by the intervention of unforeseeable factors—flaws, as it were, in the experiment, or by the failure of the general argument itself? That is, is the argument generally untrue or merely specifically untrue?

Such an essay can be approached in many different ways. You may wish to consider including some of the following elements: a history of the Malthusian controversy; a definition of over-population; an outline of current population problems; a summary and assessment of possible causes and remedies for these problems; an estimate of the most promising remedy's chances of success; a concluding passage discussing the larger implications revealed by your analysis. Probably you should focus your discussion on a limited number of these elements— perhaps on one only, and bring in the others only as you find them relevant and useful to your central discussion.

A quite different way to attack the compositional problem would be to focus on a specific illustrative case, within which the essential elements you wish to speak of are clear. Such a composition might use the plight of India, or a crowded slum, or a housing project, or even the rat cage in a children's zoo as a compositional center. A composition that makes use of an extended illustration as a way of phrasing an argument tends, generally, toward description: The writer's job is partly to render the meaning of that description by rendering it in significant detail.

2 Current efforts to limit the population of the world give rise to a number of interesting questions. What can one learn from the history of societies that already have had to cope with the problems of an overly large population? To what degree is the limiting of population a function of government, and thus of law? What social consequences will governmental efforts to limit population have—for individual liberty, for education, for equality of opportunity, for economic prosperity, for the structure of family life? How could such a control be exercised? Are any efforts likely to be both adequate in the short run and durable in the long? Do stringent efforts to curb the birthrate mean the violation of the Darwinian principle that continuous competition for survival is the only way to ensure the survival of the fittest? Must birth control include eugenics? What will the world be like in a hundred years if current efforts to lower the birthrate fail? What will be the effect on political life? On private life? On the landscape?

In composing your essay, you may find it useful to begin with a simple series of statements expressing your basic reasoning; this series can serve you as an argumentative outline. Beside each statement make a brief note of the most serious objections that can be raised against it. These objections, and your answers to them, also should be part of your composition. If you now find your outline becoming too bulky, you have two options. Your first option is to narrow your subject further—

for example, (*a*) by concentrating on the definition of a key term, e.g., "subsistence," and allowing your argument to group around that definition; or (*b*) by making a crucial distinction, e.g., between the biological and the social environments, or between living and living well; or (*c*) by focusing on the analysis of a crucial case, e.g., the case of India.

Your second option is to keep your discussion on a highly general level. Two cautions: No general argument can be successfully based on premises open to challenge; and no general argument can afford to dispense with illustration, as a way of anchoring general truths to specific facts.

M. C. TYLER

THE LITERARY RECORD OF SEVENTEENTH— CENTURY VIRGINIA

There were in Virginia, during the first twenty years of its existence, as many as six authors who there produced writings that live yet and deserve to live. But at the end of that period and for the remainder of the century, nearly all literary activity in Virginia ceased; the only exception to this statement being the brief anonymous literary memorials which have come down to us from the wrathful and calamitous uprising of the people under Nathaniel Bacon. Even of those six writers of the first two decades, all excepting one, Alexander Whitaker, flitted back to England after a brief residence in Virginia: so that besides Whitaker, the colony had during all that period no writer who gave his name to her as being willing to identify himself permanently with her fate, and to live and die in her immediate service. This is in startling contrast to the contemporaneous record of New England, which, even in that early period, had a great throng of writers, nearly all of whom took root in her soil.

These, then, are the salient facts in the early literary history of Virginia.

They are certainly very remarkable facts.   How do we account for them?

First of all, we need to ask, who were the people who during that great epoch founded the Old Dominion of Virginia?   What sort of people were they?   Of what texture of body and brain and spirit?   What were they as regards industry, enterprise, thrift?   What were their predominant notions concerning church and state?   Especially, what did they come to America for?   And what were they living for, principally, whether in America or anywhere else?   If we can work out for ourselves the true answers to these questions, we shall be able to see why we might expect to get out of the people of Virginia, during the seventeenth century and afterward, no great amount of literature: hospitality, courtly manners, military leadership, political acumen, statesmanship, but not many books.

A foolish boast still floats on the current of talk, to the effect that Virginia was originally populated to a large extent by families of wealth and of aristocratic rank in England.   On the other hand a cruel taunt is sometimes heard in response to this boast, to the effect that the first families of Virginia have really sprung from the loins of bastards, bankrupts, fugitives, transported criminals, and other equivocal Englishmen, who in the seventeenth century left their country for their country's good.   The truth seems to lie in neither of these statements alone, but in both of them mixed together and mutually modified.   For the first forty years the larger portion of the settlers in Virginia were of inferior quality, personally and socially: many of them were tramps from the pavements of London; vagrants who wandered to Virginia because they had to wander somewhere; gentlemen of fashion who were out at the elbow; aristocrats gone to seed; " 'broken men,' adventurers, bankrupts, criminals." [1]   Indeed, for some time after the first few ship-loads had gone out to Virginia, and the news had come back to England of the perils and distresses that the colonists were fallen into, not even paupers and knaves would any longer go there of their own accord, and the company in London became "humble suitors to his Majesty" to compel "vagabonds and condemned men to go thither.   Nay, . . . some did choose to be hanged before they would go thither, and were." [2]   In the year 1611, Sir Thomas Dale sailed out to Virginia with three hundred emigrants, whom, to use his own words, he gathered "in riotous, lazy, and infected places: such disordered persons, so profane, so riotous, so full of mutiny and treasonable intendments, that in a parcel of three

[1] J. R. Green, "A Short Hist. of the English People," Harper's ed. 498.
[2] Capt. J. Smith, "Gen. Hist." in Pinkerton, XIII. 240.

hundred not many gave testimony, beside their names, that they were Christians; and besides, were of such diseased and crazed bodies that the sea-voyage hither and the climate here, but a little scratching them, render them so unable, faint, and desperate of recovery, that . . . not three score may be employed upon any labor or service." [3]   But by the year 1617, and thenceforward for many years, the cultivation of tobacco in Virginia became so profitable that the labor even of English convicts was welcome; and they were accordingly transported thither in large numbers and became gradually merged in the general population of the country.   In 1619, the first negro slaves were imported into the colony; and thereafter their presence contributed a new element of prosperity and of woe to Virginia.   From about the year 1640 to the year 1660, that is during the period of the civil war and of the commonwealth in England, many persons of much finer and stronger quality emigrated to Virginia; men of force and weight in England, churchmen, cavaliers, who, especially when the cause of the king became hopeless, very naturally moved away to Virginia to find there a permanent home, and a refuge from the odious ascendency of Cromwell and his Puritans.   At the restoration in 1660, still another class of emigrants, also forceful and worthy, passed over to Virginia, men of the Cromwellian party, a few even of his iron-sided troopers, who did not care to abide in sight of the jubilant cavaliers, and who chose Virginia in preference to New England, on account of its more genial climate.   Moreover, long before the close of the seventeenth century, Virginia had placed severe restrictions upon the importation of malefactors into the colony.   Of course, from the first these colonists, whether of weak type or strong, were mostly of the party of the English church, and of royalist views in politics.   Unlike the first colonists in New England, they had no dispute with the established order of things in old England; and made Virginia, not a digression from English society, but, as George Bancroft happily describes it, "a continuation of English society."[4]   As compared with the people of New England, they of Virginia were less austere, less enterprising, less industrious, more worldly, more self-indulgent; they were impatient of asceticism, of cant, of long faces, of long players; they rejoiced in games, sports, dances, merry music, and in a free, jovial, roistering life.

In close connection with this study of the people who in our earliest age came to Virginia, we need to observe the most characteristic features of the social organization that they formed after they got there.

[3] Aspinwall Papers, 4 Mass. Hist. Coll. IX. ı, note.
[4] Bancroft, "Hist. U. S." II. 190.

Though they were of the same stock and speech as the founders of New England, in ideas they were very different; and at once proceeding to incarnate their ideas in the visible frame of society, they erected in Virginia a fabric of church and state which was of course a veracious expression of themselves, and which presents an almost perfect antithesis to the fabric of church and state which at about the same time began to be erected in New England.   The germ of the whole difference between them lay in their different notions concerning the value of vicinity among the units of society.   The founders of New England were inclined to settle in groups of families forming neighborhoods, villages, and at last cities; from which it resulted that among them there was a constant play of mind upon mind; mutual stimulation, mutual forbearance also; likewise an easier and more frequent reciprocation of the social forces and benefits; facility in conducting the various industries and trades; facility in maintaining churches, schools, and higher literary organizations; facility in the interchange of books, letters, and the like.   The course chosen by the founders of Virginia was precisely the opposite of this: they were inclined to settle not in groups of families forming neighborhoods, but in detached establishments forming individualized domestic centres.   They brought with them, as a type of the highest human felicity, the memory of the English territorial lord, seated proudly in his own castle, breasting back all human interference by miles and miles of his own land, which lay outspread in all directions from the view of his cattle-windows.   Their ambition was to become territorial lords in Virginia; to own vast tracts of land, even though unimproved; to set up imitations—crude and cheap imitations they necessarily were—of the vast and superb baronial establishments which they had gazed at in the mother-country.   And many things united to favor them in this wish.   It was extremely easy to get large tracts of land in Virginia.   Every settler received at the outset a king's grant of fifty acres for himself and for each person transported by him to Virginia; and in addition to this, by a fee of a few shillings to a clerk in the secretary's office, grants could be accumulated upon grants.[5]   Moreover Virginia is veined by a multitude of navigable rivers; so that every man who wished to segregate himself in his own mansion, amid a vast territorial solitude, needed not to wait for the construction of a public road to enable him to get to it, and occasionally to get from it; but by erecting his house near to a river bank, he could find almost at his door a convenient shipping-point for the productions of his farm, and a con-

[5] C. Campbell, "Hist. Va." 350.   Also "Virginia's Cure," 1662, in Force Hist. Tracts, III, No. 15, 8.

venient means of ingress and egress for himself and his friends. Thus, from the first, while the social structure of New England was that of concentration, the social structure of Virginia was that of dispersion. The one sought personal community, the other domestic isolation: the one developed coöperation in civil affairs, in mechanism, in trade, in culture, in religion; the other developed solitary action in all these, and consequently made but little progress in any of them: the one tended to mitigate individualism by a thousand social compromises; the other tended to stimulate individualism through an indulgence of it untempered by any adequate colliding personal force. Let any one cast his eye on a map of Virginia for the seventeenth century. He will find local names on that map; but those local names do not indicate cities, or even villages, but merely theoretic organizations of church and state— parishes, over which the inhabitants were so widely scattered that no man could have seen his neighbor without looking through a telescope, or be heard by him without firing off a gun. George Bancroft does not exaggerate when, in speaking of Virginia for the latter part of the seventeenth century, he says, "There was hardly such a sight as a cluster of three dwellings." [6] Even Jamestown, the capital, had but a state-house, one church, and eighteen private houses.

Since the units of this dispersed community inclined thus to isolation rather than to close fellowship, it followed that all those public tasks which depend on coöperation were ill done, or not done at all: the making of high roads, bridges; the erection of court-houses, schoolhouses, churches; the promotion of commercial and manufacturing establishments; postal communication; literary interchanges, the involuntary traffic of ideas. In short, the tendency of the social structure in Virginia was from the first toward a sort of rough extemporaneous feudalism, toward the grandeur and the weakness of the patriarchal state, rather than toward those complex, elaborate, and refined results which are the achievements of an advanced modern civilization, and which can be procured only by the units of society pulling together, instead of pulling apart. There was considerable individual prosperity: there was no public thrift. Manual labor was of course scorned by the man who owned slaves, and was the master of a baronial hall with its far-stretching empire of wild lands. From him likewise descended to his inferiors the sentiment of contempt for labor,—the notion that labor was not any man's glory, but his shame. Their earliest historian born in Virginia, Robert Beverley, himself of a distinguished Virginian family,

[6] Bancroft, "Hist. U. S." II. 212.

writing just at the dawn of the eighteenth century, fills his book with sarcasms at the indolence and shiftlessness of his fellow-countrymen. Naming Virginia, he says: "I confess I am ashamed to say anything of its improvements, because I must at the same time reproach my country-men with a laziness that is unpardonable." [7] "They are such abomi-nable ill-husbands,[8] that though their country be overrun with wood, yet they have all their wooden ware from England—their cabinets, chairs, tables, stools, chests, boxes, cart-wheels, and all other things, even so much as their bowls and birchen brooms, to the eternal reproach of their laziness." [9] Thus they depend altogether upon the liberality of nature, without endeavoring to improve its gifts by art or industry. They sponge upon the blessings of a warm sun and a fruitful soil, and almost grutch the pains of gathering in the bounties of the earth." [10]

The dispersed social organization of Virginia had effects as evil in the direction of religious institutions, as in the direction of material enter-prise and thrift. "The Virginia parishes," says Charles Campbell, "were so extensive that parishioners sometimes lived at the distance of fifty miles from the parish church;" hence, "paganism, atheism, or sectaries." [11]

But the result which immediately concerns us in our present studies has to do with the intellectual development of the people.   First of all, then, in those highly rarefied communities, where almost nothing was in com-mon, how could there be common schools? [12]   To have included within a school-district a sufficient number of families to constitute a school, the distances for many of the pupils would have been so great as to render attendance impracticable.   For the first three generations there were almost no schools at all in Virginia.   The historian Burk says that "until the year 1688 no mention is anywhere made in the records, of schools or of any provision for the instruction of youth." [13]   Who can wonder that under such circumstances the children in most cases grew up in ignorance; and that the historian Campbell should be obliged to testify that the first and second generations of those born in Virginia were inferior in knowledge to their ancestors? [14]

[7] Beverley, "Hist. Va." Book IV. 59.
[8] i. e., bad economists.
[9] Beverley, "Hist. Va." Book IV. 58.
[10] Ibid. 83.
[11] "Hist. Va." 382.   Also "Va.'s. Cure," in Force, III. No. 15, 4, 5.
[12] "Va.s Cure," in Force, Hist. Tracts, III. No. 15, 6.
[13] "Hist. Va." II. Appendix, xxxi.   But the author of "A Perfect Descrip. of Va.," A. D. 1648, mentions "a free school and other petty schools."   Force, Hist. Tracts, II. No. 8, 13.
[14] "Hist. Va." 352.

If primary education was so grossly neglected in Virginia during the seventeenth century, we hardly need to ask what could have been the condition of higher education there during the same period. Near the end of this century, when all English-speaking communities were finally delivered from the Stuart incubus, and when all those communities on both sides of the ocean seemed to take a fresh start toward nobler things in civilization, we find traces of an educational awakening in Virginia. Among other traces of this awakening was the suggestion of a college, which in 1692 took tangible form in the establishment of the institution named in honor of the monarchs, William and Mary. In the eighteenth century this college did much to stimulate and guide the intellectual life of the colony; but we must not be misled by its imposing name. It was called a college; but during its earlier years it was only a boarding-school for very young boys in very rudimental studies.

Thus it must be seen that Virginia in the seventeenth century was entitled to the description which Sir Philip Sidney gave to Ireland in the sixteenth century,—a place "where truly learning goeth very bare." [15] Indeed, so late as the year 1715, Governor Spotswood dissolved the colonial assembly of Virginia with this taunt upon the educational defects of a body composed of their principal gentry: "I observe that the grand ruling party in your house has not furnished chairmen of two of your standing committees who can spell English or write common sense, as the grievances under their own handwriting will manifest." [16]

It must not be supposed that the people of Virginia were generally indifferent to the intellectual disadvantages accruing to them from their peculiar social organization. Especially did they grieve over the lack of educational privileges for their children; and from time to time they suggested methods for the establishment of accessible public schools. But they were in the gripe of hostile circumstances, and all their efforts were for that day vain. Besides, during a large portion of the seventeenth century, they had the affliction of a royal governor, Sir William Berkeley, who threw the whole weight of his office and the whole energy of his despotic will in favor of the fine old conservative policy of keeping subjects ignorant in order to keep them submissive. This policy, which he most consistently maintained throughout his entire administration, from 1641 to 1677, was frankly avowed by him in his celebrated reply to the English commissioners who in 1670 questioned him concerning the condition of Virginia: "I thank God there are no free schools, nor

[15] "Apologie for Poetrie," Arber's ed. 22.
[16] C. Campbell, "Hist. Va." 395.

printing; and I hope we shall not have, these hundred years: for learning has brought disobedience, and heresy, and sects into the world, and printing has divulged them, and libels against the best government. God keep us from both." [17]   We owe to Sir William the meed of our cordial acknowledgment that at least in this article of his creed he never failed to show his faith by his works, and that he did his best while governor of Virginia to secure the answer of his own dark prayer.   And unfortunately when he was recalled from Virginia, his policy for the encouragement of popular ignorance was not recalled with him: on the contrary it was continued by the government at home, and was prescribed in the official instructions laid upon his successors.   There is no record of a printing-press in Virginia earlier than 1681; and soon after a printing-press was set up, the printer was summoned before Lord Culpepper and required to enter into bonds "not to print anything hereafter, until his majesty's pleasure shall be known," [18]—a gracious way of intimating a perpetual prohibition.   In 1683, when Lord Effingham came out as governor of Virginia, he received from the ministry instructions "to allow no person to use a printing-press on any occasion whatsoever." [19]   From that date onward till about the year 1729, no printing was done in Virginia; and from 1729 until ten years before the Declaration of Independence, Virginia had but one printing-house, and even that "was thought to be too much under the control of the governor." [20] What a base extremity of intolerance!   And how base the popular listlessness which could permit it!   In other countries it has been thought hard enough to have the printing-press clogged by the interference of official licensers and spies; in Virginia the printing-press was forbidden to work at all.   There, even the first thrust of the pressman's lever was a crime.

The whole truth with reference to the intellectual condition of Virginia in the seventeenth century will not become manifest to us, unless we rest our eyes on still another trait.   Thought was not free in Virginia; religion was not free in Virginia; and this by the explicit and reiterated choice of the people of Virginia.   The Puritan zealots of New England have for a hundred years borne the just censure of mankind for their religious intolerance,—their ungentle treatment of Baptists, Quakers, and witches.   These pages are not to be stained by any apology for religious intolerance in New England.   But in simple fairness we may

[17] Hening, II. 511.
[18] Thomas, "Hist. Printing in Am." I. 331.
[19] Chalmers, "Political Annals," I. 345.
[20] Thomas, "Hist. Printing in Am." I. 332.

not close our eyes to the fact—seldom mentioned and little known—
that the jovial fox-hunters of Virginia, the cant-despising cavaliers of
the Old Dominion, were not a whit less guilty of religious intolerance.
We are informed by Burk [21] of the burning of witches in Virginia; and
as to the molestation of men for their religious opinions, we are told by
Campbell that so early as the year 1632 an act of the assembly of Virginia laid upon all who dissented from the Episcopal Church as there
established "the penalty of the pains and forfeitures in that case appointed." [22]   Just thirty years later, the same assembly imposed a fine
of two thousand pounds of tobacco on "schismatical persons" that
would not have their children baptized; and on persons who attended
other religious meetings than those of the established church, a penalty
of two hundred pounds of tobacco for the first offence, of five hundred
pounds of tobacco for the second offence, and of banishment for the
third offence.[23]   Marriage was not tolerated under any other form than
that of the Prayer Book.   No one, unless a member of the established
church, might instruct the young, even in a private family.   Any ship-
master who should convey non-conformist passengers to Virginia was
to be punished.   Against Quakers as well as Baptists the severest laws
were passed; and in 1664 large numbers of the former were prosecuted.
Indeed, religious persecution remained rampant and flourishing in Virginia long after it had died of its own shame in New England.   As late
as 1741 penal laws were enacted in Virginia against Presbyterians and
all other dissenters.[24]   As late as 1746 the most savage penalties were
denounced there against Moravians, New Lights, and Methodists.[25]
In the presence of this array of facts relating to the people of Virginia
in its primal days, and to the social organization that they created there,
is not the phenomenon of the comparative literary barrenness of Virginia fully explained?   How could literature have sprouted and thriven
amid such conditions.   Had much literature been produced there,
would it not have been a miracle?   The units of the community isolated;
little chance for mind to kindle mind; no schools; no literary institutions
high or low; no public libraries; no printing-press; no intellectual free-

---

[21] "Hist. Va." II. Appendix, xxxi.
[22] "Hist. Va." 185.
[23] Ibid. 258.
[24] Ibid. 442.
[25] Burk, "Hist. Va." III. 125.   For other authorities upon early religious intolerance in Va., see Bancroft, "Hist. U. S." II. 190, 192, 201, 202; Beverley,
"Hist. Va." ed. of 1855, 210, 212; R. R. Howison, "Hist. Va." I. 317–321;
Hildreth, "Hist. U. S." I. 126, 336; W. C. Rives, "Life of Madison," I. 41–55;
Writings of Washington. II. 481; Works of Jefferson, I. 38, 39, 174, VIII. 398–402.

dom; no religious freedom; the forces of society tending to create two
great classes,—a class of vast landowners, haughty, hospitable, indolent,
passionate, given to field-sports and politics, and a class of impoverished
white plebeians and black serfs;—these constitute a situation out of
which may be evolved country-gentlemen, loud-lunged and jolly fox-
hunters, militia heroes, men of boundless domestic heartiness and social
grace, astute and imperious politicians, fiery orators, and by and by,
here and there, some men of elegant literary culture, mostly acquired
abroad; here and there, perhaps, after a while, a few amateur literary
men; but no literary class, and almost no literature.

Lines of Inquiry

1 Outline briefly the essential structure of Tyler's analysis.

a Where in the essay is that structure summed up?

b How does Tyler introduce his subject? How does he conclude? What is the relationship between (*1*) his introduction and his conclusion, (*2*) his introduction and the essential structure of his analysis, (*3*) his conclusion and the
essential structure of his analysis?

c Why is his last sentence so long? How do you account for
its structure?

d Work out a chart classifying by type the factors Tyler points
to as responsible for Virginia's literary poverty in the seventeenth century. Give to all categories parallel titles, e.g.,
political factors and social factors. Move the individual
categories about on the chart—does it make any difference
to the value of the chart? Now consider the sequence in
which Tyler actually discusses these factors. Can that sequence be changed as easily as the classification can, and
with as little effect? What is the difference between a classification and an analysis?

2 What are the functions of quotation in this selection? In order
to answer this question you will have to consider (*a*) where
the quotations occur, (*b*) whether or not these quotations could
have been paraphrased or their sense summed up with no loss
to the outline of facts, (*c*) what kinds of things the quotations
say, and (*d*) what kinds of people are quoted.

3 *a* What is Tyler's attitude toward the Virginians? Toward the
New Englanders? What evidence can you adduce to support
your judgment?

b Why does Tyler mention New England at all in this description of the literary record of early Virginia? Could he have
spoken of England, instead of New England, with equal
effect?

c If one were to argue that Tyler's emotions enter so openly into this account that the account itself is untrustworthy, what might be said in reply?

4 What do the italicized words in the following passages add to the bare meaning of their context?

a "Even of those six writers of the first two decades, all excepting one, Alexander Whitaker, *flitted* back to England after a brief residence in Virginia. . . ."

b "They brought with them, as a type of the highest human felicity, the memory of the English territorial lord, *seated proudly in his own castle, breasting back* all human interference by miles and miles of his own land, *which lay outspread in all directions from the view of his castle-windows.*"

c "He will find local names on that map; but those local names do not indicate cities, or even villages, but merely theoretic organizations of church and state—parishes, over which the inhabitants were *so widely* scattered *that no man could have seen his neighbor without looking through a telescope, or be heard by him without firing off a gun.*"

d "Thus it must be seen that Virginia in the seventeenth century was *entitled to the description which Sir Philip Sidney gave to Ireland in the sixteenth century—a place 'where truly learning goeth very bare.'* "

e "In other countries it has been thought hard enough to have the printing-press *clogged* by the interference of official licensers and spies; in Virginia the printing-press was forbidden to work at all. *There, even the first thrust of the press-man's lever was a crime.*"

5 Suppose that Tyler were attempting to show why so many of the early nation's most serviceable and influential leaders came from Virginia. What changes would you expect to see in his analysis? In order to answer this question systematically, consult your list of the categories by which he classifies his material (see *1* above).

a Would any of these categories become superfluous? Would any others have to be added?

b What changes would you expect to see, in order and emphasis, among the categories that would still be important?

6 *a* What points in Tyler's analysis seem strongest? What points seem weakest? In each case, why? What makes for strength; what makes for weakness?

b Tyler attributes the thin literary accomplishment of seventeenth-century Virginia to certain specific and certain general factors. Suppose that one were to argue that Tyler's process of inference is all wrong, that he is following the classic fallacious pattern of *post hoc ergo propter hoc* (after this, therefore because of this) reasoning. How might one test the validity of his reasoning, or the truth of his conclusions?

Lines of Experiment

1 Essentially, this analysis starts with a situation and attempts to explain how it came about, *first* by enumerating the factors that created the situation, and *second* by showing how these factors were connected—in effect, first by classification, second by analysis. Begin with an analogous situation concerning which you either have or are prepared to acquire information, and explain how it came about. Such subjects as the following may be illustrative:

a Why no great writers come from my home town
b Why the *Daily Bugle* is a bad newspaper
c Why I am in college
d Why Putris was elected
e Why the United States intervened in Vietnam
f Why science fiction is popular

2 Choose the single most important element in the life of something you are thoroughly familiar with. The something may be a family, a neighborhood, a club, a group of friends, a city, a county, a region, a factory, etc. Some areas are dominated by a college community; others by a racial conflict; still others by an industry, a crop, a religious sect, a rich or poor residential district, a military base, a political machine, a winter sport, and so on. Write an analysis of the impact of this single element on the life you have chosen to describe.

In thinking through your essay, you may find it useful to start with a rough classification of the phenomena of life within the area you have chosen—its business, its politics, its recreation, etc. This classification will give you a frame within which you can show the impact of a specific, dominant element on the pattern of that life. The sequence of your discussion, in turn, will be determined by your judgment of what causes what. For example, because a political machine dominates political life, it can dominate business as well; because it can dominate business, it can dominate communication; because it can dominate communication, it can dominate intellectual activity, and so on. Ultimately, of course, your analysis must have a point; it must explain why the life of your area, or a part of that life, is at it is; and it must present the facts not only for their own sake but also for the sake of their larger implications. This last consideration may suggest to you a point to begin with, a point to end with, and a touchstone with which to measure the importance of specific facts.

GEORGE COLLINGWOOD

PROGRESS AS CREATED BY HISTORICAL THINKING

The term "progress," as used in the nineteenth century when the word was much in people's mouths, covers two things which it is well to distinguish: progress in history, and progress in nature. For progress in nature the word "evolution" has been so widely used that this may be accepted as its established sense; and in order not to confuse the two things I shall restrict my use of the word "evolution" to that meaning, and distinguish the other by the name "historical progress."

"Evolution" is a term applied to natural processes in so far as these are conceived as bringing into existence new specific forms in nature. This conception of nature as evolution must not be confused with the conception of nature as process. Granted the latter conception, two views of natural process are still possible: that events in nature repeat one another specifically, the specific forms remaining constant through the diversity of their individual instances, so that "the course of nature is uniform" and "the future will resemble the past," or that the specific forms themselves undergo change, new forms coming into existence by modification of the old. The second conception is what is meant by evolution.

In one sense, to call a natural process evolutionary is the same thing as calling it progressive. For if any given specific form can come into existence only as a modification of one already established, the establishment of any given form presupposes that of which it is a modification, and so on. If a form *b* is a modification of *a*, and *c* of *b*, and *d* of *c*, the forms *a, b, c, d,* can only come to exist in that order.   The order is progressive in the sense that it is a series of terms which can come into existence only in that order.   To say this, of course, implies nothing as to why the modifications arise, or whether they are large or small.   In this sense of the word "progress," progressive only means orderly, that is, exhibiting order.

But progress in nature, or evolution, has often been taken to mean more than this: namely the doctrine that each new form is not only a modification of the last but an improvement on it.   To speak of improvement is to imply a standard of valuation.   This, in the case of breeding new forms of domestic animals or plants, is intelligible enough: the value implied is the new form's utility for human purposes.   But no one supposes that natural evolution is designed to produce such utilities; the standard implied, therefore, cannot be that.   What is it?

Kant held that there was one form of value, and only one, that was independent of human purposes, namely the moral value of the good will.   All other kinds of goodness, he argued, are merely goodness for some postulated purpose, but the goodness of morality does not depend on any postulated purpose, and thus moral goodness, as he put it, is an end in itself.   On this view the evolutionary process has been truly progressive, because it has led through a determinate series of forms to the existence of man, a creature capable of moral goodness.

If this view is rejected, it is very doubtful whether any other standard of valuation can be found which would entitle us to call evolution progressive except merely in the sense of being orderly.   Not because the idea of value finds no place in our view of nature, for it is difficult to think of any organism except as striving to maintain its own existence, and such effort implies that, at least for itself, its existence is not a mere matter of fact but something of value; but because all values seem merely relative.   The archaeopteryx may in fact have been an ancestor of the bird, but what entitles us to call the bird an improvement on the archaeopteryx?   A bird is not a better archaeopteryx, but something different that has grown out of it.   Each is trying to be itself.

But the view of human nature as the noblest outcome of the evolutionary process did undoubtedly underlie the nineteenth-century conception of historical progress as guaranteed by a law of nature.   That conception, in fact, depended on two assumptions or groups of assumptions.   First, that man is or contains in himself something of absolute value, so that the process of nature in its evolution has been a progress in so far as it has been an orderly process leading to the existence of man. From this it followed that, since man obviously did not control the process leading to his own existence, there was in nature as such an inherent tendency towards the realization of this absolute value: in other words, "progress is a law of nature." Secondly, the assumption that man, as a child of nature, is subject to natural law, and that the laws of historical process are identical with the laws of evolution: that historical process is of the same kind as natural process. It followed that human history was subject to a necessary law of progress, in other words that of the new specific forms of social organization, art and science, and so forth, which it brings into existence each is necessarily an improvement on the last.

The idea of a "law of progress" may be attacked by denying either of these two assumptions. It may be denied that man has in him anything of absolute value. His rationality, it may be said, only serves to make him the most maleficent and destructive of the animals, and is rather a blunder or a cruel joke of nature than her noblest work; his morality is only (as the modern jargon goes) a rationalization or ideology which he has devised to conceal from himself the crude fact of his bestiality. From this point of view, the natural process that has led to his existence can no longer be regarded as a progress. But further: if the conception of historical process as a mere extension of natural process is denied, as it must be by any sound theory of history, it follows that there is no natural and in that sense necessary law of progress in history. The question whether any particular historical change has been an improvement must consequently be a question to be answered on its merits in each particular case.

The conception of a "law of progress," by which the course of history is so governed that successive forms of human activity exhibit each an improvement on the last, is thus a mere confusion of thought, bred of an unnatural union between man's belief in his own superiority to nature and his belief that he is nothing more than a part of nature. If either belief is true, the other is false: they cannot be combined to produce logical offspring.

Nor can the question, whether in a given case an historical change has or has not been progressive, be answered until we are sure that such questions have a meaning. Before they are raised, we must ask what is meant by historical progress, now that it has been distinguished from natural progress; and, if anything is meant, whether the meaning is one applicable to the given case we are considering. For it would be hasty to assume that, because the conception of historical progress as dictated by a law of nature is nonsensical, the conception of historical progress itself is therefore nonsensical.

Assuming, then, that the phrase "historical progress" may still have a meaning, we must ask what it means. The fact that it has suffered confusion through contamination with the idea of evolution does not prove it meaningless; on the contrary, it suggests that it has a certain basis in historical experience.

As a first attempt to define its meaning, we might suggest that historical progress is only another name for human activity itself, as a succession of acts each of which arises out of the last. Every act whose history we may study, of whatever kind it is, has its place in a series of acts where one has created a situation with which the next has to deal. The accomplished act gives rise to a new problem; it is always this new problem, not the old problem over again, which the new act is obliged to solve. If a man has discovered how to get a meal, next time he is hungry he must find out how to get another, and the getting of this other is a new act arising out of the old. His situation is always changing, and the act of thought by which he solves the problems it presents is always changing too.

This is no doubt true, but it is not to our purpose. It is just as true of a dog as of a man, that every meal must be a different meal: just as true, that every time a bee gathering honey visits a flower, it must be a different flower; just as true, that every time a body in a straight line or an open curve comes to a part of space, it must be a different part. But these processes are not historical processes, and to quote them as throwing light on the historical process would betray the old fallacy of naturalism. Moreover, the novelty of the new situation and the new act is not a specific novelty, for the new act may be a new act of exactly the same kind (for example, setting the same snare again in the same place); so that we are not even discussing the evolutionary aspect of natural process, which is the point at which that process seems most akin to the historical. The search for a fresh meal takes place even in the most completely static or non-progressive society.

The idea of historical progress, then, if it refers to anything, refers to the coming into existence not merely of new actions or thoughts or situations belonging to the same specific type, but of new specific types. It therefore presupposes such specific novelties, and consists in the conception of these as improvements.   Suppose, for example, a man or a community had lived on fish, and, the fish-supply failing, had sought food in a new way, by digging for roots: this would be a change in the specific type of situation and activity, but it would not be regarded as a progress, because the change does not imply that the new type is an improvement on the old.   But if a community of fish-eaters had changed their method of catching fish from a less to a more efficient one, by which an average fisherman could catch ten fish on an average day instead of five, this would be called an example of progress.

But from whose point of view is it an improvement?   The question must be asked, because what is an improvement from one point of view may be the reverse from another; and if there is a third from which an impartial judgement can be passed on this conflict, the qualifications of this impartial judge must be determined.

Let us first consider the change from the point of view of the persons concerned in it: the older generation still practising the old method while the younger has adopted the new.   In such a case the older generation will see no need for the change, knowing as it does that life can be lived on the old method.   And it will also think that the old method is better than the new; not out of irrational prejudice, but because the way of life which it knows and values is built round the old method, which is therefore certain to have social and religious associations that express the intimacy of its connexion with this way of life as a whole. A man of the older generation only wants his five fish a day, and he does not want half a day's leisure; what he wants is to live as he has lived.   To him, therefore, the change is no progress, but a decadence.

It might seem obvious that by the opposite party, the younger generation, the change is conceived as a progress.   It has given up the life of its fathers and chosen a new one for itself: it would not do this (one might suppose) without comparing the two and deciding that the new is better.   But this is not necessarily the case.   There is no choice except for a person who knows what both the things are between which he is choosing.   To choose between two ways of life is impossible unless one knows what they are; and this means not merely looking on one as a spectacle, and practising the other, or practising one and conceiving the other as an unrealized possibility, but knowing both in the only way in which ways of life can be known: by actual experience, or by the sympathetic insight which may take its place for such a purpose.   But experience shows that nothing is harder than for a given generation in a changing society, which is living in a new way of its own, to enter sympathetically into the life of the last. It sees that life as a mere incomprehensible spectacle, and seems driven to escape from sympathy with it by a kind of instinctive effort to free itself from parental influences and bring about the change on which it is blindly resolved. There is here no genuine comparison between the two ways of life, and therefore no judgement that one is better than the other, and therefore no conception of the change as a progress.

For this reason, the historical changes in a society's way of life are very rarely conceived as progressive even by the generation that makes them. It makes them in obedience to a blind impulse to destroy what it does not comprehend, as bad, and substitute something else as good. But progress is not the replacement of the bad by the good, but of the good by the better. In order to conceive a change as a progress, then, the person who has made it must think of what he has abolished as good, and good in certain definite ways. This he can only do on condition of his knowing what the old way of life was like, that is, having historical knowledge of his society's past while he is actually living in the present he is creating: for historical knowledge is simply the re-enactment of past experiences in the mind of the present thinker. Only thus can the two ways of life be held together in the same mind for a comparison of their merits, so that a person choosing one and rejecting the other can know what he has gained and what he has lost, and decide that he has chosen the better. In short: the revolutionary can only regard his revolution as a progress in so far as he is also an historian, genuinely re-enacting in his own historical thought the life he nevertheless rejects.

Let us now consider the change in question, no longer from the standpoint of those concerned in it, but from that of an historian placed outside it. We might hope that, from his detached and impartial point of view, he would be able to judge with some chance of fairness whether it was a progress or not. But this is a difficult matter. He is only deceived if he fastens on the fact that ten fish are caught where five were caught before, and uses this as a criterion of progress. He must take into account the conditions and consequences of that change. He must ask what was done with the additional fish or the additional leisure. He must ask what value attached to the social and religious institutions that were sacrificed for them. In short, he must judge the relative value of two different ways of life, taken as two wholes. Now, in order to do this, he must be able to enter with equal sympathy into the essential features and values of each way of life: he must re-experience them both in his own mind, as objects of historical knowledge.   What makes him a qualified judge, therefore, is just the fact that he does not look at his object from a detached point of view, but re-lives it in himself.

We shall see, later, that the task of judging the value of a certain way of life taken in its entirety is an impossible task, because no such thing in its entirety is ever a possible object of historical knowledge.   The attempt to know what we have no means of knowing is an infallible way to generate illusions; and this attempt to judge whether one period of history or phase of human life, taken as a whole, shows progress as compared with its predecessor, generates illusions of an easily recognizable type.   Their characteristic feature is the labelling of certain historical periods as good periods, or ages of historical greatness, and of others as bad periods, ages of historical failure or poverty.   The so-called good periods are the ones into whose spirit the historian has penetrated, owing either to the existence of abundant evidence or to his own capacity for re-living the experience they enjoyed; the so-called bad periods are either those for which evidence is relatively scanty, or those whose life he cannot, for reasons arising out of his own experience and that of his age, reconstruct within himself.

At the present day we are constantly presented with a view of history as consisting in this way of good and bad periods, the bad periods being divided into the primitive and the decadent, according as they come before or after the good ones.   This distinction between periods of primitiveness, periods of greatness, and periods of decadence, is not and never can be historically true.   It tells us much about the historians who study the facts, but nothing about the facts they study.   It is characteristic of an age like our own, where history is studied widely and successfully, but eclectically.   Every period of which we have competent knowledge (and by competent knowledge I mean insight into its thought, not mere acquaintance with its remains) appears in the perspective of time as an age of brilliance: the brilliance being the light of our own historical insight.   The intervening periods are seen by contrast as, relatively speaking and in different degrees, "dark ages": ages which we know to have existed, because there is a gap of time for them in our chronology, and we have possibly numerous relics of their work and thought, but in which we can find no real life because we cannot re-enact that thought in our own minds.   That this pattern of light and darkness is an optical illusion proceeding from the distribution of the historian's knowledge and ignorance is obvious from the different ways in which it is drawn by different historians and by the historical thought of different generations.

The same optical illusion in a simpler form affected the historical thought of the eighteenth century, and laid the foundations for the dogma of progress, as that was accepted in the nineteenth. When Voltaire laid it down that "all history is modern history," [1] and that nothing could be genuinely known before about the end of the fifteenth century, he was saying two things at once: that nothing earlier than the modern period could be known, and that nothing earlier deserved to be known. These two things came to the same thing. His inability to reconstruct genuine history from the documents of the ancient world and the Middle Ages was the source of his belief that those ages were dark and barbarous. The idea of history as a progress from primitive times to the present day was, to those who believed in it, a simple consequence of the fact that their historical outlook was limited to the recent past.

The old dogma of a single historical progress leading to the present, and the modern dogma of historical cycles, that is, of a multiple progress leading to "great ages" and then to decadence, are thus mere projections of the historian's ignorance upon the screen of the past. But, setting dogmas aside, has the idea of progress no other basis than this? We have already seen that there is one condition on which that idea can represent a genuine thought, and not either a blind feeling or a mere state of ignorance. The condition is that the person who uses the word should use it in comparing two historical periods or ways of life, both of which he can understand historically, that is, with enough sympathy and insight to reconstruct their experience for himself. He must satisfy himself and his readers that no blind spot in his own mind, and no defect in his equipment of learning, prevents him from entering into the experience of either less fully than into the other's. Then, having fulfilled that condition, he is entitled to ask whether the change from the first to the second was a progress.

But when he asks this, what exactly is he asking? Obviously, he is not asking whether the second comes nearer to the way of life which he accepts as his own. By re-enacting the experience of either in his own mind he has already accepted it as a thing to be judged by its own standards: a form of life having its own problems, to be judged by its success in solving those problems and no others. Nor is he assuming

---

[1] *Dictionnaire philosophique,* art. 'Histoire'; *Œuvres* (1748), vol. xli, p. 45.

that the two different ways of life were attempts to do one and the same thing, and asking whether the second did it better than the first.   Bach was not trying to write like Beethoven and failing; Athens was not a relatively unsuccessful attempt to produce Rome; Plato was himself, not a half-developed Aristotle.

There is only one genuine meaning for this question.   If thought in its first phase, after solving the initial problems of that phase, is then, through solving these, brought up against others which defeat it; and if the second solves these further problems without losing its hold on the solution of the first, so that there is gain without any corresponding loss, then there is progress.   And there can be progress on no other terms.   If there is any loss, the problem of setting loss against gain is insoluble.

According to this definition, it would be idle to ask whether any one period of history taken as a whole showed a progress over its predecessor.   For the historian can never take any period as a whole.   There must be large tracts of its life for which he has either no data, or no data that he is in a position to interpret.   We cannot, for example, know what the Greeks enjoyed in the way of musical experience, though we know that they greatly valued it; we have not enough material; and on the other hand, though we have no lack of data about Roman religion, our own religious experience is not of such a kind as to qualify us for reconstructing in our own minds what it meant to them.   We must select certain aspects of experience and confine our search for progress to these.

Can we speak of progress in happiness or comfort or satisfaction?   Obviously not.   Different ways of life are differentiated by nothing more clearly than by differences between the things that people habitually enjoy, the conditions which they find comfortable, and the achievements they regard as satisfactory.   The problem of being comfortable in a medieval cottage is so different from the problem of being comfortable in a modern slum that there is no comparing them; the happiness of a peasant is not contained in the happiness of a millionaire.

Nor does it mean anything to ask whether there is progress in art.   The artist's problem, so far as he is an artist, is not the problem of doing what his predecessor has done and going on to do something further which his predecessor failed to do.   There is development in art, but no progress: for though in the technical processes of art one man learns from another, Titian from Bellini, Beethoven from Mozart, and so on,

the problem of art itself consists not in mastering these technical processes but in using them to express the artist's experience and give it
reflective form, and consequently every fresh work of art is the solution
of a fresh problem which arises not out of a previous work of art but out
of the artist's unreflective experience.   Artists do better or worse work
in so far as they solve these problems well or ill; but the relation between good and bad art is not an historical relation, because the problems arise out of the flow of unreflective experience, and that flow is not
an historical process.

In one sense, there is no progress in morality.   The life of morality consists not in the development of moral codes, but in their application to
individual problems of conduct, and to a great extent these problems,
like those of art, arise out of unreflective experience.   The course of
our moral life is conditioned by the succession of our desires; and,
though our desires change, they do not change historically.   They arise
out of our animal nature, and though this may change from youth to old
age, or vary in different peoples and climates, its differences are part
of the process of nature, not of history.

In another sense, however, there is or may be moral progress.   Part of
our moral life consists of coping with problems arising not out of our
animal nature but out of our social institutions, and these are historical
things, which create moral problems only in so far as they are already
the expression of moral ideals.   A man who asks himself whether he
ought to take voluntary part in his country's war is not struggling with
personal fear; he is involved in a conflict between the moral forces
embodied in the institution of the State, and those embodied not merely
in the ideal, but in the equally actual reality, of international peace and
intercourse.   Similarly the problem of divorce arises not out of the
whims of sexual desire, but out of an unresolved conflict between the
moral ideal of monogamy and the moral evils which that ideal, rigidly
applied, brings in its train.   To solve the problem of war or of divorce
is only possible by devising new institutions which shall recognize in full
the moral claims recognized by the State or by monogamy, and shall
satisfy these claims without leaving unsatisfied the further claims to
which, in historical fact, the old institutions have given rise.

The same double aspect appears in the economic life.   So far as that
consists in finding from moment to moment the means of satisfying demands which spring not from our historical environment but from our
nature as animals with certain desires, there can be no progress in it;

that would be a progress in happiness or comfort or satisfaction, which we have seen to be impossible. But not all our demands are for the satisfaction of animal desires. The demand for investments in which I can put my savings to support me in old age is not an animal desire; it arises out of an individualistic economic system in which the old are supported neither statutorily by the State nor customarily by their families, but by the fruits of their own labour, and in which capital commands a certain rate of interest. That system has solved a good many problems, and therein lies its economic value; but it gives rise to a good many others which as yet it has failed to solve. A better economic system, one whose substitution for this would be a progress, would continue to solve the same problems which are solved by individualist capitalism, and solve these others as well.

The same considerations apply to politics and law, and I need not work out the application in detail. In science, philosophy, and religion the conditions are rather different. Here, unless I am mistaken, the question of coping with our animal nature and satisfying its needs does not arise. The problem is a single one instead of a double.

Progress in science would consist in the supersession of one theory by another which served both to explain all that the first theory explained, and also to explain types or classes of events or "phenomena" which the first ought to have explained but could not. I suppose that Darwin's theory of the origin of species was an example. The theory of fixed species explained the relative permanence of natural kinds within the recorded memory of man; but it ought to have held good for the longer stretch of geological time, and it broke down, too, for the case of selectively-bred animals and plants under domestication. Darwin propounded a theory whose claim to merit rested on its bringing these three classes under one conception. I need hardly quote the now more familiar relation between Newton's law of gravitation and that of Einstein, or that between the special and general theories of relativity. The interest of science, in relation to the conception of progress, seems to be that this is the simplest and most obvious case in which progress exists and is verifiable. For this reason, those who have believed most strongly in progress have been much in the habit of appealing to the progress of science as the plainest proof that there is such a thing, and often, too, have based their hope of progress in other fields on the hope of making science the absolute mistress of human life. But science is and can be mistress only in her own house, and forms of activity which cannot progress (such as art) cannot be made to do so by subjecting them, if that phrase meant anything, to the rule of science; whereas those which can must progress by finding out for themselves how to improve in doing their own work.

Philosophy progresses in so far as one stage of its development solves the problems which defeated it in the last, without losing its hold on the solutions already achieved. This, of course, is independent of whether the two stages are stages in the life of a single philosopher, or are represented by different men. Thus, suppose it true that Plato grasped the necessity for an eternal object, the world of Ideas or Idea of the Good, and also for an eternal subject, the soul in its double function of knower and mover, as solutions for the problems with which his predecessors' work had left him confronted: but was baffled to say how these two were related; and suppose Aristotle saw that the problem of the relation between them, as Plato had stated it, or rather as he himself saw it in his long apprenticeship to Plato's teaching, could be solved by thinking of them as one and the same, pure intellect being identical with its own object, and its knowledge of that object being its knowledge of itself; then, so far (though conceivably not in other respects) Aristotle's philosophy would mark a progress on Plato's, granted that by that new step Aristotle sacrificed nothing that Plato had achieved by his theory of Ideas and his theory of soul.

In religion, progress is possible on the same terms. If Christianity, bating no jot or tittle of what Judaism had won by its conception of God as one God, just and terrible, infinitely great over against man's infinite littleness and infinitely exacting in his demands on man, could bridge the gulf between God and man by the conception that God became man in order that we might become God, that was a progress, and a momentous one, in the history of the religious consciousness.

In such senses and in such cases as these, progress is possible. Whether it has actually occurred, and where and when and in what ways, are questions for historical thought to answer. But there is one other thing for historical thought to do: namely to create this progress itself. For progress is not a mere fact to be discovered by historical thinking: it is only through historical thinking that it comes about at all.

The reason for this is that progress, in those cases (common or rare) when it happens, happens only in one way: by the retention in the mind, at one phase, of what was achieved in the preceding phase. The two phases are related not merely by way of succession, but by way of continuity, and continuity of a peculiar kind.   If Einstein makes an advance on Newton, he does it by knowing Newton's thought and retaining it within his own, in the sense that he knows what Newton's problems were, and how he solved them, and disentangling the truth in those solutions from whatever errors prevented Newton from going further, embodying these solutions as thus disentangled in his own theory.   He might have done this, no doubt, without having read Newton in the original for himself; but not without having received Newton's doctrine from someone.   Thus Newton stands, in such a context, not for a man but for a theory, reigning during a certain period of scientific thought. It is only in so far as Einstein knows that theory, as a fact in the history of science, that he can make an advance upon it.   Newton thus lives in Einstein in the way in which any past experience lives in the mind of the historian, as a past experience known as past—as the point from which the development with which he is concerned started—but re-enacted here and now together with a development of itself that is partly constructive or positive and partly critical or negative.

Similarly with any other progress.   If we want to abolish capitalism or war, and in doing so not only to destroy them but to bring into existence something better, we must begin by understanding them: seeing what the problems are which our economic or international system succeeds in solving, and how the solution of these is related to the other problems which it fails to solve.   This understanding of the system we set out to supersede is a thing which we must retain throughout the work of superseding it, as a knowledge of the past conditioning our creation of the future.   It may be impossible to do this; our hatred of the thing we are destroying may prevent us from understanding it, and we may love it so much that we cannot destroy it unless we are blinded by such hatred.   But if that is so, there will once more, as so often in the past, be change but no progress; we shall have lost our hold on one group of problems in our anxiety to solve the next.   And we ought by now to realize that no kindly law of nature will save us from the fruits of our ignorance.

Lines of Inquiry

1 Frequently logically organized discourse begins with a distinction that defines the subject.   Collingwood begins his essay on progress with a distinction between progress in nature and progress in history.

   a How important is this distinction to his subsequent line of thought?   Why does he discuss evolution at all?

b Mark the three chief divisions in Collingwood's argument. How does the process of definition bear upon these structural divisions?

c Could any of these three divisions be omitted without damage to the "wholeness" of Collingwood's argument?

d At what points does Collingwood resort to classification in order to press his argument further? Why must he do so?

e How is his concluding sentence related to the first question he discusses? If he had ended his essay without the last sentence, what would he have lost?

2 a What aspect of Collingwood's subject forces him into considering the point of view from which an event is seen? What points of view does he distinguish?

b Is he able to resolve his inquiry by analyzing the possible points of view from which an event may be judged to be either progressive or not progressive? If he is, why does he go on? If he is not, what is the use of analyzing those points of view at all?

c How many times in the essay does Collingwood appear to come to a dead end? What process does this coming to a dead end represent?

3 Collingwood's line of reasoning in this essay could be represented by means of extended paraphrases of the type illustrated here on pages 114–115, but the process of representing it by this means would be extremely clumsy—and would not show the actual current of Collingwood's thought. That current might be represented better by a series of questions and answers:

Q First, what is meant ordinarily by the term progress?
A Both natural progress and historical progress.

Q But what is meant ordinarily by the term natural progress?
A Not process but evolution.

Q But what is meant ordinarily by the term evolution?
A Not order but improvement.

Q But what is meant ordinarily by improvement?
A An absolute increase in value, not a relative increase.

Q But what is an absolute increase in value?
A An increase in morality, not an increase in utility.

Q But how can morality be said to increase?
A Only with the evolution of man, a creature capable of moral goodness.

a The argument tacks at this point. Why?

b How is Collingwood's thought as outlined here reflected in the structure and linking of his first five paragraphs?

c What common features do you see in the series of questions? In the series of answers?

d Work out the series of questions and answers by means of which Collingwood arrives at a defensible definition of historical progress. Can you formulate that definition? How do you account for the fact that it takes him far longer to answer this series of questions than to answer the first series?

4 Define the phrase "theory of history." It is often said that (*1*) nothing really changes, or (*2*) history repeats itself, or (*3*) things are getting worse all the time, or (*4*) things are getting better all the time. In abstract terms one can classify the theories of history behind such phrases as (*1*) static, (*2*) cyclical, (*3*) degenerative, (*4*) progressive.

a Does Collingwood allude to these common ways of interpreting events?

b How would you classify his own theory of history?

c He remarks that "any sound theory of history" must deny that historical process is an extension of natural process. Why must it?

d How can a theory of history be sound?

e Why does Collingwood use this word, instead of the word "true"? Is soundness the same as truth? The same as value? What value can a theory of history have?

f How would you test either the soundness or the value of a theory of history?

5 At one point Collingwood remarks that "the question, whether in a given case, an historical change has or has not been progressive, [cannot] be answered *until we are sure that such questions have a meaning*." At another, he says, "But science is and can be mistress only in her own house, and forms of activity which cannot progress (such as art) cannot be made to do so by subjecting them, *if that phrase meant anything,* to the rule of science." (Italics added)

a What distinguishes a meaningful question or phrase from a meaningless one?

b Here are several phrases—two from Collingwood's own essay. In each case, what must you determine before you can say whether they are meaningful or meaningless?

(*1*) Progress is the law of nature.

(*2*) Thought is the shadow of life.

(3) "But progress is not the replacement of the bad by the good, but of the good by the better. . . ."

(4) Who really won the Civil War?

(5) The ultimate heresy is the denial of Being.

(6) "The attempt to know what we have no means of knowing is an infallible way to generate illusions."

(7) Is patriotism dead, or does it merely sleep?

(8) The task before us today is to bring chance under the rule of law.

(9) "Poets are the unacknowledged legislators of the world."

Lines of Experiment

1 Collingwood suggests that progress is possible in the areas of morality, economics, politics, science, philosophy, religion. Choosing an appropriate but much more specifically focused subject—one relatively clear in outline and well known to you—write an essay presenting the problems current practice attempts to solve, and the problems created in turn by that attempt at solution. You may conclude at this point, if you wish (your analysis should give you a clear view of your subject's larger implications, and thus a chance to round off your essay), or you may pass beyond analysis to a proposal for an historically progressive change. The following categories may suggest a suitable topic.

Home design	Student government
The lecture system	Social security
Selective service	Marriage
Interurban road systems	Professional sports
Mass education	Democracy
Dormitories	

One caution: None of these suggestions is more than a category. Each one needs to be defined in such a way as to pose an answerable question before it can provide the focus for a composition. It may help you if you bear in mind that analysis frequently uses the methods of narrative.

2 Use the method of definition to give structure to a discussion of a difficult concept. A standard and widely used strategy is: *First,* show that the usual definition of the concept is inadequate; *second,* formulate an adequate definition; *third,* present the implications of that adequate definition for a wider field of ideas.

Almost any highly general concept may suggest to you an appropriate topic, even though you doubtless will be unable to discuss an entire range of meanings in a single essay. Your job will be to clarify one aspect of an idea invoked without any awareness of the assumptions behind it or of the possibility that in one or another of its uses it may be meaningless. A close look at the ordinary meaning attached to any one of the following concepts can suggest a specific line of inquiry:

Equality   Literature
Democracy   Human rights
Sanity   Justice
Education   Intelligence

THOMAS HOBBES

OF THE
NATURAL CONDITION
OF MANKIND

Men by nature equal   Nature hath made men so equal, in the faculties of the body, and mind; as that though there be found one man sometimes manifestly stronger in body, or of quicker mind than another; yet when all is reckoned together, the difference between man, and man, is not so considerable, as that one man can thereupon claim to himself any benefit, to which another may not pretend, as well as he. For as to the strength of body, the weakest has strength enough to kill the strongest, either by secret machination, or by confederacy with others, that are in the same danger with himself.

And as to the faculties of the mind, setting aside the arts grounded upon words, and especially that skill of proceeding upon general, and infallible rules, called science; which very few have, and but in few things; as being not a native faculty, born with us; not attained, as prudence, while we look after somewhat else, I find yet a greater equality amongst men, than that of strength. For prudence, is but experience; which equal time, equally bestows on all men, in those things they equally apply themselves unto. That which may perhaps make such equality incredible, is but a vain conceit of one's own wisdom, which almost all men think they have in a greater degree, than the vulgar; that is, than all men but themselves, and a few others, whom by fame, or for concurring with themselves, they approve.   For such is the nature of men, that howsoever they may acknowledge many others to be more witty, or more eloquent, or more learned; yet they will hardly believe there be many so wise as themselves; for they see their own wit at hand, and other men's at a distance.   But this proveth rather that men are in that point equal, than unequal.   For there is not ordinarily a greater sign of the equal distribution of any thing, than that every man is contented with his share.

From equality proceeds diffidence   From this equality of ability, ariseth equality of hope in the attaining of our ends.   And therefore if any two men desire the same thing, which nevertheless they cannot both enjoy, they become enemies; and in the way to their end, which is principally their own conservation, and sometimes their delectation only, endeavour to destroy, or subdue one another.   And from hence it comes to pass, that where an invader hath no more to fear, than another man's single power; if one plant, sow, build, or possess a convenient seat, others may probably be expected to come prepared with forces united, to dispossess, and deprive him, not only of the fruit of his labour, but also of his life, or liberty.   And the invader again is in the like danger of another.

From diffidence war   And from this diffidence of one another, there is no way for any man to secure himself, so reasonable, as anticipation; that is, by force, or wiles, to master the persons of all men he can, so long, till he see no other power great enough to endanger him: and this is no more than his own conservation requireth, and is generally allowed. Also because there be some, that taking pleasure in contemplating their own power in the acts of conquest, which they pursue farther than their security requires; if others, that otherwise would be glad to be at ease within modest bounds, should not by invasion increase their power, they would not be able, long time, by standing only on their defence, to subsist.   And by consequence, such augmentation of dominion over men being necessary to a man's conservation, it ought to be allowed him.

Again, men have no pleasure, but on the contrary a great deal of grief, in keeping company, where there is no power able to over-awe them all. For every man looketh that his companion should value him, at the same rate he sets upon himself: and upon all signs of contempt, or undervaluing, naturally endeavours, as far as he dares, (which amongst them that have no common power to keep them in quiet, is far enough to make them destroy each other), to extort a greater value from his contemners, by damage; and from others, by the example.

So that in the nature of man, we find three principal causes of quarrel. First, competition; secondly, diffidence; thirdly, glory.

The first, maketh men invade for gain; the second, for safety; and the third, for reputation. The first use violence, to make themselves masters of other men's persons, wives, children, and cattle; the second, to defend them; the third, for trifles, as a word, a smile, a different opinion, and any other sign of undervalue, either direct in their persons, or by reflection in their kindred, their friends, their nation, their profession, or their name.

Out of civil states, there is always war of every one against every one Hereby it is manifest, that during the time men live without a common power to keep them all in awe, they are in that condition which is called war; and such a war, as is of every man, against every man. For WAR, consisteth not in battle only, or the act of fighting; but in a tract of time, wherein the will to contend by battle is sufficiently known: and therefore the notion of *time,* is to be considered in the nature of war; as it is in the nature of weather. For as the nature of foul weather, lieth not in a shower or two of rain; but in an inclination thereto of many days together: so the nature of war, consisteth not in actual fighting; but in the known disposition thereto, during all the time there is no assurance to the contrary. All other time is peace.

The incommodities of such a war Whatsoever therefore is consequent of a time of war, where every man is enemy to every man; the same is consequent to the time, wherein men live without other security, than what their own strength, and their own invention shall furnish them withal. In such condition, there is no place for industry; because the fruit thereof is uncertain; and consequently no culture of the earth; no navigation, nor use of the commodities that may be imported by sea; no commodious building; no instruments of moving, and removing, such things as require much force; no knowledge of the face of the earth; no account of time; no arts; no letters; no society; and which is worst of all, continual fear, and danger of violent death; and the life of man, solitary, poor, nasty, brutish, and short.

It may seem strange to some man, that has not well weighed these things; that nature should thus dissociate, and render men apt to invade, and destroy one another: and he may therefore, not trusting to this inference, made from the passions, desire perhaps to have the same confirmed by experience. Let him therefore consider with himself, when taking a journey, he arms himself, and seeks to go well accompanied; when going to sleep, he locks his doors; when even in his house he locks his chests; and this when he knows there be laws, and public officers, armed, to revenge all injuries shall be done him; what opinion he has of his fellow-subjects, when he rides armed; of his fellow citizens, when he locks his doors; and of his children, and servants, when he locks his chests. Does he not there as much accuse mankind by his actions, as I do by my words? But neither of us accuse man's nature in it. The desires, and other passions of man, are in themselves no sin. No more are the actions, that proceed from those passions, till they know a law that forbids them: which till laws be made they cannot know: nor can any law be made, till they have agreed upon the person that shall make it.

It may peradventure be thought, there was never such a time, nor condition of war as this; and I believe it was never generally so, over all the world: but there are many places, where they live so now. For the savage people in many places of America, except the government of small families, the concord whereof dependeth on natural lust, have no government at all; and live at this day in that brutish manner, as I said before. Howsoever, it may be perceived what manner of life there would be, where there were no common power to fear, by the manner of life, which men that have formerly lived under a peaceful government, use to degenerate into, in a civil war.

But though there had never been any time, wherein particular men were in a condition of war one against another; yet in all times, kings, and persons of sovereign authority, because of their independency, are in continual jealousies, and in the state and posture of gladiators; having their weapons pointing, and their eyes fixed on one another; that is, their forts, garrisons, and guns upon the frontiers of their kingdoms; and continual spies upon their neighbours; which is a posture of war. But because they uphold thereby, the industry of their subjects; there does not follow from it, that misery, which accompanies the liberty of particular men.

In such a war nothing is unjust   To this war of every man, against every man, this also is consequent; that nothing can be unjust. The notions of right and wrong, justice and injustice have there no place. Where there is no common power, there is no law: where no law, no injustice. Force, and fraud, are in war the two cardinal virtues. Justice, and injustice are none of the faculties neither of the body, nor mind. If they were, they might be in a man that were alone in the world, as well as his senses, and passions. They are qualities, that relate to men in society, not in solitude. It is consequent also to the same condition, that there be no propriety, no dominion, no *mine* and *thine* distinct; but only that to be every man's, that he can get: and for so long, as he can keep it. And thus much for the ill condition, which man by mere nature is actually placed in. . . .

Lines of Inquiry

1 This selection is taken from Chapter 13 of *Leviathan,* Hobbes's celebrated study of the state.

   a What is the importance of the natural condition of mankind to such a study?

   b What does Hobbes mean by "natural condition"?

   c Hobbes argued on behalf of a strong central government under an absolute ruler: In what way does his analysis of man's natural condition seem related to this argument?

2 Outline the structure of Hobbes's analysis of man's natural condition.

   a Does he break from analysis at any point? Why?

   b Attach the concluding paragraph of this selection to the sentence "All other time is peace," omitting the material between. The essay is obviously damaged—in what way?

   c Could the material you have just omitted be placed *after* the current concluding paragraph and leave the logic of Hobbes's thought intact? If logic would not suffer, what would?

3 a Look at the subtitle and first sentence of each section: What principle of sequence underlies this structure?

   b Now imagine a description of the natural condition of mankind organized according to the sequence of time: What would be its divisions? What kind of attitude toward human life would such a sequence seem best able to reflect?

   c What kind of attitude, by contrast, does the sequence employed by Hobbes seem best able to reflect?

4 a In what sections of the selection does Hobbes employ classification as a device for furthering his discussion? What would be left of the essay if the passages involving classification were deleted?

   b Where in the essay does its development depend on definition? What is the consequence of this definition for his argument? For opposing arguments?

5 Mark in the essay every occasion on which Hobbes appears to be answering an objection raised by an invisible adversary.

  a How do you explain the location of the most important of these "replies"?

  b What technique of exposition does Hobbes put to major use in these passages?

6 The climax of Hobbes's prose is reached in his discussion of the incommodities of war:

> In such condition, there is no place for industry, because the fruit thereof is uncertain: and consequently no culture of the earth; no navigation, nor use of the commodities that may be imported by sea; no commodious building; no instruments of moving, and removing, such things as require much force; no knowledge of the face of the earth; no account of time; no arts; no letters; no society; and which is worst of all, continual fear, and danger of violent death; and the life of man, solitary, poor, nasty, brutish, and short.

What is there in this sentence that accounts for its powerful effect? Consider the following: (*a*) the order of ideas, (*b*) the effects of repetition, (*c*) the length of clauses, (*d*) the actual individual words.

  a If you find this difficult, revision may help you to appreciate the original: Scramble the order of ideas, eliminate the repetitions, change the length of each clause, and substitute other words, close synonyms, for the words Hobbes actually employs.

  b In the original, do one further thing: Place a slanted stress line (') *over* each syllable that must be heavily stressed when the passage is read aloud, one vertical line *between* each syllable where the voice pauses briefly when the passage is read aloud, and two vertical lines between each syllable where the voice pauses for a longer time. What does the frequency of these three kinds of lines suggest? What does your revision do to their pattern?

7 Scan the first clause of each sentence in the selection.

  a How many of them contain a logical connective, or pivot term—an "and," "but," "therefore," etc.? What is the effect of Hobbes's explicit use of these terms?

  b Read the first two paragraphs aloud, omitting all the logical connectives; what is the result?

8 Hobbes's opinion of human character is rather low.   How is that opinion mediated in the following phrases?

a "For as to strength of body, the weakest has strength enough to kill the strongest, either by secret machination, or by confederacy with others, that are in the same danger as himself."

b ". . . there is not ordinarily a greater sign of the equal distribution of any thing, than that every man is contented with his share."

c "But because they [the kings] uphold thereby [by a warlike posture] the industry of their subjects; there does not follow from it, that misery, which accompanies the liberty of particular men."

Lines of Experiment

1 Hobbes's argument deals essentially with the old question "What is human nature really like?" Hobbes and Thomas Jefferson, author of the Declaration of Independence, begin from a common premise—that all men are created equal—but arrive at different estimates of human character and at different theories of government.   Because Hobbes's argument is conducted on a highly abstract level and each point of it is scrupulously and logically connected to the next, its structure is easy to see.

In this argument, you doubtless will find much to argue about. Among the questions raised by the selection, the following are merely a few about which good essays could be written:

a Is there such a thing as a natural man?

b Are men created equal, or nearly so?

c Is prudence merely experience?

d Do some men damage others for pleasure only?

e Is power the only restraint on war?

In developing an essay from any such question, the problem of definition is foremost.   What does one mean by "natural," "equal," "experience," "pleasure," "justice," and "power"?   All these terms are vague in themselves; their context, however, helps to distinguish the meaning Hobbes himself has in mind. Thus "power," as Hobbes uses the word, means governmental power, specifically law backed by force; "justice" means the principles of judgment enforced by law, and so forth.   Unless the way in which any such term is used is made explicit, an argument focusing on the concept named by that term can hardly find firm ground.

But any such term can mean, quite legitimately, a number of different things; the process of definition, then, is in part a

process of isolating the sense of the term important in a particular discussion. General questions of the kind illustrated
above often conceal several different meanings within the same
term, and so have to be rephrased before they can be answered.
The process of definition in such cases implies the defining of
an answerable question. One way of testing the adequacy of a
logical question is to ask if it conceivably can be answered; if
it cannot, it may still be meaningful but it needs to be rephrased.

2 Essentially, Hobbes starts by establishing a single general premise about human nature and, with the help of a series of less
important premises, follows its implications through to a theory
of government. Here are some familiar premises concerning
the conduct and character of human beings and their institutions. Select some such statement that you personally believe
to be true, and trace its implications for a single area of human
activity—government, economics, education, family life, styles
of dress, the relations between the sexes, religion, etc. One
caution: Do not try to write like Hobbes. You can learn
much from a study of his style, but you cannot and should not
learn to copy his private turn with the language.
a Human beings are significantly unequal in intelligence.
b Character is fixed by the age of ten.
c We are the products of our heredity and our environment.
d There is a sucker born every minute.
e The chief passion of mankind is greed.
f Power corrupts; absolute power corrupts absolutely.
g People believe what it is profitable for them to believe.
h Gentlemen prefer blondes.

HENRY DAVID THOREAU

ON THE DUTY
OF CIVIL
DISOBEDIENCE

I heartily accept the motto,—"That government is best which governs
least"; and I should like to see it acted up to more rapidly and systematically. Carried out, it finally amounts to this, which also I be-

lieve,—"That government is best which governs not at all", and when men are prepared for it, that will be the kind of government which they will have.   Government is at best but an expedient; but most governments are usually, and all governments are sometimes, inexpedient. The objections which have been brought against a standing army, and they are many and weighty, and deserve to prevail, may also at last be brought against a standing government.   The standing army is only an arm of the standing government. The government itself, which is only the mode which the people have chosen to execute their will, is equally liable to be abused and perverted before the people can act through it.   Witness the present Mexican war, the work of comparatively a few individuals using the standing government as their tool; for, in the outset, the people would not have consented to this measure.

This American government,—what is it but a tradition, though a recent one, endeavoring to transmit itself unimpaired to posterity, but each instant losing some of its integrity?   It has not the vitality and force of a single living man; for a single man can bend it to his will.   It is a sort of wooden gun to the people themselves; and, if ever they should use it in earnest as a real one against each other, it will surely split. But it is not the less necessary for this; for the people must have some complicated machinery or other, and hear its din, to satisfy that idea of government which they have.   Governments show thus how successfully men can be imposed on, even impose on themselves, for their own advantage.   It is excellent, we must all allow; yet this government never of itself furthered any enterprise, but by the alacrity with which it got out of its way.   *It* does not keep the country free.   *It* does not settle the West.   *It* does not educate.   The character inherent in the American people has done all that has been accomplished; and it would have done somewhat more, if the government had not sometimes got in its way.   For government is an expedient by which men would fain succeed in letting one another alone; and, as has been said, when it is most expedient, the governed are most let alone by it.   Trade and commerce, if they were not made of India rubber, would never manage to bounce over the obstacles which legislators are continually putting in their way; and, if one were to judge these men wholly by the effects of their actions, and not partly by their intentions, they would deserve to be classed and punished with those mischievous persons who put obstructions on the railroads.

But, to speak practically and as a citizen, unlike those who call themselves no-government men, I ask for, not at once no government, but *at once* a better government.   Let every man make known what kind of government would command his respect, and that will be one step toward obtaining it.

After all, the practical reason why, when the power is once in the hands of the people, a majority are permitted, and for a long period continue, to rule, is not because they are most likely to be in the right, nor because this seems fairest to the minority, but because they are physically the strongest. But a government in which the majority rule in all cases cannot be based on justice, even as far as men understand it. Can there not be a government in which majorities do not virtually decide right and wrong, but conscience?—in which majorities decide only those questions to which the rule of expediency is applicable? Must the citizen ever for a moment, or in the least degree, resign his conscience to the legislator? Why has every man a conscience, then? I think that we should be men first, and subjects afterward. It is not desirable to cultivate a respect for the law, so much as for the right. The only obligation which I have a right to assume, is to do at any time what I think right. It is truly enough said, that a corporation has no conscience; but a corporation of conscientious men is a corporation *with* a conscience. Law never made men a whit more just; and, by means of their respect for it, even the well-disposed are daily made the agents of injustice. A common and natural result of an undue respect for law is, that you may see a file of soldiers, colonel, captain, corporal, privates, powder-monkeys, and all, marching in admirable order over hill and dale to the wars, against their wills, aye, against their common sense and consciences, which makes it very steep marching indeed, and produces a palpitation of the heart. They have no doubt that it is a damnable business in which they are concerned; they are all peaceably inclined. Now, what are they? Men at all? or small moveable forts and magazines, at the service of some unscrupulous man in power? Visit the Navy Yard, and behold a marine, such a man as an American government can make, or such as it can make a man with its black arts, a mere shadow and reminiscence of humanity, a man laid out alive and standing, and already, as one may say, buried under arms with funeral accompaniments, though it may be

> Not a drum was heard, nor a funeral note,
>   As his corse to the ramparts we hurried;
> Not a soldier discharged his farewell shot
>   O'er the grave where our hero we buried.

The mass of men serve the State thus, not as men mainly, but as machines, with their bodies. They are the standing army, and the

militia, jailers, constables, *posse comitatus,* etc.   In most cases there
is no free exercise whatever of the judgment or of the moral sense; but
they put themselves on a level with wood and earth and stones; and
wooden men can perhaps be manufactured that will serve the purpose
as well.   Such command no more respect than men of straw, or a lump
of dirt.   They have the same sort of worth only as horses and dogs.
Yet such as these even are commonly esteemed good citizens.   Others,
as most legislators, politicians, lawyers, ministers, and office-holders,
serve the State chiefly with their heads; and, as they rarely make any
moral distinctions, they are as likely to serve the devil, without intending it, as God.   A very few, as heroes, patriots, martyrs, reformers in
the great sense, and *men,* serve the State with their consciences also,
and so necessarily resist it for the most part; and they are commonly
treated by it as enemies.   A wise man will only be useful as a man,
and will not submit to the "clay," and "stop a hole to keep the wind
away," but leave that office to his dust at least:—

I am too high-born to be propertied,
To be a secondary at control,
Or useful serving-man and instrument
To any sovereign state throughout the world.

He who gives himself entirely to his fellow-men appears to them useless
and selfish; but he who gives himself partially to them is pronounced
a benefactor and philanthropist.

How does it become a man to behave toward this American government
to-day?   I answer that he cannot without disgrace be associated with
it.   I cannot for an instant recognize that political organization as *my*
government which is the *slave's* government also.

All men recognize the right of revolution; that is, the right to refuse
allegiance to and to resist the government, when its tyranny or its inefficiency are great and unendurable.   But almost all say that such is
not the case now.   But such was the case, they think, in the Revolution
of '75.   If one were to tell me that this was a bad government because
it taxed certain foreign commodities brought to its ports, it is most
probable that I should not make an ado about it, for I can do without
them: all machines have their friction; and possibly this does enough
good to counterbalance the evil.   At any rate, it is a great evil to make
a stir about it.   But when the friction comes to have its machine, and
oppression and robbery are organized, I say, let us not have such a
machine any longer.   In other words, when a sixth of the population

of a nation which has undertaken to be the refuge of liberty are slaves, and a whole country is unjustly overrun and conquered by a foreign army, and subjected to military law, I think that it is not too soon for honest men to rebel and revolutionize.   What makes this duty the more urgent is the fact, that the country so overrun is not our own, but ours is the invading army.

Practically speaking, the opponents to a reform in Massachusetts are not a hundred thousand politicians at the South, but a hundred thousand merchants and farmers here, who are more interested in commerce and agriculture than they are in humanity, and are not prepared to do justice to the slave and to Mexico, *cost what it may.*   I quarrel not with far-off foes, but with those who, near at home, co-operate with, and do the bidding of those far away, and without whom the latter would be harmless.   We are accustomed to say, that the mass of men are unprepared; but improvement is slow, because the few are not materially wiser or better than the many.   It is not so important that many should be as good as you, as that there be some absolute goodness somewhere; for that will leaven the whole lump.   There are thousands who are *in opinion* opposed to slavery and to the war, who yet in effect do nothing to put an end to them; who, esteeming themselves children of Washington and Franklin, sit down with their hands in their pockets, and say that they know not what to do, and do nothing; who even postpone the question of freedom to the question of free-trade, and quietly read the prices-current along with the latest advices from Mexico, after dinner, and, it may be, fall asleep over them both.   What is the price-current of an honest man and patriot to-day?   They hesitate, and they regret, and sometimes they petition; but they do nothing in earnest and with effect.   They will wait, well disposed, for others to remedy the evil, that they may no longer have it to regret.   At most, they give only a cheap vote, and a feeble countenance and God-speed, to the right, as it goes by them.   There are nine hundred and ninety-nine patrons of virtue to one virtuous man; but it is easier to deal with the real possessor of a thing than with the temporary guardian of it.

All voting is a sort of gaming, like chequers or backgammon, with a slight moral tinge to it, a playing with right and wrong, with moral questions; and betting naturally accompanies it.   The character of the voters is not staked.   I cast my vote, perchance, as I think right; but I am not vitally concerned that that right should prevail.   I am willing to leave it to the majority.   Its obligation, therefore, never exceeds that of expediency.   Even voting *for the right* is *doing* nothing for it.   It is only expressing to men feebly your desire that it should prevail.   A wise man will not leave the right to the mercy of chance, nor wish it to prevail through the power of the majority.   There is but little virtue in the action of masses of men.   When the majority shall at length vote for the abolition of slavery, it will be because they are indifferent to slavery, or because there is but little slavery left to be abolished by their vote.   *They* will then be the only slaves.   Only *his* vote can hasten the abolition of slavery who asserts his own freedom by his vote.

I hear of a convention to be held at Baltimore, or elsewhere, for the selection of a candidate for the Presidency, made up chiefly of editors, and men who are politicians by profession; but I think, what is it to any independent, intelligent, and respectable man what decision they may come to, shall we not have the advantage of his wisdom and honesty, nevertheless?   Can we not count upon some independent votes?   Are there not many individuals in the country who do not attend conventions?   But no: I find that the respectable man, so called, has immediately drifted from his position, and despairs of his country, when his country has more reason to despair of him.   He forthwith adopts one of the candidates thus selected as the only *available* one, thus proving that he is himself *available* for any purposes of the demagogue.   His vote is of no more worth than that of any unprincipled foreigner or hireling native, who may have been bought.   Oh for a man who is a *man,* and, as my neighbor says, has a bone in his back which you cannot pass your hand through!   Our statistics are at fault: the population has been returned too large.   How many *men* are there to a square thousand miles in this country?   Hardly one.   Does not America offer any inducement for men to settle here?   The American has dwindled into an Odd Fellow,—one who may be known by the development of his organ of gregariousness, and a manifest lack of intellect and cheerful self-reliance; whose first and chief concern, on coming into the world, is to see that the alms-houses are in good repair; and, before yet he has lawfully donned the virile garb, to collect a fund for the support of the widows and orphans that may be; who, in short, ventures to live only by the aid of the mutual insurance company, which has promised to bury him decently.

It is not a man's duty, as a matter of course, to devote himself to the eradication of any, even the most enormous wrong; he may still properly have other concerns to engage him; but it is his duty, at least, to wash his hands of it, and, if he gives it no thought longer, not to give it practically his support.   If I devote myself to other pursuits and contemplations, I must first see, at least, that I do not pursue them sitting upon another man's shoulders. I must get off him first, that he may pursue his contemplations too. See what gross inconsistency is tolerated. I have heard some of my townsmen say, "I should like to have them order me out to help put down an insurrection of the slaves, or to march to Mexico,—see if I would go;" and yet these very men have each, directly by their allegiance, and so indirectly, at least, by their money, furnished a substitute. The soldier is applauded who refuses to serve in an unjust war by those who do not refuse to sustain the unjust government which makes the war; is applauded by those whose own act and authority he disregards and sets at nought; as if the State were penitent to that degree that it hired one to scourge it while it sinned, but not to that degree that it left off sinning for a moment. Thus, under the name of order and civil government, we are all made at last to pay homage to and support our own meanness. After the first blush of sin, comes its indifference; and from immoral it becomes, as it were, *un*moral, and not quite unnecessary to that life which we have made.

How can a man be satisfied to entertain an opinion merely, and enjoy *it?* Is there any enjoyment in it, if his opinion is that he is aggrieved? If you are cheated out of a single dollar by your neighbor, you do not rest satisfied with knowing that you are cheated, or with saying that you are cheated, or even with petitioning him to pay you your due; but you take effectual steps at once to obtain the full amount, and see that you are never cheated again. Action from principle,—the perception and the performance of right,—changes things and relations; it is essentially revolutionary, and does not consist wholly with any thing which was. It not only divides states and churches, it divides families; aye, it divides the *individual,* separating the diabolical in him from the divine.

Unjust laws exist: shall we be content to obey them, or shall we endeavor to amend them, and obey them until we have succeeded, or shall we transgress them at once? Men generally, under such a government as this, think that they ought to wait until they have persuaded the majority to alter them. They think that, if they should resist, the remedy would be worse than the evil. But it is the fault of the government itself that the remedy *is* worse than the evil. *It* makes it worse. Why is it not more apt to anticipate and provide for reform? Why does it not cherish its wise minority? Why does it cry and resist before it is hurt? Why does it not encourage its citizens to be on the alert to point out its faults, and *do* better than it would have them? Why does it always crucify Christ, and excommunicate Copernicus and Luther, and pronounce Washington and Franklin rebels?

If the injustice is part of the necessary friction of the machine of government, let it go, let it go: perchance it will wear smooth,—certainly the machine will wear out. If the injustice has a spring, or a pulley, or a rope, or a crank, exclusively for itself, then perhaps you may consider whether the remedy will not be worse than the evil; but if it is of such a nature that it requires you to be the agent of injustice to another, then, I say, break the law. Let your life be a counter friction to stop the machine. What I have to do is to see, at any rate, that I do not lend myself to the wrong which I condemn.

I do not hesitate to say, that those who call themselves abolitionists should at once effectually withdraw their support, both in person and property, from the government of Massachusetts, and not wait till they constitute a majority of one, before they suffer the right to prevail through them. I think that it is enough if they have God on their side, without waiting for that other one. Moreover, any man more right than his neighbors, constitutes a majority of one already.

I meet this American government, or its representative the State government, directly, and face to face, once a year, no more, in the person of its tax-gatherer; this is the only mode in which a man situated as I am necessarily meets it; and it then says distinctly, Recognize me; and the simplest, the most effectual, and, in the present posture of affairs, the indispensablest mode of treating with it on this head, of expressing your little satisfaction with and love for it, is to deny it then. My civil neighbor, the tax-gatherer, is the very man I have to deal with,—for it is, after all, with men and not with parchment that I quarrel,—and he has voluntarily chosen to be an agent of the government. How shall he ever know well what he is and does as an officer of the government, or as a man, until he is obliged to consider whether he shall treat me, his neighbor, for whom he has respect, as a neighbor and well-disposed man, or as a maniac and disturber of the peace, and see if he can get over this obstruction to his neighborliness without a ruder and more impetuous thought or speech corresponding with his action? I know this well, that if one thousand, if one hundred, if ten men whom I could name,—if ten *honest* men only,—aye, if one HONEST man, in this State of Massachusetts, *ceasing to hold slaves,* were actually to withdraw from this copartnership, and be locked up in the county jail therefor, it would be the abolition of slavery in America.   For it matters not how small the beginning may seem to be: what is once well done is done for ever.   But we love better to talk about it: that we say is our mission. Reform keeps many scores of newspapers in its service, but not one man.   If my esteemed neighbor, the State's ambassador, who will devote his days to the settlement of the question of human rights in the Council Chamber, instead of being threatened with the prisons of Carolina, were to sit down the prisoner of Massachusetts, that State which is so anxious to foist the sin of slavery upon her sister,—though at present she can discover only an act of inhospitality to be the ground of a quarrel with her,—the Legislature would not wholly waive the subject the following winter.

Under a government which imprisons any unjustly, the true place for a just man is also a prison.   The proper place to-day, the only place which Massachusetts has provided for her freer and less desponding spirits, is in her prisons, to be put out and locked out of the State by her own act, as they have already put themselves out by their principles.   It is there that the fugitive slave, and the Mexican prisoner on parole, and the Indian come to plead the wrongs of his race, should find them; on that separate, but more free and honorable ground, where the State places those who are not *with* her but *against* her,—the only house in a slave-state in which a free man can abide with honor.   If any think that their influence would be lost there, and their voices no longer afflict the ear of the State, that they would not be as an enemy within its walls, they do not know by how much truth is stronger than error, nor how much more eloquently and effectively he can combat injustice who has experienced a little in his own person.   Cast your whole vote, not a strip of paper merely, but your whole influence.   A minority is powerless while it conforms to the majority; it is not even a minority then; but it is irresistible when it clogs by its whole weight. If the alternative is to keep all just men in prison, or give up war and slavery, the State will not hesitate which to choose.   If a thousand men were not to pay their tax-bills this year, that would not be a violent and bloody measure, as it would be to pay them, and enable the State to commit violence and shed innocent blood.   This is, in fact, the definition of a peaceable revolution, if any such is possible.   If the tax-gatherer, or any other public officer, asks me, as one has done, "But what shall I do?" my answer is, "If you really wish to do any thing, resign your office."   When the subject has refused allegiance, and the officer has resigned his office, then the revolution is accomplished.   But even suppose blood should flow. Is there not a sort of blood shed when the conscience is wounded? Through this wound a man's real manhood and immortality flow out, and he bleeds to an everlasting death. I see this blood flowing now.

I have contemplated the imprisonment of the offender, rather than the seizure of his goods,—though both will serve the same purpose,—because they who assert the purest right, and consequently are most dangerous to a corrupt State, commonly have not spent much time in accumulating property. To such the State renders comparatively small service, and a slight tax is wont to appear exorbitant, particularly if they are obliged to earn it by special labor with their hands. If there were one who lived wholly without the use of money, the State itself would hesitate to demand it of him. But the rich man—not to make any invidious comparison—is always sold to the institution which makes him rich. Absolutely speaking, the more money, the less virtue; for money comes between a man and his objects, and obtains them for him; and it was certainly no great virtue to obtain it. It puts to rest many questions which he would otherwise be taxed to answer; while the only new question which it puts is the hard but superfluous one, how to spend it. Thus his moral ground is taken from under his feet. The opportunities of living are diminished in proportion as what are called the "means" are increased. The best thing a man can do for his culture when he is rich is to endeavour to carry out those schemes which he entertained when he was poor. Christ answered the Herodians according to their condition. "Show me the tribute-money," said he;—and one took a penny out of his pocket;—If you use money which has the image of Cæsar on it, and which he has made current and valuable, that is, *if you are men of the State,* and gladly enjoy the advantages of Cæsar's government, then pay him back some of his own when he demands it; "Render therefore to Cæsar that which is Cæsar's, and to God those things which are God's,"—leaving them no wiser than before as to which was which; for they did not wish to know.

When I converse with the freest of my neighbors, I perceive that, whatever they may say about the magnitude and seriousness of the question, and their regard for the public tranquillity, the long and the short of the matter is, that they cannot spare the protection of the existing government, and they dread the consequences of disobedience to it to their property and families. For my own part, I should not like to think that I ever rely on the protection of the State. But, if I deny the authority of the State when it presents its tax-bill, it will soon take and waste all

my property, and so harass me and my children without end. This
is hard. This makes it impossible for a man to live honestly and at
the same time comfortably in outward respects. It will not be worth
the while to accumulate property; that would be sure to go again. You
must hire or squat somewhere, and raise but a small crop, and eat that
soon. You must live within yourself, and depend upon yourself, always tucked up and ready for a start, and not have many affairs. A
man may grow rich in Turkey even, if he will be in all respects a good
subject of the Turkish government. Confucius said,—"If a State is
governed by the principles of reason, poverty and misery are subjects
of shame; if a State is not governed by the principles of reason, riches
and honors are the subjects of shame." No: until I want the protection of Massachusetts to be extended to me in some distant southern
port, where my liberty is endangered, or until I am bent solely on building up an estate at home by peaceful enterprise, I can afford to refuse
allegiance to Massachusetts, and her right to my property and life. It
costs me less in every sense to incur the penalty of disobedience to the
State, than it would to obey. I should feel as if I were worth less in
that case.

Some years ago, the State met me in behalf of the church, and commanded me to pay a certain sum toward the support of a clergyman
whose preaching my father attended, but never I myself. "Pay it," it
said, "or be locked up in the jail." I declined to pay. But, unfortunately, another man saw fit to pay it. I did not see why the schoolmaster should be taxed to support the priest, and not the priest the
schoolmaster; for I was not the State's schoolmaster, but I supported
myself by voluntary subscription. I did not see why the lyceum should
not present its tax-bill, and have the State to back its demand, as well as
the church. However, at the request of the selectmen, I condescended
to make some such statement as this in writing:—"Know all men by
these presents, that I, Henry Thoreau, do not wish to be regarded as a
member of any incorporated society which I have not joined." This
I gave to the town-clerk; and he has it. The State, having thus learned
that I did not wish to be regarded as a member of that church, has never
made a like demand on me since; though it said that it must adhere to
its original presumption that time. If I had known how to name them,
I should then have signed off in detail from all the societies which I
never signed on to; but I did not know where to find a complete list.

I have paid no poll-tax for six years. I was put into a jail once on this
account, for one night; and, as I stood considering the walls of solid
stone, two or three feet thick, the door of wood and iron, a foot thick,

and the iron grating which strained the light, I could not help being struck with the foolishness of that institution which treated me as if I were mere flesh and blood and bones, to be locked up. I wondered that it should have concluded at length that this was the best use it could put me to, and had never thought to avail itself of my services in some way. I saw that, if there was a wall of stone between me and my townsmen, there was a still more difficult one to climb or break through, before they could get to be as free as I was. I did not for a moment feel confined, and the walls seemed a great waste of stone and mortar. I felt as if I alone of all my townsmen had paid my tax. They plainly did not know how to treat me, but behaved like persons who are underbred. In every threat and in every compliment there was a blunder; for they thought that my chief desire was to stand the other side of that stone wall. I could not but smile to see how industriously they locked the door on my meditations, which followed them out again without let or hindrance, and *they* were really all that was dangerous. As they could not reach me, they had resolved to punish my body; just as boys, if they cannot come at some person against whom they have a spite, will abuse his dog. I saw that the State was half-witted, that it was timid as a lone woman with her silver spoons, and that it did not know its friends from its foes, and I lost all my remaining respect for it, and pitied it.

Thus the State never intentionally confronts a man's sense, intellectual or moral, but only his body, his senses. It is not armed with superior wit or honesty, but with superior physical strength. I was not born to be forced. I will breathe after my own fashion. Let us see who is the strongest. What force has a multitude? They only can force me who obey a higher law than I. They force me to become like themselves. I do not hear of *men* being *forced* to live this way or that by masses of men. What sort of life were that to live? When I meet a government which says to me, "Your money or your life," why should I be in haste to give it my money? It may be in a great strait, and not know what to do: I cannot help that. It must help itself; do as I do. It is not worth the while to snivel about it. I am not responsible for the successful working of the machinery of society. I am not the son of the engineer. I perceive that, when an acorn and a chestnut fall side by side, the one does not remain inert to make way for the other, but both obey their own laws, and spring and grow and flourish as best they can, till one, perchance, overshadows and destroys the other. If a plant cannot live according to its nature, it dies; and so a man.

I have never declined paying the highway tax, because I am as desirous of being a good neighbor as I am of being a bad subject; and, as for supporting schools, I am doing my part to educate my fellow-country-men now.   It is for no particular item in the tax-bill that I refuse to pay it.   I simply wish to refuse allegiance to the State, to withdraw and stand aloof from it effectually.   I do not care to trace the course of my dollar, if I could, till it buys a man, or a musket to shoot one with—the dollar is innocent—but I am concerned to trace the effects of my allegiance.   In fact, I quietly declare war with the State, after my fashion, though I will still make what use and get what advantage of her I can, as is usual in such cases.

I think sometimes, Why, this people mean well; they are only ignorant; they would do better if they knew how: why give your neighbors this pain to treat you as they are not inclined to?   But I think, again, this is no reason why I should do as they do, or permit others to suffer much greater pain of a different kind.   Again, I sometimes say to myself, When many millions of men, without heat, without ill-will, with-out personal feeling of any kind, demand of you a few shillings only, without the possibility, such is their constitution, of retracting or alter-ing their present demand, and without the possibility, on your side, of appeal to any other millions, why expose yourself to this overwhelming brute force?   You do not resist cold and hunger, the winds and the waves, thus obstinately; you quietly submit to a thousand similar neces-sities.   You do not put your head into the fire.   But just in proportion as I regard this as not wholly a brute force, but partly a human force, and consider that I have relations to those millions as to so many mil-lions of men, and not of mere brute or inanimate things, I see that ap-peal is possible, first and instantaneously, from them to the Maker of them, and, secondly, from them to themselves.   But, if I put my head deliberately into the fire, there is no appeal to fire or to the Maker of fire, and I have only myself to blame.   If I could convince myself that I have any right to be satisfied with men as they are, and to treat them accordingly, and not according, in some respects, to my requisitions and expectations of what they and I ought to be, then, like a good Mussulman and fatalist, I should endeavor to be satisfied with things as they are, and say it is the will of God.   And, above all, there is this difference between resisting this and a purely brute or natural force, that I can resist this with some effect; but I cannot expect, like Orpheus, to change the nature of the rocks and trees and beasts.

I do not wish to quarrel with any man or nation.   I do not wish to split hairs, to make fine distinctions, or set myself up as better than my neighbors. I seek rather, I may say, even an excuse for conforming to the laws of the land. I am but too ready to conform to them. Indeed I have reason to suspect myself on this head; and each year, as the tax-gatherer comes round, I find myself disposed to review the acts and position of the general and state governments, and the spirit of the people, to discover a pretext for conformity. I believe that the State will soon be able to take all my work of this sort of my hands, and then I shall be no better a patriot than my fellow-countrymen. Seen from a lower point of view, the Constitution, with all its faults, is very good; the law and the courts are very respectable; even this State and this American government are, in many respects, very admirable and rare things, to be thankful for, such as a great many have described them; but seen from a point of view a little higher, they are what I have described them; seen from a higher still, and the highest, who shall say what they are, or that they are worth looking at or thinking of at all?

However, the government does not concern me much, and I shall bestow the fewest possible thoughts on it. It is not many moments that I live under a government, even in this world. If a man is thought-free, fancy-free, imagination-free, that which *is not* never for a long time appearing *to be* to him, unwise rulers or reformers cannot fatally interrupt him.

I know that most men think differently from myself; but those whose lives are by profession devoted to the study of these or kindred subjects, content me as little as any. Statesmen and legislators, standing so completely within the institution, never distinctly and nakedly behold it. They speak of moving society, but have no resting-place without it. They may be men of a certain experience and discrimination, and have no doubt invented ingenious and even useful systems, for which we sincerely thank them; but all their wit and usefulness lie within certain not very wide limits. They are wont to forget that the world is not governed by policy and expediency. Webster never goes behind government, and so cannot speak with authority about it. His words are wisdom to those legislators who contemplate no essential reform in the existing government; but for thinkers, and those who legislate for all time, he never once glances at the subject. I know of those whose serene and wise speculations on this theme would soon reveal the limits of his mind's range and hospitality. Yet, compared with the cheap professions of most reformers, and the still cheaper wisdom and eloquence of politicians in general, his are almost the only sensible and valuable words, and we thank Heaven for him. Comparatively, he is always strong, original, and, above all, practical. Still, his quality is not wisdom, but prudence. The lawyer's truth is not Truth, but consistency, or a consistent expediency. Truth is always in harmony with herself, and is not concerned chiefly to reveal the justice that may consist with wrong-doing. He well deserves to be called, as he has been called, the Defender of the Constitution. There are really no blows to be given by him but defensive ones. He is not a leader, but a follower. His leaders are the men of '87. "I have never made an effort," he says, "and never propose to make an effort; I have never countenanced an effort, and never mean to countenance an effort, to disturb the arrangement as originally made, by which the various States came into the Union." Still thinking of the sanction which the Constitution gives to slavery, he says, "Because it was a part of the original compact,—let it stand." Notwithstanding his special acuteness and ability, he is unable to take a fact out of its merely political relations, and behold it as it lies absolutely to be disposed of by the intellect,—what, for instance, it behoves a man to do here in America to-day with regard to slavery, but ventures, or is driven, to make some such desperate answer as the following, while professing to speak absolutely, and as a private man,— from which what new and singular code of social duties might be inferred?—"The manner," says he, "in which the government of those States where slavery exists are to regulate it, is for their own consideration, under their responsibility to their constituents, to the general laws of propriety, humanity, and justice, and to God. Associations formed elsewhere, springing from a feeling of humanity, or any other cause, have nothing whatever to do with it. They have never received any encouragement from me, and they never will."

They who know of no purer sources of truth, who have traced up its stream no higher, stand, and wisely stand, by the Bible and the Constitution, and drink at it there with reverence and humility; but they who behold where it comes trickling into this lake or that pool, gird up their loins once more, and continue their pilgrimage toward its fountain-head.

No man with a genius for legislation has appeared in America. They are rare in the history of the world. There are orators, politicians, and eloquent men, by the thousand; but the speaker has not yet opened his mouth to speak, who is capable of settling the much-vexed questions of the day. We love eloquence for its own sake, and not for any truth which it may utter, or any heroism it may inspire. Our legislators have not yet learned the comparative value of free-trade and of freedom, of union, and of rectitude, to a nation. They have no genius or talent for comparatively humble questions of taxation and finance, commerce and manufactures and agriculture. If we were left solely to the wordy wit of legislators in Congress for our guidance, uncorrected by the seasonable experience and the effectual complaints of the people, America would not long retain her rank among the nations. For eighteen hundred years, though perchance I have no right to say it, the New Testament has been written; yet where is the legislator who has wisdom and practical talent enough to avail himself of the light which it sheds on the science of legislation?

The authority of government, even such as I am willing to submit to,— for I will cheerfully obey those who know and can do better than I, and in many things even those who neither know nor can do so well—is still an impure one: to be strictly just, it must have the sanction and consent of the governed. It can have no pure right over my person and property but what I concede to it. The progress from an absolute to a limited monarchy, from a limited monarchy to a democracy, is a progress toward a true respect for the individual. Is a democracy, such as we know it, the last improvement possible in government? Is it not possible to take a step further towards recognizing and organizing the rights of man? There will never be a really free and enlightened State, until the State comes to recognize the individual as a higher and independent power, from which all its own power and authority are derived, and treats him accordingly. I please myself with imagining a State at last which can afford to be just to all men, and to treat the individual with respect as a neighbor; which even would not think it inconsistent with its own repose, if a few were to live aloof from it, not meddling with it, nor embraced by it, who fulfilled all the duties of neighbors and fellow-men. A State which bore this kind of fruit, and suffered it to drop off as fast as it ripened, would prepare the way for a still more perfect and glorious State, which also I have imagined, but not yet anywhere seen.

Lines of Inquiry

1 Both the content and the style of this essay's opening sentence are remarkable. Consider it by itself, as if you had not read Thoreau's full argument.

    a What premises seem to lie beneath the conclusion that "that government is best that governs least"? How would you go about testing the truth of these premises?

    b Why does Thoreau begin his essay with a quotation—why not simply begin with a similar statement of his own?

    c Thoreau says that he would like to see this principle "acted up to *more rapidly and systematically.*" (Italics added.) How are the italicized words related to the preceding judgment of government? What difference do you see between "acted up to" and "acted on"?

d What might be the advantages of opening an essay in this fashion, with the pronoun "I"?

2 It has been said that every sentence solves a problem or answers a question raised by the preceding sentence. If this assertion is even partially true,

a What can be said of the first sentence of any given essay?

b What problems does Thoreau have to solve as a consequence of his first sentence?

c How many of these problems does he attack directly in the rest of the essay?

3 Mark the points where this essay appears to make a transition from one subject to another.

a Where does the introductory section end? Does the section that immediately succeeds it appear to answer a question raised by the introduction?

b How do you explain the sequence of topics?

c On what aspect of his subject does Thoreau spend the most time? How is this aspect related to the essay's opening sentence and its general point?

4 In describing Daniel Webster, Thoreau says "The lawyer's truth is not Truth, but consistency, or a consistent expediency."

a What definition of truth does Thoreau appear to have in mind? Is this definition convertible? Does it matter if it is or is not convertible?

b What distinction is he pointing at in writing truth without, and then with, an initial capital?

c Does Thoreau make a distinction between consistency and consistent expediency? If so, what is the distinction? If not, why does he appear to be making one?

d There appears to be a contradiction between Thoreau's point here and the point made concerning truth and consistency, in the introduction to this part of the text. Is this apparent contradiction also substantial?

5 Any assertion may be *judged* to be true, or to be false, or to be true in one respect yet false in another, or to be obscure. It may also be *accounted for,* as part of a system of ideas. Account for the following assertions as part of Thoreau's system of ideas on civil disobedience, and judge their truth.

a "Government is an expedient by which men would fain succeed in letting one another alone."

b "Law never made men a whit more just."

c "Action from principle,—the perception and the performance of right,—changes things and relations; it is essentially revolutionary, and does not consist wholly with any thing which was."

d "The rich man . . . is always sold to the institution which makes him rich. Absolutely speaking, the more money, the less virtue. . . ."

6 Though in actual fact we often do not reason from premises to conclusions, but rather find our way back from conclusions to premises, the truth of any conclusion must be judged finally not on the motives of the person urging it, nor on the psychological maneuvering that got him from premises to conclusion, but on the validity of his argument in its final state. Psychologically, premises are often the products of conclusions; logically, conclusions must be the products of premises.

Both "Civil Disobedience" and the preceding essay by Thomas Hobbes make assumptions about human nature; these assumptions lie beneath their arguments.

a How do their premises about human nature differ?

b What is the evidence given to support each view?

c How important is each to the subsequent argument?

d Is either set of assumptions true, in your opinion? What arguments would you use to support your answer? What opposing arguments would you anticipate?

7 One of the central logical problems presented by Thoreau's argument is the apparent inconsistency between attributing a conscience to every man ("Why has every man a conscience, then?") and asserting nonetheless that "there is but little virtue in the actions of masses of men." Suppose one were to urge that the inconsistency is more apparent than real, that Thoreau is actually contrasting the ability of the individual to act virtuously with the inability of the group to do so.

a Is this interpretation of Thoreau's position confirmed or denied by the total essay?

b What theory of action would seem to flow from such an interpretation?

c Can you formulate a clearer and more satisfying interpretation of Thoreau's point?

d Is the inconsistency in his argument apparent or real?

8 Thoreau's conscience serves him as a touchstone for the moral quality of action. List the five issues of your own time and place that most clearly are moral in their implications and

most urgently demand a solution. (You need not take the overriding international issues.)

a What kind of issue is easiest for you to judge on the basis of conscience, and what kind is hardest? Or are all equally easy?

b What kind of knowledge does your conscience provide you with concerning these issues?

c Does anyone in your class have a different list? A different sense of priority? A different kind of knowledge?

d How do you account for the fact that there are any moral problems at all? And that the solution to any given problem is not always universally known?

e How does Thoreau account for the widespread presence of moral problems and the widespread ignorance of proper solutions?

Lines of Experiment

1 The subject of civil disobedience is likely to be relevant no matter what the time or place. Write a brief essay focused not on the concept of civil disobedience but on one way in which that concept is used (or proposed for use) in your immediate world. Out of a specific focus on event, of course, will arise at least an implied judgment of what lies behind that event—a judgment of the concept itself. You may find it valuable to narrow your focus very sharply—to consider the aspect of an event that reflects most clearly on a single assumption behind the theory of civil disobedience, or on a single effect of it. Choose a crucial matter, however; take one of the points most heatedly debated. And despite the pressure of the times, try not to arrive at a conclusion before you have considered the evidence you are able to muster. It is precisely in the matters most heatedly debated that you can least afford to be trapped within unexamined thoughts, to be the victim of other people's convictions and not the master of your own.

2 Write a brief narrative essay illustrating the value or lack of value, the truth or lack of truth, in a specific premise of the theory of civil disobedience. You need not focus on an overtly political event: Human nature, group nature, or the immediate and final consequences of various modes of action manifest themselves everywhere, even in the home. Yet if the arena of the event is not political, be careful: The home is not a political state, and to generalize from one kind of situation to another must be done with caution.

THE MIDDLE GROUND: ILLUSTRATION

Illustration occupies a kind of middle ground between mimetically and logically ordered discourse: By becoming illustrations of ideas, factual events take on meaning; by anchoring themselves to illustrative facts, ideas take on substance.

The following passage opens Letwin's essay, "Four Fallacies about Economic Development." The illustrations that he uses are italicized, for our purposes here; they will form the basis for the discussion and analysis that follow.

By fallacy I mean truism that has been misunderstood. It is a statement which, if hedged in by enough qualifications, would be correct, but which, as commonly understood, is false.

It cannot be demonstrated that the human mind is especially given to fallacies when exercising itself on problems of economic development. But the idea of economic development is so vague that it invites confusion. Development is generally understood as the going from an underdeveloped economy to a developed economy, and an underdeveloped economy is generally supposed to be less developed than a developed economy. This circularity in definition leads to quite unnecessary paradoxes. *For instance, the national income of Nepal (the most underdeveloped economy presently on record) has been growing recently; despite that, Nepal must now be considered more underdeveloped than ever before—because the highly developed economy of the United States has been growing faster.* Nobody would be satisfied to *have it said that a growing boy was becoming less developed because a bigger boy was growing faster.* Such a paradox is not essential to the subject.

Economic development can be spoken of simply as the process by which a nation grows richer. An underdeveloped economy, then, is an economy that is poor in a special sense—by comparison with its own economic potential in the foreseeable future. *A nation founded on a tiny island in the Antarctic wastes, its land consisting of naked volcanic rock, snow-bound, ice-locked, and wind-swept eleven months of the year; peopled by a race that is unskilled, untaught and unteachable, possessing no capital—that nation would be poor but not underdeveloped, for it might have reached the limits of its economic capacity.* Most poor nations are not poor in quite so ultimate and hopeless a sense.

If we try to read the passage without its illustrative details, we can see how important they are: The specific makes the general real. Both writer and reader need to know what facts an idea stands for, the writer in order to conform his thought to the real world, the reader in order to understand and to judge that thought. Thought itself has sometimes been described (perhaps too simply) as a constant oscillation between image and idea; and in this, illustration imitates its movement.

The sequence of thought apparent in this passage, then, appears to be fairly fundamental: Idea swings toward image, then back again to idea. In discussing this sequence, at least three questions are important. First, what determines the idea to be illustrated? Second, what accounts for the pattern of each illustrative sequence? Third, what accounts for the kinds of illustration used?

SEQUENCE AND PURPOSE IN ILLUSTRATION

Each of the illustrative sequences in Letwin's opening paragraphs mediates between a general idea and the specific things behind that idea. Thus the general statement that a particular definition of economic underdevelopment leads to quite unnecessary paradoxes is illustrated by a specific case: the folly of a particular kind of comparison between

Nepal and the United States. But that illustration itself is still pretty far from general experience; most of us are not economists, and we find thinking in these terms rather difficult. So Letwin suggests a homely analogy: the case of the two growing boys. The least technically inclined among his readers can hardly help but see the point now; in consequence, the illustrative chain can end by returning to its original level of abstraction: "Such a paradox is not essential to the subject."

The next illustrative sequence circles from the general to the specific and back to the general in a similar way. First, Letwin makes a general statement: An economy can properly be thought underdeveloped only by comparison with its own economic potential, and if it has no further potential, it may be poor but is not underdeveloped. But the content of the statement is hard to grasp clearly; therefore, the author illustrates his point: "A nation founded on a tiny island in the Antarctic wastes. . . ." The sequence then returns to its original level of abstraction, and in effect, to its original point: Most nations are not poor in so absolute a sense (i.e., they are economically underdeveloped).

The method used in this excerpt suggests several important features of illustration. First, an illustration need not be drawn from the world actually located in time and space: "The national economy of Nepal" may be more specific than 'the underdeveloped nation," but the phrase is still highly abstract—nobody can point to that economy. Similarly, the two growing boys have parallels in the real world, but are themselves not real; the hopelessly poor island is a deliberate fiction. Yet all are successful as illustrations. We can conclude that the purpose of an illustrative chain is not so much to make an abstract or general idea specific or concrete as to make it *visible* and *definite.*

But to say so much is not to say that illustration is or can be out of touch with fact. We hardly ever actually produce concrete things themselves as illustrations (*"This* is what I mean by a cow"), but we do use illustration to *suggest* the concrete and to link a general idea to its specific contents. "The national economy of Nepal" suggests fishermen, farmers, and so on; the hopelessly poor island suggests what such an island would be like. In this respect, an illustration suggests a classification of the things it tries to represent—of the kinds of activity that make up Nepal's economy, for instance. We need to know what an idea contains in order to illustrate it; and we generally illustrate it by going to a more nearly specific level within the idea. Thus one might illustrate *life* more specifically as *fish, mammal,* etc., and illustrate *fish,* in turn, as *herring.* In the example, we take *Nepal* as illustration of its superior category, *economically underdeveloped nations.* But once the world of things in time and space becomes visible, we need go no further: The case of the two growing boys illustrates convincingly what Letwin is talking about, and the sequence ends there.

The second point, then, is that illustration depends on our knowing the contents of the idea we are speaking of, and also knowing how those contents can be classified. The third point is that illustration is *focused:* Not all ideas in a given context need to be illustrated. Obviously, there are many unillustrated ideas in the passage under discussion, but these ideas need no explanation in this context. Such words as "capital" and "race" are clear enough in meaning to be understood as they stand and as they are used here. If Letwin had tried to illustrate them, he would merely have blurred his focus. Illustration lights up a central idea or line of thought; when ideas are already visible and definite enough in their context to serve the purposes of their enlistment, they need no illustration.

Fourth, an illustrative chain usually ends by restating in direct or indirect fashion the idea that was its starting point, the idea that needed clarification. The main line of a discussion preserves one level of abstraction throughout; illustration shifts that level only temporarily, in order to anchor ideas to facts.

Fifth, the kind of audience we write for determines whether or not we need an illustrative chain: What they already know about, we do not need to tell them. The kind of audience will also decide for us how long we must make that chain, and what kinds of illustrations we must use in it. The illustrations based on the typical case of two growing boys would be superfluous to an audience used to the abstractions of economics. A more general audience needs the more familiar illustration, in order to see the point easily and clearly.

A distinction must be drawn here between *visibility* and *vividness.* The illustrations of the first paragraph are visible but not especially vivid. Letwin is trying to show not the economy of Nepal but the kinds of paradoxes that result from a circular definition of economic underdevelopment; therefore, he is uninterested in making his readers *see* Nepal's economy. The important thing is that they grasp the idea (the kinds of paradoxes one can get into, and so on), not the actual fact (Nepal's workaday world).

On the other hand, the illustration in the second paragraph—the hopelessly poor country in the Antarctic wastes—is made extremely vivid: We can almost see that miserable island. Why? Letwin had several perfectly legitimate alternatives. He could have illustrated the idea of a hopelessly poor country in a fairly abstract way:

A nation with no natural resources, highly unfavorable climate, no persons of superior intelligence, no stored purchasing power, would be poor but not underdeveloped. . . .

Indeed, he could have illustrated directly not a hopelessly poor country but an underdeveloped and poor one—his real subject, after all:

A poor nation founded on an unsuspected mountain of high-grade iron ore might be said properly to be economically underdeveloped, poor only in a special sense. . . .

But the vivid details of the actual illustration—dry volcanic rock, Antarctic wastes, wind, ice—make the idea of poverty important in human terms: one feels one ought to do something about poverty-stricken countries. Letwin's choice of illustration, then, depends on how he wants his audience to *feel*. It has an emotional as well as a rational value.

ILLUSTRATION
AS ARGUMENT

To illustrate an idea is, in a way, to document it—to show that it is consistent with fact. The illustrations in Letwin's two paragraphs suggest as much, for they not only make us understand what is being said, but also persuade us that what is being said holds true for and is important in the real world. In Part II we distinguished between two kinds of consistency: consistency among statements (validity) and consistency of statements with fact (truth). Illustration can be described as a primary means of demonstrating consistency of statements with fact. For this reason, illustration is indispensable in logical discourse.

A given writer obviously must choose among many possible illustrations for any given idea. What determines his choice? Two considerations, aside from his knowledge and his material: the audience he writes for and the point he wants to make. A third consideration is the relative value in logically ordered discourse of different kinds of illustration. Flatly, a writer has to consider what kind of illustration will help him to secure his point against contest.

TYPES
OF ILLUSTRATION

The passage from Letwin's essay contains several kinds of illustration: *example, comparison and contrast,* and *analogy.* Their boundaries overlap, of course; the contrast of Nepal and the United States is used as an example of a particular kind of inappropriate reasoning; the example of the hopelessly poor country is really in contrast to that of the simply underdeveloped country; the analogy of the two growing boys is both contrast and example.   But each of these kinds of illustration has a special character: An example that is not an analogy, for instance, has a different effect from one that is.   The important questions are: why an imaginary poor country with nothing to hope for, instead of an actual poor country with some hope; why two growing boys, instead of two growing weeds—or two growing economies; why Nepal and the United States, instead of Brazil and Germany or China and Russia?

In short, what makes a good illustration?

Example
A nation founded on a tiny island in the Antarctic wastes, its land consisting of naked volcanic rock, snow-bound, ice-locked, and wind-swept eleven months of the year; peopled by a race that is unskilled, untaught, and unteachable; possessing no capital— that nation would be poor but not underdeveloped.

No example can work well unless it represents the class it is taken from.   In order to represent that class, it must make the significant features of the class visible—as, for example, the illustration above makes visible what is meant by a hopelessly poor but not under-developed nation.   The real problem is to decide what can represent adequately the significant features of the class we are trying to illustrate.

Now the class of economically fully developed but poor nations will include some nations and exclude all others.   But within that class there will be some extreme cases—nations much poorer or much richer than the others—and there will also be some more or less average cases. Further, nations may be distributed along the range rather evenly, or may clump up; some will be poor for one reason, some for another;

some will be poor some of the time, others will be poor all the time; some will be poor in one way, others in another.   In fact, a "representative case" will depend on what kind of representativeness is necessary. No single case will represent the total group in all ways, and no two cases will represent it in exactly the same way.   For convenience, let me name two kinds of examples: the average and the extreme.

The Average Case

The average of a class is its most direct and simple representative. But we have to know what we are averaging in order to know when we have found an average—if we can find it.   What is an average economically underdeveloped nation? Mathematical averages are easy, but are not always meaningful; how much does it mean to say the average line of blank verse has ten syllables? Everyone knows the difficulties from his ordinary experience: What does an average student think on this subject or on that? In the end, we may answer such a question by reporting the ideas of the average business major and the average humanities major, of the average freshman and the average senior, and so on.   In doing so, we recognize that, where a class has diverse kinds of members, a series of averages reflecting its interior divisions may represent it better than a single average can.   Thus— had this been his purpose—Letwin might have instanced one ordinary nation impoverished by poor soil, another by paralytic climate, still another by ignorance, and so forth, and so arrive at something like a representative series.

Such a series of averages has its drawbacks, of course, as well as its virtues.   It may do a better job than the simple average in representing the divisions of a class; but with many subjects, once we begin slicing the end may never come—our limits are still arbitrary, and the effort to represent everything may lead us to try to pack everything in.   A series of averages, then, can easily get too bulky.   It can also be hard to establish.   The average of all nations impoverished by climate, after all, may be almost as hard to find as the average of all nations that are just plain impoverished.

The Extreme Case

Where average cases are clear, obviously they make strong illustrations. But in some cases they are not clear.   In yet other cases, they may not represent the ideas we are after.

The extreme case is usually much easier than the average to locate. We may not be sure what the average economically underdeveloped nation is, but we can be sure that "Nepal is the most underdeveloped economy presently on record." A further advantage of the extreme case is that it exaggerates, shows the basic, irreducible features of a class almost in caricature, and thus makes them more obvious. A "totally impoverished nation" has this illustrative value: Once we have seen it, we know what is meant by total poverty, we know what kinds of riches and poverty there are: soil, climate, capital, and labor.

Extreme cases, too, have a drawback that is precisely the reverse of their advantage: They are *not* typical, and they have, therefore, limited value as tests of consistency with fact. To point out that heroes exist is not to show that men are heroic. But even here, where it is logically weakest, the extreme case can sometimes help us over a difficulty: If we can show that the least heroic of men is capable of courage, then we have shown that all men are; if we can show that the wisest of men is sometimes stupid, then we have shown that stupidity is part of the inevitable for us all; if we can show that a particular definition of economic underdevelopment will lead to our overlooking the real progress made even by the miserable economy of Nepal, where such progress ought to be most striking, then we have shown that such a definition will be useless in dealing with cases whose progress is less striking. If a definition will not work where it ought to work best, then it will not work at all.

We use this kind of illustration in our ordinary lives all the time. We say, "If ever a man ought to have flunked out in his freshman year, George was that man"—implying that if George can succeed, anybody can.

The Hypothetical Case

The extreme case, then, has real value as illustration. But it is often as hard to find as an average case. Indeed, actual circumstances are full of clutter: Not only was George a phenomenally hard worker, but also he was paid a princely sum by his father to stay in school. Similarly, the totally impoverished nation turns out to be a prime candidate for foreign aid from a neighboring rich country, and the economy impoverished by poor soil is also impoverished by lack of capital—but has a tremendous supply of labor.

There are two ways of handling the problem of clutter. One is to find a case whose clutter is irrelevant to the point at issue. This indeed is what we do when we search for a clear illustration. The other way is to make up the example: "A hopelessly poor country in the Antarctic wastes. . . ." (There is a third way: to take so many examples that the clutter of one cancels out the clutter of another. This method of avoiding clutter is possible for the scientist but difficult for the writer.)

Hypothetical examples have one clear defect—they are out of touch with fact. But they offer a number of clear advantages in return. First, a made-up example can eliminate all irrelevance: The average student is exactly an average student, because we declare him to be— his health is average, his parents are average, his grades are average, his brains are average, his emotions are average; similarly, our hopelessly poor country is really and thoroughly hopeless. Second, the writer can be swift: He need not justify his choice of, say, Germany, as the average developed nation, for the case is precisely what he calls it— average or extreme. Third, he runs very little risk of distracting a reader with any special or private problems about a real example: The government of a hypothetical country will not rise to denounce its creator in the UN, the least heroic man will not breathe heavily at him over the phone, the missionary to that country and the friend of that man will not hurl the essay away in disgust. The hypothetical example is emotionally far more controllable than the real example.

Last, and most important, in some kinds of speculation only hypothetical cases can point to clear questions and answers. If a man is in a burning building and has a choice between saving the Mona Lisa and saving a tomcat, which should he save? The answer tells us nothing about the Mona Lisa or the cat, but it does suggest how that man— presumably like all men—weighs the greatest art against the meanest life visibly like our own. Yet nobody would want to put the matter to an actual test, any more than he would want to find out if, robbed of all four limbs, he would still want to live.

Comparison and Contrast

For instance, the national income of Nepal (the most underdeveloped economy presently on record) has been growing recently; despite that, Nepal must now be considered more underdeveloped than ever before—because the highly developed economy of the United States has been growing faster. . . . An underdeveloped economy, then, is an economy that is poor in a special sense—by comparison with its own economic potential in the foreseeable future.

Comparison and contrast as a technique of illustration does not make use of kinds of examples that differ from those just discussed—it simply groups them in a slightly different fashion. Nepal, instead of standing alone, is contrasted to the United States: extreme to extreme. Just as easily, one might contrast two average cases, or two hypothetical cases—for example, the average nation impoverished by poor soil and the average nation impoverished by lack of capital.

Comparison and contrast illustrates the significance of the thing being discussed by setting next to it another thing that can act as its measure. But the examples compared must be sufficiently alike to make their similarities or differences significant: They must belong to the same class. (What would a comparison between the economy of Nepal and the literature of Russia accomplish?) Within the same class, the comparison and contrast of extremes has particular value, for the extremes allow us to see the full range of possibility—not only the features that all members of the class have in common, but also the range of separation. In effect, such an illustration can provide not only a strong pattern of emphasis but also a kind of subject inventory. Let us put side by side a rich economy and a poor one, a decent war and an indecent one, a beautiful building and an ugly one, a good student and a bad one, a champion boxer and one who never made it out of the Golden Gloves. We do not change the individual cases, but we are likely to see what there is to talk about a little more clearly, and to judge each pair with greater sureness. Comparison and contrast is a primary means of establishing the structure of analysis and evaluation. A beauty contest with only one candidate makes the judge's decision both easy and meaningless. With two candidates, criteria begin to emerge.

But it is possible to make a misleading comparison or contrast, as well as to make a fruitful one. Letwin's point in his actual passage is that the comparison between the United States and Nepal is of no use in a definition of economic underdevelopment—that the proper comparison here is between a given country's actual and its potential wealth.

Analogy

Nobody would be satisfied to have it said that a growing boy was becoming less developed because a bigger boy was growing faster.

An analogy is a form of comparison in which we try to understand a thing not in terms of its own significant features or by contrast to something in the same class, but in terms of the features of something in another but parallel class, better known or more observable. Thus one might describe the development of economies in terms of the development of boys, a heart in terms of a pump, a government in terms of a well-balanced machine, poetry in terms of painting or music.

Analogies have certain marked advantages. They can make difficult or abstract ideas visible in homely terms: A national economy is a fairly vague notion, but a growing boy is not. Further, because of its homeliness, an analogy can develop a point very swiftly—as in the example above. Third, analogies can be suggestive, can lead toward the possibility of resemblances we had never dreamed of. Thus the wave theory of light began its career in a speculative analogy between the behavior of light and that of water; thus, also, modern fiction takes much of its character from analogies with the structure and technique of painting. Fourth, analogies—like other forms of illustration—are useful in argument. One might argue that because government is like a machine, its parts should show interdependence and differentiation of function, and it should occasionally be overhauled or traded in for a later model.

Analogy is valuable in argument, however, only when the things compared are alike in the area under discussion—when the analogy is "true" or "close." We might make an analogy between men and rats, and find the analogy useful in biological research; we would be unlikely to find it of use in discussions of human society or of art. Similarly, the analogy between growing boys and growing economies is close in the single respect necessary for Letwin's argument: The only useful measure of development for boy or economy is the potential for that boy or that economy. In most other respects, the analogy breaks down (boys must grow, in order to live; economies can stagnate forever).

As a rule, the further an analogy is pushed, the less parallel it runs; its greatest use, therefore, is in giving visible shape to difficult ideas, in introducing or explaining more direct kinds of illustration—and—like all forms of comparison and contrast—in suggesting new directions for analytic thought.

Illustration as Inquiry

Ordinarily, a writer illustrates in order to make statements visible, and not in order to find out what to say; but the illustrative case, be it extreme, average, or whatever, frequently can be extended into a technique of inquiry. If we have a class of events but do not know much about them, the analysis of an illustrative case may actually provide useful answers. If the question is "What makes an under-developed nation underdeveloped?" an answer may arise from the detailed analysis of Nepal's economy.

Such extended analytic studies have their greatest uses where little is known. Why do some brilliant students drop out of school and others stay forever? Why do some people fear change, and why does change occur even when people most fear it? The chief advantage of the extended case study is that it makes possible an immense concentration and focusing of ideas, and so a just treatment of the complexity of real events. The most frequent weakness of such studies is that the illus-trations chosen fail to be representative. But when a case is carefully chosen for its simplicity and clarity, for its lack of clutter, an extended illustrative analysis can often lead to the discovery of general truths.

Illustration as Structural Center and Metaphor
Such extended illustrations serve, in effect, as compositional centers. They determine much of the sequence, point, and style of an essay by determining its focus. (Only the *scale* of the extended illustration sets it apart from the kind explored earlier; in every instance, illustration is a way of concentrating and of focusing ideas.)

In this way, the illustrative case helps to solve one of the chief problems of the writer: his need to find a way of condensing what he has to say, without becoming in the process either so abstract as to lose his audience or so concrete as to lose his point. The illustrative case, treated in detail, provides him with a way of showing what he is talking about and of analyzing it, at the same time. A carefully chosen and limited series of illustrations, offered as illustrations only and not as covering every contingency, can become the backbone of a composition: Three scenes in a novel can illustrate all scenes, two houses can illustrate a city, five flowers a landscape, one action the entire quality of a culture, and so on. In such structures illustration becomes metaphorical, the representing of a total entity by means of one of its parts.

This is especially true of the case study, which passes over naturally and almost inevitably into narrative or description, and thus creates in an image the visible face of an idea. When specific images are made to stand for ideas so complex that they cannot be recovered or duplicated by paraphrase, we probably should acknowledge that we have passed beyond illustration into metaphor and symbol. In a metaphor, the relation between image and idea is made explicit: A ship is made to stand for the state, a womb for chaos, a book for learning, and so on.   In a symbol, the relation is left implicit, is not expressed, and the potential meanings are therefore multiple: The ship may stand for mankind, the state, progress, learning, or a dozen such ideas together, and the womb for anything that generates.   The mark of metaphor and symbol is that they cannot be paraphrased, they exist primarily and uniquely in their own terms, an equation of idea and image.

It frequently happens that a writer will take as his subject something finally too difficult to render in a satisfactory paraphrase or analysis, will find that some emotional shading, some nuance, some unity, escapes him, and so will decide to present it at one point in metaphor or symbol. He may draw his subject loosely around a single narrative center—a visit to a city, a conversation—or around a single descriptive center— a building, a landscape.   He may place two such centers in contrast. Frequently he will break from analysis altogether at such moments, changing style and tone as he does.   Such an approach, in which the image becomes the only full statement of the idea and its value, gives a special quality to prose, and can produce an effective blend of logically and mimetically ordered discourse.

WILLIAM LETWIN

 FOUR FALLACIES
ABOUT ECONOMIC
DEVELOPMENT

By fallacy I mean a truism that has been misunderstood. It is a statement which, if hedged in by enough qualifications, would be correct, but which, as commonly understood, is false.

It cannot be demonstrated that the human mind is especially given to fallacies when exercising itself on problems of economic development. But the idea of economic development is so vague that it invites confusion.   Development is generally understood as the going from an underdeveloped economy to a developed economy, and an underdeveloped economy is generally supposed to be less developed than a developed economy. This circularity in the definition leads to quite unnecessary paradoxes. For instance, the national income of Nepal (the most underdeveloped economy presently on record) has been growing recently; despite that, Nepal must now be considered more underdeveloped than ever before—because the highly developed economy of the United States has been growing faster. Nobody would be satisfied to have it said that a growing boy was becoming less developed because a bigger boy was growing faster. Such a paradox is not essential to the subject.

Economic development can be spoken of simply as the process by which a nation grows richer. An underdeveloped economy, then, is an economy that is poor in a special sense—by comparison with its own economic potential in the foreseeable future. A nation founded on a tiny island in the Antarctic wastes, its land consisting of naked volcanic rock, snow-bound, ice-locked, and wind-swept eleven months of the year; peopled by a race that is unskilled, untaught and unteachable, possessing no capital—that nation would be poor but not underdeveloped, for it might have reached the limits of its economic capacity. Most poor nations are not poor in quite so ultimate and hopeless a sense.

The practical problem of economic development is how to make poor countries richer absolutely. To make them as rich or nearly as rich as the United States or any other rich country is irrelevant and meaningless: are they to be made as rich as the United States is now, was some time ago, or will be hence? We can hope to help the underdeveloped nations eradicate hunger; it is fatuous to hope that the citizens of all nations will some day eat the same amount of food; it is utopian to hope that all men will some day have the same incomes. In any event, to eliminate hunger and misery is a far more commendable and humane goal than to aim for mathematical equality.

The question then is how nations have become richer in the past and how others can become richer in the future. Much is known about this and much more surmised. The four fallacies cover only a small part of the ground, although all alike are fundamental and popular.

The first fallacy: Manufacturing is more productive than agriculture.

This fallacy underlies the widespread belief that the prime or exclusive cure for national poverty lies in industrialization.

Folklore has it that human beings, when they first appeared on the earth, earned their living by hunting. Later, understanding how efficient it would be to keep their prey in easy reach, men supposedly turned to grazing. As communities formed, peace and order were established, and with them the likelihood that a man could reap without hindrance where he sowed; thus cultivation began. And finally—so the legend goes—when farmers had become so proficient that they could raise more food than they needed themselves, the surplus was used to sustain urban workers who earned their claim to food by exchanging for it fabricated things, or manufactures, as they are still called.

Some such broad historical scheme—sketching a development from husbandry to industry—has been borrowed from folklore by social philosophers and social scientists, who by endorsing it and systematizing it have reinforced the public faith. This picture underlies the schematic views on economic history of men as diverse as Adam Smith, Thomas Jefferson and Thorstein Veblen, to mention only a few. It underlies also, for instance, the classification of goods that is part of an economist's everyday vocabulary: "primary" goods being those produced by agriculture and extractive industries; "secondary" goods, manufactures; and "tertiary" goods, those commodities and services generated by "service industries."

Although the notion of the historical priority of agriculture is embedded in folklore, it is not false. On the contrary, the fundamental assertion —leaving aside the details of the story—is more nearly correct than its opposite: it is certain that industry did not predate the extractive occupations, including agriculture. But the historical doctrine in its ordinary form is nevertheless fallacious, for the truth is that agriculture and industry have always coexisted; extraction and fabrication both have gone on together ever since the beginning.

Endless evidence exists for the early practice of manufacturing. Stone-Age arrowheads show that the act of capture was preceded by handicrafts; Stone-Age scrapers and knives show that the act of capture was immediately succeeded by acts of fabrication. Man is, among other things, a tool-making animal; and tools are essential because men are neither strong nor agile enough to capture many animals without tools, and also because Nature does not provide many raw materials that human beings can use, without first transforming them, for food, shelter, or especially clothing. Even the life of men as primitive as can be, is cluttered with spears, knives, pots, bags, huts, ropes and cloths—all fabricated things. Taking things from the earth and molding those things to human ends are equally essential parts of human activity.

History cannot clearly distinguish between agriculture and manufacture according to the order of their appearance; theory cannot more sharply distinguish between their natures. Both activities use land, labor, and capital in the production of commodities. The way each uses them and the character of the commodities that each produces do not fall into the neat and expected categories.

Does manufacture use more capital relative to labor than agriculture? Quite the contrary; it turns out that now, at least, and in many places, agriculture is more capital-intensive than manufacturing. Does manufacture use more power than agriculture? Some forms of it probably do; but on the other hand, the highly mechanized branches of agriculture use more power than an industry as advanced and complex as electronic-components manufacturing. Is the planning period for agricultural production longer than for manufactures? Possibly; but whereas it takes about four or five years from the time a particular automobile model begins to be planned until it comes off the assembly lines, agricultural processes such as mushroom culture take only a few weeks from seed to fruit. Does agriculture produce food, and manufacture other sorts of things? Obviously not, since manufacture produces bread, whereas agriculture produces jute, indigo, and beeswax. Does agriculture produce necessities, and manufacture luxuries? No; manufacture produces boots and brooms, but agriculture produces silk, strawberries, and orchids.

Everyone knows the difference between a farmer and a mill hand, but for the purposes of economic policy too much is usually made of that difference.

These caveats having been entered, it should be pointed out that all underdeveloped economies depend heavily on agriculture, whereas all highly developed economies generate very little of their income by agriculture. Only 5 per cent of the income of the United States arises in agriculture, forestry and fishery; and only 8 per cent of the American labor force is engaged in those activities. In Nepal, by contrast, 93 per cent of the labor force is engaged in agriculture. In India, about half of the national income derives from agriculture, forestry and fishery. But in New Zealand, whose citizens enjoy the third highest average income in the world, only one-sixth of the labor force is engaged in agriculture, and they produce only one-fifth of the national income. The other countries of the world arrange themselves more or less neatly on this scale, neatly enough so that one would be warranted in betting that a country which specializes in agriculture is a poor country and that a country which does not is relatively rich.

That this is not a mere happenstance, but an outcome of the general process of enrichment can be seen by examining the long history of the American economy. In 1840 probably more than half of American output was being produced in the agricultural sector; by the end of the Civil War the contribution of agriculture had shrunk to one-fifth; by the end of World War I to about one-tenth, and by now to less than one-twentieth. The same pattern could be exhibited in the history of the United Kingdom or of any other industrialized society. An inevitable concomitant of national enrichment is that agriculture ceases to be the single greatest contributor to national income and in time becomes, instead, one of the lesser contributors.

But the evidence should not be misread. Agriculture ultimately becomes less important when a nation has become fairly rich; although its agricultural output may continue to rise absolutely, the *fraction* of the national income produced by agriculture steadily declines because other forms of production take on greater significance. But this does not mean that agriculture is a crutch that can be abandoned. Although agriculture is superseded in rich nations, there is good reason to think that during the period of its primacy it was agriculture, above all, in nations such as the United States or New Zealand or Great Britain, which established the base for enrichment. At some points in the development of any economy, agriculture rather than manufacture *may* be the best means of enrichment.

Agriculture, then, though neither historically prior nor analytically distinguishable, tends to be superseded by manufacture in the course of enrichment. And it should be added, manufacture in turn tends to be displaced somewhat by service industries. For what reason?

The fundamental cause of this sequence is a fairly universal human taste for refinement. In the history of the Western world, for instance, white wheaten bread has always been preferred to whole-grain wheaten bread. But white bread is inevitably more expensive than dark—all else being equal—because the former uses up more wheat per ounce of bread; in consequence, the bread of the rich was always whiter than that of the poor. For similar reasons the linens of the rich have always been finer and whiter, their furnishings more delicate, their manners more elaborate. To refine nature's products to the standards which the human imagination invents requires much transformation, that is, much manufacture, which is costly.   Hence, as men's incomes rise, they spend an increasing fraction of their incomes on the manufacturing processes that turn the immediate products of nature into the goods and services that fancy requires.

A poor savage, for want of better, sits in the sand eating meat of the bear that he has himself slain, quartered, and roasted over fire.   The wealthy aesthete eats the meat of a duckling that has been reared in domestic tranquility, which has been pressed and cooked with the aid of ingenious machinery and talented labor and in the presence of artfully contrived wines, and which is served to him in a setting far from natural. The former, whose income is small, eats a meal the main ingredient of whose cost is an agricultural or extractive effort.   The latter, in paying for his meal, pays mainly for the labor and capital that went into setting the dish before him, the refined dish in its refined setting; only a minuscule part of the cost is accounted for by the effort of producing the duckling, that is, by specifically agricultural costs.

The technical terms describing this behavior are that the income-elasticity of demand for agricultural products is low.   It is not, of course, as low as all that.   "Food" is not a homogeneous stuff.   As their incomes rise, men choose to consume foods of the more tender and delectable sorts: spareribs and lamb forequarters are replaced by tender-loin, in the American version; in France, ordinary wine gives way to Burgundy; among Indian peasants, millet is abandoned in favor of rice. Nevertheless, in all places, the *fraction* of income devoted to the raw— that is, purely agricultural—ingredients of the diet falls as income rises. That is the chief reason why the fraction of income generated by agri-culture—as "income" and "agriculture" are defined in national income statistics—is lower in rich countries than in poor countries.

This indisputable fact has been widely misinterpreted after the *post hoc ergo propter hoc* fashion.   If rich countries do much manufacturing, does it not follow that a country wishing to be rich should expand its manufactures?   Such reasoning is part of the doctrine, albeit only part, which suggests to impoverished nations throughout the world that to erect a steel mill is to make the first step toward national opulence.

It is easy enough to specify circumstances in which it would be anything but reasonable to set up a steel mill, or any other manufacturing enter-prise.   Imagine a very poor nation, very sparsely settled, absolutely closed off from the rest of the world; and suppose that each inhabitant had the same income, an income hardly sufficient to keep his family alive.   In those circumstances agriculture and other extractive occupations would be the only ones; everyone would farm and fish and hunt, and in his spare hours everyone would be busy making clothing and housing, preparing meals, and fashioning implements.   In such a setting, were incomes miraculously to rise a bit, nobody would think of spending the increase on anything but extra food.   Nobody would think of buying any manufactured goods whatsoever, unless his income were to rise vastly beyond its existing range.   Even if a foreign expert could demonstrate that the same effort required to increase the output of rice by one pound could produce instead one hundred pounds of steel, the demonstration would fall on deaf ears—for the inhabitants would want rice so badly that no amount of steel, or gold, would be an acceptable substitute.   In a very poor and utterly closed economy, manufacture would be an inimical luxury.

Underdeveloped nations are neither so poor nor so closed as that hypothetical one.   Since at least some of their inhabitants are not on the verge of starvation, the nation is already consuming a certain amount of manufactured goods, which may be made inside the country or imported from abroad.   At that point it becomes plausible to ask whether the most efficient way to raise the average incomes of inhabitants is by investing capital—supposing there be some to invest—in agriculture or in manufacturing.   The manufactured goods might, of course, find no buyers within the country; but that would be immaterial as long as the goods could be exchanged elsewhere in the world for additional food, if additional food were wanted.   On the other hand, the manufactured goods might be of such a sort that they could find no buyers abroad; but that would be no fatal objection if they could be sold domestically to persons who until then had been buying similar goods imported from abroad.   Whether the manufactured goods increased the nation's exports or decreased its imports, either way the foreign exchange acquired in the process could be used to buy extra food, if extra food were wanted.

In an open economy, in short, manufacturing may be a better way of getting food than the practice of agriculture.   Similarly, agriculture may be a more efficient way of getting manufactured goods.   The rational rule, then, is to pursue that activity which is most efficient.   A nation that wants steel should not produce steel unless producing it is the cheapest way to get it; the possibility of international trade means that the cheapest way for some nations to get their steel is by producing butter or by catching fish.

Whether manufacturing is more productive than agriculture is therefore a question that cannot be answered in general, but only when one knows which branches of either group are being considered, and where, and when, and at what prices and costs. If an underdeveloped nation can produce radio circuits at a price far below world prices, but cannot produce its staple breadstuff as cheaply as others can, it will enrich itself more quickly by making the former and buying the latter. But which of these two, or of any other form of production it can carry on most efficiently, depends on the intricate relations, at each given moment, between such variables as the levels of income and rates of change of incomes throughout the world; of wage rates, interest rates, and rents at home and everywhere; of private tastes and diplomatic relations at home and abroad; and many more considerations of that sort.

All such qualifications being made, and in view of the fact that incomes have been rising throughout the world—despite the fears of neo-Malthusians who warn that the world's population will soon outrun the world's capacity to grow food—it is a safe general rule that *eventually* it will pay every nation to devote an increasing fraction of its productive efforts to manufacturing. But this is not all. The day may come when incomes have risen so high everywhere that manufactured goods too, like agricultural goods now, despite being more plentiful become insignificant in the budgets of consumers, who will begin to satisfy increasingly their desire for services.

The second fallacy: More capital is better than less capital.

This fallacy underlies the supposition that the problems of under-developed countries can be overcome merely by providing them with more capital.

A simple example will demonstrate the nature of the fallacy. Consider a small farm cultivated by farmer and ox. The man follows the plow from morning until night, under a hot sun: his life is hard. Imagine that the farmer acquires a tractor. The tractor chugs merrily through the day's work in an hour, the farmer driving it comfortably under an awning: his life has become easy and leisurely. The picture rightly comforts all humanitarian observers. The only difficulty is that the farmer is now starving.   True, he has more leisure, but his crop is no larger than before, and the cost of keeping up the tractor (including as its main ingredient the interest charges on the loan with which he bought the tractor) is eating up a great deal of the food he previously had. The handy, efficient piece of machinery is impoverishing him.

The case of the farmer and his tractor, translated into technical terms, shows that the use of more rather than less capital is economically rational only if the labor saved by introducing an additional capital good is worth more than the costs added by using the capital good.   As underdeveloped economies typically suffer from considerable unemployment, overt or disguised, the labor saved by introducing *certain* capital goods into *certain* occupations has a proper economic value of zero.   That is to say that the real economic cost of using an hour's labor in any given enterprise is measured by its "opportunity cost," the additional output which that hour's labor would have produced in alternative employment.   If Robinson Crusoe can gather a pound of brambleberries in an hour or catch half a pound of fish, then what the pound of fish really costs him is the two pounds of brambleberries he must forego for it.   To return to the peasant and the tractor, the opportunity cost to the peasant of the hours of labor that the tractor saves him may be zero because he cannot use the saved time productively.   In that case, the use of labor-saving capital goods is sheer waste.

The more general rule under which the peasant's case falls is that the most efficient combination of resources—efficiency being measured by costs—in the production of any goods is that which uses but little of the most costly resources and much of the cheaper resources.   In an economy where wages are high and the use of machinery is cheap, goods that technically could be produced either by hand work or by machine work, will tend to be produced by machine.   The converse would naturally hold in an economy where wages are low relative to the price of machinery.

The application of this rule explains, for instance, why Americans buy so many new cars.   The American motorists' buying habits are generally thought to be a manifestation of lightheadedness, a proof that the consumer is enslaved by advertisers, and an illustration of conformism.   By contrast, the tendency of motorists elsewhere to keep their cars for much longer stretches is supposed to result from a higher sobriety or more elevated taste.   All that may be; yet the contrast can be explained simply in terms of economic rationality.   In countries where labor is plentiful in comparison with producers' capital goods, the cheapest way to repair a car is by hand labor, that is, labor equipped with a minimal supply of simple tools. In a country like the United States, where labor is more expensive relative to capital goods, the cheapest way to keep a car up to a certain standard of performance is regularly to buy a new one from an automobile factory, where relatively little labor is combined with a vast supply of highly mechanized tools. The most efficient way to repair a car in the United States is to build a new car; the most efficient way to build a new car in most other places is to repair an old one.

In the same way it is equally sensible to build roads in the United States with bulldozers and diesel earthmovers and to build roads in China by using large gangs of laborers shifting gravel with no equipment other than picks, shovels and buckets. From the purely economic standpoint, to save much of that labor in China by using many bulldozers would be a sheer waste.

It is a fallacy, therefore, to believe that using more capital in any given enterprise is economically more efficient than using less. Capital goods, like other productive factors, are efficient only when they are properly allocated among all of the various uses to which they can be put.

The decision as to how much capital should be invested in any particular enterprise cannot be divorced from another decision, how much total capital a nation should accumulate, create or use.

At any given moment, to be sure, the amount of capital at a nation's disposal is not a matter of choice but of fact. Over any stretch of time, however, the amount can be expanded or contracted. Capital goods are produced, like all other goods, by the use of land, labor and capital. The only way a nation can by its own efforts expand its stock of capital goods, therefore, is by using resources that could otherwise have been devoted to making additional consumption goods. This interchangeability, in the production process, of capital goods and consumption goods is illustrated in a farmer's choice between eating his harvest and planting it as seed; the more he eats, the less he can plant; the more he uses for current consumption, the less he can use as capital. The monetary counterpart of this choice is that income can be spent on consumption goods, or set aside as savings; and in an economy that is working smoothly, the relative outputs of consumption goods and capital goods will match the ratio of consumption expenditures to savings.   All that the people of an underdeveloped economy need do to expand the national stock of capital is to consume less than they produce.   Leaving aside economic perturbations and peculiarities, the less they consume relative to current output, the faster their supply of capital will grow.

A slight defect in this prescription is that underdeveloped nations are so poor that they cannot generate much capital.   The income of a very poor man hardly suffices for the ordinary needs of life; he cannot be expected to restrict his consumption in favor of future benefits; his needs press too urgently to allow much concern for the future.   A man who is twenty and starving would be whimsical to invest in an annuity payable at sixty.   A nation full of such men would not rationally do much saving, hence would not generate much capital.   It would not, that is, if the voluntary individual choices of its citizens were allowed to prevail.

But the rate of capital formation in an underdeveloped economy can be speeded up by its government.   Suppose the citizens are on the average currently saving 5 per cent of their incomes.   If the government increases the tax rate and spends the added revenue on capital goods it can push the *national* savings rate, and the national rate of capital formation, up to any level it chooses short of the limit imposed by the size of national income.   Programs of forced savings have been instituted by the governments of many underdeveloped nations.   Insofar as the tax burden falls on the relatively wealthy citizens of those nations, the policy of forced savings is in effect a program of redistribution, open to approval or disapproval on the grounds generally applicable to schemes for equalizing income and wealth.   Unfortunately, however, in very poor economies the national rate of capital formation cannot be raised much by any level of taxation applied to the wealthy few.   Where that is the case, and it is probably a fairly typical case, the regime of forced savings may be extended to citizens who are poor absolutely, with the result that those who were already underfed are required to reduce their consumption further.   The offer held out to them is that by making this coerced sacrifice now, by foregoing current consumption in order that extra capital may be created, they are guaranteeing themselves a higher income at some future time.   But if it would be whimsical or mad for a very poor man voluntarily to save too much, it is surely whimsical or inhumane for a government to force him to save too much.   One reads with shock of the aged bachelor brothers discovered lying dead of starvation on mattresses stuffed with money;

the spectacle would be hardly more edifying had they died so because the state commandeered their income to build, for the national good, a splendid atomic power station.

There is still another way in which a nation can increase the supply of capital at its disposal, which is to borrow it from foreigners. This method, which has been used by underdeveloped nations for many centuries, is especially suitable since it can put at their disposal, quickly, capital far in excess of the amounts they could generate at home. Moreover, it is made feasible not only by the benevolence of foreign governments; the self-interest of foreign capitalists moves them, too, to invest in underdeveloped countries, for the rate of return in countries that as yet possess little capital is apt to be much higher than the rate capital can earn in richer economies. Unfortunately capital borrowed from private lenders is seldom or never received so warmly by the underdeveloped nation as when it is proffered to the government by other governments or international agencies. The reason is not only that public lenders are more likely to offer bargain rates. More often reluctance is dictated by the feeling that when foreigners invest in and own a country's facilities, especially its public services, they acquire too great a power in its political affairs. Whether this fear is realistic, and if realistic, so compelling that a nation should forego possibilities of more rapid enrichment in order to exclude the threat, is a question fruitless to consider in the abstract. It can be usefully answered, in concrete instances, only by the exercise of fine political prudence. As to the purely economic issue, there is no doubt that foreign financing is the quickest way for underdeveloped nations to expand their supply of capital. It is convenient, also, that transfers of capital, conceived as loans, sometimes end life as gifts.

To accumulate capital, no matter how a nation comes by it, means necessarily to defer current consumption. As men can be short-sighted, so too can they be excessively long-sighted; they can cheat the present as easily as they can cheat the future, and in that sense more capital is no better than less.

The third fallacy: More roads are better than fewer roads.

In this fallacy, "roads" stands as a symbol for all installations having to do with transportation and communications, or more broadly, all those commonly called public works. The fallacy urges that economic development is peculiarly dependent on a dense network of avenues and wires.

As all public works are capital goods, the general arguments given earlier as to getting and spending capital apply to them also.   It is urged in extenuation, however, that public works have a special character, indicated by the technical titles commonly assigned them, Infrastructure or Social Overhead Capital.

Roads are called "Social" capital not only because they are generally owned by and used by the public, but mainly because a road bestows benefits on persons who have never seen it, much less travelled it.   The parson in farthest Utah, as he drinks his morning's orange juice, drinks it cheaper because of a little road in Florida that enables the oranges to reach their market with less effort.   It can be said, of course, that though he has not travelled that road in the flesh, he has travelled it vicariously by the motion of those oranges he consumes.   Yet similar benefits will be realized also by persons who are utter strangers to the public improvement, such as the driver of a car who finds his journey to work eased because so many other commuters have taken to travel by subway, or the village gossip who sparing the expense of a telephone nevertheless feasts on the news it carries.   Every public facility does social good far outside the circle of its users.

A road is "Overhead" capital because the cost of the road does not vary with the services it provides.   Its cost is overhead in the same way that the cost of maintaining a factory building is no less or greater when the factory is working overtime than when it is standing idle. It is overhead cost by contrast with variable costs, such as the cost of the wood or labor that goes into table making, the total amount of it varying with the number of tables the factory constructs.

Because a road is overhead capital, and the amount of it required cannot be meted out in accordance with how intensely it is used, the investment required for it is said to be "lumpy."   Some considerable investment is needed to build a length of road, whether one man or a hundred were expected to walk on it during any day.   Moreover, the investment may take a long time to yield fruit.   From the first moment capital begins to be sunk in the building of the road until the road is bearing enough traffic to justify its cost, years may elapse.

Now because of these three characteristics imputed to roads and other such facilities—the large investment, the long time elapsing before the investment yields commensurate benefits, and the enjoyment of benefits by people who do not in any direct or ordinary sense "use" the facility —some experts argue that social overhead capital must necessarily be provided or subsidized by the state. They argue that private investors cannot or will not make such big investments, that they cannot or will not wait so long to start earning a return on their investment, and that in any event they cannot get a sufficient return on their investment because so many of the beneficiaries are unknown, or even if known, could not be required to pay for their benefits.

Let us consider the arguments in order. A road needs a big invest-ment, but private investors do not make big investments. But surely a big investment is only required for big roads. A short and narrow path does not need much capital. A long superhighway needs very much capital. But is it not surprising, then, that many of the biggest and longest superhighways in the United States, built by huge invest-ments of capital, were financed by private capital, accumulated by the sale of turnpike-authority bonds in the open, competitive, private bond market? If it is said that in no underdeveloped economy could private citizens provide the capital to finance such a project, it might be answered that no underdeveloped country needs such roads at this point in its development—its scarce stocks of capital can be put to much more efficient uses.

The second argument is that private individuals will not wait as long as is required to realize returns on such investments. There is much evidence to the contrary. A young man freshly awarded his Ph.D. can be thought of as a capital good into which investment has been poured for a quarter of a century before it even begins to yield any monetary return. Shortly thereafter, the young man will begin investing about 5 per cent of his income in life-insurance, an investment guaranteed, on the average, to pay no return until half a century later. Orchards bear no fruit for five to fifteen years after planting; yet many private men invest in orchards. Private lumber companies plant seedlings that will not be harvested for thirty years. It is not clear that the state has a monopoly of patience.

The third argument is that the benefits of roads leak off, as it were, to many people who do not use them; hence the private investor could not capture an adequate return from investment in roads. The premise that leakage of benefits takes place is undeniable; but in the context it is fallacious because it implies that this is a special characteristic of roads as contrasted with other capital goods or other commodities.   It is not special at all.   A small boy who buys a chocolate for a penny may feel that he has been favored by a gift from the gods; he would gladly have given three cents or seven, had it been demanded.   Every bargain in the eye of the buyer represents a leakage of benefits in the eye of the seller; the seller is prevented from charging a price exactly equal to the benefit only by force of the competition that presses prices down toward the cost of production.   Moreover, in private production it also regularly happens that benefits leak off to persons that were not privy to the transaction.   When the lady of fashion walks out in her latest creation, the boulevardier glories at the sight, but Mme. Chanel knows no way to levy a charge on him for the pleasure that her creation is occasioning.   Neither can my neighbor who plants a beautiful garden.

If leakage of benefits were a fatal objection to private industry, there could not be any private industry at all.   But private investors do not base their calculations on whether they can charge for *all* the utility their efforts give rise to, but only whether they can charge for enough to yield a suitable rate of return for the investment.   It is true that were the leakage exceptionally severe, private investors would be dissuaded from investing, *even though* the total of all benefits realized by the whole community might amply justify the investment.   In such cases, where the social benefit of an undertaking vastly exceeds the rate of return that the private investor could make it yield to him, there is occasion for the state to invest in the facility.   A prime instance is a lighthouse.

Yet the abstract case that can be made for state investment in such projects encounters one great difficulty in practical application.   The value of leaked benefits—or non-pecuniary social income—is difficult or impossible to assess: they are spread widely and nobody knows what precise value, in dollars, to attach to any one of them.   To make investments in such cases is risky because the poverty of information subjects government officials to error, but safe because the critics of government investment cannot conclusively demonstrate that the investment was wasteful.   For both reasons, the presumption ought to run against government investment in roads and other social facilities.   The existence of privately financed railroads, turnpikes, airlines, canals, telegraph companies, newspapers, radio and the like demonstrates that private investors have not refused to construct social overhead capital.

Although, if the building of all public facilities were left to private enterprise, there would almost certainly be somewhat too few of them; if government builds and operates them on a subsidy basis—that is, in such a way that the charges to direct users do not completely cover the costs —there will almost certainly be too many of them. This tendency will result inevitably from the fact that every individual has a private incentive to be subsidized by government, that is to have benefits conferred on him at the expense of other citizens. This incentive operates all the more forcibly to the extent that the citizens have been taught to make a sharp distinction between subsidies from government and subsidies from their fellow citizens; the former can be claimed proudly as of right; taking the latter could not fail to have an ethically dubious tone when the grantee knows that his fellow citizens are giving the gift under compulsion. It would be too much to say that every man looks forward with delight and an ardent sense of righteousness to receiving public subsidies; yet many do. Does the man living on top of a remote mountain doubt that his letters have an immutable right to be transported to the other end of the country for 5 cents, if that is the fee required of all other Americans, for instance of a New Yorker mailing an announcement to his next-door neighbor?

The private citizen demands that his government build better roads, better schools, better facilities of all sorts. There are many private citizens; taken together, they issue commands for facilities far beyond the resources available to satisfy them. Each, after all, is asking for something that would in fact benefit him considerably but that would cost him little or nothing. Would not the total demand for foodstuffs, housing, or automobiles be exorbitant if the price to the individual demanding it were a negligible part of its cost?

Faced with such demands, may not the government provide too much road? It is possible; to answer whether it is true would require a most exquisite calculation to determine whether the benefits to be realized by the community from an additional dollar invested in roads are at any moment greater or less than the benefits from that dollar's investment in any other capital good. The question cannot be answered.

But, since every one who talks about roads says that there are not enough roads, it is important to notice that there *can* be too many roads and that a democratic government may systematically err in favor of too many roads.

The fourth fallacy: Rapid economic development is better than slow economic development.

The need for rapidity is emphasized by those who point out that the impoverished masses in underdeveloped areas are impatient and that public impatience must lead to political disorder and perhaps to communism, unless it is soothed by quick and dramatic improvements in the standard of living.

Leaving aside important doubts as to whether the citizenry of the underdeveloped nations really are as impatient as all that, and whether the inevitable outcome of impatience is more likely to be political chaos than increased economic effort, one should nevertheless point out that the remedy proposed is impossible to achieve. It is impossible to accomplish simultaneously the *greatest* possible increase in the standard of living and the *speediest* increase.

The most feasible means—though neither a certain nor a unique means —to improve the standard of living is to build up one's stock of capital. But every addition to capital is necessarily made at the expense of current consumption; it is therefore impossible simultaneously to consume as much as possible in the present and to make the best possible arrangements for increasing future income. If a man wants to maximize consumption *this year,* he should consume all his current income and more: that behavior would reflect the extreme of impatience. If another one wants to maximize his consumption next year, ten years hence, or at any future date, he should consume nothing this year, next year, or any year up to the final one, but invest, invest, and invest; in the year when he finally turns to consumption, the income available to him will be the highest possible, a proper reward for uncommon patience. If one compares the standard of living of the two, it is clear that the first one is better off for each of the years while the other is biding his time and building his fortune, and after that the second is able to live much better. In short the *level* of consumption that can be achieved and the *speed* with which it is achieved stand in direct opposition to one another.

Economic policy, to be meaningful, must be based on a choice as to *when* the maximum level of consumption that the system is capable of producing should be achieved. To decide *when* is also to decide on *how high* the attainable level will be. These two variables are linked; they are the pans of a scale, and to raise one is necessarily to lower the other.

The choice of how much economic growth a nation should aim for and when it should start enjoying the fruits of that growth in increased consumption is not a single choice but a never-ending succession of choices. In order to make those choices rationally, a great array of tastes must be consulted. Each individual knows more or less well his own tastes about how much of his income he prefers to use now and how much he prefers to set aside for the future. It is not essential that this matter of individual choice be turned into a political question, to be decided by majority vote or the judgment of experts.

If rapidity of economic growth were not costly in terms of other human objectives, everyone should endorse it without qualification; as it is, no reasonable man can prefer it to the exclusion of all other goals. It is one of many objectives, and must be weighed against the rest.

However difficult and complex the whole problem of economic development is, one of its most confusing aspects is the difficulty of ascertaining exactly how poor the poor nations are.

There is no doubt that the standard methods of national-income accounting exaggerate their poverty. In rural and simple economies, people make for themselves many of the things that the inhabitants of complex industrialized economies do not make for themselves but buy from others. National income statistics usually and necessarily differentiate between goods exchanged in markets and identical goods that do not enter the market; the value of the former appearing in the total, the latter not. The textbook instance is that national income falls when a man marries his housekeeper, and rises when instead of shaving himself he goes to a barber. But in African villages, householders build their own huts; and throughout the underdeveloped world, neighbors sing and dance for each others' entertainment instead of going to concert halls to buy the services of paid performers. National income statistics cannot easily register the value of unbought services since those do not leave tangible traces in accounting records. The standard of living in non-industrial nations is therefore much understated by ordinary statistics.

This is all the more true because national income statistics cannot and do not take into account the value of leisure. Imagine two identical farms, each producing one thousand bushels of wheat in a year, the only difference being that one farmer works fourteen hours each day and the other somehow manages to do the work in six; from the standpoint of national income statistics, the two farmers would be enjoying identical incomes even though it is obvious that the true income of the second is very much greater if he attaches any positive value to leisure. Time free from labor is not necessarily leisure, as it may yield nothing but boredom or frustration; but it should be remembered that men who live in industrialized societies have very assiduously trained themselves to attach a lower value to leisure than men have at other times and places. To the extent that people in underdeveloped nations do attach a high value to leisure, the statistics badly understate their total incomes by leaving out of account the psychic, non-pecuniary components of their incomes.

A further consideration suggesting that the poverty of underdeveloped nations is different in character than we suppose, arises from the reflection that the poorest nations are almost all tropical and tropical nations are poor. Not much is made of this beyond the platitude that men do not thrive in extreme heat, but insects and bacteria do. It seems a more plausible generalization, however, that a perpetually warm climate is highly favorable to human life; it reduces man's need for food, clothing and shelter; and at the same time it puts in his hands throughout the year—and not only in one short season—a plentiful supply of plants and animals.

From this standpoint the economic civilization that northern peoples have developed is a colossal exercise in irony. Having deliberately planted themselves in inhospitable regions, they have been forced to overcome the hazards of nature by donning heavy clothing, erecting bulky housing, and forcing crops from a reluctant earth. Then, having made all those things, the need for which was imposed only by the unsuitable setting in which they perversely decided to live, they have weighed all those goods, and finding them many, they call themselves rich.

But, if by contrast the inhabitants of perpetually warm places have Nature as an ally, why are they in fact so poor? The answer, perhaps, is that only in warm places can people as poor as they continue to live.

It cannot be denied that in the underdeveloped nations, however high a value the inhabitants may assign to leisure and the other pleasures of a simple life, many of them are too poor to enjoy anything at all. The entirely laudable desire to help relieve them will not have been very effective if, in the rush for a remedy, it urges cures that eradicate old miseries only to install new miseries in their place. A physician carried away by the pain of the victim and the impatience of the victim's friends does not work at his best.

Lines of Inquiry
1 Letwin calls a fallacy "a truism that has been misunderstood."
Read the entry under "Fallacious Reasoning" in the Glossary.

a Could the fallacies discussed there be called "truisms that have been misunderstood"?

b Would it be logical or illogical to conclude that one should be suspicious of truisms?

c What kinds of statements need one not view with suspicion?

2 Letwin discusses four fallacies: (*1*) Manufacturing is more productive than agriculture. (*2*) More capital is better than less capital. (*3*) More roads are better than fewer roads. (*4*) Rapid economic development is better than slow economic development.

a Do you see any reason behind this specific sequence? (If you do not, try rearranging it.)

b Look at the opening paragraphs of each section in turn. What appears to be their function?

c The "four fallacies" are framed by an introductory and a concluding section: How are introduction and conclusion related to each other?

d How is the discussion of the last fallacy related to the point made in the conclusion?

3 Make an outline of the discussion of the first fallacy.

a How does Letwin connect one point of his argument to the next?   Bracket the pivotal sentences, and try reading through the sequence breaks without them.

b Look at the "historical sketch" that begins his discussion. How are its paragraphs linked?

4 What method of exposition is central to Letwin's opening paragraphs?   How does the sequence of discussion relate to that method?

5 Determine roughly the proportion of illustrations in this essay that make use of comparison and contrast.   How do you explain the result?

6 Go through this essay and mark all the illustrations that are clearly hypothetical.

a In what general circumstances do they occur?

b How many of them are phrased in terms of the activity of individuals (peasants, ladies of fashion, etc.)?

c How many of them represent extremes?   Why?

d Does there seem to be a characteristic *tone* to most of these hypothetical examples? (Note the illustration that begins "A poor savage. . . .")

e Is this tone related in any way to the introduction and/or conclusion?

7 The essay ends with an analogy. To what effect? Try a few other analogies in its place. Do they work as well? Why, or why not?

8 This essay first appeared in *Daedalus,* the journal of the American Academy of Arts and Sciences. *Daedalus* is published for an intelligent but diversely trained and interested audience. How does this audience appear to affect Letwin's use of illustrations? Suppose that the audience consisted of trained economists. What would happen to the pattern of illustrations?

Lines of Experiment

1 Review the discussion of fallacies, in the Glossary. Write a brief essay exposing and evaluating a fallacious idea well known to you. Suggestion: Look for truisms such as "clothes make the man," "there are two sides to every question," "education is the gateway of success," "honesty is the best policy."

2 Imagine an essay entitled "Three Fallacies about Education." List five such fallacies, then choose three to write about. Why those three? Under each fallacy, outline the sequence of ideas you would write about and the illustrations you would use to clarify and support those ideas before you begin. *Then* write the appropriate introduction.

3 Choose a specific subject—e.g., The Population Explosion, Automobiles, Food at School, Saddle Horses, Summer Vacations, Gardening, Basketball—and write down about that subject at least three general ideas that you feel prepared to defend (e.g., there are far too many people in the world; food at school is a never-ending surprise; the automobile is a necessity; vacations are boring). Then give five illustrations for each statement, each of a different kind (extreme case, average case, series of averages, hypothetical case, comparison or contrast, or analogy). For each statement choose those that seem most successful: Why are they so? What relationship does this type have to the type of statement it illustrates? Why did the others fail? At what point did you have too many illustrations for a given idea?

You now have the best part of three original compositions. Choose the statement for which you have found the best illustrations, and write.

ALDOUS HUXLEY

 USUALLY
DESTROYED

Our guide through the labyrinthine streets of Jerusalem was a young Christian refugee from the other side of the wall which now divides the ancient city from the new, the non-viable state of Jordan from the non-viable state of Israel.   He was a sad, embittered young man—and well he might be.   His prospects had been blighted, his family reduced from comparative wealth to the most abject penury, their house and land taken away from them, their bank account frozen and devaluated. In the circumstances, the surprising thing was not his bitterness, but the melancholy resignation with which it was tempered.

He was a good guide—almost too good, indeed; for he was quite remorseless in his determination to make us visit all those deplorable churches which were built, during the nineteenth century, on the ruins of earlier places of pilgrimage.   There are tourists whose greatest pleasure is a trip through historical associations and their own fancy. I am not one of them.   When I travel, I like to move among intrinsically significant objects, not through an absence peopled only by literary references, Victorian monuments and the surmises of archaeologists. Jerusalem, of course, contains much more than ghosts and architectural monstrosities.   Besides being one of the most profoundly depressing of the earth's cities, it is one of the strangest and, in its own way, one of the most beautiful.   Unfortunately our guide was far too conscientious to spare us the horrors and the unembodied, or ill-embodied, historical associations.   We had to see everything—not merely St. Anne's and St. James's and the Dome of the Rock, but the hypothetical site of Caiaphas's house and what the Anglicans had built in the seventies, what the Tsar and the German Emperor had countered with in the eighties, what had been considered beautiful in the early nineties by the Copts or the French Franciscans.   But, luckily, even at the dreariest moments of our pilgrimage there were compensations.   Our sad young man spoke English well and fluently, but spoke it as eighteenth-century virtuosi played music—with the addition of *fioriture* and even whole cadenzas of their own invention.   His most significant contribution to colloquial English (and, at the same time, to the science and art of history) was the insertion into almost every sentence of the word "usually." What he actually meant by it, I cannot imagine.   It may be, of course, that he didn't mean anything at all, and that what sounded like an adverb was in fact no more than one of those vocalized tics to which nervous persons are sometimes subject. I used to know a professor whose lectures and conversations were punctuated, every few seconds, by the phrase, "With a thing with a thing." "With a thing with a thing" is manifestly gibberish.   But our young friend's no less compulsive "usually" had a fascinating way of making a kind of sense —much more sense, very often, than the speaker had intended.   "This area," he would say as he showed us one of the Victorian monstrosities, "this area" [it was one of his favorite words] "is very rich in antiquity. St. Helena built here a very vast church, but the area was usually destroyed by the Samaritans in the year 529 after Our Lord Jesus Christ.   Then the Crusaders came to the area, and built a new church still more vast.   Here were mosaics the most beautiful in the world. In the seventeenth century after Our Lord Jesus Christ the Turks usually removed the lead from the roof to make ammunition; consequently rain entered the area and the church was thrown down.   The present area was erected by the Prussian Government in the year 1879 after Our Lord Jesus Christ and all these broken-down houses you see over there were usually destroyed during the war with the Jews in 1948."

Usually destroyed and then usually rebuilt, in order, of course, to be destroyed again and then rebuilt, *da capo ad infinitum*.   That vocalized tic had compressed all history into a four-syllabled word.   Listening to our young friend, as we wandered through the brown, dry squalor of the Holy City, I felt myself overwhelmed, not by the mere thought of man's enduring misery, but by an obscure, immediate sense of it, an organic realization.   These pullulations among ruins and in the dark of what once were sepulchers; these hordes of sickly children; these galled asses and the human beasts of burden bent under enormous loads; these mortal enemies beyond the dividing wall; these priest-conducted groups of pilgrims befuddling themselves with the vain repetitions, against which the founder of their religion had gone out of his way to warn them—they were dateless, without an epoch.   In this costume or that, under one master or another, praying to whichever God was temporarily in charge, they had been here from the beginning. Had been here with the Egyptians, been here with Joshua, been here when Solomon in all his glory ordered his slaves in all their misery to build the temple, which Nebuchadnezzar had usually demolished and Zedekiah, just as usually, had put together again. Had been here during the long pointless wars between the two kingdoms, and at the next destruction under Ptolemy, the next but one under Antiochus and the next rebuilding under Herod and the biggest, best destruction of all by Titus. Had been here when Hadrian abolished Jerusalem and built a brand-new Roman city, complete with baths and a theater, with a temple of Jupiter, and a temple of Venus, to take its place. Had been here when the insurrection of Bar Cocheba was drowned in blood. Had been here while the Roman Empire declined and turned Christian, when Chosroes the Second destroyed the churches and when the Caliph Omar brought Islam and, most unusually, destroyed nothing. Had been here to meet the Crusaders and then to wave them good-by, to welcome the Turks and then to watch them retreat before Allenby. Had been here under the Mandate and through the troubles of '48, and were here now and would be here, no doubt, in the same brown squalor, alternately building and destroying, killing and being killed, indefinitely.

"I do not think," Lord Russell has recently written, "that the sum of human misery has ever in the past been so great as it has been in the last twenty-five years." One is inclined to agree. Or are we, on second thoughts, merely flattering ourselves? At most periods of history moralists have liked to boast that theirs was the most iniquitous genera-tion since the time of Cain—the most iniquitous and therefore, since God is just, the most grievously afflicted. Today, for example, we think of the thirteenth century as one of the supremely creative periods of human history. But the men who were actually contemporary with the cathedrals and Scholastic Philosophy regarded their age as hopelessly degenerate, uniquely bad and condignly punished. Were they right, or are we? The answer, I suspect is: Both. Too much evil and too much suffering can make it impossible for men to be creative; but within very wide limits greatness is perfectly compatible with organized insanity, sanctioned crime and intense, chronic unhappiness for the majority. Every one of the great religions preaches a mixture of pro-found pessimism and the most extravagant optimism. "I show you sorrow," says the Buddha, pointing to man in his ordinary unregenerate condition. And in the same context Christian theologians speak of the Fall, of Original Sin, of the Vale of Tears, while Hindus refer to the workings of man's home-made destiny, his evil karma. But over against the sorrow, the tears, the self-generated, self-inflicted disasters, what superhuman prospects! If he so wishes, the Hindu affirms, a man can realize his identity with Brahman, the Ground of all being; if he so wishes, says the Christian, he can be filled with God; if he so wishes, says the Buddhist, he can live in a transfigured world where nirvana and samsara, the eternal and the temporal, are one. But, alas—and from optimism based on the experience of the few, the saints and sages return to the pessimism forced upon them by their observation of the many— the gate is narrow, the threshold high, few are chosen because few choose to be chosen. In practice man usually destroys himself—but has done so up till now a little less thoroughly than he has built himself up. In spite of everything, we are still here. The spirit of destruction has been willing enough, but for most of historical time its technological flesh has been weak. The Mongols had only horses as transport, only bows and spears and butchers' knives for weapons; if they had possessed our machinery, they could have depopulated the planet. As it was, they had to be content with small triumphs—the slaughter of only a few millions, the stamping out of civilization only in Western Asia.

In this universe of ours nobody has ever succeeded in getting anything for nothing. In certain fields, progress in the applied sciences and the arts of organization has certainly lessened human misery; but it has done so at the cost of increasing it in others. The worst enemy of life, freedom and the common decencies is total anarchy; their second worst enemy is total efficiency. Human interests are best served when society is tolerably well organized and industry moderately advanced. Chaos and ineptitude are anti-human; but so too is a superlatively efficient government, equipped with all the products of a highly developed technology. When such a government goes in for usually destroying, the whole race is in danger.

The Mongols were the aesthetes of militarism; they believed in gratuitous massacre, in destruction for destruction's sake. Our malice is less pure and spontaneous; but, to make up for this deficiency, we have ideals. The end proposed, on either side of the Iron Curtain, is nothing less than the Good of Humanity and its conversion to the Truth. Crusades can go on for centuries, and wars in the name of God or Humanity are generally diabolic in their ferocity. The unprecedented depth of human misery in our time is proportionate to the unprecedented height of the social ideals entertained by the totalitarians on the one side, the Christians and the secularist democrats on the other.

And then there is the question of simple arithmetic. There are far more people on the earth today than there were in any earlier century. The miseries which have been the usual consequence of the usual course of nature and the usual behavior of human beings are the lot today, not of the three hundred millions of men, women and children who were contemporary with Christ, but of more than two and a half billions. Obviously, then, the sum of our present misery cannot fail to be greater than the sum of misery in the past. Every individual is the center of a world, which it takes very little to transform into a world of un-adulterated suffering. The catastrophes and crimes of the twentieth century can transform almost ten times as many human universes into private hells as did the catastrophes and crimes of two thousand years ago. Moreover, thanks to improvements in technology, it is possible for fewer people to do more harm to greater numbers than ever before.

After the capture of Jerusalem by Nebuchadnezzar, how many Jews were carried off to Babylon? Jeremiah puts the figure at four thousand six hundred, the compiler of the Second Book of Kings at ten thousand. Compared with the forced migrations of our time, the Exile was the most trivial affair. How many millions were uprooted by Hitler and the Communists? How many more millions were driven out of Pakistan into India, out of India into Pakistan? How many hundreds of thousands had to flee, with our young guide, from their homes in Israel? By the waters of Babylon ten thousand at the most sat down and wept. In the single refugee camp at Bethlehem there are more exiles than that. And Bethlehem's is only one of dozens of such camps scattered far and wide over the Near East.

So it looks, all things considered, as though Lord Russell were right— that the sum of misery is indeed greater today than at any time in the past. And what of the future? Germ warfare and the H-bomb get all the headlines and, for that very reason, may never be resorted to. Those who talk a great deal about suicide rarely commit it. The greatest threat to happiness is biological. There were about twelve hundred million people on the planet when I was born, six years before the turn of the century. Today there are two thousand seven hundred millions; thirty years from now there will probably be four thousand millions. At present about sixteen hundred million people are underfed. In the nineteen-eighties the total may well have risen to twenty-five hundred millions, of whom a considerable number may actually be starving. In many parts of the world famine may come even sooner. In his Report on the Census of 1951 the Registrar General of India has summed up the biological problem as it confronts the second most populous country of the world. There are now three hundred and seventy-five million people living within the borders of India, and their numbers increase by five millions annually. The current production of basic foods is seventy million tons a year, and the highest production that can be achieved in the foreseeable future is ninety-four million tons. Ninety-four million tons will support four hundred and fifty million people at the present substandard level, and the population of India will pass the four hundred and fifty million mark in 1969. After that, there will be a condition of what the Registrar General calls "catastrophe."

In the index at the end of the sixth volume of Dr. Toynbee's *A Study of History,* Popilius Laenas gets five mentions and Porphyry of Batamaea, two; but the word you would expect to find between these names, Population, is conspicuous by its absence. In his second volume, Mr. Toynbee has written at length on "the stimulus of pressures"—but without ever mentioning the most important pressure of them all, the pressure of population on available resources. And here is a note in which the author describes his impressions of the Roman Campagna after twenty years of absence. "In 1911 the student who made the pilgrimage of the Via Appia Antica found himself walking through a wilderness almost from the moment when he passed beyond the City Walls. . . . When he repeated the pilgrimage in 1931, he found that, in the interval, Man had been busily reasserting his mastery over the whole stretch of country that lies between Rome and the Castelli Romani. . . . The tension of human energy on the Roman Campagna is now beginning to rise again for the first time since the end of the third century B.C." And there the matter is left, without any reference to the compelling reason for this "rise of tension." Between 1911 and 1931 the population of Italy had increased by the best part of eight millions. Some of these eight millions went to live in the Roman Campagna. And they did so, not because Man with a large M had in some mystical way increased the tension of human energy, but for the sufficiently obvious reason that there was nowhere else for them to go. In terms of a history that takes no cognizance of demographical facts, the past can never be fully understood, the present is quite incomprehensible and the future entirely beyond prediction.

Thinking, for a change, in demographic as well as in merely cultural, political and religious terms, what kind of reasonable guesses can we make about the sum of human misery in the years to come?   First, it seems pretty certain that more people will be hungrier and that, in many parts of the world, malnutrition will modulate into periodical or chronic famine.   (One would like to know something about the Famines of earlier ages, but the nearest one gets to them in Mr. Toynbee's index is a blank space between Muhammad Falak-al-Din and Gaius Fannius.) Second, it seems pretty certain that, though they may help in the long run, remedial measures aimed at reducing the birthrate will be powerless to avert the miseries lying in wait for the next generation.   Third, it seems pretty certain that improvements in Agriculture (not referred to in Mr. Toynbee's index, though Agrigentum gets two mentions and Agis IV, King of Sparta, no less than forty-seven) will be unable to catch up with current and foreseeable increases in population.   If the standard of living in industrially backward countries is to be improved, agricultural production will have to go up every single year by at least two and a half per cent, and preferably by three and a half per cent. Instead of which, according to the FAO, Far Eastern food production per head of population will be ten per cent less in 1956 (and this assumes that the current Five-Year Plans will be fully realized) than it was in 1938.

Fourth, it seems pretty certain that, as a larger and hungrier population "mines the soil" in a desperate search for food, the destructive processes of erosion and deforestation will be speeded up.   Fertility will therefore tend to go down as human numbers go up.   (One looks up Erosion in Mr. Toynbee's index but finds only Esarhaddon, Esotericism and Esperanto; one hunts for Forests, but has to be content, alas, with Formosus of Porto.)

Fifth, it seems pretty certain that the increasing pressure of population upon resources will result in increasing political and social unrest, and that this unrest will culminate in wars, revolutions and counter-revolutions.

Sixth, it seems pretty certain that, whatever the avowed political principles and whatever the professed religion of the societies concerned, increasing pressure of population upon resources will tend to increase the power of the central government and to diminish the liberties of individual citizens.   For, obviously, where more people are competing for less food, each individual will have to work harder and longer for his ration, and the central government will find it necessary to intervene more and more frequently in order to save the rickety economic machine from total breakdown, and at the same time to repress the popular discontent begotten by deepening poverty.

If Lord Russell lives to a hundred and twenty (and, for all our sakes, I hope most fervently that he will), he may find himself remembering these middle decades of the twentieth century as an almost Golden Age.   In 1954, it is true, he decided that the sum of human misery had never been so great as it had been in the preceding quarter century. On the other hand, "you ain't seen nuthin' yet." Compared with the sum of four billion people's misery in the eighties, the sum of two billion miseries just before, during and after the Second World War may look like the Earthly Paradise.

But meanwhile here we were in Jerusalem, looking at the usually destroyed antiquities and rubbing shoulders with the usually poverty-stricken inhabitants, the usually superstitious pilgrims.   Here was the Wailing Wall, with nobody to wail at it; for Israel is on the other side of a barrier, across which there is no communication except by occasional bursts of rifle fire, occasional exchanges of hand grenades.   Here, propped up with steel scaffolding, was the Church of the Holy Sepulchre —that empty tomb to which, for three centuries, the early Christians paid no attention whatsoever, but which came, after the time of Constantine, to be regarded, throughout Europe, as the most important thing in the entire universe.   And here was Siloam, here St. Anne's, here the Dome of the Rock and the site of the Temple, here, more ominous than Pompeii, the Jewish quarter, leveled, usually, in 1948 and not yet usually reconstructed.   Here, finally, was St. James's, of the Armenians, gay with innumerable rather bad but charming paintings, and a wealth of gaudily colored tiles.   The great church glowed like a dim religious merry-go-round.   In all Jerusalem it was the only oasis of cheerfulness.   And not alone of cheerfulness.   As we came out into the courtyard, through which the visitor must approach the church's main entrance, we heard a strange and wonderful sound.   High up, in one of the houses surrounding the court, somebody was playing the opening Fantasia of Bach's Partita in A Minor—playing it, what was more, remarkably well.   From out of the open window, up there on the third floor, the ordered torrent of bright pure notes went streaming out over the city's immemorial squalor.   Art and religion, philosophy and science, morals and politics—these are the instruments by means of which men have tried to discover a coherence in the flux of events, to impose an order on the chaos of experience. The most intractable of our experiences is the experience of Time—the intuition of duration, combined with the thought of perpetual perishing. Music is a device for working directly upon the experience of Time. The composer takes a piece of raw, undifferentiated duration and extracts from it, as the sculptor extracts the statue from his marble, a complex pattern of tones and silences, of harmonic sequences and contrapuntal interweavings. For the number of minutes it takes to play or listen to his composition, duration is transformed into something intrinsically significant, something held together by the internal logics of style and temperament, of personal feelings interacting with an artistic tradition, of creative insights expressing themselves within and beyond some given technical convention. This Fantasia, for example—with what a tireless persistence it drills its way through time! How effectively—and yet with no fuss, no self-conscious heroics—it transfigures the mortal lapse through time into the symbol, into the very fact, of a more than human life! A tunnel of joy and understanding had been driven through chaos and was demonstrating, for all to hear, that perpetual perishing is also perpetual creation. Which was precisely what our young friend had been telling us, in his own inimitable way, all the time. Usually destroyed—but also, and just as often, usually rebuilt. Like the rain, like sunshine, like the grace of God and the devastations of Nature, his verbalized tic was perfectly impartial. We walked out of the courtyard and down the narrow street. Bach faded, a donkey brayed, there was a smell of undisposed sewage. "In the year of Our Lord 1916," our guide informed us, "the Turkish Government usually massacred approximately seven hundred and fifty thousand Armenians."

Lines of Inquiry

1 Read the introductory (first two) and concluding (last) paragraphs of Huxley's essay.

a How is introduction related to conclusion?

b What happens to the essay after the second paragraph?

c What would be the effect on the essay if the last paragraph were left out?

d Underline the phrase "usually destroyed" each time it occurs in these paragraphs. Why does Huxley quote the guide's use of the phrase several times in the first paragraph—would once have served as well? Why does he use it again at the end? Is its effect there different from its effect in the beginning?

2 a What is the central illustration of the essay, and how is it related to the essay's total structure?

b For convenience we may distinguish emotional significance from rational significance. Which kind of significance does this central illustration illustrate? The introduction to this section discusses several different types of illustration: Is the kind of point this central illustration tries to make connected in any way to its type?

c Some of Huxley's illustrations have an emotional point and others have a rational point. Some of them spring directly from his personal experience, are personal in nature, and others are impersonal in nature. Which kind of illustration, the personal or the impersonal, would seem best adapted to carry an emotional significance?

3 a Of the types of illustration discussed in the introduction to this part—the average, the extreme, the hypothetical, and so on—which type is most frequent in this essay, and why?

b How does the last paragraph reflect Huxley's predominant use of the one type of illustration?

4 a The central part of this essay makes a great deal of use of gross numbers; why?

b Why is the last sentence the only point in the essay in which the guide himself offers a quantitative measure of catastrophe? What would be lost if the last sentence were changed to read, " 'In the year of Our Lord 1916,' our guide informed us, 'the Turkish government usually massacred many Armenians' "?

5 Huxley makes considerable use of the index to Toynbee's *A Study of History.*

a Why does Huxley illustrate his point about Toynbee's several oversights by citing the historian's index, instead of simply saying that Toynbee omitted to discuss population, famine, agriculture, etc. Would the latter kind of illustration be weaker *logically* than that actually employed by Huxley?

b Why does Huxley refer to Toynbee at all? Try omitting all the references to Toynbee; what are the consequences? Try grouping them together in a single paragraph; what are the consequences?

6 Go through the essay and mark the paragraphs with the largest number of incomplete sentences.

a Where in the essay do these paragraphs occur?

b What happens to the emotional tension of the essay at these points?

c Do you find anything else unusual in the syntax or vocabulary of these passages—repetition, for example?

7 One might express the line of emotional tension in a tragedy by a gradually rising and swiftly descending line, in this fashion:

The initial ascent is the opening or exposition of the drama. The slowly ascending plateau is its development or complication.   The highest point of the line is its climax, and the abrupt descent is its catastrophe.   Can you draw a line of like type— though perhaps showing a different kind of emotional movement—to reflect the development of emotional tension in this essay?

8 Huxley's essay is essentially about the meaning of history. One of the faults he finds with Toynbee's study is that it takes "no cognizance of demographical facts" and therefore is unequipped to understand past, present, and future—to perform the task of the historian. How is the sequence of Huxley's own essay related to this task?

9 The following details of Huxley's tour of Jerusalem are not given. Why?
a The number and identity of the people in Huxley's party
b The name and appearance of the guide, and how Huxley came to hire him
c How Huxley happened to be in Jerusalem and where he stayed while there
d How long his tour took
e What they traveled around the city in
f What Jerusalem's government was like

Lines of Experiment
1 In "Usually Destroyed" Huxley tries to answer possibly the largest question we have to ask: What is the ultimate worth of all the tragedies of human history? For both question and answer, Jerusalem provides a complex illustrative frame.

Frequently an extended illustrative frame of this kind—a city, a church, a group of government buildings, a reform school, a college campus, a convention, a military campaign—can provide the most effective way of rendering such a theme in specific terms.   Here are five somewhat less grand but still highly general subjects that may suggest a congenial topic:
a Is democracy worthwhile?

b Why children leave home.
c The use of poetry.
d What is education for?
e Freedom of speech.
f Love and happiness.

For the one you choose, find an illustrative frame that will permit you to give to your central idea some kind of vivid appearance.

The structure of "Usually Destroyed" may well offer useful hints in your own composition. What illustration can you use to pose the question you intend to answer? What illustration can you use to answer it? (Illustrations that spring from your own experience can bring fairly abstract questions and answers down to a real, immediate, and personal level.)

2 Take a memorable experience in your own life—a trip to a national park, an adventure in a rowboat, a session in court, a championship game, a tour of a foreign country, a transfer to a new school, an embarrassing accident—and decide what made it memorable. Your analysis should produce a kernel of ideas that can serve well as the center for an essay. The experience itself can provide you with an illustrative frame for the larger discussion of those ideas—even as Huxley's tour of Jerusalem offers him a frame for discussing the meaning of history. The important things here will be: (*a*) the selection of a few central illustrative scenes, (*b*) the rendering of those scenes in vivid detail, so that what ordinarily would seem strange to the reader is made familiar, and (*c*) a broadening of the discussion and a drawing out of its large implications. Prior to everything, of course, is thought about the experience itself; but if you do not know what you think, try to write the illustrative frame first. Once you have found your answer, cut out the inessential parts of your illustration.

H. M. TOMLINSON

 A LOST WOOD

A critic of letters was explaining the French Romantics and he dismissed, with but an impatient gesture, a suggestion by one of us that Rousseau was a harbinger of the Revolution. Literature, so the critic said, could do less to cause a general uproar than dear bread. Books, one gathered from the critic, and he knew more of them than did we who listened, were quite unrelated to the emotions of the multitude, which discharged in thunder and lightning provoked no more by letters than by daisy-chains.

The critic may have been right. I expect the change in us wrought by poetry is so slow in showing that when the transmutation is complete we know of no change. We cannot see what has happened to us. The poet, having done in his brief life his best, may get what comfort he can out of that. We are certainly obstinate in our old ways, conservative with flint arrowheads or any other familiar notion, and unmoved by revolutions which come about in imperceptible degrees. Could Sinai itself impose its revelation on a climber who was no Moses? All most of us would know at the summit of Sinai would be the uncomfortable draught sweeping barren rocks.

It is probable, we are forced to confess, that a few years of petrol have made a greater difference in the world of men than all the poets since Homer. To judge by the reformed highways and byways of England, and the talk of our neighbours, petrol has moved us more than all our converse with great literature. Petrol is more popular than religion, and whirls to delight a vast multitude of people who would remain as unaffected by Bach as a congregation of penguins. If the test were made, perhaps a little argument directed towards the choice of the right sort of motor-car might more easily raise a group of people to eloquence than an insult to the Trinity. Petrol is even dissolving the face of the English landscape. We are exchanging our woodlands for tarmac, and although tarmac is known to be kind to rubber tyres, yet its tolerance is hardly sufficient to compensate for the loss of swathes of orchards, meadows, and ancient buildings. One does not complain about this, for it would be just as foolish to complain of the untimeliness of a change in the wind.

Yet regret and disquietude, despite the improvements we are making in our condition, remain with us, for occasionally we remember our poets, and what inspired them to sing to us. Once there was a scrap of Surrey, which I had grown to accept as casually as one does those things whose importance is seen when they are gone. I think it was only common English countryside. There was nothing in it that a building contractor should desire it. Nobody with an eye to the future saw anything there. Its gravel soil was not worth an advertisement. It had only a desultory lane, with walnut, lime, and beech trees, and on a morning in late summer you were not likely to meet anything in it but a farm wagon laden with dried peppermint; mint and lavender were cultivated locally, and our only factories had stills for the extraction of the essences of herbs. The smell in the wake of that wagon on a hot day was a surprising suggestion of the virtue of Surrey earth.

I could not say the war began to change it, but it seems so. I do know that one part of the land, and corn grew there, through which the lane meandered, became very swiftly an aerodrome; and the aerodrome has not yet convinced me that it is better to see flying machines at their graceful evolutions than a field of wheat with a little wind and much sun on it. Alas, we were too busy then to consider in calmness the nature of the changes we were bringing about. I remember that, in the years of long ago, before we were even educated as far as the signs of Zeppelins by night, we had neighbouring ponds fed by springs in the chalk. At the bottom of one deep, transparent pool you could see a spring uprising; shadows coiled in the beryl. That was where, within twelve miles of Charing Cross, we watched a pair of kingfishers feeding their six youngsters; the babies sat in a row on an osier twig, which was oblique with their weight. The darting blue and chestnut of those neighbours of ours greatly distinguished us. One lucky young friend of mine saw in the same secluded grove, and as late as the days of the air-raids, a golden oriole. He still remembers it. To hear him talk of that wonderful visitor you might suppose that one day on his way home from school, where he had been learning of the brave things that were, he had surprised a dryad, who slipped into the bushes, but not before he could name her. Does Apollo live? So much was possible to him, that day.

Does he live? Well, not there; not now. Petrol has acted like magic on the place. Miraculous stuff, petrol! But the kingfishers do not like it. Nor does the lane wander any more. It has been disciplined, and we know how good is discipline. The lane is broad, it is direct. It has no dust, and has lost its smell of herbs. The old walnut trees do not lean over broken pales there. There are no trees. The lane has become a straight road with a surface like polished ebony. It is, in fact, a highway for motor-cars. It becomes dangerous every Sunday morning with an endless flying procession of engines on their way to the coast; the chain reverses towards evening. We do not hear the corncrake any more, when coolness and silence fall at eventide; we hear klaxons. We have no peppermint fields; we have filling stations. Our springs and ponds, owing to an increase in the value of gravel sites, have lapsed into areas of mud which cannot determine to dry completely, and are desolate with discarded tins. As for the golden oriole, you might as well look for a seraph. Petrol has achieved all that. We do not say a word against it, but merely point to the fact. It would be just as useful to interrupt, as a protest, the line of cars flying to the coast on a Sunday, in a moment of desperation and anger. There the cars are; they move faster than peppermint wagons, and modern youth often steers them in a fashion that mocks mortality.

It is easy to understand the popularity of petrol. As a stimulant it is taking the place of beer and whisky. Rousseau may not have helped to cause a revolution, but there is no doubt about the common emotion which petrol evokes. Petrol is taken, not in the hope that it will transport us to any better place, but merely that it will remove us swiftly from where we are. It is the latest anodyne in these years of discontent and irresolution. It would be ridiculous to expect us to know what we ought to do, for we do not always know what we want to do. Petrol settles the difficulty. We get into a car, and start the explosions within its powerful engine; then we are compelled to do something. We join an endless line of headlong vehicles, and to continue to be irresolute would be perilous. Last summer I trudged over a road, once a by-path in the West of England which a tramp could have to himself for most of a long day. I hoped to meet there a ghost or two from the past, because they used to know that road very well; and they might turn up, if the news got to them that I was there again. But I did not meet them. I met instead a procession of astonishing charabancs, some from Manchester, others from Birmingham, and one from as far as Glasgow. There was no room for a pedestrian but in the drains by the roadside, where he had to stride for safety through soiled nettles and briars. The local inns were no longer places of refreshment and gossip. About one of those inns, and I had had my mind set on it for an hour, a dozen huge social cars were parked. The road was bright with pools of black grease. The orchard of the inn was sad, through traffic for which orchards are not grown. And no room could be had at the bar, nor elsewhere within, for an idle traveller who had time to waste; other travellers were there, continually arriving and departing. They had no time to waste. Yet these travellers of the new kind appeared to be satisfied merely with travelling. They knew not why they were there; they had paid their fares. They stood about, waiting for the signal that they were to be whirled on again, with their backs to a land which is as good as most in Europe. They did not look at it. It did not exist in its reality for them; it was only on their route. They were satisfied with the knowledge that they were there; they could prove it with picture-postcards which could be bought at the inn counter.

Very early one morning, when on a voyage from the East, I was startled from sleep by a seaman. He had switched on my cabin light; it was summer, but he stood there chilling the cabin with his wet overcoat. What was wrong?

"Nothing, sir; the chief officer wants you on the bridge."

I went up hurriedly, in pyjamas and oilskins. Day had not come, but it was not night; night was lifted slightly in the east on a wedge of rose, though the wind was still bleak out of darkness. We were somewhere near the Burlings. What was this? My friend the chief officer pointed astern without a word. We were passing a ghost ship, under all canvas. The barque was so close that I could see the length of her deck. She was silent, and more pale than the twilight. She was tall, and tinctured faintly with rose. Had we steamed back into another age? Was the past so near? I could see two men on her poop, but they were not looking at us. Only my friend, and the bridge of our liner, were material. My friend spoke. "I thought you would like to see her; it may be the last time. Isn't she a beauty?"

Even with my eye still on the receding barque I felt that sailor's behaviour was more curious than what he had wakened me to watch.

His jacket, I had noticed, bore a row and a half of decorations won in war; he was a hard and busy officer; he infested that great liner like a stern challenge whose whereabouts was uncertain until he strode round a corner, and then he never stopped unless there was something which must be said. This unexpected tenderness of his for what was hardly more than a gracious apparition in a delusive hour surprised me; yet he had been so sure, without reason, that I, too, would have the eye to see the spectre, that he had summoned me from bed into the hour when there is no courage. We stood talking up aloft till the sun came and saw us.

So, though I dare not deny the critic who mocked the power of poetry to work upon us to as good a purpose as starvation, yet perhaps he was too trifling with the spell of what is imponderable. Our mutability, like the wind which bloweth where it listeth, is subject to sorceries having the necessity of the very laws which send zephyrs or hurricanes out of the immane. How often has a fond memory or sentiment, so doubtfully valid in garish daylight that we would not show it to a friend, decided us to an enterprise? And we were right. For that reason, the older we get, the more we doubt the obvious clue to any story; we have found too often that what was unrevealed at the time was more potent than anything we heard when the knowing people were explaining it. But for a barque appearing near us one morning, I should have thought my friend the chief officer was no more open to zephyrs and faint hints than the steel under us. That steel was obvious and compelling, and he was part of it. And after that voyage he sent a letter to me, disclosing a burden which not for a moment did I suspect a modern liner to carry. He was glad, he explained, to get out of London again. He called his steamer's bridge, which to me seemed to govern affairs large and complex enough to require a borough council for their management, his sanctuary. He showed a repulsion from our city which was as spontaneous and unreasonable as would be a mahatma's from a riot. He said his bridge, in the morning watch, was the only place where he could meet himself. He warned me that in London I should never meet myself. London frightened him. London was on no course. London was adrift. Its size and unrest were so like delirium that he ran from it. "Those new buildings you've got, they're Egyptian I tell you, they're horrible. Something has gone wrong with you if you like them. You'd better look out. They squat on the mind, ugly square masses, like tombs. I don't want to be under them as though

I had no name, drifting at the bottom of them with the drainage of life which doesn't know where it is going. It doesn't, does it?" He said he only found himself again when watching his ship's head grow bright in the dawn, and nothing in sight but the empty sea and the sun. Then he knew his name belonged to him, and what he was doing, and why he was doing it, to some extent.

Perhaps rebellion comes as much as anything from the sense that, as a unit in the paraphernalia of the State, one's identity is lost. A slave may have a soul, and possess it in patience, but not an automaton. Made homogenous by machinery, we are the nation, and anonymous. And when our governing machines, multiplying and expanding, claiming greater space for their wheels, flatten and unify still more the ancient, varied, and familiar things which we did not know were good till they had gone, we learn why the soul is now a myth. We become a little fearful and desperate. It is as though a chilling air were felt from unseen ice gradually advancing, warning of another glacial age, to put our name and works with the Neanderthalers. We rebel from the suggestion that we must go under the cold mass of a mindless necessity.

It was April; and that was a disturbing letter to receive when the primroses were due. I had no chance to reassure myself of my name by watching a ship's head grow bright in a broad dawn. It was Egypt for me, and the compelling rod. All I could do was to rebel for a day. I would decline to make a single brick. I began to walk away from the arid masses of London's honeycombed concrete, monuments of servitude, though I was careful to begin my escape at the tenmile radius. I remembered that it was some years since I had walked in that direction, for the paths I used to know appeared to have been mislaid. Escape was not so easy from new, wide and straight thoroughfares dangerous with swift engines. Aeroplanes were chanting overhead, but no larks. A raw inflammation of villas was spreading through a valley, which was all verdant when last I saw it. Then my companion, he who once met a golden oriole, remembered a little wood in a hollow, aside from the traffic. That, he told me, would certainly be there. Nobody would have interfered with that. He found the lane to it, after some bewilderment with his bearings, which had shifted somewhat. There was no doubt that this was the lane, he declared at last, dubiously. It was? Then we must suffer it, erupted and raw. Its hedges, bearing the first leaves of the year, were displaced, and their roots were higher than their boughs. In some lengths of the lane granite kerbs had replaced the hedges, and an iron sinkhole or two improved the ditches. A new path, a motor-lorry careened midway in its deep mud, went straight into the wood. On the verge of the wood the hazels had been crushed and splintered, and their golden tassels hung disconsolate, as though we were on the track of a recent and lusty mastodon.

Improvement had come. In the heart of the wood oaks were being felled, and by the torn roots of one was a dead hedgehog, which had been evicted from its hibernaculum into the frigid blast of reform. Unseen but near a saw was at work, and its voice was like the incessant growling of a carnivore which had got its teeth into a body and would never let go. This Easter, by all the signs, was the last the wood would see. The bluebells had been coming, expecting no evil, and, had they been allowed the grace of a few more weeks, they would have put the depth of the sky between the trees; but carts and engines had crushed them, and had exposed even their white bulbs, as though the marrow of the earth were bared.

I do not say the Easter message of that wood was especially deplorable. I knew it was possible and even right to see those granite kerbs and the cleared foundations as an urgent message of life and growth. The children of men would play in new gardens there, in another Easter. Still, somehow that direct and unquestioning attack by our machines, especially on the fragile windflowers, was more dismaying than inclement weather. A mastodon might really have been there, with no mind but in its tusks, irresistible and forthright. "I thought you would like to see her; it may be the last time. Isn't she a beauty?" It may be that the sense of beauty has no survival value, to use a term of our biological appraisers; nevertheless, it does survive, so we may suppose there is something as primordial in it as in acquisitiveness. When we see the defacement of beauty we continue to feel as though light were put out in ignorance. And what we want, as certainly as new villas, is more light. Is there a light to check us when we are steering our wheels over the windflowers, the Pasque blossoms, and are replacing them with stones?

There were Greek pagans long ago, and some of their work clearly had a value by which, though not useful, it has survived; and the idle fancy was theirs that the windflower was stained with the blood of Adonis, slain by a boar, and that its pallor was from the tears of Aphrodite, who sorrowed over the beautiful youth. Even our own pagans, before Augustine gave their thoughts another direction, felt bound to conclude that the windflower was painted by the elves. Who else could have veined so delicately that fabric? Who else would have inspired daintiness with that modesty in the half-light of the woods?

Behind me I heard the motor-lorry heaving itself out of the mire it had made. It backed and crashed like a hippopotamus into another tracery of mist and emerald, and Adonis died again. I buttoned up my coat against the northerly blast. Let Adonis die. We cannot help him. The tears of Aphrodite are of no avail against the tusks of boars. Only the bolts of Zeus could prevail against the progress of our engines; and Olympus, we have been most credibly informed for many Easters past, is "to let"; and if we must believe the reports of our busy agents of estates, then it is about the only place that is to let.

Yet one of the things I clearly remember of the war was a bluebell. It was in Thièpval wood. Men who have reason to keep in mind the valley of the Ancre will smile at that. Thièpval had come to its end. Our engines had been there, had gone over it, and were loudly progressing elsewhere on the eastern hills. It was April, but there was no wood, no village, and no old château, though a little down the slope towards St. Pierre Divion was a tank on its side; one of the automata, too, had died. Life had gone; nothing was there but mud, bones, rags, helmets, broken rifles, and skulls. Thièpval was Golgotha. We were turning from it, but were stopped by a fleck of colour in the drab wreckage; life had already returned to Thièpval? It was a wild hyacinth. One bluebell to all April! What, still there and unafraid?

One may dare to hope that the marrow of earth has a more stubborn vitality than our dismay allowed; it may survive our engines. It survived the glaciers. After all, there may be in the frail windflower a virtue that will outlast the lorries. We have been surprised, before this, by the shy patience of what may have been lovely and of good report, yet otherwise was inexcusable. The slight but haughty gesture of my sailor friend, one dawn, saluting from the bridge of his ship the beauty of the world, no more valuable though it was than the pagan thought which celebrated Adonis in the petals of the windflower, may have been a sign that nothing could deflect a barque he knew from her right course. And how else could he prove his faith? He summoned me as a witness, he was so sure of fellowship. Yet there are no mathematics to support him.

Lines of Inquiry

1 At first the structure of "A Lost Wood" may appear ramshackle, a mere collection of episodes loosely tied together at best. List these episodes.

a What is the point of each one?

b What do the contemptuous critic, the petrol (gasoline), the tarmac (macadam), the automobiles, the steamships, and the tanks have in common?

c What do Rousseau, orioles, sailing ships, windflowers, and gentians have in common?

d The episodes are all illustrative—what do they illustrate?

2 a How do you account for the sequence of episodes in this essay? Could that sequence be changed—could the essay begin with the sailing ship and end with the critic?

b Which is the central episode? Where does it stand in the sequence of illustrations, and why there?

c Look at the movement from illustration to illustration— how are they linked?

d Taking London as the geographic center of the essay, how could you describe its movement as a whole? What does this movement have to do with Tomlinson's point?

e Follow Tomlinson's references to the seasons throughout the essay. What pattern is he making use of? Why does the essay end in April?

3 A succinct statement of Tomlinson's point would take no more than a paragraph; what acconts for the length of this essay?

a Is there any development of idea from one illustration to the next?

b Could any part of the essay be skipped, without damage to the theme?

4 a Do any of the illustrations Tomlinson employs fall within the categories under which illustration is discussed earlier (see pp. 266–272)? Are his illustrations actual or hypothetical? Which of Tomlinson's episodes can be said to illustrate the average? Is there a series of averages? Are there extremes?

b Do such categorical ways of viewing Tomlinson's illustrations help to explain the sequence in which he arranges them?

c Take two episodes you are willing to accept as illustrating respectively the average and the extreme and consider the difference in emotional impact between a movement from extreme to average and a movement from average to ex-

treme.   What are the probable advantages of each sequence?
What are the probable disadvantages?

5 *a* If one were to divide meaning arbitrarily into meaning concerning fact and meaning concerning value, which kind of
meaning would you say that Tomlinson is attempting to
communicate?

   b How is his effort to communicate one kind of meaning rather
than another related in turn to the structural importance of
specific, actual illustrations, as distinct from hypothetical
ones, in this essay?

6 This essay makes continuous use of metaphor and analogy.

   a What metaphor dominates Tomlinson's concluding description of machinery?   Underline the phrases in which this
metaphor is followed up.   Do you see any development
from the first to the last?

   b Why does Tomlinson refer in his last lines to "the marrow
of earth"?   Is the metaphor implicit here exploited also in
the earlier sections of the essay?

   c In a sense, Tomlinson's essay is based on conflict.   What are
the sides?

7 Much of the poignant tone of this essay derives from allusions
Tomlinson expects his reader to catch.   In this connection,

   a Why does Tomlinson underscore the officer's judgment that
London's new buildings are Egyptian?

   b What are Sinai, Golgotha, and Olympus?   Why is Olympus
"to let"?

   c What is a mahatma?

   d Who are Rousseau, Bach, Adonis, and Aphrodite?   What
importance do they have in this context?

   e Why should a golden oriole remind us of Apollo?

8 Tomlinson's attitude toward the technological changes that are
destroying his "Lost Wood" is fairly clear.

   a His references to "reformed highways," the delights of
motoring, his education in "the signs of Zeppelins by night,"
the goodness of discipline, and so forth, are obviously ironical.   What does he gain by this irony?

   b Considered as a kind of argument, what does irony offer the
writer that a "straightforward" statement would not—e.g.
what is the *argumentative* advantage of "reformed highways"
over "ugly, straight highways" and of "we all know how
good is discipline" over "we all know how destructive is
discipline"?

Lines of Experiment

1 "A Lost Wood" is not the earliest nor yet the latest essay about the impact on the natural world of industrialism and its associated phenomena. The scientific revolution has compounded that impact and accelerated its pace. The impact of these two revolutions together on our lives provides a large body of raw material for a composition: Take some aspect of that impact for your general subject.

In shaping your essay, remember that you cannot say everything. You may find it useful to write a trial conclusion first to get your central idea down on paper. If you cannot write such a conclusion, it may be that you do not know yet what you think; in that case your essay will be an act of discovery as well as a composition (in a sense, the essay always is), and perhaps you should consider following through an extended illustration as a mode of inquiry.

Once you find out what you think—seldom as easy a job as it seems—you have to decide how to approach your subject. If you are concerned largely with facts and not with values— with simply showing how and why these revolutions have affected modern life—your essay's structure probably will be based directly on classification and analysis, and illustrations of the kind employed by Tomlinson will be of limited value. If your concern is largely with the value of fact, the actual, extended illustration may have a greater importance to you than the brief, typical or hypothetical one; you may even pass over entirely to narrative and description.

In any case, your choice of illustrations and your arrangement of those illustrations in a sequence will be a critically important part of your job. No essay can be fully planned in advance of its writing—the final composition is itself the final plan.

Consider also the effect of various possible sequences before you fix irrevocably on one. Any change in sequence inevitably means a change in effect.

2 Take a subject about which you are both experienced and knowledgeable and write an essay constructed around a series of illustrations. Illustrations, of course, are not ends in themselves: An illustration is the visible form of an idea. Theoretically, you may approach such a composition, in two fundamentally different ways. The first approach asks, "What is the idea I am trying to illustrate?" and proceeds thence to appropriate illustrations, a sequence, introduction, and conclusion. The second approach asks, "What scenes stand out here as really important, for the specific subject?" and proceeds thence to the discovery of what those scenes mean and so to introduction, sequence, and conclusion.

In practical fact most writers ask both questions at once and work out the answers in the process of composition. Only after a first draft, usually, is a writer sure of what he really wants to say.

The following general subjects may suggest a suitable topic. Note, however, that none of these subjects poses an answerable question, and therefore each of them is too indefinite to serve, without further shaping, as a topic for a composition.

a Baseball	*e* Friendship
b Cooking	*f* Elementary school
c The scientific revolution	*g* Summer camp
d Highways	*h* Toy stores

ELTING E. MORISON

A CASE
STUDY
OF INNOVATION

In the early days of the last war, when armaments of all kinds were in short supply, the British, I am told, made use of a venerable field piece that had come down to them from previous generations. The honorable past of this light artillery stretched back, in fact, to the Boer War. In the days of uncertainty after the fall of France, these guns, hitched to trucks, served as useful mobile units in the coast defense. But it was felt that the rapidity of fire could be increased. A time-motion expert was, therefore, called in to suggest ways to simplify the firing procedures. He watched one of the gun crews of five men at practice in the field for some time. Puzzled by certain aspects of the procedures, he took some slow-motion pictures of the soldiers performing the loading, aiming, and firing routines.

When he ran these pictures over once or twice, he noticed something that appeared odd to him. A moment before the firing, two members of the gun crew ceased all activity and came to attention for a three-second interval, extending throughout the discharge of the gun. He summoned an old colonel of artillery, showed him the pictures, and pointed out this strange behavior. What, he asked the colonel, did it mean? The colonel, too, was puzzled. He asked to see the pictures again. "Ah," he said when the performance was over, "I have it. They are holding the horses."

This story, true or not, and I am told it is true, suggests nicely the pain with which the human being accommodates himself to changing conditions. The tendency is apparently involuntary and immediate to protect oneself against the shock of change by continuing in the presence of altered situations the familiar habits, however incongruous, of the past.

Yet, if human beings are attached to the known, to the realm of things as they are, they also, regrettably for their peace of mind, are incessantly attracted to the unknown and to things as they might be. As Ecclesiastes glumly pointed out, men persist in disordering their settled ways and beliefs by seeking out many inventions.

The point is obvious. Change has always been a constant in human affairs; today, indeed, it is one of the determining characteristics of our civilization. In our relatively shapeless social organization, the shifts from station to station are fast and easy. More important for our immediate purpose, America is fundamentally an industrial society in a time of tremendous technological development. We are thus constantly presented with new devices or new forms of power that, in their refinement and extension, continually bombard the fixed structure of our habits of mind and behavior. Under such conditions, our salvation, or at least our peace of mind, appears to depend upon how successfully we can in the future become what has been called in an excellent phrase a completely "adaptive society."

It is interesting, in view of all this, that so little investigation, relatively, has been made of the process of change and human responses to it. Recently psychologists, sociologists, and cultural anthropologists have addressed themselves to the subject with suggestive results. But we are still far from a full understanding of the process, and still farther from knowing how we can set about simplifying and assisting an individual's or a group's accommodation to new machines or new ideas.

With these things in mind, I thought it might be interesting and perhaps useful to examine historically a changing situation within a society; to see if from this examination we can discover how the new machines or ideas that introduced the changing situation developed; to see who introduces them, who resists them, what points of friction or tension in the social structure are produced by the innovation, and perhaps why they are produced and what, if anything, may be done about it.   For this case study, the introduction of continuous-aim firing in the United States Navy has been selected.   The system, first devised by an English officer in 1898, was introduced into our Navy in the years 1900–1902.

I have chosen to study this episode for two reasons.   First, a navy is not unlike a society that has been placed under laboratory conditions. Its dimensions are severely limited; it is beautifully ordered and articulated; it is relatively isolated from random influences.   For these reasons the impact of change can be clearly discerned, the resulting dislocations in the structure easily discovered and marked out.   In the second place, the development of continuous-aim firing rests upon mechanical devices.   It, therefore, presents for study a concrete, durable situation.   It is not like many other innovating reagents—a Manichean heresy, or Marxism, or the views of Sigmund Freud—that can be shoved and hauled out of shape by contending forces or conflicting prejudices.   At all times we know exactly what continuous-aim firing really is.   It will be well now to describe, as briefly as possible, *what* it is.

The governing fact in gunfire at sea is that the gun is mounted on an unstable platform—a rolling ship.   This constant motion obviously complicates the problem of holding a steady aim.   Before 1898 this problem was solved in the following elementary fashion.   A gun pointer estimated the range of the target—ordinarily about 2800 yards.   He then raised the gun barrel to give the gun the elevation to carry the shell to the target at the estimated range.   This was accomplished by turning a small wheel on the gun mount that operated the elevating gears. With the gun thus fixed for range, the gun pointer peered through open sights, not unlike those on a small rifle, and waited until the roll of the ship brought the sights on the target.   He then pressed the firing button that discharged the gun.   There were, by 1898, on some naval guns, telescope sights which naturally enlarged the image of the target for the gun pointer.   But these sights were rarely used by gun pointers.   They were lashed securely to the gun barrel and, recoiling with the barrel, jammed back against the unwary pointer's eye.   Therefore, when used at all, they were used only to take an initial sight for purposes of estimating the range before the gun was fired.

Notice now two things about the process. First of all, the rapidity of fire was controlled by the rolling period of the ship. Pointers had to wait for the one moment in the roll when the sights were brought on the target. Notice also this: There is in every pointer what is called a "firing interval"—the time lag between his impulse to fire the gun and the translation of this impulse into the act of pressing the firing button. A pointer, because of this reaction time, could not wait to fire the gun until the exact moment when the roll of the ship brought the sights onto the target; he had to will to fire a little before, while the sights were off the target. Since the firing interval was an individual matter, varying obviously from man to man, each pointer had to estimate, from long practice, his own interval and compensate for it accordingly.

These things, together with others we need not here investigate, conspired to make gunfire at sea relatively uncertain and ineffective. The pointer, on a moving platform, estimating range and firing interval, shooting while his sight was off the target, became in a sense an individual artist.

In 1898, many of the uncertainties were removed from the process—and the position of the gun pointer radically altered—by the introduction of continuous-aim firing. The major change was that which enabled the gun pointer to keep his sight and gun barrel on the target throughout the roll of the ship. This was accomplished by altering the gear ratio in the elevating gear to permit a pointer to compensate for the roll of the vessel by rapidly elevating and depressing the gun. From this change another followed. With the possibility of maintaining the gun always on the target, the desirability of improved sights became immediately apparent. The advantages of the telescope sight, as opposed to the open sight, were for the first time fully realized. But the existing telescope sight, it will be recalled, moved with the recoil of the gun and jammed back against the eye of the gunner. To correct this, the sight was mounted on a sleeve that permitted the gun barrel to recoil through it without moving the telescope.

These two improvements—in elevating gear and sighting—eliminated the major uncertainties in gunfire at sea and greatly increased the possibilities of both accurate and rapid fire.

You must take my word for it that this changed naval gunnery from an art to a science, and that gunnery accuracy in the British and our Navy increased about 3000 percent in six years. This doesn't mean much except to suggest a great increase in accuracy. The following comparative figures may mean a little more. In 1899 five ships of the North Atlantic Squadron fired five minutes each at a lightship hulk at the conventional range of 1600 yards. After twenty-five minutes of banging away 2 hits had been made on the sails of the elderly vessel. Six years later one naval gunner made 15 hits in one minute at a target 75 x 25 feet at the same range; half of them hit in a bull's eye 50 inches square.

Now with the instruments (the gun, elevating gear, and telescope), the method, and the results of continuous-aim firing in mind, let us turn to the subject of major interest: how was the idea, obviously so simple an idea, of continuous-aim firing developed; who introduced it; and what was its reception?

Introduction of an idea   The idea was the product of the fertile mind of the English officer, Admiral Sir Percy Scott. He arrived at it in this way, while, in 1898, he was the captain of H.M.S. *Scylla.* For the previous two or three years he had given much thought, independently and almost alone in the British Navy, to means of improving gunnery. One rough day when the ship, at target practice, was pitching and rolling violently, he walked up and down the gun deck watching his gun crews. Because of the heavy weather they were making very bad scores. Scott noticed, however, that one pointer was appreciably more accurate than the rest. He watched this man with care and saw, after a time, that he was unconsciously working his elevating gear back and forth in a partially successful effort to compensate for the roll of the vessel. It flashed through Scott's mind at that moment that here was the sovereign remedy for the problems of inaccurate fire. What one man could do partially and unconsciously, perhaps all men could be trained to do consciously and completely.

Acting on this assumption, he did three things. First, in all the guns of the *Scylla,* he changed the gear ratio in the elevating gear, previously used only to set the gun in fixed position for range, so that a gunner could easily elevate and depress the gun to follow a target throughout the roll. Second, he rerigged his telescopes so that they would not be influenced by the recoil of the gun. Third, he rigged a small target at the mouth of the gun, which was moved up and down by a crank to simulate a moving target. By following this target as it moved, and firing at it with a subcalibre rifle rigged in the breech of the gun, the pointer could practice every day. Thus equipped, the ship became a training ground for gunners. Where before the good pointer was an individual artist, pointers now became trained technicians, fairly uniform in their capacity to shoot. The effect was immediately felt. Within a year the *Scylla* established records that were remarkable.

At this point I should like to stop a minute to notice several things directly related to, and involved in, the process of innovation. First, the personality of the innovator. I wish there were space to say a good deal about Admiral Sir Percy Scott. He was a wonderful man. Three small bits of evidence must suffice, however. First, he had a certain mechanical ingenuity. Second, his personal life was shot through with frustration and bitterness. There was a divorce, and a quarrel with the ambitious Lord Charles Beresford—the sounds of which, Scott liked to recall, penetrated to the last outposts of empire. Finally, he possessed, like Swift, a savage indignation directed ordinarily at the inelastic intelligence of all constituted authority—especially the British Admiralty.

There are other points worth mention here. Notice first that Scott was not responsible for the invention of the basic instruments that made the reform in gunnery possible. This reform rested upon the gun itself, which as a rifle had been in existence on ships for at least forty years; the elevating gear, which had been, in the form Scott found it, a part of the rifled gun from the beginning; and the telescope sight, which had been on shipboard at least eight years. Scott's contribution was to bring these three elements, appropriately modified, into a combination that made continuous-aim firing possible for the first time. Notice also that he was allowed to bring these elements into combination by accident, by watching the unconscious action of a gun pointer endeavoring through the operation of his elevating gear to correct partially for the roll of his vessel.

The prepared mind is not enough   Scott, as we have seen, had been interested in gunnery; he had thought about ways to increase accuracy by practice and improvement of existing machinery; but able as he was, he had not been able to produce on his own initiative and by his own thinking the essential idea and to modify instruments to fit his purpose. Notice here, finally, the intricate interaction of chance, the intellectual climate, and Scott's mind. Fortune (in this case the unaware gun pointer) indeed favors the prepared mind, but even fortune and the prepared mind need a favorable environment before they can conspire to produce sudden change. No intelligence can proceed very far above the threshold of existing data or the binding combinations of existing data.

All these elements that enter into what may be called "original thinking" interest me as a teacher. Deeply rooted in the pedagogical mind often enough is a sterile infatuation with "inert ideas"; there is thus always present in the profession the tendency to be diverted from the *process* by which these ideas, or indeed any ideas, are really produced. I well remember with what contempt a class of mine, which was reading Leonardo da Vinci's *Notebooks,* dismissed the author because he appeared to know no more mechanics than, as one wit in the class observed, a Vermont Republican farmer of the present day. This is perhaps the result to be expected from a method of instruction that too frequently implies that the great generalizations were the result, on the one hand, of chance—an apple falling in an orchard or a teapot boiling on 'the hearth—or, on the other hand, of some towering intelligence proceeding in isolation inexorably toward some prefigured idea, such as evolution, for example.

This process by which new concepts appear—the interaction of fortune, intellectual climate, and the prepared imaginative mind—is an interesting subject for examination offered by any case study of innovation. It was a subject that momentarily engaged the attention of Horace Walpole, whose lissome intelligence glided over the surface of so many ideas. In reflecting upon the part played by chance in the development of new concepts, he recalled the story of the three princes of Serendip who set out to find some interesting object on a journey through their realm. They did not find the particular object of their search, but along the way they discovered many new things simply because they were looking for *something.* Walpole believed this intellectual method ought to be given a name—in honor of the founders —Serendipity; and Serendipity certainly exerts a considerable influence in what we call original thinking. There is an element of Serendipity, for example, in Scott's chance discovery of continuous-aim firing in that he was, and had been, looking for some means to improve his target practice and stumbled upon a solution, by observation, that had never entered his head.

Educating the Navy It was in 1900 that Percy Scott went out to the China Station as commanding officer of H.M.S. *Terrible.* In that ship he continued his training methods and his spectacular successes in naval gunnery. On the China Station he met up with an American junior officer, William S. Sims. Sims had little of the mechanical ingenuity of Percy Scott, but the two were drawn together by temperamental similarities that are worth noticing here. Sims had the same intolerance for what is called spit-and-polish and the same contempt for bureaucratic inertia as his British brother officer. He had for some years been concerned, as had Scott, with what he took to be the inefficiency of his own Navy. Just before he met Scott, for example, he had shipped out to China in the brand new pride of the fleet, the battleship *Kentucky*. After careful investigation and reflection he had informed his superiors in Washington she was not a battleship at all— "but a crime against the white race."

The spirit with which he pushed forward his efforts to reform the naval service can best be stated in his own words to a brother officer: "I am perfectly willing that those holding views different from mine should continue to live, but with every fibre of my being I loathe indirection and shiftiness, and where it occurs in high place, and is used to save face at the expense of the vital interests of our great service (in which silly people place such a childlike trust), I want that man's blood and I will have it no matter what it costs me personally."

From Scott in 1900 Sims learned all there was to know about continuous-aim firing. He modified, with the Englishman's active assistance, the gear on his own ship and tried out the new system. After a few months' training, his experimental batteries began making remarkable records at target practice. Sure of the usefulness of his gunnery methods, Sims then turned to the task of educating the Navy at large. In 13 great official reports he documented the case for continuous-aim firing, supporting his arguments at every turn with a mass of factual data. Over a period of two years, he reiterated three principal points: First, he continually cited the records established by Scott's ships, the *Scylla* and the *Terrible,* and supported these with the accumulating data from his own tests on an American ship; second, he described the mechanisms used and the training procedures instituted by Scott and himself to obtain these records; third, he explained that our own mechanisms were not generally adequate without modification to meet the demands placed on them by continuous-aim firing. Our elevating gear, useful to raise or lower a gun slowly to fix it in position for the proper range, did not always work easily and rapidly enough to enable a gunner to follow a target with his gun throughout the roll of the ship. Sims also explained that such few telescope sights as there were on board our ships were useless. Their cross wires were so thick or coarse that they obscured the target, and the sights had been attached to the gun in such a way that the recoil system of the gun plunged the eyepiece against the eye of the gun pointer.

This was the substance not only of the first but of all the succeeding reports written on the subject of gunnery from the China Station. It will be interesting to see what response these met with in Washington. The response falls roughly into three easily identifiable stages.

First stage: no response. Sims had directed his comments to the Bureau of Ordnance and the Bureau of Navigation; in both bureaus there was dead silence. The thing—claims and records of continuous-aim firing—was not credible. The reports were simply filed away and forgotten. Some indeed, it was later discovered to Sims' delight, were half eaten away by cockroaches.

Second stage: rebuttal. It is never pleasant for any man to have his best work left unnoticed by superiors, and it was an unpleasantness that Sims suffered extremely ill. In his later reports, beside the accumulating data he used to clinch his argument, he changed his tone. He used deliberately shocking language because, as he said, "They were furious at my first papers and stowed them away. I therefore made up my mind I would give these later papers such a form that they would be dangerous documents to leave neglected in the files." To another friend he added, "I want scalps or nothing and if I can't have 'em I won't play."

Sims gets attention Besides altering his tone, he took another step to be sure his views would receive attention. He sent copies of his reports to other officers in the fleet. Aware, as a result, that Sims' gunnery claims were being circulated and talked about, the men in Washington were then stirred to action. They responded—notably through the Chief of the Bureau of Ordnance, who had general charge of the equipment used in gunnery practice—as follows: (1) Our equipment was in general as good as the British; (2) since our equipment was as good, the trouble must be with the men, but the gun pointer and the training of gun pointers were the responsibility of the officers on the ships; (3) and most significant—continuous-aim firing was impossible. Experiments had revealed that five men at work on the elevating gear of a six-inch gun could not produce the power necessary to compensate for a roll of five degrees in ten seconds. These experiments and calculations demonstrated beyond peradventure or doubt that Scott's system of gunfire was not possible.

Only one difficulty is discoverable in these arguments; they were wrong at important points. To begin with, while there was little difference between the standard British equipment and the standard U.S. equipment, the instruments on Scott's two ships, the *Scylla* and the *Terrible,* were far better than the standard equipment on our ships. Second, all the men could not be trained in continuous-aim firing until equipment was improved throughout the fleet. Third, the experiments with the elevating gear had been ingeniously contrived at the Washington Navy Yard—on solid ground. It had, therefore, been possible in the Bureau of Ordnance calculation, to dispense with Newton's first law of motion, which naturally operated at sea to assist the gunner in elevating or depressing a gun mounted on a moving ship. Another difficulty was of course that continuous-aim firing was in use on Scott's and some of our own ships at the time the Chief of the Bureau of Ordnance was writing that it was a mathematical impossibility. In every way I find this second stage, the apparent resort to reason, the most entertaining and instructive in our investigation of the responses to innovation.

Third stage: name calling. Sims, of course, by the high temperature he was running and by his calculated overstatement, invited this. He was told in official endorsements on his reports that there were others quite as sincere and loyal as he and far less difficult; he was dismissed as a crack-brain egotist; he was called a deliberate falsifier of evidence.

Sims gets action   The rising opposition and the character of the opposition was not calculated to discourage further efforts by Sims. It convinced him that he was being attacked by shifty, dishonest men who were the victims, as he said, of insufferable conceit and ignorance. He made up his mind, therefore, that he was prepared to go to any extent to obtain the "scalps" and the "blood" he was after. Accordingly he, a lieutenant, took the extraordinary step of writing the President of the United States, Theodore Roosevelt, to inform him of the remarkable records of Scott's ships, of the inadequacy of our own gunnery routines and records, and of the refusal of the Navy Department to act. Roosevelt, who always liked to respond to such appeals when he conveniently could, brought Sims back from China late in 1902 and installed him as Inspector of Target Practice, a post the naval officer held throughout the remaining six years of the Administration.

With this sequence of events (the chronological account of the innovation of continuous-aim firing) in mind, it is possible now to examine the evidence to see what light it may throw on our present interest—the origins of and responses to change in a society.

First, the origins. We have already analyzed briefly the origins of the idea. We have seen how Scott arrived at his notion. We must now ask ourselves, I think, why Sims so actively sought, almost alone among his brother officers, to introduce the idea into his service. It is particularly interesting here to notice again that neither Scott nor Sims invented the instruments on which the innovation rested. They did not urge their proposal because of pride in the instruments of their own design.

The engineer and the entrepreneur   The telescope sight had first been placed on shipboard in 1892 by Bradley Fiske, an officer of great inventive capacity. In that year Fiske had even sketched out on paper the vague possibility of continuous-aim firing, but his sight was condemned by his commanding officer, Robley D. Evans, as of no use. Instead of fighting for his telescope Fiske turned his attention to a range finder. But six years later Sims took over and became the engineer of the revolution.

I would suggest, with some reservations, this explanation: Fiske, as an inventor, took his pleasure in great part from the design of the device. He lacked not so much the energy as the overriding sense of social necessity that would have enabled him to *force* revolutionary ideas on the service. Sims possessed this sense. In Fiske we may here find the familiar plight of the engineer who often enough must watch the products of his ingenuity being organized and promoted by other men. These other promotional men, when they appear in the world of commerce, are called entrepreneurs. In the world of ideas they are still entrepreneurs.

Sims was one, a middle-aged man caught in the periphery (as a lieutenant) of the intricate webbing of a precisely organized society. Rank, the exact definition and limitation of a man's capacity at any given moment in his own career, prevented Sims from discharging all his exploding energies into the purely routine channels of the peacetime Navy. At the height of his powers he was a junior officer standing watches on a ship cruising aimlessly in friendly foreign waters. The remarkable changes in systems of gunfire to which Scott introduced him gave him the opportunity to expend his energies quite legitimately against the encrusted hierarchy of his society. He was moved, it seems to me, in part by his genuine desire to improve his own profession but also in part by rebellion against tedium, against inefficiency from on high, and against the artificial limitations placed on his actions by the social structure, in his case junior rank.

Responding to change   Now having briefly investigated the origins of the change, let us examine the reasons for what must be considered the weird response we have observed to this proposed change.   Here was a reform that greatly and demonstrably increased the fighting effectiveness of a service that maintains itself almost exclusively to fight.   Why then this refusal to accept so carefully documented a case, a case proved incontestably by records and experience?   Why should virtually all the rulers of a society so resolutely seek to reject a change that so markedly improved its chances for survival in any contest with competing societies?

There are the obvious reasons that will occur to everyone—the source of the proposed reform was an obscure junior officer 8000 miles away; he was, and this is a significant factor, criticizing gear and machinery designed by the very men in the bureaus to whom he was sending his criticisms.   And furthermore, Sims was seeking to introduce what he claimed were improvements in a field where improvements appeared unnecessary.   Superiority in war, as in other things, is a relative matter, and the Spanish-American War had been won by the old system of gunnery.   Therefore, it was superior even though of the 9500 shots fired, at varying but close ranges, only 121 had found their mark.

A less obvious cause appears by far the most important one. It has to do with the fact that the Navy is not only an armed force; it is a society. In the forty years following the Civil War, this society had been forced to accommodate itself to a series of technological changes—the steam turbine, the electric motor, the rifled shell of great explosive power, case-hardened steel armor, and all the rest of it.   These changes wrought extraordinary changes in ship design and, therefore, in the concepts of how ships were to be used: that is, in fleet tactics, and even in naval strategy.   The Navy of this period is a paradise for the historian or sociologist in search of evidence of a society's responses to change.

To these numerous innovations, producing as they did a spreading disorder throughout a service with heavy commitments to formal organization, the Navy responded with grudging pain.   It is wrong to assume, as civilians frequently do, that this blind reaction to technological change springs exclusively from some causeless Bourbon distemper that invades the military mind.   There is a sounder and more attractive base.   The opposition, where it occurs, of the soldier and the sailor to such change springs from the normal human instinct to protect oneself and more especially one's way of life.   Military organizations are societies built around and upon the prevailing weapon systems.   Intuitively and quite correctly the military man feels that a change in weapon portends a change in the arrangements of his society.

Think of it this way.   Since the time that the memory of man runneth not to the contrary, the naval society has been built upon the surface vessel.   Daily routines, habits of mind, social organization, physical accommodations, conventions, rituals, spiritual allegiances have been conditioned by the essential fact of the ship.   What then happens to your society if the ship is displaced as the principal element by such a radically different weapon as the plane? The mores and structure of the society are immediately placed in jeopardy.   They may, in fact, be wholly destroyed.   It was the witty cliché of the 20's that those naval officers who persisted in defending the battleship against the apparently superior claims of the carrier did so because the battleship was a more comfortable home.   What, from one point of view, is a better argument?

This sentiment would appear to account in large part for the opposition to Sims; it was the product of an instinctive protective feeling, even if the reasons for this feeling were not overt or recognized.   The years after 1902 proved how right, in their terms, the opposition was.   From changes in gunnery flowed an extraordinary complex of changes: in shipboard routines, ship design, and fleet tactics.   There was, too, a social change.   In the days when gunnery was taken lightly, the gunnery officer was taken lightly.   After 1903, he became one of the most significant and powerful members of a ship's company, and this shift of emphasis naturally was shortly reflected in promotion lists.   Each one of these changes provoked a dislocation in the naval society, and with man's troubled foresight and natural indisposition to break up classic forms, the men in Washington withstood the Sims onslaught as long as they could.   It is very significant that they withstood it until an agent from outside—outside and above—who was not clearly identified with the naval society, entered to force change.

This agent, the President of the United States, might reasonably and legitimately claim the credit for restoring our gunnery efficiency.   But this restoration by *force majeure* was brought about at great cost to the service and men involved.   Bitternesses, suspicions, wounds were caused that it was impossible to conceal or heal.

Now this entire episode may be summed up in five separate points:

1 The essential idea for change occurred in part by chance, but in an environment that contained all the essential elements for change, and to a mind prepared to recognize the possibility of change.

2 The basic elements—the gun, gear, and sight—were put in the environment by other men; men interested in designing machinery to serve different purposes, or simply interested in the instruments themselves.

3 These elements were brought into successful combination by minds not interested in the instruments for themselves but in what they could do with them.   These minds were, to be sure, interested in good gunnery, overtly and consciously.   They may also, not so consciously, have been interested in the implied revolt that is present in the support of all change.   Their temperaments and careers indeed support this view.   From gunnery, Sims went on to attack ship designs, existing fleet tactics, and methods of promotion.   He lived and died, as the service said, a stormy petrel, a man always on the attack against higher authority, a rebellious spirit.

4 He and his colleagues were opposed on this occasion by men who were apparently moved by three considerations: honest disbelief in the dramatic but substantiated claims of the new process; protection of the existing devices and instruments with which they identified themselves; and maintenance of the existing society with which they were identified.

5 The deadlock between those who sought change and those who sought to retain things as they were was broken only by an appeal to superior force; a force removed from and unidentified with the mores, conventions, devices of the society.   This seems to me a very important point.   The naval society in 1900 broke down in its effort to accommodate itself to a new situation.   The appeal to Roosevelt is documentation for Mahan's great generalization that no military service should or can undertake to reform itself.   It must seek assistance from outside.

Now, with these five summary points in mind, it may be possible to seek, as suggested at the outset, a few larger implications from this story.   What, if anything, may it suggest about the general process by which any society attempts to meet changing conditions?

No society can reform itself? There is, to begin with, a disturbing inference half concealed in Mahan's statement that no military organization can reform itself. Certainly civilians would agree with this. We all know now that war and the preparation of war is too important, as Clemenceau said, to be left to the generals. But military organizations are really societies—more rigidly structured, more highly integrated than most communities, but still societies. What then if we make this phrase to read, "No society can reform itself"? Is the process of adaptation to change, for example, too important to be left to human beings? This is a discouraging thought, and historically there is some cause to be discouraged.

This is a subject to which we may well address ourselves. Our society, especially, is built, as I have said, just as surely upon a changing technology as the Navy of the 90's was built upon changing weapon systems. How then can we find the means to accept with less pain to ourselves and less damage to our social organization the dislocations in our society that are produced by innovation? I cannot, of course, give any satisfying answer to these difficult questions. But in thinking about the case study before us, an idea occurred to me that at least might warrant further investigation by men far more qualified than I.

A primary source of conflict and tension in our case study appears to lie in this great word I have used so often in the summary—the word *identification*. It cannot have escaped notice that some men identified themselves with their creations—sights, gun, gear, and so forth—and thus obtained a presumed satisfaction from the thing itself, a satisfaction that prevented them from thinking too closely on either the use or the defects of the thing; that others identified themselves with a settled way of life they had inherited or accepted with minor modification and thus found their satisfaction in attempting to maintain that way of life unchanged; and that still others identified themselves as rebellious spirits, men of the insurgent cast of mind, and thus obtained a satisfaction from the act of revolt itself.

This purely personal identification with a concept, a convention, or an attitude would appear to be a powerful barrier in the way of easily acceptable change. Here is an interesting primitive example. In the years from 1864–1871 ten steel companies in the country began making steel by the new Bessemer process. All but one of them at the outset imported from Great Britain English workmen familiar with the process. One, the Cambria Company, did not. In the first few years those companies with British labor established an initial superiority. But by the end of the 70's, Cambria had obtained a commanding lead over all competitors.

The Bessemer process, like any new technique, had been constantly improved and refined in this period from 1864–1871. The British laborers of Cambria's competitors, secure in the performance of their own original techniques, resisted and resented all change. The Pennsylvania farm boys, untrammeled by the rituals and traditions of their craft, happily and rapidly adapted themselves to the constantly changing process. They ended by creating an unassailable competitive position for their company.

How then can we modify the dangerous effects of this word *identification?* And how much can we tamper with this identifying process? Our security, much of it, after all, comes from giving our allegiance to something greater than ourselves. These are difficult questions to which only the most tentative and provisional answers may here be proposed for consideration.

The danger of limited identifications   If one looks closely at this little case history, one discovers that the men involved were the victims of *severely limited* identifications. They were presumably all part of a society dedicated to the process of national defense, yet they persisted in aligning themselves with separate parts of that process—with the existing instruments of defense, with the existing customs of the society, or with the act of rebellion against the customs of the society. Of them all, the insurgents had the best of it. They could, and did, say that the process of defense was improved by a gun that shot straighter and faster, and since they wanted such guns, they were unique among their fellows—patriots who sought only the larger object of improved defense. But this beguiling statement—even when coupled with the recognition that these men were right, and extremely valuable and deserving of respect and admiration—cannot conceal the fact that they were interested too in scalps and blood. They were so interested, in fact, that they made their case a militant one and thus created an atmosphere in which self-respecting men could not capitulate without appearing either weak or wrong or both. So these limited identifications brought men into conflict with each other, and the conflict prevented them from arriving at a common acceptance of a change that presumably, as men interested in our total national defense, they would all find desirable.

It appears, therefore, if I am correct in my assessment, that we might spend some time and thought on the possibility of enlarging the sphere of our identifications from the part to the whole. For example, those Pennsylvania farm boys at the Cambria Steel Company were, apparently, much more interested in the manufacture of steel than in the preservation of any particular way of making steel. So I would suggest that in studying innovation we look further into this possibility: the possibility that any group that exists for any purpose—the family, the factory, the educational institution—might begin by defining for itself its grand object, and see to it that that grand object is communicated to every member of the group. Thus defined and communicated, it might serve as a unifying agent against the disruptive local allegiances of the inevitable smaller elements that compose any group. It may also serve as a means to increase the acceptability of any change that would assist in the more efficient achievement of the grand object.

There appears also a second possible way to combat the untoward influence of limited identifications. We are, I may repeat, a society based on technology in a time of prodigious technological advance, and a civilization committed irrevocably to the theory of evolution. These things mean that we believe in change; they suggest that if we are to survive in good health we must become an "adaptive society." By the word "adaptive" is meant the ability to extract the fullest possible returns from the opportunities at hand; the ability of Sir Percy Scott to select judiciously from the ideas and material presented both by the past and present and to throw them into a new combination. "Adaptive," as here used, also means the kind of resilience that will enable us to accept fully and easily the best promises of changing circumstances without losing our sense of continuity or our essential integrity.

We are not yet emotionally an adaptive society, though we try systematically to develop forces that tend to make us one. We encourage the search for new inventions; we keep the mind stimulated, bright, and free to seek out fresh means of transport, communication, and energy; yet we remain, in part, appalled by the consequences of our ingenuity and, too frequently, try to find security through the shoring up of ancient and irrelevant conventions, the extension of purely physical safeguards, or the delivery of decisions we ourselves should make into the keeping of superior authority like the state. These solutions are not necessarily unnatural or wrong, but historically they have not been enough, and I suspect they never will be enough to give us the serenity and competence we seek.

A new view of ourselves   If the preceding statements are correct, they suggest that we might give some attention to the construction of a new view of ourselves as a society which in time of great change identified itself with and obtained security and satisfaction from the wise and creative accommodation to change itself.   Such a view rests, I think, upon a relatively greater reverence for the mere *process* of living in a society than we possess today, and a relatively smaller respect for and attachment to any special *product* of a society—a product either as finite as a bathroom fixture or as conceptual as a fixed and final definition of our Constitution or our democracy.

Historically such an identification with *process* as opposed to *product,* with adventurous selection and adaptation as opposed to simple retention and possessiveness, has been difficult to achieve collectively.   The Roman of the early republic, the Italian of the late fifteenth and early sixteenth century, the Englishman of Elizabeth's time appear to have been most successful in seizing the new opportunities while conserving as much of the heritage of the past as they found relevant and useful to their purpose.

We seem to have fallen on times similar to theirs, when many of the existing forms and schemes have lost meaning in the face of dramatically altering circumstances.   Like them we may find at least part of our salvation in identifying ourselves with the adaptive process and thus share with them some of the joy, exuberance, satisfaction, and security with which they went out to meet their changing times.

Lines of Inquiry

1 a Where in the essay does Morison justify his choice of this particular "case study" as an illustration of the process of change?

b Why does he have to justify his choice at all?

c What objections does Morison find to the use as illustration of such "innovating reagents" as Marxism?

d What system of classifying such illustrative episodes seems implied in his contrast of continuous aim firing to Marxism, the Manichean heresy, and "the views of Sigmund Freud"?

e Considering your answers, list the criteria by which one can determine the suitability of a specific subject for a "case study."

2 "Change" is a big word.   Many kinds of things can be said to produce changes: plague, earthquake, soil erosion, war, elections, etc.

a Could Morison have used an episode of some such kind to illustrate his point?

b What kind of change is he really interested in, and why is this kind of change particularly interesting to the historian?

c What conception of the historian's task seems to lie behind Morison's choice of a subject in this essay?

3 a What is the Manichean heresy?

b Why is it relevant to discussion of the process of change?

c Why is it useless for Morison's purposes?

d What do you conclude concerning systematic thought from the fact that a given set of facts and ideas can be thoroughly relevant to an inquiry, yet useless?

4 The essential point of the anecdote with which the essay begins is obvious: Human beings resist change instinctively. The point is common; so are anecdotes illustrating it.

a What does Morison gain from this particular anecdote, besides its essential point?

b How is the subject of the anecdote related to the subject of the essay as a whole? What can you conclude from this resemblance about anecdotes that serve to introduce?

c Here are three illustrations that might have been used instead; how would the use of each change Morison's introduction? Would any of them tend to change your attitude toward Admiral Sims and his problem? Can you match these illustrations with others?

   (*1*) In the nineteenth century large bands of English workers displaced by machinery broke into factories and attempted to destroy the machines.

   (*2*) The French lost battle after battle in the Hundred Years War through stubborn refusal to adapt their tactics to the challenge of the English longbow.

   (*3*) Until recently, church architecture has slavishly imitated the forms developed in the Middle Ages, though the functional necessity of buttresses, bell towers, etc., has long since disappeared.

5 The case of the "venerable fieldpiece" supplies one element in Morison's introduction.

a What other matters does he take up before returning to the body of his analysis?

b Do any of these other matters seem essential, and if so, why?

c What is the point of the allusion to Ecclesiastes, and what does this allusion illustrate?

d The author of Ecclesiastes ("the preacher") was also fond of remarking, "Vanity of vanities, all is vanity." Would this quotation be more or less apposite to Morison's point than the quotation he uses?

6 At the end of the first section, Morison remarks that through two improvements in elevating gear and sighting, gunnery accuracy was increased by 3,000 percent.

    a Eliminate the illustration that follows; what happens to this simple statistic?

    b Now eliminate the statistic instead; what happens to the following illustration?

    c What do you conclude about the illustrative value of statistics and the statistical value of illustrations?

    d Within the illustration itself, why does Morison identify not only the number of ships involved but also the squadron to which they belonged and the exact character of the target they were firing at. Why does he use the phrase "banging away"?

    e How many points of contrast between the first firing practice and the second does Morison introduce? Are any of these points of contrast logically unnecessary to his point—merely there for emphasis?

7 *a* Why does Morison give the *result* of continuous aim firing before he describes how it was introduced?

    b Would the essay be dramatically more effective if he had brought it to a climax with the firing test of 1905?

    c Had he done so, what would have happened to the focus of the essay?

    d Why does Morison "throw away" the potentially grand scene in which President Roosevelt summons Sims to Washington, and to his proper reward?

8 In his conclusion, Morison refers to "the Roman of the early republic, the Italian of the late fifteenth and early sixteenth century, the Englishman of Elizabeth's time."

    a Why does he choose these particular examples?

    b Why would the Puritan of early America, the Englishman of Victoria's time, the Italian of the late 1930s, be less appropriate examples?

    c What would be the effect of Morison's conclusion had he made no such allusions whatever?

9 *a* Why does Morison discuss even briefly the personalities of Scott and Sims—what is the importance of their personalities to Morison's argument?

    b Why does Morison tell us that Scott "liked to recall" that his quarrel with Lord Beresford "penetrated to the last outposts of empire"? Why does Morison use that particular phrase to describe its notoriety?

c Morison could easily have summarized Sims's attitudes instead of quoting him. Omit from Morison's opening account of Sims's character all the quotations from Sims himself; what would be lost?

d Why does Morison scrupulously give the names of ships and dates of actions? Follow those dates through the essay; what is their function?

Lines of Experiment

1 In one form or another, change comes constantly to everything and to everyone. Morison's study is focused on the process of change as it affects an institution that in some respects can serve as a model for society at large. From your own experience, undertake a parallel—though necessarily more limited —case study. Your case may be within an institution, a business, a profession, a process, a personality, a sport, a group; and the kind of change you will consider will vary appropriately, of course, with the kind of case you choose.

In choosing your specific case study, bear in mind that your focus is not on the case itself but on what it means as an illustration of the process of change, and that the good case study is (*a*) "relatively isolated from random influences" and (*b*) easily measurable. Ordinarily, the narration of the case will precede its analysis, but the narrative itself should set forth clearly the factors to be analyzed.

2 Write an essay on change that does not depend on the extended case study. You may restrict yourself to mimetically ordered discourse (the narration or description of a specific or typical case). Or you may use as a frame for a larger discussion either definition (what is change?) or classification (from a given, significant point of view, how can changes be classified usefully —and of the changes so classified, which are important and which are not?). You are free, of course, to take any attitude toward change that you wish, and to adopt any focus that you choose (see Collingwood's "Progress as a Result of Historical Thinking," p. 219). One of your first jobs will be to decide what kind of question you are answering; otherwise, you are likely to be unable to pull your thoughts together. Morison answers one kind of inquiry; you may choose to answer quite another.

3 Write an essay relying on the analytic technique of the case study, but focus on some such subject as the following:

a The purpose of college athletics

b Why people fight

c How the military mind is shaped

d Why the younger generation is fed up

e How to campaign for office

f Why men like to hunt

g Why the divorce rate rises

h Why our moral standards are shifting

Obviously, a question—direct or indirect—is imbedded in each title. A case study is an effort to answer a question, and in every instance listed above the question really asks for the analysis of a pattern.

JAMES THURBER

 DOC MARLOWE

I was too young to be other than awed and puzzled by Doc Marlowe when I knew him. I was only sixteen when he died. He was sixty-seven. There was that vast difference in our ages and there was a vaster difference in our backgrounds. Doc Marlowe was a medicine-show man. He had been a lot of other things, too: a circus man, the proprietor of a concession at Coney Island, a saloon-keeper; but in his fifties he had traveled around with a tent-show troupe made up of a Mexican named Chickalilli, who threw knives, and a man called Professor Jones, who played the banjo. Doc Marlowe would come out after the entertainment and harangue the crowd and sell bottles of medicine for all kinds of ailments. I found out all this about him gradually, toward the last, and after he died. When I first knew him, he represented the Wild West to me, and there was nobody I admired so much.

I met Doc Marlowe at old Mrs. Willoughby's rooming house.   She had been a nurse in our family, and I used to go and visit her over weekends sometimes, for I was very fond of her.   I was about eleven years old then.   Doc Marlowe wore scarred leather leggings, a bright-colored bead vest that he said he got from the Indians, and a ten-gallon hat with kitchen matches stuck in the band, all the way around.   He was about six feet four inches tall, with big shoulders, and a long, drooping mustache.   He let his hair grow long, like General Custer's.   He had a wonderful collection of Indian relics and six-shooters, and he used to tell me stories of his adventures in the Far West.   His favorite expressions were "Hay, boy!" and "Hay, boy-gie!," which he used the way some people now use "Hot dog!" or "Doggone!"   He told me once that he had killed an Indian chief named Yellow Hand in a tomahawk duel on horseback.   I thought he was the greatest man I had ever seen.   It wasn't until he died and his son came on from New Jersey for the funeral that I found out he had never been in the Far West in his life.   He had been born in Brooklyn.

Doc Marlowe had given up the road when I knew him, but he still dealt in what he called "medicines."   His stock in trade was a liniment that he had called Snake Oil when he traveled around.   He changed the name to Blackhawk Liniment when he settled in Columbus.   Doc didn't always sell enough of it to pay for his bed and board, and old Mrs. Willoughby would sometimes have to "trust" him for weeks at a time.   She didn't mind, because his liniment had taken a bad kink out of her right limb that had bothered her for thirty years.   I used to see people whom Doc had massaged with Blackhawk Liniment move arms and legs that they hadn't been able to move before he "treated" them.   His patients were day laborers, wives of streetcar conductors, and people like that.   Sometimes they would shout and weep after Doc had massaged them, and several got up and walked around who hadn't been able to walk before.   One man hadn't turned his head to either side for seven years before Doc soused him with Blackhawk.   In half an hour he could move his head as easily as I could move mine.   "Glory be to God!" he shouted.   "It's the secret qualities in the ointment, my friend," Doc Marlowe told him, suavely. He always called the liniment ointment.

News of his miracles got around by word of mouth among the poorer classes of town—he was not able to reach the better people (the "tony folks," he called them)—but there was never a big enough sale to give Doc a steady income.   For one thing, people thought there was more

magic in Doc's touch than in his liniment, and, for another, the ingredients of Blackhawk cost so much that his profits were not very
great.   I know, because I used to go to the wholesale chemical company once in a while for him and buy his supplies.   Everything that
went into the liniment was standard and expensive (and well-known, not
secret).   A man at the company told me he didn't see how Doc could
make much money on it at thirty-five cents a bottle.   But even when
he was very low in funds Doc never cut out any of the ingredients or
substituted cheaper ones.   Mrs. Willoughby had suggested it to him
once, she told me, when she was helping him "put up a batch," and
he had got mad.   "He puts a heap of store by that liniment being right
up to the mark," she said.

Doc added to his small earnings, I discovered, by money he made
gambling.   He used to win quite a few dollars on Saturday nights at
Freck's saloon, playing poker with the marketmen and the railroaders
who dropped in there.   It wasn't for several years that I found out Doc
cheated.   I had never heard about marked cards until he told me
about them and showed me his.   It was one rainy afternoon, after he
had played seven-up with Mrs. Willoughby and old Mr. Peiffer, another
roomer of hers.   They had played for small stakes (Doc wouldn't play
cards unless there was some money up, and Mrs. Willoughby wouldn't
play if very much was up).   Only twenty or thirty cents had changed
hands in the end.   Doc had won it all.   I remember my astonishment
and indignation when it dawned on me that Doc had used the marked
cards in playing the old lady and the old man.   "You didn't cheat
them, did you?" I asked him.   "Jimmy, my boy," he told me, "the man
that calls the turn wins the money."   His eyes twinkled and he seemed
to enjoy my anger.   I was outraged, but I was helpless.   I knew I
could never tell Mrs. Willoughby about how Doc had cheated her at
seven-up.   I liked her, but I liked him, too.   Once he had given me
a whole dollar to buy fireworks with on the Fourth of July.

I remember once, when I was staying at Mrs. Willoughby's, Doc
Marlowe was roused out of bed in the middle of the night by a poor
woman who was frantic because her little girl was sick.   This woman
had had the sciatica driven out of her by his liniment, she reminded
Doc.   He placed her then.   She had never been able to pay him a
cent for his liniment or his "treatments," and he had given her a great
many.   He got up and dressed, and went over to her house.   The child
had colic, I suppose.   Doc couldn't have had any idea what was the
matter, but he sopped on liniment; he sopped on a whole bottle.   When

he came back home, two hours later, he said he had "relieved the distress." The little girl had gone to sleep and was all right the next day, whether on account of Doc Marlowe or in spite of him I don't know. "I want to thank you, Doctor," said the mother, tremulously, when she called on him that afternoon. He gave her another bottle of liniment, and he didn't charge her for it or for his "professional call." He used to massage, and give liniment to, a lot of sufferers who were too poor to pay. Mrs. Willoughby told him once that he was too generous and too easily taken in. Doc laughed—and winked at me, with the twinkle in his eye that he had had when he told me how he had cheated the old lady at cards.

Once I went for a walk with him out Town Street on a Saturday afternoon. It was a warm day, and after a while I said I wanted a soda. Well, he said, he didn't care if he took something himself. We went into a drugstore, and I ordered a chocolate soda and he had a lemon phosphate. When we had finished, he said, "Jimmy, my son, I'll match you to see who pays for the drinks." He handed me a quarter and he told me to toss the quarter and he would call the turn. He called heads and won. I paid for the drinks. It left me with a dime.

I was fifteen when Doc got out his pamphlets, as he called them. He had eased the misery of the wife of a small-time printer and the grateful man had given him a special price on two thousand advertising pamphlets. There was very little in them about Blackhawk Liniment. They were mostly about Doc himself and his "Life in the Far West." He had gone out to Franklin Park one day with a photographer—another of his numerous friends—and there the photographer took dozens of pictures of Doc, a lariat in one hand, a six-shooter in the other. I had gone along. When the pamphlets came out, there were the pictures of Doc, peering around trees, crouching behind bushes, whirling the lariat, aiming the gun. "Dr. H. M. Marlowe Hunting Indians" was one of the captions. "Dr. H. M. Marlowe after Hoss-Thieves" was another one. He was very proud of the pamphlets and always had a sheaf with him. He would pass them out to people on the street.

Two years before he died Doc got hold of an ancient, wheezy Cadillac somewhere. He aimed to start traveling around again, he said, but he never did, because the old automobile was so worn out it wouldn't hold up for more than a mile or so. It was about this time that a man named Hardman and his wife came to stay at Mrs. Willoughby's. They were farm people from around Lancaster who had sold their place. They got to like Doc because he was so jolly, they said, and they enjoyed his stories. He treated Mrs. Hardman for an old complaint in the small of her back and wouldn't take any money for it. They thought he was a fine gentleman. Then there came a day when they announced that they were going to St. Louis, where they had a son. They talked some of settling in St. Louis. Doc Marlowe told them they ought to buy a nice auto cheap and drive out, instead of going by train—it wouldn't cost much and they could see the country, give themselves a treat. Now, he knew where they could pick up just such a car.

Of course, he finally sold them the decrepit Cadillac—it had been stored away somewhere in the back of a garage whose owner kept it there for nothing because Doc had relieved his mother of a distress in the groins, as Doc explained it. I don't know just how the garage man doctored up the car, but he did. It actually chugged along pretty steadily when Doc took the Hardmans out for a trial spin. He told them he hated to part with it, but he finally let them have it for a hundred dollars. I knew, of course, and so did Doc, that it couldn't last many miles.

Doc got a letter from the Hardmans in St. Louis ten days later. They had had to abandon the old junk pile in West Jefferson, some fifteen miles out of Columbus. Doc read the letter aloud to me, peering over his glasses, his eyes twinkling, every now and then punctuating the lines with "Hay, boy!" and "Hay, boy-gie!" "I just want you to know, Dr. Marlowe," he read, "what I think of low-life swindlers like you [Hay, boy!] and that it will be a long day before I put my trust in a two-faced lyer and imposture again [Hay, boy-gie!]. The garrage man in W. Jefferson told us your old rattle-trap had been doctored up just to fool us. It was a low down dirty trick as no swine would play on a white man [Hay, boy!]." Far from being disturbed by the letter, Doc Marlowe was plainly amused. He took off his glasses, after he finished it and laughed, his hand to his brow and his eyes closed. I was pretty mad, because I had liked the Hardmans, and because they had liked him. Doc Marlowe put the letter carefully back into its envelope and tucked it away in his inside coat pocket, as if it were something precious. Then he picked up a pack of cards and began to lay out a solitaire hand. "Want to set in a little seven-up game, Jimmy?" he asked me. I was furious. "Not with a cheater like you!" I shouted, and stamped out of the room, slamming the door. I could hear him chuckling to himself behind me.

The last time I saw Doc Marlowe was just a few days before he died. I didn't know anything about death, but I knew that he was dying when I saw him. His voice was very faint and his face was drawn; they told me he had a lot of pain. When I got ready to leave the room, he asked me to bring him a tin box that was on his bureau. I got it and handed it to him. He poked around in it for a while with unsteady fingers and finally found what he wanted. He handed it to me. It was a quarter, or rather it looked like a quarter, but it had heads on both sides. "Never let the other fella call the turn, Jimmy, my boy," said Doc, with a shadow of his old twinkle and the echo of his old chuckle. I still have the two-headed quarter. For a long time I didn't like to think about it, or about Doc Marlowe, but I do now.

Lines of Inquiry

1 Doc Marlowe, as Thurber presents him, is a highly anomalous personality; the structure of the essay is based on his internal contradictions.

    a Where in the essay are the contradictions in his character first introduced?

    b One might classify Doc Marlowe's actions as honest and dishonest or as charitable and uncharitable. How is this contrast exploited in the structure of the essay? (What do his honest acts have to do with? What do his dishonest acts have to do with?) What point is Thurber trying to make by means of this contrast?

2 List the stages by which Thurber reveals Doc Marlowe's dishonesty: his dishonesty about his past, his dishonesty about his liniment, etc.

    a What kind of progression does the sequence show?

    b What would be the effect if Doc Marlowe's treacherous dealings with the Hardmans were placed first?

    c The two-headed quarter appears twice in the essay—where? Could the essay have begun with the first anecdote about that quarter?

    d Of all the anecdotes, which is longest? Why? Where in the sequence of anecdotes is it placed?

3 Read the first two and the last two paragraphs of the essay. How are they related? With what effect?

4 *a* Marlowe's attempts to cheat Thurber himself seem particularly infuriating—why? How does Marlowe refer to Thurber in the essay?

    b Thurber ends, "For a long time I didn't like to think about it, or about Doc Marlowe, but I do now." Why? Does he suggest any reason for his change of attitude? How is that change prepared for in the essay? What does the change mean?

c Can you describe the significance of Doc Marlowe as young Thurber views him?

d What would be lost if Thurber were to write about Doc Marlowe impersonally—without referring to himself? How old is Thurber within the essay? What kind of person is he? How does the character of this "internal" Thurber affect the kind of thing Thurber writes about—and does not write about?

e How is Thurber's internal point of view—that of a young boy—related to the last sentence, to the fact that Thurber never presses his sketch into overt analysis?

5 What is the value to Thurber's account of each of the following:

a "He told me once he had killed an Indian chief *named Yellow Hand* in a tomahawk duel *on horseback*."

b " 'Glory be to God!' he shouted. *'It's the secret qualities in the ointment, my friend,'* Doc Marlowe told him, suavely."

c "Doc couldn't have had any idea what was the matter, but he sopped on liniment, *he sopped on a whole bottle*."

d "They thought he was *a fine gentleman*."

e "Of course he finally sold them the decrepit Cadillac. It had been stored away somewhere in the back of a garage whose owner kept it there for nothing because Doc had relieved his mother of *a distress in the groins,* as Doc explained it."

f "I was pretty sad, because I had liked the Hardmans, *and because they had liked him*."

Lines of Experiment

1 Although Doc Marlowe represents a type now extinct, most people know in their adolescence men or women who, like him, represent unfamiliar and even glamorous ways of life. Write a brief essay in narrative form on some such person. Probably you will be best off by choosing a figure you knew well over a fairly long period, but close observation of a striking figure for only a few hours can provide you with the material for this kind of essay. The world represented need not be that of the con man, tramp, or dope peddler; the world of the banker, the professional soldier, or the farmer can be equally strange.

In writing, remember that because you cannot possibly tell

everything, what you tell must be representative, illustrative of the meaning you wish to present. You will find it useful to select as a subject someone whose outline is definite: Thurber did not write about Mrs. Willoughby, nor about the Hardmans. After you have selected someone as a subject, make a brief list of the things about him that you recall as most characteristic, most illustrative. What do they illustrate? In what sequence will you arrange them? How will you tie them together? Of the episodes that strike you as important, which seems most revealing? If you know that your subject is meaningful but you do not know what the meaning is, make your first draft work for you; the act of composition itself is a way of discovering meaning.

2 Thurber restricts himself to the narrative style in this essay, but he could have launched into a full-scale analysis of the meaning of Doc Marlowe, taken as a case study in social responsibility, or honesty, or hero worship. The difference between "Doc Marlowe" as it stands and an analytic study of social responsibility springing from the same illustrative material is one of focus: In the first, the question of meaning—of what can be said logically—is subordinate to the image of a moving and speaking Marlowe; in the second, that image is subordinate to what can be said of it. Write the second kind of essay.

Your major problem in such an essay will be to decide what the meaning of your central illustrative case is. Because all real cases (see Doc Marlowe's) illustrate many ideas, not merely one, you will have to isolate the meaning you are after from the meanings you are not after. This isolation of the central meaning will make your illustration "thinner," in a sense, but more usable. In order to maintain an analytic focus, you may find it useful (*a*) to use more than one illustration, (*b*) to employ definition to establish your subject, and (*c*) to classify the important elements in your central case, and so to separate them for study.

EDWARD GIBBON

THE SLAVERY
OF THE
ROMANS

If a man were called to fix the period in the history of the world during which the condition of the human race was most happy and prosperous, he would, without hesitation, name that which elapsed from the death of Domitian to the accession of Commodus.   The vast extent of the Roman empire was governed by absolute power, under the guidance of virtue and wisdom.   The armies were restrained by the firm but gentle hand of four successive emperors whose characters and authority commanded involuntary respect.   The forms of the civil administration were carefully preserved by Nerva, Trajan, Hadrian, and the Antonines, who delighted in the image of liberty and were pleased with considering themselves as the accountable ministers of the laws. Such princes deserved the honour of restoring the republic, had the Romans of their days been capable of enjoying a rational freedom.

The labours of these monarchs were overpaid by the immense reward that inseparably waited on their success; by the honest pride of virtue and by the exquisite delight of beholding the general happiness of which they were the authors.   A just but melancholy reflection embittered, however, the noblest of human enjoyments.   They must often have recollected the instability of a happiness which depended on the character of a single man.   The fatal moment was perhaps approaching when some licentious youth or some jealous tyrant would abuse, to the destruction, that absolute power which they had exerted for the benefit of their people.   The ideal restraints of the senate and the laws might serve to display the virtues, but could never correct the vices, of the emperor.   The military force was a blind and irresistible instrument of oppression; and the corruption of Roman manners would always supply flatterers eager to applaud and ministers prepared to serve the fear or the avarice, the lust or the cruelty, of their masters.

These gloomy apprehensions had been already justified by the experience of the Romans.   The annals of the emperors exhibit a strong and various picture of human nature, which we should vainly seek among the mixed and doubtful characters of modern history. In the conduct of those monarchs we may trace the utmost lines of vice and virtue, the most exalted perfection and the meanest degeneracy of our own species. The golden age of Trajan and the Antonines had been preceded by an age of iron. It is almost superfluous to enumerate the unworthy successors of Augustus. Their unparalleled vices, and the splendid theatre on which they were acted, have saved them from oblivion. The dark unrelenting Tiberius, the furious Caligula, the feeble Claudius, the profligate and cruel Nero, the beastly Vitellius, [1] and the timid, inhuman Domitian are condemned to everlasting infamy. During fourscore years (excepting only the short and doubtful respite of Vespasian's reign) Rome groaned beneath an unremitting tyranny, which exterminated the ancient families of the republic and was fatal to almost every virtue and every talent that arose in that unhappy period.

Under the reign of these monsters the slavery of the Romans was accompanied with two peculiar circumstances, the one occasioned by their former liberty, the other by their extensive conquests, which rendered their condition more completely wretched than that of the victims of tyranny in any other age or country. From these causes were derived: I. the exquisite sensibility of the sufferers: and II. the impossibility of escaping from the hand of the oppressor.

I. When Persia was governed by the descendants of Sefi, a race of princes whose wanton cruelty often stained their divan, their table, and their bed with the blood of their favourites, there is a saying recorded of a young nobleman that he never departed from the sultan's presence without satisfying himself whether his head was still on his shoulders. The experience of every day might almost justify the scepticism of Rustan. Yet the fatal sword, suspended above him by a single thread, seems not to have disturbed the slumbers or interrupted the tranquillity of the Persian. The monarch's frown, he well knew, could level him with the dust; but the stroke of lightning or apoplexy might be equally fatal; and it was the part of a wise man to forget the inevitable calamities of human life in the enjoyment of the fleeting hour. He was dignified with the appellation of the king's slave; had, perhaps, been purchased from obscure parents in a country which he had never known; and was trained up from his infancy in the severe discipline of the seraglio. His

---

[1] Vitellius consumed, in mere eating, at least six millions of our money in about seven months. It is not easy to express his vices with dignity or even decency. Tacitus fairly calls him a hog; but it is by substituting to a coarse word a very fine image. (Gibbon.)

name, his wealth, his honours were the gift of a master who might, without injustice, resume what he had bestowed. Rustan's knowledge, if he possessed any, could only serve to confirm his habits by prejudices. His language afforded not words for any form of government except absolute monarchy. The history of the East informed him that such had ever been the condition of mankind. The Koran, and the interpreters of that divine book, inculcated to him that the sultan was the descendant of the prophet and the vice-regent of heaven, that patience was the first virtue of a Mussulman, and unlimited obedience the great duty of a subject.

The minds of the Romans were very differently prepared for slavery. Oppressed beneath the weight of their own corruption and of military violence, they for a long while preserved the sentiments, or at least the ideas, of their free-born ancestors. The education of Helvidius and Thrasea, of Tacitus and Pliny, was the same as that of Cato and Cicero. From Grecian philosophy they had imbibed the justest and most liberal notions of the dignity of human nature and the origin of civil society. The history of their own country had taught them to revere a free, a virtuous, and a victorious commonwealth; to abhor the successful crimes of Cæsar and Augustus; and inwardly to despise those tyrants whom they adored with the most abject flattery. As magistrates and senators, they were admitted into the great council which had once dictated laws to the earth, whose name still gave a sanction to the acts of the monarch, and whose authority was so often prostituted to the vilest purposes of tyranny. Tiberius and those emperors who adopted his maxims attempted to disguise their murders by the formalities of justice, and perhaps enjoyed a secret pleasure in rendering the senate their accomplice as well as their victim. By this assembly the last of the Romans were condemned for imaginary crimes and real virtues. Their infamous accusers assumed the language of independent patriots, who arraigned a dangerous citizen before the tribunal of his country; and the public service was rewarded by riches and honours. The servile judges professed to assert the majesty of the commonwealth, violated in the person of its first magistrate, whose clemency they most applauded when they trembled the most at his inexorable and impending cruelty.[2] The tyrant beheld their baseness with just contempt and encountered their secret sentiments of detestation with sincere and avowed hatred for the whole body of the senate.

[2] After the virtuous and unfortunate widow of Germanicus had been put to death, Tiberius received the thanks of the senate for his clemency. She had not been publicly strangled; nor was the body drawn with a hook to the Gemoniæ, where those of common malefactors were exposed. (Gibbon.)

II.   The division of Europe into a number of independent states, connected, however, with each other by the general resemblance of religion, language, and manners, is productive of the most beneficial consequences to the liberty of mankind.   A modern tyrant, who should find no resistance either in his own breast or in his people, would soon experience a gentle restraint from the example of his equals, the dread of present censure, the advice of his allies, and the apprehension of his enemies.   The object of his displeasure, escaping from the narrow limits of his dominions, would easily obtain, in a happier climate, a secure refuge, a new fortune adequate to his merit, the freedom of complaint, and perhaps the means of revenge.   But the empire of the Romans filled the world, and when that empire fell into the hands of a single person, the world became a safe and dreary prison for his enemies. The slave of Imperial despotism, whether he was condemned to drag his gilded chain in Rome and the senate, or to wear out a life of exile on the barren rock of Seriphus or the frozen banks of the Danube, expected his fate in silent despair.   To resist was fatal, and it was impossible to fly.   On every side he was encompassed with a vast extent of sea and land, which he could never hope to traverse without being discovered, seized, and restored to his irritated master.   Beyond the frontiers his anxious view could discover nothing except the ocean, inhospitable deserts, hostile tribes of barbarians of fierce manners and unknown language, or dependent kings who would gladly purchase the emperor's protection by the sacrifice of an obnoxious fugitive. "Wherever you are," said Cicero to the exiled Marcellus, "remember that you are equally within the power of the conqueror."

Lines of Inquiry

1 In this selection, Gibbon describes the condition of a free
   Roman under the Empire, but his larger subject is the tragic
   collapse of a great civilization.   In Gibbon's view, the constitution of the Roman Empire was deliberately destroyed by the
   first emperors—even the virtue of the Antonines could not
   restore it.   This selection, the concluding passage from his
   chapter on the erosion of Roman liberty, uses comparison and
   contrast to illustrate the melancholy situation in which the
   Romans found themselves.

   a What essential difference between the situation of the Ro-
      mans and that of the Persians accounts for the "exquisite
      sensibility" of the former?   Why is the sensibility of the
      Persian to his situation so much less acute?

   b What would have been the effect if Gibbon had compared
      the slavery of the Romans not to that of the Persians but to

(*1*) the ancient freedom of the Athenians, (*2*) the freedom of the German Barbarians, (*3*) the slavery of Roman slaves? What special advantages derive from the use of the Persians as a point of comparison?   Can you think of other possible points of comparison or contrast?

c Why, in the second part of Gibbon's analysis, does he shift his ground to contrast the situation of the oppressed Roman not to that of the oppressed Persian but to that of an oppressed contemporary of Gibbon himself?

d Which element in each comparison does Gibbon deal with first?   Why?

2 Gibbon uses the slavery of the Persians as a way of illustrating the slavery of the Romans; but the slavery of the Persians itself is illustrated by the attitude of a single legendary young nobleman.   Is there a parallel reduction in scale in his description of Roman slavery?   Why is Gibbon not content with a general illustration—why does he try to make it specific?   Why does he give the Persian a name?

3 This concluding passage begins with an encomium of four successive virtuous emperors, only to revert to the condition of the Romans under their predecessors.   A more obviously historical sequence would describe the slavery of the Romans under Tiberius et al., and then stop; the corruption of the Romans was then complete.

a Why does Gibbon mention the four virtuous emperors at all?

b Why does he mention them out of the obvious historical order?   (The easiest way to see his motive is to transpose the first two paragraphs from beginning to end and consider the consequence.)

c What technique of illustration does Gibbon's practice here represent?

4 Construct a system of classification reflecting Gibbon's discussion of the differences between Persian and Roman slavery.

a Would this passage be more effective if the system of classification were more explicitly outlined?

b Many possible points of comparison and contrast are omitted —military obligations, legal recourse, property rights, etc. Why?   What is the focus of Gibbon's comparison, as it stands?

5 Gibbon uses only one quotation in the passage.   Where?   At what points in his composition might he have placed it with equal logic?   Why does he place it where he does?

6 The greatness of Gibbon's history derives not only from the sweep of his historical imagination but also from the quality of his prose. Study the construction of the following sentences, first by substituting reasonably close synonyms for the italicized words, and second by rearranging the sequence of clauses, with what minor grammatical changes you must make in order to do so. In each case, how would you describe the methods by which Gibbon obtains his stylistic effects?

  a "The *ideal restraints* of the senate and the laws might serve to *display* the *virtues,* but could never correct the *vices,* of the emperor."

  b "In the conduct of those monarchs we may trace the *utmost lines* of vice and virtue, the most *exalted perfection* and the *meanest degeneracy* of our own species."

  c "The *dark* unrelenting Tiberius, the *furious* Caligula, the *feeble* Claudius, the *profligate and cruel* Nero, the *beastly* Vitellius, and the *timid, inhuman* Domitian are condemned to everlasting infamy."

  d "By *this assembly* the *last* of the Romans were condemned for *imaginary crimes* and *real virtues.*"

  e "To resist was *fatal,* and it was impossible to fly."

7 Here are six subjects; find two useful points of comparison and contrast for each. What do you have to decide about each subject before you can find a point of comparison or of contrast for it? What reasons lie behind your choice in each case?

  a Modern American courtship
  b The hunter
  c The situation of the American Negro
  d The presidential election of 1968
  e The conscientious objector
  f City life today

8 One might chart Gibbon's use of comparison and contrast in this selection in some such way as this:

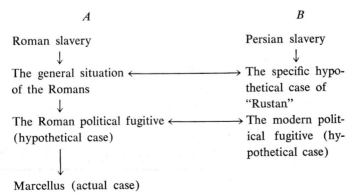

A	B
Roman slavery ↓	Persian slavery ↓
The general situation of the Romans ⟷	The specific hypothetical case of "Rustan"
↓	
The Roman political fugitive (hypothetical case) ⟷	The modern political fugitive (hypothetical case)
↓	
Marcellus (actual case)	

Such a chart illuminates the fact that comparison and contrast often achieves its special vividness by phrasing the general case in terms of specific cases, by passing from the hypothetical to the actual, and by varying one "side" of the contrast as necessary to illuminate the other—the real, continuous subject. The development of idea under *A* is continuous; under *B*, by contrast, each illustration ends with itself. Take one of the comparisons and contrasts you worked out for *8* above, and draw up a similar chart, showing how you would develop it.

Lines of Experiment

1 Make use of the technique of comparison and contrast in an essay illustrating a type of character, situation, or predicament. Be careful to choose a subject lying firmly within your experience and knowledge. The suggestions in *7* and *8* may be useful to you in isolating a specific subject and in planning your composition.

A few general ideas to keep in mind: *First,* get a clear sense of what you wish to illustrate—not only the fact, but also, and especially, the significance of the fact. *Second,* give yourself a choice: List several possible points of comparison and contrast before choosing one to exploit, and make your final choice with the significance of your main subject clearly in mind. *Third,* be sure that you are comparing aspects of your subject that are really central—the political aspects, if you are making a point about politics, the emotional aspects, if you are making a point about emotion, etc. *Fourth,* make the aspect of your subject that you are throwing into a comparison as vivid as you can: The major function of comparison and contrast is emphasis, and a subject can be made emphatic only as its significance for actual human life is illustrated in concrete, specific terms. *Fifth,* arrange the parts of your comparison and contrast in a dramatically effective pattern: Try out several sequences in your mind, before you fix on one.

2 Only too frequently there is a strong contrast between the way things are and the way they ought to be—between the real and the ideal—and this kind of contrast is more poignant than any other. The Roman citizen's enslavement by the emperors was far bitterer for him than it would have been had he known no history of freedom: His laws, his schools, even his forms of government suggested continuously a contrasting ideal of liberty. We often call such contrasts ironical. We find irony in a phrase ("That great statesman and profound political philosopher, Calvin Coolidge"), in a situation (Commodore Leon Smith's bombardment of the Union flotilla blockading

Galveston in 1863 killed, among others, Lieutenant Leon Smith, Jr., of the Union Navy), and in an idea (Joe Hill was lynched in a thoroughly democratic fashion). As these illustrations themselves make clear, the elements of the contrast are not always completely explicit; irony often relies on our recognizing a contrast without its being pointed out to us ("For Brutus is an honorable man").

Write an ironical essay on one of the following subjects. You may make the contrast explicit or implicit, as you choose. Three cautions: (*1*) Like other essays, ironical essays need to be thought through; (*2*) the most effective irony is not always hammered home with a sledge; (*3*) the greatest risk the ironist runs is that of being taken "straight." The suggested subjects are:

a Good old mother love
b The electoral process in a democracy
c News and the newspaper
d A man and his car
e "In God We Trust"
f How to cross a street
g "Till Death do us part"
h Education: myth and fact
i "A good time was had by all"

If none of these subjects suits you, choose your own. In order to be successfully ironical, however, you must keep clearly before your eyes the contrast between truth and pretence, faith and fact, reality and dream, aims and results, etc. You will have no trouble in discerning such differences.

HENRY ADAMS

THE COURT
OF THE
QUEEN OF HEAVEN

All artists love the sanctuary of the Christian Church, and all tourists love the rest. The reason becomes clear as one leaves the choir, and goes back to the broad, open hall of the nave. The choir was made not for the pilgrim but for the deity, and is as old as Adam, or perhaps older; at all events old enough to have existed in complete artistic and theological form, with the whole mystery of the Trinity, the Mother and Child, and even the Cross, thousands of years before Christ was born; but the Christian Church not only took the sanctuary in hand, and gave it a new form, more beautiful and much more refined than the Romans or Greeks or Egyptians had ever imagined, but it also added the idea of the nave and transepts, and developed it into imperial splendour. The pilgrim-tourist feels at home in the nave because it was built for him; the artist loves the sanctuary because he built it for God.

Chartres was intended to hold ten thousand people easily, or fifteen thousand when crowded, and the decoration of this great space, though not a wholly new problem, had to be treated in a new way. Sancta Sofia was built by the Emperor Justinian, with all the resources of the Empire, in a single violent effort, in six years, and was decorated throughout with mosaics on a general scheme, with the unity that Empire and Church could give, when they acted together. The Norman Kings of Sicily, the richest princes of the twelfth century, were able to carry out a complete work of the most costly kind, in a single sustained effort from beginning to end, according to a given plan. Chartres was a local shrine, in an agricultural province, not even a part of the royal domain, and its cathedral was the work of society, without much more tie than the Virgin gave it. Socially Chartres, as far as its stone-work goes, seems to have been mostly rural; its decoration, in the porches and transepts, is royal and feudal; in the nave and choir it is chiefly bourgeois. The want of unity is much less surprising than the unity, but it is still evident, especially in the glass. The mosaics of Monreale begin and end; they are a series; their connection is artistic and theological at once; they have unity. The windows of Chartres have no sequence, and their charm is in variety, in individuality, and sometimes even in downright hostility to each other, reflecting the picturesque society that gave them. They have, too, the charm that the world has made no attempt to popularize them for its modern uses, so that, except for the useful little guide-book of the Abbé Clerval, one can see no clue to the legendary chaos; one has it to one's self, without much fear of being trampled upon by critics or Jew dealers in works of art; any Chartres beggar-woman can still pass a summer's day here, and never once be mortified by ignorance of things that every dealer in bric-à-brac is supposed to know.

Yet the artists seem to have begun even here with some idea of sequence, for the first window in the north aisle, next the new tower, tells the story of Noah; but the next plunges into the local history of Chartres, and is devoted to Saint Lubin, a bishop of this diocese who died in or about the year 556, and was, for some reason, selected by the Wine-Merchants to represent them, as their interesting medallions show. Then follow three amusing subjects, charmingly treated: Saint Eustace . . . ; Joseph and his brethren; and Saint Nicholas, the most popular saint of the thirteenth century, both in the Greek and in the Roman Churches. The sixth and last window on the north aisle of the nave is the New Alliance.

Opposite these, in the south aisle, the series begins next the tower with John the Evangelist, followed by Saint Mary Magdalen, given by the Water-Carriers. The third, the Good Samaritan, given by the Shoe-makers, has a rival at Sens which critics think even better. The fourth is the Death, Assumption, and Coronation of the Virgin. Then comes the fifteenth-century Chapel of Vendôme, to compare the early and later glass. The sixth is, or was, devoted to the Virgin's Miracles at Chartres; but only one complete subject remains.

These windows light the two aisles of the nave and decorate the lower walls of the church with a mass of colour and variety of line still practically intact in spite of much injury; but the windows of the transepts on the same level have almost disappeared, except the Prod-igal Son and a border to what was once a Saint Lawrence, on the north; and, on the south, part of a window to Saint Apollinaris of Ravenna, with an interesting hierarchy of angels above: seraphim and cherubim with six wings, red and blue; Dominations; Powers; Principali-ties; all, except Thrones.

All this seems to be simple enough, at least to the people for whom the nave was built, and to whom the windows were meant to speak. There is nothing esoteric here; nothing but what might have suited the great hall of a great palace. There is no difference in taste between the Virgin in the choir, and the Water-Carriers by the doorway. Blanche, the young Queen, liked the same colours, legends, and lines that her Grocers and Bakers liked. All equally loved the Virgin. There was not even a social difference. In the choir, Thibaut, the Count of Chartres, immediate lord of the province, let himself be put in a dark corner next the Belle-Verrière, and left the Bakers to display their wealth in the most serious spot in the church, the central window of the central chapel, while in the nave and transepts all the lower windows that bear signatures were given by trades, as though that part of the church were abandoned to the commons.   One might suppose that the feudal aristocracy would have fortified itself in the clerestory and upper windows, but even there the bourgeoisie invaded them, and you can see, with a glass, the Pastrycooks and Turners looking across at the Weavers and Curriers and Money-Changers, and the "Men of Tours." Beneath the throne of the Mother of God, there was no distinction of gifts; and above it the distinction favoured the commonalty.   Of the seven immense windows above and around the high altar, which are designed as one composition, none was given by a prince or a noble. The Drapers, the Butchers, the Bakers, the Bankers are charged with the highest duties attached to the Virgin's service.   Apparently neither Saint Louis, nor his father Louis VIII, nor his mother Blanche, nor his uncle Philippe Hurepel, nor his cousin Saint Ferdinand of Castile, nor his other cousin Pierre de Dreux, nor the Duchess Alix of Brittany, cared whether their portraits or armorial shields were thrust out of sight into corners by Pastrycooks and Teamsters, or took a whole wall of the church to themselves.   The only relation that connects them is their common relation to the Virgin, but that is emphatic, and dominates the whole.

It dominates us, too, if we reflect on it, even after seven hundred years that its meaning has faded.   When one looks up to this display of splendour in the clerestory, and asks what was in the minds of the people who joined to produce, with such immense effort and at such self-sacrifice, this astonishing effect, the question seems to answer itself like an echo.   With only half of an atrophied imagination, in a happy mood we could still see the nave and transepts filled with ten thousand people on their knees, and the Virgin, crowned and robed, seating herself on the embroidered cushion that covered her imperial throne; sparkling with gems; bearing in her right hand the sceptre, and in her lap the infant King; but, in the act of seating herself, we should see her pause a moment to look down with love and sympathy on us—her people—who pack the enormous hall, and throng far out beyond the open portals; while, an instant later, she glances up to see that her great lords, spiritual and temporal, the advisers of her judgment, the supports of her authority, the agents of her will, shall be in place; robed, mitred, armed; bearing the symbols of her authority and their office; on horseback, lance in hand; all of them ready at a sign to carry out a sentence of judgment or an errand of mercy; to touch with the sceptre or to strike with the sword; and never err.

There they still stand! unchanged, unfaded, as alive and complete as when they represented the real world, and the people below were the unreal and ephemeral pageant! Then the reality was the Queen of Heaven on her throne in the sanctuary, and her court in the glass; not the queens or princes who were prostrating themselves, with the crowd, at her feet.   These people knew the Virgin as well as they knew their own mothers; every jewel in her crown, every stitch of gold-embroidery in her many robes; every colour; every fold; every expression on the perfectly familiar features of her grave, imperial face; every care that lurked in the silent sadness of her power; repeated over and over again, in stone, glass, ivory, enamel, wood; in every room, at the head of every bed, hanging on every neck, standing at every street-corner, the Virgin was as familiar to every one of them as the sun or the seasons; far more familiar than their own earthly queen or countess, although these were no strangers in their daily life; familiar from the earliest childhood to the last agony; in every joy and every sorrow and every danger; in every act and almost in every thought of life, the Virgin was present with a reality that never belonged to her Son or to the Trinity, and hardly to any earthly being, prelate, king, or kaiser; her daily life was as real to them as their own loyalty which brought to her the best they had to offer as the return for her boundless sympathy; but while they knew the Virgin as though she were one of themselves, and because she had been one of themselves, they were not so familiar with all the officers of her court at Chartres; and pilgrims from abroad, like us, must always have looked with curious interest at the pageant.

Far down the nave, next the western towers, the rank began with saints, prophets, and martyrs, of all ages and countries; local, like Saint Lubin; national, like Saint Martin of Tours and Saint Hilary of Poitiers; popular like Saint Nicholas; militant like Saint George; without order; symbols like Abraham and Isaac; the Virgin herself, holding on her lap the Seven Gifts of the Holy Ghost; Christ with the Alpha and Omega; Moses and Saint Augustine; Saint Peter; Saint Mary the Egyptian; Saint Jerome; a whole throne-room of heavenly powers, repeating, within, the pageant carved on the porches and on the portals without. From the croisée in the centre, where the crowd is most dense, one sees the whole almost better than Mary sees it from her high altar, for there all the great rose windows flash in turn, and the three twelfth-century lancets glow on the western sun.   When the eyes of the throng are directed to the north, the Rose of France strikes them almost with a physical shock of colour, and, from the south, the Rose of Dreux challenges the Rose of France.

Every one knows that there is war between the two! The thirteenth century has few secrets.   There are no outsiders.   We are one family as we are one Church. Every man and woman here, from Mary on her throne to the beggar on the porch, knows that Pierre de Dreux detests Blanche of Castile, and that their two windows carry on war across the very heart of the cathedral. Both unite only in asking help from Mary; but Blanche is a woman, alone in the world with young children to protect, and most women incline strongly to suspect that Mary will never desert her. Pierre, with all his masculine strength, is no courtier. He wants to rule by force. He carries the assertion of his sex into the very presence of the Queen of Heaven.

The year happens to be 1230, when the roses may be supposed just finished and showing their whole splendour for the first time. Queen Blanche is forty-three years old, and her son Louis is fifteen. Blanche is a widow these four years, and Pierre a widower since 1221. Both are regents and guardians for their heirs. They have necessarily carried their disputes before Mary. Queen Blanche claims for her son, who is to be Saint Louis, the place of honour at Mary's right hand; she has taken possession of the north porch outside, and of the north transept within, and has filled the windows with glass, as she is filling the porch with statuary. Above is the huge rose; below are five long windows; and all proclaim the homage that France renders to the Queen of Heaven.

The Rose of France shows in its centre the Virgin in her majesty, seated, crowned, holding the sceptre with her right hand, while her left supports the infant Christ-King on her knees; which shows that she, too, is acting as regent for her Son. Round her, in a circle, are twelve medallions; four containing doves; four six-winged angels or Thrones; four angels of a lower order, but all symbolizing the gifts and endowments of the Queen of Heaven. Outside these are twelve more medallions with the Kings of Judah, and a third circle contains the twelve lesser prophets. So Mary sits, hedged in by all the divinity that graces earthly or heavenly kings; while between the two outer circles are twelve quatrefoils bearing on a blue ground the golden lilies of France; and in each angle below the rose are four openings, showing alternately the lilies of Louis and the castles of Blanche. We who are below, the common people, understand that France claims to protect and defend the Virgin of Chartres, as her chief vassal, and that this ostentatious profusion of lilies and castles is intended not in honour of France, but as a demonstration of loyalty to Notre Dame, and an assertion of her rights as Queen Regent of Heaven against all comers, but particularly against Pierre, the rebel, who has the audacity to assert rival rights in the opposite transept.

Beneath the rose are five long windows, very unlike the twelfth-century pendants to the western rose. These five windows blaze with red, and their splendour throws the Virgin above quite into the background. The artists, who felt that the twelfth-century glass was too fine and too delicate for the new scale of the church, have not only enlarged their scale and coarsened their design, but have coarsened their colour-scheme also, discarding blue in order to crush us under the earthly majesty of red. These windows, too, bear the stamp and seal of Blanche's Spanish temper as energetically as though they bore her portrait. The great central figure, the tallest and most commanding in the whole church, is not the Virgin, but her mother Saint Anne, standing erect as on the trumeau of the door beneath, and holding the infant Mary on her left arm. She wears no royal crown, but bears a flowered sceptre. The only other difference between Mary and her mother, that seems intended to strike attention, is that Mary sits, while her mother stands; but as though to proclaim still more distinctly that France supports the royal and divine pretensions of Saint Anne, Queen Blanche has put beneath the figure a great shield blazoned with the golden lilies on an azure ground.

With singular insistence on this motive, Saint Anne has at either hand a royal court of her own, marked as her own by containing only figures from the Old Testament. Standing next on her right is Solomon, her Prime Minister, bringing wisdom in wordly counsel, and trampling on human folly. Beyond Wisdom stands Law, figured by Aaron with the Book, trampling on the lawless Pharaoh. Opposite them, on Saint Anne's left, is David, the energy of State, trampling on a Saul suggesting suspicions of a Saul de Dreux; while last, Melchisedec who is Faith, tramples on a disobedient Nebuchadnezzar Mauclerc.

How can we, the common people, help seeing all this and much more, when we know that Pierre de Dreux has been for years in constant strife with the Crown and the Church? He is very valiant and lion-hearted;—so say the chroniclers, priests though they are;—very skilful and experienced in war whether by land or sea; very adroit, with more sense than any other great lord in France; but restless, factious, and regardless of his word.   Brave and bold as the day; full of courtesy and "largesse"; but very hard on the clergy; a good Christian but a bad churchman! Certainly the first man of his time, says Michelet! "I have never found any that sought to do me more ill than he," says Blanche, and Joinville gives her very words; indeed, this year, 1230, she has summoned our own Bishop of Chartres among others to Paris in a court of peers, where Pierre has been found guilty of treason and deposed. War still continues, but Pierre must make submission. Blanche has beaten him in politics and in the field! Let us look round and see how he fares in theology and art!

There is his rose—so beautiful that Blanche may well think it seeks to do hers ill! As colour, judge for yourselves whether it holds its own against the flaming self-assertion of the opposite wall! As subject, it asserts flat defiance of the monarchy of Queen Blanche. In the central circle, Christ as King is seated on a royal throne, both arms raised, one holding the golden cup of eternal priesthood, the other, blessing the world. Two great flambeaux burn beside Him. The four Apocalyptic figures surround and worship Him; and in the concentric circles round the central medallion are the angels and the kings in a blaze of colour, symbolizing the New Jerusalem.

All the force of the Apocalypse is there, and so is some of the weakness of theology, for, in the five great windows below, Pierre shows his training in the schools. Four of these windows represent what is called, for want of a better name, the New Alliance; the dependence of the New Testament on the Old; but Pierre's choice in symbols was as masculine as that of Blanche was feminine. In each of the four windows, a gigantic Evangelist strides the shoulders of a colossal Prophet. Saint John rides on Ezekiel; Saint Mark bestrides Daniel; Saint Matthew is on the shoulders of Isaiah; Saint Luke is carried by Jeremiah. The effect verges on the grotesque. The balance of Christ's Church seems uncertain. The Evangelists clutch the Prophets by the hair, and while the synagogue stands firm, the Church looks small, feeble, and vacillating. The new dispensation has not the air of mastery either physical or intellectual; the old gives it all the support it has, and, in the absence of Saint Paul, both old and new seem little concerned with the sympathies of Frenchmen. The synagogue is stronger than the Church, but even the Church is Jew.

That Pierre could ever have meant this is not to be dreamed; but when the true scholar gets thoroughly to work, his logic is remorseless, his art is implacable, and his sense of humour is blighted. In the rose above, Pierre had asserted the exclusive authority of Christ in the New Jerusalem, and his scheme required him to show how the Church rested on the Evangelists below, who in their turn had no visible support except what the Prophets gave them. Yet the artist may have had a reason for weakening the Evangelists, because there remained the Virgin! One dares no more than hint at a motive so disrespectful to the Evangelists; but it is certainly true that, in the central window, immediately beneath the Christ, and His chief support, with the four staggering Evangelists and Prophets on either hand, the Virgin stands, and betrays no sign of weakness.

The compliment is singularly masculine; a kind of twelfth-century flattery that might have softened the anger of Blanche herself, if the Virgin had been her own; but the Virgin of Dreux is not the Virgin of France. No doubt she still wears her royal crown, and her head is circled with the halo; her right hand still holds the flowered sceptre, and her left the infant Christ, but she stands, and Christ is King. Note, too, that she stands directly opposite to her mother Saint Anne in the Rose of France, so as to place her one stage lower than the Virgin of France in the hierarchy. She is the Saint Anne of France, and shows it. "She is no longer," says the official Monograph, "that majestic queen who was seated on a throne, with her feet on the stool of honour; the personages have become less imposing and the heads show the decadence." She is the Virgin of Theology; she has her rights, and no more; but she is not the Virgin of Chartres.

She, too, stands on an altar or pedestal, on which stands a shield bearing the ermines, an exact counterpart of the royal shield beneath Saint Anne. In this excessive display of armorial bearings—for the two roses above are crowded with them—one likes to think that these great princes had in their minds not so much the thought of their own importance—which is a modern sort of religion—as the thought of their devotion to Mary. The assertion of power and attachment by one is met by the assertion of equal devotion by the other, and while both loudly proclaim their homage to the Virgin, each glares defiance across the church. Pierre meant the Queen of Heaven to know that, in case of need, her left hand was as good as her right, and truer; that the ermines were as well able to defend her as the lilies, and that Brittany would fight her battles as bravely as France. Whether his meaning carried with it more devotion to the Virgin or more defiance to France depends a little on the date of the windows, but, as a mere point of history, every one must allow that Pierre's promise of allegiance was kept more faithfully by Brittany than that of Blanche and Saint Louis has been kept by France.

The date seems to be fixed by the windows themselves. Beneath the Prophets kneel Pierre and his wife Alix, while their two children, Yolande and Jean, stand. Alix died in 1221. Jean was born in 1217. Yolande was affianced in marriage in 1227, while a child, and given to Queen Blanche to be brought up as the future wife of her younger son John, then in his eighth year. When John died, Yolande was contracted to Thibaut of Champagne in 1231, and Blanche is said to have written to Thibaut in consequence: "Sire Thibauld of Champagne, I have heard that you have covenanted and promised to take to wife the daughter of Count Perron [1] of Brittany. Wherefore I charge you, if you do not wish to lose whatever you possess in the kingdom of France, not to do it. If you hold dear or love aught in the said kingdom, do it not." Whether Blanche wrote in these words or not, she certainly prevented the marriage, and Yolande remained single until 1238 when she married the Comte de la Marche, who was, by the way, almost as bitter an enemy of Blanche as Pierre had been; but by that time both Blanche and Pierre had ceased to be regents. Yolande's figure in the window is that of a girl, perhaps twelve or four-teen years old; Jean is younger, certainly not more than eight or ten years of age; and the appearance of the two children shows that the window itself should date between 1225 and 1230, the year when Pierre de Dreux was condemned because he had renounced his homage to King Louis, declared war on him, and invited the King of England into France. As already told, Philippe Hurepel de Boulogne, the Comte de la Marche, Enguerrand de Couci—nearly all the great nobles—had been leagued with Pierre de Dreux since Blanche's regency began in 1226.

That these transept windows harmonize at all, is due to the Virgin, not to the donors. At the time they were designed, supposing it to be during Blanche's regency (1226–36), the passions of these donors brought France to momentary ruin, and the Virgin in Blanche's Rose de France, as she looked across the church, could not see a single friend of Blanche. What is more curious, she saw enemies in plenty, and in full readiness for battle. We have seen in the centre of the small rose in the north transept, Philippe Hurepel still waiting her orders; across the nave, in another small rose of the south transept, sits Pierre de Dreux on his horse. The upper windows on the side walls of the choir are very interesting but impossible to see, even with the best glasses, from the floor of the church. Their sequence and dates have already been discussed; but their feeling is shown by the character of the Virgin, who in French territory, next the north transept, is still the Virgin of France, but in Pierre's territory, next the Rose de Dreux, becomes again the Virgin of Dreux, who is absorbed in the Child—not

1 That is, Pierre.

the Child absorbed in her—and accordingly the window shows the chequers and ermines.

The figures, like the stone figures outside, are the earliest of French art, before any school of painting fairly existed. Among them, one can see no friend of Blanche. Indeed, outside of her own immediate family and the Church, Blanche had no friend of much importance except the famous Thibaut of Champagne, the single member of the royal family who took her side and suffered for her sake, and who, as far as books tell, has no window or memorial here. One might suppose that Thibaut, who loved both Blanche and the Virgin, would have claimed a place, and perhaps he did; but one seeks him in vain. If Blanche had friends here, they are gone. Pierre de Dreux, lance in hand, openly defies her, and it was not on her brother-in-law Philippe Hurepel that she could depend for defence.

This is the court pageant of the Virgin that shows itself to the people who are kneeling at high mass. We, the public, whoever we are— Chartrain, Breton, Norman, Angevin, Frenchman, Percherain, or what not—know our local politics as intimately as our lords do, or even better, for our imaginations are active, and we do not love Blanche of Castile. We know how to read the passions that fill the church. From the north transept Blanche flames out on us in splendid reds and flings her Spanish castles in our face. From the south transept Pierre retorts with a brutal energy which shows itself in the Prophets who serve as battle-chargers and in the Evangelists who serve as knights— mounted warriors of faith—whose great eyes follow us across the church and defy Saint Anne and her French shield opposite. Pierre was not effeminate; Blanche was fairly masculine. Between them, as a matter of sex, we can see little to choose; and, in any case, it is a family quarrel; they are all cousins; they are all equals on earth, and none means to submit to any superior except the Virgin and her Son in heaven. The Virgin is not afraid. She has seen many troubles worse than this; she knows how to manage perverse children, and if necessary she will shut them up in a darker room than ever their mothers kept open for them in this world. One has only to look at the Virgin to see!

There she is, of course, looking down on us from the great window above the high altar, where we never forget her presence! Is there a thought of disturbance there? Around the curve of the choir are seven great windows, without roses, filling the whole semicircle and the whole vault, forty-seven feet high, and meant to dominate the nave as far as the western portal, so that we may never forget how Mary fills her church without being disturbed by quarrels, and may understand why Saint Ferdinand and Saint Louis creep out of our sight, close by the Virgin's side, far up above brawls; and why France and Brittany hide their ugly or their splendid passions at the end of the transepts, out of sight of the high altar where Mary is to sit in state as Queen with the young King on her lap.   In an instant she will come, but we have a moment still to look about at the last great decoration of her palace, and see how the artists have arranged it.

Since the building of Sancta Sofia, no artist has had such a chance. No doubt, Rheims and Amiens and Bourges and Beauvais, which are now building, may be even finer, but none of them is yet finished, and all must take their ideas from here.   One would like, before looking at it, to think over the problem, as though it were new, and so choose the scheme that would suit us best if the decoration were to be done for the first time.   The architecture is fixed; we have to do only with the colour of this mass of seven huge windows, forty-seven feet high, in the clerestory, round the curve of the choir, which close the vista of the church as viewed from the entrance.   This vista is about three hundred and thirty feet long.   The windows rise about a hundred feet. How ought this vast space to be filled? Should the perpendicular upward leap of the architecture be followed and accented by a perpendicular leap of colour? The decorators of the fifteenth and sixteenth centuries seem to have thought so, and made perpendicular architectural drawings in yellow that simulated gold, and lines that ran with the general lines of the building.   Many fifteenth-century windows seem to be made up of florid Gothic details rising in stages to the vault.   No doubt critics complained, and still complain, that the monotony of this scheme, and its cheapness of intelligence, were objections; but at least the effect was light, decorative, and safe.   The artist could not go far wrong and was still at liberty to do beautiful work, as can be seen in any number of churches scattered broadcast over Europe and swarming in Paris and France.   On the other hand, might not the artist disregard the architecture and fill the space with a climax of colour? Could he not unite the Roses of France and Dreux above the high altar in an overpowering outburst of purples and reds? The seventeenth century might have preferred to mass clouds and colours, and Michael Angelo, in the sixteenth, might have known how to do it.   What we want is not the feeling of the artist so much as the feeling of Chartres.   What shall it be—the jewelled brilliancy of the western windows, or the fierce self-assertion of Pierre Mauclerc, or the royal splendour of Queen

Blanche, or the feminine grace and decorative refinement of the Charlemagne and Santiago windows in the apse?

Never again in art was so splendid a problem offered, either before or since, for the artist of Chartres solved it, as he did the whole matter of fenestration, and later artists could only offer variations on his work. You will see them at Bourges and Tours and in scores of thirteenth and fourteenth and fifteenth and sixteenth century churches and windows, and perhaps in some of the twentieth century—all of them interesting and some of them beautiful—and far be it from us, mean and ignorant pilgrims of art, to condemn any intelligent effort to vary or improve the effect; but we have set out to seek the feeling, and while we think of art in relation to ourselves, the sermon of Chartres, from beginning to end, teaches and preaches and insists and reiterates and hammers into our torpid minds the moral that the art of the Virgin was not that of her artists but her own.   We inevitably think of our tastes; they thought instinctively of hers.

In the transepts, Queen Blanche and Duke Perron, in legal possession of their territory, showed that they were thinking of each other as well as of the Virgin, and claimed loudly that they ought each to be first in the Virgin's favour; and they stand there in place, as the thirteenth century felt them.   Subject to their fealty to Mary, the transepts belonged to them, and if Blanche did not, like Pierre, assert herself and her son on the Virgin's window, perhaps she thought the Virgin would resent Pierre's boldness the more by contrast with her own good taste. So far as is known, nowhere does Blanche appear in person at Chartres; she felt herself too near the Virgin to obtrude a useless image, or she was too deeply religious to ask anything for herself.   A queen who was to have two children sainted, to intercede for her at Mary's throne, stood in a solitude almost as unique as that of Mary, and might ignore the raw brutalities of a man-at-arms; but neither she nor Pierre has carried the quarrel into Mary's presence, nor has the Virgin condescended even to seem conscious of their temper.   This is the theme of the artist—the purity, the beauty, the grace, and the infinite loftiness of Mary's nature, among the things of earth, and above the clamour of kings.

Therefore, when we, and the crushed crowd of kneeling worshippers around us, lift our eyes at last after the miracle of the mass, we see, far above the high altar, high over all the agitation of prayer, the passion of politics, the anguish of suffering, the terrors of sin, only the figure of the Virgin in majesty, looking down on her people, crowned, throned, glorified, with the infant Christ on her knees. She does not assert herself; probably she intends to be felt rather than feared. Compared with the Greek Virgin, as you see her, for example, at Torcello, the Chartres Virgin is retiring and hardly important enough for the place. She is not exaggerated either in scale, drawing, or colour. She shows not a sign of self-consciousness, not an effort for brilliancy, not a trace of stage effect—hardly even a thought of herself, except that she is at home, among her own people, where she is loved and known as well as she knows them. The seven great windows are one composition; and it is plain that the artist, had he been ordered to make an exhibition of power, could have overwhelmed us with a storm of purple, red, yellows, or given us a Virgin of Passion who would have torn the vault asunder; his ability is never in doubt, and if he has kept true to the spirit of the western portal and the twelfth century, it is because the Virgin of Chartres was the Virgin of Grace, and ordered him to paint her so. One shudders to think how a single false note—a suggestion of meanness, in this climax of line and colour—would bring the whole fabric down in ruins on the eighteenth-century meanness of the choir below; and one notes, almost bashfully, the expedients of the artists to quiet their effects. So the lines of the seven windows are built up, to avoid the horizontal, and yet not exaggerate the vertical. The architect counts here for more than the colourists; but the colour, when you study it, suggests the same restraint. Three great windows on the Virgin's right, balanced by three more on her left, show the prophets and precursors of her Son; all architecturally support and exalt the Virgin, in her celestial atmosphere of blue, shot with red, calm in the certainty of heaven. Any one who is prematurely curious to see the difference in treatment between different centuries should go down to the church of Saint Pierre in the lower town, and study there the methods of the Renaissance. Then we can come back to study again the ways of the thirteenth century. The Virgin will wait; she will not be angry; she knows her power; we all come back to her in the end.

Or the Renaissance, if one prefers, can wait equally well, while one kneels with the thirteenth century, and feels the little one still can feel of what it felt. Technically these apsidal windows have not received much notice; the books rarely speak of them; travellers seldom look at them; and their height is such that even with the best glass, the quality of the work is beyond our power to judge. We see, and the artists meant that we should see, only the great lines, the colour, and the Virgin. The mass of suppliants before the choir look up to the light, clear blues and reds of this great space, and feel there the celestial peace and beauty of Mary's nature and abode. There is heaven! and Mary looks down from it, into her church, where she sees us on our knees, and knows each one of us by name. There she actually is—not in symbol or in fancy, but in person, descending on her errands of mercy and listening to each one of us, as her miracles prove, or satisfying our prayers merely by her presence which calms our excitement as that of a mother calms her child. She is there as Queen, not merely as intercessor, and her power is such that to her the difference between us earthly beings is nothing. Her quiet, masculine strength enchants us most. Pierre Mauclerc and Philippe Hurepel and their men-at-arms are afraid of her, and the Bishop himself is never quite at his ease in her presence; but to peasants, and beggars, and people in trouble, this sense of her power and calm is better than active sympathy. People who suffer beyond the formulas of expression—who are crushed into silence, and beyond pain—want no display of emotion—no bleeding heart—no weeping at the foot of the Cross—no hysterics—no phrases! They want to see God, and to know that He is watching over His own. How many women are there, in this mass of thirteenth-century suppliants, who have lost children? Probably nearly all, for the death rate is very high in the conditions of mediaeval life. There are thousands of such women here, for it is precisely this class who come most; and probably every one of them has looked up to Mary in her great window, and has felt actual certainty, as though she saw with her own eyes—there, in heaven, while she looked—her own lost baby playing with the Christ-Child at the Virgin's knee, as much at home as the saints, and much more at home than the kings. Before rising from her knees, every one of these women will have bent down and kissed the stone pavement in gratitude for Mary's mercy. The earth, she says, is a sorry place, and the best of it is bad enough, no doubt, even for Queen Blanche and the Duchess Alix who has had to leave her children here alone; but there above is Mary in heaven who sees and hears me as I see her, and who keeps my little boy till I come; so I can wait with patience, more or less! Saints and prophets and martyrs are all very well, and Christ is very sublime and just, but Mary *knows!*

It was very childlike, very foolish, very beautiful, and very true—as art, at least: so true that everything else shades off into vulgarity, as you see the Persephone of a Syracusan coin shade off into the vulgarity of a Roman emperor; as though the heaven that lies about us in our infancy too quickly takes colours that are not so much sober as sordid, and would be welcome if no worse than that. Vulgarity, too, has feeling, and its expression in art has truth and even pathos, but we shall have time enough in our lives for that, and all the more because, when we rise from our knees now, we have finished our pilgrimage. We have done with Chartres. For seven hundred years Chartres has seen pilgrims, coming and going more or less like us, and will perhaps see them for another seven hundred years; but we shall see it no more, and can safely leave the Virgin in her majesty, with her three great prophets on either hand, as calm and confident in their own strength and in God's providence as they were when Saint Louis was born, but looking down from a deserted heaven, into an empty church, on a dead faith.

Lines of Inquiry

1 a Some understanding of cathedral architecture is essential to the analysis of this essay. Look up and draw the usual ground plan of a gothic cathedral, and identify on it the nave, the choir, the transepts, the sanctuary, and the altar.

   b Adams's vocabulary is somewhat difficult. If you do not know the meanings of the following words, look them up: bourgeois, mosaic, medallion, esoteric, clerestory, armorial, mitred, croisée, lancet, regent, rose window, apse.

2 a What pattern does Adams appear to be following in describing the cathedral at Chartres? You will find it useful, in answering this question, to break the essay down into internal units, and to examine these units in relation to the diagram you drew for *1* above.

   b How is the title of the essay related to its structure?

   c How is the first paragraph related to this structure?

   d How is the last paragraph related to the first paragraph?

3 a In earlier introductions, we have seen that description and narration are in a sense illustrative. Consider this essay as a whole; what does it illustrate?

    (1) Why does Adams give so much of the history of the cathedral?

    (2) Why does he spend so much time describing the strife between Pierre de Dreux and Queen Blanche?

   b The point was made in the introduction to this part that illustration is frequently a component of argument, a sign that the premises and conclusions of a logical process are consistent with fact. What value would Adams's essay have as part of an argument on any of the following points:

    (1) Medieval artists were skilled craftsmen.

    (2) Chartres Cathedral is a great work of art.

(*3*) Chartres Cathedral reflects vividly the history and spirit of the epoch in which it was built.

(*4*) In the Middle Ages life was more satisfying than it is now.

(*5*) The figure of the Virgin dominated and unified the medieval sense of life.

c For which of the above assertions would this chapter stand as the best illustration?

d Arrange the five assertions above in a congruent order, from most specific (i.e., concrete) to most general (i.e., abstract). Is your order related to the actual sequence of ideas in the essay?

4 The handling of time in this essay is unusual.

a What pattern of movement through time do you note? How is that pattern indicated?

b In what tense is most of the essay written? At what points in the essay does Adams shift tenses? What are his transitional devices in moving from one time to another?

c Why does Adams treat time in this essay as he does? Could he have written the whole thing just as well in the simple past tense? What would he have had to omit had he done so?

5 *a* What point of view does Adams appear to be following?

b Who is the "pilgrim-tourist" to whom he refers in the first paragraph? How essential is this phrase to the definition of Adams's point of view?

c Adams seems to ask us to see the cathedral from different angles or different times: We look, as it were, at first through one set of eyes then through another. What set of eyes is dominant?

d How is this shift in angle of vision related to the sequence of Adams's description of the cathedral?

e How does point of view enter into the introduction and the conclusion?

6 Mark in the essay every sentence that ends with an exclamation mark or a question mark.

a Where are exclamations and questions most frequent?

b Are the questions real or merely rhetorical?

c What effect do these exclamations and questions have on the tone of the essay?

7 This essay refers to many figures from history and religious legend. How many of the following do you recognize?

a "St. Sophia was built by the emperor *Justinian* with all the resources of the *Empire*. . . ."

b "The new tower tells the story of *Noah*. . . ."

c "*Joseph and his brethren.*"

d "*The Good Samaritan.*"

e "The *Death, Assumption, and Coronation* of the Virgin."

f "The *Prodigal Son.*"

g "*St. Louis.*"

h "Christ with the *Alpha and Omega*. . . ."

i "*Aaron* with *the book,* trampling on the lawless pharaoh. . . ."

j "*David* . . . trampling on a Saul suggesting suspicions of a Saul de Dreux; while last, *Melchisedec,* who is Faith, tramples on a disobedient *Nebuchadnezzar* Mauclerc."

k "The *four Apocalyptic figures* surround and worship Him."

l "In each of the four windows a gigantic *evangelist* strides the shoulders of a colossal prophet.   St. John rides on Ezekiel; St. Mark bestrides Daniel; St. Matthew is on the shoulders of Isaiah; St. Luke is carried by Jeremiah."

8 The artists who designed the glass of Chartres Cathedral are frequently referred to in this essay, although mere description of the windows would require no such references.

a What would have been lost had all reference to the artists been omitted?

b What view of the function of art appears to underlie Adams's discussion of the problems faced by the designers of the apsidal windows?

9 a At two points in the essay, Adams refers to the Jews.   In what spirit?

b What effect do these references have on you, as a reader?

c What effect does Adams expect them to have?

d What assumptions underlie Adams's use of "Jew" in this essay?

e Adams says, "One has it [the Cathedral] to oneself, without much fear of being trampled on by critics or Jew dealers in works of art. . . ."   Substitute for "Jew" each of the following words in turn, and judge the effect: homosexual, American, international, rich, female, German, hungry, academic, vulgar, conceited, Republican, Texan.

(1) Which words in this list seem more "legitimate"?   Why?

(2) Attempt to place yourself 200 years in the future: Do you imagine that your judgments of the appropriateness of any of these words will have changed by that time?

(3) How do you distinguish between a prejudiced and an unprejudiced judgment?

(*4*) Which kind of judgment appears inherent in Adams's use of the word "Jew"?

Lines of Experiment

1 In a sense, Adams presents Chartres Cathedral as symbolic of the medieval spirit.   The Cathedral itself makes this treatment possible, for its windows depict both the history and the faith of its time.   Adams's essay is unlikely to serve you as a close model for an essay of your own, however, for it is unlikely that you will find any contemporary building rich enough in historic and artistic fact to put successfully to a parallel symbolic use.   (It is unlikely also that you have presently the historical background to write an essay of such complexity and range.)

Adams's handling of time and of point view, however, can offer useful models for almost any descriptive essay contrasting a past to a present state.   An essay about a childhood gang, for example, might begin in the past tense—that gang being far away, long gone—and shift in midstream to the present tense.   It might begin with a personal point of view ("I") and shift to a collective point of view ("we").   Similarly an effort to contrast a present to a past landscape—city to village, tract to wilderness—might "fold" time and shift point of view in analogous ways.   The purpose of such shifts, of course, would be to make the past "come alive."

Choose some such subject—a contrast between two stages in your own life, between a past and a present landscape, etc.— and develop it in ways similar to those employed by Adams. One caution: Do not choose too large a subject, but do try to choose one that you know well.   Corollary: Do not choose a subject with a long historical foreground.

2 The essential point of Adams's *Mont St. Michel and Chartres,* the book from which "The Court of the Queen of Heaven" is taken, is that in the thirteenth century the world was able to unify itself around the figure of the Virgin.   By contrast Adams felt that the twentieth century was unable to unify itself —except around the idea of mindless force.   In his autobiography, *The Education of Henry Adams* (written, by the way, in the third person singular), Adams used his own life as the frame for a contrast between thirteenth-century unity and twentieth-century multiplicity, and found for the twentieth century a sufficient symbol in the dynamo.

The first of these books is descriptive; the second, narrative.

It is also possible, of course, to write about the changes of the past several centuries and about the significance of those changes within the framework of logically ordered discourse. One might, for example, classify the changes that seem to have taken place in the last 300 or 400 years, show how one change has led to another, and conclude with some general predictions about the future: Such an analytic essay would use various illustrations, of course, to make the process of change vivid, but would be unlikely to focus on a single symbolic center such as Chartres Cathedral.

The problem of such an analytic essay is to find a way of keeping it within reasonable boundaries. Focus on one kind of change might help: One might show how vastly a specific human activity—transportation, or farming, or communication —has changed as a result of modern industrial technology. Or one might reduce the scale still further, to a specific case study of the individual farm, factory, newspaper, or whatever. Write an essay of this last kind—one close in focus, distinct in subject, but rich in implication.

HERBERT J. MULLER

ST. SOPHIA
AND THE USES
OF THE PAST

I

When Henry Adams studied the great medieval cathedrals, he was inspired to work out his "dynamic theory of history," and in particular his famous contrast between the Virgin and the Dynamo, as the symbols of medieval unity and modern anarchy. He came to feel that the love of the Virgin Mary, which had raised the cathedral of Chartres, was "the greatest force the Western world ever felt," or even "the highest energy ever known to man." As a philosopher of history, he resolved to concentrate on the Virgin's "mental and physical energy of creation," and not to yield to the charm of the "adorable mistress"; but he was obviously smitten.   He ended by drawing his wistful, loving picture of the Middle Ages, which has become still more charming as men have grown appalled by the folly and evil of our own age.   Many writers are now saying that the thirteenth century was the greatest of all centuries, the apex of Western civilization; and a chorus swells with the obvious religious moral.

I thought of Henry Adams last year when I was working in the cathedral of St. Sophia, in Istanbul.   Here was the great monument of Eastern Christendom, in which the Virgin had also been the favorite object of worship.   From its famous dome one might get a still longer and larger view of history; for it was completed by the Emperor Justinian in the year 537—six centuries before Chartres—and it looks down on both Europe and Asia.   And so I too began to ponder the meanings of the past.   Unfortunately, however, my reflections did not lead to a neat theory of history, or to any simple, wholesome moral.   The cathedral of "Sancta Sophia," or the "Holy Wisdom," gave me only a fuller sense of the complexities, incongruities, and ambiguities of human history.   Yet I propose to dwell on these messy meanings.   They may be, after all, the most wholesome meanings for us today.   For the only use of the past is in the service of the present, and a simplified, glorified view of the past may serve only to make the present more unintelligible or more intolerable.

At least I begin in simple piety.   Although St. Sophia lacks the soaring grandeur of the Gothic cathedrals and today is rather shabby in its ornateness, like an overdressed dowager in decay, it remains a magnificent monument.   It is not a degenerate form of classic architecture but a bold creation in a new style; among other things, its architects were the first to solve, on a grand scale, the problems of setting a spherical dome on a square chamber.   Despite its ornateness there is a majestic simplicity in its basic design, with the vast nave lined by towering columns of porphyry and verd antique, and crowned by the great dome.   One can still get a vivid idea of its original splendor, when the sunlight streaming in through the high windows of the dome made a glory of the acres of goldleaf mosaic on its vaulted ceilings, and of the black, red, green, purple, and yellow marble of its paneled walls. And St. Sophia would be impressive enough simply because it has stood up for fourteen centuries, in constant use, withstanding hundreds of earthquakes, surviving the rise and fall of empires—living out a longer history than any other great building in Christendom.
Hence it is rich with the associations of all that has made Constantinople

so memorable in history. For nine hundred years St. Sophia was the stage for the high pageantry of the Byzantine Empire. Here presided the Patriarchs of the Orthodox Church—the Bishops of Constantinople who struggled with the Bishops of Rome, and established their supremacy in the East. Here the emperors were crowned and consecrated to the service of the true faith, and here they gave thanks for their victories over the enemies of Byzantium and God. In a real sense they owed their power to St. Sophia, for the Orthodox Church was the chief unifying force of a heterogeneous empire. It was the Church that inspired the heroic resistance to the all-conquering Arabs, which preserved Christendom in the East. Or it might be called the power of the Virgin; for more than once, in popular belief, it was only a miracle of the Virgin that saved Constantinople from conquest by the heathens.

Yet simple piety is hardly the key to the history of this worldly city, or even of St. Sophia. The Virgin no doubt had sufficient reason for allowing her cathedral to fall to the Turks; in its subsequent history, at any rate, there is an insistent irony of the obvious Thomas Hardy type; and thereby hangs my incongruous tale. Under the Ottoman Empire, Sancta Sophia served as a mosque, resounding with praise of the very masculine Mohammed. A few years ago this desecration was at last ended by the godless Kemal Ataturk, who was himself attempting the miracle of creating a new Turkey on the Western model; he made the cathedral into a museum, in keeping with his policy of discouraging religion. An American architect was granted permission to make the first thorough study of the world-famous building. I relieved the architect of some routine work by making rubbings or copies of masons' marks—the initials of the ancient builders, cut into the stones. This simple task gave me the opportunity of crawling all over the stately monument, feeling my way back through the centuries, and working up a curious, fond acquaintance with the anonymous masons. From these simple workmen I learned more about the complexities of history.

II

According to Henry Adams, it was the "attraction of power in a future life" that raised St. Sophia and the Gothic cathedrals. This motive might seem as selfish or vain as it did to St. Bernard, who was horrified by the ostentation of church-towers; but the more popular idea of Gothic art is that expressed by Ralph Adams Cram. Cram drew an ideal picture of the medieval artists and artisans, working freely together in a common love of beauty and of God. He contrasted their exalted piety with the crass materialism that raises the modern skyscraper, built by gangs of hired laborers to the greater glory of big business. And certainly we should be chastened by the glorious medieval cathedrals, especially when we consider that the Virgin of Chartres, the adorable Mother who was Notre Dame, or "Our Lady," is known to most Americans today only for her football team. Nevertheless the humble artisans who built St. Sophia—which Cram called "the everlasting wonder of all Christendom"—gave me chastening ideas of a different kind.

From all appearances, these artisans did not work in a holy, dedicated spirit. On some of the finer marble panels they left proud signatures, fancy monograms cut with loving care; but on most of the stones they chiseled out very crude initials. Apparently they made these marks in order to claim payment for their work; sometimes they signed a stone twice to make sure, with one signature upside down. I gathered that their primary motive was to get a job done and a living made, just as it is with workmen today. They differed from contemporary builders most obviously in that they did not work to exact specifications, but improvised as they went along. Their stones are generally rough-hewn, irregular in size or shape, and sometimes strangely imperfect. Instead of discarding, for example, a floor slab that had a broken corner or a crooked side, the masons cut the next one crooked so as to fit them together.

Upon close inspection, indeed, St. Sophia is an everlasting wonder in its anomalies. Quite apart from the wear and tear of centuries, there is hardly a straight line or a true curve in the majestic structure. Everywhere one finds an exquisite care in the refinements of decoration, and an amateurish crudeness in the rudiments. The splendid columns of porphyry and verd antique are typical. Their capitals, and the arches resting on them, are elaborately carved; their bases are so roughly finished as to shame an apprentice. And in inconspicuous places even their ornamented capitals are apt to be unfinished. Everything stands; but everything is wavering, bulging, or askew.

The obvious excuse for such slovenliness is the haste with which St. Sophia was erected: by a mighty effort, the Emperor Justinian succeeded in completing it in less than six years. This haste, however, suggests an unseemly impatience in his hopes of power in a future life. Justinian's piety is unquestionable—it is further proved by his savage persecution of heretics and his wars to extend the true faith. But it appears that he was also inspired by the hope of worldly fame that has led ordinary kings and capitalists to erect great monuments. At the dedication of his cathedral, he raised his hands to heaven and cried, "Glory to God, who has judged me worthy of accomplishing such a work as this! O Solomon, I have outdone you!" In other words, glory to God, and to the Emperor Justinian. Carved all over St. Sophia is the monogram of Justinian and Theodora, the brilliant courtesan who became his empress. Outside the cathedral he set up a colossal equestrian statue of himself, as a modern Achilles. In his palace nearby he required all officials to swear loyalty to "our divine and pious despots," Justinian and Theodora; all who entered the royal presence had to prostrate themselves and call themselves slaves. And to meet the worldly costs of his zeal in extending and adorning his holy empire, he imposed atrocious taxes—a fiscal tyranny that made him more hated by his Christian subjects than by his heathen enemies. Altogether, his reign was the most brilliant and glorious in Byzantine history, and the most disastrous. The builder of St. Sophia left an exhausted empire that quickly fell to pieces after his death, and took a century and a half to recover.

The succeeding generations of worshippers in St. Sophia left humbler tokens of their own aspirations to immortality. Scratched on the columns and balustrades in the galleries, where the women sat, are many ancient initials, sketches, and doodlings, including satirical drawings of bishops in their ceremonial robes. On the main floor the piety was purer, though of a superstitious kind. Hollows worn in the pavement beside the columns indicate where countless worshippers stood to kiss the holy ikons; a deep hole worn into the "perspiring column" of St. Gregory betokens the faith of countless more, who rubbed their fingers here to cure or prevent eye trouble. But less edifying are the memorials of royal worshippers. Among the superb mosaics, for example, is a portrait of the Empress Zoe, who ascended the throne as a middle-aged virgin and devoted herself chiefly to making amends for her prolonged chastity. Beside her is her husband Constantine Monomachos, who looks somewhat strange because his head is set on shoulders belonging to somebody else; he had been preceded by two husbands who turned out badly.

On the whole, the history enacted in the cathedral of the Holy Wisdom seems little holier or wiser than the goings on in most worldly capitols. Justinian the Great had strengthened the claim of the emperor to appoint and control the Patriarchs; his successors received a kind of divine right from the ceremonial of consecration in St. Sophia, wearing haloes in their official portraits; and whether or not they were pious and divine despots, they usually dominated the Orthodox Church. Occasionally a high-minded Patriarch defied an unprincipled emperor, or a bigoted Patriarch defied a wise emperor. More often the spiritual father accepted the policy of his worldly master, whose support he was pleased to enlist in struggles against rival bishops and the Roman Popes.

The one notable triumph of the Church was in its long struggle with the Iconoclasts, the emperors who tried to restore the purity of early Christianity by suppressing the worship of images. One result of this triumph is the beautiful mosaic of the Virgin that adorns the entrance to St. Sophia. Another result was the canonization of the Empress Irene—the imperious beauty who, as regent, brought up her son in utter dissipation, in order to unfit him for the exercise of his royal prerogatives and, when he nevertheless asserted himself, had him dethroned and blinded. She later became St. Irene because the Church remembered only her devotion to images: she had assembled the Council of Nicaea that pronounced "anathema on all who communicate with them who do not worship images," and that thereby reversed the Council of Constantinople of some thirty years earlier, in which 348 bishops had unanimously decreed that images were inventions of the devil. Although two more Councils later assembled in St. Sophia, to reverse each other, the images were finally restored once and for all, in the year 843, by a solemn ceremony which thereafter was annually commemorated in the cathedral.

Altogether, the Byzantine Empire is apt to look strange and unattractive to the Western eye. It was a nation without nationality—an artificial empire that called itself Roman, that we call Greek, and that in fact was made up chiefly of assorted Asiatics, of some twenty different nationalities. Culturally, it had little of the glory that was Greece. It maintained a brilliant capital, produced a notable architecture and ornamental art, and educated the Slavic East; but it contributed nothing of importance to literature, philosophy, science, or the life of reason generally. Politically, it was an Oriental despotism that had something of the grandeur of Rome but more of its rottenness. Its haloed emperors were above all law, subject only to the wiles of eunuchs or other court favorites, and to the plots of ambitious generals. Although many of them were able statesmen and brave warriors, hardly one was distinguished for Christian virtue; most were unscrupulous and cruel—ruthless adventurers or dissolute weaklings who alike earned the assassination that was commonly their fate. Their brilliant capital

was usually turbulent and licentious, the more so because it was never
free. Its history in this aspect is a drama of incessant intrigue and
brawl, centered about St. Sophia, the Sacred Palace, and the Hippo-
drome. In almost every scene some leading actors are executed or
murdered, and lesser ones have their noses cut off or their eyes put out.

In this whole drama, the historian Arnold Toynbee finds a wholesome
moral. He declares that the Byzantine Empire broke down about the
year 1000 A.D. (though it took four more centuries in dying), and
that the cause of its crumbling, just when Western Christendom was
starting a vigorous growth, was the imperial domination of the Orthodox
Church. The imperial ideal, a relic of old Rome, not only smothered
the vitality and creativeness of the Church but led to a fierce war with
the Bulgarians, fellow Orthodox Christians who refused to be dominated;
though the empire finally won this war, it was softened up for the
oncoming Seljuk Turks. Toynbee's moral is "the universal nemesis
of idolatry," the "perverse and sinful" idolatry of an ephemeral institution, in which worship is transferred "from the Creator to the creature."

Unhappily, Toynbee proves too little—or too much. The Byzantine
Empire was always fighting wars, for one reason or another, and almost
any war might have served to destroy it. The victorious one against
the Bulgarians appears no more inevitable, or inevitably fatal, than
countless others that have been waged in the name of either the Creator
or his creatures. If anything, Toynbee seems to prove the universal
failure of religion. The sinful idolatry of worldly institutions has been
common to all civilizations; established religions have typically been
allied with imperial or aristocratic interests. The fact remains that
the Orthodox Church approved of the Bulgarian war. Despite its
subservience to the throne it always retained great power and prestige,
which it seldom exerted in behalf of purer worship of the Creator. Because of its power it often weakened the empire, by its violent factional-
ism, and by its political conflict with the Roman Church.

In the closing scenes of Byzantine history, at any rate, one may also
remark the nemesis of the orthodox kind of idolatry. On the night
before the final Turkish onslaught on Constantinople, in 1453, the
Emperor Constantine Palæologus, the last of the Constantines, received
communion in St. Sophia. Then, accompanied by the Patriarch and a
large crowd, he proceeded to the church of St. Theodosia, to pray to
this martyr who had been manufactured in the struggle against the
Iconoclasts, and whose relics were famous for exceptionally miraculous

powers.   At dawn of the next day, which was St. Theodosia's day, he returned with a small band to the city walls, to fight and die gallantly. The great majority of his subjects spent the day in the churches, praying to their saints for another miracle instead of aiding their emperor. When the Turks fought their way into Constantinople, they found ten thousand persons in St. Sophia, still praying.   Legend has it that when Sultan Mehmet made his triumphal entrance he illustrated the lesson of nemesis with the head of the last Constantine, which he exposed at the foot of Justinian's statue.   In any event, he transformed Sancta Sophia into a mosque.

III

The future now belonged to Western Christendom, which had failed to come to the aid of Constantinople; but the Turks suggested another unwholesome moral.   As pious Moslems, they plastered over the mosaics in St. Sophia, because all representations of the human form were sacrilegious, and they obliterated the sculptured crosses of the infidel Christians.   They even effaced the crude little crosses in the signatures of some of the old masons.   They were almost as careless of detail, however, as the original builders: they overlooked quite a few crosses and did not bother with the inconspicuous ones.   Likewise they did not destroy the unholy mosaics but merely covered them with plaster, enabling their restoration in recent years.   More important, the Turks preserved St. Sophia for posterity by thorough, skilful repair. For they respected the magnificent capital of Eastern Christendom. They respected even the Patriarchate, granting it civil authority over Orthodox Christians throughout the Ottoman Empire; and by their conquests they gave it a wider jurisdiction than it had had in its heyday.   The unwholesome moral is that the terrible Turks were more civilized and humane than the Christians of the Fourth Crusade, who had captured Constantinople before them.

Setting out to fight infidels, with the blessing of the great Pope Innocent III, these Crusaders were more inspired by the attraction of wealth and power in this world, and they ended by fighting the Byzantine Empire.   When they took Constantinople they fired large sections of the city, massacred thousands of their fellow Christians, and for some days wantonly pillaged and destroyed.   They looted the churches as they did other monuments, carrying off some treasures, melting down others to make coinage.   (Thus some famous bronze statues of antiquity, which Constantine the Great had collected to adorn the first capital of the Christian world, were made into pennies to pay off the common soldiers.)   The priceless accumulations of nine centuries were part of the price of the Fourth Crusade.   And this happened in the year 1204, the beginning of the glorious thirteenth century, when the Virgin was at the height of her power.

So in fairness to St. Sophia, whose history we have been looking at from a possibly prejudiced, Western point of view, we might now look at the happenings in and around the cathedrals of the West. The thirteenth century also saw the founding of the Inquisition, the increasingly systematic persecution of Jews and dissenters, the atrocious extermination of the Albigenses.   Such violent intolerance was no doubt logical, given the Devil.   The Devil too was very real at this time; he was known to command a formidable army of witches, goblins, werewolves, and assorted demons, all in human shape.   Nevertheless the violence raises some question about an age supposedly united in a loving faith.   As for the great multitude, the social records of the period make clear that their faith was woefully impure, shot through with pagan superstitions, and at that was not sufficient solace for their hard lot on earth.   Although churchmen rarely protested against the principle of serfdom (and to Ralph Adams Cram feudalism is the truly "Christian social system"), they were constantly attacking village dance and song, constantly complaining that drunkenness and crime were most prevalent on Sundays and holy-days.   As for the churchmen themselves, there was notorious venality among the lower orders, and at the top a fierce struggle for worldly power.   And so Dante—now regarded as the symbol of this greatest of ages—believed that it was morally and spiritually bankrupt, and consoled himself by torturing its leaders in the ghastliest of hells.

The thirteenth century was in fact extraordinary in its twin cults of the Virgin and the Devil, its blend of chivalry and brutality, love and lust, faith and fear.   Yet it was a tragic century for Western Christendom.   In Toynbee's sympathetic account, its main outcome was the failure of the ideal proclaimed by the Hildebrandine Papacy—the lofty ideal of a universal Christian society, united under the spiritual dominion of the Church; and the failure was due to the arrogance of the Church.   From the beginning, this holy end had been corrupted by the use of violent means, and it steadily degenerated into a lust for power.   By the thirteenth century, the Papacy was engaged in a bloody, vindictive struggle with the emperors.   It was fatally injured even by its victories, having undermined its spiritual cause and armed the worldly powers that were to overthrow it. The aftermath—the Great Schism and the Reformation—only emphasized the spiritual disaster that had already occurred.

According to Toynbee, then, the Eastern Christian Society failed because the throne dominated the Church, and the Western Christian Society failed because the Church tried to dominate the throne. Or one might say that the power of the Virgin—"the highest energy ever known to man"—was not high enough to create a really Christian society. Neither Chartres nor St. Sophia inspired any notable holiness or wisdom in political and economic life. In both, the masses of men were taught to seek their well-being in the life to come, and to endure without complaint the hard lot that enabled the ruling classes to enjoy well-being in this life. The Eastern and the Western Churches clashed because both were politically ambitious, and because both—unlike the religions of the Far East—taught that salvation was possible only to their own followers, thereby automatically condemning the overwhelming majority of mankind to eternal torment. As for the conspicuous differences between the two societies, the pious Westerner may remark that Byzantium produced no Aquinas, no Dante, no Innocent III. The impious may remark that the West became the dominant civilization in the world after it had shaken off the domination of the Church, and set about cultivating natural sources of power; while Byzantium, trusting its Virgin and its saints to the end, went down ignominiously.

Yet St. Sophia still stands, eloquent in its massive silence; and its long history raises a final mystery before which all Westerners might be humble. Despite its apparently rotten foundation, this Eastern Roman-Byzantine empire had an astonishing vitality. It survived the fall of Rome, the "Eternal City," by a thousand years, maintaining a high civilization despite constant pressure from barbarians and infidels, and outlasting all contemporary empires, such as the Persian, the Arabian, and the Frankish. Why? What kept it going? I can see no very good reason, or at least none that illustrates a satisfying philosophy of history. It had a strong walled capital, with an excellent location for purposes of trade and defense. It had the secret of "Greek fire," the diabolic weapon that scattered or destroyed enemy fleets besieging Constantinople; possibly this military secret did more to preserve the empire than did its whole Greek heritage. Above all, it had good luck in its emperors during its worst crises, being periodically saved by the emergence of a strong, able ruler. This looks like mere luck because the rise of such saviors was not provided for by any peculiar wisdom in its political institutions; it was facilitated by the customary turbulence, intrigue, and corruption that also enabled worthless adventurers to seize power.   One is tempted to think that it was indeed the Virgin who kept saving the empire, for some unfathomable feminine reason.

Or one who wishes to be philosophical may note that the kind of despotism established by Constantine the Great, and cemented by Justinian, seems to be naturally congenial to the East, where, throughout history, there has been little spirit of liberty or faith in the power of reason.   In all the great Eastern empires the peasant masses have had little or no voice, and little will but to work and to worship.   To a democratic Western eye, accordingly, there is always an instructive moral in the eventual collapse of these empires; but the trouble remains that they often flourished for centuries.   So Egypt endured for more than two thousand years after its despots, in their monstrous obsession with power in a future life, took to building pyramids out of the blood of their people; and their pyramids are quite likely to outlast Western civilization, or possibly the human race itself.

IV

What, then, does St. Sophia have to tell us? I should not restrict its meaning to the few implications I have chosen to stress, from the drama of fourteen hundred years.   I should insist only that there is no one simple meaning, and that we must realize the profound incongruities of the drama if we hope to rise on stepping stones of our dead selves to higher things.   St. Sophia remains an inspiring monument, glorious and vainglorious.   It is a symbol of humility and pride, of holiness and worldliness, of the power of faith and the limitations of faith.   It is an everlasting triumph, of a society that failed.   So with Greece, or Rome, or the Middle Ages: as we rhapsodize over any golden age, we must add that it did not last, it did not do.   Especially as we feel that our own society may be damned and doomed, we must remember that all the great societies of the past were sufficiently damned, and were certainly doomed.

This is to say that the past should be regarded in the spirit of the great tragic poets, with reverence and with irony.   For most contemporaries, I suppose, the chief need is more reverence.   An American lady who paid ten cents to visit St. Sophia was so disappointed that she wanted her money back.   "They call it a museum," she exclaimed, "and there's nothing in it."   So there is nothing in the past for too many Americans, except for a notion of the holiness of their own brief history; and so they cannot really know who they are or where they are going, any more than one can live intelligently without memory.   Yet a sentimental view of the past or an infatuation with a dead self may also unfit men to deal intelligently with the present. Memory is apt to sentimentalize, especially in times of trouble.   As the simple man talks of his happy, carefree childhood days, which were actually full of childish cares, so the intellectual writes of some great age of the past, forgetting that it also had its follies and its vices, and was not great enough to master them.   On the most obvious issue raised by St. Sophia—the religious one—I should stress the need of irony.

Again I take Toynbee for my text.   From his remarkably bold, imaginative, stimulating study of the world's civilizations, he draws a remarkably simple conclusion about our own.   The decay of religious belief, he declares, is the "supreme danger" to our society—"a deadlier danger, by far, than any of our hotly canvassed . . . political and economic maladies"; our one hope of salvation is a return to the "One True God."   For the individual, this may indeed be the way to peace of mind—and the individual is no doubt entitled to whatever peace he can find these days.   But as a solution for the world's problems Toynbee's pious hope is hardly supported by his own study. He shows that the "higher religions" all developed in disintegrating societies, and did not prevent their collapse.   He shows that when Christian belief was strongest, it bred the sin of worldly pride from which it is supposed to deliver us, and was most deeply involved in the moral failures of both Eastern and Western Christendom.

Hence I conclude that if it is religion the world needs, it is a rather different kind from historic religion.   Perhaps it should be not so high a religion; we may welcome the increasing concern of the churches with the creation of a better society on this earth, instead of the salvation of the private soul in another world.   Certainly it should be a less exclusive and aggressive religion than historic Christianity.   Since the world order that men have long dreamed of has become a desperate necessity, the first duty of the Christian is not to convert the rest of the world to the True God but to tolerate, or even to learn from the great religions of the East.   For Christianity has not only failed to bring peace and good will on earth; until the decay of belief it was a major cause of war and ill will.   Even the medieval ideal of a united Christendom was provincial, and at worst barbarous; heathens and heretics—the vast majority of mankind—remained fair game for the pious. We may be grateful for the growth of tolerance, even though it means some loss of certitude in these high matters. And here Toynbee seems surprisingly provincial in his apparent implication that the True God is known only to Christians. He explains the triumph of Jehovah over all his ancient rivals by his jealousy, his relentless intolerance, his demand for nothing less than total victory; he concludes that only through this spirit of "uncompromising exclusiveness" can man grasp "the profound and elusive truth of the unity of God." If so, I conclude that this truth will continue to elude most of God's creatures, and that the price of His unity will remain the disunity of mankind.

Meanwhile our imperious problems are political and economic, and must be solved in those terms. In our efforts to solve them, we shall need all the good will that religion may inspire. But we shall also need intelligence, resolution, and social responsibility, which a religious revival might weaken. Today this revival often looks like what Toynbee calls "archaism"—a futile response to times of troubles which is animated by mere aversion or fear, and amounts to "a withdrawal according to plan rather than a pilgrimage inspired by faith." His own response amounts to a prayer: "we may and must pray" that God will grant our society a reprieve if we ask for it "in a humble spirit and with a contrite heart." In effect, he is saying that only a miracle can save us. I think he may be right. But I think we had better not live on this assumption, or give up faith in our own efforts. The plainest lesson I get from the history of St. Sophia is that men cannot count on miracles.

Lines of Inquiry

1 Muller's essay is broken into four sections.

   a What is the major subject of each section?

   b Underline in each section the sentence that seems to sum up the best its focal idea. Try changing the sequence of these focal ideas—for example, put the first section's central idea last, the last section's first. Could such an order be made to work well? What attitude toward St. Sophia and toward Christianity itself would such an order suggest?

2 Muller's title tells us that his essay discusses in part "the uses of the past." What are those uses? What use does he find in St. Sophia particularly? Is his discussion about the Church itself, about Byzantine history, about the religious spirit—or about all those things?

3 *a* Delete from the essay all references to Henry Adams—the first two paragraphs of the first section, the first clause in the second section, etc. In what ways does the essay suffer, if at all, from such surgery?

b What illustrative technique does Muller's use of Adams's theories exemplify?

c In what way is the focus of the essay on St. Sophia itself a necessary part of that technique?

d In your judgment, what might have been the effect if Muller had used as an illustrative center, instead of St. Sophia:

(*1*) A neo-gothic cathedral, such as St. Patrick's, New York

(*2*) A medieval English cathedral, such as that at Canterbury

(*3*) Chartres cathedral itself

(*4*) A modern church

e What special advantages does Muller derive from the use of St. Sophia in particular?

4 *a* What accounts for Muller's references to Toynbee?

b Why does Muller begin with a reference to Adams and end with a reference to Toynbee? What would have been the probable effect were the discussion to begin with Toynbee and end with Adams?

c How would you describe Muller's theory of history? (Compare R. G. Collingwood, "Progress as a Result of Historical Thinking," p. 219.)

5 Mark in the essay each paragraph specifically focused on St. Sophia as a building.

a What appears to be the function of these paragraphs?

b What relationship do these paragraphs seem to have to their immediately preceding and following paragraphs?

c What attitude does each such descriptive passage attempt to communicate?

d In what way does the sequence in which Muller has arranged these descriptive passages reflect his central point about the Middle Ages?

6 *a* How does the sequence of time enter into Muller's discussion?

b In what sections is that sequence most dominant, and why?

c What is used to bridge the gap between one time and another? From one topic to another?

d The third section begins with a reference to the Turks—why?

If that section were to open with a direct reference to the
Crusades of 1204 (e.g., "The Christians of the Fourth Crusade had captured Constantinople before then. . . .") would
anything be lost?

d Why does Muller turn in the third section to "the happenings
in and around the cathedrals of the West"? Muller does
not focus here on a specific cathedral—say Chartres—as he
did on St. Sophia; why not?

7 The last half of the second paragraph in the first section offers
a clear statement of Muller's attitude toward his subject—an
anticipation of his conclusions, as it were. Read the section
rapidly, omitting these sentences. Is the essay made stronger
or weaker by the omission?

8 Each of the following sentences preserves the bare sense of its
original. The original sentence follows in parentheses. In
each case, what is lost—or gained—in the revision?

a I begin in simple piety. "(At least I begin in simple piety.)"

b And St. Sophia would be impressive enough simply because
it has stood up for fourteen centuries, in constant use, despite
all calamities—because it is the oldest great building of the
Christian world. ("And St. Sophia would be impressive
enough simply because it has stood up for fourteen centuries,
in constant use, withstanding hundreds of earthquakes, surviving the rise and fall of empires—living out a longer history than any other great building in Christendom.")

c The splendid marble columns are typical. ("The splendid
columns of porphyry and verd antique are typical.")

d Beside her is her husband Constantine Monomachos, whose
figure is out of proportion because his head is set on the
body of a preceding husband. ("Beside her is her husband
Constantine Monomachos, who looks somewhat strange because his head is set on shoulders belonging to somebody
else; he had been preceded by two husbands who turned out
badly.")

e When Justinian died, the empire was exhausted, and broke
apart for a century and a half. ("The builder of St. Sophia
left an exhausted empire that quickly fell to pieces after his
death, and took a century and a half to recover.")

f Politically, the Byzantine Empire was an Oriental despotism,
splendid but corrupt. ("Politically, it was an Oriental despotism that had something of the grandeur of Rome but
more of its rottenness.")

9 St. Sophia forms a specific, nuclear image, around which

Muller builds his essay. For each of the following topics, identify three buildings that might serve analogous purposes. In each case, which building of the three seems the best choice? Why? What do you have to decide about the subject before you can identify a best choice? Do you discover *two* best choices in any of these cases?

a City life in the mid-twentieth century

b Country life in the mid-twentieth century

c The local state of the arts

d Local politics

e The local economy

Lines of Experiment

1 Go to a public building in your immediate area at a time when you can examine it thoroughly. Before you go, make a brief general list of the notable things about any building: its appearance, external and internal; its construction; its workmanship; its design; its surroundings; its furnishings, etc. (Much of this list you can construct from a study of what Muller talks about.) If you are at a loss as to how to proceed to study the building, walk through it swiftly once. What are its purposes? Has it more than one purpose? An unofficial as well as an official purpose? An emotional purpose as well as a rational one? What kind of people use it? How are its purposes reflected in its architectural details? Is the outside strikingly different from the inside? Are the back rooms strikingly different from the front ones? In short, what does its general architecture tell you about the meaning and quality of the life lived there?

Now you may wish to go through the building again, considering its details closely in relation to the general judgments you have come to. You may find it useful to make an outline of your ideas and to note the details that seem to reenforce those ideas. These judgments, and their supporting details, are the materials for your composition.

2 A building is not the only thing that can serve as the focal image for an analytic essay; a park, a street, a railway yard, a factory complex, a boat, a classroom, a book, a sport, a work of art, or a game often can serve as well.

In writing an essay centering on some such object, your essential problem is to find the object that will stand for what you want to say—that will serve as an image of your meaning. If you already know what you want to say, you can search systematically for the image that best expresses it. If you do not, you can look for the object that seems to mean the most— even if that meaning is not clear to you; by examining the object carefully, you should be able to find out what you think about it.

In your composition, keep your central object in the fore-ground: Use it as a bridge between ideas, as a way of passing through time and space, etc.; use it also as a way of establishing and maintaining an appropriate tone. The movement of an internal "I" is a valuable way of introducing a central image.

One caution: Choose for the center of your essay something you know well, and preferably something you can examine closely before you write your final draft. You cannot be specific about a building you know little about, for example, and you may not have noticed already all the details that will become important to you as you develop your theme.

ANGLE AND VOICE: POINT OF VIEW

"**Point of view**" can mean several different things—in ordinary talk, often "somebody's ideas about something"—Darwin's ideas about life, for example.   In this ordinary sense, point of view furnishes the materials for composition, but is not part of its technique, and therefore lies beyond the boundaries of this text.

In two other senses of the term, however, point of view is important to the writer as a way of ordering and presenting his ideas.   If we refer to "the scientific point of view," we use the term to mean a typical angle of approach to or attitude in dealing with a characteristic kind of fact.   Point of view in this sense is external to the act of writing but influences it greatly.   In another sense, the term is used to identify the typical kind of voice or person most present within the composition, whose way of organizing facts we are asked to follow, whose eyes we are asked to look through.   This sense is most familiar to us from fiction: In *Huckleberry Finn,* for example, Huckleberry himself is the internal point of view—we hear his voice, we see through his eyes.

Here are three passages illustrating different external and internal points of view.

1 The Crow universe was narrowly bounded. To the north and east flowed the "Great River" on which their kin, the Hidatsa, lived with their fellow agriculturalists, the Mandan and Arikara. But that far to the south there were Indians planting corn to the practical exclusion of hunting, people who dwelt in stone houses, made painted pottery, wove cotton fabrics, and, among many strange calendric festivals, also danced with snakes in their mouths—that was something wholly beyond the Crow ken. In 1916 I once sketched to a few elderly Lodge Grass men what I had seen among the Hopi; they listened with interest but without the slightest sense of kinship with these weird folk: I might have been telling of a trip to the moon. Nor did any Crow divine that on the coast of British Columbia there were members of their race who traveled in forty-foot canoes, built solid wooden houses, and recognized sharply separated social castes. Crow geography was of the Northern Plains, sweeping within their ethnographic horizon only a few marginal parasites like the "Pierced Noses" (Nez Percé) and "Bad Lodges" (Shoshone).
(Robert Lowie, "The World View of the Crow Indian," p. 405)

2 The Emperor Augustus would sometimes say to his Senate: "Words fail me, my Lords; nothing I can say could possibly indicate the depth of my feelings in this matter." But in this matter of mass culture, of the mass media, I am speaking not as an emperor but as a fool, a suffering, complaining, helplessly non-conforming poet-or-artist-of-a-sort, far off at the obsolescent rear of things; what I say will indicate the depth of my feelings and the shallowness and one-sidedness of my thoughts. If those English lyric poets who went mad during the eighteenth century had told you why the Age of Enlightenment was driving them crazy, it would have had a kind of documentary interest; what I say may have a kind of documentary interest. *The toad beneath the harrow knows/Exactly where each tooth-point goes:* if you tell me that the field is being harrowed to grow grain for bread, and to create a world in which there will be no more famines, or toads either, I will say: "I know"; but let me tell you where the tooth-points go, and what the harrow looks like from below.
(Randall Jarrell, "A Sad Heart at the Supermarket," p. 414)

3 In his paper, *The Tribune of the People,* he [Babeuf] denounced the new constitution of 1795, which had abolished universal suffrage and imposed a high property qualification.

He demanded not merely political but also economic equality. He declared that he would prefer civil war itself to "this horrible concord which strangles the hungry." But the men who had expropriated the nobles and the Church remained loyal to the principle of property itself. *The Tribune of the People* was stopped, and Babeuf and his associates were sent to prison.

While Babeuf was in jail, his seven-year-old daughter died of hunger. He had managed to remain poor all his life. His popularity had been all with the poor. Now, as soon as he was free again, he proceeded to found a political club. . . .

(Edmund Wilson, "Babeuf's Defense," pp. 433–434)

Each of these passages presents "somebody's ideas about something" —a point of view in the first, vague sense of the term. But each passage also deals with a characteristic kind of fact—Lowie with the facts of Crow Indian culture; Jarrell with poets, poetry, emperors, and fools; Wilson, with the stages in Babeuf's career. Further, each organizes his facts in a characteristic way, by a characteristic sequence: Lowie defines and illustrates; Jarrell constructs metaphors; Wilson records a series of events. To sum up, we say that Lowie is an ethnographer, Jarrell a poet, and Wilson an historian; these are the angles from which they write.

But a point of view in this sense, external to a composition, can show itself to us only in the way it is presented within that composition. Looked at in this light, the three passages not only are written from different angles but also present their subjects internally in different voices. In fact, the writers themselves seem to stand in quite different relations to the reader. Lowie speaks once, as an "I," but the sentence in which he does so tells us almost nothing about him; we must infer his point of view from the way in which he handles his facts, and we adopt that view ourselves without being especially aware of it. Jarrell also speaks as an "I"—but he declares his point of view, defines it openly and in forceful tones, and we cannot escape being constantly aware of it. Wilson presents still another case: He stands almost out of sight in the shadow of Babeuf, and it is Babeuf's angle of vision that we seem to see from, his voice that we seem to hear.

In sum, each of the passages reflects the controlling view of its author in a different way, corresponding roughly to the degree to which the author himself stands in the foreground of his composition. Jarrell's voice is highly *personal*. Lowie's voice is relatively *impersonal.*

Wilson's voice is the most impersonal of all, for in his essay he makes so consistent a use of a *secondary* point of view—a secondary voice, as it were—that it seems almost to displace his own.

These are the categories within which this introduction takes up point of view.

EXTERNAL POINT OF VIEW: THE ANGLE OF APPROACH

A carefully defined external point of view, or angle of approach, is important to the writer because it enables him to decide the relevance or irrelevance of specific aspects of his subject matter and the appropriateness of different ways of arranging and judging facts.

All subjects offer far more material, and suggest many more angles of approach, than any writer can use in any single composition. We can assume confidently, for example, that in writing each of the passages above the writer found details at hand that he made no use of: the physical appearance of the Lodge Grass men in their astonishment, the immense quantity of wood pulp digested daily by the mass media, the name of Babeuf's daughter.

Why were such details rejected? Nothing in the mass media as a subject demanded that Jarrell find poetry more relevant than wood pulp; nothing about the Lodge Grass men demanded that Lowie find their appearance less relevant than their age; nothing about Babeuf demanded that we know the name of his newspaper but not that of his daughter. Such facts are irrelevant not because the subjects are as they are but because the writers approach them as they do. To the ethnographer, the age of his informants is significant (the elderly speak more directly for a culture in its original state), although their physical appearance is not; to the poet, a line of poetry is relevant, although a ton of wood pulp is not; to the historian of ideas, the name of the newspaper is relevant, although the name of the daughter is not. A painter, an economist, a biographer, each might make different choices.

At first glance, the angle from which a given set of facts is approached may seem inevitable. Thus Lowie had to write from some point of view, and Lowie sees things and writes about them as an ethnographer because an ethnographer is what he is. Things seem the way we see them because we see them as they seem—the notion has an obvious, tautological truth to it.

The very obviousness of this idea, however, conceals the fact that men often change their points of view to fit their circumstances, the things they are trying to set in order, the results they hope for.   The medical student who dissects a cadaver in the morning and takes his girl friend for a stroll in the evening is careful to change his angle of approach to fit his circumstances and his purposes: He looks for the point of view that works.   Lowie writes characteristically as an ethnographer because the ethnographer's point of view permits the successful organization of certain kinds of facts for certain ends.   In another connection, however, that point of view may not serve him—he may have to assume the viewpoint of a taxpayer, an academic, a citizen.

It is hard, nonetheless, for us to imagine Jarrell or Lowie or Wilson writing from a point of view different from the one each actually uses. A hypothetical example, therefore, may illustrate the problem of choice more conveniently.   The man whose professional career has hardened writes, generally, from the angle established by his profession: Lowie is an ethnographer.   But the average student's education typically apprentices him to different points of view—the historical, the military, the legal, and so forth.   Let us suppose him writing about the draft.   If he takes the historian's view, he will probably be concerned with the origins of the system, its influence on political and social institutions, and so on—and he will find less relevant the system's treatment of individuals, its impact on medical standards, present deferment policies, and alternatives to military service—unless it is specifically the history of those things that he is writing about.   If he takes the military point of view, the military value of the draft would be the most important thing to discuss, and its history would be relatively unimportant; alternatives to military service would be totally irrelevant.   If he takes the legal view, or his own view as a young man about to be drafted, the relative importance of each aspect of the subject would shift again. Of the many points of view open to him, no two will produce quite the same order of ideas, quite the same standard of relevance.   He cannot take all points of view at the same time.

Once a writer has chosen his material, then he must define the specific angle from which he intends to approach it.   That angle will largely determine what aspects of his material are relevant and what aspects irrelevant, what topics are central and what topics peripheral.

Often, of course, the appropriate angle is defined by circumstance: In a history class, the student will assume an historian's point of view for

the simple reason that no other will satisfy his audience. If he assumes some other point of view—the artist's, for example—he must
be careful to identify it; otherwise, he runs the grave risk of misleading or even confusing his reader.

This last point is worth some emphasis. A careful *identification* of
the angle from which a composition is written is important, of course,
to the writer, as a way of establishing a standard of relevance and order.
But it is equally important to the reader, who must be able to recognize
that standard in order to appreciate the development of the writer's
ideas.

A general *consistency* in point of view is important to the reader for
the same reason. Any change in point of view always changes the
standard of relevance by which facts must be judged; therefore, such
a change can be thoroughly confusing unless explicitly identified and
carefully planned. Let us imagine Lowie confusing the ethnographer's
way of seeing things with the painter's:

> In 1916 I once sketched to a few elderly Lodge Grass men what
> I had seen among the Hopi; they listened with interest but with-
> out the slightest sense of kinship with these weird folk: I might
> have been telling of a trip to the moon. The firelight fell in star-
> tling patterns, reddish-yellow and smoke grey, through the lodge.
> The chief, the oldest man there, sat almost naked and cross-legged,
> his head thrown back, his scant squirrelly beard jutting out, his
> nostrils dark pits, fissures running from eyes to mouth like a pair
> of calipers, black edging into ochre; and two fiery spots where
> the eyes themselves caught the light. . . .

The images have been deliberately overdone, but clearly the point of
the paragraph is drastically altered—the ethnographer has disappeared.
Even slight uncertainty in the angle of vision, however, can blur the
focus and order of ideas:

> The military efficiency of the Selective Service system is open to
> serious question. The draft began in this country in the Civil
> War. After that conflict ended, the system was discontinued for
> over fifty years. The war of 1914–1918 saw it reestablished, and
> since 1941 it has been a permanent fact in American life. Vet-
> erans' benefits have pumped untold billions into the national
> economy, providing many avenues for Federal influence over
> education, medicine, home construction, farming—practically all

aspects of American life.   Still, an army recruited from volunteers could easily meet this country's current and foreseeable military needs.

Here, the focus appears to blur in the second sentence, and to be totally lost by the fourth; the last sentence, taking up again the point of the first, seems nonetheless to hang in midair.   Had a military point of view been maintained throughout, it could have illuminated the relevant aspect of each fact and thus established a much clearer structure:

The military efficiency of the Selective Service system is open to serious question.   The immense demand for men in this country's past large-scale wars—the Civil War, the First and Second World Wars—made some system of mass conscription an absolute necessity.   And the present economic importance of a huge military establishment with its economic afterlife in billions and billions of dollars' worth of veterans' benefits, makes the abandonment of Selective Service almost unthinkable.   Still, from the purely military point of view, an army recruited solely from volunteers could easily meet this country's current and foreseeable military needs.

In the second version, the overall point of view is consistently maintained; the historical and economic points of view are mentioned only to set off and define the military, by deliberate contrast.

To sum up: The standard by which the relevance and value of fact and idea can be determined in any given composition is largely a function of the writer's point of view or angle of approach.   This choice among points of view, in turn, depends partly on his material, partly on his audience, and partly on his purposes.   He looks for the point of view that works and sticks to it.

INTERNAL POINT
OF VIEW

The impersonal voice   That Lowie writes as an ethnographer determines his use of a relatively impersonal voice:

The Crow universe was narrowly bounded.   To the north and east flowed the "Great River" on which their kin, the Hidatsa, lived with their fellow-agriculturalists, the Mandan and Arikara.

But that far to the south there were Indians planting corn to the practical exclusion of hunting, people who dwelt in stone houses, made painted pottery, wove cotton fabrics, and, among many strange calendric festivals, also danced with snakes in their mouths—that was something wholly beyond the Crow ken.   In 1916 I once sketched to a few elderly Lodge Grass men what I had seen among the Hopi; they listened with interest but without the slightest sense of kinship with these weird folk: I might have been telling of a trip to the moon.   Nor did any Crow divine that on the coast of British Columbia there were members of their race who traveled in forty-foot canoes, built solid wooden houses, and recognized sharply separated social castes.   Crow geography was of the Northern Plains, sweeping within their ethnographic horizon only a few marginal parasites like the "Pierced Noses" (Nez Percé) and "Bad Lodges" (Shoshone).

The passage is clearly expository.   It forms a neat illustrative sequence, moving from general statement ("The Crow universe was narrowly bounded") through illustrative evidence (the Crow knew nothing of such diverse Indian cultures as those of the Hopi and the Northwest Coast tribes) to restatement of the original point.   Within this sequence, the Hopi and the Northwest Coast Indians constitute extreme illustrative cases, working to confirm the judgment with which the paragraph opens.

Even the systems of classification within the illustrative chain follow obvious divisions.   The surrounding cultures are classified by the four points of the compass: "To the north and east . . . to the south . . . on the coast of British Columbia."   The directions are called off in a systematic, clockwise order (not "north, west, south, east," or "north, east, west, south"), providing both sequence and linkage.   The points of difference between the Crow and the surrounding cultures are equally clear and simple: method of gaining food, method of building, social structure, and so forth.   Throughout, the reader feels no uncertainty about what classes of fact are relevant, about how they should be linked, or about what they mean.   The compositional game that Lowie plays is in a sense already common property.   His angle of approach contains no peculiarly private reactions, interpretations, or linking systems.

Throughout the passage, one further related fact stands out: Lowie himself is not part of the subject.   Only at one point does he appear to become part of it:

In 1916 I once sketched to some elderly Lodge Grass men what
I had seen among the Hopi; they listened with interest but without
the slightest sense of kinship with these weird folk: I might have
been telling of a trip to the moon.

But all we can infer from this is that Lowie observed as an ethnographer; his point of view does not become personal. We know
nothing of *his* reactions either to the Hopi or to the Lodge Grass men:
Lowie appears merely as a recording instrument for the Crows' astonishment—as part of the documentation. He could have kept himself out
out of it altogether:

The Crow knew nothing of the Hopi; when the way of life of
these Pueblo Indians was described to them, they reacted with
interest and astonishment, but without any sense of kinship. Nor
could any Crow divine. . . .

But Lowie's direct testimony to the degree of the Crows' astonishment
would be lost: "I might have been telling of a trip to the moon."

Lowie assumes a relatively impersonal voice, then, because both his
subject and his angle of approach are impersonal—are public property;
where his own testimony has value to such a discussion, he steps
forward—but he himself is not the focus. Obviously, Lowie's experience is necessarily private, like all experience, and there is much more
to it than appears in his report. But the specific area of experience
that he is after can be rendered in satisfactory public terms, within a
publicly recognized and accepted system of explanation known as
ethnography; therefore, although we obviously hear his voice, we do
not need to know about his peculiarly private reactions.

The strength of the impersonal voice in exposition and argument comes
from its implicit statement that private experience is rendered in public
terms: It suggests a broad common ground in fact and procedure, an
agreement about terms, a firm principle of relevance supported by
tradition. It avoids any suggestion of eccentricity, of a private quirk of
perception and judgment. If we imagine Lowie organizing his material
by a more personal, private test of the relevance of facts—telling us
of the line from *Hamlet* that entered his mind as he listened to
the Lodge Grass men, of his attitude toward snake dances, of his
regret that a fellow anthropologist was disabled by dysentery—the focus
changes instantly: We become conscious of a personal point of view
not our own, not public, not defined by general consent, but dependent

on, focused on, Lowie's special experience and concerns. Lowie becomes part of the subject simply because he has made us conscious of himself as observer.

In the original, by contrast, the impersonal voice restricts the focus to what could be said or found true by any man; in doing so, it appears almost to eliminate point of view as a factor in the ordering of ideas, and so to increase the certainty of the results. Those angles of approach that set up standard methods of dealing with limited kinds of facts—those adopted by the physical and social sciences, for example —are by nature impersonal.

One further element in Lowie's paragraph is important here: the handling of emotion. What has been said may suggest that the impersonal voice is not emotional; but this is not so. Gibbon's "The Slavery of the Romans" (see p. 346) is heavy with the judgment of history, expressed in deeply emotional phrasing and illustration. But that expression is indirect; we are made conscious of the judgment, but not of Gibbon the private man. To the historian, an ultimate judgment on history is both relevant and necessary—and entails the rendering of emotion. To the ethnographer, a further kind of emotion is relevant: the emotion of the people he describes. Such phrases as "strange calendric festivals," "weird folk," "members of their race who traveled in forty-foot canoes"—even such slight things as the "far" in "far to the south" or the use of "the Great River" instead of "the Missouri" move us because they suggest something of the value system of the Crow. But if Lowie had written "fascinating calendric festivals" or "a few disgusting parasites," the peculiarly personal emotion such phrases suggest would shift our attention immediately to the writer himself, who thereby would become part of the subject, fail in consistency of point of view, and blur the ethnographic record.

As it is, we see the Crow from two sides. The ethnographer's report remains impersonal, as it must; but the Crow speaks for himself:

> When Young-cottontail's mates have gone a certain distance, they turn back crying and offer to take him along. A second time he bids them leave and save themselves. When they return, the youth's father finds out all about his whereabouts and at once starts out with a rescuing party. "How is he getting on, I wonder? Is he still alive?" he said, and went off crying.

In such ways the ethnographer's necessarily impersonal voice can transmit an authentic personal record.

Emotion, value, and tone are discussed as a single subject in the introduction to the last part of this text. Here the relevant point is that the impersonal voice can carry emotion or avoid carrying it; the real question again is one of the standard of relevance implied by a specific angle of approach. An engineer's discussion of atomic weapons may well be unemotional; an historian's cannot be. The question most often is, what kind of emotion should be reported, and how can it be reported without a confusion of focus?

Thus, if, in a given discussion, the kinds of facts, the connections among facts, and the standards of judgment to be brought to bear on them can all be identified and agreed to readily by a reader—if they do not depend on the writer's special experience and vision, then that writer has strong reason to speak in an impersonal voice, for he is writing within a publicly acknowledged and understood framework of fact, method, and value. His own state of mind is not in question.

The personal voice Not all angles of approach can be adequately transmitted in composition by an impersonal voice, for the simple reason that some things are not public knowledge, and some angles are inescapably private. Jarrell writes in a personal voice because he writes about how he feels as a poet and as a private man:

The Emperor Augustus would sometimes say to his Senate: "Words fail me, my Lords; nothing I can say could possibly indicate the depth of my feelings in this matter." But in this matter of mass culture, the mass media, I am speaking not as an emperor but as a fool, a suffering, complaining, helplessly nonconforming poet-or-artist-of-a-sort, far off at the obsolescent rear of things; what I say will indicate the depth of my feelings and the shallowness and one-sidedness of my thoughts. If those English lyric poets who went mad during the eighteenth century had told you why the Age of Enlightenment was driving them crazy, it would have had a kind of documentary interest; what I say may have a kind of documentary interest. *The toad beneath the harrow knows/Exactly where each tooth-point goes:* if you tell me that the field is being harrowed to grow grain for bread, and to create a world in which there will be no more famines, or toads either, I will say: "I know"; but let me tell you where the tooth-points go, and what the harrow looks like from below.

Merely as a cluster of ideas, this paragraph is notable in several ways. First, its elements are remarkably diverse; it combines a quotation from the Emperor Augustus, a reference to certain mad eighteenth-century poets, a line of contemporary poetry, an analogy based on that line, and a concluding couplet.   Second, though some of these elements are offered us as if part of a common body of fact and opinion, no such common body is there: The quotation is spurious; the assertion that the Age of Enlightenment was responsible for the madness of certain lyric poets is not supported by a single illustration; the analogy between Jarrell's relation to his society and the toad's relation to the harrow is valuable only as an expression of Jarrell's own feelings.

Further, the connections among these details are tortuous: Only a close reader, remembering that the Age of Enlightenment was also called the Augustan Age and the Age of Reason, is likely to follow Jarrell's thought easily from sentence to sentence and to see that Jarrell is attacking modern culture as excessively rational, too little concerned with emotion.   The stuffy Augustan (and British) cliché links Roman rationalism of the first century to neo-classic English rationalism of the eighteenth; the Augustan esteem of the rational is then linked to the madness of certain eighteenth-century poets; and the poet Jarrell's own condition in the twentieth century is pressed, with the help of a line of poetry, into a modern analogy.

But as we understand from the moment we run into the blatantly spurious quotation with which the essay begins, a literal reading is entirely beside the point: The phony quotation, the shaky facts, the subjective analogy, are actually all illustrations of the way Jarrell feels.   The real focus of the passage is not on the "facts" that Jarrell adduces, but on his own state of mind—his private angle of vision:

> I am speaking not as an emperor but as a fool, a suffering, complaining, helplessly non-conforming poet-or-artist-of-a-sort. . . .
> What I say will indicate the depth of my feelings and the shallowness and one-sidedness of my thoughts.

That angle of vision is not only within the subject, in a sense it *is* the subject: "what the harrow looks like from below." The subject itself makes a personal angle and voice inevitable, for only the toad can know or say what he feels when the harrow hits him.   Jarrell does not expect to find any common ground with his reader ("If you tell me . . . I will say, 'I know'; but let me tell you. . . ."). And the function of that deliberately absurd quotation with which that essay opens is to announce that the logic of the passage is a poet's logic, its facts are facts of the imagination, its connections are metaphorical, its point of view is private. The first sentence establishes a class of relevant fact for the rest of the essay—and wood pulp simply is not in it. The personal voice, in turn, can identify and define that angle of vision, supply the necessary linkage among ideas, and justify the method, as an impersonal voice could not. In order to achieve his ends, Jarrell must create a kind of common ground out of a highly private stock of ideas and emotions, by making them public. Only a strenuous personal voice can do this job.

One important element in making public what is private is vividness of report. Consider the following:

> The ruler of a rationally organized society naturally speaks of his reasons, not of his emotions. The victims of that rational society, however, can speak only of their emotions, for reason is on the other side. Their testimony to the emotional damage done by a rationally-organized mass society has value, however, to those who want to understand their world; for only the victim can speak of what he feels.

Some readers may find this kind of prose clearer, in a sense, than the highly metaphorical prose written by Jarrell. Yet its clarity is more apparent than real; the original has far greater impact:

> The ruler of a rational, organized society
> The Emperor Augustus used to remark. . . .
>
> Only the victim can speak of what he feels.
> Let me tell you where the tooth-points go. . . .

Further, because ordinarily a personal voice is able to stay very close to image even when dealing with highly general ideas, it can suggest highly complex clusters of meaning and judgment with greater economy than can the impersonal voice: It can say "toads," instead of "victims," allude slyly to the role of the wise fool at the emperor's court (the fool has fool's freedom to tell the rude truth), and exploit without comment the condensed irony of "poets who went insane during the eighteenth century."

Such advantages as these clearly bear on the reader's emotions; viewed solely in a rational light, of course, many of Jarrell's statements are suspect. Perhaps the greatest strength of the personal voice is that it can present private emotion with something like its real force. Jarrell's title itself, "A Sad Heart at the Supermarket," tells us the subjective kind of fact he is most concerned with.

The personal voice, then, has great advantages. It can link highly disparate kinds of fact without seeming incongruent. Its informality permits sudden transitions, equally sudden shifts from anecdote to generalization, easy use of metaphor—in effect, great flexibility in tone. In organizing subjects essentially private in nature—subjects whose meaning lies in nuances or intensities of emotion, whose understanding is dependent on special insight or momentary and unrecoverable evidence, whose facts and values fall into no publicly agreed-on pattern—the personal voice offers the writer an indispensable liberty.

But it has also one weakness: By definition, the ideas it expresses are merely the author's:

> I am speaking not as an emperor but as a fool. . . . What I say will indicate the depth of my feelings and the shallowness and one-sidedness of my thoughts. . . .

If our experience of the mass media and of mass culture sorts with Jarrell's, if our reading is wide enough to enable us to catch and to understand his allusions, we may accept his judgments as valid.   If our experience differs from his—if we cannot adopt his angle of vision, Jarrell's conclusions remain merely his own.

The essential job of the personal voice, then, is to render an inescapably private world as vividly as possible—to make it over to the reader so thoroughly, so authentically, that it forms a common ground where none existed before.   Its aim is testimony, and only indirectly proof.

The secondary voice   In "Babeuf's Defense," Wilson writes as an historian.   In order to show one segment of the past as a significant pattern of events, he makes use of a point of view located within that pattern:

> In his paper, *The Tribune of the People,* he [Babeuf] denounced the new constitution of 1795, which had abolished universal suffrage and imposed a high property qualification. He demanded not merely political but also economic equality. He declared that he would prefer civil war itself to "this horrible concord which strangles the hungry." But the men who had expropriated the nobles and the Church remained loyal to the

principle of property itself. *The Tribune of the People* was stopped, and Babeuf and his associates were sent to prison.

While Babeuf was in jail, his seven-year-old daughter died of hunger. He had managed to remain poor all his life. His popularity had been all with the poor. Now, as soon as he was free again, he proceeded to found a political club. . . .
(Edmund Wilson, "Babeuf's Defense," pp. 433–434)

Such a point of view may be called secondary: Though Wilson is the writer, we appear to see the events of Revolutionary France as if we were in Babeuf's shoes, and the impersonal "I" of the author seems largely subordinated if not displaced.

Much of what has already been said of other internal points of view is true here also: The point of view we are asked to follow is identified at the beginning of the passage; it is consistently maintained; it provides the necessary transitions from event to event, from idea to idea. Things happen to Babeuf, and he responds, in "natural" (i.e., mimetic) sequence: First he founds a paper, then he condemns the constitution of 1795, then he is sent to jail, and so on. This natural sequence forms also a sequence of cause and effect, and thus Babeuf's life and thought form an illustration of the historical meaning of his time, and his point of view apparently, a test for the relevance of fact and idea.

Yet there is a distinct and obvious difference between Babeuf and Jarrell. Babeuf, after all, is not really in control of this paragraph. Babeuf's daughter dies of hunger—but we do not know her name, nor his personal feelings at her death; we do not know his wife's reactions, either—nor even if he had a wife. We hear about the constitution of 1795 not when Babeuf presumably heard about it—when it was promulgated, but rather when Babeuf reacted to it significantly and publicly—when he entered history in that connection. We witness not the career of Babeuf the entire man but that of Babeuf the Socialist; and it is Wilson's judgment that chooses and arranges the facts. Wilson provides a framework of idea; Babeuf is essentially his illustration.

This is the great value of the secondary point of view in description and narrative: It makes possible a compounding of the impersonal and the personal in such a way as to gain the special strength of each—the certainty that comes from dealing with public facts in ways publicly recognized and accepted and the value that comes from showing how those facts impinge in real terms on real lives. In a parallel way, an essay on the theory of democracy might use Thomas Jefferson as a secondary voice within the essay in order to present the abstract issues in moving terms, and within the frame of a specific, significant life.

Secondary points of view also enter frequently into expository narrative. In this form of discourse a writer may choose to follow a hypothetical secondary point of view through a sequence of actions—a sawmill manager through the sequence of lumber production, a lobbyist through a day's lobbying—in order to connect and explain that sequence. He may even decide to adopt the "point of view" of an inanimate object: an atom passing through an atom smasher, a white blood cell fighting an infection. Narratives of this last kind usually have very little emotional element, for evident reasons: An effort to show us how an atom feels as it is being smashed can only fail. By contrast, an expository narrative designed to illustrate the life cycle of the duck may well use a secondary point of view not only to link one stage of that life cycle to another, but also to suggest something of its pathos.

In all these instances, clearly any point of view will not do as well as any other. The mill hand will not pass through the experience of the manager, nor the manager pass through that of the mill hand; the duck lover and the duck will see things from different angles. Any point of view automatically limits the field of vision, sets boundaries to the subject and establishes an order among the facts within those boundaries. If it is to represent its subject well, a secondary point of view must lie not only *within* the real subject but also *close to its center of meaning*. Neither Charles de Gaulle nor Louis XVI could have served Wilson's turn.

Ultimately, it is the dramatic power latent in ideas that the secondary point of view elicits; for this reason, it is especially valuable in persuasion. Wilson's impersonal explanation of socialist thought in Revolutionary France might be lucidity itself, but it would remain, after all, only the view of a man at a distance. Babeuf's view is that of a man who paid his life for the socialist ideal. Especially where, as with Babeuf, the immediate human record is that of a man himself capable of powerful thought and expression, the use of a secondary point of view can create great dramatic tension at no expense to lucidity of idea. In such instances the writer himself can afford to stay fully in the background, for he is able to present the rational and the emotional in their original, fused state.

ROBERT LOWIE

THE WORLD VIEW
OF THE
CROW INDIAN

The Crow universe was narrowly bounded. To the north and east flowed the "Great River" on which their kin, the Hidatsa, lived with their fellow-agriculturists, the Mandan and Arikara. But that far to the south there were Indians planting corn to the practical exclusion of hunting, people who dwelt in stone houses, made painted pottery, wove cotton fabrics, and, among many strange calendric festivals, also danced with snakes in their mouths,—that was something wholly beyond the Crow ken. In 1916 I once sketched to a few elderly Lodge Grass men what I had seen among the Hopi; they listened with interest but without the slightest sense of kinship with these weird folk: I might have been telling of a trip to the moon. Nor did any Crow divine that on the coast of British Columbia there were members of their race who traveled in forty-foot canoes, built solid wooden houses, and recognized sharply separated social castes. Crow geography was of the Northern Plains, sweeping within their ethnographic horizon only a few marginal parasites like the "Pierced Noses" (Nez Percé) and "Bad Lodges" (Shoshone).

Within the radius, then, of a few hundred miles the gunless, horseless Crow of pre-Caucasian days sought to preserve his existence. It was a sorry kind of life. "Savages," says Dr. Marett, "live at but one remove from death." The ancient tales are charged with that theme: "In the early days the Crow were moving camp, they were roaming about seeking food." And Old Man Coyote is forever pictured going about, racked with hunger, "looking for food." But to seek and to find were not the same. Again and again a band was reduced to rabbit fare and threatened with starvation when big game capriciously stayed

away.   But even at best foraging was no light task.   Individual hunters
were gored by buffalo; the tribal hunt failed unless there was perfect
coöperation; women on a berrying-bee were surprised by bears or
abducted by enemies; even a fair-sized party of men were liable to find
themselves surrounded by a superior force of Cheyenne or Dakota.

Sorry, indeed, was the plight of the disabled or orphaned.   We hear
of a man with failing sight; his wife goes digging up roots and follows
in the wake of the camp, picking up what food others have scorned.
More circumstantial is the legend of two kinless boys: "Whenever the
camp moved, they followed behind; when the camp was pitched they
made a shelter for themselves, that is where *they* stayed.   Whenever
meat was plentiful, they picked up what had been left and dried it.
When the camp moved, they [the boys] took the discarded moccasins;
the best part of these they would sew together and put on. . . ."

Emergencies at times presented a grim alternative.   Should a crippled
tribesman be shielded at the risk of peril to his mates or abandoned to
his fate? On-top-of-the-bull goes on a war party and a shot fractures
his shinbone.   His friends drag him into a wood and discuss what
ought to be done.   But the hero grasps the situation with relentless
objectivity: "You had better leave me, you can't help me, you had
better go home."   So they put up a shelter, fill a paunch with water,
bring him firewood, and leave what provisions they can spare.   This
legendary episode was almost duplicated in the life of my informant
Yellow-brow's maternal uncle, Young-cottontail.   As a youth of
eighteen he went on a raid organized by Twitching-eyes.   An arrow
pierced his knee-pan and would not come out; his knee swelled up—
"There was nothing like it."   His fellows were helpless, and he himself urged them to abandon him.   So they made him a shelter, stocked
it with buffalo flesh and water paunches, and went away.

Yet in both cases the human spirit rises superior to the urge of self-
preservation.   Among On-top-of-the-bull's comrades is his own younger
brother.   When this lad has gone a little way, he bursts out crying:
"If I leave my brother while he is still alive, I'll never forget that.   I
will not go, I'll stay with him."   So he goes back to tend his brother
and hunt game for him.   Nor is this all.   When the party gets home,
On-top-of-the-bull's sweetheart learns of his plight and decides to rescue
him.   One of the warriors tells her the route, but with scant encouragement: "If you don't freeze and are not killed, you can get to him."   She
steals away with provisions, crosses river after river on the ice, finds

her lover, and brings him her food. Yet another trial awaits her. The brother sights a hostile party advancing toward them, and the older man bids his mistress conceal herself. She answers: "I have come a long way to see you and shall die with you now." By a lucky chance the enemy turns in another direction, and the rescue is consummated. The historical parallel holds similar acts of devotion. When Young-cottontail's mates have gone a certain distance, they turn back crying and offer to take him along. A second time he bids them leave him and save themselves. When they return, the youth's father finds out all about his whereabouts and at once starts out with a rescuing party. " 'How is he getting on, I wonder? Is he still alive?' he said and went off crying." They reach the hero and bring him back in safety.

Tales like these explain what social bonds mean where there is no paternalistic State to guard its wards. The single human being is a mere worm at the mercy of the elements. A man may be a champion marksman, but when there is no game to shoot he falls back on the pemmican his wife has stored against that very emergency; and even in the chase he is most efficient when he hunts in company. His robes and leggings are the work of his wives or kinswomen; his very arrows are not of his own making but the handiwork of skilled craftsmen. If he seeks renown, what are his chances as a lonely raider? Even a well-organized party was likely to be cut to pieces or be hard put to it when fleeing from superior numbers. Crisis lowered on every side, and it meant everything to be able to face life not alone but with a comrade, shielded by one's family and clan, in the bosom of one's club. That is why the kinless man was an outcast and byword of shame, the target for the brutality of sadistic tribesmen, forced to throw himself on the mercy of benign supernaturals.

Yet here is a curious fact. Battered by natural forces and surrounded by enemies, the Crow managed to wrest from existence his portion of happiness. Ask an Indian of the old school whether he prefers modern security to the days of his youth: he will brush aside all recent advantages for a whiff of the buffalo-hunting days. If there was starvation then, there were buffalo tongues, too,—supreme among earthly dishes; if you were likely to be killed, you had a chance to gain glory. What is a Crow to look forward to nowadays? Shall he enter unequal competition with white farmers? And his sister aspire to wash the laundry of frontier towns? Under the old régime, harassed as he might be, the Crow was owner of his soul. He had somehow hammered out for himself standards that lifted him above the sordid animal-like fray for survival. So with all the grossness of his sex life there evolved awe-inspired reverence for immaculate virtue; the callous egotism of the daily struggle for existence could be transmuted into purest self-sacrifice; above the formalized and sometimes tricky competition for honor emerged the loftiest defiance of relentless destiny.

We have found the Indians a mass of contradictions; and nowhere more so than in the matter of bravery. On the one side, old age is decried and youthful death alone looms as a man's proper lot in life. Yet more often than not discretion seems the better part of valor. More than one character in the tales lives to be "so old that his flesh cracked whenever he moved." The visions that mirror so faithfully the hidden longings of the soul again and again bring out the same urge for longevity. Hillside's protector appears with gray hair in earnest of the visionary's old age; a buffalo opens his toothless mouth to show Humped-wolf that he need not fear death until he has lost his teeth; and so forth. So the commonest form of prayer asks for life to be continued until such and such a season. Again, a warrior *could* scry[1] before setting out on a raid: if he saw his image with wrinkled face in a mixture of buffalo and badger blood, all was well; if he saw himself scalped or bloodstained, evil awaited him. But, Gray-bull admitted, people in his heyday were afraid to use this kind of divination; and his grandfather had become very brave *after* seeing his reflection with white hair and wrinkled face.

But as in every generation there were women who would not yield to the temptations of the flesh and fulfilled the qualifications of a Tree-notcher in the Sun Dance, so there were men to whom the traditional ideals were more than empty words to be sung at a dance to impress the young women. "I do not want to be old . . . I don't want to be afraid of anything . . . I'll do something to die," said one Rides-a-white-horse-down-a-bank. He went on four parties and dug himself a hole. When the enemy surrounded it, he leapt out and drove them back. Once there was a Lumpwood dance, and he allowed himself to be led about camp by a man who declared: "If any young women want this man for a sweetheart, let them do it forthwith, he does not want to live long." The young man painted himself white, mounted his white horse, covered its eyes, and made it jump down a steep and rocky bank, so that both of them were crushed.

Such aversion from life was sufficiently common to be pressed into a

[1] Attempt to see an image of the future.

fixed pattern. A man no longer interested in living became a "Crazy-Dog-wishing-to-die"; he wore sashes and other trappings for regalia, carried a rattle, danced and sang distinctive songs as he rode about camp. He "talked crosswise," i.e., he said the opposite of what he meant and expected to be addressed correspondingly. Above all, he was pledged to foolhardiness. In this as in other features he conformed to the pattern of the military clubs. But while the officers in these societies were in the main obliged merely to hold their ground, a Crazy Dog deliberately courted death, recklessly dashing up to the enemy so as to be killed within the space of one season. Whenever one of them rode through camp, the old women cheered him lustily and younger ones came to comfort him at night. But his own kin naturally tried to dissuade him and grieved over his resolve to die. "Why have you done that?" Spotted-rabbit's mother asked: "you are one of the best-situated young men . . . you are one of the most fortunate men who ever lived . . . and were always happy." But Spotted-rabbit was bored with life because he could not get over his father's death. Similarly, Cottontail's sister tried to dissuade him: "This is a bad thing for you to do. Even if you want to die without good cause, there are plenty of enemies and if you are not afraid you can get killed without special effort. If men become Crazy Dogs and are not killed, they become a laughingstock, . . . they are said to be worthless." The account continues: "He did not say 'Yes,' he said nothing at all, but one night some time after this when the people had gone to bed he came out, shouting, and sang the Crazy Dog songs. His sisters fell a-crying, but there was nothing they could do." Cottontail, too, had a motive: he had never wholly recovered from the injury to his knee. "Whenever young men went afoot on a raid or hunting, whenever they undertook anything, he was handicapped and felt envious."

Such men grew restive if the days passed and their longing remained unfulfilled. When Spotted-rabbit received a gift of plums, he said, "I began to be a Crazy Dog early in the spring and did not think I should live so long; yet here am I today eating plums." And Cottontail would complain, "Methinks, we'll *never* meet the enemy." But he, like Spotted-rabbit before him, had his wish. Once the Crow made the enemy fortify himself in a trench. Cottontail said, "Already I was thinking I was not to see the enemy . . . ; yonder I see some. This is what I am looking for." He advanced, shot down at the Dakota, and was instantly killed. That night it rained violently, and the corpse lay in the water until daybreak. Then the Crow hung it over Cottontail's horse.

"Then they brought him home, grieving they took him to the camp, all the Crow, the entire camp cried. They laid him on a scaffold, they stuck a tipi pole into the ground and tied his sashes to it, his drum and rattle they tied to it. Above they were blowing in the breeze. Then without him they moved."

The respect paid to a Crazy Dog was probably not altogether due to admiration for egotistical recklessness. It was a foregone conclusion that a man who had renounced life would do the utmost damage possible to the enemy. More than a mere paragon of valor, he was thus at least potentially a source of power to the tribe. But the altruistic value of intrepidity appears in more explicit fashion. There were men willing to make a stand to rescue a fleeing fellow-Crow and honored accordingly. A bereaved mother would go about wailing and implore brave men to avenge her wrongs: "The Dakota have killed my . . . child, who is going to kill one of them for me?" And the warrior's mentor would encourage him with such words as: "A child has been killed, a woman has asked you for help, that is why I want you to help." In the herald's speeches the appeal is constantly to human sympathy with the pitiable captives subjected to humiliation by a cruel chief and casting wistful glances toward their possible liberators.

The same narrative contains an extraordinary human document exposing at once human frailty and grandeur in the same individual and culminating in a magnificent blending of patriotic fervor on behalf of the oppressed tribesfolk and the spirit of the Crazy Dog who has faced reality and turns his back upon this vale of tears. Double-face has been one of the young braves publicly presented to the tribe by the herald as their champions in the impending battle. But when the crowd has dispersed, Double-face is racked with doubts. To quote Yellow-brow:

"Then this day Double-face was lying around; he stripped, he was nervous, he was uncomfortable. Whatever he undertook turned out ill. The reason he was upset was that there was to be a battle and he was nervous: whether because of eagerness or fear, whatever the cause, that is why he was upset. He would smoke, he would sit up, he lay down, he got up and bathed, he would return and stroll about, then he sat down. Now he had an elder brother, Deer-necklace, and him he sent for. He came and entered. 'Sit there.' This man who had just entered said, 'Well, why are you calling me?' 'Well, I am upset now, that is why I am calling you. There are three things I am now eager to do: I want to sing a sacred song; I want to sing a Big Dog song; I want to cry. Why is it thus?' Double-face asked. This man answered: 'You are about to go to battle, your medicines are anxious, that is why. Wait!' He boiled wild-carrot root . . . and mixed it with a little white clay. He [Double-face] took it . . . and swallowed it. 'That is all, I'll go now.' This man went out and away.

"Double-face got very hot, he began to perspire. His horse had been standing. 'I have been upset, but I shall accomplish my purpose,' he said and went out. He took his horse, marked it, fitted on his medicines, painted himself, and went out mounted to wail within the camp-circle:

" 'I used to think that since my birth I had had many sorrows. It turns out that there was something in store for me. I was grieving, but I did not know that today all manner of sorrow would be coming to a head. The women at my home are miserable, I daresay. 'How are the captive Crow faring?' they are ever thinking to themselves. My poor dear housemates, my distressed kin, the enemy makes them sit under the dripping water, he is ever abusing them, he thinks his men are the only ones to be brave. What can I do to distress him, I wonder?

" 'You Above, if there be one who knows what is going on, repay me today for the distress I have suffered. Inside the Earth, if there be any one there who knows what is going on, repay me for the distress I have suffered. The One Who causes things, Whoever he be, I have now had my fill of life. Grant me death, my sorrows are overabundant. Though children are timid, they die harsh deaths, it is said. Though women are timid, You make them die harsh deaths. *I* do not want to live long; were I to live long, my sorrows would be overabundant, I do not want it!'

"He went crying," the tale continues, "and those who heard him all cried."

We have here reached the peak of the Crow spirit. With a splendid gesture the hero turns away from the earthly goods that figure so largely in Crow prayer; he has no thought even of glory, he thinks only of his suffering kin in a hostile camp. Bruised by the problem of evil that in retrospect seems to have dogged him from infancy, he asks only for release from his torture. Why linger? Earth and sky are everlasting, but men must die; old age is a scourge and death in battle a blessing.

Lines of Inquiry

1 In the introduction to this part, Lowie's point of view was identified as that of the ethnographer.

   a What kinds of facts does the ethnographer appear to think most relevant to the understanding of a world view?

    b Can you name five classes of fact that the ethnographer does *not* consider relevant?

    c What definition of the term "world view" seems to underlie Lowie's discussion?

2 *a* What is the major class of fact that Lowie makes use of in this essay?

    b How is this class of fact related to his subject?

    c Can you distinguish different types of illustration within this class?

    d Why does the story about On-top-of-the-bull precede the story about Young-cottontail?   Could their order be reversed with no loss?

    e Why does the story about Rides-a-white-horse-down-a-bank precede the stories of Spotted-rabbit and Cottontail?

    f Why do the stories of Spotted-rabbit and Cottontail precede that of Double-face?

3 *a* What appears to be Lowie's audience?

    b Would it be possible for Lowie to write about the Crow attitude toward life and death from any point of view other than that of the ethnographer?

    c What changes would you expect to see in the essay if it were to be rewritten for an audience of (*1*) psychologists, (*2*) classicists, (*3*) musicians, (*4*) clergymen, (*5*) teachers, (*6*) soldiers.

4 Each of Lowie's paragraphs is focused on a particular idea, usually announced in the first or second sentence.   List these ideas in their actual sequence, and mark off on your list the points at which one group of related ideas—one superparagraph—gives place to another.

    a How would you characterize the movement of ideas within the first group?

    b Could the sequence of main ideas in this first group be shifted?

    c What is the movement of ideas within the last sequence?

    d Why does the story of Double-face end without a clear statement of his fate?

5 What seems to be the most important of Lowie's illustrations, where is it placed in the sequence of the essay, and why there?

6 In previous essays, we have often noted a relationship between the first and the last paragraphs—a kind of circling back, an expansion at the end of a statement made at the beginning. Is there any such relationship between the opening and the closing of Lowie's essay on the world view of the Crow?

How would you characterize the movement of the essay as a whole?

Lines of Experiment

1 Write an essay describing the characteristic world view of a kind of person you know well: the athlete, the professional military officer, the politician, the college professor, the suburban housewife, the would-be writer, etc. Be sure to choose as your subject a group that is fairly homogenous in its views; otherwise, you may not be able to isolate a strongly defined common world view.

Some of the questions important to answer in a discussion of any such topic are these:

a How can you define the world view of the group you have chosen—what kinds of ideas does it contain?

b What form of evidence will you use? Narratives? Myths? Songs? Cliches? Characteristic actions?

c What specific illustration can serve as a center for your essay?

d How can you introduce your subject so as to make it interesting to a reader, and how can you end it so as to make the end more important than the beginning?

e What determines the order in which you present the main ideas in this world view?

2 Take three or four stories about the same subject—"the war," a sport, school plays, teachers, etc.—and make these stories the center of an analytic essay. Your focus here is not on a world view so much as on the significance of a specific subject to a specific group. You do not have to restrict yourself to stories that you know to be historically true; fiction can be just as descriptive as history.

a What do these stories have in common, besides their subject?

b What do they say?

c Who tells them?

d In what circumstances are they told?

e What do they mean?

3 Choose a poet, a short story writer, a journalist, an historian, or the author of one of the essays in this volume—the sole condition being that you are familiar with the work of your subject —and describe the world view expressed in that work. In shaping your composition, you may find the questions under *1* and *2* above useful to you. If "world view" seems too large a focus, narrow it. You may restrict yourself to the writer's attitudes toward art, industrialism, sex, violence, or whatever. The essential problem of the composition is to find, in written

material, evidences of a specific attitude and to group those
evidences in an effective and revealing way.

RANDALL JARRELL

A SAD HEART
AT THE
SUPERMARKET

The Emperor Augustus would sometimes say to his Senate: "Words
fail me, my Lords; nothing I can say could possibly indicate the depth
of my feelings in this matter."   But in this matter of mass culture, the
mass media, I am speaking not as an emperor but as a fool, a suffering,
complaining, helplessly non-conforming poet-or-artist-of-a-sort, far off
at the obsolescent rear of things; what I say will indicate the depth of
my feelings and the shallowness and one-sidedness of my thoughts.   If
those English lyric poets who went mad during the eighteenth century
had told you why the Age of Enlightenment was driving them crazy, it
would have had a kind of documentary interest: what I say may have a
kind of documentary interest. *The toad beneath the harrow knows/
Exactly where each tooth-point goes:* if you tell me that the field is being
harrowed to grow grain for bread, and to create a world in which there
will be no more famines, or toads either, I will say: "I know"; but let
me tell you where the tooth-points go, and what the harrow looks like
from below.

Advertising men, businessmen speak continually of *media* or *the media*
or *the mass media*.   One of their trade journals is named, simply,
Media.   It is an impressive word: one imagines Mephistopheles offering
Faust *media that no man has ever known;* one feels, while the word is
in one's ear, that abstract, overmastering powers, of a scale and intensity unimagined yesterday, are being offered one by the technicians
who discovered and control them—offered, and at a price.   The word
has the clear fatal ring of that new world whose space we occupy so
luxuriously and precariously; the world that produces mink stoles,
rockabilly records, and tactical nuclear weapons by the million; the
world that Attila, Galileo, Hansel and Gretel never knew.

And yet, it's only the plural of *medium*. *"Medium,"* says the dictionary, "that which lies in the middle; hence, middle condition or degree . . . A substance through which a force acts or an effect is transmitted . . . That through or by which anything is accomplished; as, an advertising *medium* . . . *Biol.* A nutritive mixture or substance, as broth, gelatin, agar, for cultivating bacteria, fungi, etc."

Let us name *our* trade journal *The Medium*. For all these media— television, radio, movies, newspapers, magazines, and the rest—are a single medium, in whose depths we are all being cultivated. This Medium is of middle condition or degree, mediocre; it lies in the middle of everything, between a man and his neighbor, his wife, his child, his self; it, more than anything else, is the substance through which the forces of our society act upon us, and make us into what our society needs.

And what does it need? For us to need.

Oh, it needs for us to do or be many things: workers, technicians, executives, soldiers, housewives. But first of all, last of all, it needs for us to be buyers; consumers; beings who want much and will want more —who want consistently and insatiably. Find some spell to make us turn away from the stoles, the records, and the weapons, and our world will change into something to us unimaginable. Find some spell to make us see that the product or service that yesterday was an unthinkable luxury today is an inexorable necessity, and our world will go on. It is the Medium which casts this spell—which is this spell. As we look at the television set, listen to the radio, read the magazines, the frontier of necessity is always being pushed forward. The Medium shows us what our new needs are—how often, without it, we should not have known!—and it shows us how they can be satisfied: they can be satisfied by buying something. The act of buying something is at the root of our world; if anyone wishes to paint the genesis of things in our society, he will paint a picture of God holding out to Adam a check-book or credit card or Charge-A-Plate.

But how quickly our poor naked Adam is turned into a consumer, is linked to others by the great chain of buying!

No outcast he, bewildered and depressed:
Along his infant veins are interfused
The gravitation and the filial bond
Of nature that connect him with the world.

Children of three or four can ask for a brand of cereal, sing some soap's commercial; by the time that they are twelve or thirteen they are not children but teen-age consumers, interviewed, graphed, analyzed.   They are well on their way to becoming that ideal figure of our culture, the knowledgeable consumer.   Let me define him: the knowledgeable consumer is someone who, when he comes to Weimar, knows how to buy a Weimaraner.

Daisy's voice sounded like money; everything about the knowledgeable consumer looks like or sounds like or feels like money, and informed money at that.   To live is to consume, to understand life is to know what to consume: he has learned to understand this, so that his life is a series of choices—correct ones—among the products and services of the world.   He is able to choose to consume something, of course, only because sometime, somewhere, he or someone else produced something —but just when or where or what no longer seems to us of as much interest.   We may still go to Methodist or Baptist or Presbyterian churches on Sunday, but the Protestant ethic of frugal industry, of production for its own sake, is gone.

Production has come to seem to our society not much more than a condition prior to consumption.   "The challenge of today," an advertising agency writes, "is to make the consumer raise his level of demand."   This challenge has been met: the Medium has found it easy to make its people feel the continually increasing lacks, the many specialized dissatisfactions (merging into one great dissatisfaction, temporarily assuaged by new purchases) that it needs for them to feel. When in some magazine we see the Medium at its most nearly perfect, we hardly know which half is entertaining and distracting us, which half making us buy: some advertisement may be more ingeniously entertaining than the text beside it, but it is the text which has made us long for a product more passionately.   When one finishes *Holiday* or *Harper's Bazaar* or *House and Garden* or *The New Yorker* or *High Fidelity* or *Road and Track* or—but make your own list—buying something, going somewhere seems a necessary completion to the act of reading the magazine.

Reader, isn't buying or fantasy-buying an important part of your and my emotional life?   (If you reply, *No,* I'll think of you with bitter envy as more than merely human; as deeply un-American.)   It is a standard joke that when a woman is bored or sad she buys something, to cheer herself up; but in this respect we are all women together, and can hear complacently the reminder of how feminine this consumer-world of ours has become. One imagines as a characteristic dialogue of our time an interview in which someone is asking of a vague gracious figure, a kind of Mrs. America: "But while you waited for the intercontinental ballistic missiles what did you *do?*" She answers: "I bought things."

She reminds one of the sentinel at Pompeii—a space among ashes, now, but at his post: she too did what she was supposed to do. Our society has delivered us—most of us—from the bonds of necessity, so that we no longer struggle to find food to keep from starving, clothing and shelter to keep from freezing; yet if the ends for which we work and of which we dream are only clothes and restaurants and houses, possessions, consumption, how have we escaped?—we have exchanged man's old bondage for a new voluntary one. It is more than a figure of speech to say that the consumer is trained for his job of consuming as the factory-worker is trained for his job of producing; and the first can be a longer, more complicated training, since it is easier to teach a man to handle a tool, to read a dial, than it is to teach him to ask, always, for a name-brand aspirin—to want, someday, a stand-by generator.

What is that? You don't know? I used not to know, but the readers of *House Beautiful* all know, so that now I know. It is the electrical generator that stands in the basement of the suburban house-owner, shining, silent, till at last one night the lights go out, the furnace stops, the freezer's food begins to—

Ah, but it's frozen for good, the lights are on forever; the owner has switched on the stand-by generator.

But you don't see that he really needs the generator, you'd rather have seen him buy a second car? He has two. A second bathroom? He has four. When the People of the Medium doubled everything, he doubled everything; and now that he's gone twice round he will have to wait three years, or four, till both are obsolescent—but while he waits there are so many new needs that he can satisfy, so many things a man can buy. "Man wants but little here below/Nor wants that little long," said the poet; what a lie! Man wants almost unlimited quantities of almost everything, and he wants it till the day he dies.

Sometimes in *Life* or *Look* we see a double-page photograph of some family standing on the lawn among its possessions: station-wagon, swimming-pool, power-cruiser, sports-car, tape-recorder, television sets, radios, cameras, power lawn-mower, garden tractor, lathe, barbecue-set, sporting equipment, domestic appliances—all the gleaming, grotesquely imaginative paraphernalia of its existence. It was hard to get everything on two pages, soon it will need four.   It is like a dream, a child's dream before Christmas; yet if the members of the family doubt that they are awake, they have only to reach out and pinch something.   The family seems pale and small, a negligible appendage, beside its possessions; only a human being would need to ask: "Which owns which?" We are fond of saying that something is not just something but "a way of life"; this too is a way of life—our way, the way.

Emerson, in his spare stony New England, a few miles from Walden, could write: "Things are in the saddle/And ride mankind."   He could say more now: that they are in the theater and studio, and entertain mankind; are in the pulpit and preach to mankind.   The values of business, in a business society like our own, are reflected in every sphere: values which agree with them are reinforced, values which disagree are cancelled out or have lip service paid to them.   In business what sells is good, and that's the end of it—that is what *good* means; if the world doesn't beat a path to your door, your mouse-trap wasn't better.   The values of the Medium—which is both a popular business itself and the cause of popularity in other businesses—are business values: money, success, celebrity.   If we are representative members of our society, the Medium's values are ours; and even if we are unrepresentative, non-conforming, our hands are—too often—subdued to the element they work in, and our unconscious expectations are all that we consciously reject.   Darwin said that he always immediately wrote down evidence against a theory because otherwise, he'd noticed, he would forget it; in the same way, we keep forgetting the existence of those poor and unknown failures whom we might rebelliously love and admire.

If you're so smart why aren't you rich? is the ground-bass of our society, a grumbling and quite unanswerable criticism, since the society's non-monetary values *are* directly convertible into money.   Celebrity turns into testimonials, lectures, directorships, presidencies, the capital gains of an autobiography *Told To* some professional ghost who photographs the man's life as Bachrach photographs his body.   I read in the newspapers a lyric and perhaps exaggerated instance of this direct conversion of celebrity into money: his son accompanied Adlai Stevenson on a trip to Russia, took snapshots of his father, and sold them (to accompany his father's account of the trip) to *Look* for $20,000.   When Liberace said that his critics' unfavorable reviews hurt him so much that he cried all the way to the bank, one had to admire the correctness and penetration of his press-agent's wit—in another age, what might not such a man become!

Our culture is essentially periodical: we believe that all that is deserves to perish and to have something else put in its place. We speak of planned obsolescence, but it is more than planned, it is felt; is an assumption about the nature of the world. We feel that the present is better and more interesting, more real, than the past, and that the future will be better and more interesting, more real, than the present; but, consciously, we do not hold against the present its prospective obsolescence. Our standards have become to an astonishing degree the standards of what is called the world of fashion, where mere timeliness —being orange in orange's year, violet in violet's—is the value to which all other values are reducible. In our society the word *old-fashioned* is so final a condemnation that someone like Norman Vincent Peale can say about atheism or agnosticism simply that it is old-fashioned; the homely recommendation of the phrase *Give me that good old-time religion* has become, after a few decades, the conclusive rejection of the phrase *old-fashioned atheism.*

All this is, at bottom, the opposite of the world of the arts, where commercial and scientific progress do not exist; where the bone of Homer and Mozart and Donatello is there, always, under the mere blush of fashion; where the past—the remote past, even—is responsible for the way that we understand, value, and act in, the present. (When one reads an abstract expressionist's remark that Washington studios are "eighteen months behind" those of his colleagues in New York, one realizes something of the terrible power of business and fashion over those most overtly hostile to them.) An artist's work and life presuppose continuing standards, values extended over centuries or millennia, a future that is the continuation and modification of the past, not its contradiction or irrelevant replacement. He is working for the time that wants the best that he can do: the present, he hopes—but if not that, the future. If he sees that fewer and fewer people are any real audience for the serious artists of the past, he will feel that still fewer are going to be an audience for the serious artists of the present: for those who, willingly or unwillingly, sacrifice extrinsic values to intrinsic ones, immediate effectiveness to that steady attraction which, the artist hopes, true excellence will always exert.

The past's relation to the artist or man of culture is almost the opposite of its relation to the rest of our society. To him the present is no more than the last ring on the trunk, understandable and valuable only in terms of all the earlier rings. The rest of our society sees only that great last ring, the enveloping surface of the trunk; what's underneath is a disregarded, almost mythical foundation. When Northrop Frye

writes that "the preoccupation of the humanities with the past is sometimes made a reproach against them by those who forget that we face
the past: it may be shadowy, but it is all that is there," he is saying
what for the artist or man of culture is self-evidently true.   Yet for the
Medium and the People of the Medium it is as self-evidently false: for
them the present—or a past so recent, so quick-changing, so soon-
disappearing, that it might be called the specious present—is all that is
there.

In the past our culture's body of common knowledge—its frame of
reference, its possibility of comprehensible allusion—changed slowly
and superficially; the amount added to it or taken away from it, in any
ten years, was surprisingly small.   Now in any ten years a surprisingly
large proportion of the whole is replaced.   Most of the information
people have in common is something that four or five years from now
they will not even remember having known.   A newspaper story remarks in astonishment that television quiz-programs "have proved that
ordinary citizens can be conversant with such esoterica as jazz, opera,
the Bible, Shakespeare, poetry, and fisticuffs."   You may exclaim:
"Esoterica!   If the Bible and Shakespeare are esoterica, what is there
that's common knowledge?"   The answer, I suppose, is that Elfrida von
Nordroff and Teddy Nadler—the ordinary citizens on the quiz-programs—are common knowledge; though not for long.   Songs disappear
in two or three months, celebrities in two or three years; most of the
Medium is little felt and soon forgotten.   Nothing is as dead as day-
before-yesterday's newspaper, the next-to-the-last number on the roulette
wheel; but most of the knowledge people have in common and lose in
common is knowledge of such newspapers, such numbers.   Yet the
novelist or poet or dramatist, when he moves a great audience, depends
upon the deep feelings, the living knowledge, that the people of that
audience share; if so much has become contingent, superficial, ephemeral, it is disastrous for him.

New products and fashions replace the old, and the fact that they replace them is proof enough of their superiority.   Similarly, the Medium
does not need to show that the subjects which fill it are interesting or
timely or important; the fact that they are its subjects makes them so.
If *Time, Life,* and the television shows are full of Tom Fool this month,
he's no fool.   And when he has been gone from them a while, we do
not think him a fool—we do not think of him at all.   He no longer
exists, in the fullest sense of the word *exist:* to be is to be perceived, to
be a part of the Medium of our perception.   Our celebrities are not

kings, romantic in exile, but Representatives who, defeated, are forgotten; they had, always, only the qualities that we delegated to them.

After driving for four or five minutes along the road outside my door,
I come to a row of one-room shacks about the size of kitchens, made
out of used boards, metal signs, old tin roofs. To the people who live
in them an electric dishwasher of one's own is as much a fantasy as an
ocean liner of one's own. But since the Medium (and those whose
thought is molded by it) does not perceive them, these people are
themselves a fantasy. No matter how many millions of such exceptions to the general rule there are, they do not really exist, but have a
kind of anomalous, statistical subsistence; our moral and imaginative
view of the world is no more affected by them than by the occupants
of some home for the mentally deficient a little farther along the road.
If some night one of these out-moded, economically deficient ghosts
should scratch at my window, I could say only: "Come back twenty or
thirty years ago." And if I myself, as an old fashioned, one-room poet,
a friend of "quiet culture," a "meek lover of the good," should go out
some night to scratch at another window, shouldn't I hear someone's
indifferent or regretful: "Come back a century or two ago"?

When those whose existence the Medium recognizes ring the chimes
of the writer's doorbell, fall through his letter-slot, float out onto his
television-screen, what is he to say to them? A man's unsuccessful
struggle to get his family food is material for a work of art—for tragedy,
almost; his unsuccessful struggle to get his family a stand-by generator
is material for what? Comedy? Farce? Comedy on such a scale,
at such a level, that our society and its standards seem, almost, farce?
And yet it is the People of the Medium—those who struggle for and
get, or struggle for and don't get, the generator—whom our society
finds representative: they are there, there primarily, there to be treated
first of all. How shall the artist treat them? And the Medium itself
—an end of life and a means of life, something essential to people's
understanding and valuing of their existence, something many of their
waking hours are spent listening to or looking at—how is *it* to be treated
as subject-matter for art? The artist cannot merely reproduce it; should
he satirize or parody it? But by the time the artist's work reaches its
audience, the portion of the Medium which it satirized will already have
been forgotten; and parody is impossible, often, when so much of the
Medium is already an unintentional parody. (Our age might be defined as the age in which real parody became impossible, since any
parody had already been duplicated, or parodied, in earnest.) Yet

the Medium, by now, is an essential part of its watchers.   How can you explain those whom Mohammedans call the People of the Book in any terms that omit the Book?   We are people of the television-set, the magazine, the radio, and are inexplicable in any terms that omit them.

Oscar Wilde said that Nature imitates Art, that before Whistler painted them there were no fogs along the Thames.   If his statement were not false, it would not be witty.   But to say that Nature imitates Art, when the Nature is human nature and the Art that of television, radio, motion-pictures, magazines, is literally true.   The Medium shows its People what life is, what people are, and its People believe it: expect people to be that, try themselves to be that.   Seeing is believing; and if what you see in *Life* is different from what you see in life, which of the two are you to believe?   For many people it is what you see in *Life* (and in the movies, over television, on the radio) that is real life; and everyday existence, mere local or personal variation, is not real in the same sense.

The Medium mediates between us and raw reality, and the mediation more and more replaces reality for us.   Many radio-stations have a news-broadcast every hour, and many people like and need to hear it. In many houses either the television set or the radio is turned on during most of the hours the family is awake.   It is as if they longed to be established in reality, to be reminded continually of the "real," "objective" world—the created world of the Medium—rather than to be left at the mercy of actuality, of the helpless contingency of the world in which the radio-receiver or television set is sitting.   And surely we can sympathize: which of us hasn't found a similar refuge in the "real," created world of Cézanne or Goethe or Verdi?   Yet Dostoievsky's world is too different from Wordsworth's, Piero della Francesca's from Goya's, Bach's from Wolf's, for us to be able to substitute one homogeneous mediated reality for everyday reality in the belief that it *is* everyday reality.   For many watchers, listeners, readers, the world of events and celebrities and performers—the Great World—has become the world of primary reality: how many times they have sighed at the colorless unreality of their own lives and families, and sighed for the bright reality of, say, Elizabeth Taylor's.   The watchers call the celebrities by their first names, approve or disapprove of "who they're dating," handle them with a mixture of love, identification, envy, and contempt.   But however they handle them, they *handle* them: the Medium has given everyone so terrible a familiarity with everyone that it takes great magnanimity of spirit not to be affected by it.   These celebrities are not heroes to us, their valets.

Better to have these real ones play themselves, and not sacrifice too much of their reality to art; better to have the watcher play himself, and not lose too much of himself in art.   Usually the watcher is halfway between two worlds, paying full attention to neither: half distracted from, half distracted by, this distraction; and able for the moment not to be too greatly affected, have too great demands made upon him, by either world.   For in the Medium, which we escape to from work, nothing is ever *work,* makes intellectual or emotional or imaginative demands which we might find it difficult to satisfy.   Here in the half-world everything is homogeneous—is, as much as possible, the same as everything else: each familiar novelty, novel familiarity has the same treatment on top and the same attitude and conclusion at bottom; only the middle, the particular subject of the particular program or article, is different.   If it *is* different: everyone is given the same automatic "human interest" treatment, so that it is hard for us to remember, unnecessary for us to remember, which particular celebrity we're reading about this time—often it's the same one, we've just moved on to a different magazine.

Francesco Caraccioli said that the English have a hundred religions and one sauce; so do we; and we are so accustomed to this sauce or dye or style of presentation, the aesthetic equivalent of Standard Brands, that a very simple thing can seem obscure or perverse without it.   And, too, we find it hard to have to shift from one genre to another, to vary our attitudes and expectations, to use our unexercised imaginations.   Poetry disappeared long ago, even for most intellectuals; each year fiction is a little less important.   Our age is the age of articles: we buy articles in stores, read articles in magazines, exist among the interstices of articles: of columns, interviews, photographic essays, documentaries; of facts condensed into headlines or expanded into non-fiction best-sellers; of real facts about real people.

Art lies to us to tell us the (sometimes disquieting) truth.   The Medium tells us truths, facts, in order to make us believe some reassuring or entertaining lie or half-truth.   These actually existing celebrities, of universally admitted importance, about whom we are told directly authoritative facts—how can fictional characters compete with these?   These *are* our fictional characters, our Lears and Clytemnestras.   (This is ironically appropriate, since many of their doings and sayings are fictional, made up by public relations officers, columnists, agents, or other affable familiar ghosts.)   And the Medium gives us such facts, such tape-recordings, such clinical reports not only about the great but also about (representative samples of) the small.   When we have been shown so much about so many—*can* be shown, we feel, anything about anybody—does fiction seem so essential as it once seemed?   Shakespeare or Tolstoy can show us all about someone, but so can *Life;* and when *Life* does, it's someone real.

The Medium is half life and half art, and competes with both life and art.   It spoils its audience for both; spoils both for its audience.   For the People of the Medium life isn't sufficiently a matter of success and glamor and celebrity, isn't entertaining enough, distracting enough, *mediated* enough; and art is too difficult or individual or novel, too much a matter of tradition and the past, too much a matter of special attitudes and aptitudes—its mediation sometimes is queer or excessive, and sometimes is not even recognizable as mediation.   The Medium's mixture of rhetoric and reality, in which people are given what they know they want to be given in the form in which they know they want to be given it, is something more efficient and irresistible than any real art.   If a man has all his life been fed a combination of marzipan and ethyl alcohol—if eating, to him, is a matter of being knocked unconscious by an ice cream soda—can he, by taking thought, come to prefer a diet of bread and wine, apples and well-water?   Will a man who has spent his life watching gladiatorial games come to prefer listening to chamber music?   And those who produce the bread and the wine and the quartets for him—won't they be tempted either to give up producing them, or else to produce a bread that's half sugar and half alcohol, a quartet that ends with the cellist at the violist's bleeding throat?

Any outsider who has worked for the Medium will have observed that the one thing which seems to its managers most unnatural is for someone to do something naturally, to speak or write as an individual speaking or writing to other individuals, and not as a sub-contractor supplying a standardized product to the Medium.   It is as if producers and editors and supervisors—middle men—were particles forming a screen between maker and public, one which will let through only particles of their own size and weight (or as they say, the public's).   As you look into their strained puréed faces, their big horn-rimmed eyes, you despair of Creation itself, which seems for the instant made in their own owl-eyed image.   There are so many extrinsic considerations involved in the presentation of his work, the maker finds, that by the time it is presented almost any intrinsic consideration has come to seem secondary.   No wonder that the professional who writes the ordinary commercial success—the ordinary script, scenario, or best seller—resembles imaginative writers less than he resembles editors, producers, executives.   The supplier has come to resemble those he supplies, and what he supplies them resembles both.   With an artist you never know what you will get; with him you know what you will get.   He is a reliable source for a standard product.   He is almost exactly the opposite of the imaginative artist: instead of stubbornly or helplessly sticking to what he sees and feels—to what is right for him, true to his reality, regardless of what the others think and want —he gives the others what they think and want, regardless of what he himself sees and feels.

The Medium represents, to the artist, all that he has learned not to do: its sure-fire stereotypes seem to him what any true art, true spirit, has had to struggle past on its way to the truth.   The artist sees the values and textures of this art-substitute replacing those of his art, so far as most of society is concerned; conditioning the expectations of what audience his art has kept.   Mass culture either corrupts or isolates the writer.   His old feeling of oneness—of speaking naturally to an audience with essentially similar standards—is gone; and writers no longer have much of the consolatory feeling that took its place, the feeling of writing for the happy few, the kindred spirits whose standards are those of the future.   (Today they feel: the future, should there be one, will be worse.)   True works of art are more and more produced away from or in opposition to society.   And yet the artist needs society as much as society needs him: as our cultural enclaves get smaller and drier, more hysterical or academic, one mourns for the artists inside and the public outside.   An incomparable historian of mass culture, Ernest van den Haag, has expressed this with laconic force: "The artist who, by refusing to work for the mass market, becomes marginal, cannot create what he might have created had there been no mass market. One may prefer a monologue to addressing a mass meeting.   But it is still not a conversation."

Even if the rebellious artist's rebellion is whole-hearted, it can never be whole-stomach'd, whole-unconscious'd.   Part of him wants to be like his kind, is like his kind; longs to be loved and admired and successful. Our society—and the artist, in so far as he is truly a part of it—has no place set aside for the different and poor and obscure, the fools for Christ's sake: they all go willy-nilly into Limbo.   The artist is tempted, consciously, to give his society what it wants—or if he won't or can't, to give it nothing at all; is tempted, unconsciously, to give it superficially independent or contradictory works which are at heart works of the Medium. But it is hard for him to go on serving both God and Mammon when God is so really ill-, Mammon so really well-organized. "Shakespeare wrote for the Medium of his day; if Shakespeare were alive now he'd be writing *My Fair Lady;* isn't *My Fair Lady,* then, our *Hamlet?* shouldn't you be writing *Hamlet* instead of sitting there worrying about your superego? I need my *Hamlet!*" So society speaks to the artist, reasons with the artist; and after he has written it its *Hamlet* it is satisfied, and tries to make sure that he will never do it again. There are many more urgent needs that it wants him to satisfy: to lecture to it; to be interviewed; to appear on television programs; to give testimonials; to attend book luncheons; to make trips abroad for the State Department; to judge books for Book Clubs; to read for publishers, judge for publishers, be a publisher for publishers; to edit magazines; to teach writing at colleges or conferences; to write scenarios or scripts or articles—articles about his home town for *Holiday,* about cats or clothes or Christmas for *Vogue,* about "How I Wrote *Hamlet*" for anything; to—

But why go on? I once heard a composer, lecturing, say to a poet, lecturing: "They'll pay us to do *anything,* so long as it isn't writing music or writing poems." I knew the reply that as a member of my society I should have made: "As long as they pay you, what do you care?" But I didn't make it: it was plain that they cared . . . But how many more learn not to care, to love what they once endured! It is a whole so comprehensive that any alternative seems impossible, any opposition irrelevant; in the end a man says in a small voice: "I accept the Medium." The Enemy of the People winds up as the People—but where there is no enemy, the people perish.

The climate of our culture is changing. Under these new rains, new suns, small things grow great, and what was great grows small; whole species disappear and are replaced. The American present is very different from the American past: so different that our awareness of the extent of the changes has been repressed, and we regard as ordinary what is extraordinary—ominous perhaps—both for us and for the rest of the world. The American present is many other peoples' future: our cultural and economic example is to much of the world mesmeric, and it is only its weakness and poverty that prevent it from hurrying with us into the Roman future. But at this moment of our power and success, our thought and art are full of a troubled sadness, of the conviction of our own decline. When the President of Yale University writes that "the ideal of the good life has faded from the educational process, leaving only miscellaneous prospects of jobs and joyless hedonism," are we likely to find it unfaded among our entertainers and executives? Is the influence of what I have called the Medium likely to lead us to any good life? to make us love and try to attain any real excellence, beauty, magnanimity? or to make us understand these as obligatory but transparent rationalizations behind which the realities of money and power are waiting?

The tourist Matthew Arnold once spoke about our green culture in terms that have an altered relevance—but are not yet irrelevant—to our ripe one. He said: "What really dissatisfies in American civilization is the want of the *interesting,* a want due chiefly to the want of those two great elements of the interesting, which are elevation and beauty." This use of *interesting*—and, perhaps, this tone of a curator pointing out what is plain and culpable—shows how far along in the decline of West Arnold came: it is only in the latter days that we ask to be interested. He had found the word, he tells us, in Carlyle. Carlyle is writing to a friend to persuade him not to emigrate to the United States; he asks: "Could you banish yourself from all that is interesting to your mind, forget the history, the glorious institutions, the noble principles of old Scotland—that you might eat a better dinner, perhaps?" We smile, and feel like reminding Carlyle of the history, the glorious institutions, the noble principles of new America—of that New World which is, after all, the heir of the Old.

And yet . . . Can we smile as comfortably, today, as we could have smiled yesterday? Nor could we listen as unconcernedly, if on taking leave of us some other tourist should conclude, with the penetration and obtuseness of his kind:

"I remember reading somewhere: that which you inherit from your fathers you must earn in order to possess. I have been so much impressed with your power and your possessions that I have neglected, perhaps, your principles. The elevation or beauty of your spirit did not equal, always, that of your mountains and skyscrapers: it seems to me that your society provides you with 'all that is interesting to the mind' only exceptionally, at odd hours, in little reservations like those of your Indians. But as for your dinners, I've never seen anything like them: your daily bread comes *flambé.* And yet—wouldn't you say—

the more dinners a man eats, the more comforts he possesses, the hungrier and more uncomfortable some part of him becomes: inside every fat man there is a man who is starving. Part of you is being starved to death, and the rest of you is being stuffed to death. But this will change: no one goes on being stuffed to death or starved to death forever.

"This is a gloomy, an equivocal conclusion? Oh yes, I come from an older culture, where things are accustomed to coming to such conclusions; where there is no last-paragraph fairy to bring one, always, a happy ending—or that happiest of all endings, no ending at all. And have I no advice to give you as I go? None. You are too successful to need advice, or to be able to take it if it were offered; but if ever you should fail, it is there waiting for you, the advice or consolation of all the other failures."

Lines of Inquiry

1 Jarrell's essay is written from the point of view of "a fool, a suffering, complaining, helplessly non-conforming poet-or-artist-of-a-sort far off at the obsolescent rear of things."

   a What are the most important words in this description?

   b Why does Jarrell employ such an apparently self-deprecating phrase?

   c Is the character of this phrase in any way connected to the fact that this essay first appeared in an issue of *Daedalus* (the Journal of the American Academy of Sciences) that was specifically devoted to the mass media?

   d Does this fact have any discernible bearing on:

      (*1*) The structure of Jarrell's introduction

      (*2*) The kinds of illustrations he uses

      (*3*) His choice of a specific internal voice

2 a What kind of evidence does Jarrell employ to support his generalizations about the mass media?

   b How is his use of the personal voice related to this kind of evidence, and to the kinds of generalizations he permits himself? Can you illustrate your point?

   c Suppose that Jarrell had identified his angle of vision as that of a teacher; in what ways would you expect his essay to change?

3 Scan the allusions that Jarrell employs in the essay.

   a "The knowledgeable consumer is someone who when he comes to Weimar knows how to buy a Weimaraner." (*Faust* is a great German dramatic poem by Goethe; Goethe

lived in Weimar and was virtually an object of cultural
pilgrimage; a Weimaraner is a dog.)   How is the use of
this kind of allusion related to Jarrell's point of view?

b Other aspects of the essay's verbal style are reflected in:

(*1*) The obviously fictional quotation from the Emperor
Augustus with which the essay opens

(*2*) The suggestion that a modern painting of Genesis would
show God handing Adam a Charge-A-Plate

(*3*) The phrase "the people of the medium"

Are such aspects of Jarrell's style related to his use of the personal voice, or only to his distaste for modern commercial
culture?   (Imagine a different kind of voice—say, that of a
social scientist; would the same style be appropriate?)

4 As the answer to *3* above will have suggested, much of the
force of this essay depends upon allusions to figures in history
and literature.   But history and literature are packed with
figures capable of being alluded to.   In the following, what
accounts for the particular allusions Jarrell employs?   What
patterns do you see in each cluster?

a "The word has the clear fatal ring of that new world whose
space we occupy so luxuriously and precariously; the world
that produces mink stoles, rockabilly records, and tactical
nuclear weapons by the million; the world that *Attila,
Galileo, Hansel and Gretel* never knew."

b She ["Mrs. America"] reminds one of the *sentinel at Pompeii*
—a space among ashes, now, but at his post. . . ."

c "All this is, at bottom, the opposite of the world of the arts,
where commercial and scientific progress do not exist; where
the bone of *Homer* and *Mozart* and *Donatello* is there, always, under the mere blush of fashion. . . ."

d "And surely we can sympathize: which of us hasn't found a
similar refuge in the 'real,' created world of *Cézanne or
Goethe or Verdi*?   Yet *Dostoievsky*'s world is too different
from *Wordsworth's, Piero della Francesca's* from *Goya's,
Bach's* from *Wolf's,* for us to be able to substitute one
homogeneous mediated reality for everyday reality in the
belief that it *is* everyday reality."

5 Jarrell's indignation is often communicated obliquely.   What
is the oblique meaning of each of the following:

a " 'Medium,' says the dictionary, 'that which lies in the
middle . . . *Biol.*   A nutritive mixture of substance, as
broth, gelatin, agar, for cultivating bacteria, fungi, etc.' "

b " 'The challenge of today,' an advertising agency writes, 'is to make the consumer raise his level of demand.' This challenge has been met . . ."

c "'Man wants but little here below/nor wants that little long,' said the poet; what a lie! Man wants almost unlimited quantities of almost everything, and he wants it till the day he dies."

d "When Liberace said that his critics' unfavorable reviews hurt him so much that he cried all the way to the bank, one had to admire the correctness and penetration of his press-agent's wit—in another age, what might not such a man have become!"

e "Our culture is essentially periodical: we believe that all that is deserves to perish. . . ."

6 a How does Jarrell employ comparison and contrast to give structure to this essay?

b What contrasts dominate the introductory paragraphs?

c Which of these contrasts becomes central to the entire essay?

d At what point in the essay does this central contrast emerge most clearly? (Look at the opening sentence of each paragraph.)

e When in the essay does Jarrell employ hypothetical examples, and why?

7 At the end of the essay Jarrell quotes first from Matthew Arnold, then from "some other tourist."

a Who is this last person?

b Why is the passage presented to us as a quotation?

c Are there any quotations of a similar character earlier in the essay?

d What would happen to those quotations if Jarrell had employed an impersonal point of view?

8 Much of Jarrell's thesis about mass culture cannot be understood without an understanding of his attitude toward art. The following two passages express that attitude; what does each passage mean?

a "Oscar Wilde said that Nature imitates Art, that before Whistler painted them there were no fogs along the Thames. If his statement were not false, it would not be witty."

b "Art lies to us to tell us the (sometimes disquieting) truths."

9 At one point (p. 424) Jarrell writes, "Any outsider who has worked for the Medium will have observed that the one thing which seems to its managers most unnatural is for someone to do something naturally, to speak or write as an individual speaking or writing to other individuals. . . ."

a Is Jarrell saying that everything should be written from a personal angle and in a personal voice? If he is not saying that, what *is* he saying?

b How do the transitions in his own essay reflect this principle that one should "speak or write as an individual speaking or writing to other individuals"? (Look at the paragraph openings: Roughly what proportion of them begin with direct address to the reader, or contain the first person plural?)

Lines of Experiment

1 Choose a topic whose importance you feel strongly and whose facts you are familiar with. Write your essay in the personal voice. Because one chief value of the personal voice is its ability to communicate states of feeling, and because states of feeling are necessarily private, only your own emotions can identify an appropriate specific subject for such an essay. The central thing in locating such a subject is perhaps to distinguish subjects you really feel to be important from those that you think you ought to feel important.

As you write, consider the advantages in flexibility of approach that are inherent in the personal voice: its capacity to draw naturally upon private experience as well as upon public experience for its illustrations and allusions, to shift focus and idea without extended explanations, to make emotion itself justify the development of one idea into another, to use all the resources of personal as distinct from impersonal language—including sentence fragments, run-on sentences, slang, etc.—in the creation of an appropriate tone. The flexibility inherent in the personal voice, indeed, is so great that one of your chief concerns must be to use it responsibly, deliberately, as a way of expressing what you think and feel, and not as a way of sending up a pointless shower of verbal sparks.

2 You doubtless have observed some of the effects of mass culture—in education, if nowhere else. Write an essay analyzing the impact of mass culture on a specific aspect of the life you know well.

Some procedural suggestions may be in order. *First,* consider your role as a writer: Choose an external point of view, an angle, that can provide you with a principle by which you can judge the relevance of specific facts and their relations to one another.

Second, consider your specific subject: Focus on a relatively limited area, in order to give density to your thought and to provide you with clear transitional materials. You may be able to use contrast effectively by focusing on a subject whose state before mass culture hit it can be contrasted to its state afterward: a wilderness now a housing project, a country schoolhouse become a consolidated school, a corner store become a supermarket, an empty lot become a filling station, etc.

Third, consider how the effects of mass culture on your subject can be classified: physical effects, psychological effects, moral effects, aesthetic effects, or whatever. Such a classification can provide you with much of the structure of an analysis.

Fourth, select a point of main emphasis, distinguishing the less from the more important, and determine a sequence of illustration and idea that will place the emphasis where you want it to fall.

Last, choose an internal voice that will carry your point of view into the essay effectively—that will enable you to present your materials clearly, in the patterns you see as really important, without irrelevance or loss.

EDMUND WILSON

ORIGINS OF
SOCIALISM:
BABEUF'S DEFENSE

The years of relaxation under the Directory which followed the fall of Robespierre were troubled by the activities of a man who called himself Gracchus Babeuf.

With the Directory the French Revolution had passed into the period of reaction which was to make possible the domination of Bonaparte. The great rising of the bourgeoisie, which, breaking out of the feudal forms of the monarchy, dispossessing the nobility and the clergy, had presented itself to society as a movement of liberation, had ended by depositing the wealth in the hands of a relatively small number of people and creating a new conflict of classes.   With the reaction against the Terror, the ideals of the Revolution were allowed to go by the board. The five politicians of the Directory and the merchants and financiers allied with them were speculating in confiscated property, profiteering in army supplies, recklessly inflating the currency and gambling on the falling gold louis.   And in the meantime, during the winter of 1795–96, the working people of Paris were dying of hunger and cold in the streets.

Babeuf was the son of a Protestant who had been sent abroad by the Calvinists to negotiate a union with the Lutherans and who had remained to serve as a major in the army of Maria Theresa and later to tutor her children.   Returned to France, he had fallen into misery, and the son had had to learn his letters, he said, from papers picked up in the street.   His father taught him Latin and mathematics.   On his deathbed, the old man gave him a Plutarch and told him that he himself could have wished to play the role of Caius Gracchus.   He made the boy swear on his sword that he would defend to the death the interests of the people.

This was in 1780.   When the Revolution occurred, Babeuf was twenty-nine.   He was present at the taking of the Bastille.   He had been employed as a clerk to a registrar of seignorial rights in the little town of Roye in the Somme, and now he burned the seignorial archives. Thereafter, as journalist and official, he threw himself into the work of the Revolution with an earnestness that kept him in continual hot water. He incited the tavern-keepers of the Somme to rebel against paying the old wine tax, which the Constituent Assembly had abolished; he sold up the expropriated estates and divided the village common among the poor.   Babeuf went too fast for his province.   The landlords and the local authorities kept arresting him and clapping him in jail.   At last in 1793 he was given a post in Paris in the Bureau of Subsistence of the Commune.   The privation in Paris was terrible, and Babeuf found a leak in the bureau's accounts.   He came to the conclusion that the authorities were deliberately producing a famine in order to exploit the demand for foodstuffs, and he had a commission of investigation appointed.   The government suppressed the commission, and Babeuf soon found himself pursued for what were apparently framed charges of fraud in connection with his administration in the provinces.

After Thermidor, he rallied around him those elements of the Revolution who were trying to insist on its original aims.   In his paper, *The Tribune of the People,* he denounced the new constitution of 1795, which had abolished universal suffrage and imposed a high property qualification. He demanded not merely political but also economic equality. He declared that he would prefer civil war itself to "this horrible concord which strangles the hungry." But the men who had expropriated the nobles and the Church remained loyal to the principle of property itself. *The Tribune of the People* was stopped, and Babeuf and his associates were sent to prison.

While Babeuf was in jail, his seven-year-old daughter died of hunger. He had managed to remain poor all his life. His popularity had been all with the poor. His official posts had earned him only trouble. Now, as soon as he was free again, he proceeded to found a political club, which opposed the policies of the Directory and which came to be known as the Society of the Equals. They demanded in a *Manifesto of the Equals* (not, however, at that time made public) that there should be "no more individual property in land; the land belonged to no one. . . . We declare that we can no longer endure, with the enormous majority of men, labor and sweat in the service and for the benefit of a small minority. It has now been long enough and too long that less than a million individuals have been disposing of that which belongs to more than twenty millions of their kind. . . . Never has a vaster design been conceived or put into execution. Certain men of genius, certain sages, have spoken of it from time to time in a low and trembling voice. Not one of them has had the courage to tell the whole truth. . . . People of France! open your eyes and your heart to the fullness of happiness. Recognize and proclaim with us the Republic of Equals!"

The Society of Equals was also suppressed; Bonaparte himself closed the club. But, driven underground, they now plotted an insurrection; they proposed to set up a new directory. And they drafted a constitution that provided for "a great national community of goods" and worked out with some precision the mechanics of a planned society. The cities were to be deflated and the population distributed in villages. The State was to "seize upon the new-born individual, watch over his early moments, guarantee the milk and care of his mother and bring him to the *maison nationale,* where he was to acquire the virtue and enlightenment of a true citizen." There was thus to be equal education for all. All able-bodied persons were to work, and the work that was unpleasant or arduous was to be accomplished by everybody's taking turns. The necessities of life were to be supplied by the government, and the people were to eat at communal tables. The government was to control all foreign trade and to pass on everything printed.

In the meantime, the value of the paper money had depreciated almost to zero. The Directory tried to save the situation by converting the currency into land warrants, which were at a discount of 82 per cent the day they were issued; and there was a general belief on the part of the public that the government had gone bankrupt. There were in Paris alone some five hundred thousand people in need of relief. The Babouvistes placarded the city with a manifesto of historical importance; they declared that Nature had given to every man an equal right to the enjoyment of every good, and it was the purpose of society to defend that right; that Nature had imposed on every man the obligation to work, and that no one could escape this obligation without committing a crime; that in "a true society" there would be neither rich nor poor; that the object of the Revolution had been to destroy every inequality and to establish the well-being of all; that the Revolution was therefore "not finished," and that those who had done away with the Constitution of 1793 were guilty of *lèse-majesté* against the people.

In the cafés, they were singing a song composed by a member of the society: "Dying of hunger, dying of cold, the people robbed of every right . . . newcomers gorged with gold, who have given neither work nor thought, are laying hold on the hive; while you, the toiling people, eat iron like an ostrich. . . . A brainless double council, five frightened directors; the soldier pampered and petted, the democrat crushed: *Voilà la République!"*

Babeuf's "insurrectionary committee" had agents in the army and the police, and they were doing such effective work that the government tried to send its troops out of Paris, and, when they refused to obey, disbanded them. During the early days of May, 1796, on the eve of the projected uprising, the Equals were betrayed by a stool pigeon and their leaders were arrested and put in jail. The followers of Babeuf made an attempt to rally a sympathetic police squadron, but were cut down by a new Battalion of the Guard which had been pressed into service for the occasion.

Babeuf was made a public example by being taken to Vendôme in a cage—an indignity which not long before had filled the Parisians with fury when the Austrians had inflicted it on a Frenchman.

His defense, which lasted for six sittings of the court and fills more than three hundred pages, is an impressive and moving document. Babeuf knew well that he was facing death and that the Revolution was doomed. The French had been finally exhausted by the birth-throes of the seven years that had passed since the taking of the Bastille. All the fervor of which they were still capable was siphoned off into the revolutionary army, which that spring was being led by Bonaparte to the victories of the Italian campaign. At home, since the Terror, they were shy of violence. Babeuf had united with the last of the Jacobins, and the people had had enough of *them*. Uncompromising principles and the guillotine were inextricably associated in their minds; they were glad to be free to live, and a period of frivolity had set in. And the bourgeois instinct for property was already becoming the overmastering motive, taking the place of other instincts and ideals; all those who had succeeded in getting anything clung to it with desperate tenacity; the idea of redistribution frightened them out of their wits. And the poor were no longer prepared to fight. Babeuf knew all this, and his defense has a realism and a sobriety which suggest much later phases of socialism. It is no longer the rhetoric of the Revolution, grandiose, passionate and confusing. At a time when people in general were able to think only of the present, Babeuf looked both backward and forward; at the moment when a society still talking the language of the ideals of the Revolution, libertarian, equalitarian and fraternal, had passed completely into the hands of a new owning class, with its new privileges, injustices and constraints, Babeuf, with great courage and insight, was able to analyze the ambiguous situation. His defense is like a summing-up of the unrealized ideas of the Enlightenment and a vindication of their ultimate necessity. And it has moments of grandeur which it is not absurd to compare to Socrates' *Apology*.

The real issue in this case, says Babeuf, is less the question of conspiracy against the government than the spreading of certain ideas subversive to the dominating class. He has seen under the Directory, he says, the sovereignty of the people disregarded, and the right to elect and be elected reserved to certain castes. He has seen privilege brought back again. He has seen the people deprived of freedom of the press and assembly, and the right to petition and the right to carry arms. He has seen even the right to ratify the laws taken away from the citizens and vested in a second chamber. He has seen an executive power set up which is out of the reach of the people and independent of popular control. He has seen relief and education forgotten. And finally he has seen the Constitution of 1793, which had been approved by nearly five million votes with genuine popular feeling behind them, replaced by an unpopular constitution, put over by scarcely a million dubious ones. So that if it were true that he had conspired (it *was* true, though at the trial he denied it), it would have been against an illegitimate authority. The cause of revolutions is the bending beyond what they can bear of the human springs of society. The people rebel against the pressure; and they are right, because the aim of society is the good of the greatest number. If the people still finds itself bent double, it doesn't matter what the rulers say: the revolution is not finished yet. Or if it is, the rulers have committed a crime.

Happiness, in Europe, is a new idea. But today we know that the unhappy are the really important powers of the earth; they have the right to speak as the real masters of the governments that neglect them. We know that every man has an equal right to the enjoyment of every benefit, and that the real purpose of society is to defend that right and to increase the common benefits. And work, like enjoyment, should be shared by all. Nature has decreed that we all must work: it is a crime to evade this duty. And it is a crime to take for oneself at the expense of other people the products of industry or the earth. In a society which was really sound, there would be neither poor nor rich. There would be no such system of property as ours. Our laws of heredity and inalienability are "humanicide" institutions. The monopoly of the land by individuals, their possession of its produce in excess of their wants, is nothing more nor less than theft; and all our civil institutions, our ordinary business transactions, are the deeds of a perpetual brigandage, authorized by barbarous laws.

But you say that it is my ideas, he goes on, which would send society back to barbarism. The great philosophers of the century did not think so; and it is they whose disciple I am. You should be arraigning the monarchy for having shown itself so much less inquisitorial than the government of our present Republic; you should arraign it for not having prevented me from getting hold of the pernicious books of the Mablys, the Helvétius, the Diderots, the Jean-Jacques. Philanthropists of today! if it had not been for the poisons of these older philanthropists, I might share your moral principles and your virtues: I might have been moved by the tenderest solicitude for the minority of the mighty of this world; I might have been pitiless for the suffering mass. Didn't you know that you had included in your indictment a passage I had quoted from Rousseau, which was written in 1758? He had spoken of "men so odious as to dare to have more than enough while other men are dying of hunger." I do not hesitate to make this revelation because I am not afraid of compromising this new conspirator: he is beyond the jurisdiction of your tribunal. And Mably, the popular, the sensitive, the human, was not he an even deeper-dyed conspirator? "If you follow the chain of our vices," he said, "you will find that the first link is fastened to the inequality of wealth." The Manifesto of the Equals, which had never been brought out of the dust of the box where we had put it but about which so much fuss has been made, went no further than Mably and Rousseau. And Diderot, who said that from the scepter to the crozier, humanity was ruled by personal interest, and that personal interest arose from property, and that it was idle for philosophers to argue about the best possible form of government so long as the ax had not been laid to the roots of property itself—Diderot, who asked whether the instability, the periodic vicissitudes of empires, would be possible if all goods were held in common, and who asserted that every citizen should take from the community what he needed and give to the community what he could and that anyone who should try to restore the detestable principle of property should be locked up as an enemy of humanity and a dangerous lunatic!—Citizens, "dangerous lunatic" is precisely what you have called *me* for trying to introduce equality!

And Tallien and Armand de la Meuse, who are now sitting in the Directory and the legislature—why have they not been called to the bar? Tallien, only a few years ago when he was editing *The Sans-Culottes' Friend,* was telling us that "the anarchy would cease as soon as wealth was less unequal." And Armand de la Meuse was assuring the Convention that "every candid person must admit that political equality without real equality is only a tantalizing illusion," and that the "cruelest error of the revolutionary bodies has been their failure to mark the limits of property rights and their consequent abandonment of the people to the greedy speculations of the rich."

Christ has told us to love our neighbor and to do as we would be done by; but I admit that Christ's code of equality caused him to be prosecuted for conspiracy.

The way that things were going would have been brought home to me even if I had not been able to see them. When I was sent to jail for my writings, I left my wife and my three unfortunate children helpless during the horrible famine. My little girl of seven died when the allowance of bread was cut down to two ounces; and the others grew so thin that when I saw them again, I could hardly recognize them. And we were only one among thousands of families—the greater part of Paris, in fact—whose faces were blighted by the famine, who tottered when they walked.

And if I have desired for them a better system, it is not that I have expected to impose it by force. All I want is that the people should be enlightened and convinced of their own omnipotence, of the inviolability of their rights, and that the people should demand their rights. I want, if need be, that they should be shown the way to demand their rights; but I want nothing except subject to the people's consent.

But where Mably and Diderot and Rousseau and Helvétius have failed, how should I have hoped to succeed? I am a lesser disciple of theirs, and the Republic is less tolerant than the monarchy.

He reminded them of the fact that the royalists of the Vendémiaire conspiracy had all been pardoned and set free, and that the party of the Pretender had been openly saying that the new constitution would suit them very well if there were one director instead of five. The Society of Equals had reason to believe that a massacre was being plotted against them, like the massacres of republicans in the Midi, and Babeuf launched upon so provocative a picture of the hounding of the republicans by the forces of reaction that the judges made him stop his speech and would not let him go on till the next day.

Babeuf declared in conclusion that the death sentence would not surprise or frighten him. He had got used to prison and violent death in the course of his revolutionary mission. It was abundant consolation, he said, that his own wife and children and those of his followers had never been ashamed of what had happened to their husbands and fathers, but had come there to the courtroom to sustain them.

"But, oh, my children," he concluded, "I have from my place above these benches—the only place from which my voice can reach you, since they have even, contrary to law, made it impossible for me to see you—I have only one bitter regret to express to you: that, though I have wanted so much to leave you a heritage of that liberty which is the source of every good, I foresee for the future only slavery, and that I am leaving you a prey to every ill. I have nothing at all to give you! I would not leave you even my civic virtues, my profound hatred of tyranny, my ardent devotion to the cause of Liberty and Equality, my passionate love of the People. I should make you too disastrous a present. What would you do with it under the monarchic oppression which is infallibly going to descend on you? I am leaving you slaves, and it is this thought alone which will torture my soul in its final moments. I should equip you, in this situation, with advice as to how to bear your chains more patiently, but I do not feel that I am capable of it."

The vote, after much disagreement, went against Babeuf. One of his sons had smuggled in to him a tin dagger made out of a candlestick; and when he heard the verdict pronounced, he stabbed himself in the Roman fashion, but only wounded himself horribly and did not die. The next morning (May 27, 1797) he went to the guillotine. Of his followers thirty were executed and many sentenced to penal servitude or deportation.

Before he died, Babeuf had written to a friend, to whom he had confided his wife and children: "I believe that in some future day men will give thought again to the means of procuring for the human race the happiness which we have proposed for it."

His defense did not reach the world for almost a hundred years. The newspapers reported only part of it, and the full text was never published till 1884. His name remained a bugbear for decades.

Lines of Inquiry

1 Wilson's title indicates clearly both the purpose and the focus of his essay. Here are five different titles. What differences in purpose, focus, and tone do you see between each of these and Wilson's actual title? In each case, what directions would you expect to see the following essay take?

a The Man Called Babeuf

b Origins of Socialism

c Origins of Socialism: The Society of Equals

d Babeuf's Defense

e The Citizen Babeuf: A Case Study in the Revolutionary Temperament

2 Reading an opening paragraph is a little like looking through an open door into an unfamiliar room: Even though the details of the room elude us, our initial glimpse will tell us roughly what to expect.

a What does the opening paragraph of Wilson's essay tell you about his attitude toward his subject? What, in consequence, do you expect? What is the significance of the phrase "a man *who called himself* Gracchus Babeuf"?

b What relationship, if any, do you see between the introduction (taking the title as part of the introduction) and the conclusion of this essay?

c Suppose the essay began with the second paragraph; what would be lost? Now suppose that the second paragraph were omitted—suppose the essay skipped from the end of the first to the beginning of the third paragraph; what would be lost, if anything? Could the order of these first two paragraphs be reversed? With what effect?

3 a Much of this essay is given over to a report not of Babeuf's life but of his statement at his trial; why? What would be the effect on the essay had Wilson merely summarized Babeuf's defense in court as "an eloquent plea on behalf of equal rights for all"?

b Where in the essay does Wilson quote Babeuf's defense in full, and why there? (Obviously he could have given the outcome of Babeuf's trial *before* quoting his defense, i.e., "Babeuf's trial ended with a death sentence. But his defense, which lasted for six sittings of the court. . . .")

c Part way through Wilson's summary of Babeuf's statement in court, both tense and pronoun suddenly change; why?

d Suppose the first half of the essay, concerning Babeuf's early life and career before his arrest, to be condensed to a few sentences or paragraphs, while the account of his defense itself retained its present size. That defense would lose none of its clarity; what would it lose, if anything?

e In Babeuf's statement to the court he speaks of his daughter's death by starvation. Wilson, earlier, also referred to this event. Why does Wilson allow this simple fact to enter the essay twice?

f At his trial, Babeuf denied involvement in a conspiracy. Wilson mentions this fact only in a parenthesis. Why? What would have happened to the essay if Wilson had given an entire paragraph to Babeuf's denial—perhaps had even quoted him denying the charge? (Consider that the charge was actually true.)

g Immediately before reporting the substance of Babeuf's defense, Wilson points out in a long paragraph its historical importance. Skip from the first sentence in that paragraph to the report of the defense itself; what, if anything, is lost? Could Wilson have put this passage at the end of Babeuf's defense, instead of at the beginning, with no loss of dramatic effect?

h What accounts for the place assigned in the essay to "a song composed by a member of the Society"? Why does Wilson refer to this song at all? Why does he quote it, instead of merely paraphrasing it, e.g., "a member of the society composed a song lamenting the condition of the poor and the corruption of the government; it went the rounds of Paris." Why, in the actual passage, does Wilson refer to the singers as "they"? Who are "they"?

4 In the introduction to this part of the text, it was pointed out that Wilson follows Babeuf's point of view in this essay—that we "see" events as if we were looking through Babeuf's eyes, or over his shoulder.

   a How is Wilson's decision to use a secondary point of view related to Babeuf's history and character? If, for example, Babeuf had been an inarticulate man, could Wilson have followed his point of view as successfully as he does here? On the basis of your answer to this and similar questions, can you generalize about the conditions under which a secondary point of view may be useful? Can you generalize about the kind of person most likely to be valuable as a secondary point of view?

   b Suppose that Wilson had followed the point of view of Babeuf's wife, rather than that of Babeuf himself. What would happen to the following elements in the essay?

   (*1*) Its focus

   (*2*) Its central idea

   (*3*) Its opening and closing

   (*4*) Babeuf's statement to the court

   (*5*) The death of his daughter

   (*6*) The suffering of the poor

   (*7*) Babeuf's legacy

5 Underline each date given in the essay. (As a central date, take that of the French Revolution: 1789.)

   a How old was Babeuf when his father died? Why does Wilson refer to Babeuf as "the boy" in describing his father's deathbed scene?

   b How old was Babeuf when he himself was executed? How long was he in prison before his execution?

   c Considering the sequence of dates as Wilson gives them, how do you account for Wilson's rearrangement of "natural" sequence; i.e., what paragraphs are placed out of their "natural" sequence, and why those paragraphs in particular?

   d How is the first paragraph of the essay related to that rearrangement? How is the last paragraph related to it?

   e What is the most precise date given? How do you account for Wilson's precision at this particular point?

   f Why does Wilson *not* give the date on which the French Revolution began?

6 Despite the spareness of Wilson's prose, he manages frequently to create a remarkably vivid picture of Babeuf and his times. Some of the information on which that vividness depends will seem at first glance unnecessary. Why does Wilson tell that *a* Babeuf's father was a Protestant, taught him Latin and mathematics, gave him a copy of Plutarch and made him swear "on his sword" to defend the interests of the people.

b The Manifesto of the Equals was not made public "at that time."

c "Bonaparte himself" closed the club of Babeuf's society of equals.

d Babeuf stabbed himself with "a tin dagger made out of a candlestick."

e His daughter was seven years old when she died.

f Babeuf's defense "did not reach the world for almost a hundred years, and his name remained a bugbear for decades."

7 Let us suppose that you take as the general material for an essay a famous battle of the Civil War, say Gettysburg or Chancellorsville. What might the following secondary points of view offer you, in grouping and interpreting the meaning of such a battle? What kinds of information, what central idea, would each seem most "likely" to transmit?

a A private soldier in the Union army

b A private soldier in the Confederate army

c The Union commander

d A nearby noncombatant

e A field surgeon

f A newspaper illustrator

g A slave

8 Let us suppose that you are to write an essay about each of the following topics, and that you decide to employ a secondary point of view if you can find one that is suitable. What kind of person will you look for, in each case, to act as your secondary point of view? Try to think of at least two possible points of view before making your choice; on what basis will you choose? What must you decide about each topic before you can choose any point of view at all?

a The western gunfighter

b The exploration of outer space

c Military life

d University life

e The Vietnam War

f The American adolescent

g Advances in medicine

h The contemporary house

Lines of Experiment

1 Wilson's subject in "Babeuf's Defense" is really the development of socialist thought in Revolutionary France. For that

subject he found an appropriate focus and voice in "the man who called himself Gracchus Babeuf." In a parallel way, one might present the founding of the American Republic by following the career of Franklin; ordinarily, Franklin's point of view would imply the use of Franklin's voice in documents, letters, etc. Or one might present the controversy over slavery by focusing on the violently debated Fugitive Slave Act of 1850, and by employing as a secondary point of view and voice one of the great figures in that debate—Daniel Webster, for example.

Such huge historical episodes require too much background reading, a too extensive acquaintance with actual people, actual documents, actual events, to make good subjects for short compositions; unless you have real interest, a good deal of time, and a fair acquaintance with your subject already, you should not choose to write on so large a subject.

But the secondary point of view often can bring into useful focus less intimidating, more familiar kinds of subjects. One might write about the racial conflicts of contemporary America, for example, by following a secondary point of view, say, that of a typical policeman, a typical minister, a typical businessman, a boy from some racial ghetto, through a race riot or even through an average day's life. One might describe a certain kind of business ethics by following a used-car salesman through a fast sale. One might find small-town life reflected in the career of an ambitious bookstore owner.

Use a secondary point of view to organize an essay about some such subject of your own choosing. As the above examples should make clear, your secondary point of view need not be that of an actual person—a typical person frequently will do just as well. The sole condition that you must observe is that the secondary point of view you follow should enable you to organize your subject and to help you to reveal its meaning economically, clearly, and dramatically.

2 Choose an episode you know a good deal about and organize it by means of a secondary point of view. The episode may be either within your personal experience (e.g., the defeat of a football team, the collapse of a business, the founding of a motorcycle club, the breakup of a family, the staging of a play, the carrying through of a political protest) or even a matter of historical record, if you are ambitious and interested in history (e.g., the drawing up of the Constitution, the Battle of

Cannae, the assassination of J. F. Kennedy, the Watts race riot, etc.).

Again, consider your audience. What subject will seem most important to them? What way of getting at that subject will have, for them, the greatest dramatic and persuasive power? If you cannot think of any other audience, write for your class.

3 The secondary point of view finds one of its chief uses in expository narrative: in organizing how and why a mechanism, an institution, a process functions as it does. Point of view here, of course, is strictly a device of focus, not an essential part of the subject: The *personality* of that point of view is completely subordinate to its ability to organize the subject so as to show how it works or why it works as it does. In expository narrative, we do not care whether the point of view has heartburn, ambition, or even intelligence: We do care whether he allows us to pass from one element to another of a deliberate pattern of event in such a way as to make clear why that pattern is arranged as it is.

Listed below are eight subjects for expository narrative. If you do not like any of them, choose your own. Organize your subject by means of a secondary point of view. *Note:* Exactly because the personality of a secondary point of view does not enter into expository narrative, at times such narratives can be constructed best not around human beings but around objects—a log passing from forest to housing tract, a rifle passing from Springfield National Armory to the hands of an Asian guerilla, etc.

a How the Nuclear Reactor Works
b Detroit Iron: The Making of the American Automobile
c How to Catch a Fish
d Snowing the Teacher
e Rock Climbing
f Engineering a Protest
g Escape from Home
h How to Live on Nothing a Year
i Courtship in College: How to Do Well

THUCYDIDES

THE MELIAN
DEBATE

Next summer Alcibiades sailed to Argos with twenty ships and seized 300 Argive citizens who were still suspected of being pro-Spartan. These were put by the Athenians into the nearby islands under Athenian control.

The Athenians also made an expedition against the island of Melos. They had thirty of their own ships, six from Chios, and two from Lesbos; 1,200 hoplites, 300 archers, and twenty mounted archers, all from Athens; and about 1,500 hoplites from the allies and the islanders.

The Melians are a colony from Sparta.   They had refused to join the Athenian empire like the other islanders, and at first had remained neutral without helping either side; but afterwards, when the Athenians had brought force to bear on them by laying waste their land, they had become open enemies of Athens.

Now the generals Cleomedes, the son of Lycomedes, and Tisias, the son of Tisimachus, encamped with the above force in Melian territory and, before doing any harm to the land, first of all sent representatives to negotiate.   The Melians did not invite these representatives to speak before the people, but asked them to make the statement for which they had come in front of the governing body and the few.   The Athenian representatives then spoke as follows:

Athenians: So we are not to speak before the people, no doubt in case the mass of the people should hear once and for all and without interruption an argument from us which is both persuasive and incontrovertible, and should so be led astray.   This, we realize, is your motive in bringing us here to speak before the few.   Now suppose that you who sit here should make assurance doubly sure.   Suppose that you, too, should refrain from dealing with every point in detail in a set speech, and should instead interrupt us whenever we say something controversial and deal with that before going on to the next point? Tell us first whether you approve of this suggestion of ours.

The Council of the Melians replied as follows:

Melians: No one can object to each of us putting forward our own views in a calm atmosphere.   That is perfectly reasonable.   What is scarcely consistent with such a proposal is the present threat, indeed the certainty, of your making war on us.   We see that you have come prepared to judge the argument yourselves, and that the likely end of it all will be either war, if we prove that we are in the right, and so refuse to surrender, or else slavery.

Athenians: If you are going to spend the time in enumerating your suspicions about the future, or if you have met here for any other reason except to look the facts in the face and on the basis of these facts to consider how you can save your city from destruction, there is no point in our going on with this discussion.   If, however, you will do as we suggest, then we will speak on.

Melians: It is natural and understandable that people who are placed as we are should have recourse to all kinds of arguments and different points of view.   However, you are right in saying that we are met together here to discuss the safety of our country and, if you will have it so, the discussion shall proceed on the lines that you have laid down.

Athenians: Then we on our side will use no fine phrases saying, for example, that we have a right to our empire because we defeated the Persians, or that we have come against you now because of the injuries you have done us—a great mass of words that nobody would believe. And we ask you on your side not to imagine that you will influence us by saying that you, though a colony of Sparta, have not joined Sparta in the war, or that you have never done us any harm.   Instead we recommend that you should try to get what it is possible for you to get, taking into consideration what we both really do think; since you know as well as we do that, when these matters are discussed by practical people, the standard of justice depends on the equality of power to compel and that in fact the strong do what they have the power to do and the weak accept what they have to accept.

Melians: Then in our view (since you force us to leave justice out of account and to confine ourselves to self-interest)—in our view it is at any rate useful that you should not destroy a principle that is to the general good of all men—namely, that in the case of all who fall into danger there should be such a thing as fair play and just dealing, and that such people should be allowed to use and to profit by arguments that fall short of a mathematical accuracy. And this is a principle which affects you as much as anybody, since your own fall would be visited by the most terrible vengeance and would be an example to the world.

Athenians: As for us, even assuming that our empire does come to an end, we are not despondent about what would happen next. One is not so much frightened of being conquered by a power which rules over others, as Sparta does (not that we are concerned with Sparta now), as of what would happen if a ruling power is attacked and defeated by its own subjects. So far as this point is concerned, you can leave it to us to face the risks involved. What we shall do now is to show you that it is for the good of our own empire that we are here and that it is for the preservation of your city that we shall say what we are going to say. We do not want any trouble in bringing you into our empire, and we want you to be spared for the good both of yourselves and of ourselves.

Melians: And how could it be just as good for us to be the slaves as for you to be the masters?

Athenians: You, by giving in, would save yourselves from disaster; we, by not destroying you, would be able to profit from you.

Melians: So you would not agree to our being neutral, friends instead of enemies, but allies of neither side?

Athenians: No, because it is not so much your hostility that injures us; it is rather the case that, if we were on friendly terms with you, our subjects would regard that as a sign of weakness in us, whereas your hatred is evidence of our power.

Melians: Is that your subjects' idea of fair play—that no distinction should be made between people who are quite unconnected with you and people who are mostly your own colonists or else rebels whom you have conquered?

Athenians: So far as right and wrong are concerned they think that there is no difference between the two, that those who still preserve their independence do so because they are strong, and that if we fail to attack them it is because we are afraid. So that by conquering you we shall increase not only the size but the security of our empire. We rule the sea and you are islanders, and weaker islanders too than the others; it is therefore particularly important that you should not escape.

Melians: But do you think there is no security for you in what we suggest? For here again, since you will not let us mention justice, but tell us to give in to your interests, we, too, must tell you what our interests are and, if yours and ours happen to coincide, we must try to persuade you of the fact. Is it not certain that you will make enemies of all states who are at present neutral, when they see what is happening here and naturally conclude that in course of time you will attack them too? Does not this mean that you are strengthening the enemies you have already and are forcing others to become your enemies even against their intentions and their inclinations?

Athenians: As a matter of fact we are not so much frightened of states on the continent. They have their liberty, and this means that it will be a long time before they begin to take precautions against us. We are more concerned about islanders like yourselves, who are still unsubdued, or subjects who have already become embittered by the constraint which our empire imposes on them. These are the people who are most likely to act in a reckless manner and to bring themselves and us, too, into the most obvious danger.

Melians: Then surely, if such hazards are taken by you to keep your empire and by your subjects to escape from it, we who are still free would show ourselves great cowards and weaklings if we failed to face everything that comes rather than submit to slavery.

Athenians: No, not if you are sensible. This is no fair fight, with honour on one side and shame on the other. It is rather a question of saving your lives and not resisting those who are far too strong for you.

Melians: Yet we know that in war fortune sometimes makes the odds more level than could be expected from the difference in numbers of the two sides. And if we surrender, then all our hope is lost at once, whereas, so long as we remain in action, there is still a hope that we may yet stand upright.

Athenians: Hope, that comforter in danger! If one already has solid advantages to fall back upon, one can indulge in hope. It may do harm, but will not destroy one. But hope is by nature an expensive commodity, and those who are risking their all on one cast find out what it means only when they are already ruined; it never fails them in the period when such a knowledge would enable them to take precautions.   Do not let this happen to you, you who are weak and whose fate depends on a single movement of the scale.   And do not be like those people who, as so commonly happens, miss the chance of saving themselves in a human and practical way, and, when every clear and distinct hope has left them in their adversity, turn to what is blind and vague, to prophecies and oracles and such things which by encouraging hope lead men to ruin.

Melians: It is difficult, and you may be sure that we know it, for us to oppose your power and fortune, unless the terms be equal.   Nevertheless we trust that the gods will give us fortune as good as yours, because we are standing for what is right against what is wrong; and as for what we lack in power, we trust that it will be made up for by our alliance with the Spartans, who are bound, if for no other reason, then for honour's sake, and because we are their kinsmen, to come to our help.   Our confidence, therefore, is not so entirely irrational as you think.

Athenians: So far as the favour of the gods is concerned, we think we have as much right to that as you have.   Our aims and our actions are perfectly consistent with the beliefs men hold about the gods and with the principles which govern their own conduct.   Our opinion of the gods and our knowledge of men lead us to conclude that it is a general and necessary law of nature to rule wherever one can.   This is not a law that we made ourselves, nor were we the first to act upon it when it was made.   We found it already in existence, and we shall leave it to exist for ever among those who come after us.   We are merely acting in accordance with it, and we know that you or anybody else with the same power as ours would be acting in precisely the same way.   And therefore, so far as the gods are concerned, we see no good reason why we should fear to be at a disadvantage.   But with regard to your views about Sparta and your confidence that she, out of a sense of honour, will come to your aid, we must say that we congratulate you on your simplicity but do not envy you your folly.   In matters that concern themselves or their own constitution the Spartans are quite remarkably good; as for their relations with others, that is a long story, but it can be expressed shortly and clearly by saying that of all people we know the Spartans are most conspicuous for believing that what they like doing is honourable and what suits their interests is just.   And this kind of attitude is not going to be of much help to you in your absurd quest for safety at the moment.

Melians: But this is the very point where we can feel most sure. Their own self-interest will make them refuse to betray their own colonists, the Melians, for that would mean losing the confidence of their friends among the Hellenes and doing good to their enemies.

Athenians: You seem to forget that if one follows one's self-interest one wants to be safe, whereas the path of justice and honour involves one in danger. And, where danger is concerned, the Spartans are not, as a rule, very venturesome.

Melians: But we think that they would even endanger themselves for our sake and count the risk more worth taking than in the case of others, because we are so close to the Peloponnese that they could operate more easily, and because they can depend on us more than on others, since we are of the same race and share the same feelings.

Athenians: Goodwill shown by the party that is asking for help does not mean security for the prospective ally. What is looked for is a positive preponderance of power in action. And the Spartans pay attention to this point even more than others do. Certainly they distrust their own native resources so much that when they attack a neighbour they bring a great army of allies with them. It is hardly likely therefore that, while we are in control of the sea, they will cross over to an island.

Melians: But they still might send others. The Cretan sea is a wide one, and it is harder for those who control it to intercept others than for those who want to slip through to do so safely. And even if they were to fail in this, they would turn against your own land and against those of your allies left unvisited by Brasidas.[1] So, instead of troubling about a country which has nothing to do with you, you will find trouble nearer home, among your allies, and in your own country.

Athenians: It is a possibility, something that has in fact happened before. It may happen in your case, but you are well aware that the Athenians have never yet relinquished a single siege operation through fear of others. But we are somewhat shocked to find that, though you announced your intention of discussing how you could preserve yourselves, in all this talk you have said absolutely nothing which could justify a man in thinking that he could be preserved. Your chief

---

[1] A Spartan general.

points are concerned with what you hope may happen in the future, while your actual resources are too scanty to give you a chance of survival against the forces that are opposed to you at this moment. You will therefore be showing an extraordinary lack of common sense if, after you have asked us to retire from this meeting, you still fail to reach a conclusion wiser than anything you have mentioned so far. Do not be led astray by a false sense of honour—a thing which often brings men to ruin when they are faced with an obvious danger that somehow affects their pride. For in many cases men have still been able to see the dangers ahead of them, but this thing called dishonour, this word, by its own force of seduction, has drawn them into a state where they have surrendered to an idea, while in fact they have fallen voluntarily into irrevocable disaster, in dishonour that is all the more dishonourable because it has come to them from their own folly rather than their misfortune. You, if you take the right view, will be careful to avoid this. You will see that there is nothing disgraceful in giving way to the greatest city in Hellas when she is offering you such reasonable terms—alliance on a tribute-paying basis and liberty to enjoy your own property. And, when you are allowed to choose between war and safety, you will not be so insensitively arrogant as to make the wrong choice. This is the safe rule—to stand up to one's equals, to behave with deference towards one's superiors, and to treat one's inferiors with moderation. Think it over again, then, when we have withdrawn from the meeting, and let this be a point that constantly recurs to your minds—that you are discussing the fate of your country, that you have only one country, and that its future for good or ill depends on this one single decision which you are going to make.

The Athenians then withdrew from the discussion. The Melians, left to themselves, reached a conclusion which was much the same as they had indicated in their previous replies. Their answer was as follows:

Melians: Our decision, Athenians, is just the same as it was at first. We are not prepared to give up in a short moment the liberty which our city has enjoyed from its foundation for 700 years. We put our trust in the fortune that the gods will send and which has saved us up to now, and in the help of men—that is, of the Spartans; and so we shall try to save ourselves. But we invite you to allow us to be friends of yours and enemies to neither side, to make a treaty which shall be agreeable to both you and us, and so to leave our country.

The Melians made this reply, and the Athenians, just as they were breaking off the discussion, said:

Athenians: Well, at any rate, judging from this decision of yours, you seem to us quite unique in your ability to consider the future as something more certain than what is before your eyes, and to see uncertainties as realities, simply because you would like them to be so. As you have staked most on and trusted most in Spartans, luck, and hopes, so in all these you will find yourselves most completely deluded.

The Athenian representatives then went back to the army, and the Athenian generals, finding that the Melians would not submit, immediately commenced hostilities and built a wall completely round the city of Melos, dividing the work out among the various states. Later they left behind a garrison of some of their own and some allied troops to blockade the place by land and sea, and with the greater part of their army returned home. The force left behind stayed on and continued with the siege.

About the same time the Argives invaded Phliasia and were ambushed by the Phliasians and the exiles from Argos, losing about eighty men.

Then, too, the Athenians at Pylos captured a great quantity of plunder from Spartan territory. Not even after this did the Spartans renounce the treaty and make war, but they issued a proclamation saying that any of their people who wished to do so were free to make raids on the Athenians. The Corinthians also made some attacks on the Athenians because of private quarrels of their own, but the rest of the Peloponnesians stayed quiet.

Meanwhile the Melians made a night attack and captured the part of the Athenian lines opposite the market-place. They killed some of the troops, and then, after bringing in corn and everything else useful that they could lay their hands on, retired again and made no further move, while the Athenians took measures to make their blockade more efficient in future. So the summer came to an end.

In the following winter the Spartans planned to invade the territory of Argos, but when the sacrifices for crossing the frontier turned out unfavourably, they gave up the expedition. The fact that they had intended to invade made the Argives suspect certain people in their city, some of whom they arrested, though others succeeded in escaping.

About this same time the Melians again captured another part of the Athenian lines where there were only a few of the garrison on guard. As a result of this, another force came out afterwards from Athens under the command of Philocrates, the son of Demeas. Siege operations were now carried on vigorously and, as there was also some treachery from inside, the Melians surrendered unconditionally to the Athenians, who put to death all the men of military age whom they took, and sold the women and children as slaves.   Melos itself they took over for themselves, sending out later a colony of 500 men.

Lines of Inquiry

1 "The Melian Debate" is a chapter from Thucydides' account of the great war between Athens and Sparta, a war that ended in the destruction of the Athenian Empire. Thucydides was an Athenian general during this war, yet refers to himself only once during the entire account.

   a Why does he not write about the Melian campaign from his own point of view?

   b What would have been the result for the description of the causes of the Melian campaign had Thucydides adopted only the point of view of the Melian Senate? Or that of the Athenian ambassadors?

   c What would have been the result if an ordinary soldier's view of the war had determined the structure?

   d We can suppose that the Melian Senate and the Athenian embassy together made up a fair number of people—perhaps twenty or thirty, at least. What does Thucydides gain by limiting his cast of speakers to "the Athenians" and "the Melians"? What would be the result if he had differentiated among Athenian speakers or among Melian speakers?

2 The conquest of Melos was of almost no military advantage to Athens in its conflict with Sparta.

   a What reasons are given in the debate for the Athenian attack? What are the real issues involved?

   b How are these issues related to Thucydides' choice of point of view?

3 Outline the sequence of argument and event as the chapter presents it.

   a How would that sequence differ if Thucydides had not used secondary points of view as he does? If he had decided to explain the campaign solely from the Athenian point of view? From the point of view of one of the generals involved?

b Would the relative scale of argument and event shift, as well as the sequence? Why?

c What do you conclude about the relationship of sequence and scale to point of view?

4 Outline the sequence of argument in the chapter. How is this sequence related to the debate form?

5 *a* Look at the transitional passages between the comments of the Athenians and those of the Melians. Suppose these transitions to be more extensive—to tell us more about the physical situation, the private consultations, the general brouhaha, that must have accompanied the debate; what would be the result?

b Consider the relative scale of the debate and the narrative of events. Is Thucydides interested in *what* happened, or in *why* it happened?

6 Thucydides often employs the device of a public debate before the total citizenry of the cities or city involved in a decision as a way of presenting the issues of the war. "The Melian Debate," by contrast, is a private affair between generals and senators. How would the form of the debate have been affected had Thucydides used the public debate, before "the many" and not "the few," as a vehicle.

Lines of Experiment

1 Take a topic—political, moral, educational—on which opinion is diverse. (Suggestions: nongraded classes, sexual mores, the effort to reach the moon, compulsory military service, the use of atomic weapons in war.) Now write an examination of the issues, using the debate form as your compositional device. Who are your principals? How abrupt are your transitions? Are you principally concerned with narrative or with argument? How does the balance between narrative and argument affect the form of your debate?

2 Formulate the issues that lay behind the Vietnam War—or behind any war. Now phrase them in debate form. How does the debate form assist you in your treatment of the issues? What advantages does it have?

3 James Reston, a popular newspaper columnist, sometimes reported the results of a computer called "Uniquack," which translated into plain and obvious language the circumlocutions of political debate, especially the public statements of heads of rival states. Process a current debate through your own Uni-

quack. What do you gain? What do you lose? What does
it tell you about political debates?

4 Imagine a war between two states. Phrase the origin, issues,
and upshot of that war in terms parallel to those of the Melian
Debate.

SACHEVERELL SITWELL

 **CUPID AND
THE JACARANDA**

In nearly every composition or work of art there is a Cupid, if it be
only to fill in a corner or populate a cloud; and Cupid, we are told, "is
generally represented as amusing himself with some childish diversion.
Sometimes he appears driving a hoop, throwing a quoit, playing with a
nymph, catching a butterfly, or trying to burn with a torch; at other
times he plays upon a horn before his mother, Venus, or closely embraces a swan, or, with one foot raised in the air, in a musing posture,
seems to meditate some trick."

That is what Dr. Lemprière has to say of him.

His, indeed, are directions for the placing of Cupid in classical compositions of any and every sort, and in obedience to that instruction
here is our picture of him. If it has no other merit, it brings our
fantasy born of fact and of imagination to an appropriate end.

I must explain that in the early summer of 1949 I was in Lisbon, and
that in one respect there is a difference or an improvement since I was
there before. It is a matter of the jacaranda. I am inclined to believe
that upon previous visits to Lisbon, the earliest was in 1926, the
jacarandas were not old enough to flower. Since then, many of the
wider streets and avenues have been planted with them, and they grow
in many gardens.

The jacaranda is a Brazilian tree and was probably brought to Europe
from Madeira. The wood is of splendid quality. But the beauty of
the jacaranda tree is when it is in blossom. Then, it is one of the most

wonderful sights of nature. It may be the loveliest of all flowering trees. I must further explain that I had been ill, and that I have never before seen a jacaranda tree in blossom.

The first that I saw was upon a steep hill, one of the seven hills of Lisbon, climbing abruptly to the British Embassy. It stood in a walled garden, to the right-hand side of the road, and was about as big as a fair-sized oak tree. Rather smaller than beech or sycamore, and with a smooth stem. Not a leaf to be seen. For the blue jacaranda was in flower. But I had little time for it. I was so late for luncheon. Coming out, I saw it again, but with difficulty because of the high wall.

This must have been one of the earliest jacaranda trees to flower in Lisbon. A morning or two later, on waking and looking out of the open window, a tree at the back of some houses opposite the hotel, had broken into blossom. The tree had been of little significance and no interest; it had shown no sign of it the day before. It had not even occurred to me that it was a jacaranda. Now, in one night, it had become a blue tree.

That morning, or the next, there were any number of jacarandas in full flower along an avenue down by the harbour, where you take the train to Estoril. But they are not seen at their best, there, because the houses in the background are washed or painted blue, and because they climb too high above the jacarandas and enclose them. Also, they are tall, dull tenements. What are wanting are the tilted roofs of Lisbon; curving eaves that give to the old houses of Lisbon the touch of Macao or Canton; walls washed with bright colours, or lined with china tiles.

One of the most beautiful of the jacarandas grows outside the Museum of Artillery, which is in an old palace of the eighteenth century along the Tagus. The Museum is a two-storey building, of just the right height, and the jacaranda is about as high as that, or a little higher, and about as wide as a plane tree or a sycamore. Here, you can walk all round the jacaranda and look at it from every angle. You can see it against the façade of the palace, or against the sky, or distant buildings; or stand right under it and look up through the boughs. Or, again, move away a few steps until you can take in the whole of the blue tree with your eyes.

And now it is time to describe a jacaranda tree in flower.

It is a blue you have not seen before. Like the blue heliotrope, in substance, that is to say, the whole head of flower, the entire jacaranda taken in at a glance, has something of the soft outline of a heliotrope. It is of powdery texture like the heliotrope, but only at the first sight of it, and only at a distance. For the individual flowers of the jacaranda have no resemblance at all to the florets of the heliotrope. It is only that they are in the same key of blue; that they strike the same note of blueness. The little separate flowers, indeed, are trumpet-shaped. We shall see that one of the flowers, by itself, can become the horn that Cupid plays while Venus listens.

I would call the flowering jacaranda powder blue, if it were not that powder-blue china is of another and darker colour altogether. Neither is it the powdered blue of the heads and necks of certain pigeons; a pale silvery blue; or a paler, more distinct blue frosted with silver; or as if powdered with flour; or a little like very fine dew or hoar frost upon blue. The jacaranda has no undertones. It strikes the note and holds it. I think the moment of first seeing it is one of the memorable sensations of a lifetime. What it evokes is a new civiliza-tion and a new music, borne to one upon the soft Brazilian airs, "the *modinhas* that Beckford loved, that Beckford wished to learn . . ." and other, newer measures of that huge sub-continent where race mingles with race but there is no enmity or persecution of minorities. I do not believe the jacaranda in Burma or in South Africa, or wherever else it grows, could evoke a civilization of its own. It could be only, and nothing but, Brazilian, for the jacaranda, as we have said, is a Brazilian tree.

I have not seen the flamboyant, which is another tropical flowering tree. But I am not prepared to think that its vermilion flowers could evoke a whole new world before you, an architecture and a music, and in-habited streets and houses. The jacaranda tree in front of the Museum of Artillery at Lisbon does all this for you, and more. It is a sensation approaching the miraculous to stand a few feet away from it and look up at the blue flowers—again I am bound to say that it has something of the heliotrope, but with the black or purple of the heliotrope left out of it, and keyed brighter, softer, clearer; or perhaps it is that the black in the heliotrope is altered to a base of red in the jacaranda. The blue note of the jacaranda is incomparable; a marvellous mid-blue, but neither mauve, nor violet; not like the plumage of any bird, nor the colour of any sky; and with the property, it seems to me, that you forget your worries and sorrows, and how old the world is, or how new and augmenting are its troubles, and have time only for the jacaranda during the few days it is in blossom.

I had seen the blue paulownia, which grows in Tuscany at the same season as the blue wistaria, but it is as nothing to the jacaranda. So I thought; at which moment the whole blue tree shook and trembled in the wind, and I saw a few of the blue flowers lying on the ground. Above them, the dovesoft boughs lifted and danced in the wind. I wondered, what would a jacaranda look like by night? Would it keep that colour, which is the promise of music not yet written, and of a harmony and a civilization as yet unborn?

Upon the evening of that same spring day we walked along the square of the Rossio with its striped pavement, up the Praça dos Restauradores, and into the long tree-lined avenue beyond it; which is a public promenade up a hillside, with bars and band kiosques on the sidewalks, and shops and cinemas. It was near midnight, and very warm. Too lovely a night, indeed, for an early bed.

So we wandered, on the left of the avenue, to a place where there were bright lights, and paid for admission at a stile and found ourselves in an enclosed space into which people were streaming out from a theatre upon one side and a cinema on the other, and taking up all the empty seats in one or other of the cafés. We were lucky to find a table and two empty chairs.

The café was half in the open and half inside, and we were sitting in the open part of it, nearly, but not quite, under a magnificent jacaranda tree. A band played in the restaurant, but for the first few moments one could do nothing but admire the jacaranda, for night made no difference to the beautiful blue flowers. Now and again they danced in a breath of wind, and as in the morning a few of the blue flowers lay on the ground.

Soon, we began to take note of the other persons in the café and it was not long before we noticed they were all young. There were a good many young men who must be students and four or five young women, sitting by themselves, at first, but who before long exchanged glances with their neighbours or recognized old admirers. A little later, two or three of the young men came and joined them at their table.

At this point the prettiest of the young women detached herself from her companions and went to sit alone. She was tall, with a thin waist; with dark eyes, dark skin, and dark, dark hair; and in Brazil would have passed for a Brazilian. In fact, more Brazilian than a native of Portugal; and with, who knows, the touch of Angola or of

Mozambique? Or of the black fishing quarter of Bahia, in Brazil, where they dance the conga and the samba, and other tropical dances under the jacaranda.   And, evidently, she wished to sit alone.

Now it so happens that in cafés and restaurants in Portugal, that is to say, in Lisbon and in Oporto, which are its only cities, there is often a little page boy to take your hat or run with messages.   There are some horrible children in a restaurant in Lisbon who wear large Eton collars, several sizes too big for them, but the child in this café wore the ordinary page's clothes, pale blue, with a pale blue pillbox hat. He was a fair child, ten or twelve years old, who should have been sent to bed hours ago; a pretty child, and not unlike a Cupid.   Only he looked so tired, which gave him a sinister air of dissipation.   For a moment, it looked in the shadow as if his eyes were painted.   But it was no more than the dark circles of fatigue.   Lisbon is without the wickedness of other cities.

The child hung about with nothing to do, walking round idly, or leaning upon a balustrade, while the prettiest of the young women sat near him at her table, still alone.

The May night grew warmer, and more warm.   The blue jacaranda had never looked so tropical by day.

Soon, one of the older students beckoned to Cupid and sent him on an errand.   I was shocked with the import of it; but I need not have worried about his messenger.   Cupid, before running to her, stooped to pick a fallen jacaranda flower from the ground, and making the blue calyx into a little horn or trumpet, blew into it between his fingers, and so playing, ran to Venus and whispered into her ear.

Lines of Inquiry

1 Most of Sitwell's essay is given over to the jacaranda tree.
  a What aspect of the jacaranda is most important to Sitwell?
  b Why does he have so much difficulty describing its color, and given that difficulty, why does he try to describe it?
  c What does Sitwell use as a linking device to connect one reference to the tree to another?
  d The jacaranda is first described in the fifth paragraph; that description is highly general.   Why?   How many trees does Sitwell mention before finally giving a precise description? Why does he mention the other trees at all?
  e Eliminate from the essay all references to the jacaranda— what remains?
  f What does the jacaranda *mean,* in this essay?

2 *a* What has the jacaranda tree to do with Brazil?

   b Why is it important to Sitwell that the girl in the café seems more Brazilian than Portuguese?

   c Why does he say of the jacaranda that "it evokes a new civilization and a new music"?

   d What is Brazil's relevance to Sitwell's point?

3 The following passage attempts to describe the jacaranda's color. What accounts for the sequence in which Sitwell arranges his descriptive phrases?

"I would call the flowering jacaranda powder blue, if it were not that powder-blue china is of another and darker colour altogether. Neither is it the powdered blue of the heads and necks of certain pigeons; a pale silvery blue; or a paler, more distinct blue frosted with silver; or as if powdered with flour; or a little like very fine dew or hoar frost upon blue."

4 Underline the word "blue" each time it appears in the essay. What is the effect of this repetition? Gertrude Stein once said "When I wrote 'a rose is a rose is a rose' the rose was red for the first time in a hundred years." What did she mean? What might one conclude about repetition as a stylistic device?

5 Sitwell's last scene introduces us to "Cupid." In this scene,

   a Why does Sitwell describe the page boy's clothes?

   b Why does Sitwell describe the boy as looking "so tired, which gave him a sinister air of dissipation"?

   c Why does he say that "The May night grew warmer, and more warm. The blue jacaranda had never looked so tropical by day"—what does this last sentence add?

   d Sitwell remarks that he "need not have worried about his [the student's] messenger." Why might he have worried? Why does he suggest in the essay that there might be something to worry about?

   e What is Sitwell trying to say in this last scene?

   f Look from the conclusion of the essay to its opening paragraph. How are the two related?

6 *a* What point of view does Sitwell employ in this essay?

   b How does that point of view affect or control the essay's structure—its subject and sequence of subjects?

   c Why does Sitwell feel that he must "explain that I had been ill, and that I have never before seen a jacaranda tree in blossom"?

7 To paraphrase the meaning of this essay is virtually impossible.

Assuming that Sitwell knows what he is doing, how do you account for the essay's obscurity?

8 "Cupid and the Jacaranda" is the last essay in Sitwell's book of
the same title.   What has the subject of the essay to do with
its position in the total book, according to Sitwell?   (Read
the first paragraph again.)

9 This essay has essentially four elements: Venus, Cupid, the
jacaranda, and Sitwell himself.   Of these four the jacaranda
tree seems clearly its descriptive center, in one sense.
  a Does this make Cupid subordinate to the jacaranda?   Or
    is the jacaranda subordinate to Cupid?
  b What does the place of Cupid in the essay—his place in the
    sequence of Sitwell's observation—suggest concerning the
    relative importance of the deity and the tree?

Lines of Experiment

1 The jacaranda is a symbol, and symbols are never entirely open
to paraphrase.   It is easy enough to call the jacaranda a tree,
and possible to describe its color with some precision, but its
final, full meaning rises only intuitively out of its circumstances, and only to a specific point of view.   Sitwell is able
to exploit the jacaranda at length partly because his point of
view is personal; his own attitudes, experiences and observations are within the subject.

The jacaranda is an unusual object; symbols are not always so.
Look about the room in which you are sitting as you read this,
and pick out what seems to you to be its most significant object—perhaps an old wall clock with a gold eagle on top; a
teacher's lectern; an elaborate radio-phonograph; a wicker sofa;
a crayon sketch done years before; a high school pennant; a
battered stuffed animal.   Study this object for what it means
to you, as student, as neophyte artist, as "growing older young
man," as rock 'n' roll addict, as member of a family.   (Be
sure you identify clearly for yourself the point of view by
means of which you "control" the object; you could successfully
compound three or four of the above—student, artist, son—
provided they are closely linked; but you might run some risk
of confusing your view of the subject were you to confuse
entirely unrelated points of view, such as the chemist's with
the artist's.   Your assignment is to write the meaningful history of that portion of your experience connected to, symbolized by, the object you have taken as a significant center.

Two cautions: *First,* try to get a feeling for the meaning of your symbol before you begin to write. *Second,* do not try to phrase that meaning directly and explicitly within your essay: Arrange your history in "scenes," let those scenes themselves stand for your meaning, and use your symbolic center—the clock, the lectern, the sketch—as a point of departure (introduction) and of return (conclusion).

Concentration of idea is one of the chief uses of the symbolic method. Can you use comparison or contrast to enhance that vividness of effect? Can you work into your essay a pattern of movement that will enhance its meaning and effect? Can you find in a single aspect of your symbol—its color, shape, ornament, movement, position—a concentrated, unified expression of its meaning?

2 To describe one's emotions directly and accurately is often almost impossible: Summary words such as "lovable," "hateful," "beautiful," or "repulsive," do little to communicate the usual complexity of emotional states. Frequently, only a symbol can represent a complex of emotions in a satisfactory, unitary way and so make them authentic. Choose three things you have seen in the past year that have made an especially deep impression on you. Of the three, the one concerning which you feel you can best answer the following questions probably will be the best subject for an essay. *Do not stop to answer such questions before you write, however:* Let the answers—and their significance—emerge as you compose.

a What was its single most obviously striking characteristic?

b Why was this single characteristic so striking?

c What was the relationship of this striking characteristic to the whole subject of which it was a part?

d What were your circumstances when you saw it, and what field of objects and actions surrounded the subject at the time?

e What relationship, if any, did your circumstances have to the way you felt about it?

f How do you feel about it now?

g What other, similar things have you seen or experienced, and in what ways were those things similar? What was the common denominator of feeling, and what were the points of difference?

WILLIAM STYRON

 THIS QUIET
DUST

You mought be rich as cream
And drive you coach and four-horse team,
But you can't keep de world from moverin' round
Nor Nat Turner from gainin' ground.

And your name it mought be Caesar sure
And got you cannon can shoot a mile or more,
But you can't keep de world from moverin' round
Nor Nat Turner from gainin' ground.

—Old-time Negro Song

My native state of Virginia is, of course, more than ordinarily conscious of its past, even for the South. When I was learning my lessons in the mid-1930s at a grammar school on the banks of the James River, one of the required texts was a history of Virginia—a book I can recall far more vividly than any history of the United States or of Europe I studied at a later time. It was in this work that I first encountered the name Nat Turner. The reference to Nat was brief; as a matter of fact, I do not think it unlikely that it was the very brevity of the allusion —amounting almost to a quality of haste—which captured my attention and stung my curiosity. I can no longer quote the passage exactly, but I remember that it went something like this: "In 1831, a fanatical Negro slave named Nat Turner led a terrible insurrection in South-ampton County, murdering many white people. The insurrection was immediately put down, and for their cruel deeds Nat Turner and most of the other Negroes involved in the rebellion were hanged." Give or take a few harsh adjectives, this was all the information on Nat Turner supplied by that forgotten historian, who hustled on to matters of greater consequence.

I must have first read this passage when I was ten or eleven years old.

At that time my home was not far from Southampton County, where the rebellion took place, in a section of the Virginia Tidewater which is generally considered part of the Black Belt because of the predominance of Negroes in the population.   (When I speak of the South and Southerners here, I speak of *this* South, where Deep South attitudes prevail; it would include parts of Maryland and East Texas.)   My boyhood experience was the typically ambivalent one of most native Southerners, for whom the Negro is simultaneously taken for granted and as an object of unending concern.   On the one hand, Negroes are simply a part of the landscape, an unexceptional feature of the local scenery, yet as central to its character as the pinewoods and sawmills and mule teams and sleepy river estuaries that give such color and tone to the Southern geography.   Unnoticed by white people, the Negroes blend with the land and somehow melt and fade into it, so that only when one reflects upon their possible absence, some magical disappearance, does one realize how unimaginable this absence would be: it would be easier to visualize a South without trees, without *any* people, without life at all.   Thus at the same time, ignored by white people, Negroes impinge upon their collective subconscious to such a degree that it may be rightly said that they become the focus of an incessant preoccupation, somewhat like a monstrous, recurring dream populated by identical faces wearing expressions of inquietude and vague reproach.   "Southern whites cannot walk, talk, sing, conceive of laws or justice, think of sex, love, the family, or freedom without responding to the presence of Negroes."   The words are those of Ralph Ellison, and, of course, he is right.

Yet there are many Souths, and the experience of each Southerner is modified by the subtlest conditions of self and family and environment and God knows what else, and I have wondered if it has ever properly been taken into account how various this response to the presence of the Negroes can be.   I cannot tell how typical my own awareness of Negroes was, for instance, as I grew up near my birthplace—a small seaside city about equally divided between black and white.   My feelings seem to have been confused and blurred, tinged with sentimentality, colored by a great deal of folklore, and wobbling always between a patronizing affection, fostered by my elders, and downright hostility.   Most importantly, my feelings were completely uninformed by that intimate knowledge of black people which Southerners claim as their special patent; indeed, they were based upon an almost total ignorance.

For one thing, from the standpoint of attitudes toward race, my upbringing was hardly unusual: it derived from the simple conviction that Negroes were in every respect inferior to white people and should be made to stay in their proper order in the scheme of things. At the same time, by certain Southern standards my family was enlightened: although my mother taught me firmly that the use of "lady" instead of "woman" in referring to a Negro female was quite improper, she writhed at the sight of the extremes of Negro poverty, and would certainly have thrashed me had she ever heard me use the word "nigger." Yet outside the confines of family, in the lower-middle-class school world I inhabited every day, this was a word I commonly used. School segregation, which was an ordinary fact of life for me, is devastatingly effective in accomplishing something that it was only peripherally designed to do: it prevents the awareness even of the existence of another race. Thus, whatever hostility I bore toward the Negroes was based almost entirely upon hearsay.

And so the word "nigger," which like all my schoolmates I uttered so freely and so often, had even then an idle and listless ring. How could that dull epithet carry meaning and conviction when it was applied to a people so diligently isolated from us that they barely existed except as shadows which came daily to labor in the kitchen, to haul away garbage, to rake up leaves? An unremarked paradox of Southern life is that its racial animosity is really grounded not upon friction and propinquity, but upon an almost complete lack of contact. Surrounded by a sea of Negroes, I cannot recall more than once—and then briefly, when I was five or six—ever having played with a Negro child, or ever having spoken to a Negro, except in trifling talk with the cook, or in some forlorn and crippled conversation with a dotty old grandfather angling for hardshell crabs on a lonesome Sunday afternoon many years ago. Nor was I by any means uniquely sheltered. Whatever knowledge I gained in my youth about Negroes, I gained from a distance, as if I had been watching actors in an all-black puppet show.

Such an experience has made me distrust any easy generalizations about the South, whether they are made by white sociologists or Negro playwrights, Southern politicians or Northern editors. I have come to understand at least as much about the Negro after having lived in the North. One of the most egregious of the Southern myths—one in this case propagated solely by Southerners—is that of the Southern white's boast that he "knows" the Negro. Certainly in many rural areas of the South the cultural climate has been such as to allow a mutual understanding, and even a kind of intimacy, to spring up between the races,

at least in some individual instances.   But my own boyhood surroundings, which were semi-urban (I suppose suburban is the best description, though the green little village on the city's outskirts where I grew
up was a far cry from Levittown), and which have become the youthful
environment for vast numbers of Southerners, tended almost totally to
preclude any contact between black and white, especially when that
contact was so sedulously proscribed by law.

Yet if white Southerners cannot "know" the Negro, it is for this very
reason that the entire sexual myth needs to be reexamined.   Surely a
certain amount of sexual tension between the races does continue to
exist, and the Southern white man's fear of sexual aggression on the
part of the Negro male is still too evident to be ignored.   But the
nature of the growth of the urban, modern South has been such as to
impose ever more effective walls between the races.   While it cannot
be denied that slavery times produced an enormous amount of inter-
breeding (with all of its totalitarianism, this was a free-for-all atmosphere far less self-conscious about carnal mingling than the Jim Crow
era which began in the 1890s) and while even now there must logically
take place occasional sexual contacts between the races—especially in
rural areas where a degree of casual familiarity has always obtained—
the monolithic nature of segregation has raised such an effective barrier
between whites and Negroes that it is impossible not to believe that
theories involving a perpetual sexual "tension" have been badly in-
flated.   Nor is it possible to feel that a desire to taste forbidden fruit
has ever really caused this barrier to be breached.   From the standpoint
of the Negro, there is indifference or uncomplicated fear; from that of
the white—segregation, the law, and, finally, indifference, too.   When
I was growing up, the older boys might crack wan jokes about visiting
the Negro whorehouse street (patronized entirely, I later discovered, by
Negroes plus a few Scandinavian sailors), but to my knowledge none
of them ever really went there.   Like Negroes in general, Negro girls
were to white men phantoms, shadows.   To assume that anything
more than a rare and sporadic intimacy on any level has existed in the
modern South between whites and Negroes is simply to deny, with a
truly willful contempt for logic, the monstrous effectiveness of that
apartheid which has been the Southern way of life for almost three-
quarters of a century.

I have lingered on this matter only to try to underline a truth about
Southern life which has been too often taken for granted, and which
has therefore been overlooked or misinterpreted.   Most Southern white

people *cannot* know or touch black people and this is because of the
deadly intimidation of a universal law.   Certainly one feels the presence
of this gulf even in the work of a writer as supremely knowledgeable
about the South as William Faulkner, who confessed a hesitancy about
attempting to "think Negro," and whose Negro characters, as marvel-
ously portrayed as most of them are, seem nevertheless to be meticu-
lously *observed* rather than *lived*.   Thus in *The Sound and the Fury,*
Faulkner's magnificent Dilsey comes richly alive, yet in retrospect one
feels this is a result of countless mornings, hours, days Faulkner had
spent watching and listening to old Negro servants, and not because
Dilsey herself is a being created from a sense of withinness: at the last
moment Faulkner draws back, and it is no mere happenstance that
Dilsey, alone among the four central figures from whose points of
view the story is told, is seen from the outside rather than from that
intensely "inner" vantage point, the interior monologue.

Innumerable white Southerners have grown up as free of knowledge
of the Negro character and soul as a person whose background is rural
Wisconsin or Maine.   Yet, of course, there is a difference, and it is a
profound one, defining the white Southerner's attitudes and causing him
to be, for better or for worse, whatever it is he is to be.   For the
Negro is *there*.   And he is there in a way he never is in the North, no
matter how great his numbers.   In the South he is a perpetual and
immutable part of history itself, a piece of the vast fabric so integral
and necessary that without him the fabric dissolves; his voice, his
black or brown face passing on a city street, the sound of his cry rising
from a wagonload of flowers, his numberless procession down dusty
country roads, the neat white church he has built in some pine grove
with its air of grace and benison and tranquillity, his silhouette behind
a mule team far off in some spring field, the wail of his blues blaring
from some jukebox in a backwoods roadhouse, the sad wet faces of
nursemaids and cooks waiting in the evening at city bus stops in pouring rain—the Negro is always *there*.

No wonder then, as Ellison says, the white Southerner can do virtually
nothing without responding to the presence of Negroes.   No wonder the white man so often grows cranky, fanciful, freakish, loony,
violent: how else respond to a paradox which requires, with the full
majesty of law behind it, that he deny the very reality of a people
whose multitude approaches and often exceeds his own; that he dis-
claim the existence of those whose human presence has marked every
acre of the land, every hamlet and crossroad and city and town, and

whose humanity, however inflexibly denied, is daily evidenced to him like a heartbeat in loyalty and wickedness, madness and hilarity and mayhem and pride and love? The Negro may feel that it is too late to be known, and that the desire to know him reeks of outrageous condescension.   But to break down the old law, to come to *know* the Negro, has become the moral imperative of every white Southerner.

II

I suspect that my search for Nat Turner, my own private attempt as a novelist to re-create and bring alive that dim and prodigious black man, has been at least a partial fulfillment of this mandate, although the problem has long since resolved itself into an artistic one—which is as it should be.   In the late 1940s, having finished college in North Carolina and come to New York, I found myself again haunted by that name I had first seen in the Virginia history textbook.   I had learned something more of Southern history since then, and I had become fascinated by the subject of Negro slavery.   One of the most striking aspects of the institution is the fact that in the 250 years of its existence in America, it was singularly free of organized uprisings, plots, and rebellions.   (It is curious that as recently as the late 1940s, scholarly insights were lagging, and I could only have suspected then what has since been made convincing by such historians as Frank Tannenbaum and Stanley Elkins: that American Negro slavery, unique in its psychological oppressiveness—the worst the world has ever known—was simply so despotic and emasculating as to render organized revolt next to impossible.)   There were three exceptions: a conspiracy by the slave Gabriel Prosser and his followers near Richmond in the year 1800, the plot betrayed, the conspirators hanged; a similar conspiracy in 1822, in Charleston, South Carolina, led by a free Negro named Denmark Vesey, who also was betrayed before he could carry out his plans, and who was executed along with other members of the plot.

The last exception, of course, was Nat Turner, and he alone in the entire annals of American slavery—alone among all those "many thousand gone"—achieved a kind of triumph.

Even today, many otherwise well-informed people have never heard the name Nat Turner, and there are several plausible reasons for such an ignorance.   One of these, of course, is that the study of our history —and not alone in the South—has been tendentious in the extreme, and has often avoided even an allusion to a figure like Nat, who inconveniently disturbs our notion of a slave system which, though morally wrong, was conducted with such charity and restraint that any organized act of insurrectory and murderous violence would be unthinkable. But a general ignorance about Nat Turner is even more understandable in view of the fact that so little is left of the actual record. Southampton County, which even now is off the beaten track, was at that period the remotest backwater imaginable. The relativity of time allows us elastic definitions: 1831 was yesterday. Yet the year 1831, in the Presidency of Andrew Jackson, lay in the very dawn of our modern history, three years before a railroad ever touched the soil of Virginia, a full fifteen years before the use of the telegraph. The rebellion itself was of such a cataclysmic nature as practically to guarantee confusion of the news, distortion, wild rumors, lies, and, finally, great areas of darkness and suppression; all of these have contributed to Nat's obscurity.

As for the contemporary documents themselves, only one survives: the *Confessions of Nat Turner,* a brief pamphlet of some five thousand words, transcribed from Nat's lips as he awaited trial, by a somewhat enigmatic lawyer named Thomas Gray, who published the *Confessions* in Baltimore and then vanished from sight. There are several discrepancies in Gray's transcript but it was taken down in haste, and in all major respects it seems completely honest and reliable. Those few newspaper accounts of the time, from Richmond and Norfolk, are sketchy, remote, filled with conjecture, and are thus virtually worthless. The existing county court records of Southampton remain brief and unilluminating, dull lists, a dry catalogue of names in fading ink: the white people slain, the Negroes tried and transported south, or acquitted, or convicted and hanged.

Roughly seventy years after the rebellion (in 1900, which by coincidence was the year Virginia formally adopted its first Jim Crow laws), the single scholarly book ever to be written on the affair was published —*The Southampton Insurrection,* by a Johns Hopkins Ph.D candidate named William S. Drewry, who was an unreconstructed Virginian of decidedly pro-slavery leanings and a man so quaintly committed to the *ancien régime* that, in the midst of a description of the ghastliest part of the uprising, he was able to reflect that "slavery in Virginia was not such to arouse rebellion, but was an institution which nourished the strongest affection and piety in slave and owner, as well as moral qualities worthy of any age of civilization." For Drewry, Nat Turner was some sort of inexplicable aberration, like a man from Mars.

Drewry was close enough to the event in time, however, to be able to interview quite a few of the survivors, and since he also possessed a bloodthirsty relish for detail, it was possible for him to reconstruct the chronology of the insurrection with what appears to be considerable accuracy. Drewry's book (it is of course long out of print) and Nat's *Confessions* remain the only significant sources about the insurrection. Of Nat himself, his background and early years, very little can be known. This is not disadvantageous to a novelist, since it allows him to speculate—with a freedom not accorded the historian—upon all the intermingled miseries, ambitions, frustrations, hopes, rages, and desires which caused this extraordinary black man to rise up out of those early mists of our history and strike down his oppressors with a fury of retribution unequaled before or since.

He was born in 1800, which would have made him at the time of the insurrection thirty-one years old—exactly the age of so many great revolutionaries at the decisive moment of their insurgency: Martin Luther,[1] Robespierre, Danton, Fidel Castro. Thomas Gray, in a footnote to the *Confessions,* describes him as having the "true Negro face" (an offhand way of forestalling an assumption that he might have possessed any white blood), and he adds that "for natural intelligence and quickness of apprehension he is surpassed by few men I have ever seen" —a lofty tribute indeed at that inflammatory instant, with antebellum racism at its most hysteric pitch. Although little is known for certain of Nat's childhood and youth, there can be no doubt that he was very precocious and that he learned not only to read and write with ease —an illustrious achievement in itself, when learning to read and write was forbidden to Negroes by law—but at an early age acquired a knowledge of astronomy, and later on experimented in making paper and gunpowder. (The resemblance here to the knowledge of the ancient Chinese is almost too odd to be true, but I can find no reason to doubt it.)

The early decades of the nineteenth century were years of declining prosperity for the Virginia Tidewater, largely because of the ruination of the land through greedy cultivation of tobacco—a crop which had

---

[1] See Erik Erikson's *Young Man Luther* for a brilliant study of the development of the revolutionary impulse in a young man, and the relationship of this impulse to the father-figure. Although it is best to be wary of any heavy psychoanalytical emphasis, one cannot help believing that Nat Turner's relationship with his father, like Luther's, was tormented and complicated, especially since this person could not have been his real father, who ran away when Nat was an infant, but the white man who owned and raised him.

gradually disappeared from the region, causing the breakup of many of the big old plantations and the development of subsistence farming on small holdings. It was in these surroundings—a flat pastoral land of modest farms and even more modest homesteads, where it was rare to find a white man prosperous enough to own more than half a dozen Negroes, and where two or three slaves to a family was the general rule—that Nat was born and brought up, and in these surroundings he prepared himself for the apocalyptic role he was to play in history. Because of the failing economic conditions, it was not remarkable that Nat was purchased and sold several times by various owners (in a sense, he was fortunate in not having been sold off to the deadly cotton and rice plantations of South Carolina and Georgia, which was the lot of many Virginia Negroes of the period); and although we do not know much about any of these masters, the evidence does not appear to be that Nat was ill-treated, and in fact one of these owners (Samuel Turner, brother of the man whose property Nat was born) developed so strong a paternal feeling for the boy and such regard for Nat's abilities, that he took the fateful step of encouraging him in the beginnings of an education.

The atmosphere of the time and place was fundamentalist and devout to a passionate degree, and at some time during his twenties Nat, who had always been a godly person—"never owning a dollar, never uttering an oath, never drinking intoxicating liquors, and never committing a theft"—became a Baptist preacher. Compared to the Deep South, Virginia slave life was not so rigorous; Nat must have been given considerable latitude, and found many opportunities to preach and exhort the Negroes. His gifts for preaching, for prophecy, and his own magnetism seem to have been so extraordinary that he grew into a rather celebrated figure among the Negroes of the county, his influence even extending to the whites, one of whom—a poor, half-cracked, but respectable overseer named Brantley—he converted to the faith and baptized in a mill pond in the sight of a multitude of the curious, both black and white. (After this no one would have anything to do with Brantley, and he left the county in disgrace.)

At about this time Nat began to withdraw into himself, fasting and praying, spending long hours in the woods or in the swamp, where he communed with the Spirit and where there came over him, urgently now, intimations that he was being prepared for some great purpose. His fanaticism grew in intensity, and during these lonely vigils in the forest he began to see apparitions:

I saw white spirits and black spirits engaged in battle, and the sun was darkened; the thunder rolled in the heavens and blood flowed in streams . . . I wondered greatly at these miracles, and prayed to be informed of a certainty of the meaning thereof; and shortly afterwards, while laboring in the fields, I discovered drops of blood on the corn as though it were dew from heaven. For as the blood of Christ had been shed on this earth, and had ascended to heaven for the salvation of sinners, it was now returning to earth again in the form of dew . . . On the twelfth day of May, 1828, I heard a loud noise in the heavens, and the Spirit instantly appeared to me and said the Serpent was loosened, and Christ had laid down the yoke he had borne for the sins of men, and that I should take it on and fight against the Serpent, for the time was fast approaching when the first should be last and the last should be first . . .

Like all revolutions, that of Nat Turner underwent many worrisome hesitations, false starts, procrastinations, delays (with appropriate irony, Independence Day, 1830, had been one of the original dates selected, but Nat fell sick and the moment was put off again); finally, however, on the night of Sunday, August 21, 1831, Nat, together with five other Negroes in whom he had placed his confidence and trust, assembled in the woods near the home of his owner of the time, a carriage maker named Joseph Travis, and commenced to carry out a plan of total annihilation. The penultimate goal was the capture of the county seat, then called Jerusalem (a connotation certainly not lost on Nat, who, with the words of the prophets roaring in his ears, must have felt like Gideon himself before the extermination of the Midianites); there were guns and ammunition in Jerusalem, and with these captured it was then Nat's purpose to sweep thirty miles eastward, gathering black recruits on the way until the Great Dismal Swamp was reached—a snake-filled and gloomy fastness in which Nat believed, with probable justification, only Negroes could survive, and no white man's army could penetrate. The immediate objective, however, was the destruction of every white man, woman, and child on the ten-mile route to Jerusalem; no one was to be spared; tender infancy and feeble old age alike were to perish by the axe and the sword. The command, of course, was that of God Almighty, through the voice of his prophet Ezekiel: *"Son of Man, prophesy and say, Thus saith the Lord; Say, a sword, a sword is sharpened, and also furbished: it is sharpened to make a sore slaughter . . . Slay utterly old and young, both maids and little children, and women . . ."* It was a scheme so wild and daring that it could only have

been the product of the most wretched desperation and frustrate misery
of soul; and of course it was doomed to catastrophe not only for whites
but for Negroes—and for black men in ways which from the vantage
point of history now seem almost unthinkable.

They did their job rapidly and with merciless and methodical determination.   Beginning at the home of Travis—where five people, including a six-month-old infant, were slain in their beds—they marched
from house to house on an eastward route, pillaging, murdering,
sparing no one.   Lacking guns—at least to begin with—they employed
axes, hatchets, and swords as their tools of destruction, and swift
decapitation was their usual method of dispatch.   (It is interesting
that the Negroes did not resort to torture, nor were they ever accused
of rape.   Nat's attitude toward sex was Christian and high-minded,
and he had said: "We will not do to their women what they have done
to ours.")

On through the first day they marched, across the hot August fields,
gaining guns and ammunition, horses, and a number of willing recruits.
That the insurrection was not purely racial, but perhaps obscurely pre-
Marxist, may be seen in the fact that a number of dwellings belonging
to poor white people were pointedly passed by.   At midday on Monday
their force had more than tripled, to the amount of nineteen, and nearly
thirty white people lay dead.   By this time, the alarm had been sounded
throughout the country, and while the momentum of the insurgent
band was considerable, many of the whites had fled in panic to the
woods, and some of the farmers had begun to resist, setting up bar-
ricades from which they could fire back at Nat's forces.   Furthermore,
quite a few of the rebels had broken into the brandy cellars of the
houses they had attacked and had gotten roaring drunk—an eventuality
Nat had feared and had warned against.   Nevertheless, the Negroes—
augmented now by forty more volunteers—pressed on toward Jerusalem,
continuing the attack into the next night and all through the following
day, when at last obstinate resistance by the aroused whites and the
appearance of a mounted force of militia troops (also, it must be
suspected, continued attrition by the apple brandy) caused the rebels to
be dispersed, only a mile or so from Jerusalem.

Almost every one of the Negroes was rounded up and brought to
trial—a legalistic nicety characteristic of a time in which it was necessary for one to determine whether *his* slave, property, after all, worth

eight or nine hundred dollars, was really guilty and deserving of the gallows. Nat disappeared immediately after the insurrection, and hid in the woods for over two months, when near-starvation and the onset of autumnal cold drove him from his cave and forced him to surrender to a lone farmer with a shotgun. Then he too was brought to trial in Jerusalem—early in November 1831—for fomenting a rebellion in which sixty white people had perished.

The immediate consequences of the insurrection were exceedingly grim. The killing of so many white people was in itself an act of futility. It has never been determined with any accuracy how many black people, not connected with the rebellion, were slain at the hands of rampaging bands of white men who swarmed all over Southampton in the week following the uprising, seeking reprisal and vengeance. A contemporary estimate by a Richmond newspaper, which deplored this retaliation, put the number at close to two hundred Negroes, many of them free, and many of them tortured in ways unimaginably horrible. But even more important was the effect that Nat Turner's insurrection had upon the institution of slavery at large. News of the revolt spread among Southern whites with great speed: the impossible, the unspeakable had at last taken place after 200 years of the ministrations of sweet old mammies and softly murmured Yassuhs and docile compliance —and a shock wave of anguish and terror ran through the entire South. If such a nightmarish calamity happened there, would it not happen *here?*—here in Tennessee, in Augusta, in Vicksburg, in these bayous of Louisiana? Had Nat lived to see the consequences of his rebellion, surely it would have been for him the cruelest irony that his bold and desperate bid for liberty had caused only the most tyrannical new controls to be imposed upon Negroes everywhere—the establishment of patrols, further restrictions upon movement, education, assembly, and the beginning of other severe and crippling restraints which persisted throughout the slaveholding states until the Civil War. Virginia had been edging close to emancipation, and it seems reasonable to believe that the example of Nat's rebellion, stampeding many moderates in the legislature into a conviction that the Negroes could not be safely freed, was a decisive factor in the ultimate victory of the proslavery forces. Had Virginia, with its enormous prestige among the states, emancipated its slaves, the effect upon our history would be awesome to contemplate.

Nat brought cold, paralyzing fear to the South, a fear that never departed. If white men had sown the wind with chattel slavery, in Nat Turner they had reaped the whirlwind for white and black alike.

Nat was executed, along with sixteen other Negroes who had figured large in the insurrection. Most of the others were transported south, to the steaming fields of rice and cotton. On November 11, 1831, Nat was hanged from a live oak tree in the town square of Jerusalem. He went to his death with great dignity and courage. "The bodies of those executed," wrote Drewry, "with one exception, were buried in a decent and becoming manner. That of Nat Turner was delivered to the doctors, who skinned it and made grease of the flesh."

III

Not long ago, in the spring of the year, when I was visiting my family in Virginia, I decided to go down for the day to Southampton County, which is a drive of an hour and a half by car from the town where I was born and raised. Nat Turner was of course the reason for this trip, although I had nothing particular or urgent in mind. What research it was possible to do on the event I had long since done. The Southampton court records, I had already been reliably informed, would prove unrewarding. It was not a question, then, of digging out more facts, but simply a matter of wanting to savor the mood and atmosphere of a landscape I had not seen for quite a few years, since the times when as a boy I used to pass through Southampton on the way to my father's family home in North Carolina. I thought also that there might be a chance of visiting some of the historic sites connected with the insurrection, and perhaps even of retracing part of the route of the uprising through the help of one of those handsomely produced guidebooks for which the Historical Commission of Virginia is famous— guides indispensable for a trip to such Old Dominion shrines as Jamestown and Appomattox and Monticello. I became éven more eager to go when one of my in-laws put me in touch by telephone with a cousin of his. This man, whom I shall call Dan Seward, lived near Franklin, the main town of Southampton, and he assured me in those broad cheery Southern tones which are like a warm embrace—and which, after long years in the chill North, are to me always so familiar, reminiscent, and therefore so unsettling, sweet, and curiously painful— that he would like nothing better than to aid me in my exploration in whatever way he could.

Dan Seward is a farmer, and prosperous grower of peanuts in a prosperous agricultural region where the peanut is the unquestioned monarch. A combination of sandy loam soil and a long growing season has made Southampton ideal for the cultivation of peanuts; over 30,000 acres are planted annually, and the crop is processed and marketed in Franklin—a thriving little town of 7,000 people—or in Suffolk and Portsmouth, where it is rendered into Planters cooking oil and stock feed and Skippy peanut butter. There are other money-making crops—corn and soybeans and cotton. The county is at the northernmost edge of the cotton belt, and thirty years ago cotton was a major source of income. Cotton has declined in importance but the average yield per acre is still among the highest in the South, and the single gin left in the county in the little village of Drewryville processes each year several thousand bales which are trucked to market down in North Carolina. Lumbering is also very profitable, owing mainly to an abundance of the loblolly pines valuable in the production of kraft wood pulp; and the Union Bag–Camp Paper Company's plant on the Blackwater river in Franklin is a huge enterprise employing over 1,600 people. But it is peanuts—the harvested vines in autumn piled up mile after mile in dumpy brown stacks like hay—which have brought money to Southampton, and a sheen of prosperity that can be seen in the freshly painted farmhouses along the monotonously flat state highway which leads into Franklin, and the new-model Dodges and Buicks parked slantwise against the curb of some crossroads hamlet, and the gaudy, eye-catching signs that advise the wisdom of a bank savings account for all those surplus funds.

The county has very much the look of the New South about it, with its airport and its shiny new motels, its insistent billboards advertising space for industrial sites, the sprinkling of housing developments with television antennas gleaming from every rooftop, its supermarkets and shopping centers and its flavor of go-getting commercialism. This is the New South, where agriculture still prevails but has joined in a vigorous union with industry, so that even the peanut when it goes to market is ground up in some rumbling engine of commerce and becomes metamorphosed into wood stain or soap or cattle feed. The Negroes, too, have partaken of this abundance—some of it, at least—for they own television sets also, and if not new-model Buicks (the Southern white man's strictures against Negro ostentation remain intimidating), then decent late-model used Fords; while in the streets of Franklin the Negro women shopping seemed on the day of my visit very proud and well-dressed compared to the shabby stooped figures I recalled from the Depression years when I was a boy. It would certainly appear that Negroes deserve some of this abundance, if only because they make up so large a part of the work force. Since Nat Turner's day the balance of population in Southampton—almost 60 per cent Negro—has hardly altered by a hair.

"I don't know anywhere that a Negro is treated better than around here," Mr. Seward was saying to the three of us, on the spring morning I visited him with my wife and my father. "You take your average person from up North, he just doesn't *know* the Negro like we do. Now for instance I have a Negro who's worked for me for years, name of Ernest. He knows if he breaks his arm—like he did a while ago, fell off a tractor—he knows he can come to me and I'll see that he's taken care of, hospital expenses and all, and I'll take care of him and his family while he's unable to work, right on down the line. I don't ask him to pay back a cent, either, that's for sure. We have a wonderful relationship, that Negro and myself. By God, I'd die for that Negro and he knows it, and he'd do the same for me. But Ernest doesn't want to sit down at my table, here in this house, and have supper with me—and he wouldn't want me in *his* house. And Ernest's got kids like I do, and he doesn't want them to go to school with my Bobby, any more than Bobby wants to go to school with *his* kids. It works both ways. People up North don't seem to be able to understand a simple fact like that."

Mr. Seward was a solidly fleshed, somewhat rangy, big-shouldered man in his early forties with an open, cheerful manner which surely did nothing to betray the friendliness with which he had spoken on the telephone. He had greeted us—total strangers, really—with an animation and uncomplicated good will that would have shamed an Eskimo; and for a moment I realized that, after years amid the granite outcroppings of New England, I had forgotten that this *was* the passionate, generous, outgoing nature of the South, no artificial display but a social gesture as natural as breathing.

Mr. Seward had just finished rebuilding his farmhouse on the outskirts of town, and he had shown us around with a pride I found understandable: there was a sparkling electric kitchen worthy of an advertisement in *Life* magazine, some handsome modern furniture, and several downstairs rooms paneled beautifully in the prodigal and lustrous hardwood of the region. It was altogether a fine, tasteful house, resembling more one of the prettier medium-priced homes in the Long Island suburbs than the house one might contemplate for a Tidewater farmer. Upstairs, we had inspected his son Bobby's room, a kid's room with books like *Pinocchio* and *The Black Arrow* and *The Swiss Family Robinson,* and here there was a huge paper banner spread across one entire wall with the crayon inscription: *"Two . . . four . . . six . . . eight! We Don't Want to Integrate!"* It was a sign which so overwhelmingly dominated the room that it could not help provoking comment, and it was this that eventually had led to Mr. Seward's reflections about *knowing* Negroes.

There might have been something vaguely defensive in his remarks but not a trace of hostility.   His tone was matter-of-fact and good-natured, and he pronounced the word Negro as *nigra,* which most Southerners do with utter naturalness while intending no disrespect whatsoever, in fact quite the opposite—the mean epithet, of course, is *nigger.*   I had the feeling that Mr. Seward had begun amiably to regard us as sympathetic but ill-informed outsiders, non-Southern, despite his knowledge of my Tidewater background and my father's own accent, which is thick as grits.   Moreover, the fact that I had admitted to having lived in the North for fifteen years caused me, I fear, to appear alien in his eyes, *déraciné,*[2] especially when my acculturation to Northern ways has made me adopt the long "e" and say Negro.   The racial misery, at any rate, is within inches of driving us mad: how can I explain that, with all my silent disagreement with Mr. Seward's paternalism, I knew that when he said, "By God, I'd die for that Negro," he meant it?

Perhaps I should not have been surprised that Mr. Seward seemed to know very little about Nat Turner.   When we got around to the subject, it developed that he had always thought that the insurrection occurred way back in the eighteenth century.   Affably, he described seeing in his boyhood the "Hanging Tree," the live oak from which Nat had been executed in Courtland (Jerusalem had undergone this change of name after the Civil War), and which had died and been cut down some thirty years ago; as for any other landmarks, he regretted that he did not know of a single one.   No, so far as he knew, there just wasn't anything.

For me, it was the beginning of disappointments which grew with every hour.   Had I *really* been so ingenuous as to believe that I would unearth some shrine, some home preserved after the manner of Colonial Williamsburg, a relic of the insurrection at whose portal I would discover a lady in billowing satin and crinoline, who for fifty cents would

2 Uprooted.

shepherd me about the rooms with a gentle drawl indicating the spot where a good mistress fell at the hands of the murderous darky? The native Virginian, despite himself, is cursed with a suffocating sense of history, and I do not think it impossible that I actually suspected some such monument. Nevertheless, confident that there would be something to look at, I took heart when Mr. Seward suggested that after lunch we all drive over to Courtland, ten miles to the west. He had already spoken to a friend of his, the Sheriff of the county, who knew all the obscure byways and odd corners of Southampton, mainly because of his endless search for illegal stills; if there was a solitary person alive who might be able to locate some landmark, or could help retrace part of Nat Turner's march, it was the Sheriff. This gave me hope. For I had brought along Drewry's book and its map which showed the general route of the uprising, marking the houses by name. In the sixty years since Drewry, there would have been many changes in the landscape. But with this map oriented against the Sheriff's detailed county map, I should easily be able to pick up the trail and thus experience, however briefly, a sense of the light and shadow that played over that scene of slaughter and retribution a hundred and thirty-four years ago.

Yet it was as if Nat Turner had never existed, and as the day lengthened and afternoon wore on, and as we searched Nat's part of the county— five of us now, riding in the Sheriff's car with its huge star emblazoned on the doors, and its radio blatting out hoarse intermittent messages, and its riot gun protectively nuzzling the backs of our necks over the edge of the rear seat—I had the sensation from time to time that this Negro, who had so long occupied my thoughts, who indeed had so obsessed my imagination that he had acquired larger spirit and flesh than most of the living people I encountered day in and day out, had been merely a crazy figment of my mind, a phantom no more real than some half-recollected image from a fairy tale. For here in the back country, this horizontal land of woods and meadows where he had roamed, only a few people had heard of Nat Turner, and of those who had—among the people we stopped to make inquiries of, both white and black, along dusty country roads, at farms, at filling stations, at crossroad stores—most of them confused him, I think, with something spectral, mythic, a black Paul Bunyan who had perpetrated mysterious and nameless deeds in millennia past. They were neither facetious nor evasive, simply unaware. Others confounded him with the Civil War—a Negro general. One young Negro field hand, lounging at an

Esso station, figured he was a white man. A white man, heavy-lidded and paunchy, slow-witted, an idler at a rickety store, thought him an illustrious racehorse of bygone days.

The Sheriff, a smallish, soft-speaking ruminative man, with the whisper of a smile frozen on his face as if he were perpetually enjoying a good joke, knew full well who Nat Turner was, and I could tell he relished our frustrating charade. He was a shrewd person, quick and sharp with countrified wisdom, and he soon became quite as fascinated as I with the idea of tracking down some relic of the uprising (although he said that Drewry's map was hopelessly out of date, the roads of that time now abandoned to the fields and woods, the homes burnt down or gone to ruin); the country people's ignorance he found irresistible and I think it tickled him to perplex their foolish heads, white or black, with the same old leading question: "You heard about old Nat Turner, ain't you?" But few of them had heard, even though I was sure that many had plowed the same fields that Nat had crossed, lived on land that he had passed by; and as for dwellings still standing which might have been connected with the rebellion, not one of these back-country people could offer the faintest hint or clue. As effectively as a monstrous and unbearable dream, Nat had been erased from memory.

It was late afternoon when, with a sense of deep fatigue and frustration, I suggested to Mr. Seward and the Sheriff that maybe we had better go back to Courtland and call it a day. They were agreeable—relieved, I felt, to be freed of this tedious and fruitless search—and as we headed east down a straight unpaved road, the conversation became desultory, general. We spoke of the North. The Sheriff was interested to learn that I often traveled to New York. He went there occasionally himself, he said; indeed, he had been there only the month before—"to pick up a nigger," a fugitive from custody who had been awaiting trial for killing his wife. New York was a fine place to spend the night, said the Sheriff, but he wouldn't want to live there.

As he spoke, I had been gazing out of the window, and now suddenly something caught my eye—something familiar, a brief flickering passage of a distant outline, a silhouette against the sun-splashed woods—and I asked the Sheriff to stop the car. He did, and as we backed up slowly through a cloud of dust, I recognized a house standing perhaps a quarter of a mile off the road, from this distance only a lopsided oblong sheltered by an enormous oak, but the whole tableau—the house and the glorious hovering tree and the stretch of woods beyond—so familiar to me that it might have been some home I passed every day. And of course now as recognition came flooding back, I knew whose house it was. For in *The Southampton Insurrection,* the indefatigable Drewry had included many photographs—amateurish, doubtless taken by himself, and suffering from the fuzzy offset reproduction of 1900. But they were clear enough to provide an unmistakable guide to the dwellings in question, and now as I again consulted the book I could see that this house—the monumental oak above it grown scant inches it seemed in sixty years—was the one referred to by Drewry as having belonged to Mrs. Catherine Whitehead. From this distance, in the soft clear light of a spring afternoon, it seemed most tranquil, but few houses have come to know such a multitude of violent deaths. There in the late afternoon of Monday, August 22, Nat Turner and his band had appeared, and they set upon and killed "Mrs. Catherine Whitehead, son Richard, and four daughters, and grandchild."

The approach to the house was by a rutted lane long ago abandoned and overgrown with lush weeds which made a soft, crushed, rasping sound as we rolled over them. Dogwood, white and pink, grew on either side of the lane, quite wild and wanton in lovely pastel splashes. Not far from the house a pole fence interrupted our way; the Sheriff stopped the car and we got out and stood there for a moment, looking at the place. It was quiet and still—so quiet that the sudden chant of a mockingbird in the woods was almost frightening—and we realized then that no one lived in the house. Scoured by weather, paintless, worn down to the wintry gray of bone and with all the old mortar gone from between the timbers, it stood alone and desolate above its blasted, sagging front porch, the ancient door ajar like an open wound. Although never a manor house, it had once been a spacious and comfortable country home; now in near-ruin it sagged, finished, a shell, possessing only the most fragile profile of itself. As we drew closer still we could see that the entire house, from its upper story to the cellar, was filled with thousands of shucked ears of corn—feed for the malevolent-looking little razorback pigs which suddenly appeared in a tribe at the edge of the house, eying us, grunting. Mr. Seward sent them scampering with a shied stick and a farmer's sharp "Whoo!" I looked up at the house, trying to recollect its particular role in Nat's destiny, and then I remembered.

There was something baffling, secret, irrational about Nat's own participation in the uprising. He was unable to kill. Time and time again in his confession one discovers him saying (in an offhand tone; one must dig for the implications): "I could not give the death blow, the hatchet glanced from his head," or, "I struck her several blows over the head, but I was unable to kill her, as the sword was dull . . ." It is too much to believe, over and over again: the glancing hatchet, the dull sword. It smacks rather, as in *Hamlet,* of rationalization, ghastly fear, an access of guilt, a shrinking from violence, and fatal irresolution. Alone here at this house, turned now into a huge corncrib around which pigs rooted and snorted in the silence of a spring afternoon, here alone was Nat finally able—or was he forced?—to commit a murder, and this upon a girl of eighteen named Margaret Whitehead, described by Drewry in terms perhaps not so romantic or farfetched after all, as "the belle of the county." The scene is apocalyptic—afternoon bedlam in wild harsh sunlight and August heat.

"I returned to commence the work of death, but those whom I left had not been idle; all the family were already murdered but Mrs. Whitehead and her daughter Margaret. As I came round the door I saw Will pulling Mrs. Whitehead out of the house and at the step he nearly severed her head from her body with his axe. Miss Margaret, when I discovered her, had concealed herself in the corner formed by the projection of the cellar cap from the house; on my approach she fled into the field but was soon overtaken and after repeated blows with a sword, I killed her by a blow on the head with a fence rail."

It is Nat's only murder. Why, from this point on, does the momentum of the uprising diminish, the drive and tension sag? Why, from this moment in the *Confessions,* does one sense in Nat something dispirited, listless, as if all life and juice had been drained from him, so that never again through the course of the rebellion is he even on the scene when a murder is committed? What happened to Nat in this place? Did he discover his humanity here, or did he lose it?

I lifted myself up into the house, clambering through a doorway without steps, pushing myself over the crumbling sill. The house had a faint yeasty fragrance, like flat beer. Dust from the mountains of corn lay everywhere in the deserted rooms, years and decades of dust, dust an inch thick in some places, lying in a fine gray powder like sooty fallen snow. Off in some room amid the piles of corn I could hear a delicate scrabbling and a plaintive squeaking of mice. Again it was very still, the shadow of the prodigious old oak casting a dark pattern of leaves, checkered with bright sunlight, aslant through the gaping door.   As in those chilling lines of Emily Dickinson, even this lustrous and golden day seemed to find its only resonance in the memory, and perhaps a premonition, of death.

> This quiet Dust was Gentlemen and Ladies,
>   And Lads and Girls;
> Was laughter and ability and sighing,
>   And frocks and curls.[3]

Outside, the Sheriff was calling in on his car radio, his voice blurred and indistinct; then the return call from the county seat, loud, a dozen incomprehensible words in an uproar of static.   Suddenly it was quiet again, the only sound my father's soft voice as he chatted with Mr. Seward.

I leaned against the rotting frame of the door, gazing out past the great tree and into that far meadow where Nat had brought down and slain Miss Margaret Whitehead.   For an instant, in the silence, I thought I could hear a mad rustle of taffeta, and rushing feet, and a shrill girlish piping of terror; then that day and this day seemed to meet and melt together, becoming almost one, and for a long moment indistinguishable.

Lines of Inquiry

1 In this essay Styron speaks in a personal voice.
  a Where does that fact become clear?
  b What purposes does the personal voice serve in the essay?
  c Could an historical essay on Nat Turner's revolt be written in the impersonal voice?   What changes in focus, structure, and tone would you expect to see in an essay so written?

2 The use of a personal voice implies, of course, a subject controlled by a private point of view, as well as an overt, personal entry of the author into his essay.
  a What are the characteristics of Styron's point of view? Where in the essay is it defined?
  b Here are three other points of view that a writer could conceivably take in describing Nat Turner's revolt.   If followed exclusively, what probable effect would each have on the organization of the essay, the kind of fact the essay would focus on, and the kind of point it would be able to make?
  (*1*) The historian's point of view

[3] The lines quoted on this page are from *The Complete Poems of Emily Dickinson,* copyright © 1914, 1942 by Martha Dickinson Bianchi, with the permission of Little, Brown and Company.

(2) The New Yorker's point of view

(3) The Southern politician's point of view

3 Points of view might be classified broadly as either simple (that of the historian, the automobile manufacturer, the physicist) or compound (that of the political radical turned conservative churchman, the automobile manufacturer entered into politics, the physicist concerned about political ethics); most actual points of view, like Styron's, are obviously compound. How is the complexity of Styron's theme related to his use of the personal voice? Could one generalize to say that all complex points of view require the use of a personal voice? How would such a generalization be borne out, or refuted, by the essays in this section?

4 Styron's essay is broken into three sections.

  a What is the essential matter—the focus—of each section?

  b How do you explain the sequence in which Styron casts his material?

  c Examine the first sentences of each section; how are they related?

  d How is the point of view Styron employs related to his sequence?

5 Styron begins with a fragment of an old-time Negro song.

  a What is the significance of that song?

  b Could Styron have begun just as effectively with a quotation from Drewry, the author of *The Southampton Insurrection* (for example, something like the "quotation" that Styron actually gives in his first paragraph)?

  c What contrast is embedded in the introduction? What is the function of that contrast in relation to the essay's total structure?

6 What is the significance of the essay's title? What is the dust to which it refers? How is the introduction related to the conclusion? (Consider title and song as part of the introduction.)

7 The third section of this essay begins with a description of Southampton county.

  a Why does Styron tell us so much about its economy?

  b Ostensibly, Dan Seward has nothing to do with the story of Nat Turner. Why, then, does Styron spend so much time describing him? What is the focus of that description?

  c Why does Styron emphasize the genuineness of Southern hospitality? Why does he contrast it to the "chill North"?

  d What function does the sheriff have in Styron's description

of his search for traces of the insurrection? Why does
Styron refer to the sheriff in his last paragraphs?

e Toward the end of his search, Styron recognizes the Whitehead house. Before he remembers its place in Nat Turner's
history, he describes the house. Why does he describe it as
he does?

f The origins and general course of Nat Turner's revolt are
described in the essay's second section. Why, then, does
Styron reserve for the concluding section his account of the
Whitehead murders?

8 In the following sentences what is the full meaning of the
italicized words? Supply for each word three possible synonyms as alternatives. What accounts for the specific word
chosen by Styron?

a "Give or take a few harsh adjectives, this was all the information on Nat Turner supplied by that *forgotten* historian, who *hustled on* to matters of greater consequence."

b "Thus at the same time, ignored by white people, Negroes
impinge upon their collective subconscious to such a degree
that it may be rightly said that they become the focus of an
incessant preoccupation. . . ."

c "I suspect my search for Nat Turner, my own private attempt as a novelist to re-create and bring alive that *dim* and
prodigious black man, has been at least a partial fulfillment
of this mandate. . . ."

d "My feelings seem to have been confused and blurred,
tinged with sentimentality, *colored by* a great deal of *folklore*."

e "His fanaticism grew in intensity, and during these lonely
vigils in the forest he began to see *apparitions*."

f "They employed axes, hatchets, and swords as their *tools
of destruction*, and swift decapitation was their usual method
of *dispatch*."

g "Had I really been so *ingenuous* as to believe that I would
unearth some shrine, some home preserved after the manner
of colonial Williamsburg, a *relic* of the *insurrection* at whose
portal I would discover a lady in *billowing* satin and crinoline . . . ?"

9 Earlier introductions have made the point that in a sense the
narrative of an event is not only the record of its facts but also
an illustration of its meaning. Consider "This Quiet Dust"
in such a light.

a What does the essay illustrate? (Check your answer: Does
it account for *all* the elements in the essay?)

b How are Styron's external point of view and his use of the personal voice related to the illustrative function of the essay?

c How would you classify the following as illustrations within Styron's essay?

(*1*) Nat Turner's revolt

(*2*) Dan Seward

(*3*) Brantley's conversion

(*4*) William Faulkner

(*5*) The Whitehead murders

(*6*) William Styron's "I"

d How does the essay's structure reflect the characteristic sequence of illustration—from abstract statement to visible image, and back again?

Lines of Experiment

1 It is unlikely that you will be able to write about an historical incident as large in scale and implication as Nat Turner's revolt. But the controlling techniques of the essay—its view of an external incident from a private point of view, its use of the personal voice, its consequent fluidity of focus and sequence— are usable on a far less apocalyptic scale. A ball game, a protest rally, a strike, a student "rumble," a family triumph or catastrophe, a courtship, a wedding—any such incident, provided that you know a good deal about it, can provide you with rich material for a composition.

Because essays built in this way are essentially illustrative, your choice of subject will depend on the point you want to make. But in framing your essay you may find it useful to bear in mind:

a That a large-scale subject generally requires a long essay

b That the angle from which any such subject is seen determines the significance that can be found in it

c That that significance will depend a good deal on the sequence in which you arrange—or rearrange—the parts of your incident

d That your choice of detail must be made with the point that you are trying to make clearly in mind

Styron's essay illustrates one other aspect of the illustrative narrative: its dependence on sensitive wording. Both the last and the most continuous job you must face in writing is to find the right word: "Vision" is not the same as "apparition," and "famous" is not the same as "prodigious." To write well, your choices among synonyms must be exact and sensitive.

Note: Styron organizes his treatment of Nat Turner's revolt by means of a special personal point of view; in a sense he conducts two case studies at once, one of Nat Turner, one of himself. *Do not* imitate him in this, unless you are extremely ambitious.

2 Styron presents in the narrative of Nat Turner's revolt a metaphor for the struggle of Black and White. One might write about that struggle in a more explicitly logical frame, paying attention, perhaps, to the problems of definition (What is "racial conflict," and what, indeed, is "race"?), of classification (What kinds of racial conflict are there and which of these kinds are basic, which superficial; which permanent, which temporary; which constructive, which destructive?), or of analysis (How are these classes of racial conflict connected causally—how do they "work" to produce one another?). Doubtless such an essay also would find a less particularized, more current pattern of illustration to connect it to the real, present world: not Nat Turner's revolt, perhaps, but last summer's race riots, the Black Power movement, the failure of an open housing or equal employment law, etc.

Let us suppose you are to write such an essay. Your ultimate job is logical: to decide what conclusions are justified by fact and evidence. But your immediate and in a sense even more important job is rhetorical: to find a way of cutting such a huge subject down to manageable size. You may wish to focus and so to give edge to your ideas through definition of a part of the problem. For example, careful definitions of "race" and "conflict" might easily lead to the conclusion that "racial conflict" is an inadequate and even deceptive name for what is going on in the United States. Or you may use classification and analysis of the forms of racial conflict as a way of focusing your ideas. For example, by dividing racial discrimination into (*a*) economic discrimination and (*b*) social discrimination, one might be able to show clearly and briefly that one form of discrimination is the long-term result of the other.

The best advice in dealing with any such subject is to limit its scale: Do not try to say everything in one essay.

JAMES BALDWIN

NOTES
OF A
NATIVE SON

On the 29th of July, in 1943, my father died.   On the same day, a few hours later, his last child was born.   Over a month before this, while all our energies were concentrated in waiting for these events, there had been, in Detroit, one of the bloodiest race riots of the century. A few hours after my father's funeral, while he lay in state in the undertaker's chapel, a race riot broke out in Harlem.   On the morning of the 3rd of August, we drove my father to the graveyard through a wilderness of smashed plate glass.

The day of my father's funeral had also been my nineteenth birthday. As we drove him to the graveyard, the spoils of injustice, anarchy, discontent, and hatred were all around us.   It seemed to me that God himself had devised, to mark my father's end, the most sustained and brutally dissonant of codas.   And it seemed to me, too, that the violence which rose all about us as my father left the world had been devised as a corrective for the pride of his eldest son.   I had declined to believe in that apocalypse which had been central to my father's vision; very well, life seemed to be saying, here is something that will certainly pass for an apocalypse until the real thing comes along.   I had inclined to be contemptuous of my father for the conditions of his life, for the conditions of our lives.   When his life had ended I began to wonder about that life and also, in a new way, to be apprehensive about my own.

I had not known my father very well.   We had got on badly, partly because we shared, in our different fashions, the vice of stubborn pride. When he was dead I realized that I had hardly ever spoken to him. When he had been dead a long time I began to wish I had.   It seems to be typical of life in America, where opportunities, real and fancied,

are thicker than anywhere else on the globe, that the second generation
has no time to talk to the first.   No one, including my father, seems to
have known exactly how old he was, but his mother had been born
during slavery.   He was of the first generation of free men.   He, along
with thousands of other Negroes, came North after 1919 and I was
part of that generation which had never seen the landscape of what
Negroes sometimes call the Old Country.

He had been born in New Orleans and had been a quite young man
there during the time that Louis Armstrong, a boy, was running errands
for the dives and honky-tonks of what was always presented to me as
one of the most wicked of cities—to this day, whenever I think of
New Orleans, I also helplessly think of Sodom and Gomorrah.   My
father never mentioned Louis Armstrong, except to forbid us to play
his records; but there was a picture of him on our wall for a long time.
One of my father's strongwilled female relatives had placed it there and
forbade my father to take it down.   He never did, but he eventually
maneuvered her out of the house and when, some years later, she was
in trouble and near death, he refused to do anything to help her.

He was, I think, very handsome.   I gather this from photographs and
from my own memories of him, dressed in his Sunday best and on his
way to preach a sermon somewhere, when I was little.   Handsome,
proud, and ingrown, "like a toe-nail," somebody said.   But he looked
to me, as I grew older, like pictures I had seen of African tribal chief-
tains: he really should have been naked, with war-paint on and barbaric
mementos, standing among spears.   He could be chilling in the pulpit
and indescribably cruel in his personal life and he was certainly the
most bitter man I have ever met; yet it must be said that there was
something else in him, buried in him, which lent him his tremendous
power and, even, a rather crushing charm.   It had something to do
with his blackness, I think—he was very black—with his blackness
and his beauty, and with the fact that he knew that he was black but
did not know that he was beautiful.   He claimed to be proud of his
blackness but it had also been the cause of much humiliation and it
had fixed bleak boundaries to his life.   He was not a young man when
we were growing up and he had already suffered many kinds of ruin;
in his outrageously demanding and protective way he loved his children, who were black like him and menaced, like him; and all these
things sometimes showed in his face when he tried, never to my knowledge with any success, to establish contact with any of us.   When he
took one of his children on his knee to play, the child always be-

came fretful and began to cry; when he tried to help one of us with our homework the absolutely unabating tension which emanated from him caused our minds and our tongues to become paralyzed, so that he, scarcely knowing why, flew into a rage and the child, not knowing why, was punished.   If it ever entered his head to bring a surprise home for his children, it was, almost unfailingly, the wrong surprise and even the big watermelons he often brought home on his back in the summertime led to the most appalling scenes.   I do not remember, in all those years, that one of his children was ever glad to see him come home. From what I was able to gather of his early life, it seemed that this inability to establish contact with other people had always marked him and had been one of the things which had driven him out of New Orleans.   There was something in him, therefore, groping and tentative, which was never expressed and which was buried with him.   One saw it most clearly when he was facing new people and hoping to impress them.   But he never did, not for long.   We went from church to smaller and more improbable church, he found himself in less and less demand as a minister, and by the time he died none of his friends had come to see him for a long time.   He had lived and died in an intolerable bitterness of spirit and it frightened me, as we drove him to the graveyard through those unquiet, ruined streets, to see how powerful and overflowing this bitterness could be and to realize that this bitterness now was mine.

When he died I had been away from home for a little over a year.   In that year I had had time to become aware of the meaning of all my father's bitter warnings, had discovered the secret of his proudly pursed lips and rigid carriage: I had discovered the weight of white people in the world.   I saw that this had been for my ancestors and now would be for me an awful thing to live with and that the bitterness which had helped to kill my father could also kill me.

He had been ill a long time—in the mind, as we now realized, reliving instances of his fantastic intransigence in the new light of his affliction and endeavoring to feel a sorrow for him which never, quite, came true.   We had not known that he was being eaten up by paranoia, and the discovery that his cruelty, to our bodies and our minds, had been one of the symptoms of his illness was not, then, enough to enable us to forgive him.   The younger children felt, quite simply, relief that he would not be coming home anymore.   My mother's observation that it was he, after all, who had kept them alive all these years meant nothing because the problems of keeping children alive are not real for children. The older children felt, with my father gone, that they could invite their friends to the house without fear that their friends would be insulted or, as had sometimes happened with me, being told that their friends were in league with the devil and intended to rob our family of everything we owned. (I didn't fail to wonder, and it made me hate him, what on earth we owned that anybody else would want.)

His illness was beyond all hope of healing before anyone realized that he was ill. He had always been so strange and had lived, like a prophet, in such unimaginably close communion with the Lord that his long silences which were punctuated by moans and hallelujahs and snatches of old songs while he sat at the living-room window never seemed odd to us. It was not until he refused to eat because, he said, his family was trying to poison him that my mother was forced to accept as a fact what had, until then, been only an unwilling suspicion. When he was committed, it was discovered that he had tuberculosis and, as it turned out, the disease of his mind allowed the disease of his body to destroy him. For the doctors could not force him to eat, either, and, though he was fed intravenously, it was clear from the beginning that there was no hope for him.

In my mind's eye I could see him, sitting at the window, locked up in his terrors; hating and fearing every living soul including his children who had betrayed him, too, by reaching towards the world which had despised him. There were nine of us. I began to wonder what it could have felt like for such a man to have had nine children whom he could barely feed. He used to make little jokes about our poverty, which never, of course, seemed very funny to us; they could not have seemed very funny to him, either, or else our all too feeble response to them would never have caused such rages. He spent great energy and achieved, to our chagrin, no small amount of success in keeping us away from the people who surrounded us, people who had all-night rent parties to which we listened when we should have been sleeping, people who cursed and drank and flashed razor blades on Lenox Avenue. He could not understand why, if they had so much energy to spare, they could not use it to make their lives better. He treated almost everybody on our block with a most uncharitable asperity and neither they, nor, of course, their children were slow to reciprocate.

The only white people who came to our house were welfare workers and bill collectors. It was almost always my mother who dealt with them, for my father's temper, which was at the mercy of his pride, was

never to be trusted.   It was clear that he felt their very presence in
his home to be a violation: this was conveyed by his carriage, almost
ludicrously stiff, and by his voice, harsh and vindictively polite.   When
I was around nine or ten I wrote a play which was directed by a young,
white schoolteacher, a woman, who then took an interest in me, and
gave me books to read and, in order to corroborate my theatrical bent,
decided to take me to see what she somewhat tactlessly referred to as
"real" plays.   Theatergoing was forbidden in our house, but, with the
really cruel intuitiveness of a child, I suspected that the color of this
woman's skin would carry the day for me.   When, at school, she
suggested taking me to the theater, I did not, as I might have done if
she had been a Negro, find a way of discouraging her, but agreed that
she should pick me up at my house one evening.   I then, very cleverly,
left all the rest to my mother, who suggested to my father, as I knew
she would, that it would not be very nice to let such a kind woman
make the trip for nothing.   Also, since it was a schoolteacher, I imagine
that my mother countered the idea of sin with the idea of "education,"
which word, even with my father, carried a kind of bitter weight.

Before the teacher came my father took me aside to ask *why* she was
coming, what *interest* she could possibly have in our house, in a boy like
me.   I said I didn't know but I, too, suggested that it had something
to do with education.   And I understood that my father was waiting
for me to say something—I didn't quite know what; perhaps that I
wanted his protection against this teacher and her "education."   I said
none of these things and the teacher came and we went out.   It was
clear, during the brief interview in our living room, that my father was
agreeing very much against his will and that he would have refused
permission if he had dared.   The fact that he did not dare caused me
to despise him: I had no way of knowing that he was facing in that
living room a wholly unprecedented and frightening situation.

Later, when my father had been laid off from his job, this woman
became very important to us.   She was really a very sweet and generous woman and went to a great deal of trouble to be of help to us,
particularly during one awful winter.   My mother called her by the
highest name she knew: she said she was a "christian."   My father
could scarcely disagree but during the four or five years of our relatively close association he never trusted her and was always trying to
surprise in her open, Midwestern face the genuine, cunningly hidden, and
hideous motivation.   In later years, particularly when it began to be
clear that this "education" of mine was going to lead me to perdition, he

became more explicit and warned me that my white friends in high school were not really my friends and that I would see, when I was older, how white people would do anything to keep a Negro down. Some of them could be nice, he admitted, but none of them were to be trusted and most of them were not even nice. The best thing was to have as little to do with them as possible. I did not feel this way and I was certain, in my innocence, that I never would.

But the year which preceded my father's death had made a great change in my life. I had been living in New Jersey, working in defense plants, working and living among southerners, white and black. I knew about the south, of course, and about how southerners treated Negroes and how they expected them to behave, but it had never entered my mind that anyone would look at me and expect *me* to behave that way. I learned in New Jersey that to be a Negro meant, precisely, that one was never looked at but was simply at the mercy of the reflexes the color of one's skin caused in other people. I acted in New Jersey as I had always acted, that is as though I thought a great deal of myself—I had to *act* that way—with results that were, simply, unbelievable. I had scarcely arrived before I had earned the enmity, which was extraordinarily ingenious, of all my superiors and nearly all my co-workers. In the beginning, to make matters worse, I simply did not know what was happening. I did not know what I had done, and I shortly began to wonder what *anyone* could possibly do, to bring about such unanimous, active, and unbearably vocal hostility. I knew about jim-crow but I had never experienced it. I went to the same self-service restaurant three times and stood with all the Princeton boys before the counter, waiting for a hamburger and coffee; it was always an extraordinarily long time before anything was set before me; but it was not until the fourth visit that I learned that, in fact, nothing had ever been set before me: I had simply picked something up. Negroes were not served there, I was told, and they had been waiting for me to realize that I was always the only Negro present. Once I was told this, I determined to go there all the time. But now they were ready for me and, though some dreadful scenes were subsequently enacted in that restaurant, I never ate there again.

It was the same story all over New Jersey, in bars, bowling alleys, diners, places to live. I was always being forced to leave, silently, or with mutual imprecations. I very shortly became notorious and children giggled behind me when I passed and their elders whispered or shouted—they really believed that I was mad. And it did begin to work on my mind, of course; I began to be afraid to go anywhere and to compensate for this I went places to which I really should not have gone and where, God knows, I had no desire to be. My reputation in town naturally enhanced my reputation at work and my working day became one long series of acrobatics designed to keep me out of trouble. I cannot say that these acrobatics succeeded. It began to seem that the machinery of the organization I worked for was turning over, day and night, with but one aim: to eject me. I was fired once, and contrived, with the aid of a friend from New York, to get back on the payroll; was fired again, and bounced back again. It took a while to fire me for the third time, but the third time took. There were no loopholes anywhere. There was not even any way of getting back inside the gates.

That year in New Jersey lives in my mind as though it were the year during which, having an unsuspected predilection for it, I first contracted some dread, chronic disease, the unfailing symptom of which is a kind of blind fever, a pounding in the skull and fire in the bowels. Once this disease is contracted, one can never be really carefree again, for the fever, without an instant's warning, can recur at any moment. It can wreck more important things than race relations. There is not a Negro alive who does not have this rage in his blood—one has the choice, merely, of living with it consciously or surrendering to it. As for me, this fever has recurred in me, and does, and will until the day I die.

My last night in New Jersey, a white friend from New York took me to the nearest big town, Trenton, to go to the movies and have a few drinks. As it turned out, he also saved me from, at the very least, a violent whipping. Almost every detail of that night stands out very clearly in my memory. I even remember the name of the movie we saw because its title impressed me as being so patly ironical. It was a movie about the German occupation of France, starring Maureen O'Hara and Charles Laughton and called *This Land Is Mine*. I remember the name of the diner we walked into when the movie ended: it was the "American Diner." When we walked in the counterman asked what we wanted and I remember answering with the casual sharpness which had become my habit: "We want a hamburger and a cup of coffee, what do you think we want?" I do not know why, after a year of such rebuffs, I so completely failed to anticipate his answer, which was, of course, "We don't serve Negroes here." This reply failed to discompose me, at least for the moment. I made some sardonic comment about the name of the diner and we walked out into the streets.

This was the time of what was called the "brown-out," when the lights in all American cities were very dim. When we re-entered the streets something happened to me which had the force of an optical illusion, or a nightmare. The streets were very crowded and I was facing north. People were moving in every direction but it seemed to me, in that instant, that all of the people I could see, and many more than that, were moving toward me, against me, and that everyone was white. I remember how their faces gleamed. And I felt, like a physical sensation, a *click* at the nape of my neck as though some interior string connecting my head to my body had been cut. I began to walk. I heard my friend call after me, but I ignored him. Heaven only knows what was going on in his mind, but he had the good sense not to touch me—I don't know what would have happened if he had—and to keep me in sight. I don't know what was going on in my mind, either; I certainly had no conscious plan. I wanted to do something to crush these white faces, which were crushing me. I walked for perhaps a block or two until I came to an enormous, glittering, and fashionable rostaurant in which I knew not even the intercession of the Virgin would cause me to be served. I pushed through the doors and took the first vacant seat I saw, at a table for two, and waited.

I do not know how long I waited and I rather wonder, until today, what I could possibly have looked like. Whatever I looked like, I frightened the waitress who shortly appeared, and the moment she appeared all of my fury flowed towards her. I hated her for her white face, and for her great, astounded, frightened eyes. I felt that if she found a black man so frightening I would make her fright worthwhile.

She did not ask me what I wanted, but repeated, as though she had learned it somewhere, "We don't serve Negroes here." She did not say it with the blunt, derisive hostility to which I had grown so acoustomed, but, rather, with a note of apology in her voice, and fear. This made me colder and more murderous than ever. I felt I had to do something with my hands. I wanted her to come close enough for me to get her neck between my hands.

So I pretended not to have understood her, hoping to draw her closer. And she did step a very short step closer, with her pencil poised incongruously over her pad, and repeated the formula: ". . . don't serve Negroes here."

Somehow, with the repetition of that phrase, which was already ring-
ing in my head like a thousand bells of a nightmare, I realized that she
would never come any closer and that I would have to strike from a
distance.   There was nothing on the table but an ordinary watermug
half full of water, and I picked this up and hurled it with all my
strength at her.   She ducked and it missed her and shattered against
the mirror behind the bar.   And, with that sound, my frozen blood
abruptly thawed, I returned from wherever I had been, I *saw,* for
the first time, the restaurant, the people with their mouths open, already,
as it seemed to me, rising as one man, and I realized what I had done,
and where I was, and I was frightened.   I rose and began running for
the door.   A round, potbellied man grabbed me by the nape of the
neck just as I reached the doors and began to beat me about the face.
I kicked him and got loose and ran into the streets.   My friend
whispered, *"Run!"* and I ran.

My friend stayed outside the restaurant long enough to misdirect my
pursuers and the police, who arrived, he told me, at once.   I do not
know what I said to him when he came to my room that night.   I
could not have said much.   I felt, in the oddest, most awful way,
that I had somehow betrayed him.   I lived it over and over and over
again, the way one relives an automobile accident after it has happened
and one finds oneself alone and safe.   I could not get over two facts,
both equally difficult for the imagination to grasp, and one was that I
could have been murdered.   But the other was that I had been ready to
commit murder.   I saw nothing very clearly but I did see this: that
my life, my *real* life, was in danger, and not from anything other
people might do but from the hatred I carried in my own heart.

II

I had returned home around the second week in June—in great haste
because it seemed that my father's death and my mother's confinement
were both but a matter of hours.   In the case of my mother, it soon
became clear that she had simply made a miscalculation.   This had
always been her tendency and I don't believe that a single one of us
arrived in the world, or has since arrived anywhere else, on time.   But
none of us dawdled so intolerably about the business of being born as
did my baby sister.   We sometimes amused ourselves, during those
endless, stifling weeks, by picturing the baby sitting within in the safe,
warm dark, bitterly regretting the necessity of becoming a part of our
chaos and stubbornly putting it off as long as possible.   I understood

her perfectly and congratulated her on showing such good sense so soon. Death, however, sat as purposefully at my father's bedside as life stirred within my mother's womb and it was harder to understand why he so lingered in that long shadow. It seemed that he had bent, and for a long time, too, all of his energies towards dying. Now death was ready for him but my father held back.

All of Harlem, indeed, seemed to be infected by waiting. I had never before known it to be so violently still. Racial tensions throughout this country were exacerbated during the early years of the war, partly because the labor market brought together hundreds of thousands of ill-prepared people and partly because Negro soldiers, regardless of where they were born, received their military training in the south. What happened in defense plants and army camps had repercussions, naturally, in every Negro ghetto. The situation in Harlem had grown bad enough for clergymen, policemen, educators, politicians, and social workers to assert in one breath that there was no "crime wave" and to offer, in the very next breath, suggestions as to how to combat it. These suggestions always seemed to involve playgrounds, despite the fact that racial skirmishes were occurring in the playgrounds, too. Playground or not, crime wave or not, the Harlem police force had been augmented in March, and the unrest grew—perhaps, in fact, partly as a result of the ghetto's instinctive hatred of policemen. Perhaps the most revealing news item, out of the steady parade of reports of muggings, stabbings, shootings, assaults, gang wars, and accusations of police brutality, is the item concerning six Negro girls who set upon a white girl in the subway because, as they all too accurately put it, she was stepping on their toes. Indeed she was, all over the nation.

I had never before been so aware of policemen, on foot, on horseback, on corners, everywhere, always two by two. Nor had I ever been so aware of small knots of people. They were on stoops and on corners and in doorways, and what was striking about them, I think, was that they did not seem to be talking. Never, when I passed these groups, did the usual sound of a curse or a laugh ring out and neither did there seem to be any hum of gossip. There was certainly, on the other hand, occurring between them communication extraordinarily intense. Another thing that was striking was the unexpected diversity of the people who made up these groups. Usually, for example, one would see a group of sharpies standing on the street corner, jiving the passing chicks; or a group of older men, usually, for some reason, in the vicinity of a barber shop, discussing baseball scores, or the numbers, or making rather chilling observations about women they had known. Women, in a general way, tended to be seen less often together—unless they were church women, or very young girls, or prostitutes met together for an unprofessional instant. But that summer I saw the strangest combinations: large, respectable, churchly matrons standing on the stoops or the corners with their hair tied up, together with a girl in sleazy satin whose face bore the marks of gin and the razor, or heavy-set, abrupt, no-nonsense older men, in company with the most disreputable and fanatical "race" men, or these same "race" men with the sharpies, or these sharpies with the churchly women. Seventh Day Adventists and Methodists and Spiritualists seemed to be hobnobbing with Holy-rollers and they were all, alike, entangled with the most flagrant disbelievers; something heavy in their stance seemed to indicate that they had all, incredibly, seen a common vision, and on each face there seemed to be the same strange, bitter shadow.

The churchly women and the matter-of-fact, no-nonsense men had children in the Army. The sleazy girls they talked to had lovers there, the sharpies and the "race" men had friends and brothers there. It would have demanded an unquestioning patriotism, happily as uncommon in this country as it is undesirable, for these people not to have been disturbed by the bitter letters they received, by the newspaper stories they read, not to have been enraged by the posters, then to be found all over New York, which described the Japanese as "yellowbellied Japs." It was only the "race" men, to be sure, who spoke ceaselessly of being revenged—how this vengeance was to be exacted was not clear—for the indignities and dangers suffered by Negro boys in uniform; but everybody felt a directionless, hopeless bitterness, as well as that panic which can scarcely be suppressed when one knows that a human being one loves is beyond one's reach, and in danger. This helplessness and this gnawing uneasiness does something, at length, to even the toughest mind. Perhaps the best way to sum all this up is to say that the people I knew felt, mainly, a peculiar kind of relief when they knew that their boys were being shipped out of the south, to do battle overseas. It was, perhaps, like feeling that the most dangerous part of a dangerous journey had been passed and that now, even if death should come, it would come with honor and without the complicity of their countrymen. Such a death would be, in short, a fact with which one could hope to live.

It was on the 28th of July, which I believe was a Wednesday, that I visited my father for the first time during his illness and for the last time in his life.   The moment I saw him I knew why I had put off this visit so long.   I had told my mother that I did not want to see him because I hated him.   But this was not true.   It was only that I *had* hated him and I wanted to hold on to this hatred.   I did not want to look on him as a ruin: it was not a ruin I had hated.   I imagine that one of the reasons people cling to their hates so stubbornly is because they sense, once hate is gone, that they will be forced to deal with pain.

We traveled out to him, his older sister and myself, to what seemed to be the very end of a very Long Island.   It was hot and dusty and we wrangled, my aunt and I, all the way out, over the fact that I had recently begun to smoke and, as she said, to give myself airs.   But I knew that she wrangled with me because she could not bear to face the fact of her brother's dying.   Neither could I endure the reality of her despair, her unstated bafflement as to what had happened to her brother's life, and her own.   So we wrangled and I smoked and from time to time she fell into a heavy reverie.   Covertly, I watched her face, which was the face of an old woman; it had fallen in, the eyes were sunken and lightless; soon she would be dying, too.

In my childhood—it had not been so long ago—I had thought her beautiful.   She had been quick-witted and quick-moving and very generous with all the children and each of her visits had been an event. At one time one of my brothers and myself had thought of running away to live with her.   Now she could no longer produce out of her handbag some unexpected and yet familiar delight.   She made me feel pity and revulsion and fear.   It was awful to realize that she no longer caused me to feel affection.   The closer we came to the hospital the more querulous she became and at the same time, naturally, grew more dependent on me.   Between pity and guilt and fear I began to feel that there was another me trapped in my skull like a jack-in-the-box who might escape my control at any moment and fill the air with screaming.

She began to cry the moment we entered the room and she saw him lying there, all shriveled and still, like a little black monkey.   The great, gleaming apparatus which fed him and would have compelled him to be still even if he had been able to move brought to mind, not beneficence, but torture; the tubes entering his arm made me think of pictures I had seen when a child, of Gulliver, tied down by the pygmies on that island.   My aunt wept and wept, there was a whistling sound in my father's throat; nothing was said; he could not speak. I wanted to take his hand, to say something. But I do not know what I could have said, even if he could have heard me. He was not really in that room with us, he had at last really embarked on his journey; and though my aunt told me that he said he was going to meet Jesus, I did not hear anything except that whistling in his throat. The doctor came back and we left, into that unbearable train again, and home. In the morning came the telegram saying that he was dead. Then the house was suddenly full of relatives, friends, hysteria, and confusion and I quickly left my mother and the children to the care of those impressive women, who, in Negro communities at least, automatically appear at times of bereavement armed with lotions, proverbs, and patience, and an ability to cook. I went downtown. By the time I returned, later the same day, my mother had been carried to the hospital and the baby had been born.

III

For my father's funeral I had nothing black to wear and this posed a nagging problem all day long. It was one of those problems, simple, or impossible of solution, to which the mind insanely clings in order to avoid the mind's real trouble. I spent most of that day at the downtown apartment of a girl I knew, celebrating my birthday with whiskey and wondering what to wear that night. When planning a birthday celebration one naturally does not expect that it will be up against competition from a funeral and this girl had anticipated taking me out that night, for a big dinner and a night club afterwards. Sometime during the course of that long day we decided that we would go out anyway, when my father's funeral service was over. I imagine *I* decided it, since, as the funeral hour approached, it became clearer and clearer to me that I would not know what to do with myself when it was over. The girl, stifling her very lively concern as to the possible effects of the whiskey on one of my father's chief mourners, concentrated on being conciliatory and practically helpful. She found a black shirt for me somewhere and ironed it and, dressed in the darkest pants and jacket I owned, and slightly drunk, I made my way to my father's funeral.

The chapel was full, but not packed, and very quiet. There were, mainly, my father's relatives, and his children, and here and there I saw faces I had not seen since childhood, the faces of my father's

one-time friends. They were very dark and solemn now, seeming
somehow to suggest that they had known all along that something like
this would happen. Chief among the mourners was my aunt, who
had quarreled with my father all his life; by which I do not mean to
suggest that her mourning was insincere or that she had not loved him.
I suppose that she was one of the few people in the world who had,
and their incessant quarreling proved precisely the strength of the
tie that bound them. The only other person in the world, as far as
I knew, whose relationship to my father rivaled my aunt's in depth was
my mother, who was not there.

It seemed to me, of course, that it was a very long funeral. But it
was, if anything, a rather shorter funeral than most, nor, since there
were no overwhelming, uncontrollable expressions of grief, could it
be called—if I dare to use the word—successful. The minister who
preached my father's funeral sermon was one of the few my father
had still been seeing as he neared his end. He presented to us in his
sermon a man whom none of us had ever seen—a man thoughtful,
patient, and forbearing, a Christian inspiration to all who knew him,
and a model for his children. And no doubt the children, in their
disturbed and guilty state, were almost ready to believe this; he had
been remote enough to be anything and, anyway, the shock of the incontrovertible, that it was really our father lying up there in that casket,
prepared the mind for anything. His sister moaned and this grief-
stricken moaning was taken as corroboration. The other faces held a
dark, non-committal thoughtfulness. This was not the man they
had known, but they had scarcely expected to be confronted with *him;*
this was, in a sense deeper than questions of fact, the man they had
not known, and the man they had not known may have been the real
one. The real man, whoever he had been, had suffered and now he
was dead: this was all that was sure and all that mattered now. Every
man in the chapel hoped that when his hour came he, too, would be
eulogized, which is to say forgiven, and that all of his lapses, greeds,
errors, and strayings from the truth would be invested with coherence
and looked upon with charity. This was perhaps the last thing human
beings could give each other and it was what they demanded, after
all, of the Lord. Only the Lord saw the midnight tears, only He was
present when one of His children, moaning and wringing hands, paced
up and down the room. When one slapped one's child in anger the
recoil in the heart reverberated through heaven and became part of the
pain of the universe. And when the children were hungry and sullen
and distrustful and one watched them, daily, growing wilder, and further

away, and running headlong into danger, it was the Lord who knew what the charged heart endured as the strap was laid to the backside; the Lord alone who knew what one *would* have said if one had had, like the Lord, the gift of the living word.   It was the Lord who knew of the impossibility every parent in that room faced: how to prepare the child for the day when the child would be despised and how to *create* in the child—by what means?—a stronger antidote to this poison than one had found for oneself.   The avenues, side streets, bars, billiard halls, hospitals, police stations, and even the playgrounds of Harlem—not to mention the houses of correction, the jails, and the morgue—testified to the potency of the poison while remaining silent as to the efficacy of whatever antidote, irresistibly raising the question of whether or not such an antidote existed; raising, which was worse, the question of whether or not an antidote was desirable; perhaps poison should be fought with poison.   With these several schisms in the mind and with more terrors in the heart than could be named, it was better not to judge the man who had gone down under an impossible burden. It was better to remember: *Thou knowest this man's fall; but thou knowest not his wrassling.*

While the preacher talked and I watched the children—years of changing their diapers, scrubbing them, slapping them, taking them to school, and scolding them had had the perhaps inevitable result of making me love them, though I am not sure I knew this then—my mind was busily breaking out with a rash of disconnected impressions.   Snatches of popular songs, indecent jokes, bits of books I had read, movie sequences, faces, voices, political issues—I thought I was going mad; all these impressions suspended, as it were, in the solution of the faint nausea produced in me by the heat and liquor.   For a moment I had the impression that my alcoholic breath, inefficiently disguised with chewing gum, filled the entire chapel.   Then someone began singing one of my father's favorite songs and, abruptly, I was with him, sitting on his knee, in the hot, enormous, crowded church which was the first church we attended.   It was the Abyssinia Baptist Church on 138th Street.   We had not gone there long.   With this image, a host of others came.   I had forgotten, in the rage of my growing up, how proud my father had been of me when I was little.   Apparently, I had had a voice and my father had liked to show me off before the members of the church.   I had forgotten what he had looked like when he was pleased but now I remembered that he had always been grinning with pleasure when my solos ended.   I even remembered certain expressions on his face when he teased my mother—had he loved her? I would never know. And when had it all begun to change? For now it seemed that he had not always been cruel. I remembered being taken for a haircut and scraping my knee on the footrest of the barber's chair and I remembered my father's face as he soothed my crying and applied the stinging iodine. Then I remembered our fights, fights which had been of the worst possible kind because my technique had been silence.

I remembered the one time in all our life together when we had really spoken to each other.

It was on a Sunday and it must have been shortly before I left home. We were walking, just the two of us, in our usual silence, to or from church. I was in high school and had been doing a lot of writing and I was, at about this time, the editor of the high school magazine. But I had also been a Young Minister and had been preaching from the pulpit. Lately, I had been taking fewer engagements and preached as rarely as possible. It was said in the church, quite truthfully, that I was "cooling off."

My father asked me abruptly, "You'd rather write than preach, wouldn't you?"

I was astonished at his question—because it was a real question. I answered, "Yes."

That was all we said. It was awful to remember that that was all we had *ever* said.

The casket now was opened and the mourners were being led up the aisle to look for the last time on the deceased. The assumption was that the family was too overcome with grief to be allowed to make this journey alone and I watched while my aunt was led to the casket and, muffled in black, and shaking, led back to her seat. I disapproved of forcing the children to look on their dead father, considering that the shock of his death, or, more truthfully, the shock of death as a reality, was already a little more than a child could bear, but my judgment in this matter had been overruled and there they were, bewildered and frightened and very small, being led, one by one, to the casket. But there is also something very gallant about children at such moments. It has something to do with their silence and gravity and with the fact that one cannot help them. Their legs, somehow, seem *exposed,* so that it is at once incredible and terribly clear that their legs are all they have to hold them up.

I had not wanted to go to the casket myself and I certainly had not wished to be led there, but there was no way of avoiding either of these forms. One of the deacons led me up and I looked on my father's face. I cannot say that it looked like him at all. His blackness had been equivocated by powder and there was no suggestion in that casket of what his power had or could have been. He was simply an old man dead, and it was hard to believe that he had ever given anyone either joy or pain. Yet, his life filled that room. Further up the avenue his wife was holding his newborn child. Life and death so close together, and love and hatred, and right and wrong, said something to me which I did not want to hear concerning man, concerning the life of man.

After the funeral, while I was downtown desperately celebrating my birthday, a Negro soldier, in the lobby of the Hotel Braddock, got into a fight with a white policeman over a Negro girl. Negro girls, white policemen, in or out of uniform, and Negro males—in or out of uniform—were part of the furniture of the lobby of the Hotel Braddock and this was certainly not the first time such an incident had occurred. It was destined, however, to receive an unprecedented publicity, for the fight between the policeman and the soldier ended with the shooting of the soldier. Rumor, flowing immediately to the streets outside, stated that the soldier had been shot in the back, an instantaneous and revealing invention, and that the soldier had died protecting a Negro woman. The facts were somewhat different—for example, the soldier had not been shot in the back, and was not dead, and the girl seems to have been as dubious a symbol of womanhood as her white counterpart in Georgia usually is, but no one was interested in the facts. They preferred the invention because this invention expressed and corroborated their hates and fears so perfectly. It is just as well to remember that people are always doing this. Perhaps many of those legends, including Christianity, to which the world clings began their conquest of the world with just some such concerted surrender to distortion. The effect, in Harlem, of this particular legend was like the effect of a lit match in a tin of gasoline. The mob gathered before the doors of the Hotel Braddock simply began to swell and to spread in every direction, and Harlem exploded.

The mob did not cross the ghetto lines. It would have been easy, for example, to have gone over Morningside Park on the west side or to have crossed the Grand Central railroad tracks at 125th Street on the east side, to wreak havoc in white neighborhoods. The mob seems to have been mainly interested in something more potent and real than the white face, that is, in white power, and the principal damage done during the riot of the summer of 1943 was to white business establishments in Harlem. It might have been a far bloodier story, of course, if, at the hour the riot began, these establishments had still been open. From the Hotel Braddock the mob fanned out, east and west along 125th Street, and for the entire length of Lenox, Seventh, and Eighth avenues. Along each of these avenues, and along each major side street—116th, 125th, 135th, and so on—bars, stores, pawnshops, restaurants, even little luncheonettes had been smashed open and entered and looted—looted, it might be added, with more haste than efficiency. The shelves really looked as though a bomb had struck them. Cans of beans and soup and dog food, along with toilet paper, corn flakes, sardines, and milk tumbled every which way, and abandoned cash registers and cases of beer leaned crazily out of the splintered windows and were strewn along the avenues. Sheets, blankets, and clothing of every description formed a kind of path, as though people had dropped them while running. I truly had not realized that Harlem *had* so many stores until I saw them all smashed open; the first time the word *wealth* ever entered my mind in relation to Harlem was when I saw it scattered in the streets. But one's first, incongruous impression of plenty was countered immediately by an impression of waste. None of this was doing anybody any good. It would have been better to have left the plate glass as it had been and the goods lying in the stores.

It would have been better, but it would also have been intolerable, for Harlem had needed something to smash. To smash something is the ghetto's chronic need. Most of the time it is the members of the ghetto who smash each other, and themselves. But as long as the ghetto walls are standing there will always come a moment when these outlets do not work. That summer, for example, it was not enough to get into a fight on Lenox Avenue, or curse out one's cronies in the barber shops. If ever, indeed, the violence which fills Harlem's churches, pool halls, and bars erupts outward in a more direct fashion, Harlem and its citizens are likely to vanish in an apocalyptic flood. That this is not likely to happen is due to a great many reasons, most hidden and powerful among them the Negro's real relation to the white American. This relation prohibits, simply, anything as uncomplicated and satisfactory as pure hatred. In order really to hate white people, one has to blot so much out of the mind—and the heart—that this hatred itself becomes an exhausting and self-destructive pose. But this does not mean, on the other hand, that love comes easily: the white world is too powerful, too complacent, too ready with gratuitous humiliation, and, above all, too ignorant and too innocent for that. One is absolutely forced to make perpetual qualifications and one's own reactions are always canceling each other out.   It is this, really, which has driven so many people mad, both white and black.   One is always in the position of having to decide between amputation and gangrene.   Amputation is swift but time may prove that the amputation was not necessary—or one may delay the amputation too long. Gangrene is slow, but it is impossible to be sure that one is reading one's symptoms right. The idea of going through life as a cripple is more than one can bear, and equally unbearable is the risk of swelling up slowly, in agony, with poison.   And the trouble, finally, is that the risks are real even if the choices do not exist.

"But as for me and my house," my father had said, "we will serve the Lord."   I wondered, as we drove him to his resting place, what this line had meant for him.   I had heard him preach it many times.   I had preached it once myself, proudly giving it an interpretation different from my father's.   Now the whole thing came back to me, as though my father and I were on our way to Sunday school and I were memorizing the golden text: *And if it seem evil unto you to serve the Lord, choose you this day whom you will serve; whether the gods which your fathers served that were on the other side of the flood, or the gods of the Amorites, in whose land ye dwell: but as for me and my house, we will serve the Lord.*   I suspected in these familiar lines a meaning which had never been there for me before.   All of my father's texts and songs, which I had decided were meaningless, were arranged before me at his death like empty bottles, waiting to hold the meaning which life would give them for me.   This was his legacy: nothing is ever escaped.   That bleakly memorable morning I hated the unbelievable streets and the Negroes and whites who had, equally, made them that way.   But I knew that it was folly, as my father would have said, this bitterness was folly.   It was necessary to hold on to the things that mattered.   The dead man mattered, the new life mattered; blackness and whiteness did not matter; to believe that they did was to acquiesce in one's own destruction.   Hatred, which could destroy so much, never failed to destroy the man who hated and this was an immutable law.

It began to seem that one would have to hold in the mind forever two ideas which seemed to be in opposition.   The first idea was acceptance, the acceptance, totally without rancor, of life as it is, and men as they are: in the light of this idea, it goes without saying that injustice is a commonplace. But this did not mean that one could be complacent, for the second idea was of equal power: that one must never, in one's own life, accept these injustices as commonplace but must fight them with all one's strength. This fight begins, however, in the heart and it now had been laid to my charge to keep my own heart free of hatred and despair. This intimation made my heart heavy and, now that my father was irrecoverable, I wished that he had been beside me so that I could have searched his face for the answers which only the future would give me now.

Lines of Inquiry

1 List in their chronological (not their compositional) order the major events referred to in this essay.

   a How does the chronological differ from the compositional order?

   b Examine the structure of the opening paragraph. How are its sentences linked?

   c How is the structure of this paragraph related to that of the essay as a whole?

   d How would the effect of the essay have been modified, had Baldwin followed the chronological order in composing his sequence? (Obviously, you must guess.)

2 Examine the first sentences of each paragraph in the first section of the essay.

   a How is the focus of the section maintained?

   b Where does that focus shift?

   c Examine the transitional paragraph; how is the focus made to shift without our being aware of a break? (Look at the first sentence of this paragraph and note what is happening in it.)

   d How is the last paragraph of this section connected to the first?

3 What is the significance of Baldwin's title? Here are four alternative titles: What differences in focus do they imply?

   a History of a Native Son

   b Notes of an American Negro

   c My Black Childhood

   d My Father

4 This essay is written from a highly personal point of view.

   a Who is James Baldwin? If you do not know, how will you find out?

b What facts from Baldwin's private life enter this essay? Can you name any class of fact that does *not* enter it? What is Baldwin's criterion of relevance?

c You have been set the task of summarizing and evaluating the significance of Baldwin's essay. What must you know before you can define the angle from which you will analyze it and the voice you will use in discussing it?

d In what sense could this essay be said to be *about* points of view? What does its overall focus have to do with the point of view Baldwin follows? Could he himself have written about the same general subject (summarize it in one comprehensive statement) in an impersonal voice? From a different angle?

5 The third part of this text suggests that in a sense all narratives are illustrative, in that their focus and detail must be selected with some principle of relevance, of significance, in mind. Baldwin's narrative here describes how he grew up to understand the black man's heritage in America and to find a personal response to it; his personal case illustrates a far more general one. This basic narrative is composed of several subsidiary narratives. Identify each of these subsiding narratives by a phrase (e.g., the Harlem riot). What does each illustrate?

6 It is often said that character is narrative, that is, that the line of any true narrative action can only be established by the characters implicated in it. If character is narrative, and all narrative illustrates something, then character too must be illustrative. What does Baldwin's father illustrate? And his mother? And the white schoolteacher? And the waitress who refused to serve him?

7 Each detail of a narrative must also illustrate something— otherwise, we can find no explanation for the presence in it of one part of reality rather than, or at the expense of, another. What do the following illustrate?

a The way the riot began

b The appearance of the looted streets after it was over

c The fact that Baldwin's father died because he was insane and refused to eat

d The whistling in his dying father's throat

e The fact that the chapel was full of his father's ex-friends

8 Much of the meaning of Baldwin's essay is obliquely put.

a How does Baldwin interpret the meaning of the biblical text with which he closes the essay? Why does he quote this text at the end, instead of elsewhere?

b What is the meaning of the last paragraph?

c What is the "something I did not want to hear concerning man, concerning the life of man" (suggested to Baldwin) by "life and death so close together, and love and hatred, and right and wrong"?

d What does he mean when he says of the children at the funeral that "their legs somehow seem exposed, so that it is at once incredible and terribly clear that their legs are all they have to hold them up"?

e Baldwin says that having "nothing black to wear" for his father's funeral was "one of those problems, simple, or impossible of solution, to which the mind insanely clings in order to avoid the mind's real trouble." What was the mind's real trouble? Why was it "simple, or impossible of solution?"

9 Since the publication of this essay, Baldwin has written extensively on the same general theme. In your library, look up *The Fire Next Time*. Do you notice a change in Baldwin's attitude in that work? How do you account for it?

10 What is Baldwin's audience?

11 "This Quiet Dust" resembles "Notes of a Native Son" in a number of respects. What parallels do you see between the narrative structures of the two essays? How are they alike in their use of point of view? In their focus? What substantial differences are there? How do you account for those differences? Could it be said that one essay is more successful than the other, in presenting the problem of racial conflict in America?

Lines of Experiment

1 In all cultures, the great moments of an individual life are the same, though the commemorations offered such moments are different. Birth, death, initiation into the adult world, marriage —each culture develops its own "rites of passage" to formalize the meaning of such occasions. Baldwin's essay begins with birth and death, formalized by a funeral; his own initiation into the adult world forms the major concluding matter of his first section; and a ghastly ritual consequence on a larger stage —the Harlem riot—testifies to the universality of what otherwise would be merely a private "rite." Such moments are the symbolic peaks of a personal history. Literature is so deeply concerned with them that, stretching a little, one might call the literary work a special rite of passage, reflecting a special meaning. The ritual may be for others as well as for oneself.

Take some such moment in your own life, and make it the center of a narrative essay. Probably you will be best off following a personal point of view (though it is not impossible. of course, to be impersonal about one's own life); in any case. the shape of event in your narrative will be determined largely by your own sense of what was, and what was not, significant. To illuminate the meaning of your central incident, you may wish to make use of one or two others, in comparison or contrast.

2 Baldwin's essay deals with perhaps the chief political and moral problem of American civilization in the mid-twentieth century. In its wider implications, indeed, the essay forces us to confront the chief political and moral problem of the contemporary world.

An essay on race relations in the national or international context would have to be pitched on a very high level of abstraction—that is, on a level far removed from the facts of your own immediate experience—in order to be both successful and brief: Such an essay would have too much country to take in, except at long range. But the issues pose themselves everywhere in urban life, and even, to the careful eye, in largely agricultural regions. In order to deal effectively with such a subject, you probably should localize the issue in a circumstance you know about, a racial conflict you are familiar with, a specific illustrative case you are competent to discuss. You need not have your conclusions handy when you begin; in a subject as complex and far-reaching as this, the case study may produce the greater and most significant return. *Be sure to formulate your real problem before you begin, however;* you will be attacking something of a straw dummy if you plead extensively for the desirability of something officially acknowledged on all sides to be desirable. A public display of piety is a poor substitute for serious thought.

V

EMOTION
AND VALUE:
TONE

Tone is the emotional element in language, the current of feeling that passes through a given description of ideas or events. A direct statement about feeling differs from a tonal statement in the same way that an abstract statement differs from an illustration; the second is necessary to make the first authentic. The great importance of tone is this: Our moral and aesthetic judgments, our ideas of beauty and of worth, depend for their intensity—if not for their character—on our emotions. Tone, the deliberate creation of emotional pressure in language, is the chief vehicle by which such judgments can be made vivid to others.

Any experiment will show that emotion is difficult to describe, and impossible to describe fully; there is always some well that is hidden or obscured. The same may be said of tone: The shades of emotion a writer may create are as numberless and impalpable as the methods by which he can create them. In such a case a contrast of extremes can be the most effective illustration. The two passages on death that follow are from the *Encyclopaedia Britannica*'s article on "Death (Biological)" and from a sermon by John Donne.

(*1*) The state of death has always been obscured by mystery and superstition and may only be truly defined biologically as the absence of potential life. More specifically, this means the lack of ability to synthesize new molecules in an integrated organized system. The usual criteria of life, such as respiration, duplication and transportation of substrates and ions, are not in themselves necessary for potential life at any given time. . . .

The diagnosis of death in the mammalian organism is usually based on the following criteria: the absence of peripheral pulse and heartbeat, the absence of respiration, the lack of corneal reflex, and the presence of a bluish color (cyanosis) that results from a lack of oxygen in the blood. The discoloration is seen most easily in the mucous membranes of the mouth and lips and in the nail beds. . . .

(*2*) Doth not man die even in his birth? The breaking of prison is death, and what is our birth but a breaking of prison? As soon as we were clothed by God, our very apparell was an emblem of death. In the skins of dead beasts he covered the skins of dying men . . . As soon as God set us on work, our very occupation was an emblem of death: it was to dig the earth, not to dig pitfalls for other men but graves for ourselves. Hath any man here forgot today that yesterday is dead. . . ? We die every day, and we die all the day long; and because we are not absolutely dead, we call that an eternity, an eternity of dying. And is there comfort in that state? Why, that is the state of hell itself, eternal dying and not dead. . . .

It [death] comes equally to us all, and makes us all equal when it comes. The ashes of an oak in the chimney are no epitaph of that oak, to tell me how high and how large that was; it tells me not what flocks it sheltered while it stood, nor what men it hurt when it fell. The dust of great persons' graves is speechless too, it says nothing, it distinguishes nothing: as soon the dust of a wretch whom thou wouldst not, as of a Prince whom thou couldst not look upon, will trouble thine eyes, if the wind blow it thither; and when a whirlwind hath blown the dust of the churchyard into the church, and the man sweeps out the dust of the church into the churchyard, who will undertake to sift those dusts again, and to pronounce, this is the patrician, this is the noble flower, and this the yeomanly, this the plebian bran?

TONE
AND POINT
OF VIEW

The most obvious difference between the two passages is a difference in focus: They are really about two very different kinds of death. The first writer is concerned with formulating the sound definition of a specific physical state, and his method is rigorously logical. He begins by making the thing to be defined as distinct as he can: not death, therefore, but the state of death, a condition capable of being physically or chemically measured, and thus placed within exact boundaries. All that is not measurable, that is local or parochial in the human concern for death, is here irrelevant. Even the description of mammalian death is kept as clinical as possible: We are not so much as reminded that we ourselves are mammals.

The final effect of such a focus is that we feel little if any emotion; the tone of the passage is flat. Should the writer's definition suggest to us (irrelevantly) that after all there is no real distinction between a dead man and a dead fish, or should it prompt us to examine our nail beds for traces of a bluish color, the scientific focus blurs in our minds, we begin to wonder what life is for, why there is death, what it all means—and exact physical definitions seem suddenly without interest. We have shifted point of view, and become concerned with value rather than with structure. But the writer's point of view here is that of a compiler of information that can be demonstrated and defined: He is writing for a reference book, and his tone is appropriately flat. No article on "Death (Spiritual)" or "Death (Meaning of)" or even "Life (Meaning of)" is to be found in the encyclopedia; and if one were, it would have to be a systematic compilation of opinion, in effect a history and analysis of beliefs—for that is the focus such a point of view would entail.

In the first passage, then, the writer's angle of approach makes for a neutral tone. (For this reason, too, his voice is highly impersonal.) The second passage is controlled by an exactly opposed standard of relevance. Donne writes as a clergyman. His angle of approach is, therefore, radically moral, focused on the spiritual meaning and worth of men, of acts, of life—and of death. To such a point of view, the physical world and its measurement are relevant only as they may illuminate the psychic world: "Life (Meaning of)" is the whole point, and the vivid illustration of a set of values relevant to the meaning of life is the purpose of the passage. If it were changed to read, "Death can be considered as the termination of life; in mammalian organisms the process finally results in a complete dispersion of molecules," most of its bare factual sense might be preserved, but its real significance would be lost.

In sum: The tone appropriate to a given discussion is closely related to the angle from which the writer approaches his subject. When his purpose is strictly to set forth the shape of fact, or theory, or opinion— to outline a structure but not to render vividly its worth—a heightened tone is a mere distraction. When, however, he wishes not only to set forth the structure of his subject but also to fuse to that structure an image, so to speak, of its value—then a heightening of tone is not only appropriate but even necessary.

The essential questions about the creation of tone remain. How is the sermon made to differ so remarkably in tone from the encyclopedia article?

DENOTATION
AND CONNOTATION

Perhaps the most immediately obvious technical difference between the two passages is in vocabulary. The vocabulary of the first reflects above all a search for precision: "death" is less precise than "the state of death"; "breathing" is less precise than "respiration"; "create" is far less precise than "synthesize"; and "failure of sight" is vagueness itself beside "lack of corneal reflex."

The vocabulary of the sermon—indeed, the whole habit of its language —is a remarkable contrast. Precision is deliberately avoided: "death" means both a spiritual and a physical state—even, apparently, something that affects totally nonliving and abstract things, such as time; and a great many other words are used in senses difficult if not impossible to capture in a definition: "prison," "eternity," "equal," "noble."

This difference in vocabulary is clearly a difference in the kind of word-meaning each passage draws on. The first passage uses words in senses that can be exactly distinguished and bounded, that refer only to a single thing, or phenomenon, or idea: thus, at an extreme, "cyanosis," "respiration," "mammal." Such words are purely denotative in meaning: They may refer to simple or complex things, pleasant or unpleasant things, but they name single ideas that can be closely

identified or defined.   Even those words in this passage that can have
several meanings, and that suggest possible uses in different contexts,
such as "pulse," "heart," "lips," are used in a way that clearly limits
their meaning to the denotative: The heart is not the seat of the emotions, but simply a blood pump.   There is only one denotative meaning
of a word in a given context, and that denotative meaning can be
clearly identified.

The second passage, by contrast, deliberately makes use of words that
even when clear in denotation (as some are not) are also rich in
associations that cling to them from other contexts of thought and are not
destroyed in this one.   The word "noble," for example, suggests vaguely
not only a fine gentleman but also a member of the feudal aristocracy
(noted for its pride of place), a moral quality, fine clothing, fine manners, fine gestures, elevated thought, and elegant assemblies—perhaps
even the gold coin once so called; and these secondary shades of meaning and association play subtly on one another to create the overtone,
the *connotation* of the word.   The connotative meanings of some words
cannot be separated from the words themselves, in any context: "Noble"
cannot be reduced to mere denotative meaning.   But even when Donne
employs words whose connotative meanings can be stripped from them,
such as "birth," he employs them in such a way as to enhance their
connotations.

His reason for doing so is easy to see.   Connotative meanings are by
nature vague, and their interplay is indefinable.   Because emotion may
be identified but not easily rendered by denotative language, the tonal
character of a word depends chiefly on its connotations; a word that
has no connotations, as "synthesis" has none, is without tonal character
—it is flat; a word that is rich in connotation, as "create" is rich, has a
proportionate tonal strength, rising from its currency in the important
thought and art of the West—it sets off showers of secondary ideas and
images in the mind.   Thus: "death."

One chief element in the heightening of tone, then, is the choice of
words rich in connotative meaning.   And one way to avoid an inappropriate heightening of tone is to choose words strong in denotation,
weak in connotation.

ALLUSION
AND METAPHOR

In a sense, a connotation is allusive: It suggests a pattern of thought
and image beyond the thing denoted, and draws indirectly on the ra-

tional and emotional texture of that pattern. But *allusion* can be far more direct than this, and thus far more controlled in effect.

The first passage alludes vaguely to "mystery and superstition." The allusion is deliberately left abstract; it does not develop into image, and what images may precipitate from it are not particularly pleasant. Such an allusion does not lead us through connotative avenues, away from a focus on "Death (Biological)"; indeed, its purpose is to poison the wells of connotation at the beginning, and thereafter we are clear that by "heart" is meant the muscle that pumps blood through the arterial system—nothing reminds us of the seat of noble emotions, or any other figurative association.

Allusion, then, can be used to close off avenues of thought. (See the first paragraph of "A Sad Heart at the Supermarket," p. 414, for an allusion specifically designed to close off purely denotative patterns of thought.) It can also be used—and is much more frequently used—to open them, and so to heighten tone. For example, Donne alludes deliberately and forcefully to ideas and images prominent within the Christian tradition. Some of these allusions may be lost on a modern reader, but Donne's audience very well knew that God gave to Adam and Eve coats of skins, on their expulsion from paradise, on which occasion (one tradition went) they were also doomed to die; thus, "In the skins of dead beasts he covered the skins of dying men." That audience would have also recognized allusions to the burial service, with its metaphor of dust and ashes; to God's speech out of the whirlwind, in the Book of Job; and to a variety of traditional metaphors—the oak as nobility and longevity, and life as a prison.

By such means the tone of the passage is greatly heightened, for Donne's subject is projected sharply upon a background of Christian thought and legend: Death is no longer merely itself, but a thing placed within a theory of what life is for, and why it is at all; it is no longer merely a concept, but an image. The specific direction of allusion is very important, to be sure: Had Donne directed us toward vanished military heroes, forgotten reputations, we might find some melancholy pleasure in considering how the glories of the world fade, but we would not be so clearly struck with the religious significance of the original version. Yet any specific pattern of allusion would have resulted in a heightening of tone.

Metaphor is a third element, closely related to verbal connotation and to allusion, by which tone can be heightened. (Here, as elsewhere, I use "metaphor" to mean the basic figure of speech.) God is a whirlwind; the oak is the king of trees; yesterday is dead—such phrases are precise in a totally unscientific sense, yet tonally remarkable, for they muster connotative meanings in peculiarly dense patterns. A whirlwind is an overpowering force; it springs, apparently, from nothing; it moves in unaccountable ways; it destroys; above all, it seems to have a weird interior purpose of its own. As a way of referring to the similarly forceful, unaccountable, sourceless, destructive, purposeful work of death, i.e., God's will, it carries intense emotional force. The same thing is true of the metaphorical habit that declares that yesterday can die: If time can die, then death is not a local state at all, but a supreme and necessary law; and each day sees us die a little. It is *our* yesterday that is dead; hence the power of the figure. Simply to say that time always passes—even to say that yesterday never comes back, is not the same thing.

The death of time is a very common metaphor; therefore, it is both easy to appreciate and, after so much use, somewhat hard to get excited about, except when its force is renewed by a good writer. The metaphor that dominates Donne's second paragraph (the body is mere dust and ash) is equally familiar; again, renewal makes the traditional metaphor powerful.

Indeed, there is little uncommon about any of these metaphors—the wind of fate is a cliché, the noble oak no less. Each seems to spring out of the matter, almost out of the very language, with which the writer is engaged, to be transformed by him. Really new metaphors, in fact, are quite rare; many times, indeed, the metaphors handiest to the expression of an idea are those buried in the words that burst into the mind. Metaphors are everywhere in language, which has been called the cemetery of metaphor for good cause: The heart *pumps,* the mind *sees,* the hand *dances* over the keyboard, and a *cemetery* is a sleeping chamber. One metaphor springs from another: If life is a prison, then death is a breaking of prison. The writer with an interest in metaphorical possibilities will find them throughout in his own speech. His job is to choose those with the proper tonal potential and to bring them back to life.

TONE
AND ILLUSTRATION

The tonal importance of illustration recurs frequently in Part III and needs only to be pointed to here. Illustrations differ not only in denotation—in their ability to represent a class, but in connotation as well.

An oak is not a pine: It lives longer, and burns slower, it is harder and stronger, its shelter is wider, its limbs are thicker and longer, its roots are deeper, the ground beneath it is more fertile, its death is slower, its wreck stands longer.   A man vainly sifting the windblown dust of a churchyard is not a man reading tombstones, much less a man looking over a hall full of cadavers.   Tonally, it makes all the difference whether one illustrates the fragility of life by flowers that fade or by a cancer ward—and whether one illustrates the qualities of tone by a passage from "Death (Biological)" or by a passage from one of John Donne's sermons.

REPETITION
AND SOUND

The contrast in sound between the two illustrative passages is as great as the contrast in vocabulary and in the use of allusions.   One might judge with some plausibility that the first passage was not written to be read aloud, even in the mind's ear, and that the second cannot be really appreciated if it is not so read.   There is, first of all, in this second passage, a heavy and sonorous repetition of key words: In the first three sentences, the word "death" or a variant of it occurs five times; "birth" occurs twice; in the last sentences of the first paragraph, emphasis falls on the phrase "eternal dying"; in the second paragraph, the word "dust" appears five times.   Words suggesting time are similarly stressed: "today," "yesterday," "day."   The central concepts thus are tonally emphasized by verbal repetitions: "death" becomes more real, "today" more perishable, "eternity" more eternal.

In addition, the passage shows frequent near-rhymes: "birth" and "death" are very close, as are "even" and "prison."   Patterns of alliteration and assonance (see the Glossary if in doubt) tie the passage even more tightly together, making its ideas seem more congruent, more inevitably connected—truer, in a sense, despite the fact that neither alliteration nor assonance has the slightest logical value.   Thus d's, b's, p's and r's dominate the first sentences.   A sentence such as "We die every day and we die all the day long; and because we are not absolutely dead we call that an eternity, an eternity of dying" uses verbal repetition, alliteration, and assonance in a pattern not less tonally effective because difficult to describe: The vowel of "die" and "day" repeats itself (the two vowels would have sounded even more alike in Donne's time than they are in our own); "all," "long," "because," "call" have the same vowel; and the sentence passes from a repetition of "day" to a repetition of "eternity," with a corresponding change of focus and heightening of tone.

Sentence rhythm contributes a further element to tone. Any comparison of the two illustrative passages shows that, although the first is completely uninterested in establishing any marked sentence rhythm, even when such a rhythm might be very easy to create (as in the last clauses, where the parallelism of ideas would lend itself to a tonally sonorous parallel phrasing), the second passage has a marked rhythm in every sentence. The fall of heavy stress on the key words ("Dóth nót mán díe, éven in his bírth?"); the tense rhythmic balance of important clausal structures ("The breaking of prison/is death//and what is death/but the breaking of prison?"); the gradual, cumulating rush of clauses in the second paragraph, ending in the completely static "weighing" of one dust against another—all this is carefully considered for its emotional impact.

It would take little skill and be of little value to show that revisions that destroy these repetitive elements, that break up this music, would also destroy the tone of Donne's prose. The pragmatic test of reading aloud will illustrate this interdependence of tone and sound.

SEQUENCE
AND STRUCTURE

The tonal devices so far discussed are most obvious in individual sentences and paragraphs, but they also can affect overall structure and sequence. For example, the passage quoted from Donne's sermon opens with a series of fairly static images and an idea of death that is deliberately abstract. We begin with the birth of the world, in Eden. As the paragraph develops it becomes more personal ("Hath any man here. . . ?"), but never concrete. The second paragraph, however, moves from an initial general statement to increasingly specific visual images, from stasis to action, in a movement rather suggesting the whirlwind itself: The oak lies in ashes; general human dust blown by the wind becomes specific dust swept into a church by a whirlwind and out again by a man, only to balance in stasis once more, in the hands of someone who presumptuously would "undertake to sift those dusts again. . . ." As noted, the sentences themselves echo this development of idea, moving from simple balance to greater and greater complexity, ending again in a balance that, however, is far from simple —like the task it describes. In emotional terms, the tension of this second paragraph increases from an initial quiet truism to a turbulent image of dust swept about by a whirlwind, only to be resolved in the final, complexly balanced clauses.   Literally, it is ashes to ashes, dust to dust, from beginning to end.

Similar effects can be obtained on an even larger scale by the repetition, or reintroduction, of single structural elements—phrase, image, metaphor—at critical points in the development of an entire composition.   The tonality of a piece can be established by a mode of transition (imagine an argument whose transitions are managed in terms of anecdotes about children); by a style of illustration (an essay on government, for instance, illustrated by scenes from military life); by deliberately recurrent judgments (as, for example, in an argument, each of whose sections concludes, "How idiotic can one be?"); by a return in the final paragraph to the tone of the opening sentences; and so on.   There is no practical limit to the number of such devices for establishing and maintaining tone.

Usually, when the chief purpose of a writer is to arouse a given emotional response toward a set of facts, the structure of his composition is almost entirely tonally determined—becomes, in effect, fully dramatic. An ability to construct an essay with a unified dramatic impact is, indeed, one of the most important tests of a writer's competence.   Our willingness to enter into the mood of an essay, to accept it as emotionally "true," depends in large part on the consistency of its tone and on the degree to which it can suggest a certain completeness of feeling, the rounding off of a subjective circle.   Tonal shifts that shatter our expectations, tonal conclusions that do not somehow round out the emotions generated in the essay, jar us out of belief and assent.   The function of a conclusion is not only to tell us what has been concluded, but also to make us feel as if the pattern is complete.

VARIETIES
OF TONE

Only one kind of heightened tone has been illustrated here, and there are obviously many kinds.   The same essential devices are at the foundations of almost every kind of tone, however; comedy is also manufactured by verbal connotation, by allusion, by metaphor, by repetition, by patterns of sound, by recurrence.   The difference between the kind of tone aimed at by Donne and the comic tone is in the congruity of the elements thrown together.   Comedy rises out of incongruity: A man in a top hat slips on a banana—so the dignified are brought low. A comic tone rises out of deliberately incongruous tonal elements—not elements put together by accident, but elements deliberately juxtaposed almost in a spirit of parody: The rattled cleric speaks like a hippie; the schoolteacher's sufferings are compared to those of Prometheus (chained to a rock, with eagles pecking at his liver); Romeo opens his mouth and says "A-a-a-ah-h . . . ," ; a politician is as disinterested as a fox in a chickencoop.

Such tonal elements must be handled with great skill in order to be effective. But an even greater risk, perhaps, than failure at the comic, is failure at the sublime. *Sentimentality* is the vice of tone. When tone is manufactured for its own sake, and the heightening of tone is not justified by the ideas actually discussed, the circumstances actually portrayed, the result will be either comedy (if the incongruity is deliberate) or sentimentality (if it is not deliberate). The only certain way to avoid sentimentality is not to press tone beyond the point where its control is difficult. Only very great writers can emulate John Donne. Most of us are better off in attempting less, until we are certain that we can render emotion as richly and as complexly as our subject demands—can create not so much a picture of *our* emotion for the reader to wonder at, but rather a picture that will lead him to his own.

D. H. LAWRENCE

 ## FLOWERY TUSCANY

Each country has its own flowers, that shine out specially there. In England it is daisies and buttercups, hawthorn and cowslips. In America, it is goldenrod, stargrass, June daisies, Mayapple and asters, that we call Michaelmas daisies. In India, hibiscus and datura and champa flowers, and in Australia mimosa, that they call wattle, and sharp-tongued strange heath flowers. In Mexico it is cactus flowers, that they call roses of the desert, lovely and crystalline among many thorns: and also the dangling yard-long clusters of the cream bells of the yucca, like dropping froth.

But by the Mediterranean, now as in the days of the Argosy, and, we hope, for ever, it is narcissus and anemone, asphodel and myrtle. Narcissus and anemone, asphodel, crocus, myrtle, and parsley, they leave their sheer significance only by the Mediterranean. There are daisies in Italy too: at Paestum there are white little carpets of daisies, in March, and Tuscany is spangled with celandine. But for all that, the daisy and the celandine are English flowers, their best significance is for us and for the North.

The Mediterranean has narcissus and anemone, myrtle and asphodel and grape hyacinth. These are the flowers that speak and are understood in the sun round the Middle Sea.

Tuscany is especially flowery, being wetter than Sicily and more homely than the Roman hills. Tuscany manages to remain so remote, and secretly smiling to itself in its many sleeves. There are so many hills popping up, and they take no notice of one another. There are so many little deep valleys with streams that seem to go their own little way entirely, regardless of river and sea. There are thousands, millions of utterly secluded little nooks, though the land has been under cultivation these thousands of years. But the intensive culture of vine and olive and wheat, by the ceaseless industry of naked human hands and winter-shod feet, and slow stepping, soft-eyed oxen does not devastate a country, does not denude it, does not lay it bare, does not uncover its nakedness, does not drive away either Pan or his children. The streams run and rattle over wild rocks of secret places, and murmur through blackthorn thickets where the nightingales sing all together, unruffled and undaunted.

It is queer that a country so perfectly cultivated as Tuscany, where half the produce of five acres of land will have to support ten human mouths, still has so much room for the wild flowers and the nightingale. When little hills heave themselves suddenly up, and shake themselves free of neighbours, man has to build his garden and his vineyard, and sculp his landscape. Talk of hanging gardens of Babylon, all Italy, apart from the plains, is a hanging garden. For centuries upon centuries man has been patiently modelling the surface of the Mediterranean countries, gently rounding the hills, and graduating the big slopes into the almost invisible levels of terraces. Thousands of square miles of Italy have been lifted in human hands, piled and laid back in tiny little flats, held up by the drystone walls, whose stones came from the lifted earth. It is a work of many, many centuries. It is the gentle sensitive sculpture of all the landscape. And it is the achieving of the peculiar Italian beauty which is so exquisitely natural, because man, feeling his way sensitively to the fruitfulness of the earth, has moulded the earth to his necessity without violating it.

Which shows that it *can* be done. Man *can* live on the earth and by the earth without disfiguring the earth. It has been done here, on all these sculptured hills and softly, sensitively terraced slopes.

But, of course, you can't drive a steam plough on terraces four yards wide, terraces that dwindle and broaden and sink and rise a little, all according to the pitch and the breaking outline of the mother hill. Corn has got to grow on these little shelves of earth, where already the grey olive stands semi-invisible, and the grape-vine twists upon its own scars. If oxen can step with that lovely pause at every little stride, they can plough the narrow field. But they will have to leave a tiny fringe, a grassy lip over the drystone wall below. And if the terraces are too narrow to plough, the peasant digging them will still leave the grassy lip, because it helps to hold the surface in the rains.

And here the flowers take refuge. Over and over and over and over has this soil been turned, twice a year, sometimes three times a year, for several thousands of years. Yet the flowers have never been driven out. There is a very rigorous digging and sifting, the little bulbs and tubers are flung away into perdition, not a weed shall remain.

Yet spring returns, and on the terrace lips, and in the stony nooks between terraces, up rise the aconites, the crocuses, the narcissus and the asphodel, the inextinguishable wild tulips. There they are, for ever hanging on the precarious brink of an existence, but for ever triumphant, never quite losing their footing. In England, in America, the flowers get rooted out, driven back. They become fugitive. But in the intensive cultivation of ancient Italian terraces, they dance round and hold their own.

Spring begins with the first narcissus, rather cold and shy and wintry. They are the little bunchy, creamy narcissus with the yellow cup like the yolk of the flower. The natives call these flowers *tazzette*, little cups. They grow on the grassy banks rather sparse, or push up among thorns.

To me they are winter flowers, and their scent is winter. Spring starts in February, with the winter aconite. Some icy day, when the wind is down from the snow of the mountains, early in February, you will notice on a bit of fallow land, under the olive trees, tight, pale-gold little balls, clenched tight as nuts, and resting on round ruffs of green near the ground.   It is winter aconite suddenly come.

The winter aconite is one of the most charming flowers.   Like all the early blossoms, once her little flower emerges it is quite naked.   No shutting a little green sheath over herself, like the daisy or the dandelion. Her bubble of frail, pale, pure gold rests on the round frill of her green collar, with the snowy wind trying to blow it away.

But without success.   The *tramontana* ceases, comes a day of wild February sunshine.   The clenched little nuggets of the aconite puff out, they become light bubbles, like small balloons, on a green base. The sun blazes on, with February splendour.   And by noon, all under the olives are wide-open little suns, the aconites spreading all their rays; and there is an exquisitely sweet scent, honey-sweet, not narcissus-frosty; and there is a February humming of little brown bees.

Till afternoon, when the sun slopes, and the touch of snow comes back into the air.

But at evening, under the lamp on the table, the aconites are wide and excited, and there is a perfume of sweet spring that makes one almost start humming and trying to be a bee.

Aconites don't last very long.   But they turn up in all odd places— on clods of dug earth, and in land where the broadbeans are thrusting up, and along the lips of terraces.   But they like best land left fallow for one winter.   There they throng, showing how quick they are to seize on an opportunity to live and shine forth.

In a fortnight, before February is over, the yellow bubbles of the aconite are crumpling to nothingness.   But already in a cosy nook the violets are dark purple, and there is a new little perfume in the air.

Like the debris of winter stand the hellebores, in all the wild places, and the butcher's broom is flaunting its last bright red berry. Hellebore is Christmas roses, but in Tuscany the flowers never come white.   They emerge out of the grass towards the end of December, flowers wintry of winter, and they are delicately pale green, and of a lovely shape, with yellowish stamens.   They have a peculiar wintry quality of invisibility, so lonely rising from the sere grass, and pallid green, held up like a little hand-mirror that reflects nothing.   At first they are single upon a stem, short and lovely, and very wintry-beautiful, with a will not to be touched, not to be noticed.   One instinctively leaves them alone.   But as January draws towards February, these hellebores, these greenish Christmas roses become more assertive.   Their pallid water-green becomes yellower, pale sulphur-yellow-green, and they rise up, they are in tufts, in throngs, in veritable bushes of greenish open flowers, assertive, bowing their faces with a hellebore assertiveness.   In some places they throng among the bushes and above the water of the stream, giving the peculiar pale glimmer almost of primroses, as you walk among them. Almost of primroses, yet with a coarse hellebore leaf and an uprearing hellebore assertiveness, like snakes in winter.

And as one walks among them, one brushes the last scarlet off the butcher's broom.   This low little shrub is the Christmas holly of Tuscany, only a foot or so high, with a vivid red berry stuck on in the middle of its sharp hard leaf.   In February the last red ball rolls off the prickly plume, and winter rolls with it.   The violets already are emerging from the moisture.

But before the violets make any show, there are the crocuses.   If you walk up through the pine-wood, that lifts its umbrellas of pine so high, up till you come to the brow of the hill at the top, you can look south, due south, and see snow on the Apennines, and on a blue afternoon, seven layers of blue-hilled distance.

Then you sit down on that southern slope, out of the wind, and there it is warm, whether it be January or February, *tramontana* or not. There the earth has been baked by innumerable suns, baked and baked again; moistened by many rains, but never wetted for long.   Because it is rocky, and full to the south, and sheering steep in the slope.

And there, in February, in the sunny baked desert of that crumbly slope, you will find the first crocuses.   On the sheer aridity of crumbled stone you see a queer, alert little star, very sharp and quite small. It has opened out rather flat, and looks like a tiny freesia flower, creamy, with a smear of yellow yolk.   It has no stem, seems to have been just lightly dropped on the crumbled, baked rock.   It is the first hill-crocus.

II

North of the Alps, the everlasting winter is interrupted by summers that struggle and soon yield; south of the Alps, the everlasting summer is interrupted by spasmodic and spiteful winters that never get a real hold, but that are mean and dogged. North of the Alps, you may have a pure winter's day in June. South of the Alps, you may have a mid-summer day in December or January or even February. The in-between, in either case, is just as it may be. But the lands of the sun are south of the Alps, for ever.

Yet things, the flowers especially, that belong to both sides of the Alps, are not much earlier south than north of the mountains. Through all the winter there are roses in the garden, lovely creamy roses, more pure and mysterious than those of summer, leaning perfect from the stem. And the narcissus in the garden are out by the end of January, and the little simple hyacinths early in February.

But out in the fields, the flowers are hardly any sooner than English flowers. It is mid-February before the first violets, the first crocus, the first primrose. And in mid-February one may find a violet, a primrose, a crocus in England, in the hedgerows and the garden corner.

And still there is a difference. There are several kinds of wild crocus in this region of Tuscany: being little spiky mauve ones, and spiky little creamy ones, that grow among the pinetrees of the bare slopes. But the beautiful ones are those of a meadow in the corner of the woods, the low hollow meadow below the steep, shadowy pine-slopes, the secretive grassy dip where the water seeps through the turf all winter, where the stream runs between thick bushes, where the nightin-gale sings his mightiest in May, and where the wild thyme is rosy and full of bees, in summer.

Here the lavender crocuses are most at home—here sticking out of the deep grass, in a hollow like a cup, a bowl of grass, come the lilac-coloured crocuses, like an innumerable encampment. You may see them at twilight, with all the buds shut, in the mysterious stillness of the grassy underworld, palely glimmering like myriad folded tents. So the Apaches still camp, and close their tepees, in the hollows of the great hills of the West, at night.

But in the morning it is quite different. Then the sun shines strong on the horizontal green cloud-puffs of the pines, the sky is clear and full of life, the water runs hastily, still browned by the last juice of crushed olives. And there the earth's bowl of crocuses is amazing. You can-not believe that the flowers are really still. They are open with such delight, and their pistil-thrust is so red-orange, and they are so many, all reaching out wide and marvellous, that it suggests a perfect ecstasy of radiant, thronging movement, lit-up violet and orange, and surging in some invisible rhythm of concerted, delightful movement.   You cannot believe they do not move, and make some sort of crystalline sound of delight.   If you sit still and watch, you begin to move with them, like moving with the stars, and you feel the sound of their radiance. All the little cells of the flowers must be leaping with flowery life and utterance.

And the small brown honey-bees hop from flower to flower, dive down, try, and off again.   The flowers have been already rifled, most of them.   Only sometimes a bee stands on his head, kicking slowly inside the flower, for some time.   He has found something.   And all the bees have little loaves of pollen, bee-bread, in their elbow-joints.

The crocuses last in their beauty for a week or so, and as they begin to lower their tents and abandon camp, the violets begin to thicken. It is already March.   The violets have been showing like tiny dark hounds for some weeks.   But now the whole pack comes forth, among the grass and the tangle of wild thyme, till the air all sways subtly scented with violets, and the banks above where the crocuses had their tents are now swarming brilliant purple with violets.   They are the sweet violets of early spring, but numbers have made them bold, for they flaunt and ruffle till the slopes are a bright blue-purple blaze of them, full in the sun, with an odd late crocus still standing wondering and erect amongst them.

And now that it is March, there is a rush of flowers.   Down by the other stream, which turns sideways to the sun, and has tangles of brier and bramble, down where the hellebore has stood so wan and dignified all winter, there are now white tufts of primroses, suddenly come. Among the tangle and near the water-lip, tufts and bunches of primroses, in abundance.   Yet they look more wan, more pallid, more flimsy than English primroses.   They lack some of the full wonder of the northern flowers.   One tends to overlook them, to turn to the great, solemn-faced purple violets that rear up from the bank, and above all, to the wonderful little towers of the grape-hyacinth.

I know no flower that is more fascinating, when it first appears, than the blue grape-hyacinth.   And yet, because it lasts so long, and keeps on coming so repeatedly, for at least two months, one tends later on to ignore it, even to despise it a little.   Yet that is very unjust.

The first grape-hyacinths are flowers of blue, thick and rich and meaningful, above the unrenewed grass.   The upper buds are pure blue, shut tight; round balls of pure, perfect warm blue, blue, blue; while the lower bells are darkish blue-purple, with the spark of white at the mouth.   As yet, none of the lower bells has withered, to leave the greenish, separate sparseness of fruiting that spoils the grape-hyacinth later on, and makes it seem naked and functional.   All hyacinths are like that in the seeding.

But, at first, you have only a compact tower of night-blue clearing to dawn, and extremely beautiful.   If we were tiny as fairies, and lived only a summer, how lovely these great trees of bells would be to us, towers of night and dawn-blue globes.   They would rise above us thick and succulent, and the purple globes would push the blue ones up, with white sparks of ripples, and we should see a god in them.

As a matter of fact, someone once told me they were the flowers of the many-breasted Artemis; and it is true, the Cybele of Ephesus, with her clustered breasts, was like a grape-hyacinth at the bosom.

This is the time, in March, when the sloe is white and misty in the hedge-tangle by the stream, and on the slope of land the peach tree stands pink and alone.   The almond blossom, silvery pink, is passing, but the peach, deep-toned, bluey, not at all ethereal, this reveals itself like flesh, and the trees are like isolated individuals, the peach and the apricot.

A man said this spring: "Oh, I *don't* care for peach blossom!   It is such a vulgar pink!"   One wonders what anybody means by a "vulgar" pink.   I think pink flannelette is rather vulgar.   But probably it's the flannelette's fault, not the pink.   And peach blossom has a beautiful sensual pink, far from vulgar, most rare and private.   And pink is so beautiful in a landscape, pink houses, pink almond, pink peach and purply apricot, pink asphodels.

It is so conspicuous and so individual, that pink among the coming green of spring, because the first flowers that emerge from winter seem always white or yellow or purple.   Now the celandines are out, and along the edges of the *podere*,[1] the big, sturdy, black-purple anemones, with black hearts.

They are curious, these great, dark-violet anemones.   You may pass them on a grey day, or at evening or early morning, and never see them. But as you come along in the full sunshine, they seem to be baying at you with all their throats, baying deep purple into the air.   It is because they are hot and wide open now, gulping the sun.   Whereas when they

[1] Cultivated field.

are shut, they have a silkiness and a curved head, like the curve of an umbrella handle, and a peculiar outward colourlessness, that makes them quite invisible.   They may be under your feet, and you will not see them.

Altogether anemones are odd flowers.   On these last hills above the plain, we have only the big black-purple ones, in tufts here and there, not many.   But two hills away, the young green corn is blue with the lilac-blue kind, still the broad-petalled sort with the darker heart.   But these flowers are smaller than our dark-purple, and frailer, more silky. Ours are substantial, thickly vegetable flowers, and not abundant.   The others are lovely and silky-delicate, and the whole corn is blue with them.   And they have a sweet, sweet scent, when they are warm.

Then on the priest's *podere* there are the scarlet, Adonis-blood anemones: only in one place, in one long fringe under a terrace, and there by a path below.   These flowers above all you will never find unless you look for them in the sun.   Their silver silk outside makes them quite invisible, when they are shut up.

Yet, if you are passing in the sun, a sudden scarlet faces on to the air, one of the loveliest scarlet apparitions in the world.   The inner surface of the Adonis-blood anemone is as fine as velvet, and yet there is no suggestion of pile, not as much as on a velvet rose.   And from this inner smoothness issues the red colour, perfectly pure and unknown of earth, no earthiness, and yet solid, not transparent.   How a colour manages to be perfectly strong and impervious, yet of a purity that suggests condensed light, yet not luminous, at least, not transparent is a problem.   The poppy in her radiance is translucent, and the tulip in her utter redness has a touch of opaque earth.   But the Adonis-blood anemone is neither translucent nor opaque.   It is just pure condensed red, of a velvetiness without velvet, and a scarlet without glow.

This red seems to me the perfect premonition of summer—like the red on the outside of apple blossom—and later, the red of the apple.   It is the premonition in redness of summer and of autumn.

The red flowers are coming now.   The wild tulips are in bud, hanging their grey leaves like flags.   They come up in myriads, wherever they get a chance.   But they are holding back their redness till the last days of March, the early days of April.

Still, the year is warming up.   By the high ditch the common magenta anemone is hanging its silky tassels, or opening its great magenta daisy-shape to the hot sun.   It is much nearer to red than the big-petalled anemones are; except the Adonis-blood.   They say these anemones spring from the tears of Venus, which fell as she went looking for Adonis.   At that rate, how the poor lady must have wept, for the anemones by the Mediterranean are common as daisies in England.

The daisies are out here too, in sheets, and they too are red-mouthed. The first ones are big and handsome.   But as March goes on, they dwindle to bright little things, like tiny buttons, clouds of them together. That means summer is nearly here.

The red tulips open in the corn like poppies, only with a heavier red. And they pass quickly, without repeating themselves.   There is little lingering in a tulip.

In some places there are odd yellow tulips, slender, spiky, and Chinese-looking.   They are very lovely, pricking out their dulled yellow in slim spikes.   But they too soon lean, expand beyond themselves, and are gone like an illusion.

And when the tulips are gone, there is a moment's pause, before summer.   Summer is the next move.

III

In the pause towards the end of April, when the flowers seem to hesitate, the leaves make up their minds to come out.   For some time, at the very ends of the bare boughs of fig trees, spurts of pure green have been burning like little cloven tongues of green fire vivid on the tips of the candelabrum.   Now these spurts of green spread out, and begin to take the shape of hands, feeling for the air of summer.   And tiny green figs are below them, like glands on the throat of a goat.

For some time, the long stiff whips of the vine have had knobby pink buds, like flower buds.   Now these pink buds begin to unfold into greenish, half-shut fans of leaves with red in the veins, and tiny spikes of flower, like seed-pearls.   Then, in all its down and pinky dawn, the vine-rosette has a frail, delicious scent of a new year.

Now the aspens on the hill are all remarkable with the translucent membranes of blood-veined leaves.   They are gold-brown, but not like autumn, rather like the thin wings of bats when like birds—call them birds—they wheel in clouds against the setting sun, and the sun glows through the stretched membrane of their wings, as through thin,

brown-red stained glass.   This is the red sap of summer, not the red
dust of autumn.   And in the distance the aspens have the tender panting glow of living membrane just come awake.   This is the beauty of
the frailty of spring.

The cherry tree is something the same, but more sturdy.   Now, in the
last week of April, the cherry blossom is still white, but waning and
passing away: it is late this year; and the leaves are clustering thick and
softly copper in their dark blood-filled glow.   It is queer about fruit
trees in this district.   The pear and the peach were out together.   But
now the pear tree is a lovely thick softness of new and glossy green,
vivid with a tender fullness of apple-green leaves, gleaming among all
the other green of the landscape, the half-high wheat, emerald, and the
grey olive, half-invisible, the browning green of the dark cypress, the
black of the evergreen oak, the rolling, heavy green puffs of the stone-
pines, the flimsy green of small peach and almond trees, the sturdy
young green of horse-chestnut.   So many greens, all in flakes and
shelves and tilted tables and round shoulders and plumes and shaggles
and uprisen bushes, of greens and greens, sometimes blindingly brilliant
at evening, when the landscape looks as if it were on fire from inside,
with greenness and with gold.

The pear is perhaps the greenest thing in the landscape.   The wheat
may shine lit-up yellow, or glow bluish, but the pear tree is green in
itself.   The cherry has white, half-absorbed flowers, so has the apple.
But the plum is rough with her new foliage, and inconspicuous, inconspicuous as the almond, the peach, the apricot, which one can no longer
find in the landscape, though twenty days ago they were the distinguished pink individuals of the whole countryside.   Now they are
gone.   It is the time of green, pre-eminent green, in ruffles and flakes
and slabs.

In the wood, the scrub-oak is only just coming uncrumpled, and the
pines keep their hold on winter.   They are wintry things, stone-pines.
At Christmas, their heavy green clouds are richly beautiful.   When
the cypresses raise their tall and naked bodies of dark green, and the
osiers are vivid red-orange, on the still blue air, and the land is
lavender; then, in mid-winter, the landscape is most beautiful in colour,
surging with colour.

But now, when the nightingale is still drawing out his long, wistful,
yearning, teasing plaint-note, and following it up with a rich and
joyful burble, the pines and the cypresses seem hard and rusty, and the

wood has lost its subtlety and its mysteriousness.   It still seems wintry in spite of the yellowing, young oaks, and the heath in flower. But hard, dull pines above, and hard, dull, tall heath below, all stiff and resistant, this is out of the mood of spring.

In spite of the fact that the stone-white heath is in full flower, and very lovely when you look at it, it does not, casually, give the impression of blossom.   More the impression of having its tips and crests all dipped in hoarfrost; or in a whitish dust.   It has a peculiar ghostly colourlessness amid the darkish colourlessness of the wood altogether, which completely takes away the sense of spring.

Yet the tall white heath is very lovely, in its invisibility.   It grows sometimes as tall as a man, lifting up its spires and its shadowy-white fingers with a ghostly fullness, amid the dark, rusty green of its lower bushiness; and it gives off a sweet honeyed scent in the sun, and a cloud of fine white stone-dust, if you touch it.   Looked at closely, its little bells are most beautiful, delicate and white, with the brown-purple inner eye and the dainty pin-head of the pistil.   And out in the sun at the edge of the wood, where the heath grows tall and thrusts up its spires of dim white next a brilliant, yellow-flowering vetch-bush, under a blue sky, the effect has a real magic.

And yet, in spite of all, the dim whiteness of all the flowering heath-fingers only adds to the hoariness and out-of-date quality of the pine-woods, now in the pause between spring and summer.   It is the ghost of the interval.

Not that this week is flowerless.   But the flowers are little lonely things, here and there: the early purple orchid, ruddy and very much alive, you come across occasionally, then the little groups of bee-orchid, with their ragged concerted indifference to their appearance. Also there are the huge bud-spikes of the stout, thick-flowering pink orchid, huge buds like fat ears of wheat, hard-purple and splendid. But already odd grains of the wheat-ear are open, and out of the purple hangs the delicate pink rag of a floweret.   Also there are very lovely and choice cream-coloured orchids with brown spots on the long and delicate lip.   These grow in the most moist places, and have exotic tender spikes, very rare-seeming.   Another orchid is a little, pretty yellow one.

But orchids, somehow, do not make a summer.   They are too aloof and individual.   The little slate-blue scabious is out, but not enough to raise an appearance.   Later on, under the real hot sun, he will bob into notice.   And by the edges of the paths there are odd rose cushions of wild thyme.   Yet these, too, are rather samples than the genuine thing.   Wait another month, for wild thyme.

The same with the irises.   Here and there, in fringes along the upper edge of terraces, and in odd bunches among the stones, the dark-purple iris sticks up.   It is beautiful, but it hardly counts.   There is not enough of it, and it is torn and buffeted by too many winds.   First the wind blows with all its might from the Mediterranean, not cold, but infinitely wearying, with its rude and insistent pushing.   Then, after a moment of calm, back comes a hard wind from the Adriatic, cold and disheartening.   Between the two of them, the dark-purple iris flutters and tatters and curls as if it were burnt: while the yellow rock-rose streams at the end of its thin stalk, and wishes it had not been in such a hurry to come out.

There is really no hurry.   By May, the great winds will drop, and the great sun will shake off his harassments.   Then the nightingale will sing an unbroken song, and the discreet, barely audible Tuscan cuckoo will be a little more audible.   Then the lovely pale-lilac irises will come out in all their showering abundance of tender, proud, spiky bloom, till the air will gleam with mauve, and a new crystalline lightness will be every-where.

The iris is half-wild, half-cultivated.   The peasants sometimes dig up the roots, iris root, orris root (orris powder, the perfume that is still used).   So, in May, you will find ledges and terraces, fields just lit up with the mauve light of irises, and so much scent in the air, you do not notice it, you do not even know it.   It is all the flowers of iris, before the olive invisibly blooms.

There will be tufts of iris everywhere, rising up proud and tender. When the rose-coloured wild gladiolus is mingled in the corn, and the love-in-the-mist opens blue: in May and June, before the corn is cut.

But as yet it is neither May nor June, but the end of April, the pause between spring and summer, the nightingale singing interruptedly, the bean-flowers dying in the bean-fields, the bean-perfume passing with spring, the little birds hatching in the nests, the olives pruned, and the vines, the last bit of late ploughing finished, and not much work to hand, now, not until the peas are ready to pick, in another two weeks or so. Then all the peasants will be crouching between the pea-rows, endlessly gathering peas, in the long pea-harvest which lasts two months.

So the change, the endless and rapid change.   In the sunny countries, the change seems more vivid, and more complete than in the grey countries. In the grey countries, there is a grey or dark permanency, over whose surface passes change ephemeral, leaving no real mark. In England, winters and summers shadowily give place to one another. But underneath lies the grey substratum, the permanency of cold, dark reality where bulbs live, and reality is bulbous, a thing of endurance and stored-up, starchy energy.

But in the sunny countries, change is the reality and permanence is artificial and a condition of imprisonment. In the North, man tends instinctively to imagine, to conceive that the sun is lighted like a candle, in an everlasting darkness, and that one day the candle will go out, the sun will be exhausted, and the everlasting dark will resume uninter-rupted sway. Hence, to the northerner, the phenomenal world is essen-tially tragical, because it is temporal and must cease to exist. Its very existence implies ceasing to exist, and this is the root of the feeling of tragedy.

But to the southerner, the sun is so dominant that, if every phenomenal body disappeared out of the universe, nothing would remain but bright luminousness, sunniness. The absolute is sunniness; and shadow, or dark, is only merely relative: merely the result of something getting between one and the sun.

This is the instinctive feeling of the ordinary southerner. Of course, if you start to *reason,* you may argue that the sun is a phenomenal body. Therefore it came into existence, therefore it will pass out of existence, therefore the very sun is tragic in its nature.

But this is just argument. We think, because we have to light a candle in the dark, therefore some First Cause had to kindle the sun in the infinite darkness of the beginning.

The argument is entirely shortsighted and specious. We do not know in the least whether the sun ever came into existence, and we have not the slightest possible ground for conjecturing that the sun will ever pass out of existence. All that we do know, by actual experience, is that shadow comes into being when some material object intervenes between us and the sun, and that shadow ceases to exist when the intervening object is removed. So that, of all temporal or transitory or bound-to-cease things that haunt our existence, shadow, or darkness, is the one which is purely and simply temporal. We can think of death, if we like, as of something permanently intervening between us and the sun: and this is at the root of the southern, under-world idea of death.

But this doesn't alter the sun at all.   As far as experience goes, in the human race, the one thing that is always there is the shining sun, and dark shadow is an accident of intervention.

Hence, strictly, there is no tragedy.   The universe contains no tragedy, and man is only tragical because he is afraid of death.   For my part, if the sun always shines, and always will shine, in spite of millions of clouds of words, then death, somehow, does not have many terrors.   In the sunshine, even death is sunny.   And there is no end to the sunshine.

That is why the rapid change of the Tuscan spring is utterly free, for me, of any sense of tragedy.   "Where are the snows of yesteryear?" Why, precisely where they ought to be.   Where are the little yellow aconites of eight weeks ago?   I neither know nor care.   They were sunny and the sun shines, and sunniness means change, and petals passing and coming.   The winter aconites sunnily came, and sunnily went.   What more?   The sun always shines.   It is our fault if we don't think so.

Lines of Inquiry

1 Lawrence's essay is called "Flowery Tuscany," but his subject evidently goes beyond the simple limits implied by that title. What is the full theme of the essay?

2 Obviously, Lawrence views the flowers of Tuscany as symbolic.   Does he appear to see the same meaning in all of them alike?   If he does, why did he bother to use so many flowers?   If he does not, what range of meanings does he appear to see in them?

3 Though the essay is formally on the flowers of Tuscany, Lawrence speaks also of English and American flowers.
a Which English and American flowers are chosen, and why?
b Why are their popular but not their botanical names given?
c In what sections of the essay are they introduced?
d What do you conclude about Lawrence's intention in using them?

4 a By what basic sequence does Lawrence unify his description of the flowers of Tuscany?   What is the emotional effect of this sequence?
b Where does the sequence end?   How do you explain the fact that the essay continues after that basic sequence has ended?

5 a How are the formal internal divisions of the essay related to Lawrence's sequence?

b What other principles of sequence can you think of, by which an essay on the flowers of Tuscany could be held together?

c Choosing one of these alternative principles, consider the effect that such a choice would have on:
  (*1*) the formal internal divisions mentioned above
  (*2*) Lawrence's voice, within the essay
  (*3*) the references within the essay to foreign flowers
  (*4*) tone

6 *a* Look at the first and last paragraphs of the essay. Do you see any relationship between them in language or in rhythm? What would happen to the essay if these paragraphs were deleted?

  b Note the number of paragraphs beginning with "and" or "yet" or "still" or "but." How do you account for the unusual prominence of these connectives? What is their effect on the reader?

7 What kinds of repetition do you find in the essay? Consider not only the obvious and continuous repetition of single words, but also the repetition of sounds, of syntactical patterns within a given paragraph, of idea, etc. How is Lawrence's heavy use of repetition connected to his theme?

8 In this essay, Lawrence describes much besides flowers.
  a How could one classify the other kinds of things that appear?
  b Why did Lawrence focus on flowers, instead of on birds?
  c Why, having decided to write about flowers—to make them his descriptive focus—did Lawrence introduce other elements into the landscape?
  d What other elements in the landscape would he have had to mention, had he been taking a complete inventory? Why are these other elements—the highways, for example —left out?

9 In the introduction to Part I, it was said that the "life" of a description depends in large part on the presence of movement.
  a What kinds of movement are there in 'Flowery Tuscany"?
  b In which sections is movement most intense?
  c In which is the essay most static?
  d Take the fourth paragraph and eliminate from it its movement: What happens?

10 Lawrence lived for some time in Tuscany. If one were to argue that Lawrence wrote about the flowers of Tuscany because he lived in Tuscany, what would you reply? What do you conclude about the relationship between the facts of a writer's life and the forms and themes of his work?

Lines of Experiment

1 Choosing a scene, city or country, with which you are very familiar, make a brief list of the kinds of important detail to be found there—e.g., flowers, cows, concrete buildings, street bums, policemen, braceros. (Recall that you must take a point of view in order to have a standard of importance.) Obviously, you will not be able to write about everything on your list; you will have to choose one class that can illustrate the importance you see in the scene. A useful way to proceed may involve: *first,* classifying the contents of that class of detail (winter flowers, spring flowers, etc.); *second,* assigning to each a value or importance, relative to the rest; *third,* arranging them in a sequence that allows that value or importance to be rendered effectively—with the most important details last, for example; *fourth,* finding a way of *connecting* them in that sequence. Do not forget, as you write, that an effective description is full of movement.

2 Take from your biology textbook or from some other simple, schematic source, a description of the life cycle of the salamander, the frog, the duck, the fish, or some other fairly simple organism. Now write a descriptive essay that attempts to make your readers (who are your readers?) feel the significance, the value, of that life cycle. On what part of the life cycle will you focus your attention? Your answer here will determine, in large part, the actual sequence into which you cast your details. What will be the key words, the key rhythmic sequences or effects, that you will try to reiterate in your essay? These words and sequences you will want to establish early (note the reiteration of "shine" in "Flowery Tuscany"). Can you employ the life cycle of some other organism, in comparison and contrast? If you decide to do this, you must introduce that other organism fairly early in your essay, and choose it carefully for the light it can shed on your real subject—not for the light it can shed on itself. You probably will do well to specify an exact species of frog, duck, fish, etc. Without doing so, you will have no opportunity to use details of color, shape, movement, and so forth, and so will cut yourself off from much of the armory of style.

3 Some descriptions describe actual things; others, typical things; still others, hypothetical things. (Lawrence's description is of typical things.) Choosing an appropriate, limited subject, plan three different descriptions of it—the first, a description of an actual thing; the second, a description of a typical thing; the third, a description of a hypothetical thing. Subjects such as the following may suggest a topic: an urban childhood day, a class in English composition, an impossible choice, an impossible date, a student election, lunch at the cafeteria, graduation, a satellite launching, a city house, a dog, a flower garden. Your final essay may follow only one of your plans, or may throw two—or even all three—into contrast. Each plan should make possible a particular tonal effect; a combination of plans should make possible a more complex tonal structure.

A. A. MILNE

 ## AN IMMORTAL
NAME

I suppose that every one of us hopes secretly for immortality; to leave, I mean, a name behind him which will live for ever in this world, whatever he may be doing, himself, in the next. There was a time when I saw myself in the happy company of Keats and Shakespeare; immortal as they; writer of deathless poetry and plays. But there were technical difficulties in the way; trifles with which I need not trouble you now. Moreover, I said to myself, "Was even Shakespeare sure? Was Keats?" And I wondered if certainty could come to any man on his death-bed that ten, fifty, a hundred years hence his name would be in the mouths of all.

So wondering, I walked one day among my flowers. And I looked at my dahlias, at the lobelia cardinalis, at the fuchsias, the rudbeckias, the camellia, the magnolia, the buddleias, all the commonplaces of the cottage garden, and I said to myself. "There is your immortality!"

For we may be sure that Dr. Lobel, who had the distinction, if it was no great pleasure, of being physician to King James the First, had already given up hope of immortality when immortality fell upon him. His new method of blood-letting brought him little comfort. His closed-window cure for diseases of the lung died with its victims. His bed-side manner might be a memory for a generation, but no longer. And then he invented the lobelia. For once his bed-side manner failed him. A lifetime of bowings and scrapings and washings of hands urged him to call it the jamesia, but the craving for immortality which works in us all was too strong for him. James was going into history anyhow; but here only was the chance of Dr. Lobel. So he called his flower the lobelia . . . and three hundred years later we are still talking of him.

Pottering round my garden with the watering-can, giving a drink here to the dahlia of M. Dahl and a drink there to the fuchsia of M. Fuchs, I have dreamed of a Milnia which the world will be watering three hun-dred years hence. Throw a stone into the sea and there is a splash, yes, and a widening ripple, but the ripple grows even fainter as it travels, and in a little while it is as if the stone had never been cast. So, it may be, with our books. How little will it mean, all that I have struggled to write, to the cottager of the twenty-second century who has decided to transplant his Milnia from the back garden to the front. "How are your Milnias doing?" they will ask each other, and I shall straighten myself proudly in my grave if they answer, "Well." For I feel that I should do well; yes, I have that feeling. Even in a north border "*Milnia grandiflora cerulia,* an interesting growth of neat habit," would do well.

Shall I ever achieve this immortality? I do not know. It should be easier, surely, to produce a new kind of flower than to produce a new kind of book. How does one begin? A nursery-gardener, called into consultation last summer, stopped in his tour of inspection and said, pointing to a group of flowers, "That's a curious sort of poppy you have there. I've never seen one like that anywhere else." I answered "No," with a faint touch of distance in my voice, as if I also had never seen one like it anywhere else, and had been compelled, there-fore, to make it for myself.

I did not make it, however. It just came; some sport of earth and air and water and sun. Perhaps this is how all the new flowers come. Dr. Lobel did not grow the lobelia out of his own head; his share in it was no more than the easy naming of an accidental bloom. He was at the bed-side of King James, during one of those small indispositions which are forced upon royalty, having brought with him the usual courtly bunch of flowers, "And what's that?" asked James, pointing to one he didn't know.   Whereupon Dr. Lobel, who had been wondering too, answered on the impulse of the moment, "The—er—lobelia, sire" . . . and the lobelia it was ever afterwards.   Alas! it is too late now to tell my nursery-gardener that the poppy he admired was *Papaver Milnia accidentalis;* yet so it should have been if I had had the readiness of Dr. Lobel.

For even to have one small shoot of the family named after us would be something; would, indeed, be much if the flower were common enough.   One often introduces a geum to the visitor without going into particulars, but one never limits oneself to the observation, "This is a rose climbing up the pergola."   Some further explanation is customary.   Is it Albertine, Carmine Pillar, or Lady Gay?

Or is it Dorothy Perkins?   She, surely, is immortal, no less than Dr. Lobel.   Perhaps she herself is still of this world.   How thrilling to shake hands with her—("Let me introduce you to Miss Perkins. Dorothy, dear—this is Mr. Milne")—and to say to her, "Are you *the* Dorothy Perkins?"   How does she feel when she walks around a garden, incognita, and hears people whispering about her?   A little *blasé* perhaps now; not as feels the author whose first book has been mentioned casually in a railway carriage, and he blushing unknown in the corner.   For there is something in one's name which seems so private to oneself that any mention of it by others brings for the moment a vague sense of discomfort, as if a liberty were threatened. But Miss Perkins has outgrown all that.   I dare say she talks to her gardener of the green-fly on the Dorothy Perkins with complete indifference now; and if you were to say to her: "Are you *the* Dorothy Perkins?" she would answer: "You mean the flower?   Yes, I was called after it."

To return to the Milnia, which we have neglected a little; I imagine it as something like Sweet William in shape and texture, but blue in colour.   Who was William, by the way?   I am jealous of him.   I doubt if he was as charming as all that.   Probably he was just William Sweet, one of two brothers living in Sussex, publicans by profession, but doing a bit of gardening in their spare time.   Having discovered this new flower, they called the June-flowering variety William, and the autumn-flowering variety, now out of fashion, John.   Sweet (William) survives, and is thus written by the pedantic.   Let us be grateful to him that we don't have to call it the Sweetia.

Which reminds me of the hard case of Professor Magnol, the only begetter of that beautiful tree, the magnolia. All his life Professor Magnol was irritated by two sorts of stupid people; those who mistakenly credited him with the invention of the magnol-wurzel, and those (like you and me) who thought that the magnolia was so called because it had a very large and magnificent flower. In a sense he is immortal, or will be when I have finished writing about him, but he has missed some of the rapture of it in the last two hundred years. Possibly he was a bad man, and this is his punishment. Each time you have looked admiringly at a friend's magnolia, his ghost has been there at your elbow, reading the thought in your mind, gnashing, as it were its teeth at your stupidity. "What a lovely large flower," you have thought; "no wonder they call it the magnolia"—and at that moment you have felt a faint cold breath at the back of your neck, and have shivered, and told yourself that already there was a touch of autumn in the air. You are wrong. It was the ghost of Professor Magnol hissing at you.

Lines of Inquiry

1 Man's longing for immortality expresses itself in religious ritual and belief, in literature, in patriotism, in family life, and in most things that we care about.

  a Why does Milne choose to focus on the immortality conferred by flowers on their discoverers?

  b How would you describe the tone that results?

  c What would happen to that tone had Milne focused instead on the immortality conferred by their actions upon

    (*1*) Founders of international religions

    (*2*) Discoverers of mountains

    (*3*) Inventors of gadgets

    (*4*) Politically important figures

2 In his second paragraph, Milne lists a number of specific flowers.

  a On what basis has he selected them?

  b How is this list reflected in the structure of the essay?

  c He does not list the rose—considering that he speaks later of roses, how do you explain this omission?

3 *a* Milne's anecdote of Dr. Lobel's lobelia, is broken in two—by what?

  b How are the two parts of the anecdote related, i.e., is the second part of the anecdote a continuation or a rephrasing of the first part?

  c Could the first part of the anecdote have followed the second without changing the effect of the anecdote? How do you account for the actual sequence?

4 In the first sentence, Milne refers to Shakespeare and Keats. How do you account for this reference? What does it contribute to the essay's tone? (If you have difficulty in answering this question, read a brief biographical sketch of each of these poets. What is their rank among English poets? How does each appear to have felt about his art, as route to immortality? Considered as illustrations of Milne's point, how would you classify them?)

5 The subject and theme of Milne's essay are somewhat like those of Lawrence's "Flowery Tuscany" (page 523)—yet the total effect of the two essays could hardly be more different. How do you account for these differences? (If you are at a loss, examine the first paragraphs of each essay. From what point of view is each written? In what voice? With what specific focus? Given Milne's focus, what would be the probable effect were he to attempt to discuss immortality with Lawrence's passionate intensity of tone?)

6 Milne suggests two flower names incorporating his own: *Milnia grandiflora cerulia* and *Papaver milnia accidentalis*. Why does he choose these specific names? (Suggestions: Look up "cerulean" in the dictionary, and reread the first sentence of the essay. Now what about "accidentalis"?)

7 Explain the tonal function of the following passages in their context. (If you are at a loss, subtract them from their context and view the result.)
  a "For once his bed-side manner failed him."
  b "For I feel that I should do well; yes, I have that feeling."
  c "I answered, 'No,' with a faint touch of distance in my voice. . . ."
  d "To return to the Milnia, which we have neglected a little. . . ."
  e "In a sense he [Magnol] is an immortal, or will be when I have finished writing about him, but he has missed some of the rapture of it in the last two hundred years."
  f ". . . at that moment you have felt a faint cold breath at the back of your neck, and have shivered, and told yourself that already there was a touch of autumn in the air."

8 a What is the characteristic device by which Milne links his paragraphs together in this essay? How is his linking system related to his point of view and tone?
  b Examine the introduction and conclusion; are they related in any way? How does the conclusion's slight shift in tone affect the entire essay?

Lines of Experiment

1 One point of Milne's essay might be put this way: Generally we are remembered, if at all, as a result of some happy or unhappy accident. Illustrations of this fact are easy to come by in our own experience. Why do some people stick in our memories, and others not? You will easily find examples from school life, local politics, sports, etc. In writing an essay on such a topic, you will find it useful to stick close to a subject matter you are thoroughly familiar with (Milne knew his flowers well). You need not agree with Milne's point, of course. You may choose to contrast the deserved fame resulting from one kind of activity with the accidental fame resulting from another. You may go further, indeed, and consider whether or not there is a real difference between the purposed and the accidental—could Shakespeare's fame be described as in any sense "accidental"? Such an essay would turn more explicitly on definition, of course, and less on narration; why?

2 The comic tone of Milne's essay arises in part from the incongruity between the sublime human wish for immortality and the trivial means by which that wish appears sometimes to be satisfied. Incongruity of some sort seems at the bottom of most comedies. A stately, top-hatted man slips on a banana peel, falls in mud, and we laugh. Our laughter is a comment on the value of a particular, formal kind of dignity.

Take a theme of some importance, e.g., love, patriotism, justice, and consider how you might write a comic essay on that theme by exploiting such incongruities. You will probably achieve the comic focus best by restricting yourself to a few illustrative anecdotes. For example, one might open an essay on love by describing the tragic passion between Tristan and Isolde, and go on to point out how shatteringly short of the sublime one's own love relationships had fallen—how, at the moment of sublimest passion, a stray dog somehow always seems to wander up.

3 Comic essays are not always gentle, and not always even funny. The essence of comedy is the contrast between the world as it is and the world as it ought to be, with the emphasis falling on the world as it is. At times, these contrasts are more painful than amusing. The comic tone thus conceals frequently a profound bitterness over the state of the world. Voltaire's Dr. Pangloss, dying of syphilis, mumbles through rotten lips his perennial "Everything is for the best in the best of all possible worlds." We may smile, but we also wince.

The best comedy has this double nature. The comic situation offered us by the assembly-line slave who defends the factory system; by the superpatriot who in the name of morality murders hundreds of innocent people; by the state that in the name of individual rights permits the old, the poor, and the unfortunate to starve, or that in the name of educational excellence herds its racial minorities into second- and third-class schools—such subjects offer the serious writer of comedy rare opportunities. There are so many subjects of this kind in the world that you should have little trouble in finding one to your taste.

CHARLES LAMB

 WITCHES, AND OTHER NIGHT FEARS

We are too hasty when we set down our ancestors in the gross for fools, for the monstrous inconsistencies (as they seem to us) involved in their creed of witchcraft. In the relations of this visible world we find them to have been as rational and shrewd to detect an historic anomaly as ourselves. But when once the invisible world was supposed to be opened, and the lawless agency of bad spirits assumed, what measures of probability, of decency, of fitness, or proportion—of that which distinguishes the likely from the palpable absurd—could they have to guide them in the rejection or admission of any particular testimony? That maidens pined away, wasting inwardly as their waxen images consumed before a fire—that corn was lodged, and cattle lamed —that whirlwinds uptore in diabolic revelry the oaks of the forests— or that spits and kettles only danced a fearful innocent vagary about some rustic's kitchen when no wind was stirring,—were all equally probable where no law of agency was understood. That the prince of the powers of darkness, passing by the flower and pomp of the earth, should lay preposterous siege to the weak fantasy of indigent eld—has neither likelihood nor unlikelihood *à priori* to us, who have no measure to guess at his policy, or standard to estimate what rate those anile souls may fetch in the devil's market. Nor, when the wicked are expressly symbolized by a goat, was it to be wondered at so much, that *he* should come sometimes in that body and assert his metaphor. That the intercourse was opened at all between both worlds, was perhaps the mistake,—but that once assumed, I see no reason for disbelieving one attested story of this nature more than another on the score of absurdity. There is no law to judge of the lawless, or canon by which a dream may be criticised.

I have sometimes thought that I could not have existed in the days of received witchcraft; that I could not have slept in a village where one of those reputed hags dwelt. Our ancestors were bolder or more obtuse. Amidst the universal belief that these wretches were in league with the author of all evil, holding hell tributary to their muttering, no simple Justice of the Peace seems to have scrupled issuing, or silly Headborough serving, a warrant upon them,—as if they should subpœna Satan! Prospero in his boat, with his books and wand about him, suffers himself to be conveyed away at the mercy of his enemies to an unknown island. He might have raised a storm or two, we think, on the passage. His acquiescence is in exact analogy to the non-resistance of witches to the constituted powers. What stops the Fiend in Spenser from tearing Guyon to pieces,—or who had made it a condition of his prey, that Guyon must take assay of the glorious bait,—we have no guess. We do not know the laws of that country.

From my childhood I was extremely inquisitive about witches and witch-stories. My maid, and more legendary aunt, supplied me with good store. But I shall mention the accident which directed my curiosity originally into this channel. In my father's book-closet, the "History of the Bible" by Stackhouse occupied a distinguished station. The pictures with which it abounds—one of the ark, in particular, and another of Solomon's temple, delineated with all the fidelity of ocular admeasurement, as if the artist had been upon the spot—attracted my childish attention. There was a picture, too, of the Witch raising up Samuel, which I wish that I had never seen. We shall come to that hereafter. Stackhouse is in two huge tomes,—and there was a pleasure in removing folios of that magnitude, which, with infinite straining, was as much as I could manage, from the situation which they occupied upon an upper shelf. I have not met with the work from that time to this, but I remember it consisted of Old Testament stories, orderly set down, with the *objection* appended to each story, and the *solution* of the objection regularly tacked to that. The *objection* was a summary of whatever difficulties had been opposed to the credibility of the history, by the shrewdness of ancient or modern infidelity, drawn up with an almost complimentary excess of candor. The *solution* was brief, modest, and satisfactory. The bane and antidote were both before you. To doubts so put, and so quashed, there seemed to be an end forever. The dragon lay dead, for the foot of the veriest babe to trample on. But—like as was rather feared than realized from that slain monster in Spenser—from the womb of those crushed errors young dragonets would creep, exceeding the prowess of so tender a Saint George as myself to vanquish. The habit of expecting objections to every passage, set me upon starting more objections, for the glory of finding a solution of my own for them. I became staggered and perplexed, a skeptic in long coats. The pretty Bible stories which I had read, or heard read in church, lost their purity and sincerity of impression, and were turned into so many historic or chronologic theses to be defended against whatever impugners. I was not to disbelieve them, but—the next thing to that—I was to be quite sure that some one or other would or had disbelieved them. Next to making a child an infidel, is the letting him know that there are infidels at all. Credulity is the man's weakness, but the child's strength. O how ugly sound scriptural doubts from the mouth of a babe and a suckling!—I should have lost myself in these mazes, and have pined away, I think, with such unfit sustenance as these husks afforded, but for a fortunate piece of ill-fortune, which about this time befell me. Turning over the picture of the ark with too much haste, I unhappily made a breach in its ingenious fabric,—driving my inconsiderate fingers right through the two larger quadrupeds,—the elephant, and the camel,—that stare (as well they might) out of the last two windows next the steerage in that unique piece of naval architecture. Stackhouse was henceforth locked up, and became an interdicted treasure. With the book, the *objections* and *solutions* gradually cleared out of my head, and have seldom returned since in any force to trouble me. But there was one impression which I had imbibed from Stackhouse, which no lock or bar could shut out, and which was destined to try my childish nerves rather more seriously. That detestable picture!

I was dreadfully alive to nervous terrors. The nighttime, solitude, and the dark, were my hell. The sufferings I endured in this nature would justify the expression. I never laid my head on my pillow, I suppose, from the fourth to the seventh or eighth year of my life—so far as memory serves in things so long ago—without an assurance, which realized its own prophecy, of seeing some frightful spectre. Be old Stackhouse then acquitted in part, if I say, that to his picture of the Witch raising up Samuel—(O that old man covered with a mantle!)—I owe—not my midnight terrors, the hell of my infancy—but the shape and manner of their visitation. It was he who dressed up for me a hag that nightly sat upon my pillow,—a sure bed-fellow, when my aunt or my maid was far from me. All day long, while the book was permitted me, I dreamed waking over his delineation, and at night (if I may use so bold an expression) awoke into sleep, and found the vision true. I durst not, even in the daylight, once enter the chamber where I slept, without my face turned to the window, aversly from the bed where my witchridden pillow was. Parents do not know what they do when they leave tender babes alone to go to sleep in the dark. The feeling about for a friendly arm—the hoping for a familiar voice—when they wake screaming—and find none to soothe them,—what a terrible shaking it is to their poor nerves! The keeping them up till midnight, through candlelight and the unwholesome hours, as they are called,— would, I am satisfied, in a medical point of view, prove the better caution. That detestable picture, as I have said, gave the fashion to my dreams,—if dreams they were,—for the scene of them was in- variably the room in which I lay. Had I never met with the picture, the fears would have come self-pictured in some shape or other,—

Headless bear, black man, or ape,—

but, as it was, my imaginations took that form. It is not book, or pic- ture, or the stories of foolish servants which create these terrors in children. They can at most but give them a direction. Dear little T. H., who of all children has been brought up with the most scrupulous exclusion of every taint of superstition—who was never allowed to hear of goblin or apparition, or scarcely to be told of bad men, or to read or hear of any distressing story,—finds all this world of fear, from which he has been so rigidly excluded *ab extra,* in his own "thick-coming fancies"; and from his little midnight pillow, this nurse-child of optimism will start at shapes, unborrowed of tradition, in sweats to which the reveries of the cell-damned murdered are tranquillity.

Gorgons, and Hydras, and Chimeras dire—stories of Calæno and the Harpies—may reproduce themselves in the brain of superstition,—but they were there before. They are transcripts, types,—the archetypes are in us, and eternal. How else should the recital of that, which we know in a waking sense to be false, come to affect us at all?—or

> Names, whose sense we see not,
> Fray us with things that be not?

Is it that we naturally conceive terror from such objects, considered in their capacity of being able to inflict upon us bodily injury? O, least of all! These terrors are of older standing. They date beyond body, —or, without the body they would have been the same. All the cruel, tormenting, defined devils in Dante,—tearing, mangling, choking, stifling, scorching demons,—are they one half so fearful to the spirit of a man as the simple idea of a spirit unembodied following him—

> Like one that on a lonesome road
> Doth walk in fear and dread,
> And having once turn'd round, walks on
> And turns no more his head;
> Because he knows a frightful fiend
> Doth close behind him tread.[1]

That the kind of fear here treated of is purely spiritual,—that it is strong in proportion as it is objectless upon earth,—that it predominates in the period of sinless infancy,—are difficulties the solution of which might afford some probable insight into our antemundane condition, and a peep at least into the shadowland of preëxistence.

My night fancies have long ceased to be afflictive. I confess an occasional nightmare; but I do not, as in early youth, keep a stud of them. Fiendish faces, with the extinguished taper, will come and look at me; but I know them for mockeries, even while I cannot elude their presence, and I fight and grapple with them. For the credit of my imagination, I am almost ashamed to say how tame and prosaic my dreams are grown. They are never romantic, seldom even rural. They are of architecture and of buildings,—cities abroad, which I have never seen and hardly have hoped to see. I have traversed, for the seeming length of a natural day, Rome, Amsterdam, Paris, Lisbon— their churches, palaces, squares, marketplaces, shops, suburbs, ruins, with an inexpressible sense of delight—a map-like distinctness of trace —and a daylight vividness of vision, that was all but being awake. I have formerly travelled among the Westmoreland fells, my highest Alps,—but they are objects too mighty for the grasp of my dreaming recognition; and I have again and again awoke with ineffectual struggles of the inner eye, to make out a shape in any way whatever, of Hel-vellyn. Methought I was in that country, but the mountains were

[1] Mr. Coleridge's *Ancient Mariner*.

gone. The poverty of my dreams mortifies me. There is Coleridge, at his will can conjure up icy domes, and Pleasure-houses for Kubla Kahn, and Abyssinian maids, and songs of Abara, and caverns,

Where Alph, the sacred river, runs,

to solace his night solitudes,—when I cannot muster a fiddle. Barry Cornwall has his tritons and his nereids gambolling before him in nocturnal visions, and proclaiming sons born to Neptune,—when my stretch of imaginative activity can hardly, in the night season, raise up the ghost of a fishwife. To set my failures in somewhat a mortifying light,—it was after reading the noble Dream of this poet, that my fancy ran strong upon these marine spectra: and the poor plastic power, such as it is, within me set to work, to humor my folly in a sort of dream that very night. Methought I was upon the ocean billows at some sea nuptials, riding and mounted high, with the customary train sounding their conchs before me, (I myself, you may be sure, the *leading god,*) and jollily we went careering over the main, till just where Ino Leucothea should have greeted me (I think it was Ino) with a white embrace, the billows gradually subsiding, fell from a sea-roughness to a sea-calm, and thence to a river motion, and that river (as happens in the familiarization of dreams) was no other than the gentle Thames, which landed me in the wafture of a placid wave or two, alone, safe, and inglorious, somewhere at the foot of Lambeth palace.

The degree of the soul's creativeness in sleep might furnish no whimsical criterion of the quantum of poetical faculty resident in the same soul waking. An old gentleman, a friend of mine, and a humorist, used to carry this notion so far, that when he saw any stripling of his acquaintance ambitious of becoming a poet, his first question would be, —"Young man, what sort of dreams have you?" I have so much faith in my old friend's theory, that when I feel that idle vein returning upon me, I presently subside into my proper element of prose, remembering those eluding nereids, and that inauspicious inland landing.

Lines of Inquiry

1 Outline Lamb's essay in as brief a form as you can by means of a list of its essential statements.

   a Where in each paragraph do you usually find its essential statement?

   b You will find a point of separation, a kind of apex dividing the slopes of the essay; where does this point of separation occur?

c How would you describe the central idea of the second section? How is that idea related to the point of the first?

d Could Lamb have reversed the sequence of these two sections —begun with what is now the concluding part of the essay and ended with what is now its beginning—without changing its point? What pattern of emphasis would have resulted had he done so? What do you conclude about the relative importance of beginnings and endings?

e Is the essay as a whole really only about witches and night fears? How would you describe its central idea?

2 Here are four hypotheses that might account for Lamb's writing an essay about witchcraft, fanciful monsters, etc.

a He wrote it for money.

b He wrote it because he liked writing essays.

c He wrote it because as a child he had had bad dreams.

d He wrote it because the subject seemed significant to him. Are these purposes mutually exclusive? Which best explains Lamb's writing this essay *in particular?*

3 Lamb employs allusion frequently in this essay. Within what general category do most of his allusions fall? (Suggestion: Consider the closing paragraphs.)

4 Look at the opening sentence of each paragraph in this essay.

a From your study what do you conclude about the function of "voice" in this essay?

b If that voice were changed—if Lamb were to speak impersonally—what would happen to the form and focus of the essay? Could it exist substantially as it does?

c Imagine an essay on nightmares, and so forth, written from one of the following external points of view. In what respects would the essays resulting differ from Lamb's?

(1) The psychologist's point of view

(2) The minister's point of view

(3) The folklorist's point of view

5 Lamb's subject is very large and, in a sense, amorphous. He easily could have rambled from witch to witch, from nightmare to nightmare.

a How does he bring this subject into focus? (What is the illustrative center by means of which Lamb brings his subject into focus?)

b How would you classify this central anecdote, considered as illustration?

c Read the essay as if the third paragraph began it, as if the first and second paragraphs followed the third instead of preceding it. What happens to the tone of the essay? What happens to its focus?

d Considering this transposition, do you judge the dominant order of the essay as Lamb wrote it to be deductive or inductive? How do you explain Lamb's practice in this respect?

6 What is the meaning of the following passages?

a "Nor, when the wicked are expressly symbolized by a goat, was it to be wondered at so much, that *he* should come sometimes in that body and assert his metaphor."

b "There is no law to judge of the lawless, or canon by which a dream can be criticised."

c "I confess an occasional nightmare; but I do not, as in early youth, keep a stud of them."

d "The degree of the soul's creativeness in sleep might furnish no whimsical criterion of the quantum of poetical faculty resident in the same soul waking."

7 Analyze the tone of the following passages. How is the tone of each established?

a "That maidens pined away, wasting inwardly as their waxen images consumed before a fire—that corn was lodged, and cattle lamed—that whirlwinds uptore in diabolic revelry the oaks of the forests—or that spits and kettles only danced a fearful innocent vagary about some rustic's kitchen when no wind was stirring—were all equally probable where no law of agency was understood."

b "Turning over the picture of the ark with too much haste, I unhappily made a breach in its ingenious fabric—driving my inconsiderate fingers right through the two larger quadrupeds—the elephant and the camel—that stare (as well they might) out of the last two windows next to the steerage in that unique piece of naval architecture."

c "Be old Stackhouse then aquitted in part, if I say, that to his picture of the Witch raising up Samuel—(O that old man covered with a mantle!)—I owe—not my midnight terrors, the hell of my infancy—but the shape and manner of their visitation."

d "Methought I was upon the ocean billows at some sea nuptials, riding and mounted high, with the customary train sounding their conchs before me, (I myself, you may be sure, the *leading god,*) and jollily we went careering over the main, till just where Ino Leucothea should have greeted me

(I think it was Ino) with a white embrace, the billows gradually subsiding, fell from a sea-roughness to a sea-calm, and thence to a river motion, and that river (as happens in the familiarization of dreams) was no other than the gentle Thames, which landed me in the wafture of a placid wave or two, alone, safe, and inglorious, somewhere at the foot of Lambeth palace."

e "I have so much faith in my old friend's theory, that when I feel that idle vein returning upon me, I presently subside into my proper element of prose, remembering those eluding nereids, and that inauspicious inland landing."

8 Lamb assumes that his readers will recognize various references. How many of the following can you identify?

a "The Prince of the Powers of Darkness"	e Gorgons, Hydras, Chimeras, Harpies
b Prospero	f Kubla Kahn
c Spenser	g Neptune
d "The Witch raising up Samuel"	h Nereids

Lines of Experiment

1 Stealing shamelessly from Lamb if you wish, write an essay about dreams, nightmares, or fantasies. (They need not necessarily be your own, though you may draw on your own inner life for material if you wish.)

In working out such a composition, you will have to consider first the point of view from which you wish to approach your subject. The psychologist, the artist, the businessman, and the politician see such matters from different angles. Second, given the point of view you adopt, you will have to fit to it either a relatively personal or a relatively impersonal voice. Each voice creates a different distance from the subject, a different style of transition between one idea and another, a different mixture of the forms of discourse. Third, you must find a clear focus, an illustrative center, that will help you to make economically the point you wish to make. Because the significance of dreams and fantasies is in large part emotional, you must be especially careful to work for a tone appropriate to your point of view and your intention. After you have finished a satisfactory draft, read it aloud; where you find your voice stumbling or hesitating, you probably should revise. Listen to the "melody" of your clauses and sentences: Make your tone an echo of your sense.

2 From one point of view Lamb appears to be decrying night-

mares; from another, he appears to regret that he now dreams only of cities—as if the "Gorgons, and Hydras, and Chimeras dire" might possibly have had some value after all. Think of a parallel case, of something thoroughly uncomfortable, unpleasant, apparently destructive, that proves on later reflection to have had some value. (Suggestions: a course of study, a tour of duty overseas, a year at a private school, loafing, a fist fight, a summer vacation, a childhood enmity, a financial catastrophe, a bully's persecution.) Take this curious opposition of good and bad within your subject as the material for an essay. Decide what was unpleasant about it, and what pleasant; choose a vivid illustrative center for its unpleasant side, and another for its pleasant side; find a way of introducing your subject, and a device for following it through to a conclusion.

3 Work toward the subject of an essay by considering fantasy from an analytic point of view. You need not write about your own experience, but you can use it as material for analysis —for discovering what fantasy means. Can you find a way of classifying the ordinary human fantasies—into fantasies of success and of failure, for example; or into love fantasies, hate fantasies, revenge fantasies; or into political fantasies and social fantasies; retrospective fantasies and prophetic fantasies; daytime fantasies and nighttime fantasies; or whatever? Have you any clue as to what in the external world sets off a particular train of fantasy? Can you find any patterns by which one fantasy develops into another?

To such large questions you may not find fully satisfactory answers. But any one of them can lead to a good subject for the essayist, for the study of fantasies can tell us much about our real wishes and fears, the dangers thrust on us by the world in which we live, and the basic patterns of our psychological, emotional, and moral life.

ROBERT GRAVES

THE DEVIL
IS A
PROTESTANT

As a child in London I was once covertly taken to High Mass by a nursemaid who had hitherto pretended to be Church of England. When my parents got wind of it they dismissed her on the spot and persuaded me that I had been given a foretaste of Hell. No, this is not a psychological short story: I cannot pretend that I became a secret Papist, intoxicated by the incense, the music, the antique ritual, and wept disconsolate for the wronged nursemaid; and that, by contrast, the matins celebrated next Sunday in our redbrick Evangelical church appeared inexpressibly drab and soulless. The truth is that what my parents disrespectfully called "the mumbojumbo of Romanism" had so dismayed and repelled me that I would have been quite willing to accept their interpretation of my experience as correct, even if I had not regarded the nursemaid as a thoroughly unprincipled person; and that a cradle-Protestant, even if he turns atheist or becomes converted to the elder faith, remains temperamentally a cradle-Protestant, however hard he may try to extirpate the heresy. Incense for me will always smell of brimstone; and this I heartily regret.

I am of course long acclimatized to the Catholic atmosphere; so much that, when the U.S. aircraft carrier *Midway* put in at Palma the other day and I was invited by the local Spanish-Protestant parson, who lives a hole-and-corner life in a suburban catacomb, to interpret the sermons —Spanish-English, English-Spanish—at a "Reunion of Solidarity" there with the *Midway's* chaplain and choir, the un-Latin atmosphere dismayed and repelled me. Ah, the pitchpine pews, the puritanical communion-table, the plain brass cross, the wheezy harmonium (operated by a fish-like U.S. mess-steward), the dusty, turkey-red Protestant hassocks and the tattered copies of *Hymns Ancient and Modern!*

Nevertheless, to be acclimatized is not to be indoctrinated. On my way home I paused outside a Catholic repository and gazed thoughtfully at a St Lucia wearing a crown of candles and carrying two glass eyes on a tray. St Lucia, who celebrates her feast on the shortest and dimmest day of the year (Old Style), helps Mallorquin girls embroider roses and palms and pansies on table linen for tourists, at two pesetas an hour. The heathen blinded her at Syracuse in the year 97 A.D., which made her the patron saint of needlewomen and gave her the power to cure ophthalmic distempers by the use of "St Lucia's eyes." These are small discs of nacre about the size of a little finger-nail, with a brown eye on one side and a spiral on the other: the artifact of a clever seasnail. In Australia, of course, the eyes are blue, as one might expect in a continent that produces black swans, and where one eats plum-pudding at Midsummer, and the water goes widdershins down the waste-pipe when one empties the bath-tub. Lucia is a hard-working saint, like St Ivo, the only lawyer who was not a thief: *Advocatus sed non latrunculus*—emblems: a quill-pen, a briefcase, and a Madonna lily. Or St Isidore, who to dig is not ashamed. Or Santa Rita, patroness of impossible wishes. Or St Fiacre, who designs the optimistic flower pictures on seed-packets and makes the seeds actually grow to sample. Or St Piran, who came drifting from Ireland on a mill-stone, accompanied by his acolyte, a girl in disguise; landed at Zabulo in Cornwall; praised God; kindled a fire, banking it up with some lumps of ore, and lo! discovered tin. Or St Benedict, who helps weary-footed house-hunters; they have only to vow him a candle, throw a stone into the garden or area of the house they most want, and it will be vacant before the next quarter-day, sure as death.

To such saints a cradle-Protestant extends a certain humorous in-dulgence, Protestantism laying heavy emphasis on the social services; and this evening I felt warmly disposed towards the entire Catholic calendar, by way of protest against Anglophile Mallorquins who sing *Onward, Christian Soldiers!* in Spanish to a harmonium, and disregard even red-letter saints. But after a while I found myself thinking despitefully of crossgrained anchorites, who lived in remote caves, like the egregious St Rule of Kylbrimont, or on the tops of pillars sixty feet high, like St Simon Stylites. Could I ever learn to love or honour these? St Simon kept himself from a tumble not by faith, but by wear-ing an iron dog-collar chained to a wooden pulpit which he also used as a desk for writing unpleasant letters to the Byzantine Emperor; and stood fast thirty-six years. And St Simon Stylites Junior spent nearly seventy years on another pillar, having cut his double-teeth up there . . .

The Catholics have a patron saint for everyone, I reflected idly.   St Simon Stylites for steeplejacks, no doubt.   St Clement for capmakers— he made the first felt-block.   St Crispin for cobblers.   St Dismas for cutpurses.   St Barbara for cannoneers.   St Joseph for carpenters, cuckolds and crosspatches.   The Spaniards call anyone they dislike a *tio,* meaning an uncle, meaning a crosspatch uncle, meaning specifically the Virgin's crosspatch uncle and husband, Tio Pepe, or St Joseph. According to the gospel of *Pseudo-Matthew* (once canonical), St Joseph refused to humour the Virgin, who had a *pica* for cherries, declaring that the child in her womb was none of his.   "And Joseph made answer in accent most wild: 'I *will* pluck no cherries to give to thy child!' " Every Mallorquin knows that to refuse a woman with a *pica,* however illegitimate, is tantamount to child murder: a pregnant woman can wander around the market from stall to stall eating whatever fruit is in season, a cherry here, a strawberry there, an apricot, a peach, and nobody will dare deny her for fear of being called a *tio.*   (Joseph Bonaparte being one of the least popular Kings of Spain, his subjects called him "Tio Pepe," but acknowledged that he had a good taste in dry sherry.)   Cap-makers, cobblers, cutpurses, cannoneers, carpenters, cuckolds and crosspatches!   And, of course, St Mary Gipsy for courtesans.   St Mary Gipsy felt impelled one day to go on a pilgrimage to the Holy Land.   But the crew of the only ship bound for Acre warned her that she must pay her fare by sleeping with all of them in turn throughout the voyage.   She accordingly made the supreme sacrifice, spending the rest of her life in penitence and good works, and was eventually passed into Heaven by St Peter on the ground that "she loved much."

Am I sneering again? Forgive me.   I did not intend to sneer.   It is the Devil's fault.   Let me explain my mood by a brief historical review of Heaven and its celestial population; for a Protestant conscience, which has outlasted my acceptance of the Thirty-nine Articles, will keep me from deliberately misinforming you.

Ezekiel, the first Evangelist, marked a number of Israelites with the *tau*-cross as a sign of redemption, so that by God's mercy they should be taken up into Heaven and become glorified; and though a remote pagan origin can be claimed for the Essenes' Western Apple Orchard which Josephus described pleasantly in his *Antiquities of the Jews,* Ezekiel's glittering vision of God's Throne and Temple is the earliest in sacred literature.   The authors of *Daniel* and the horrific *Book of Enoch* elaborated this picture, and when speculation arose in the late pre-Christian era about the nature of the celestials, and the extent of their interest in mankind, learned Pharisee doctors made a series of *ex cathedra* pronouncements. They ruled that the Recording Angel Metatron, Elias the Prophet who had ascended alive into Heaven, a few Seraphim messengers, and the seven planetary Archangels were those most active on behalf of mortals. The Archangels had been organized according to the seven days of Creation. Raphael was required to supervise Sunday (Illumination and Hygiene); Gabriel, Monday (Doom and Water Supplies); Sammael, Tuesday (Defence and Agriculture); Michael, Wednesday (Education and the Sciences); Izidkiel, Thursday (Justice and Fisheries); Hanael, Friday (Amatory and Social Relations); Kepharel, Saturday (Recreation and Hospitality). The Patriarchs, though still alive, remained comatose, the Heavenly Choir never ceased from alleluias, and the Four Beasts contented themselves with wide-eyed meditation. This was the orderly Heaven accepted by the Primitive Church at Jerusalem.

However, the Gentile Christian authorities of the second and third centuries began to reorganize Heaven on pagan lines. Each of the Olympian gods and Titans had been exceedingly jealous of his or her *timē, moira, lachos or cleros*—meaning honour, function, task, birthright, sole prerogative. Helius's function was to drive his fiery team once a day across the heavens. Hephaestus presided over forges, ovens, and all fires, except the hearth-fire, which was Hestia's. Atlas held up the sky. Hermes conducted souls to Heaven, and Hades enjoyed the sole prerogative of receiving them. Athene's many functions included weaving, and one day (so Hesiod reports) catching Aphrodite at work on a loom, she flew into a rage. "Your tasks are love-making and cosmetics," she shouted. "You have infringed my *cleros!* All right, then, keep it and be damned; but nobody will ever find me doing a hand's turn on a loom again!" The early Fathers scorned the gods and dared deny that they existed; nevertheless for fear of causing an awkward religious vacuum, they invited the souls of defunct prophets, apostles, bishops, virgins and martyrs to take over these Olympian functions. Thus John the Baptist, who had been described as a "burning and a shining light," supplanted Helius; John was Elias, and Elias had ascended to Heaven in a fiery chariot, and "Elias" sounds like "Helius." St Lucia of Syracuse supplanted Artemis Lucia— Wolfish Artemis: she could see in the dark and was a goddess of healing. St Nicolas, whose feast introduced the mid-December Halcyon

Days (Old Style), took over the temples and functions of Poseidon; this was his reward for boxing the ears of Arius, the originator of the Arian Heresy, at the Great Council of Nicaea.   St Elmo (May 10), martyred at the naval base of Puteoli, replaced Castor and Pollux, to whom sailors had formerly appealed during storms at sea.   The Nine Muses were ousted by the Holy Trinity.   Hercules, the Porter of Heaven, yielded to St Peter . . .

In the scramble for Olympian functions, distribution seems sometimes to have been made at haphazard; but there was always a certain divine logic at work.   For instance, one would have expected the patronage of bell-founders to have gone to one of the Typasas martyrs, whose tongues were cut out by Hunneric the Vandal when they refused to become Arians, and whose praise of God nevertheless continued to ring sweetly and articulately in the streets of Constantinople—Aeneas of Gaza the philosopher, Marcellinus, Procopius and Victor Tunnensis, three reputable historians, and Pope Gregory the Great, all witnessed this miracle.   Similarly one would have expected the patronage of pastry-cooks to be taken over by some such anchorite as Julian of Edessa (June 9), or Julian of Osroene (October 18), as a reward for subsisting, year in, year out, on coarse grass and water from pools fouled by the stale of camels; though tempted every night with Apician visions of puff-pastry, quince conserve and cream-cracknels.   But no, the saint of both bellfounders and pastry-cooks is St Agatha, martyred under Decius, whose persecutors hacked off her breasts and rolled her naked over live coals mixed with potsherds.   Saints, as is well known, bear little emblems as distinguishing marks: St Lawrence, a grid-iron; St Francis of the Tailors, a pair of shears; St Catalina Tomás (a peasant girl who was baptized in our parish church, and whose kitchensink I bought when her cottage was pulled down) a cone of figbread—and St Agatha of Catania, her two undraped breasts set side by side on a tray.   The embarrassing objects have been claimed as bells by the bellfounders and as sugar-cakes topped with cherries by the pastry-cooks, but only because St Agatha is patroness of furnaces and because both bell-founders and pastry-cooks need to manage theirs with exceptional care.   St Agatha's veil is carried in procession at Catania whenever Mount Etna is erupting and her "letters" are a sure charm against burns. She has, in fact, been awarded the *cleros* of Hephaestus, whose sons, the Cyclopes, used to work his Etna furnace.

Each pagan city or small town had kept a local deity or hero as a focus for its religious emotions, and Christian saints were called upon to fill these vacancies too, unless the former occupant cared to turn Christian, as did the goddess Brigit of Kildare, or the Blue Hag Annis of Leicester, or in the wilder parts of Italy, the gods Mercury and Venus. The chief difference between the saints and their pagan predecessors lay in the offerings they demanded—lighted candles instead of warm sacrificial blood, flowers instead of chopped fruit, wine and pearl-barley. Such well-tried phenomena as sweating and bleeding images, daylight visions, and miraculous interventions against drought and plague continued. Moreover, *ex voto* objects representing divinely healed parts of the human body, and the mass-produced figurines and religious charms which the Romans had exported all over the known world remained in continuous use. The *Apocalypse of St John the Divine* did, indeed, perpetuate the Jewish ban on the sea as the corrupt home of the Sea-goddess Rahab, and the Assyrio-Phoenician architecture and furnishings of the Judgement Hall were not altered; but the atmosphere of Heaven became unmistakably Graeco-Roman, and no Archangel preserved his original *cleros*. Michael and Gabriel escaped relegation to Sheol only because they happened to figure in the New Testament as, respectively, Commander-in-Chief of the Forces and Announcer—Gabriel has even been appointed official patron of television. And Raphael, now for the most part invoked to accompany travellers on lonesome journeys, owes his survival to the strong fascination that the *Book of Tobit* exercised on mediaeval church painters. The four other Archangels are forgotten.

According to cradle-Catholic gossip, to which I lend a fascinated ear, there is as much jealousy in Heaven as there ever was on Olympus. Peter and Paul are said to bicker for precedence on their common saint's day no less passionately than did Athene and Poseidon for the possession of Troezen or the Athenian Acropolis; and even the patronage of syphilis is disputed—St Christopher brought the disease to Naples from America, but St Denis claims it as the "French pox." Namesakes are said to be a constant source of trouble, SS. William of the Desert and William of Norwich accuse each other of sheep-stealing; and though John the Baptist and John the Evangelist continue to exchange beatific smiles, the Baptist scornfully rejects all Evangelical Jacks and Johnnies—"No sheep of mine," he growls; and quotes *Luke* i, 6: *"Not so: for he shall be called John."*

As for the Anthony's . . . A mason working on the roof of Palma

Cathedral once slipped from a scaffold and, as he fell, shouted "Help, St Anthony!" An invisible hand arrested him in mid-air and a voice boomed: "Which St Anthony?"

"Of Padua!"

¡Catacrok!

It was St Anthony the Abbot, whose temptations had left him as sour as a crab, and the mason hurtled another hundred feet to the flags below.

Greek gods and goddesses adopted a variety of local titles—the Virgin Artemis, for instance, could be Our Lady of Wild Things, Our Lady of the Lake, Huntress, Saviour, Spoil Winner, Strangled One, Assuager of Childbirth, Many-Breasted, Friend of Youth, Mistress of the Nets, Mistress of the Cedars, Wolfish, Light-Bringer, Persuader, Bear-Leader, Horse-Finder, and the like.   But I do not recall that there was ever the same bitter rivalry between this Artemis and that as is now presumed in Mallorca between the Black Virgin and the White.   The Black Virgin of Lluch, who seems to have inherited the *cleros* of the Syrian goddess in the *Golden Ass,* lives on the top of a mountain, among a collection of *ex voto* crutches, legbraces, suspensory bandages, and other discarded orthopaedic contraptions.   Occasionally she tours the island, collecting money for the *Acción Católica,* the new Seminary, or similar causes; whereupon the witches of the red-light district of Palma raise thunderstorms to drench her devotees.   She was appointed patroness of the island a century or two ago, because the monks of her monastery claimed that, soon after James I of Aragon drove out the infidel Moors, a bright light guided the shepherd boy Lucas to a cairn under which the image had taken refuge five centuries previously. Thus, though dated by art experts as not earlier than the close of the thirteenth century, the Black Virgin has been granted precedence of the lily-white "Virgin of Good Health" who inspired James's expedition in 1229 and saved his fleet from shipwreck, and of whom the Palma women say: "Only look at her; at once you feel better!" It is in troubled waters like these that the Devil fishes; and the Devil, the Catholics say, is a Protestant.

At times, it is claimed, even the Devil has nostalgic feelings about Heaven.   A distinguished stranger once visited St Moling in his mediaeval Irish cell and announced himself as the Man of Tribulations.

"The Devil you are!" cried the astonished Moling. "Does Christ come in purple and pomp rather than in the guise of a leper?"

"The Devil I am!" he assented.

"What is your errand?" asked Moling politely.   He was no gross ink-pot-throwing Luther.

"I come for your blessing."

"You have not deserved it, and besides, what good would it do you if I bestowed it?"

"It would be like bathing in a tub of honey with my clothes on."

"Be more explicit, pray!"

"Though your blessing would not affect me inwardly, its good luck and virtue and bloom would be fragrant on me."

"You might use it to deceive."

"Then curse me properly!"

"What good would that do? The venom and bitterness of the curse would merely scald my lips; for you are already beyond the reach of curses.   Away with you, Satan! Leave me to my meditations.   You shall be given neither blessing nor curse!"

"I should dearly have liked a blessing.   Can I not somehow earn it?"

"Certainly; by service to God."

"Alas, that is against my destiny."

"Then by study of the Scriptures."

"Your own studies have not been deeper or wider, and I am none the better for them."

"Then by fasting."

"I have fasted since Creation."

"Then by genuflexions."

"Impossible.   My knees bend backwards."

"Pray, excuse me," said Moling, reaching for his rosary.   "I fear I can do nothing for you."

Thereupon the Devil recited his famous *Blessing Upon Moling,* in Irish rhymed quatrains:

Golden sky the sun surrounding,
Silver bowl replete with wine,
Such is he, the prudent angel
Of our King Divine.

Fragrant branch, or gallon-measure
Filled with honey to the brim,
Precious stone of sovereign virtue,
Who is true to Him;

But who yields Him no obedience
Sparrow in a trap is he,
Sinking vessel, leaking goblet,
Withered apple-tree.

Five more verses have been recorded in Whitley Stokes's *Felire Oingusso,* comparing Moling with a crystal vessel, a victorious race-horse, a holy shrine, a communion table, a clean golden chalice.

But the Devil must have been trying to seduce Moling by flattery. He has always been a perfectionist, even when sick, which is indeed what provoked his expulsion from Heaven: since no human soul, not even a Moling, came up to his mercilessly high standards, he had demanded that saints should be abolished altogether. This could not be: the imperfect, all-too-human, easy-going world of capmaker, cutpurse, cobbler, cuckold and courtesan needed saints to worship, gossip about, swear by, cultivate, laugh at. So he converted only the humourless Protestants to his view; and (here I come to the point) impressed his sneer on my infant features at the very font. Forgive me therefore, St Lucia—and you, St William of the Desert—and you, St John the Baptist—and you, St Thomas the Doubter—in whose honour four of my children celebrate their name days with rockets and candled cakes.

Heaven is always early morning,
Gold sun, silver olive-trees,
Jewelled saints innumerable
Kneeling on their knees.

No more twilight, no more starlight,
Fog, nor sleet, nor hail, nor snow . . .

Were I a cradle-Catholic, or a flattering Devil, I could finish these stanzas, which swam prettily into my mind as I stood outside the repository, and dedicate them jointly to you; but alas! I am neither, and to apologize for a congenital sneer is not to wipe it off one's face.   I should be embarrassed by the honeyed blessing of a true saint (though true saints have been far more numerous than the Devil allows), nor am I destined to earn one.   I do not fast, except when I become so engrossed in my studies that I forget to eat; and my knees bend neither forwards nor backwards.   It is an unenviable situation. I am left only with a teasing historical conscience; and my mystic friends assure me that to account factually for a religious belief is not to evaluate it.

Lines of Inquiry

1 Graves' essay is distinguished by its treatment of the saints.
  a How does Graves represent the saints' style of conversation, and why?
  b What is the point of his anecdote about Mary Gipsy?   St. Agatha?   St. Anthony the Abbot?   St. Moling?
  c You probably are more familiar with saints that Graves does not mention than with those he does.   How do you account for the absence from his essay of St. Francis, St. Dominic, St. Bernard, St. Peter, St. Sebastian, etc.?
  d What in Graves' experience prompted him to think of the saints at all?   How is the essay's structure connected to this prompting fact?

2 How is the title of Graves' essay related to
  a Its first paragraph
  b Its treatment of the saints
  c Its point of view
  d Its structure
  e Its tone

3 Much in this essay is implicit, not explicit.
  a Why does Graves remark that his family church was built of red brick?
  b Why does he comment on the "fish-like appearance" of the *Midway*'s harmonium-playing steward?
  c Why does Graves give the names of his children—Lucia, John, Thomas, and William?
  d Why is the Devil made to identify himself as the Man of Tribulations?
  e What is the point of the remark that the Devil's knees bend only backward, and Graves' knees will bend neither forward nor backward?

4 What allusion is made in each of the following italicized phrases, and how is that allusion related to Graves' point?

a   *"Incense* for me will always smell of *brimstone;* and this I heartily regret."

b   "I felt warmly disposed toward the entire Catholic calendar, by way of protest against Anglophile Mallorquins who sing *Onward, Christian Soldiers!* in Spanish to a harmonium, and disregard even red-letter *saints."*

c   "The *Patriarchs,* those still alive, remained comatose, the *Heavenly Choir* never ceased from alleluias, and the *Four Beasts* contented themselves with wide-eyed meditation."

d   " 'What is your errand?' asked Moling politely. He was no gross *inkpot-throwing Luther."*

5   Tone, here as everywhere, depends largely on nuances of meaning conveyed by careful phrasing. How does the phrasing of each of the following sentences contribute to the tone of Graves' essay?

a   "Or St. Benedict, who helps weary-footed house-hunters; they have only to vow him a candle, throw a stone into the garden or area of the house they most want, and it will be vacant before the next quarter-day, sure as death."

b   "St. Mary Gipsy felt impelled one day to go on a pilgrimage to the Holy Land. But the crew of the only ship bound for Acre warned her that she must pay her fare by sleeping with all of them in turn throughout the voyage. She accordingly made the supreme sacrifice, spending the rest of her life in penitence and good works, and was eventually passed into Heaven by St. Peter on the ground that 'she loved much.' "

c   "Let me explain my mood by a brief historical review of Heaven and its celestial population. . . ."

d   "In the scramble for Olympian functions, distribution seems sometimes to have been made at haphazard; but there was always a certain divine logic at work."

e   "According to cradle-Catholic gossip, to which I lend a fascinated ear, there is as much jealousy in heaven as there ever was on Olympus."

6   At one point, Graves says that "to be acclimatized is not to be indoctrinated." What does he mean? Does this distinction hold true universally? Is there always a difference between acclimatization and indoctrination? Could it be argued that these apparently quite different categories are in fact identical —that acclimatization is indoctrination? What evidence might you adduce to support either one view or the other? (Think of your own experience and that of your friends.)

7 "My mystic friends assure me that to account factually for a religious belief is not to evaluate it."

a What is the meaning of "evaluate" in this phrase? How might one test the truth of these mystic friends' assertion?

b Might something similar be said about political belief? About moral belief? Could a parallel point be made with respect to the much-attacked belief that men are essentially rational beings?

c Here are three assertions of belief. How might one test their truth? What do you have to do before you can begin even to try to test them?

(*1*) Men are naturally good.

(*2*) Representative democracy is the best form of government.

(*3*) In modern civilization, the only way a man can save his soul is to drop out.

8 What kind of audience do you think this essay was written for? How might it be politic to change it for the following audiences? Why? *Should* the essay be so changed?

a A Catholic girls' school

b A Protestant girls' school

c A class in freshman English

d The readers of *Modern Thelogy*

e The Inter-faith Breakfast Club

Lines of Experiment

1 It takes considerable historical knowledge and a special interest in religious custom and belief to write an essay on such a subject as this. But almost any subject ordinarily treated with reverence may be treated also in a tone similar to that of Graves' essay—one hovering between parody and appreciation. One of the following titles may suggest a congenial subject to you and imply a tone (obviously none defines a subject).

a Patriotism in Elementary School

b My Friend the Eastern Mystic

c The Serious Cat Lover

d The Ritual of Clean P. E.

e A Simple Door-to-door Evangelist

f Advertising: The Salesman of the Beautiful

To deal with any subject, whether one's tone is straight or parodic, one must find a way of focusing one's ideas. Graves finds in the legends surrounding the saints an adequate metaphor for what he has to say here about religion. In your efforts to focus your own subject, consider the tone you are after.   Had Graves, like Adams, used a cathedral as his focal point, his essay necessarily would have been much different.

2 At first, Graves' essay seems anti-Catholic; however, a closer look will reveal that his attitude is far from that simple.   Write an analysis of Graves' attitude toward religion in general, and toward Catholicism in particular.   Pay attention not only to what he says about the saints, but also to how he says it. What is the final impression conveyed by all these anecdotes about the saints?   How many of them are unpleasant?   How many appreciative?   Which of the saints that he mentions does he seem most to disapprove of?   How does Graves treat himself and his Protestant background?   In focusing your analysis, do not try to deal with everything; here again, a restricted focus on a few crucial points or phrases will serve you better than a general survey.   Above all, bear in mind that the essential meaning of Graves' essay is to be found in its *tone:* Your analysis should be particularly directed to that.

JONATHAN SWIFT

 **A MODEST
PROPOSAL**

FOR

PREVENTING THE CHILDREN OF POOR PEOPLE IN
IRELAND FROM BEING A BURDEN TO THEIR
PARENTS OR COUNTRY, AND FOR MAKING THEM
BENEFICIAL TO THE PUBLIC

It is a melancholy object to those who walk through this great town, or travel in the country, when they see the streets, the roads and cabin-doors crowded with beggars of the female sex, followed by three, four, or six children, all in rags, and importuning every passenger for an alms. These mothers, instead of being able to work for their honest livelihood, are forced to employ all their time in strolling, to beg sustenance for their helpless infants, who, as they grow up, either turn thieves for

want of work, or leave their dear native country to fight for the
Pretender in Spain, or sell themselves to the Barbadoes.

I think it is agreed by all parties that this prodigious number of children, in the arms, or on the backs, or at the heels of their mothers,
and frequently of their fathers, is in the present deplorable state of the
kingdom a very great additional grievance; and therefore whoever could
find out a fair, cheap, and easy method of making these children sound
and useful members of the commonwealth would deserve so well of
the public as to have his statue set up for a preserver of the nation.

But my intention is very far from being confined to provide only for
the children of professed beggars; it is of a much greater extent, and
shall take in the whole number of infants at a certain age who are born
of parents in effect as little able to support them as those who demand
our charity in the streets.

As to my own part, having turned my thoughts for many years upon
this important subject, and maturely weighed the several schemes of
other projectors, I have always found them grossly mistaken in their
computation. It is true a child just dropped from its dam may be
supported by her milk for a solar year with little other nourishment,
at most not above the value of two shillings, which the mother may
certainly get, or the value in scraps, by her lawful occupation of begging, and it is exactly at one year old that I propose to provide for
them, in such a manner as, instead of being a charge upon their parents,
or the parish, or wanting food and raiment for the rest of their lives,
they shall, on the contrary, contribute to the feeding and partly to
the clothing of many thousands.

There is likewise another great advantage in my scheme, that it will
prevent those voluntary abortions, and that horrid practice of women
murdering their bastard children, alas, too frequent among us, sacrificing
the poor innocent babes, I doubt, more to avoid the expense than the
shame, which would move tears and pity in the most savage and inhuman breast.

The number of souls in Ireland being usually reckoned one million and
a half, of these I calculate there may be about two hundred thousand
couples whose wives are breeders, from which number I subtract thirty
thousand couples who are able to maintain their own children, although
I apprehend there cannot be so many under the present distresses of
the kingdom, but this being granted, there will remain an hundred and
seventy thousand breeders. I again subtract fifty thousand for those

women who miscarry, or whose children die by accident or disease within the year. There only remain an hundred and twenty thousand children of poor parents annually born: the question therefore is, how this number shall be reared, and provided for, which, as I have already said, under the present situation of affairs is utterly impossible by all the methods hitherto proposed, for we can neither employ them in handicraft or agriculture; we neither build houses (I mean in the country), nor cultivate land: they can very seldom pick up a livelihood by stealing until they arrive at six years old, except where they are of towardly parts, although I confess they learn the rudiments much earlier, during which time they can however be properly looked upon only as probationers, as I have been informed by a principal gentleman in the County of Cavan, who protested to me that he never knew above one or two instances under the age of six, even in a part of the kingdom so renowned for the quickest proficiency in that art.

I am assured by our merchants that a boy or a girl before twelve years old, is no saleable commodity, and even when they come to this age, they will not yield above three pounds, or three pounds and half-a-crown at most on the Exchange, which cannot turn to account either to the parents or the kingdom, the charge of nutriment and rags having been at least four times that value.

I shall now therefore humbly propose my own thoughts, which I hope will not be liable to the least objection.

I have been assured by a very knowing American of my acquaintance in London, that a young healthy child well nursed is at a year old a most delicious, nourishing and wholesome food, whether stewed, roasted, baked, or boiled, and I make no doubt that it will equally serve in a fricassee, or a ragout.

I do therefore humbly offer it to public consideration, that of the hundred and twenty thousand children already computed, twenty thousand may be reserved for breed, whereof only one fourth part to be males, which is more than we allow to sheep, black-cattle, or swine, and my reason is that these children are seldom the fruits of marriage, a circumstance not much regarded by our savages, therefore one male will be sufficient to serve four females. That the remaining hundred thousand may at a year old be offered in sale to the persons of quality, and fortune, through the kingdom, always advising the mother to let them suck plentifully in the last month, so as to render them plump, and fat for a good table. A child will make two dishes at an entertainment for friends, and when the family dines alone, the fore or hind quarter will make a reasonable dish, and seasoned with a little pepper or salt will be very good boiled on the fourth day, especially in winter.

I have reckoned upon a medium, that a child just born will weigh twelve pounds, and in a solar year if tolerably nursed increaseth to twenty-eight pounds.

I grant this food will be somewhat dear, and therefore very proper for landlords, who, as they have already devoured most of the parents, seem to have the best title to the children.

Infant's flesh will be in season throughout the year, but more plentiful in March, and a little before and after, for we are told by a grave [1] author, an eminent French physician, that fish being a prolific diet, there are more children born in Roman Catholic countries about nine months after Lent than at any other season; therefore reckoning a year after Lent, the markets will be more glutted than usual, because the number of Popish infants is at least three to one in this kingdom, and therefore it will have one other collateral advantage by lessening the number of Papists among us.

I have already computed the charge of nursing a beggar's child (in which list I reckon all cottagers, labourers, and four-fifths of the farmers) to be about two shillings *per annum,* rags included, and I believe no gentleman would repine to give ten shillings for the carcass of a good fat child, which, as I have said, will make four dishes of excellent nutritive meat, when he hath only some particular friend or his own family to dine with him.   Thus the Squire will learn to be a good landlord and grow popular among his tenants, the mother will have eight shillings net profit, and be fit for work until she produces another child.

Those who are more thrifty (as I must confess the times require) may flay the carcass; the skin of which artificially dressed, will make admirable gloves for ladies, and summer boots for fine gentlemen.

As to our city of Dublin, shambles may be appointed for this purpose, in the most convenient parts of it, and butchers we may be assured will not be wanting, although I rather recommend buying the children alive, and dressing them hot from the knife, as we do roasting pigs.

[1] Rabelais.

A very worthy person, a true lover of his country, and whose virtues I highly esteem, was lately pleased, in discoursing on this matter to offer a refinement upon my scheme. He said that many gentlemen of this kingdom, having of late destroyed their deer, he conceived that the want of venison might be well supplied by the bodies of young lads and maidens, not exceeding fourteen years of age, nor under twelve, so great a number of both sexes in every county being now ready to starve, for want of work and service: and these to be disposed of by their parents if alive, or otherwise by their nearest relations. But with due deference to so excellent a friend, and so deserving a patriot, I cannot be altogether in his sentiments. For as to the males, my American acquaintance assured me from frequent experience that their flesh was generally tough and lean, like that of our schoolboys, by continual exercise, and their taste disagreeable, and to fatten them would not answer the charge. Then as to the females, it would, I think with humble submission, be a loss to the public, because they soon would become breeders themselves: and besides, it is not improbable that some scrupulous people might be apt to censure such a practice (although indeed very unjustly) as a little bordering upon cruelty, which I confess, hath always been with me the strongest objection against any project, howsoever well intended.

But in order to justify my friend, he confessed that this expedient was put into his head by the famous Psalmanazar, a native of the island Formosa, who came from thence to London, above twenty years ago, and in conversation told my friend that in his country when any young person happened to be put to death, the executioner sold the carcass to persons of quality, as a prime dainty, and that, in his time, the body of a plump girl of fifteen, who was crucified for an attempt to poison the emperor, was sold to his Imperial Majesty's Prime Minister of State, and other great Mandarins of the Court, in joints from the gibbet, at four hundred crowns. Neither indeed can I deny that if the same use were made of several plump young girls in this town who, without one single groat to their fortunes, cannot stir abroad without a chair, and appear at the playhouse and assemblies in foreign fineries, which they never will pay for, the kingdom would not be the worse.

Some persons of a desponding spirit are in great concern about that vast number of poor people, who are aged, diseased, or maimed, and I have been desired to employ my thoughts what course may be taken to ease the nation of so grievous an encumbrance. But I am not in the least pain upon that matter, because it is very well known that they are every day dying, and rotting, by cold, and famine, and filth, and vermin, as fast as can be reasonably expected. And as to the younger labourers they are now in almost as hopeful a condition. They cannot get work, and consequently pine away from want of nourishment, to a degree that if at any time they are accidentally hired to common labour, they have not strength to perform it; and thus the country and themselves are in a fair way of being soon delivered from the evils to come.

I have too long digressed, and therefore shall return to my subject. I think the advantages by the proposal which I have made are obvious and many, as well as of the highest importance.

For first, as I have already observed, it would greatly lessen the number of Papists, with whom we are yearly over-run, being the principal breeders of the nation, as well as our most dangerous enemies, and who stay at home on purpose with a design to deliver the kingdom to the Pretender, hoping to take their advantage by the absence of so many good Protestants, who have chosen rather to leave their country than stay at home and pay tithes against their conscience to an idolatrous Episcopal curate.

Secondly, the poorer tenants will have something valuable of their own, which by law may be made liable to distress, and help to pay their landlord's rent, their corn and cattle being already seized, and money a thing unknown.

Thirdly, whereas the maintenance of an hundred thousand children, from two years old, and upwards, cannot be computed at less than ten shillings a piece *per annum,* the nation's stock will be thereby increased fifty thousand pounds *per annum,* besides the profit of a new dish, introduced to the tables of all gentlemen of fortune in the kingdom, who have any refinement in taste, and the money will circulate among ourselves, the goods being entirely of our own growth and manufacture.

Fourthly, the constant breeders, besides the gain of eight shillings sterling *per annum,* by the sale of their children, will be rid of the charge of maintaining them after the first year.

Fifthly, this food would likewise bring great custom to taverns, where the vintners will certainly be so prudent as to procure the best receipts for dressing it to perfection, and consequently have their houses frequented by all the fine gentlemen, who justly value themselves upon their knowledge in good eating; and a skilful cook, who understands how to oblige his guests, will contrive to make it as expensive as they please.

Sixthly, this would be a great inducement to marriage, which all wise nations have either encouraged by rewards, or enforced by laws and penalties. It would increase the care and tenderness of mothers towards their children, when they were sure of a settlement for life, to the poor babes, provided in some sort by the public to their annual profit instead of expense. We should soon see an honest emulation among the married women, which of them could bring the fattest child to the market. Men would become as fond of their wives, during the time of their pregnancy, as they are now of their mares in foal, their cows in calf, or sows when they are ready to farrow, nor offer to beat or kick them (as it is too frequent a practice) for fear of a miscarriage.

Many other advantages might be enumerated. For instance, the addition of some thousand carcasses in our exportation of barrelled beef; the propagation of swine's flesh, and improvement in the art of making good bacon, so much wanted among us by the great destruction of pigs, too frequent at our tables, are no way comparable in taste or magnificence to a well-grown, fat yearling child, which roasted whole will make a considerable figure at a Lord Mayor's feast, or any other public entertainment. But this and many others I omit, being studious of brevity.

Supposing that one thousand families in this city would be constant customers for infants flesh, besides others who might have it at merry meetings, particularly weddings and christenings; I compute that Dublin would take off annually about twenty thousand carcasses, and the rest of the kingdom (where probably they will be sold somewhat cheaper) the remaining eighty thousand.

I can think of no one objection that will possibly be raised against this proposal, unless it should be urged that the number of people will be thereby much lessened in the kingdom. This I freely own, and it was indeed one principal design in offering it to the world. I desire the reader will observe, that I calculate my remedy *for this one individual Kingdom of* Ireland, *and for no other that ever was, is, or, I think, ever can be upon earth.* Therefore let no man talk to me of other expedients: *Of taxing our absentees at five shillings a pound: Of using neither clothes, nor household furniture, except what is of our own growth and manufacture: Of utterly rejecting the materials and instru-*

ments that promote foreign luxury: Of curing the expensiveness of pride, vanity, idleness, and gaming in our women: Of introducing a vein of parsimony, prudence, and temperance: Of learning to love our country, wherein we differ even from Laplanders, *and the inhabitants of* Topinamboo: *Of quitting our animosities and factions, nor act any longer like the* Jews, *who were murdering one another at the very moment their city was taken: Of being a little cautious not to sell our country and consciences for nothing: Of teaching landlords to have at least one degree of mercy towards their tenants.* Lastly, *of putting a spirit of honesty, industry, and skill into our shopkeepers, who, if a resolution could now be taken to buy only our native goods, would immediately unite to cheat and exact upon us in the price, the measure and the goodness, nor could ever yet be brought to make one fair proposal of just dealing, though often and earnestly invited to it.*

Therefore I repeat, let no man talk to me of these and the like expedients, till he hath at least a glimpse of hope that there will ever be some hearty and sincere attempt to put them in practice.

But as to myself, having been wearied out for many years with offering vain, idle, visionary thoughts, and at length utterly despairing of success, I fortunately fell upon this proposal, which as it is wholly new, so it hath something solid and real, of no expense and little trouble, full in our own power, and whereby we can incur no danger in disobliging England. For this kind of commodity will not bear exportation, the flesh being of too tender a consistence to admit a long continuance in salt, *although perhaps I could name a country which would be glad to eat up our whole nation without it.*

After all I am not so violently bent upon my own opinion as to reject any offer, proposed by wise men, which shall be found equally innocent, cheap, easy and effectual. But before some thing of that kind shall be advanced in contradiction to my scheme, and offering a better, I desire the author, or authors, will be pleased maturely to consider two points. First, as things now stand, how they will be able to find food and raiment for a hundred thousand useless mouths and backs? And secondly, there being a round million of creatures in human figure, throughout this kingdom, whose whole subsistence put into a common stock would leave them in debt two millions of pounds sterling; adding those who are beggars by profession, to the bulk of farmers, cottagers, and labourers with their wives and children, who are beggars in effect; I desire those politicians who dislike my overture, and may perhaps be so bold to attempt an answer, that they will first ask the parents of these mortals whether they would not at this day think it a great happiness to have been sold for food at a year old, in the manner I prescribe, and thereby have avoided such a perpetual scene of misfortunes as they have since gone through, by the oppression of landlords, the impossibility of paying rent without money or trade, the want of common sustenance, with neither house nor clothes to cover them from the inclemencies of weather, and the most inevitable prospect of entailing the like, or greater miseries upon their breed for ever.

I profess in the sincerity of my heart that I have not the least personal interest in endeavouring to promote this necessary work, having no other motive than the *public good of my country, by advancing our trade, providing for infants, relieving the poor, and giving some pleasure to the rich.* I have no children by which I can propose to get a single penny; the youngest being nine years old, and my wife past childbearing.

Lines of Inquiry

1 "A Modest Proposal," as this essay's full title is usually abbreviated, is one of the world's most famous examples of irony. Perhaps the chief element in the marshaling of this irony is Swift's use of point of view. Swift himself was a prominent clergyman, Dean of St. Patrick's Cathedral, Dublin.

a How would you describe the character he adopts in this essay?

b How is that character related to the essay's ironic force?

c Swift instances "a very worthy person, a true lover of his country," who suggests that the want of venison could handily be supplied by the bodies of children between the ages of twelve and fourteen. The "worthy person" evidently is manufactured. But Swift could have made the suggestion through his own *persona,* or mask, only to dismiss it as impracticable. What would he have lost by doing so?

2 Some ironical statements are consciously so, as when we call someone a genius and mean that he is a fool. Others are unconsciously so, as when we speak simultaneously of the blessings of science and of the dangers of polluted air, atomic warfare, genetic deterioration, etc. Still others are both consciously and unconsciously ironical, as when Antony calls Brutus an honorable man, meaning that he is thoroughly dishonorable despite his contrary public reputation, yet missing the literal truth in the bare statement: For Brutus is indeed an honorable man. How many such levels of irony can you find in Swift's essay?

3 The "modest proposal" itself is not advanced until the ninth paragraph of Swift's essay—fairly far along.

 a What appear to be Swift's purposes in the preceding paragraphs? He speaks constantly of a solution shortly to be advanced, yet gives no explicit suggestion of its nature; with what effect?

 b When did you first suspect the nature of the proposal? Where do you find the first hint of irony? How do you account for the fact that the proposal itself, when actually flatly made, does not seem anticlimactic? (Note the exact language of the proposal.)

4 Suppose that you were to find, in some newspaper of the thirties, a heavily ironic proposal by a German politician to solve the Jewish problem by liquidating the Jews. Or, from the mid-forties, an ironical research paper advising the President of the United States to end World War II by dropping atomic bombs on large Japanese cities, one a week until the Japanese surrendered. Or. . . . (You can fill this one in.) How would such an essay seem now? Suppose that Swift's proposal actually had been adopted, in fact if not in manner. From such illustrative cases, what might one conclude to be one necessary condition for successful irony? And what might seem one of its principal (and highly ironical) dangers?

5 The following sentences are thoroughly and obviously bitter; what, in each case, makes them so?

 a "I have been assured by a very knowing American of my acquaintance in London, that a young healthy child, well nursed, is at a year old a most delicious, nourishing and wholesome food, whether stewed, roasted, baked, or boiled, and I make no doubt that it will equally serve in a fricassee, or a ragout."

 b "I have already computed the charge of nursing a beggar's child (in which list I reckon all cottagers, labourers, and four-fifths of the farmers) to be about two shillings *per annum*, rags included, and I believe no gentleman would repine to give ten shillings for the carcass of a good fat child, which, as I have said, will make four dishes of excellent nutritive meat, when he hath only some particular friend or his own family to dine with him."

 c "Secondly, the poorer tenants will have something valuable of their own, which by law may be made liable to distress, and help to pay their landlord's rent, their corn and cattle being already seized, and money a thing unknown."

d "Supposing that one thousand families in this city would be constant customers for infants flesh, besides others who might have it at merry meetings, particularly weddings and christenings, I compute that Dublin would take off annually about twenty thousand carcasses. . . ."

e "It would increase the care and tenderness of mothers towards their children, when they were sure of a settlement for life, to the poor babes, provided in some sort by the public to their annual profit instead of expense."

6 Connotation, as we have seen, is an indispensable element in tone. What differences do you see between

a "Importuning every passenger for an alms" and "asking every passenger for money"?

b "A prodigious number" of children and "a large number"?

c A "breeder" and a "mother"?

d A "body" and a "carcass"?

e "Persons of quality and fortune" and "members of the upper classes"?

f "A child dropped from its dam" and "a newborn child"?

7 Who is Swift's satire directed against? What is its purpose?

Lines of Experiment

1 Swift's essay began a durable if minor literary form: The "modest proposal" is still a favorite among ironists, as a way of calling attention to the viciousness, hopelessness, or downright insanity of things. Destroy the enemy's will to fight by dropping millions and millions of nylon stockings on his cities; solve the problem of segregated schools by doing away with education; prevent atomic war by burying a bomb large enough to blow the entire earth apart and programming it to explode at a given level of radioactivity; support the prosperity of agriculture by destroying its products. Unfortunately, some such proposals have been taken—have even been made— seriously. Some have even been implemented.

As a preliminary to the drafting of your own modest proposal, list at least four of the problems that seem critical in your own time and place. You need not take on the most apocalyptic of our national and international difficulties; a local situation or crisis may be easier for you to handle. The building of a free-way, a change in clothing fashion, widespread air pollution, a decrease in the deer harvest (note connotation)—such things offer rich possibilities to the modest proposer. Consider your four possibilities from as many directions as you can, before settling on one for a subject. If you have real trouble finding a subject, consult your local newspaper.

Any modest proposal begins from the ironic premise that the sane, decent solutions to a problem are impossible, through ill will, stupidity, selfishness, or lethargy—that only an insane proposal will stand a chance of acceptance. The insane proposal itself, then, forces the reader to confront in its logical consequences the immorality or stupidity of his own acts, or those of his society. The official premise of Swift's proposal is that the lives of the poor are of no value, and may be treated therefore as purely economic commodities; his logical conclusion from this premise discredits it, partly by revealing it, partly by showing where it leads.

In developing your own proposal, then, you should bear in mind the rational and decent solutions that you really wish to further, and you should introduce them into your essay *only to dismiss them as visionary.* No modest proposal is an end in itself; its purposes can be complex, but its central one is to reveal callousness and stupidity in their barest results, and so to make decency once more seem plausible. What you dismiss as visionary, your reader must take up as the only rational thing to do.

2 Suppose that in some troubled part of the world (past, present, or future) a new Jonathan Swift steps suddenly forward to make a modest proposal. Write a narrative essay (fantasy, of course) describing the entire circumstance: its background; the proposal itself; its reception. You may be unable to avoid a touch of the ironic. Irony seems embedded in the human condition.

H. L. MENCKEN

 ## THE CULT
OF HOPE

Of all the sentimental errors which reign and rage in this incomparable republic, the worst, I often suspect, is that which confuses the function of criticism, whether æsthetic, political or social, with the function of reform.   Almost invariably it takes the form of a protest: "The fellow condemns without offering anything better.   Why tear down without building up?" So coo and snivel the sweet ones: so wags the national tongue.   The messianic delusion becomes a sort of universal murrain. It is impossible to get an audience for an idea that is not "constructive" —*i.e.,* that is not glib, and uplifting, and full of hope, and hence capable of tickling the emotions by leaping the intermediate barrier of the intelligence.

In this protest and demand, of course, there is nothing but a hollow sound of words—the empty babbling of men who constantly mistake their mere feelings for thoughts.   The truth is that criticism, if it were thus confined to the proposing of alternative schemes, would quickly cease to have any force or utility at all, for in the overwhelming majority of instances no alternative scheme of any intelligibility is imaginable, and the whole object of the critical process is to demonstrate it.   The poet, if the victim is a poet, is simply one as bare of gifts as a herring is of fur: no conceivable suggestion will ever make him write actual poetry.   The cancer cure, if one turns to popular swindles, is wholly and absolutely without merit—and the fact that medicine offers us no better cure does not dilute its bogusness in the slightest.   And the plan of reform, in politics, sociology or what not, is simply beyond the pale of reason; no change in it or improvement of it will ever make it achieve the downright impossible.   Here, precisely, is what is the matter with most of the notions that go floating about the country, particularly in the field of governmental reform.   The trouble with them is not only that they won't and don't work; the trouble with them,

THE CULT OF HOPE

more importantly, is that the thing they propose to accomplish is intrinsically, or at all events most probably, beyond accomplishment. That is to say, the problem they are ostensibly designed to solve is a problem that is insoluble. To tackle them with a proof of that insolubility, or even with a colorable argument of it, is sound criticism; to tackle them with another solution that is quite as bad, or even worse, is to pick the pocket of one knocked down by an automobile.

Unluckily, it is difficult for a certain type of mind to grasp the concept of insolubility. Thousands of poor dolts keep on trying to square the circle; other thousands keep pegging away at perpetual motion. The number of persons so afflicted is far greater than the records of the Patent Office show, for beyond the circle of frankly insane enterprise there lie circles of more and more plausible enterprise, and finally we come to a circle which embraces the great majority of human beings. These are the optimists and chronic hopers of the world, the believers in men, ideas and things. These are the advocates of leagues of nations, wars to make the world safe for democracy, political mountebanks, "clean-up" campaigns, laws, raids, Men and Religion Forward Movements, eugenics, sex hygiene, education, newspapers. It is the settled habit of such credulous folk to give ear to whatever is comforting; it is their settled faith that whatever is desirable will come to pass. A caressing confidence—but one, unfortunately, that is not borne out by human experience. The fact is that some of the things that men and women have desired most ardently for thousands of years are not nearer realization to-day than they were in the time of Rameses, and that there is not the slightest reason for believing that they will lose their coyness on any near to-morrow. Plans for hurrying them on have been tried since the beginning; plans for forcing them overnight are in copious and antagonistic operation to-day; and yet they continue to hold off and elude us, and the chances are that they will keep on holding off and eluding us until the angels get tired of the show, and the whole earth is set off like a gigantic bomb, or drowned, like a sick cat, between two buckets.

But let us avoid the grand and chronic dreams of the race and get down to some of the concrete problems of life under the Christian enlightenment. Let us take a look, say, at the so-called drink problem, a small subdivision of the larger problem of saving men from their inherent and incurable hoggishness. What is the salient feature of the discussion of the drink problem, as one observes it going on eternally in These States? The salient feature of it is that very few honest and intelligent men ever take a hand in the business—that the best men of the nation, distinguished for their sound sense in other fields, seldom show any interest in it.   On the one hand it is labored by a horde of obvious jackasses, each confident that he can dispose of it overnight.   And on the other hand it is sophisticated and obscured by a crowd of oblique fellows, hired by interested parties, whose secret desire is that it be kept unsolved.   To one side, the professional gladiators of Prohibition; to the other side, the agents of the brewers and distillers.   But why do all neutral and clear-headed men avoid it?   Why does one hear so little about it from those who have no personal stake in it, and can thus view it fairly and accurately?   Is it because they are afraid?   Is it because they are not intrigued by it?   I doubt that it would be just to accuse them in either way.   The real reason why they steer clear of the gabble is simpler and more creditable.   It is this: that none of them—that no genuinely thoughtful and prudent man—can imagine any solution which meets the tests of his own criticism—that no genuinely intelligent man believes the thing is soluble at all.

Here, of course, I generalize a bit heavily.   Honest and intelligent men, though surely not many of them, occasionally come forward with suggestions.   In the midst of so much debate it is inevitable that even a man of critical mind should sometimes lean to one side or the other— that some salient imbecility should make him react toward its rough opposite.   But the fact still remains that not a single complete and comprehensive scheme has ever come from such a man, that no such man has ever said, in so many words, that he thought the problem could be solved, simply and effectively.   All such schemes come from idiots or from sharpers disguised as idiots to win the public confidence.   The whole discussion is based upon assumptions that even the most casual reflection must reject as empty balderdash.

And as with the drink problem, so with most of the other great questions that harass and dismay the helpless human race.   Turn, for example, to the sex problem.   There is no half-baked ecclesiastic, bawling in his galvanized-iron temple on a suburban lot, who doesn't know precisely how it ought to be dealt with.   There is no fantoddish old suffragette, sworn to get her revenge on man, who hasn't a sovereign remedy for it.   There is not a shyster of a district attorney, ambitious for higher office, who doesn't offer to dispose of it in a few weeks, given only enough help from the city editors.   And yet, by the same token, there is not a man who has honestly studied it and pondered it, bringing sound information to the business, and understanding of its inner difficulties and a clean and analytical mind, who doesn't believe and hasn't stated publicly that it is intrinsically and eternally insoluble. I can't think of an exception, nor does a fresh glance through the literature suggest one.   The latest expert to tell the disconcerting truth is Dr. Maurice Parmelee, the criminologist.   His book, "Personality and Conduct," is largely devoted to demonstrating that the popular solutions, for all the support they get from vice crusaders, complaisant legislators and sensational newspapers, are unanimously imbecile and pernicious—that their only effect in practice is to make what was bad a good deal worse.   His remedy is—what? An alternative solution? Not at all. His remedy, in brief, is to abandon all attempts at a solution, to let the whole thing go, to cork up all the reformers and try to forget it.

And in this proposal he merely echoes Havelock Ellis, undoubtedly the most diligent and scientific student of the sex problem that the world has yet seen—in fact, the one man who, above all others, has made a decorous and intelligent examination of it possible.   Ellis' remedy is simply a denial of all remedies.   He admits that the disease is bad, but he shows that the medicine is infinitely worse, and so he proposes going back to the plain disease, and advocates bearing it with philosophy, as we bear colds in the head, marriage, the noises of the city, bad cooking and the certainty of death.   Man is inherently vile—but he is never so vile as when he is trying to disguise and deny his vileness. No prostitute was ever so costly to a community as a prowling and obscene vice crusader, or as the dubious legislator or prosecuting officer who jumps as he pipes.

Ellis, in all this, falls under the excommunication of the sentimentalists. He demolishes one scheme without offering an alternative scheme.   He tears down without making any effort to build up.   This explains, no doubt, his general unpopularity; into mouths agape for peruna, he projects only paralyzing streams of ice-water.   And it explains, too, the curious fact that his books, the most competent and illuminating upon the subject that they discuss, are under the ban of the Comstocks in both England and America, whereas the hollow treatises of ignorant clerics and smutty old maids are merchanted with impunity, and even commended from the sacred desk.   The trouble with Ellis is that he tells the truth, which is the unsafest of all things to tell.   His crime is that he is a man who prefers facts to illusions, and knows what he is talking about.   Such men are never popular.   The public taste is for merchandise of a precisely opposite character.   The way to please is to proclaim in a confident manner, not what is true, but what is merely

comforting.   This is what is called building up.   This is constructive
criticism.

Lines of Inquiry

1 Mencken's title is a striking summary of his point.   Here are
four other titles; what connotative differences do you see between Mencken's and each of these?
a On Hope
b The Folly of Hope
c The Religion of Hope
d Destructive and Constructive Criticism

2 What differences do you see between
a Sentiment and sentimentality
b Stimulating and tickling
c A fool and a dolt
d A poet without talent and a poet as bare of gifts as a herring
is of fur
e A universal disease and a universal murrain
f A hopeful man and a chronic hoper

3 Mencken's prose is rich in metaphors of abuse.
a The objects of his attack here alternately coo, snivel, gabble,
babble, and bawl.   How do these words differ from one
another in connotation?   What is their common denotative
meaning?   How do the objects of Mencken's approbation
talk?   How do you account for the difference?
b Mencken refers to "the inherent and incurable hoggishness
of mankind"; at another point he refers to his opponents as
a "horde of obvious jackasses."   Metaphors that assimilate
humans to animals are common.   Make a list of several of
the commonest metaphors of this kind; how many of them
are flattering?   Can you find a categorical difference between
the flattering and unflattering comparisons?   What view of
animal character underlies the use of such metaphors?
c What connotative meaning rises from the italicized phrases
below?
(*1*) "The *Messianic delusion* becomes a sort of universal
murrain."
(*2*) "Most of the notions that *go floating about* the country."
(*3*) "Other thousands *keep pegging away* at perpetual motion."
(*4*) "Until *the angels get tired of the show,* and the whole
earth is set off like a gigantic bomb, or *drowned, like a
sick cat, between two buckets.*"
(*5*) "The *professional gladiators of prohibition.*"

(6) "The dubious legislator or prosecuting officer *who jumps as he pipes.*"

4 Take one paragraph of Mencken's essay and rewrite it carefully, sentence by sentence, so as to achieve the neutrality of tone appropriate to a social scientist. What have you had to alter? Now, without looking at the original, attempt to recreate its tone by rewriting your own bare, denotative version appropriately. How successful were you?

5 How would you characterize Mencken's essay as a form of criticism? Is such an essay worthwhile? Is the character of Mencken's essay itself related to the point he is trying to make?

6 In Part IV of this text, the possible points of view are discussed under two main categories, *angle* and *voice.*

  a What is Mencken's angle—what does he write *as?* How is that angle related to the one he establishes in the essay? To the personal voice we hear in the essay?

  b How many times in this essay does Mencken employ the first-person pronoun? Mark the passages: Why does Mencken fall back on an explicit "I" exactly at these points?

  c Rewrite the first paragraph of Mencken's essay so as to attach to every assertion whose validity is not universally recognized a clause qualifying that assertion as essentially the author's. How does the tone of your revision match with the tone of the original?

7 Mencken instances two problems that are "intrinsically and eternally insoluble"—the "drink problem" and the "sex problem."

  a What is the "sex problem"?

  b Why does Mencken deal with the "drink problem" before he deals with the "sex problem," and not after?

  c What is the common denominator of the two problems— into what category do they both fit? In what other categories of experience might one find problems that are equally insoluble?

8 The "drink problem" is still with us, though governmental attempts to deal with it have in fact been generally discontinued. The "sex problem" also appears to be a problem still. One might give parallel titles to many other problems prominent in our time. Do some of Mencken's comments on the cult of hope appear to apply to these problems as well?

  a The "population problem": How can we hope to diminish the pressure of population on natural resources?

b The "equality problem": How can we bring about equality among men?

c The "education problem": How can we educate people to become thoughtful, conscientious, skilled human beings?

d The "good government problem": How can we be sure of getting and keeping good government for everybody?

e The "morals problem": How can the younger generation be kept on the straight and narrow?

f The "tax problem": How can taxes be reduced, yet services expanded?

g The "composition problem": How can students be taught to write well?

Lines of Experiment

1 Mencken's essay is not an attack on hope so much as an attack on foolish hope—on hope cherished in the face of all fact and history, all evidence about the perennial human condition. Hope, Mencken seems to say, should be moderate, not extreme.

Consider the other traditional virtues—faith, love, chastity, prudence, courage, etc. Could Mencken's thesis concerning hope be applied to any of these? Could one write an essay capable of being titled "The Cult of Courage" or "The Cult of Love" or "The Cult of Sportsmanship"?

From some such clue, write your own brief investigation of a generally recognized virtue. You need not adopt Mencken's style, nor his point, but if the tone fits, do not be afraid of it. Mencken does not attack hope when he douses Pollyanna with ice water. (Who was Pollyanna?)

2 There is no day in our lives that passes without our criticizing something or somebody: a book, a politician, a law, a class, an automobile, a fashion in clothing. Taking as your illustrative center some such subject of special interest to you, write an essay on the function of criticism.

A preliminary comment. Criticism is an act of judgment. In any judgment, the thing being judged is of course at the center; but it is still important to know on what basis to judge it. What is the function of the thing you are judging? What should be its character? What should not be its character? Does it perform its function well? Does it conform to its essential character? The "critic's problem" then is to find proper standards of judgment before judging. In your own essay, therefore, choose as the focus for your analysis something close to home.   The answers are not always simple; an automobile is put to more human uses than transportation alone, and clothing has clearly many functions, thus many standards of value.   You may wish, in your own essay, to point out that the function usually thought of as most important in the object you are discussing is actually secondary.

VIRGINIA WOOLF

 ## TWO PARSONS

I. JAMES WOODFORDE

One could wish that the psycho-analysts would go into the question of diary-keeping.   For often it is the one mysterious fact in a life otherwise as clear as the sky and as candid as the dawn.   Parson Woodforde is a case in point—his diary is the only mystery about him. For forty-three years he sat down almost daily to record what he did on Monday and what he had for dinner on Tuesday; but for whom he wrote or why he wrote it is impossible to say.   He does not unburden his soul in his diary; yet it is no mere record of engagements and expenses.   As for literary fame, there is no sign that he ever thought of it, and finally, though the man himself is peaceable above all things, there are little indiscretions and criticisms which would have got him into trouble and hurt the feelings of his friends had they read them.   What purpose, then, did the sixty-eight little books fulfil? Perhaps it was the desire for intimacy.   When James Woodforde opened one of his neat manuscript books he entered into conversation with a second James Woodforde, who was not quite the same as the reverend gentleman who visited the poor and preached in the church.   These two friends said much that all the world might hear; but they had a few secrets which they shared with each other only.   It was a great comfort, for example, that Christmas when Nancy, Betsy, and Mr. Walker seemed to be in conspiracy against him, to exclaim in the diary, "The treatment I meet with for my Civility this Christmas is to me abominable."   The second James Woodforde sympathised and agreed.   Again, when a stranger abused his hospitality it was a relief to inform the other self who lived in the little book that he had put him to sleep in the attic story, "and I treated him as one that would be too free if treated kindly."   It is easy to understand why, in the quiet life of a country parish, these two bachelor friends became in time inseparable.   An essential part of him would have died had he been forbidden to keep his diary.   When indeed he thought himself in the grip of death he still wrote on and on. And as we read—if reading is the word for it—we seem to be listening to some one who is murmuring over the events of the day to himself in the quiet space which precedes sleep.   It is not writing, and, to speak of the truth, it is not reading.   It is slipping through half a dozen pages and strolling to the window and looking out.   It is going on thinking about the Woodfordes while we watch the people in the street below. It is taking a walk and making up the life and character of James Woodforde as we go.   It is not reading any more than it is writing— what to call it we scarcely know.

James Woodforde, then, was one of those smooth-cheeked, steady-eyed men, demure to look at, whom we can never imagine except in the prime of life.   He was of an equable temper, with only such acerbities and touchinesses as are generally to be found in those who have had a love affair in their youth and remained, as they fancy, unwed because of it.   The Parson's love affair, however, was nothing very tremendous. Once when he was a young man in Somerset he liked to walk over to Shepton and to visit a certain "sweet tempered" Betsy White who lived there.   He had a great mind "to make a bold stroke" and ask her to marry him.   He went so far, indeed, as to propose marriage "when opportunity served," and Betsy was willing.   But he delayed; time passed; four years passed indeed, and Betsy went to Devonshire, met a Mr. Webster, who had five hundred pounds a year, and married him. When James Woodforde met them in the turnpike road he could say little, "being shy," but to his diary he remarked—and this no doubt was his private version of the affair ever after—"she has proved herself to me a mere jilt."

But he was a young man then, and as time went on we cannot help suspecting that he was glad to consider the question of marriage shelved once and for all so that he might settle down with his niece Nancy at Weston Longueville, and give himself simply and solely, every day and all day, to the great business of living. Again, what else to call it we do not know.

For James Woodforde was nothing in particular. Life had it all her own way with him. He had no special gift; he had no oddity or infirmity. It is idle to pretend that he was a zealous priest. God in Heaven was much the same to him as King George upon the throne— a kindly Monarch, that is to say, whose festivals one kept by preaching a sermon on Sunday much as one kept the Royal birthday by firing a blunderbuss and drinking a toast at dinner. Should anything untoward happen, like the death of a boy who was dragged and killed by a horse, he would instantly, but rather perfunctorily exclaim, "I hope to God the Poor Boy is happy," and add, "We all came home singing"; just as when Justice Creed's peacock spread its tail—"and most noble it is"—he would exclaim, "How wonderful are Thy Works O God in every Being." But there was no fanaticism, no enthusiasm, no lyric impulse about James Woodforde. In all these pages, indeed, each so neatly divided into compartments, and each of those again filled, as the days themselves were filled, quietly and fully in a hand steady as the pacing of a well-tempered nag, one can only call to mind a single poetic phrase about the transit of Venus. "It appeared as a black patch upon a fair Lady's face," he says. The words themselves are mild enough, but they hang over the undulating expanse of the Parson's prose with the resplendence of the star itself. So in the Fen country a barn or a tree appears twice its natural size against the surrounding flats. But what led him to this palpable excess that summer's night we cannot tell. It cannot have been that he was drunk. He spoke out too roundly against such failings in his brother Jack to be guilty himself. Temperamentally he was among the eaters of meat and not among the drinkers of wine. When we think of the Woodfordes, uncle and niece, we think of them as often as not waiting with some impatience for their dinner. Gravely they watch the joint as it is set upon the table; swiftly they get their knives to work upon the succulent leg or loin; without much comment, unless a word is passed about the gravy or the stuffing, they go on eating. So they munch, day after day, year in year out, until between them they must have devoured herds of sheep and oxen, flocks of poultry, an odd dozen or so of swans and cygnets, bushels of apples and plums, while the pastries and the jellies crumble and squash beneath their spoons in mountains, in pyramids, in pagodas. Never was there a book so stuffed with food as this one is. To read the bill of fare respectfully and punctually set forth gives one a sense of repletion. Trout and chicken, mutton and peas, pork and apple sauce —so the joints succeed each other at dinner, and there is supper with more joints still to come, all, no doubt, home grown, and of the juiciest and sweetest; all cooked, often by the mistress herself, in the plainest English way, save when the dinner was at Weston Hall and Mrs. Custance surprised them with a London dainty—a pyramid of jelly, that is to say, with a "landscape appearing through it." After dinner sometimes, Mrs. Custance, for whom James Woodforde had a chivalrous devotion, would play the "Sticcardo Pastorale," and make "very soft music indeed"; or would get out her work-box and show them how neatly contrived it was, unless indeed she were giving birth to another child upstairs. These infants the Parson would baptize and very frequently he would bury them. They died almost as frequently as they were born. The Parson had a deep respect for the Custances. They were all that country gentry should be—a little given to the habit of keeping mistresses, perhaps, but that peccadillo could be forgiven them in view of their generosity to the poor, the kindness they showed to Nancy, and their condescension in asking the Parson to dinner when they had great people staying with them. Yet great people were not much to James's liking. Deeply though he respected the nobility, "one must confess," he said, "that being with our equals is much more agreeable."

Not only did Parson Woodforde know what was agreeable; that rare gift was by the bounty of Nature supplemented by another equally rare— he could have what he wanted. The age was propitious. Monday, Tuesday, Wednesday—they follow each other and each little compartment seems filled with content. The days were not crowded, but they were enviably varied. Fellow of New College though he was, he did things with his own hands, not merely with his own head. He lived in every room of the house—in the study he wrote sermons, in the diningroom he ate copiously; he looked in the kitchen, he played cards in the parlour. And then he took his coat and stick and went coursing his greyhounds in the fields. Year in, year out, the provisioning of the house and its defence against the cold of winter and the drought of summer fell upon him. Like a general he surveyed the seasons and took steps to make his own little camp safe with coal and wood and beef and beer against the enemy. His day thus had to accommodate a jumble of incongruous occupations.   There is religion to be served, and the pig to be killed; the sick to be visited and dinner to be eaten; the dead to be buried and beer to be brewed; Convocation to be attended and the cow to be bolused.   Life and death, mortality and immortality, jostle in his pages and make a good mixed marriage of it: ". . . found the old gentleman almost at his last gasp.   Totally senseless with rattlings in his Throat.   Dinner today boiled beef and Rabbit rosted."   All is as it should be; life is like that.

Surely, surely, then, here is one of the breathing-spaces in human affairs—here in Norfolk at the end of the eighteenth century at the Parsonage.   For once man is content with his lot; harmony is achieved; his house fits him; a tree is a tree; a chair is a chair; each knows its office and fulfils it.   Looking through the eyes of Parson Woodforde, the different lives of men seem orderly and settled.   Far away guns roar; a King falls; but the sound is not loud enough to scare the rooks here in Norfolk.   The proportions of things are different.   The Continent is so distant that it looks a mere blur; America scarcely exists; Australia is unknown.   But a magnifying glass is laid upon the fields of Norfolk.   Every blade of grass is visible there.   We see every lane and every field; the ruts on the roads and the peasants' faces.   Each house stands in its own breadth of meadow isolated and independent.   No wires link village to village.   No voices thread the air.   The body also is more present and more real.   It suffers more acutely.   No anaesthetic deadens physical pain.   The surgeon's knife hovers real and sharp above the limb.   Cold strikes unmitigated upon the house. The milk freezes in the pans; the water is thick with ice in the basins. One can scarcely walk from one room to another in the parsonage in winter.   Poor men and women are frozen to death upon the roads. Often no letters come and there are no visitors and no newspapers. The Parsonage stands alone in the midst of the frost-bound fields.   At last, Heaven be praised, life circulates again; a man comes to the door with a Madagascar monkey; another brings a box containing a child with two distinct perfect heads; there is a rumour that a balloon is going to rise at Norwich.   Every little incident stands out sharp and clear. The drive to Norwich even is something of an adventure.   One must trundle every step of the way behind a horse.   But look how distinct the trees stand in the hedges; how slowly the cattle move their heads as the carriage trots by; how gradually the spires of Norwich raise themselves above the hill.   And then how clear-cut and familiar are the faces of the few people who are our friends—the Custances, Mr. du Quesne.

Friendship has time to solidify, to become a lasting, a valuable possession.

True, Nancy of the younger generation is visited now and then by a flighty notion that she is missing something, that she wants something. One day she complained to her uncle that life was very dull: she complained "of the dismal situation of my house, nothing to be seen, and little or no visiting or being visited, etc.," and made him very uneasy. We could read Nancy a little lecture upon the folly of wanting that "et cetera." Look what your "et cetera" has brought to pass, we might say; half the countries of Europe are bankrupt; there is a red line of villas on every green hillside; your Norfolk roads are black as tar; there is no end to "visiting or being visited." But Nancy has an answer to make us, to the effect that our past is her present. You, she says, think it a great privilege to be born in the eighteenth century, because one called cowslips pagles and rode in a curricle instead of driving in a car. But you are utterly wrong, you fanatical lovers of memoirs, she goes on. I can assure you, my life was often intolerably dull. I did not laugh at the things that make you laugh. It did not amuse me when my uncle dreamt of a hat or saw bubbles in the beer, and said that meant a death in the family; I thought so too. Betsy Davy mourned young Walker with all her heart in spite of dressing in sprigged paduasoy. There is a great deal of humbug talked of the eighteenth century. Your delight in old times and old diaries is half impure. You make up something that never had any existence. Our sober reality is only a dream to you—so Nancy grieves and complains, living through the eighteenth century day by day, hour by hour.

Still, if it is a dream, let us indulge it a moment longer. Let us believe that some things last, and some places and some people are not touched by change. On a fine May morning, with the rooks rising and the hares scampering and the plover calling among the long grass, there is much to encourage the illusion. It is we who change and perish. Parson Woodforde lives on. It is the kings and queens who lie in prison. It is the great towns that are ravaged with anarchy and confusion. But the river Wensum still flows; Mrs. Custance is brought to bed of yet another baby; there is the first swallow of the year. The spring comes, and summer with its hay and strawberries; then autumn, when the walnuts are exceptionally fine though the pears are poor; so we lapse into winter, which is indeed boisterous, but the house, thank God, withstands the storm; and then again there is the first swallow, and Parson Woodforde takes his greyhounds out a-coursing.

II. THE REV. JOHN SKINNER

A whole world separates Woodforde, who was born in 1740 and died in 1803, from Skinner, who was born in 1772 and died in 1839.

For the few years that separated the two parsons are those momentous years that separate the eighteenth century from the nineteenth. Camerton, it is true, lying in the heart of Somersetshire, was a village of the greatest antiquity; nevertheless, before five pages of the diary are turned we read of coal-works, and how there was a great shouting at the coal-works because a fresh vein of coal had been discovered, and the proprietors had given money to the workmen to celebrate an event which promised such prosperity to the village. Then, though the country gentlemen seemed set as firmly in their seats as ever, it happened that the manor house at Camerton, with all the rights and duties pertaining to it, was in the hands of the Jarretts, whose fortune was derived from the Jamaica trade. This novelty, this incursion of an element quite unknown to Woodforde in his day, had its disturbing influence no doubt upon the character of Skinner himself. Irritable, nervous, apprehensive, he seems to embody, even before the age itself had come into existence, all the strife and unrest of our distracted times. He stands, dressed in the prosaic and unbecoming stocks and pantaloons of the early nineteenth century, at the parting of the ways. Behind him lay order and discipline and all the virtues of the heroic past, but directly he left his study he was faced with drunkenness and immorality; with indiscipline and irreligion; with Methodism and Roman Catholicism; with the Reform Bill and the Catholic Emancipation Act, with a mob clamouring for freedom, with the overthrow of all that was decent and established and right. Tormented and querulous, at the same time conscientious and able, he stands at the parting of the ways, unwilling to yield an inch, unable to concede a point, harsh, peremptory, apprehensive, and without hope.

Private sorrow had increased the natural acerbity of his temper. His wife had died young, leaving him with four small children, and of these the best-loved, Laura, a child who shared his tastes and would have sweetened his life, for she already kept a diary and had arranged a cabinet of shells with the utmost neatness, died too. But these losses, though they served nominally to make him love God the better, in practice led him to hate men more. By the time the diary opens in 1822 he was fixed in his opinion that the mass of men are unjust and malicious, and that the people of Camerton are more corrupt even than the mass of men. But by that date he was also fixed in his profession. Fate had taken him from the lawyer's office, where he would have been in his element, dealing out justice, filling up forms, keeping strictly to the letter of the law, and had planted him at Camerton among church-wardens and farmers, the Gullicks and the Padfields, the old woman who had dropsy, the idiot boy, and the dwarf. Nevertheless, however sordid his tasks and disgusting his parishioners, he had his duty to them; and with them he would remain. Whatever insults he suffered, he would live up to his principles, uphold the right, protect the poor, and punish the wrongdoer. By the time the diary opens, this strenuous and unhappy career is in full swing.

Perhaps the village of Camerton in the year 1822, with its coal-miners and the disturbance they brought, was no fair sample of English village life. Certainly it is difficult, as one follows the Rector on his daily rounds, to indulge in pleasant dreams about the quaintness and amenity of old English rural life. Here, for instance, he was called to see Mrs. Gooch—a woman of weak mind, who had been locked up alone in her cottage and fallen into the fire and was in agony. "Why do you not help me, I say? Why do you not help me?" she cried. And the Rector, as he heard her screams, knew that she had come to this through no fault of her own. Her efforts to keep a home together had led to drink, and so she had lost her reason, and what with the squabbles be-tween the Poor Law officials and the family as to who should support her, what with her husband's extravagance and drunkenness, she had been left alone, had fallen into the fire, and so died. Who was to blame? Mr. Purnell, the miserly magistrate, who was all for cutting down the allowance paid to the poor, or Hicks the Overseer, who was notoriously harsh, or the ale-houses, or the Methodists, or what? At any rate the Rector had done his duty. However he might be hated for it, he always stood up for the rights of the down-trodden; he always told people of their faults, and convicted them of evil. Then there was Mrs. Somer, who kept a house of ill fame and was bringing up her daughters to the same profession. Then there was Farmer Lippeatt, who, turned out of the Red Post at midnight, dead drunk, missed his way, fell into a quarry, and died of a broken breastbone. Wherever one turned there was suffering, wherever one looked one found cruelty behind that suffering. Mr. and Mrs. Hicks, for example, the Overseers, let an infirm pauper lie for ten days in the Poor House without care, "so that maggots had bred in his flesh and eaten great holes in his body." His only attendant was an old woman, who was so failing that she was unable to lift him. Happily the pauper died. Happily poor Garratt, the miner, died too. For to add to the evils of drink and poverty and the cholera there was constant peril from the mine itself. Accidents were common and the means of treating them elementary. A fall of coal had broken Garratt's back, but he lingered on, though exposed to the crude methods of country surgeons, from January to November, when at last death released him. Both the stern Rector and the flippant Lady of the Manor, to do them justice, were ready with their half-crowns, with their soups and their medicines, and visited sick-beds without fail. But even allowing for the natural asperity of Mr. Skinner's temper, it would need a very rosy pen and a very kindly eye to make a smiling picture of life in the village of Camerton a century ago. Half-crowns and soup went a very little way to remedy matters; sermons and denunciations made them perhaps even worse.

The Rector found refuge from Camerton neither in dissipation like some of his neighbours, nor in sport like others. Occasionally he drove over to dine with a brother cleric, but he noted acrimoniously that the entertainment was "better suited to Grosvenor Square than a clergyman's home—French dishes and French wines in profusion," and records with a note of exclamation that it was eleven o'clock before he drove home. When his children were young he sometimes walked with them in the fields, or amused himself by making them a boat, or rubbed up his Latin in an epitaph for the tomb of some pet dog or tame pigeon. And sometimes he leant back peacefully and listened to Mrs. Fenwick as she sang the songs of Moore to her husband's accompaniment on the flute. But even such harmless pleasures were poisoned with suspicion. A farmer stared insolently as he passed; some one threw a stone from a window; Mrs. Jarrett clearly concealed some evil purpose behind her cordiality. No, the only refuge from Camerton lay in Camalodunum. The more he thought of it the more certain he became that he had the singular good fortune to live on the identical spot where lived the father of Caractacus, where Ostorius established his colony, where Arthur had fought the traitor Modred, where Alfred very nearly came in his misfortunes. Camerton was undoubtedly the Camalodunum of Tacitus. Shut up in his study alone with his documents, copying, comparing, proving indefatigably, he was safe, at rest, even happy. He was also, he became convinced, on the track of an important etymological discovery, by which it could be proved that there was a secret significance "in every letter that entered into the composition of Celtic names."

No archbishop was as content in his palace as Skinner the antiquary was content in his cell.   To these pursuits he owed, too, those rare and delightful visits to Stourhead, the seat of Sir Richard Hoare, when at last he mixed with men of his own calibre, and met the gentlemen who were engaged in examining the antiquities of Wiltshire.   However hard it froze, however high the snow lay heaped on the roads, Skinner rode over to Stourhead; and sat in the library, with a violent cold, but in perfect content, making extracts from Seneca, and extracts from Diodorum Siculus, and extracts from Ptolemy's *Geography,* or scornfully disposed of some rash and ill-informed fellow-antiquary who had the temerity to assert that Camalodunum was really situated at Colchester.   On he went with his extracts, with his theories, with his proofs, in spite of the malicious present of a rusty nail wrapped in paper from his parishioners, in spite of the laughing warning of his host: "Oh, Skinner, you will bring everything at last to Camalodunum; be content with what you have already discovered, if you fancy too much you will weaken the authority of real facts."   Skinner replied with a sixth letter thirty-four pages long; for Sir Richard did not know how necessary Camalodunum had become to an embittered man who had daily to encounter Hicks the Overseer and Purnell the magistrate, the brothels, the ale-houses, the Methodists, the dropsies and bad legs of Camerton. Even the floods were mitigated if one could reflect that thus Camalodunum must have looked in the time of the Britons.

So he filled three iron chests with ninety-eight volumes of manuscript. But by degrees the manuscripts ceased to be entirely concerned with Camalodunum; they began to be largely concerned with John Skinner. It was true that it was important to establish the truth about Camalodunum, but it was also important to establish the truth about John Skinner.   In fifty years after his death, when the diaries were published, people would know not only that John Skinner was a great antiquary, but that he was a much wronged, much suffering man.   His diary became his confidante, as it was to become his champion.   For example, was he not the most affectionate of fathers, he asked the diary? He had spent endless time and trouble on his sons; he had sent them to Winchester and Cambridge, and yet now when the farmers were so insolent about paying him his tithes, and gave him a broken-backed lamb for his share, or fobbed him off with less than his due of cocks, his son Joseph refused to help him.   His son said that the people of Camerton laughed at him; that he treated his children like servants; that he suspected evil where none was meant.   And then he opened a letter by chance and found a bill for a broken gig; and then his sons lounged about smoking cigars when they might have helped him to mount his drawings.   In short, he could not stand their presence in his house.   He dismissed them in a fury to Bath.   When they had gone he could not help admitting that perhaps he had been at fault.   It was his querulous temper again—but then he had so much to make him querulous.   Mrs. Jarrett's peacock screamed under his window all night.   They jangled the church bells on purpose to annoy him.   Still, he would try; he would let them come back.   So Joseph and Owen came back.   And then the old irritation overcame him again.   He "could not help saying" something about being idle, or drinking too much cider, upon which there was a terrible scene and Joseph broke one of the parlour chairs.   Owen took Joseph's part.   So did Anna. None of his children cared for him.   Owen went further.   Owen said "I was a madman and ought to have a commission of lunacy to investigate my conduct."   And, further, Owen cut him to the quick by pouring scorn on his verses, on his diaries and archaeological theories. He said: "No one would read the nonsense I had written.   When I mentioned having gained a prize at Trinity College . . . his reply was that none but the most stupid fellows ever thought of writing for the college prize."   Again there was a terrible scene; again they were dismissed to Bath, followed by their father's curses.   And then Joseph fell ill with the family consumption.   At once his father was all tenderness and remorse.   He sent for doctors, he offered to take him for a sea trip to Ireland, he took him indeed to Weston and went sailing with him on the sea.   Once more the family came together.   And once more the querulous, exacting father could not help, for all his concern, exasperating the children whom, in his own crabbed way, he yet genuinely loved. The question of religion cropped up.   Owen said his father was no better than a Deist or a Socinian.   And Joseph, lying ill upstairs, said he was too tired for argument; he did not want his father to bring drawings to show him; he did not want his father to read prayers to him, "he would rather have some other person to converse with than me." So in the crisis of their lives, when a father should have been closest to them, even his children turned away from him.   There was nothing left to live for.   Yet what had he done to make every one hate him? Why did the farmers call him mad?   Why did Joseph say that no one would read what he wrote?   Why did the villagers tie tins cans to the tail of his dog?   Why did the peacocks shriek and the bells ring?   Why was there no mercy shown to him and no respect and no love?   With agonising repetition the diary asks these questions; but there was no answer.   At last, one morning in December 1839, the Rector took his gun, walked into the beech wood near his home, and shot himself dead.

Lines of Inquiry

1 In the introduction to Part III of this text, the point was made that narration frequently can be viewed as illustrative of some idea or set of ideas.

  a Taking this view of "Two Parsons," can you paraphrase its point in a single sentence?

  b If you find that it illustrates a set of ideas not reducible to a single paraphrasing sentence, can you arrange the ideas you find it to illustrate in a pattern ranging from the one closest to the concrete, i.e., the plain narrative of events to the one furtherest away, i.e., most abstracted from that plain narrative? Can you say of this order that any given idea, or level of idea, is "truer" than the others?

  c How do you account for the sequence in which Woolf arranges her two, essentially distinct, narratives?

2 a Woolf's comparison is between two *parsons*.   What special value does she derive from a focus on this particular occupational group?

  b In "Two Parsons" *occupation* is kept constant: Both men are parsons.   What is varied?   If you were to vary occupation in such an essay, what kind of thing might you keep constant, in order to preserve the principle that useful comparisons can only be made between things sufficiently similar to make the differences significant?

3 This essay, with others, was collected by Woolf in a book called *The Common Reader.*

  a How is the voice employed by Woolf in this essay related to "the common reader"?

  b In which section does that voice enter most obviously, and why?

  c If one were to make the point that these two brief biographies originally appeared separately, as book reviews, would the assumption that Woolf is writing from the point of view of a "common reader" be proved wrong?

4 Study the use of tense in this essay.

  a Where in the first section does the tense shift, and why there?

  b Why is there no corresponding shift of tense in the second section?

  c How is this treatment of tense related to Woolf's handling of internal point of view?

5 In Woolf's sketch of Skinner's life, his obsession with Camalodunum looms large.
a Why?
b Camalodunum is now considered to have been Colchester;
i.e., Skinner was wrong. Why doesn't Woolf say so?
c Camalodunum could have been dealt with either earlier in
Woolf's narrative or later; how do you account for its actual
position?

6 Why is it so much harder to make a satisfactory outline of
Woodforde's life than of Skinner's?

7 Examine the concluding sentences of each section.
a What tone does each create, and how is that tone related
to the theme of each section?
b How in each case does Woolf's handling of the following
contribute to that tone?
(1) Sentence structure   (5) Specificity of date and
(2) Sentence rhythm   focus
(3) Tense   (6) Specificity of fact
(4) Repetition

c Of the two brief biographies, which has most clearly a beginning, a middle, and an end? Which rises to a point of actual crisis?
d Considering Woolf's stylistic treatment of the two lives, what
relationship do you see between the structure of each biography and its point?

8 Frequently in this essay our grasp of Woolf's full meaning depends on our ability to recognize the significance of relatively
small details. In the following passages, what is the point of
each of the italicized phrases?
a "And as we read—if reading is the word for it—we seem to
be listening to someone who is murmuring over the events of
the day to himself in the quiet space which precedes sleep.
It is not writing, and, to speak of the truth, it is not reading.
It is slipping through half a dozen pages and *strolling to the
window and looking out.* It is going on thinking about the
Woodfordes *while we watch the people in the street below.*"
b "True, Nancy *of the younger generation,* is visited now and
then by a flighty notion that she is missing something, that
she wants something."
c "He stands, *dressed in the prosaic and unbecoming stocks
and pantaloons of the early nineteenth century,* at the parting
of the ways."
d "When his children were young he sometimes walked with

them in the fields, or amused himself by making them a
boat, or *rubbed up his Latin in an epitaph for the tomb of
some pet dog or tame pigeon.*"

e "And Joseph, lying ill upstairs, said he was too tired for
argument; *he did not want his father to bring drawings to
show him;* he did not want his father to read prayers to him,
'*he would rather have some other person to converse with
than me.*'"

f "At last, *one morning in December, 1839,* the rector took
his gun, *walked into the beech wood near his home,* and
shot himself dead."

9 Each of the following sentences is a revision of Woolf's original. That original follows immediately in parentheses. In
each case, what differences do you note between the two?
What is the effect of those differences?

a Diary-keeping is often the one mysterious fact in a man's
life. ("For often it [diary-keeping] is the one mysterious
fact in a life otherwise as clear as the sky and as candid as
the dawn.")

b James Woodforde was one of those men whom we can never
imagine except in middle age. ("James Woodforde, then,
was one of those smooth-cheeked, steady-eyed men, demure
to look at, whom we can never imagine except in the prime
of life.")

c He was not an energetic clergyman. ("It is idle to pretend
that he was a zealous priest.")

d So they ate, for years, until between them they must have
eaten hundreds of sheep and oxen, thousands of chickens,
and huge quantities of fruit and dessert. ("So they munch,
day after day, year in year out, until between them they
must have devoured herds of sheep and oxen, flocks of
poultry, an odd dozen or so of swans and cygnets, bushels
of apples and plums, while the pastries and the jellies
crumble and squash beneath their spoons in mountains, in
pyramids, in pagodas.")

e The ninety-eight volumes of his diary filled three trunks.
("So he filled three iron chests with ninety-eight volumes of
manuscript.")

Lines of Experiment

1 Perhaps the most remarkable thing about Woolf's essay is its
successful evocation of the quality of two lives. That evocation depends largely on the use of Woodforde's and Skinner's
diaries, as ways of revealing their private worlds—the tone of
their experience. Below are listed the names of several famous

English and American diarists. Choose one (or another not on the list, if you prefer) and make it the focus of a narrative essay on its author's life. You may take from Woolf—or from anybody else—any tonal or structural device useful to you in showing the significance of that life. Obviously, you will have to be particularly careful to find a tone that can carry your sense of that life's significance; for establishing that tone, two elements will be crucial: the language of the diarist himself and the pattern of events that you choose as the focal point of his life and experience. For some of these men the diaristic materials are very extensive. (Skim those materials rapidly before selecting a specific pattern of events as your central narrative forcus.)

a Samuel Pepys   d James Boswell
b William Byrd II of Westover   e Ralph Waldo Emerson
c Samuel Sewall   f Robert Falcon Scott

2 The transition from an essentially agricultural to an essentially industrial world, as we have seen earlier in this text, is one of the great themes or motifs of modern literature. H. M. Tomlinson's "A Lost Wood" (see p. 306) illustrates this change through its effect on the English countryside; Woolf illustrates the change through its effect on two men of barometric sensibility. Perhaps the most obvious way to approach this transition, however, is in the terms of personal experience; indeed, in both Tomlinson's and Woolf's essays, the personal reaction shapes and colors the prose. Employing your own experience, your own feelings, your own background, write your own statement on this theme.

MAX BEERBOHM

SOME WORDS ON ROYALTY

In the memoirs of Count————, privately printed last year, you will find, if you can gain access to them, many secrets told in a sprightly, yet most authoritative, manner; little that is incredible, little that is not amazing, nothing refutable.   The Count has cast upon *la haute politique,*[1] that stage without footlights, many lurid "limes," illuminating for us the faces of all the players and even enabling us to understand something of the plot.   For years the trusted Minister of the late Emperor ———— of ————, the Count has much court-lore to communicate, and is terribly frank about the master whom he served so faithfully until, in 188–, he was ousted from favour by the machinations of a jealous and not too scrupulous cabal.   I, who had always been taught to regard this monarch as a wise, gifted, and courageous gentleman, if not actually as a hero, am pleasantly shocked to find him designated with such unkind terms as *"fainéant,"* [2]—the memoirs are written in the Volapuk of diplomacy—and *"roi de paille,"* [3] and *"petit bonhomme à tête montée."* [4]   Indeed, it is undoubtedly when he is describing the life and the character of the Emperor that my author is at his most intimate, his best.   Seldom has so realistic a portrait of a modern monarch been painted for our pleasure.   Much as we talk and read about royal personages, we know really less about them than about any other kind of human beings.   We see the princes of our country caracoling past us in pageants, illustrious monsters whose breasts are all agleam and aglimmer with the symbols of fifty victories at which they were not present, and bunt with enough ribandry to trick forth fifty dairy-maids for a fair.   We tell ourselves that beneath all their frippery they are human beings.   We have heard that one is industrious, another is genial, another plays the fiddle or collects stamps.   And then, maybe, we see them at Newmarket, and we know that, for all the elaborate simplicity of their tweeds and billycocks, they are not as we are, but, rather, creatures of another order, "specimens of an unrelated species." We note the curious uniformity of their faces, almost wondering whether they are masked.   Those heavy, handsome, amiable, uninteresting and uninterested faces, are they indeed (not masks but) true mirrors of souls which a remote and esoteric life has gradually impoverished?   We know that there is a crimson drugget which underlies their every footstep from the cradle to the mausoleum; we know that their progress is beneath an awning, along that level drugget, through an unbroken avenue of bare and bowed heads.   They cannot mingle with their fellows.   They are kept from all contact with realities.   For them there is no reciprocity, no endeavour, no salt of life.   "It is a miserable State

[1] International politics.
[2] Lazy bones.
[3] Straw king.
[4] Little man with a swelled head.

of Minde," wrote a philosopher who was also a courtier, "to have few Things to desire and many Things to feare. And yet that commonly is the case of Princes." Fear kept human the Princes of other days. We have taken away their fear now, and we still leave them no loophole for desire. What, we might well wonder, will be the descendants of this race apart, of these men who neither marry nor give in marriage save among their own order? Would anyone choose to be born, in their purple, to their life of morbid and gaudy humdrum? Better, surely, to be thrown, like the ordinary child, into a life of endeavour, with unforeseen chances of success or failure. It is this scroll of chances that makes life tolerable, makes it wonderful. The life of every royal person in England begins and must needs end on the same high, smooth plane. But who shall cast the horoscope of an ordinary child? Who knows the vicissitudes of his journey? Be he suckled in a pit, or in a castle on a mountain, who shall prophesy the level of his last bed? Cast him up naked to the pit's edge, send him in purple down the wide steps of his father's castle, you know not how long he shall fare in the gloom or light of his origin, nor whither, and by what hostelries, he shall pass. He may come to a dark woodland, where, all night long, the ferns snap under the feet of elusive Dryads, and the moon is privy to the whole grief of Philomel. He may never leave that gentle labyrinth of leaves, or he may tarry there but for one night. Mocked and footsore, he may shuffle along the highways, till he come to that city whose people stone him or make him ruler over them. Exile or empery may be his, flowers or ashes, an aureole or a noose. There are seas for his drowning, and whirlwinds for his overwhelming, and sheer rocks for his ascent. He shall clutch and falter and be afraid. No bloodhounds but shall follow swiftly on his track, nor any nets but shall enmesh him. He shall laugh and conquer. He shall prosper in a great dominion. In strength and scorn there shall not be his equal. But the slaves whom he tortured shall prick him in his exultation. His wine-cup shall be a cup of gall, and a harpy shall lurk in the canopy of his bridal bed. In the blood of his children they shall bathe him. From a clear sky the lightning shall slant down on him. And the ground shall yawn for him in the garden of his design.

That, despite certain faults of exaggeration, is a piece of quite admirable prose; but let it not decoy the reader from consideration of the main theme. Count ———, whose memoirs are my cue, does not seem to have weighed the conditions of royal life. Had he done so, he would have cooled his caustic pen in the lymph of charity, and one would have lost many of his most delightful *mots*[5] and anecdotes.   He simply records, out of the fulness and intimacy of his knowledge, many suggestive facts about a monarch in whom a royal environment had not paralysed the ordinary, bright instincts of human nature.   In recording with gusto the little strategies used by his master in the pursuit of fun or the flight from duty, the Count moves his reader to tears rather than to laughter.

One of his anecdotes I must really make known, not merely because it is a good sample and deals with a famous incident, but also because it has a suggestive symbolism of its own.   Many of my readers can remember the sensation caused in the spring of a late seventy by the attempted assassination of Emperor———.   As his Imperial Majesty was being driven out of the palace gates for his daily progress through the capital, a man in the crowd fired at him with a revolver.   The miscreant was immediately seized, and, but for the soldiery, would have been torn limb from limb.   "Luckily," wrote Reuter's correspondent, "the Emperor, who was accompanied as usual by Count ——— and an aide-de-camp, was untouched.   As so often happens in such cases, the assassin, doubtless through excitement, entirely missed his aim.   The remarkable thing was the coolness and courage displayed by the Emperor.   So far from evincing any alarm, he continued to salute the crowd on either side, smilingly as ever, as though nothing at all had happened; nor was his drive in any way curtailed.   As the news spread, a vast crowd of people collected round the palace, and the Emperor, in answer to their continued cheers, at length appeared upon the balcony and bowed repeatedly."

In the light of the Count's version the Emperor's "coolness and courage" are somewhat discounted.   It seems that, about three years before, the Emperor had declared that he was going to give up the custom of the daily drive: he hated driving, he hated saluting, he hated being stared at.   The Count represented to him how unwise it would be to disappoint the people.   Finding the Emperor obstinate in his distaste, he conceived the idea of a waxen figure, made in the likeness of his master, with practicable joints worked by interior mechanism.   The Emperor promised to endure his drives for the present, and, after secret negotiations with a famous firm in England (conducted by the Count himself, who came over incognito), the figure was completed and duly delivered at the Imperial Palace.   It was so constructed that, when wound up,

---

[5] Witticisms, clever remarks.

it turned its head slowly from side to side, with a slight bend of the body, raising its hand in salute. It was considered an admirable likeness, though the Count declares that *"la figure était un peu trop distinguée."* [6] At any rate, arrayed as a Colonel of the ——— Dragoons and driven quickly through the capital, it was good enough to deceive the Emperor's loyal subjects. As I need hardly say, it was at this automaton that the revolver was fired. According to the memoirs, the Emperor himself, in a false beard, was standing near the assassin, and was actually arrested on suspicion, but managed to escape his captor in the *mêlée* [7] and reached the palace in ample time to bow from the balcony. The Count argues that the only sufferer in the affair is the poor wretch who was hanged merely for shooting at a dummy, and who has never even got the credit he deserved for a very good shot; the bullet pierced right through the dummy's chest, and says the Count, had it but lodged one-eighth of an inch lower down, it must have inevitably stopped the mechanism.

Even if the whole of this tale be but the naughty figment of a favourite in disfavour, it is, at any rate, suggestive. A mob doffing its head-gear, day after day, to a dummy! How easily, after all, could one get a dummy so constructed as to hold a *levée* [8] or sit through an opera, to open a bridge or lay a stone "well and truly." There are some persons who would fain abolish altogether the institution of royalty. I do not go so far as they. Our royal family is a rather absurd institution, no doubt. But then, humanity itself is rather absurd. A State can never be more than a kindergarten, at best, and he who would fain rule men according to principles of right reason will fare no better than did poor dear Plato at Syracuse. Put the dream of the *doctrinaire* into practice, and it will soon turn to some such nightmare as modern France or modern America. Indeed, fallacies and anomalies are the basis of all good government. A Crown, like a Garter, implies no "damned merit"; else were it void of its impressive magic for most creatures. Strictly, there is no reason why we should worship the House of Hanover more than we worship any other family. Strictly, there was no reason why the Children of Israel should bow down before brazen images. But man is not rational, and the spirit of idolatry is strong in him. And, if you take away his idol, that energy which would otherwise be spent in kotowing will probably be spent in some less harmless manner. In

---

[6] The face was a little too distinguished.
[7] Confused struggle.
[8] A reception.

every free public there is a fund of patriotic emotion which must, somehow, be worked off. I may be insular, but I cannot help thinking it better that this fund should be worked off, as in England, by cheering the members of the royal family, rather than by upsetting the current ministry, as in France.

The main good of royalty, then, and the justification of those fabulous sums of money that we sacrifice annually for its support, lie in its appeal to that idolatrous instinct which is quite unmoved by the cheap and nasty inmates of the Elysée or of the White House. In this century we have greatly restricted the sphere of royal power, insomuch that royalty cannot, as it once could, guide directly the trend of politics: politically, it does but "act by its presence." But one should not forget that a Court is for ornament, as well as for use. A capital without a Court, be the streets never so beautiful, is even as a garden where the sun shines not. As a flock of sheep without a shepherd, so is the Society that has no royal leader to set its fashions, chasten its follies, or dignify its whims with his approval. Gaiety, wit, beauty, some measure even of splendour, may be compassed in the *salons* of a republic; but distinction comes not in save with one who must be received at the foot of the staircase. In fact, royalty is indispensable: we cannot spare it. But, you may well ask, are we justified in preserving an institution which ruins the lives and saps the human nature of a whole family? What of those royal victims whom we sacrifice to our expediency? I have suggested that royal functions could be quite satisfactorily performed by automata made of wax. There, I think, lies the solution of our difficulty. Perhaps, even now, did we but know, it is the triumphs of Tussaud at whose frequent sight our pulses beat with so quick an enthusiasm. If it is so, I do not blame our royal family for its innocent subterfuge. I should welcome any device to lighten the yoke that is on their necks. I should be glad if more people would seriously examine the conditions of royalty, with a view to ameliorating the royal lot. Would that every one could gain access to the memoirs of Count ———! They might serve as an excellent manual, containing, as they do, so much that is well-observed. But they are so frankly written that they cannot, I fear, be made public before many, many years have elapsed. Perhaps the brief trumpet-note which I have sounded will be enough to rouse humanitarianism, in the meantime.

Lines of Inquiry

1 The memoirs of Count ——— are nothing if not frank. As it happens, however, the names of the king, the country concerned, and even of the Count himself are suppressed. By whom? Why?

a Suppose that Count ——, Emperor ——, and the realm of —— were all fictitious. What would be the point and value of such an essay?

b Suppose that everything in the essay is true, except the central anecdote, which we shall define arbitrarily as the slander of a disappointed, slightly malicious courtier. What would become the point of the essay, were we to know that?

2 How would you characterize the point of view adopted by Beerbohm in this essay?

a What pronoun or pronouns does he use to express that point of view?

b How is the point of view related to the tone established in this essay?

c How important to tone and point of view is it that Count —— is not identified?

d Why, in quoting from "a philosopher who was also a courtier," does Beerbohm use the archaic spellings "minde" and "feare," and employ the archaic convention of capitalizing substantives?

e Why does Beerbohm quote the Reuter's correspondent?

f Suppose Beerbohm's tone were obviously more sarcastic than it is; would a change in pronoun, or in the handling of point of view, be appropriate? (Compare "A Modest Proposal," p. 568, and "The Cult of Hope," p. 580.)

3 What is the difference between

a A memoir and an auto-   d Dummies and automata
biography   e A grave and a mausoleum

b A dryad and a nymph   f A cabal and a conspiracy

c Empery and empire

4 Many of the most cutting ideas in Beerbohm's essay are expressed by implication, rather than directly. What are the implications of the following?

a The fact that Beerbohm is "pleasantly shocked" to find the emperor designated with unkind terms

b His remark that the "curious uniformity" of the faces of royalty makes us wonder "whether they are masked"

c The fact that the emperor himself, in a false beard, was standing near his would-be assassin at the time of the shot

d The remark that "A Crown, like a Garter, implies no 'damned merit'; else were it void of its impressive magic for most creatures"

5 In the introduction to this part of the text, it was pointed out that allusion is an important element in the creation of tone. What lies behind each of the italicized phrases in the following?

a "Would anyone choose to be born, *in their purple,* to their life of morbid and gaudy humdrum?"

b "He may come to a dark woodland, where . . . the moon is privy to the *whole grief of Philomel.*"

c ". . . he who would fain rule according to principles of right reason will fare no better than did *poor dear Plato at Syracuse.*"

d "The main good of royalty . . . lies in its appeal to that idolatrous instinct which is quite unmoved by the cheap and nasty inmates of the *Elysée* or of the White House."

e "As a *flock of sheep without a shepherd,* so is the society that has no royal leader. . . ."

f "Perhaps, even now, did we but know, it is the *triumphs of Tussaud.* . . ."

6 Let us suppose that instead of mingling with the crowd from which the would-be assassin shot, the Emperor ———— of ———— had been

a Eating napoleons in the throne room

b Disguised as one of the dragoons escorting the carriage

c Skiing in Switzerland

d Participating in a secret council of war

What would be the effect on the tone of each of these changes? What is the effect of the Emperor's being where he actually is?

7 a What kind of man is the Count?

b What effect does it have on us that he is quoted in French?

c Why does Beerbohm go out of his way to tell us that it was the Count himself who suggested replacing the Emperor by an automaton?

8 At one point, Beerbohm breaks into what he calls "a piece of quite admirable prose."

a How admirable is the prose?

b Why does Beerbohm break into it?

c What is the effect of this passage on the immediately following paragraph, and on the essay as a whole?

d What relationship does this passage have to the theme of the essay—to the point that Beerbohm is trying to make about royalty?

Lines of Experiment

1 Let us suppose that the memoirs of Secretary X, an official recently released from high place in governmental life, have

just been published. You are at liberty to make up the government, the official, and the substance of his memoirs (if you do not make them up, you will get nowhere). Select from those memoirs an anecdote illustrative of political life in the good Secretary's time and place, and make it the center of an essay.

Some important questions:

a What point are you trying to illustrate?

b What type of illustration—extreme or average—will best serve that point?

c What tone do you wish to strike—savage anger, whimsical despair, contempt? (Why is a hypothetical illustration a poor vehicle for *hope?*)

d How will you frame your illustration properly, so as to place it in its larger perspective—how reduce it, how round it off? (Think of the movement between idea and image, logical and mimetic structure, so frequently spoken of in this book; ordinarily one frames the other.).

e What internal point of view will best serve to mediate the special tone you are trying to achieve? (Do not be afraid to assume an obviously fictitious identity; Swift does in "A Modest Proposal.")

Do not try to find answers to all such problems before you start to write. Be conscious of them as you go and solve them in the process itself—as all writers finally do.

2 The processes of government, and our suspicions concerning them, display similarities from age to age. Beerbohm's point in "Some Words on Royalty" is still largely valid, though costumes have changed. (A national newspaper recently ran a feature story under the title "The Robot That Sits in for the President." The "robot" was a signature-making machine.)

Write a paper on the theme touched by Beerbohm but more directly related to the politics of your own time and place. Two cautions: First write about something you know well (college, city—something close to home) in preference to something less familiar. Second, as the official images ride by, look carefully; do not mistake the dummy for the real thing.

JOHN RUSKIN

 WAR [1]

Young soldiers, I do not doubt but that many of you came unwillingly to-night, and many in merely contemptuous curiosity, to hear what a writer on painting could possibly say, or would venture to say, respecting your great art of war.   You may well think within yourselves that a painter might, perhaps without immodesty, lecture younger painters upon painting, but not young lawyers upon law, nor young physicians upon medicine—least of all, it may seem to you, young warriors, upon war.   And, indeed, when I was asked to address you, I declined at first, and declined long; for I felt that you would not be interested in my special business, and would certainly think there was small need for me to come to teach you yours.   Nay, I knew that there ought to be *no* such need, for the great veteran soldiers of England are now men every way so thoughtful, so noble, and so good, that no other teaching than their knightly example, and their few words of grave and tried counsel, should be either necessary for you, or even, without assurance of due modesty in the offerer, endured by you.

But being asked, not once nor twice, I have not ventured persistently to refuse; and I will try, in very few words, to lay before you some reason why you should accept my excuse, and hear me patiently.   You may imagine that your work is wholly foreign to, and separate from, mine.   So far from that, all the pure and noble arts of peace are founded on war; no great art ever yet rose on earth, but among a nation of soldiers.   There is no art among a shepherd people, if it remains at peace.   There is no art among an agricultural people, if it remains at peace.   Commerce is barely consistent with fine art; but

---

[1] This essay was delivered as a lecture to the cadets of the Royal Military Academy, Woolwich, England, in 1865.

cannot produce it. Manufacture not only is unable to produce it, but invariably destroys whatever seeds of it exist. There is no great art possible to a nation but that which is based on battle.

Now, though I hope you love fighting for its own sake, you must, I imagine, be surprised at my assertion that there is any such good fruit of fighting. You supposed, probably, that your office was to defend the works of peace, but certainly not to found them: nay, the common course of war, you may have thought, was only to destroy them. And truly, I, who tell you this of the use of war, should have been the last of men to tell you so, had I trusted my own experience only. Hear why: I have given a considerable part of my life to the investigation of Venetian painting; and the result of that enquiry was my fixing upon one man as the greatest of all Venetians, and therefore, as I believed, of all painters whatsoever. I formed this faith (whether right or wrong matters at present nothing) in the supremacy of the painter Tintoret, under a roof covered with his pictures; and of those pictures, three of the noblest were then in the form of shreds of ragged canvas, mixed up with the laths of the roof, rent through by three Austrian shells. Now, it is not every lecturer who *could* tell you that he had seen three of his favourite pictures torn to rags by bomb-shells. And after such a sight, it is not every lecturer who *would* tell you that, nevertheless, war was the foundation of all great art.

Yet the conclusion is inevitable, from any careful comparison of the states of great historic races at different periods. Merely to show you what I mean, I will sketch for you, very briefly, the broad steps of the advance of the best art of the world. The first dawn of it is in Egypt; and the power of it is founded on the perpetual contemplation of death, and of future judgment, by the mind of a nation of which the ruling caste were priests, and the second, soldiers. The greatest works produced by them are sculptures of their kings going out to battle, or receiving the homage of conquered armies. And you must remember also, as one of the great keys to the splendour of the Egyptian nation, that the priests were not occupied in theology only. Their theology was the basis of practical government and law; so that they were not so much priests as religious judges; the office of Samuel, among the Jews, being as nearly as possible correspondent to theirs.

All the rudiments of art then, and much more than the rudiments of all science, were laid first by this great warrior-nation, which held in contempt all mechanical trades, and in absolute hatred the peaceful life of shepherds.   From Egypt art passes directly into Greece, where all poetry, and all painting, are nothing else than the description, praise, or dramatic representation of war, or of the exercises which prepare for it, in their connection with offices of religion.   All Greek institutions had first respect to war; and their conception of it, as one necessary office of all human and divine life, is expressed simply by the images of their guiding gods.   Apollo is the god of all wisdom of the intellect; he bears the arrow and the bow, before he bears the lyre.   Again, Athena is the goddess of all wisdom in conduct.   Yet it is by the helmet and the shield, oftener than by the shuttle, that she is distinguished from other deities.

There were, however, two great differences in principle between the Greek and the Egyptian theories of policy.   In Greece there was no soldier caste; every citizen was necessarily a soldier.   And, again, while the Greeks rightly despised mechanical arts as much as the Egyptians, they did not make the fatal mistake of despising agricultural and pastoral life; but perfectly honoured both.   These two conditions of truer thought raise them quite into the highest rank of wise manhood that has yet been reached; for all our great arts, and nearly all our great thoughts, have been borrowed or derived from them.   Take away from us what they have given; and we hardly can imagine how low the modern European would stand.

Now, you are to remember, in passing to the next phase of history, that—though you *must* have war to produce art—you must also have much more than war; namely, an art-instinct or genius in the people; and that, though all the talent for painting in the world won't make painters of you, unless you have a gift for fighting as well, you may have the gift for fighting, and none for painting.   Now, in the next great dynasty of soldiers, the art-instinct is wholly wanting.   I have not yet investigated the Roman character enough to tell you the causes of this; but I believe, paradoxical as it may seem to you, that however truly the Roman might say of himself that he was born of Mars, and suckled by the wolf, he was nevertheless, at heart, more of a farmer than a soldier.   The exercises of war were with him practical, not poetical; his poetry was in domestic life only, and the object of battle, "pacis imponere morem."[2]   And the arts are extinguished in his hands, and do not rise again, until, with Gothic chivalry, there comes back into the mind of Europe a passionate delight in war itself, for the sake

[2] Virgil: "To impose the ways of peace."

of war.   And then, with the romantic knighthood which can imagine no other noble employment,—under the fighting kings of France, England, and Spain; and under the fighting dukeships and citizenships of Italy, art is born again, and rises to her height in the great valleys of Lombardy and Tuscany, through which there flows not a single stream, from all their Alps or Apennines, that did not once run dark red from battle; and it reaches its culminating glory in the city which gave to history the most intense type of soldiership yet seen among men;—the city whose armies were led in their assault by their king,[3] led through it to victory by their king, and so led, though that king of theirs was blind, and in the extremity of his age.

And from this time forward, as peace is established or extended in Europe, the arts decline.   They reach an unparalleled pitch of costliness, but lose their life, enlist themselves at last on the side of luxury and various corruption, and, among wholly tranquil nations, wither utterly away; remaining only in partial practice among races who, like the French and us, have still the minds, though we cannot all live the lives, of soldiers.

"It may be so," I can suppose that a philanthropist might exclaim. "Perish then the arts, if they can flourish only at such a cost.   What worth is there in toys of canvas and stone, if compared to the joy and peace of artless domestic life?"   And the answer is—truly, in themselves, none.   But as expressions of the highest state of the human spirit, their worth is infinite.   As results they may be worthless, but, as signs, they are above price.   For it is an assured truth that, whenever the faculties of men are at their fulness, they *must* express themselves by art; and to say that a state is without such expression, is to say that it is sunk from its proper level of manly nature.   So that, when I tell you that war is the foundation of all the arts, I mean also that it is the foundation of all the high virtues and faculties of men.

It is very strange to me to discover this; and very dreadful—but I saw it to be quite an undeniable fact.   The common notion that peace and the virtues of civil life flourished together, I found to be wholly untenable.   Peace and the *vices* of civil life only flourish together.   We talk of peace and learning, and of peace and plenty, and of peace and civilisation; but I found that those were not the words which the Muse of History coupled together: that, on her lips, the words were—peace, and sensuality—peace, and selfishness—peace, and death.   I found,

---

[3] Henry Dandolo.

in brief, that all great nations learned their truth of word, and strength of thought, in war; that they were nourished in war, and wasted by peace; taught by war, and deceived by peace; trained by war, and betrayed by peace;—in a word, that they were born in war, and expired in peace.

Yet now note carefully, in the second place, it is not *all* war of which this can be said—nor all dragon's teeth, which, sown, will start up into men. It is not the rage of a barbarian wolf-flock as under Genseric or Suwarrow; nor the habitual restlessness and rapine of mountaineers, as on the old borders of Scotland; nor the occasional struggle of a strong peaceful nation for its life, as in the wars of the Swiss with Austria; nor the contest of merely ambitious nations for extent of power, as in the wars of France under Napoleon, or the just terminated war in America. None of these forms of war build anything but tombs. But the creative, or foundational, war is that in which the natural restlessness and love of contest among men are disciplined, by consent, into modes of beautiful—though it may be fatal—play: in which the natural ambition and love of power of men are disciplined into the aggressive conquest of surrounding evil: and in which the natural instincts of self-defence are sanctified by the nobleness of the institutions, and purity of the households which they are appointed to defend. To such war as this all men are born; in such war as this any man may happily die; and out of such war as this have arisen throughout the extent of past ages, all the highest sanctities and virtues of humanity.

I shall therefore divide the war of which I would speak to you into three heads. War for exercise or play; war for dominion; and, war for defense.

And first, of war for exercise or play. I speak of it primarily in this light, because, through all past history, manly war has been more an exercise than anything else, among the classes who cause and proclaim it. It is not a game to the conscript, or the pressed sailor; but neither of these are the causers of it. To the governor who determines that war shall be, and to the youths who voluntarily adopt it as their profession, it has always been a grand pastime; and chiefly pursued because they had nothing else to do. And this is true without any exception. No king whose mind was fully occupied with the development of the inner resources of his kingdom, or with any other sufficing subject of thought, ever entered into war but on compulsion. No youth who was earnestly busy with any peaceful subject of study, or set on any serviceable course of action, ever voluntarily became a soldier. Occupy him, early and wisely, in agriculture or business, in science or in literature, and he will never think of war otherwise than as a calamity. But leave him idle; and, the more brave and active and capable he is by nature, the more he will thirst for some appointed field for action; and find, in the passion and peril of battle, the only satisfying fulfilment of his unoccupied being. And from the earliest incipient civilization until now, the population of the earth divides itself, when you look at it widely, into two races; one of workers, and the other of players—one tilling the ground, manufacturing, building, and otherwise providing for the necessities of life; the other part proudly idle, and continually therefore needing recreation, in which they use the productive and laborious orders partly as their cattle, and partly as their puppets or pieces in the game of death.

Now, remember, whatever virtue or goodliness there may be in this game of war, rightly played, there is none when you thus play it with a multitude of human pawns.

If you, the gentlemen of this or any other kingdom, choose to make your pastime of contest, do so, and welcome; but set not up these unhappy peasant-pieces upon the chequer of forest and field. If the wager is to be of death, lay it on your own heads, not theirs. A goodly struggle in the Olympic dust, though it be the dust of the grave, the gods will look upon, and be with you in; but they will not be with you, if you sit on the sides of the amphitheatre, whose steps are the mountains of earth, whose arena its valleys, to urge your peasant millions into gladiatorial war. You also, you tender and delicate women, for whom, and by whose command, all true battle has been, and must ever be; you would perhaps shrink now, though you need not, from the thought of sitting as queens above set lists where the jousting game might be mortal. How much more, then, ought you to shrink from the thought of sitting above a theatre pit in which even a few condemned slaves were slaying each other only for your delight! And do you *not* shrink from the *fact* of sitting above a theatre pit, where,—not condemned slaves,—but the best and bravest of the poor sons of your people, slay each other,—not man to man,—as the coupled gladiators; but race to race, in duel of generations? You would tell me, perhaps, that you do not sit to see this; and it is, indeed, true that the women of Europe—those who have no heart-interest of their own at peril in the contest—draw the curtains of their boxes, and muffle the openings;

so that from the pit of the circus of slaughter there may reach them only at intervals a half-heard cry, and a murmur as of the wind's sighing, when myriads of souls expire. They shut out the death-cries; and are happy, and talk wittily among themselves. That is the utter literal fact, of what our ladies do in their pleasant lives.

Nay, you might answer, speaking with them—"We do not let these wars come to pass for our play, nor by our carelessness; we cannot help them. How can any final quarrel of nations be settled otherwise than by war?"

I cannot now delay to tell you how political quarrels might be otherwise settled. But grant that they cannot. Grant that no law of reason can be understood by nations; no law of justice submitted to by them; and that, while questions of a few acres, and of petty cash, can be determined by truth and equity, the questions which are to issue in the perishing or saving of kingdoms can be determined only by the truth of the sword, and the equity of the rifle. Grant this, and even then, judge if it will always be necessary for you to put your quarrel into the hearts of your poor, and sign your treaties with peasants' blood. You would be ashamed to do this in your own private position and power. Why should you not be ashamed also to do it in public place and power? If you quarrel with your neighbour, and the quarrel be indeterminable by law, and mortal, you and he do not send your footmen to Battersea fields to fight it out; nor do you set fire to his tenants' cottages, nor spoil their goods. You fight out your quarrel yourselves, and at your own danger, if at all. And you do not think it materially affects the arbitrament that one of you has a larger household than the other; so that, if the servants or tenants were brought into the field with their masters, the issue of the contest could not be doubtful? You either refuse the private duel, or you practise it under laws of honour, not of physical force; that so it may be, in a manner, justly concluded. Now the just or unjust conclusion of the private feud is of little moment, while the just or unjust conclusion of the public feud is of eternal moment: and yet, in this public quarrel, you take your servants' sons from their arms to fight for it, and your servants' food from their lips to support it; and the black seals on the parchment of your treaties of peace are the deserted hearth, and the fruitless field.

There is a ghastly ludicrousness in this, as there is mostly in these wide and universal crimes. Hear the statement of the very fact of it in the most literal words of the greatest of our English thinkers:—
"What, speaking in quite unofficial language, is the net purport and

upshot of war? To my own knowledge, for example, there dwell and toil, in the British village of Dumdrudge, usually some five hundred souls. From these, by certain 'natural enemies' of the French there are successively selected, during the French war, say thirty able-bodied men: Dumdrudge, at her own expense, has suckled and nursed them: she has, not without difficulty and sorrow, fed them up to manhood, and even trained them to crafts, so that one can weave, another build, another hammer, and the weakest can stand under thirty stone avoirdupois. Nevertheless, amid much weeping and swearing, they are selected; all dressed in red; and shipped away, at the public charges, some two thousand miles, or say only to the south of Spain; and fed there till wanted.

"And now to that same spot in the south of Spain are thirty similar French artisans, from a French Dumdrudge, in like manner wending; till at length, after infinite effort, the two parties come into actual juxtaposition; and Thirty stands fronting Thirty, each with a gun in his hand.

"Straightway the word 'Fire!' is given, and they blow the souls out of one another; and in place of sixty brisk useful craftsmen, the world has sixty dead carcases, which it must bury, and anon shed tears for. Had these men any quarrel? Busy as the Devil is, not the smallest! They lived far enough apart; were the entirest strangers; nay, in so wide a Universe, there was even, unconsciously, by Commerce, some mutual helpfulness between them. How then? Simpleton! their Governors had fallen out; and instead of shooting one another, had the cunning to make these poor blockheads shoot." [4]

Positively, then, gentlemen, the game of battle must not, and shall not, ultimately be played this way. But should it be played any way? Should it, if not by your servants, be practised by yourselves? I think, yes. Both history and human instinct seem alike to say, yes. All healthy men like fighting, and like the sense of danger; all brave women like to hear of their fighting, and of their facing danger. This is a fixed instinct in the fine race of them; and I cannot help fancying that fair fight is the best play for them; and that a tournament was a better game than a steeplechase. The time may perhaps come, in France, as well as here, for universal hurdle-races and cricketing: but I do not think universal cricket will bring out the best qualities of the nobles of either country. I use, in such question, the test which I have adopted, of the connection of war with other arts; and I reflect

---

[4] From *Sartor Resartus* by Thomas Carlyle.

how, as a sculptor, I should feel, if I were asked to design a monument for a dead knight, in Westminster Abbey, with a carving of a bat at one end, and a ball at the other. It may be the remains in me only of savage Gothic prejudice; but I had rather carve it with a shield at one end, and a sword at the other. And this, observe, with no reference whatever to any story of duty done, or cause defended. Assume the knight merely to have ridden out occasionally to fight his neighbour for exercise; assume him even a soldier of fortune, and to have gained his bread, and filled his purse, at the sword's point. Still, I feel as if it were, somehow, grander and worthier in him to have made his bread by sword play than any other play; I had rather he had made it by thrusting than by batting;—*much* rather than by betting. Much rather that he should ride war horses, than back race horses; and—I say it sternly and deliberately—much rather would I have him slay his neighbour than cheat him.

But remember, so far as this may be true, the game of war is only that in which the *full personal power of the human creature* is brought out in management of its weapons. And this for three reasons:—

First, the great justification of this game is that it truly, when well played, determines *who is the best man;*—who is the highest bred, the most self-denying, the most fearless, the coolest of nerve, the swiftest of eye and hand. You cannot test these qualities wholly, unless there is a clear possibility of the struggle's ending in death. It is only in the fronting of that condition that the full trial of the man, soul and body, comes out. You may go to your game of wickets, or of hurdles, or of cards, and any knavery that is in you may stay unchallenged all the while. But if the play may be ended at any moment by a lance-thrust, a man will probably make up his accounts a little before he enters it. Whatever is rotten and evil in him will weaken his hand more in holding a sword-hilt than in balancing a billiard-cue; and on the whole, the habit of living lightly hearted, in daily presence of death, always has had, and must have, power both in the making and testing of honest men. But for the final testing, observe, you must make the issue of battle strictly dependent on fineness of frame, and firmness of hand. You must not make it the question, which of the combatants has the longest gun, or which has got behind the biggest tree, or which has the wind in his face, or which has gunpowder made by the best chemists, or iron smelted with the best coal, or the angriest mob at his back. Decide your battle, whether of nations or individuals, on *those* terms;—and you have only multiplied confusion, and added slaughter to iniquity. But decide your battle by pure trial which has the strongest arm, and steadiest heart,—and you have gone far to decide a great many matters besides, and to decide them rightly.

And the other reasons for this mode of decision of cause, are the diminution both of the material destructiveness, or cost, and of the physical distress of war. For you must not think that in speaking to you in this (as you may imagine) fantastic praise of battle, I have overlooked the conditions weighing against me. I pray all of you, who have not read, to read with the most earnest attention Mr. Helps' two essays, on War, and Government, in the first volume of the last series of *Friends in Council.* Everything that can be urged against war is there simply, exhaustively, and most graphically stated. And all, there urged, is true. But the two great counts of evil alleged against war by that most thoughtful writer, hold only against modern war. If you have to take away masses of men from all industrial employment,—to feed them by the labour of others,—to provide them with destructive machines, varied daily in national rivalship of inventive cost; if you have to ravage the country which you attack,—to destroy, for a score of future years, its roads, its woods, its cities and its harbours;—and if, finally, having brought masses of men, counted by hundreds of thousands, face to face, you tear those masses to pieces with jagged shot, and leave the living creatures, countlessly beyond all help of surgery, to starve and parch, through days of torture, down into clots of clay—what book of accounts shall record the cost of your work;—What book of judgment sentence the guilt of it?

That, I say, is *modern* war,—scientific war,—chemical and mechanic war,—how much worse than the savage's poisoned arrow! And yet you will tell me, perhaps, that any other war than this is impossible now. It may be so; the progress of science cannot, perhaps, be otherwise registered than by new facilities of destruction; and the brotherly love of our enlarging Christianity be only proved by multiplication of murder. Yet hear, for a moment, what war was, in Pagan and ignorant days;—what war might yet be, if we could extinguish our science in darkness, and join the heathen's practice to the Christian's creed. I read you this from a book which probably most of you know well, and all ought to know—Müller's *Dorians;*—but I have put the points I wish you to remember in closer connection than in his text.

"The chief characteristic of the warriors of Sparta was great composure and a subdued strength; the violence of Aristodemus and Isadas being considered as deserving rather of blame than praise; and these qualities in general distinguished the Greeks from the northern Barbarians, whose boldness always consisted in noise and tumult.   The conduct of the Spartans in battle denotes a high and noble disposition, which rejected all the extremes of brutal rage.   The pursuit of the enemy ceased when the victory was completed; and after the signal for retreat had been given, all hostilities ceased.   The spoiling of arms, at least during the battle, was also interdicted; and the consecration of the spoils of slain enemies to the gods, as, in general, all rejoicings for victory, were considered as ill-omened. . . . For the same reason the Spartans *sacrificed to the Muses* before an action; these goddesses being expected to produce regularity and order in battle; as they *sacrificed on the same occasion in Crete to the god of love,* as the confirmer of mutual esteem and shame. . . . Every man put on a crown, when the band of flute-players gave the signal for attack; all the shields of the line glittered with their high polish, and mingled their splendour with the dark red of the purple mantles, which were meant both to adorn the combatant, and to conceal the blood of the wounded; to fall well and decorously being an incentive the more to the most heroic valour."

Such was the war of the greatest soldiers who prayed to heathen gods. What Christian war is, preached by Christian ministers, let any one tell you, who saw the sacred crowning, and heard the sacred flute-playing, and was inspired and sanctified by the divinely-measured and musical language, of any North American regiment preparing for its charge.   And what is the relative cost of life in pagan and Christian wars, let this one fact tell you;—the Spartans won the decisive battle of Corinth with the loss of eight men; the victors at indecisive Gettysburg confess to the loss of 30,000.

I pass now to our second order of war, the commonest among men, that undertaken in desire of dominion.   And let me ask you to think for a few moments what the real meaning of this desire of dominion is —first in the minds of kings—then in that of nations.

Now, mind you this first,—that I speak either about kings, or masses of men, with a fixed conviction that human nature is a noble and beautiful thing; not a foul nor a base thing.   All the sin of men I esteem as their disease, not their nature; as a folly which may be prevented, not a necessity which must be accepted.   And my wonder, even when things are at their worst, is always at the height which this human nature can attain. Thinking it high, I find it always a higher thing than I thought it; while those who think it low, find it, and will find it, always, lower than they thought it: the fact being, that it is infinite, and capable of infinite height and infinite fall; but the nature of it—and here is the faith which I would have you hold with me— the *nature* of it is in the nobleness, not in the catastrophe.

Take the faith in its utmost terms. When the captain of the *London* shook hands with his mate, saying, "God speed you! I will go down with my passengers," *that* I believe to be "human nature." He does not do it from any religious motive,—from any hope of reward, or any fear of punishment; he does it because he is a man. But when a mother, living among the fair fields of merry England, gives her two-year-old child to be suffocated under a mattress in her inner room, while the said mother waits and talks outside: *that* I believe to be *not* human nature. You have the two extremes there, shortly. And you, men, and mothers, who are here face to face with me to-night, I call upon you to say which of these is human, and which inhuman,—which "natural" and which "unnatural." Choose your creed at once, I beseech you:—choose it with unshaken choice,—choose it for ever. Will you take, for foundation of act and hope, the faith that this man was such as God made him, or that this woman was such as God made her? Which of them has failed from their nature,—from their present, possible, actual nature;—not their nature of long ago, but their nature of now? Which has betrayed it—falsified it? Did the guardian who died in his trust die inhumanly, and as a fool; and did the murderess of her child fulfil the law of her being? Choose, I say; infinitude of choices hang upon this. You have had false prophets among you,— for centuries you have had them,—solemnly warned against them though you were; false prophets, who have told you that all men are nothing but fiends or wolves, half beast, half devil. Believe that, and indeed you may sink to that. But refuse that, and have faith that God "made you upright," though *you* have sought out many inventions; so, you will strive daily to become more what your Maker meant and means you to be, and daily gives you also the power to be,—and you will cling more and more to the nobleness and virtue that is in you, saying, "My righteousness I hold fast, and will not let it go."

I have put this to you as a choice, as if you might hold either of these creeds you liked best. But there is in reality no choice for you; the facts being quite easily ascertainable. You have no business to *think* about this matter, or to choose in it.   The broad fact is, that a human creature of the highest race, and most perfect as a human thing, is invariably both kind and true; and that as you lower the race, you get cruelty and falseness as you get deformity: and this so steadily and assuredly, that the two great words which, in their first use, meant only perfection of race, have come, by consequence of the invariable connection of virtue with the fine human nature, both to signify benevolence of disposition.   The word "generous," and the word "gentle," both, in their origin, meant only "of pure race," but because charity and tenderness are inseparable from this purity of blood, the words which once stood only for pride, now stand as synonyms for virtue.

Now, this being the true power of our inherent humanity, and seeing that all the aim of education should be to develop this;—and seeing also what magnificent self-sacrifice the higher classes of men are capable of, for any cause that they understand or feel,—it is wholly inconceivable to me how well-educated princes, who ought to be of all gentlemen the gentlest, and of all nobles the most generous, and whose title of royalty means only their function of doing every man *"right"*—how these, I say, throughout history, should so rarely pronounce themselves on the side of the poor, and of justice, but continually maintain themselves and their own interests by oppression of the poor, and by wresting of justice; and how this should be accepted as so natural, that the word loyalty, which means faithfulness to law, is used as if it were only the duty of a people to be loyal to their king, and not the duty of a king to be infinitely more loyal to his people.   How comes it to pass that a captain will die with his passengers, and lean over the gunwale to give the parting boat its course; but that a king will not usually die with, much less *for,* his passengers—thinks it rather incumbent on his passengers, in any number, to die for *him?*

Think, I beseech you, of the wonder of this.   The sea captain, not captain by divine right, but only by company's appointment;—not a man of royal descent, but only a plebeian who can steer;—not with the eyes of the world upon him, but with feeble chance, depending on one poor boat, of his name being ever heard above the wash of the fatal waves; not with the cause of a nation resting on his act, but helpless to save so much as a child from among the lost crowd with whom he resolves to be lost,—yet goes down quietly to his grave, rather than break his faith to these few emigrants.   But your captain by divine right,—your captain with the hues of a hundred shields of kings upon his breast,—your captain whose every deed, brave or base, will be illuminated or branded for ever before unescapable eyes of men, —your captain whose every thought and act are beneficent, or fatal, from sunrising to setting, blessing as the sunshine, or shadowing as the night,—this captain, as you find him in history, for the most part thinks only how he may tax his passengers, and sit at most ease in his state cabin!

For observe, if there had been indeed in the hearts of the rulers of great multitudes of men any such conception of work for the good of those under their command, as there is in the good and thoughtful masters of any small company of men, not only wars for the sake of mere increase of power could never take place, but our idea of power itself would be entirely altered. Do you suppose that to think and act even for a million of men, to hear their complaints, watch their weaknesses, restrain their vices, make laws for them, lead them, day by day, to purer life, is not enough for one man's work? If any of us were absolute lord only of a district of a hundred miles square and were resolved on doing our utmost for it; making it feed as large a number of people as possible; making every clod productive, and every rock defensive, and every human being happy; should we not have enough on our hands, think you?

But if the ruler has any other aim than this; if, careless of the result of his interference, he desires only the authority to interfere; and, regardless of what is ill-done or well-done, cares only that it shall be done at his bidding;—if he would rather do two hundred miles' space of mischief, than one hundred miles' space of good, of course he will try to add to his territory; and to add illimitably. But does he add to his power? Do you call it power in a child, if he is allowed to play with the wheels and bands of some vast engine, pleased with their murmur and whirl, till his unwise touch, wandering where it ought not, scatters beam and wheel into ruin? Yet what machine is so vast, so incognizable, as the working of the mind of a nation; what child's touch so wanton, as the word of a selfish king? And yet, how long have we allowed the historian to speak of the extent of the calamity a man causes, as a just ground for his pride; and to extol him as the greatest prince, who is only the centre of the widest error. Follow out this thought by yourselves; and you will find that all power, properly so called, is wise and benevolent. There may be capacity in a drifting fire-ship to destroy a fleet; there may be venom enough in a dead body to infect a nation:—but which of you, the most ambitious, would desire a drifting kinghood, robed in consuming fire, or a poison-dipped sceptre whose touch was mortal? There is no true potency, remember, but that of help; nor true ambition, but ambition to save.

And then, observe farther, this true power, the power of saving, depends neither on multitude of men, nor on extent of territory. We are continually assuming that nations become strong according to their numbers. They indeed become so, if those numbers can be made of one mind; but how are you sure you can stay them in one mind, and keep them from having north and south minds? Grant them unanimous, how know you they will be unanimous in right? If they are unanimous in wrong, the more they are, essentially the weaker they are. Or, suppose that they can neither be of one mind, nor of two minds, but can only be of *no* mind? Suppose they are a mere helpless mob; tottering into precipitant catastrophe, like a waggon-load of stones when the wheel comes off. Dangerous enough for their neighbours, certainly, but not "powerful."

Neither does strength depend on extent of territory, any more than upon number of population. Take up your maps when you go home this evening,—put the cluster of British Isles beside the mass of South America; and then consider whether any race of men need care how much ground they stand upon. The strength is in the men, and in their unity and virtue, not in their standing room: a little group of wise hearts is better than a wilderness full of fools; and only that nation gains true territory, which gains itself.

And now for the brief practical outcome of all this. Remember, no government is ultimately strong, but in proportion to its kindness and justice; and that a nation does not strengthen, by merely multiplying and diffusing itself. We have not strengthened as yet, by multiplying into America. Nay, even when it has not to encounter the separating conditions of emigration, a nation need not boast itself of multiplying on its own ground, if it multiplies only as flies or locusts do, with the god of flies for its god. It multiplies its strength only by increasing as one great family, in perfect fellowship and brotherhood. And lastly, it does not strengthen itself by seizing dominion over races whom it cannot benefit. Austria is not strengthened, but weakened, by her grasp of Lombardy; and whatever apparent increase of majesty and of wealth may have accrued to us from the possession of India, whether these prove to us ultimately power or weakness, depends wholly on the degree in which our influence on the native race shall be benevolent and exalting.

But, as it is at their own peril that any race extends their dominion in mere desire of power, so it is at their own still greater peril that they refuse to undertake aggressive war, according to their force, whenever they are assured that their authority would be helpful and protective. Nor need you listen to any sophistical objection of the impossibility of knowing when a people's help is needed, or when not. Make your national conscience clean, and your national eyes will soon be clear. No man who is truly ready to take part in a noble quarrel will ever stand long in doubt by whom, or in what cause, his aid is needed. I hold it my duty to make no political statement of any special bearing in this presence; but I tell you broadly and boldly, that, within these last ten years, we English have, as a knightly nation, lost our spurs: we have fought where we should not have fought, for gain; and we have been passive, where we should not have been passive, for fear. I tell you that the principle of non-intervention, as now preached among us, is as selfish and cruel as the worst frenzy of conquest, and differs from it only by being, not only malignant, but dastardly.

I know, however, that my opinions on this subject differ too widely from those ordinarily held, to be any farther intruded upon you; and therefore I pass lastly to examine the conditions of the third kind of noble war;—war waged simply for defence of the country in which we were born, and for the maintenance and execution of her laws, by whomsoever threatened or defied. It is to this duty that I suppose most men entering the army consider themselves in reality to be bound, and I want you now to reflect what the laws of mere defence are; and what the soldier's duty, as now understood, or supposed to be understood. You have solemnly devoted yourselves to be English soldiers, for the guardianship of England. I want you to feel what this vow of yours indeed means, or is gradually coming to mean.

You take it upon you, first, while you are sentimental schoolboys; you go into your military convent, or barracks, just as a girl goes into her convent while she is a sentimental schoolgirl; neither of you then know what you are about, though both the good soldiers and good nuns make the best of it afterwards. You don't understand perhaps why I call you "sentimental" schoolboys, when you go into the army? Because, on the whole, it is the love of adventure, of excitement, of fine dress and of the pride of fame, all which are sentimental motives, which make a boy like going into the Guards better than into a counting-house. You fancy, perhaps, that there is a severe sense of duty mixed with these peacocky motives? And in the best of you there is; but do not think that it is principal.   If you cared to do your duty to your country in a prosaic and unsentimental way, depend upon it, there is now truer duty to be done in raising harvests, than in burning them; more in building houses, than in shelling them—more in winning money by your own work, wherewith to help men, than in other people's work, taxing for money wherewith to slay men;—more duty finally, in honest and unselfish living than in honest and unselfish dying, though that seems to your boys' eyes the bravest.   So far, then, as for your own honour, and the honour of your families, you choose brave death in a red coat before brave life in a black one, you are sentimental; and now see what this passionate vow of yours comes to.   For a little while you ride, and you hunt tigers or savages, you shoot, and are shot; you are happy, and proud, always, and honoured and wept if you die; and you are satisfied with your life, and with the end of it; believing, on the whole, that good rather than harm of it comes to others, and much pleasure to you.

But as the sense of duty enters into your forming minds, the vow takes another aspect.   You find that you have put yourselves into the hand of your country as a weapon.   You have vowed to strike, when she bids you, and to stay scabbarded when she bids you; all that you need answer for is, that you fail not in her grasp.   And there is goodness in this, and greatness, if you can trust the hand and heart of the Britomart who has braced you to her side, and are assured that when she leaves you sheathed in darkness, there is no need for your flash to the sun.   But remember, good and noble as this state may be, it is a state of slavery.   There are different kinds of slaves and different masters.   Some slaves are scourged to their work by whips, others are scourged to it by restlessness or ambition.   It does not matter what the whip is; it is none the less a whip, because you have cut thongs for it out of your own souls: the fact, so far, of slavery, is in being driven to your work without thought, at another's bidding.   Again, some slaves are bought with money, and others with praise.   It matters not what the purchase-money is.   The distinguishing sign of slavery is to have a price, and be bought for it.   Again, it matters not what kind of work you are set on; some slaves are set to forced diggings, others to forced marches; some dig furrows, others field-works, and others graves.   Some press the juice of reeds, and some the juice of vines, and some the blood of men.   The fact of the captivity is the same, whatever work we are set upon, though the fruits of the toil may be different.

But, remember, in thus vowing ourselves to be the slaves of any master, it ought to be some subject of forethought with us, what work he is likely to put us upon. You may think that the whole duty of a soldier is to be passive, that it is the country you have left behind who is to command, and you have only to obey. But are you sure that you have left *all* your country behind, or that the part of it you have so left is indeed the best part of it? Suppose—and, remember, it is quite conceivable—that you yourselves are indeed the best part of England; that you, who have become the slaves, ought to have been the masters; and that those who are the masters, ought to have been the slaves! If it is a noble and whole-hearted England, whose bidding you are bound to do, it is well; but if you are yourselves the best of her heart, and the England you have left be but a half-hearted England, how say you of your obedience? You were too proud to become shop-keepers: are you satisfied, then, to become the servants of shop-keepers? You were too proud to become merchants or farmers yourselves: will you have merchants or farmers, then, for your field-marshals? You had no gifts of special grace for Exeter Hall: will you have some gifted person thereat for your commander-in-chief, to judge of your work, and reward it? You imagine yourselves to be the army of England: how, if you should find yourselves at last, only the police of her manufacturing towns, and the beadles of her Little Bethels?

It is not so yet, nor will be so, I trust, for ever; but what I want you to see, and to be assured of, is, that the ideal of soldiership is not mere passive obedience and bravery; that, so far from this, no country is in a healthy state which has separated, even in a small degree, her civil from her military power. All states of the world, however great, fall at once when they use mercenary armies; and although it is a less instant form of error (because involving no national taint of cowardice), it is yet an error no less ultimately fatal—it is the error especially of modern times, of which we cannot yet know all the calamitous consequences,—to take away the best blood and strength of the nation, all the soul-substance of it that is brave, and careless of reward, and scornful of pain, and faithful in trust; and to cast that into steel, and make a mere sword of it; taking away its voice and will; but to keep the worst part of the nation—whatever is cowardly, avaricious, sensual, and faithless—and to give to this the voice, to this the authority, to this the chief privilege, where there is least capacity of thought.

The fulfilment of your vow for the defence of England will by no means consist in carrying out such a system. You are not true soldiers, if you only mean to stand at a shop-door, to protect shop-boys who are cheating inside. A soldier's vow to his country is that he will die for the guardianship of her domestic virtue, of her righteous laws, and of her any-way challenged or endangered honour.   A state without virtue, without laws, and without honour, he is bound *not* to defend; nay, bound to redress by his own right hand that which he sees to be base in her.

So sternly is this the law of Nature and life, that a nation once utterly corrupt can only be redeemed by a military despotism—never by talking, nor by its free effort.   And the health of any state consists simply in this; that in it, those who are wisest shall also be strongest; its rulers should be also its soldiers; or, rather, by force of intellect more than of sword, its soldiers also its rulers.   Whatever the hold which the aristocracy of England has on the heart of England, in that they are still always in front of her battles, this hold will not be enough, unless they are also in front of her thoughts.   And truly her thoughts need good captain's leading now, if ever! Do you know what, by this beautiful division of labour (her brave men fighting, and her cowards thinking), she has come at last to think?   Here is a paper in my hand, a good one too, and an honest one; quite representative of the best common public thought of England at this moment; and it is holding forth in one of its leaders upon our "social welfare,"—upon our "vivid life"— upon the "political supremacy of Great Britain."   And what do you think all these are owing to?   To what our English sires have done for us, and taught us, age after age?   No: not to that.   To our honesty of heart, or coolness of head, or steadiness of will?   No: not to these. To our thinkers, or our statesmen, or our poets, or our captains, or our martyrs, or the patient labour of our poor?   No: not to these; or at least not to these in any chief measure.   Nay, says the journal, "more than any agency, it is the cheapness and abundance of our coal which have made us what we are."   If it be so, then "ashes to ashes" be our epitaph! and the sooner the better.

Gentlemen of England, if ever you would have your country breathe the pure breath of heaven again, and receive again a soul into her body, instead of rotting into a carcase, blown up in the belly with carbonic acid (and great *that* way), you must think, and feel, for your England, as well as fight for her: you must teach her that all the true greatness she ever had, she won while her fields were green and her faces ruddy; and that greatness is still possible for Englishmen, even though the ground be not hollow under their feet, nor the sky black over their heads.

And bear with me, you soldier youths,—who are thus in all ways the hope of your country, or must be, if she have any hope—if I urge you with rude earnestness to remember that your fitness for all future trust depends upon what you are now. No good soldier in his old age was ever careless or indolent in his youth. Many a giddy and thoughtless boy has become a good bishop, or a good lawyer, or a good merchant; but not such an one ever became a good general. I challenge you, in all history, to find a record of a good soldier who was not grave and earnest in his youth. And, in general, I have no patience with people who talk of "the thoughtlessness of youth" indulgently. I had infinitely rather hear of thoughtless old age, and the indulgence due to *that*. When a man has done his work, and nothing can any way be materially altered in his fate, let him forget his toil, and jest with his fate, if he will; but what excuse can you find for wilfulness of thought, at the very time when every crisis of future fortune hangs on your decisions? A youth thoughtless! when all the happiness of his home for ever depends on the chances, or the passions, of an hour! A youth thoughtless! when the career of all his days depends on the opportunity of a moment! A youth thoughtless! when his every act is as a torch to the laid train of future conduct, and every imagination a fountain of life or death! Be thoughtless in *any* after years, rather than now—though, indeed, there is only one place where a man may be nobly thoughtless,—his death-bed. No thinking should ever be left to be done *there*.

Having, then, resolved that you will not waste recklessly, but earnestly use, these early days of yours, remember that all the duties of her children to England may be summed in two words—industry, and honour. I say, first, industry, for it is in this that soldier youth are especially tempted to fail. Yet, surely, there is no reason, because your life may possibly or probably be shorter than other men's, that you should therefore waste more recklessly the portion of it that is granted you; neither do the duties of your profession, which require you to keep your bodies strong, in any wise involve the keeping of your minds weak. So far from that, the experience, the hardship, and the activity of a soldier's life render his powers of thought more accurate than those of other men; and while, for others, all knowledge is often little more than a means of amusement, there is no form of science which a soldier may not at some time or other find bearing on business of life and death. A young mathematician may be excused for languor in studying curves to be described only with a pencil; but not in tracing those which are to be described with a rocket. Your knowledge of a wholesome herb may involve the feeding of an army;

and acquaintance with an obscure point of geography, the success of a campaign. Never waste an instant's time, therefore: the sin of idleness is a thousand-fold greater in you than in other youths; for the fates of those who will one day be under your command hang upon your knowledge; lost moments now will be lost lives then, and every instant which you carelessly take for play, you buy with blood. . . .

First, then, by industry you must fulfil your vow to your country; but all industry and earnestness will be useless unless they are consecrated by your resolution to be in all things men of honour; not honour in the common sense only, but in the highest. Rest on the force of the two main words in the great verse, *"integer* vitæ, scelerisque *purus."* You have vowed your life to England; give it her wholly;—a bright, stainless, perfect life—a knightly life. Because you have to fight with machines instead of lances, there may be a necessity for more ghastly danger, but there is none for less worthiness of character, than in olden time. You may be true knights yet, though perhaps not *equites;* you may have to call yourselves "canonry" instead of "chivalry," but that is no reason why you should not call yourselves true men. So the first thing you have to see to in becoming soldiers is that you make yourselves wholly true. Courage is a mere matter of course among any ordinarily well-born youths; but neither truth nor gentleness is matter of course. You must bind them like shields about your necks; you must write them on the tables of your hearts. Though it be not exacted of you, yet exact it of yourselves, this vow of stainless truth. Your hearts are, if you leave them unstirred, as tombs in which a god lies buried. Vow yourselves crusaders to redeem that sacred sepulchre. And remember, before all things—for no other memory will be so protective of you—that the highest law of this knightly truth is that under which it is vowed to women. Whomsoever else you deceive, whomsoever you injure, whomsoever you leave unaided, you must not deceive, nor injure, nor leave unaided, according to your power, any woman, of whatever rank. Believe me, every virtue of the higher phases of manly character begins in this;—in truth and modesty before the face of all maidens; in truth and pity, or truth and reverence, to all womanhood.

And now let me turn for a moment to you,—wives and maidens, who are the souls of soldiers; to you,—mothers, who have devoted your children to the great hierarchy of war. Let me ask you to consider what part you have to take for the aid of those who love you; for if you fail in your part they cannot fulfil theirs; such absolute helpmates you are that no man can stand without that help, nor labour in his own strength.

I know your hearts, and that the truth of them never fails when an hour of trial comes which you recognize for such. But you know not when the hour of trial first finds you, nor when it verily finds you. You imagine that you are only called upon to wait and to suffer; to surrender and to mourn. You know that you must not weaken the hearts of your husbands and lovers, even by the one fear of which those hearts are capable,—the fear of parting from you, or of causing you grief. Through weary years of separation; through fearful expectancies of unknown fate; through the tenfold bitterness of the sorrow which might so easily have been joy, and the tenfold yearning for glorious life struck down in its prime;—through all these agonies you fail not, and never will fail. But your trial is not in these. To be heroic in danger is little;—you are Englishwomen. To be heroic in change and sway of fortune is little;—for do you not love? To be patient through the great chasm and pause of loss is little;—for do you not still love in heaven? But to be heroic in happiness; to bear yourselves gravely and righteously in the dazzling of the sunshine of morning; not to forget the God in whom you trust, when He gives you most; not to fail those who trust you, when they seem to need you least; this is the difficult fortitude. It is not in the pining of absence, not in the peril of battle, not in the wasting of sickness, that your prayer should be most passionate, or your guardianship most tender. Pray, mothers and maidens, for your young soldiers in the bloom of their pride; pray for them, while the only dangers round them are in their own wayward will; watch you, and pray, when they have to face, not death, but temptation. But it is this fortitude also for which there is the crowning reward. Believe me, the whole course and character of your lovers' lives is in your hands: what you would have them be, they shall be, if you not only desire to have them so, but deserve to have them so; for they are but mirrors in which you will see yourselves imaged. If you are frivolous, they will be so also; if you have no understanding of the scope of their duty, they also will forget it; they will listen,—they *can* listen,—to no other interpretation of it than that uttered from your lips. Bid them be brave;—they will be brave for you: bid them be cowards:—and how noble soever they be, they will quail for you. Bid them be wise, and they will be wise for you; mock at their counsel, they will be fools for you—such and so absolute is your rule over them. Your fancy, perhaps, as you have been told so often, that a wife's rule should only be over her husband's house, not over his mind. Ah, no! the true rule is just the reverse of that; a true wife, in her husband's house, is his servant; it is in his heart that she is queen. Whatever of best he can conceive, it is her part to be; whatever of highest he can hope, it is hers to promise; all that is dark in him she must purge into purity; all that is failing in him she must strengthen into truth; from her, through all the world's clamour, he must win his praise; in her, through all the world's warfare, he must find his peace.

And, now, but one word more. You may wonder, perhaps, that I have spoken all this night in praise of war. Yet, truly, if it might be, I for one, would fain join in the cadence of hammer-strokes that should beat swords into ploughshares: and that this cannot be, is not the fault of us men. It is *your* fault. Wholly yours. Only by your command, or by your permission, can any contest take place among us. And the real, final reason for all the poverty, misery, and rage of battle throughout Europe, is simply that you women, however good, however religious, however self-sacrificing for those whom you love, are too selfish and too thoughtless to take pains for any creature out of your own immediate circles. You fancy that you are sorry for the pain of others. Now I just tell you this, that if the usual course of war, instead of unroofing peasants' houses, and ravaging peasants' fields, merely broke the china upon your own drawing-room tables, no war in civilized countries would last a week. I tell you more, that at whatever moment you chose to put a period to war, you could do it with less trouble than you take any day to go out to dinner. You know, or at least you might know if you would think, that every battle you hear of has made many widows and orphans. We have, none of us, heart enough truly to mourn with these. But at least we might put on the outer symbols of mourning with them. Let but every Christian lady who has conscience toward God, vow that she will mourn, at least outwardly, for His killed creatures. Your praying is useless, and your church-going mere mockery of God, if you have not plain obedience in you enough for this. Let every lady in the upper classes of civilized Europe simply vow that, while any cruel war proceeds, she will wear *black;*—a mute's black,—with no jewel, no ornament, no excuse for, or evasion into, prettiness—I tell you again, no war would last a week.

And, lastly. You women of England are all now shrieking with one voice,—you and your clergymen together,—because you hear of your

Bibles being attacked. If you choose to obey your Bibles, you will never care who attacks them. It is just because you never fulfil a single downright precept of the Book, that you are so careful for its credit: and just because you don't care to obey its whole words, that you are so particular about the letters of them. The Bible tells you to dress plainly,—and you are mad for finery; the Bible tells you to have pity on the poor,—and you crush them under your carriage-wheels; the Bible tells you to do judgment and justice,—and you do not know, nor care to know, so much as what the Bible word "justice" means. Do but learn so much of God's truth as that comes to; know what He means when He tells you to be just; and teach your sons, that their bravery is but a fool's boast and their deeds but a firebrand's tossing, unless they are indeed Just men, and Perfect in the Fear of God:—and you will soon have no more war, unless it be indeed such as is willed by Him, of whom, though Prince of Peace, it is also written, "In Righteousness He doth judge, and make war."

Lines of Inquiry

1 a Ruskin begins by identifying explicitly his audience and his point of view. Why? Would he do so if he were himself a career military officer? "War" was delivered originally as a speech; is the demand on a speaker for this kind of explicit identification different from the demand on a writer?

b Suppose that Ruskin had set out in his speech to condemn war; would it still be necessary for him to identify his point of view and to contrast it to that of his audience?

c Under what circumstances, in your judgment, would the explicit identification of the point of view from which an essay is written and the audience to which it is addressed be most necessary?

2 a Suppose each of the following kinds of speaker delivering a speech on war to a group of military cadets and defining his point of view explicitly. In each case what elements in the resulting speech can you hope to predict on hearing the speaker's definition of his point of view? What can you not predict?

 (*1*) A psychologist

 (*2*) A politician

 (*3*) A physician

 (*4*) A pacifist

b Why might the superintendent of a military academy think of inviting a clergyman to speak to his cadets? Why might he think of inviting a scientist? A painter? A pacifist?

c You are now such a superintendent. Compose a list of
speakers, and account for your choices. (You may list
them by class, as above.) In what order would you ask
them to speak? Why?

3 Mark Ruskin's essay off into sections.

a Can it be said of each section that its ideas are *generated* by
the ideas of the preceding section? For example, is Ruskin's
discussion of the three kinds of noble warfare generated
by his discussion of the historical relationship between the
warfare and the artistic accomplishments of various civilizations?

b Examine one part of Ruskin's discussion of noble warfare
carefully: Are its ideas generated internally, B from A, C
from B, and so on?

c What accounts for the order in which he deals with the
three types of noble war? Could that order be reversed with
no loss of emphasis? Could his concluding address to
women, "the souls of soldiers," have been generated by his
discussion of warfare as play?

d How does Ruskin use point of view to generate the ideas of
his first, introductory section?

4 Much of the greatness of Ruskin's essay depends upon the
magnificent sonority and color of his prose. Each of the following passages is preceded by a summary statement of its
point. In each case what is lost and why? In each case,
what accounts for the sequence of Ruskin's thought? By
what typical rhetorical devices does Ruskin obtain his effects?

a The arts of peace are the product of war.

. . . all the pure and noble arts of peace are founded on
war; no great art ever yet rose on earth, but among a nation
of soldiers. There is no art among a shepherd people, if it
remains at peace. There is no art among an agricultural
people, if it remains at peace. Commerce is barely consistent with fine art; but cannot produce it. Manufacture
not only is unable to produce it, but invariably destroys
whatever seeds of it exist. There is no great art possible
to a nation but that which is based on battle.

b Modern war is horrible, involving the destruction of trade, of
the natural world, and of large numbers of human beings,
Those who bring about war in modern times incur great
guilt.

If you have to take away masses of men from all industrial employment,—to feed them by the labour of others,—to provide them with destructive machines, varied daily in national rivalship of inventive cost; if you have to ravage the country which you attack,—to destroy, for a score of future years, its roads, its woods, its cities and its harbours;—and if, finally, having brought masses of men, counted by hundreds of thousands, face to face, you tear those masses to pieces with jagged shot, and leave the living creatures, countlessly beyond all help of surgery, to starve and parch, through days of torture, down into clots of clay—what book of accounts shall record the cost of your work;— What book of judgment sentence the guilt of it?

c Any man who had absolute power over only a hundred square miles of territory would have a difficult time keeping it happy, prosperous, and secure.

If any of us were absolute lord only of a district of a hundred miles square and were resolved on doing our utmost for it; making it feed as large a number of people as possible; making every clod productive, and every rock defensive, and every human being happy; should we not have enough on our hands, think you?

d The strength of a country is in the character of its people, not in the extent of its lands.

The strength is in the men, and in their unity and virtue, not in their standing room: a little group of wise hearts is better than a wilderness full of fools; and only that nation gains true territory, which gains itself.

e A man who, with the thought of his reputation and that of his family's, chooses to die bravely as a soldier instead of living bravely as a civilian, is essentially sentimental. Such a life is dramatic but trivial.

So far, then, as for your own honour, and the honour of your families, you choose brave death in a red coat before brave life in a black one, you are sentimental; and now see what this passionate vow of yours comes to. For a little while you ride, and you hunt tigers or savages, you shoot, and are shot; you are happy, and proud, always, and honoured and wept if you die; and you are satisfied with your life, and with the end of it; believing, on the whole, that good rather than harm of it comes to others, and much pleasure to you.

5 a At one point, Ruskin appears to say that a man with a clean conscience and a noble spirit can always tell a just war from an unjust one. ("No man who is truly ready to take part in a noble quarrel will ever stand long in doubt by whom, or in what cause, his aid is needed.") List those wars with whose backgrounds you are fairly familiar (according to Ruskin, you need no great familiarity in order to arrive at a judgment, in such cases). Does an intuitive test of their moral worth fail with any one of them? If the proper judgment is clear with the extreme cases, is it clear with the less extreme ones? How do you recognize an extreme case in your list? How do you account for the apparently widespread confusion about the justice of most wars?

b At the center of Ruskin's analysis lies a definition of "the just war." Can you find several clear tests by which you can distinguish the just war from the unjust one? (Why do you need more than one test?) Apply your tests against several actual cases—World War II, the Korean War, the Vietnam War, the American Civil War. Do the tests hold up? Can you tell if they hold up or not? Are some more nearly certain, therefore more usable, than others?

6 In reading Ruskin's essay, you may have had no difficulty in accepting his argument. On the other hand, you may have had a hunch that "something" was wrong. Hunches of one kind or another often if not always precede and accompany systematic thought; they are thoroughly respectable, though not convincing in themselves. Arguments and counterarguments need to be systematic.

Let us suppose that a number of people wish to attack Ruskin's argument, feeling that "something" is wrong with it and that their objections are those outlined below. What follows from each objection? Which of these objections seems most sound, most destructive to Ruskin's argument, and which least?

a Ruskin's argument assumes that the Romans did not produce great art. On the contrary, now they are generally conceded to have produced a very remarkable art indeed. Therefore. . . .

b According to Ruskin's argument, England in his time was engaged in ignoble wars. Therefore, Victorian England should have produced no good art. But in fact the Victorian age is acknowledged to be one of the greatest periods in English literature. Therefore. . . .

c Ruskin is highly emotional; he never loses a chance to go for the reader's belly. Therefore. . . .

d In an age when warfare threatens not merely local but even universal annihilation, · an argument such as Ruskin's is totally unacceptable. Therefore. . . .

e War does not in itself create great art. Ambition creates both war and art. Therefore. . . .

f To say that a corrupt country can only be regenerated by military rule is to endorse despotism as a moral tonic. No man not in the clutch of a fixed idea could arrive at such a conclusion. Therefore. . . .

g There is no such thing as playful or morally noble warfare. The Spartans were not playing, and Gothic chivalry was out for plunder. Therefore. . . .

Lines of Experiment

1 Write a counterargument to Ruskin's. Your answers to 6 above may help you solve the problems of such an essay. *First,* you must determine where the weakest points of Ruskin's argument lie; like dragons, arguments are killed with greatest economy when struck in a vital spot. *Second,* do not be afraid to dispose of Ruskin's argument swiftly, in order to be able to develop one of your own; an argument that is all rebuttal, all the demolition of somebody else's theory, is likely to be far less interesting than an argument that suggests a theory of its own. *Third,* decide which of your really effective lines of argument are likely to be most effective with the audience you have chosen to write for (remember, there is no way of writing for an audience you know nothing about). *Fourth,* arrange your arguments in a sequence that will lead from the smaller to the greater, the less powerful to the more powerful, the merely plausible to the thoroughly conclusive. The emotionally most powerful argument, generally, should be placed last.

In writing, you can do worse than to learn from Ruskin's technique. Do not be afraid of extreme illustrations; the subject itself is extreme, and the extreme instance is always more powerful than the average. Use the most vigorous and vivid language you can; your job in an essay of this kind is to make the reader *see* what you are talking about and thus make him *feel* the importance of your ideas. Give your abstractions a specific face, a color, a movement,—a human relevance. Do not fear metaphor. First and last, speak to your audience in a voice it will understand.

2 Arguments contain illustrations; illustrations also contain arguments. Write a narrative essay that can illustrate one or another of the points that Ruskin makes here, about the relationship between nobility of sentiment and violence, between art and struggle, between sentimentality and the military character, between the approval of women and the acts of men, etc.

Your essay will be most convincing, probably, if you base it on personal experience: the behavior of someone you know, the emotions you have felt yourself, those you have observed in others. The wars of neighborhood gangs—even of families—can suggest analogies with the wars of nations; the behavior of the individual can often provide a clue to the behavior of the state. You need not draw any explicit moral, in such an essay; in a carefully constructed narrative the statement that remains implicit is often more satisfying, because more full of nuance, of life, than the statement trotted out at the beginning and end, like a Biblical text. Your job here will be largely to make your narrative as authentic as you can: to help us to see the person or event you are dealing with and to understand it as we would if we saw it in our own lives.

GLOSSARY

Abstract and concrete, general and specific   Both sets of terms assume
a vertical continuum of thought, rising from sense impression to idea—a
kind of ladder of ideas created by us from the raw data transmitted by the
senses.   An *abstract* idea is one that can be formed from sense experience
but that by consent cannot be noted directly except as an idea.   "Honor,"
"truth," "value," "justice," are all *high* abstractions; "honesty," "validity,"
"worth," "law" are perhaps lower.   In this set of terms, anything that can
be noted directly is concrete: A man who offers to sell stock in the United
States Postal Service performs a concrete act involving both higher and
lower abstractions.

A *general* idea, by contrast, represents categories or classes of things that
appear directly to the senses.   All general ideas group *specific* entities, and
any general idea can be noted in the form of a member of the genus.   A
given St. Bernard dog is a specific entity belonging to the somewhat more
general class of St. Bernard dogs.   That class in turn belongs to the still
more general class of just plain dogs, who belong in turn to the class of
mammals, and so on.   There is a mammal on my porch; more specifically,
a dog; more specifically still, a St. Bernard; in fact, dear old Champion

Bottle himself. General ideas are both illustrated and emphasized by specific entities, and abstract ideas are both illustrated and emphasized by concrete cases.

It should be clear that a fully concrete entity is also fully specific—that is, it is unique—and that generalization and abstraction represent two somewhat different but not entirely distinct ways of moving from a world of unique objects and acts to a world of thought. It should also be clear that the idea of *levels* of abstraction or of generalization, though convenient, describes the structure of our thought and not necessarily the structure of reality. Language as a system of meanings is already fully abstract, and the general ideas "mammal" and "St. Bernard dog," the abstract ideas "honor" and "honesty," are equally distant from—or close to—the real world.

See also the introductions to Parts II and III of this text and notes here on *Deductive and Inductive Reasoning* and *Logic*.

Alliteration and assonance   These two terms denote tonal devices fairly obvious in poetry but important in prose as well. In *alliteration*, a notable proportion of the accented syllables in a brief sequence (phrase, sentence, verse) contain the same or closely similar sounds, as in "I should have been a pair of ragged claws Scuttling across the floors of silent seas," or "a little more than kin and less than kind," or "a bulb of brain wired to a bush of dendrites." The illustrations show that alliteration serves essentially to bind words together and to emphasize their connotative meanings, hence their emotional effect. Alliteration can be made to support almost any tonal effect. Gibbon uses it to heighten the sense of order and balance in his history; Lawrence uses it to heighten the sensuousness of his descriptions of the Tuscan landscape; Mencken uses it to hone the edge of satire; Beerbohm uses it to point up irony. Because alliteration is among the most common and formal of tonal devices, it is especially easy to overdo in prose. It can emphasize sentimentality, cuteness, and bathos as readily as it can more valuable qualities; and used solely as an attention getter ("Dr. Pepper's Pleasant Pellets"), it forces language to the level of advertising copy.

Alliteration and *assonance* are commonly found together. In assonance, a notable proportion of the syllables in a brief sequence contain the same or closely similar vowel sounds, but different consonants. Lamb's concluding clauses illustrate a particularly rich and complex use of the two tonal techniques: "remembering those elusive nereids, and that inauspicious inland landing." Note the repetitions of e, i, and a, and of m, n, and l.

See also the introduction to Part V of this text and notes here on *Emphasis; Figures of Speech;* and *Sound*.

Allusion and reference   In *allusion,* a glancing or indirect reference is made to a well-known story, figure, phrase, doctrine, etc., in order to create a counterpoint of feeling or idea to the subject actually under discussion. Donne, in his sermon on death (see page 514), alludes to the story of the garden of Eden: "In the skins of dead beasts he clothed the bodies of dying men." C. G. Darwin's essay on happiness alludes, in its title, to the Declaration of Independence.

By the usual distinction, allusion is implicit, *reference* is explicit. Had Donne said, "as in the garden of Eden, he clothed the bodies of dying men," he would have referred to the garden rather than alluded to it. The distinction is one of degree.

See also the introduction to Part V of this text.

Analogy   An *analogy* is a form of illustration in which something whose features are generally known and appreciated is compared to something whose features are not so known and appreciated, in order to bring out the latter's characteristics: A heart is a pump. In other forms of comparison and contrast, it is assumed that the parts compared belong essentially to the same class or category: two movies, two writers, two birds, two landscapes. In analogy, it is acknowledged in advance that the parts compared do not belong to the same class—that their resemblances are to some degree metaphorical.

Though analogies are frequently found in logically ordered discourse, their function is not proof; they are weaker than other forms of illustration in demonstrating the consistency of ideas with facts. Peirce proves nothing by declaring that instinct is to argument what bedrock is to the foundations of the cathedral (see page 156), but the illustration is forceful and tonally important. Analogy often contributes to the tone and even to the central structure of a composition. Synge builds "An Autumn Night in the Hills" around several anecdotes deliberately thrown into analogical relations; Letwin concludes his essay on the economic development of poor nations with a tonally powerful analogy; Tomlinson's "A Lost Wood" breaks continually from abstract statement to analogical illustration; and Swift savagely extends an analogy into absurdity.

See also the introduction to Part III of this text and notes here under *Figures of Speech* and *Image.*

Analysis   *Analysis* is a method of exposition in which a subject is divided into its dissimilar parts, in order to show either how those parts are connected (*functional analysis*), or why they are connected as they are (*causal analysis*). Berelson (page 146) separates for study the elements of a particular kind of political behavior; Wald (page 178) separates for study the stages of a biological process; Tyler (page 207) separates for study the causes of a phenomenon in American literary history; and Collingwood (page 219) separates for study the meanings of an idea.

See also the introduction to Part II of this text and notes here on *Analogy* (which can offer a particularly valuable frame for analysis) and *Classification and Division*.

Anecdote   An *anecdote* is a brief illustrative narrative, usually informal and personal in tone and voice.   Many essays are strings of related anecdotes, more or less explicitly interpreted: see Orwell, Synge, Henderson, Tomlinson, Sitwell, and Lamb.   Some essays are made up of single anecdotes, closely rendered, with their meanings left implicit: see Greene.   Still other essays use a single anecdote as a narrative frame for an essentially expository or argumentative center: see Huxley.   Even in the most impersonal exposition, the brief illustrative narrative has great value: see Lowie, Wald, Tyler.   At times, the anecdote is not even true: see Beerbohm.

Argument   *Argument* is that form of logically ordered discourse that seeks to establish the truth of a contested statement.   See also the introduction to Part II of this text and notes here on *Analogy; Common Ground, Assumptions and Premises; Deductive and Inductive Reasoning; Dilemma; Evidence and Proof; Fallacies and Fallacious Reasoning; Generalization; Logic; Objectivity and Subjectivity;* and *Refutation.*

Audience   A writer's *audience* consists of those persons he writes for; others may read his work, and he should be aware of this fact, but essentially he must compose with a specific audience in mind.   Without a fairly distinct idea of what that audience knows and thinks, a writer is badly handicapped: He cannot assume a common ground, either in idea or in experience; he cannot anticipate his own effect; he cannot even be sure that he will be understood.

In a deeper sense, a writer must write only to his own best standards: He cannot adapt his judgment, his facts, his style, to suit any audience whatever, without destroying his special value as a writer.   But a concern for the experience and knowledge of that audience is not only decent—it is essential.   Haldane, Wald, Styron, Baldwin, Ruskin, and Woolf address audiences with different backgrounds and different concerns.   Their methods as writers differ accordingly, though each writer is finally only himself.

Background   See *Introduction and Background.*

Classification and division   These terms denote the grouping (*classification*) and separation (*division*) of ideas and objects according to their category relations: "dogs, cows, and horses are quadrupeds" reflects an incomplete classification; "dogs are quadrupeds" represents merely a partial definition; "the domesticated quadrupeds are . . ." represents the beginning of a division.

As methods of exposition, classification and division operate together to establish the territory of discussion—or rather, to draw its map and to locate the real subject on that map.

See the introduction to Part II of this text. Ellis illustrates a complex use of classification and division; Peirce and Collingwood, simpler uses. The sorting-out process implicit in classification and division underlies both definition and analysis, and justifies illustration.

Climax and anticlimax: dramatic structure in discourse *Climax* and *anticlimax* are terms borrowed from dramatic criticism. The climax of an action is the scene in which the conflict that gave rise to the action reaches its most intense point and turns toward resolution. An anticlimax represents a conscious or unconscious failure to realize or to maintain the level of importance implied by the preceding matter. In the last scene of *Hamlet* nearly every principal character is killed, one by another; were they to decide instead to seek psychotherapy together, the effect would be anticlimactic.

These terms have obvious relevance to description and narration, where sequence, scale, focus, tone, point of view, and essentially mimetic order conduce to a strongly dramatic structure. (See Part I of this text and, as illustrative extremes, the essays by Thurber, Adams and Wilson.) But even logically organized discourse is greatly influenced by such nonlogical considerations. The sequence by which arguments are presented is a great part of their persuasiveness; the relative scale of various elements in an analysis is an index of their relative importance; and so on. In a metaphorical sense, an argument can come to a climax—or to an anticlimax, and demands a dramatic as well as a logical resolution. See the sequence of argument in Darwin, the sequence of analysis in Tyler, the concluding passage in Wald. For an essay dominated by dramatic principles of development, see Ruskin.

Coherence, linkage, and transition An essay is *coherent* when each part leads clearly and consistently to the succeeding part. Coherence is largely the product of the careful use of bridging words and phrases, tieing ideas together sentence by sentence, paragraph by paragraph, section by section. The more limited and purely verbal of these bridging devices are usually called *links*. The sentences and paragraphs of mimetically ordered discourse are commonly linked by such imitative terms as "near," "far," "after," and the like; the sentences and paragraphs of logically ordered discourse are commonly linked by terms pointing to logical relations, such as "and," "but," "because," and the like. These basic linking systems are discussed in the introductions to Parts I and II of this text. Reiteration is another linking device: The first phrase of one unit (sentence or paragraph) picks up, directly or in slightly altered but easily recognizable form, a key word or phrase from the preceding unit. Thus a paragraph ending with the sentence, "Dancing came first," might be followed by one that begins, "The art of dancing," or "Dancing is first not only in time, but also. . . ." Boldly rhetorical pieces often link one sentence or paragraph to another by means of such reiterated phrases as "I do not ask" or "Brutus is an honorable man!" Much more subtle linking effects are possible than any of these: See Synge's description of the bridge across the flooding river, page 35. In argument cast as dramatic dialogue (see Thucydides), the regular change of voice becomes a powerful if mechanical linking device.

The more extensive and sometimes quite elaborate bridges between ideas are usually called *transitions,* rather than links. Shifts from argument to anecdote (see Huxley), or from past to present time (see Styron), or from impersonal to personal narrative (see Ruskin), are all effective methods of transition from one section of a piece to another; ingenuity will find not only parallel types of transition, but quite different types as well. Such transitions can have considerable tonal effect. The essential element in any transition is a signal of change, of redirection. The simplest—and least meaningful—transitions between sections are made with roman numerals or with extra white space.

See also the note here on *Unity.*

Common ground, assumptions, and premises   These three terms reflect the fact that every discussion is based on an at least rudimentary agreement among the participants concerning the meaning of words, the truth of some facts, the validity of some inferences from those facts, and so forth. The *common ground* of a discussion is, in the broadest sense, this area of agreement; in a narrower sense, it is that group of relevant statements necessary to the discussion and agreed to by all participants. The *assumptions* of the discussion are those relevant points of agreement that are taken for granted and so are neither explained nor argued; its *unconscious assumptions* are those points that even the participants (or the writers) are unaware of, have absorbed unknowingly, from the historical or rhetorical context; its *hidden assumptions* are those that are either unconscious or concealed. The *premises* of an argument are those statements already agreed to be true from which the conclusions of that argument are said to be validly derived. An *unspoken premise* is a premise that is not put forward, that is assumed. The terms overlap. All logically ordered discourse is built on a common ground, composed partly of assumptions and partly of premises. Some assumptions are premises, some premises are assumptions. Generally, mere economy suggests that those stages in an argument that can be assumed, in relation to a given audience, should be.

See also the introduction to Part II of this text and notes here under *Deductive and Inductive Reasoning* and *Logic.*

Comparison and contrast In comparison and contrast, two or more members of the same class are placed side by side, in order to illustrate their basic similarities or differences and so make their significance clear. As a mental operation, comparison and contrast is basic to the formation of categories, hence basic to thought. In one way or another, every essay in this collection employs comparison and contrast; in Gibbon, Tyler, Woolf, and Thucydides it is structurally central.

See also the introduction to Part III of this text and notes here on *Analogy* and *Irony.*

Connotation See *Denotation and Connotation.*

Context The historical backgrond or the logical or rhetorical setting of a particular passage, idea, discussion, etc., is its context. The meaning of a given word or idea depends partly on the context in which it is used. Thus the political theories and vocabularies of both Thoreau and Hobbes require interpretation in the light of the (quite different) philosophical and historical contexts from which they spring; and the real character of Swift's "modest proposal" is best understood within the historical context of eighteenth-century Ireland's economic condition. Part of the job of an introduction is to establish the context within which a subject is important: Thus Muller outlines the context within which he will discuss Santa Sophia, and Styron the context within which the story of Nat Turner seems significant.

The interplay between context and subject is often of great and indeed central importance: Baldwin's father's death falls in the context of the Harlem riots: the one incident illuminates the other—and both illuminate the problem Baldwin himself faces.

Deductive and inductive reasoning *Deductive reasoning* moves from a generalization (all men are mortal) to a particular case (Socrates is a man) to a conclusion (Socrates is mortal.) All deductive reasoning is based on the study of category relations and applies general truths to particular cases. The syllogistic reasoning we are all familiar with (the illustration just given comprises a syllogism) is deductive.

Inductive reasoning moves from particular cases (Socrates is mortal, Alcibiades is mortal, Thucydides is mortal, Pericles is mortal) to a general truth about the categories to which those cases belong (all men are mortal). Clearly each form of reasoning implies and requires the other, and the two forms do and must alternate. A deductive chain that pays attention to particulars only in its conclusions is bound to be unconvincing to those interested in the truth of its premises; and an inductive chain that arrives at generalizations only after all the facts are known and sorted can never hope to arrive even at the principles by which that knowing and sorting can be done. The reasoning process moves from limited fact to limited hypothesis, and thence back to limited fact once more; that process is far more subtle than such extreme terms as deduction and induction can imply.

Nonetheless, many essays may be classified fairly accurately as generally deductive or as generally inductive in structure. In an inductively organized essay, the data are presented before the conclusions are; the case study (see Morison) is a good illustration. In a deductively organized essay, the conclusions are followed by the data that suport them; Malthus bases his study of the law of population increase on a series of general statements. Hobbes and Thoreau form an interesting contrast between the inductive and the deductive mind. Ruskin's essay on war rehearses the intricate relations in his own mind between the observation of fact and the formation of hypothesis.

See also the introduction in Part II of this text and notes here under *Common Ground, Assumptions, and Premises* and *Logic*.

Definition and identification   Identification names or describes something in such a way that it may be recognized, even though not closely distinguished from similar things: Atlantic City is a famous resort on the eastern seaboard.   An extended identification might show us how the city was built, what its history has been, what it has meant as a symbol of American civilization, what kinds of people go there, etc.   Such an identification is almost an inventory of significant characteristics.   Nabokov so identifies his boyhood school, Styron so identifies the county in which Nat Turner's revolt occurred, Muller so identifies Santa Sophia, Adams so identifies the spiritual center of the Middle Ages.

Definition fixes the thing to be defined within its general class and points out the characteristics that distinguish that thing from other members of its class: First the *genus* is named, and then the *differentiae*.   Such definitions are *logical, convertible,* and *real*.   A *verbal* definition is a definition employing mere synonym: A house is a domicile.   Dictionaries commonly offer both real and verbal definitions.

Extended or rhetorical definitions are much less schematic and more elaborate explorations of meaning.   Characteristically, an extended definition works by presenting illustrations of the thing to be defined and analyzing them in such a way as to show the points of differentiation, the boundaries, in concrete form. Frequently the final formulation of results is left to the reader; and many narrative or descriptive essays are, quite literally, metaphorical definitions. Haldane uses extended definition as a way of arguing for a certain view of life, and against other views. Collingwood bases a difficult discussion of the value of historical thinking on an extended definition of "progress." Peirce uses extended definition to examine the very concept of definition itself, when applied to the indefinable.

See also the introduction to Part II of this text and notes here under *Classification and Division* and *Comparison and Contrast*.

Denotation and connotation The denotative meaning of a word is its precise meaning, the ground actually bounded by its definition within a given context of discussion. The connotative meaning of that word is the aura of meaning and value that surrounds it in that context, by virtue of its traditional associations. Denotatively, "red-gold hair" is merely hair of a particular shade; connotatively, "red-gold" suggests beauty, youth, desirability, etc. The importance of context in eliciting connotative meaning cannot be exaggerated: "He is a very rational man" can suggest either admiration or contempt, depending on the context. Connotative meanings are the chief avenues by which the emotional charge of thought—its pressure, so to speak —is transmitted.

See also the introduction to Part V of this text and notes here under *Alliteration and Assonance; Context; Diction; Figures of Speech;* and *Sound*.

Description Anything may be described, and almost any composition can be called a description; as a form of discourse, however, *description* attempts to render the spatial appearance of a given subject, as that appearance is taken in and, so to speak, organized by the eye, as if in a frozen moment. All the essays in Part I of this text make important use of description, to varying ends: Contrast Orwell's description of Marrakech to Nabokov's description of his childhood home. Distinctness in point of view and voice is crucial to description: see Dos Passos, Styron, Baldwin, Adams, Lawrence.

See further the introductions to Parts I and IV of this text and notes here under *Coherence, Linkage, and Transition; Scale;* and *Rendering*.

Diction A writer's diction is that element in his style that results from his specific choices among words roughly similar in denotation but different in connotation, in degree of precision, and in force. No specific kind of diction is abstractly either good or bad; each is good or bad only as a vehicle for establishing a particular tone, in relation to a particular audience, subject, and circumstance. The diction of the Army barracks is not often suited to the maternal living room—nor that of the maternal living room to the Army barracks. Highly concrete language is a necessity in the rendering of appearance, movement, event; it may not be suited to the analysis of highly abstract ideas. Highly connotative language is suited to discourse that seeks an emotional response; it may not be suited to discourse that seeks to avoid emotion. Highly figurative language carries great force, but it may be out of place where a strong response is not wanted. Here too, the writer finally cannot make over his personal judgment and responsibility to a set of rules; he must consult his purposes. Even within a single essay a writer may deliberately change his diction to suit his purpose: see Beerbohm. Jarrell's diction plays curiously between the formal and the informal, the poetic and the flat; even the stale language of copywriters and politicians is put to work. Collingwood's hypothetical illustrations are put forward in carefully abstract language, while Ruskin's are powerfully concrete.

See also the introduction to Part V of this text and notes here under *Abstract and Concrete, General and Specific; Denotation and Connotation; Emphasis; Levels of Usage; Rendering;* and *Style.*

Digression   In well-organized prose, there are no digressions: the passages that seem to digress (and even those that are *said* to digress) actually do not. Synge's "An Autumn Night in the Hills" can illustrate apparently artless, actually very artful, "digression" in narrative. Swift, Milne, and Beerbohm use apparent digression for ironical purposes.

Dilemma   To be in a dilemma is to be confronted by a necessary choice between two things that are almost equally desirable or undesirable. To pose a dilemma is a standard device of argument: *either* one must agree to A *or* one must agree to B—there is no third choice. Wald presents in this form the problem facing scientists who attempted to explain the origin of life: *either* one accepted the theory of spontaneous generation, disproved by Pasteur, or one accepted the theory of supernatural creation, repugnant to scientific method. Usually, though not always, there is a third choice, and the dilemma is false.

Emphasis   To emphasize something is to give it the emotional importance that seems its due. Within the sentence, emphasis can be achieved by verbal repetitions and echoes ("We call death a breaking of prison and what is birth but a breaking of prison?"); by breaks from common verbal or clausal order (contrast "The month following, the cow died," to "The cow died the following month"); by position (contrast "Jackson and Ney were both pure cavalrymen" to "Ney and Jackson were both pure cavalrymen"); by shifts in diction (contrast "MacArthur and Truman disliked one another" to "MacArthur and Truman hated each other's guts"); by, in short, every tonal device discussed in the introduction to Part V of this text. Emphasis can be got most cheaply by punctuation; contrast "I came, I saw, I conquered" to "I came! I saw! I conquered!" Punctuational emphasis is obvious, like alliterative emphasis; both should be used with caution and restraint. Emphasis can be got most directly by flat statement: "Most important of all. . . ."

Within paragraphs and sections, emphasis can be got in analogous ways. First and last sentences, first and last paragraphs, accrue emphasis by mere position; an essay that ends with an unimportant sentence or paragraph falls, wittingly or unwittingly, into anticlimax. Crucial passages can attain emphasis by shifts in diction, by apparent digression, by changes in sentence length and rhythm, by reiteration, by increased figurativeness of language, by sudden transition from one form of discourse to another. Illustration, too, can become a potent method of emphasis. See Nabokov, Thoreau, Hobbes, Jarrell, and especially Ruskin.

Emphasis is not a trick. Any verbal construction, no matter what its type, implies a pattern of emphasis.

See the introduction to Part V of this text and notes here under *Alliteration and Assonance; Analogy; Climax and Anticlimax; Diction; Digression; Figures of Speech;* and *Sound.*

Essay. A usually brief factual discourse in prose: see page xiii. Though often disprized, the essay has a long and splendid history; it is fact displayed by imagination—and, at its best, it is great art.

Evidence and proof Categorical statements are supported by *evidence*. The amount and character of evidence necessary to support any given statement will depend on the degree to which that statement is open to doubt: No supporting evidence is required for a statement already accepted as true. Specific evidence of the applicability of a general statement to a given case may well be required, if the general statement is accepted as usually but not invariably true; and specific evidence is needed to establish a categorical statement not as yet credited. Thus no evidence is needed to prove that men need food to live; specific evidence is needed to prove that population tends to outrun subsistence; and a good deal of specific evidence is necessary to prove that everywhere population is forced to a level with subsistence, by means of war, famine, and vice.

Evidence may come from fact—which requires interpretation, in every case; from customary judgment—which is not necessarily based on the careful study of fact; from expert opinion—which sometimes disagrees; and from personal experience and judgment—which is limited but at least authentic. A careful reasoner and writer will bear in mind the limitations and values of each kind of evidence and not claim for one kind of evidence the virtues of another kind. Except in aggregate, evidence is seldom fully conclusive: Where fact, customary judgment, expert opinion, and personal experience all support a given statement, that statement is probably sound. (But not always: consider the old belief that the earth is flat.)

The *proof* of a conclusion is composed of the arguments that support it, each of which in turn depends for its value on the truth of (i.e., evidence for) its premises and the validity of its inferences from those premises. A statement may be considered proved when (1) its supporting arguments are sound, (2) no serious objections have been left out of its account, and (3) the balance of probabilities is clearly in its favor. Proof nearly always requires the refutation of the strongest opposing arguments, and nearly always is incomplete.

See the introductions to Parts II and III of this text and notes here under *Common Ground, Assumptions, and Premises; Deductive and Inductive Reasoning; Fallacies and Fallacious Reasoning; Logic;* and *Refutation.*

Example Any illustration may be called an example. In this text, examples are distinguished fram illustrations involving comparison and contrast, or analogy, or metaphor. An example is a representative drawn from the class being spoken of; a good example represents the class fairly, a bad example does not. See pages 266–267.

Exposition Exposition is that form of logically organized discourse whose aim is to explain to an unaware audience systems of fact and idea already accepted as true by those competent to judge. In effect, exposition rehearses the conclusion of an argument already settled and usually must rehearse some of its evidence also, in order to make those conclusions plausible. See Haldane, Tyler, Wald. See also the introduction to Part II of this text and notes here under *Analysis; Classification and Division; Comparison and Contrast; Definition and Identification; Example; Expository Narrative;* and *Focus.*

Narratives pretending to a dramatic structure also have an "expository" element—that section of the narrative that establishes the setting or frame for the action to follow. See *Introduction and Background.*

Expository narrative Mimetically organized narrative is concerned with unique events; its focus is on character, scene, symbol, act, and its aim is representation. Logically organized or expository narrative is concerned with processes; its focus is on functional or causal patterns of development, and its aim is systematic explanation. Wald, in summarizing the controversy over life's origins, writes expository narratives. In well-written history, the logical and the mimetic frequently fuse, the former providing systematic explanation and the latter providing rhetorical power: see Gibbon, Green, Muller, Lowie.

Fallacies and fallacious reasoning   Fallacious or erroneous reasoning can take many forms; the recurrent ways in which people reason falsely are generally called fallacies.   Some errors are easy to detect, others are hard; some persons reason falsely out of knowledge, others out of ignorance.   The following discussion corresponds only in part to the categories of formal logic.

1 To mistake fact is an obvious and general source of erroneous reasoning.   No valid conclusion can be drawn from erroneous fact, and any conclusion so drawn can easily be shot down.   The only safeguard is the checking of any fact about which there may be doubt.

2 To mistake opinion for fact is a second common source of error.   Much that we ordinarily think of as fact is actually opinion.   That the Civil War ended legal slavery in America, for example, is fact, and certain; but that the Civil War was fought over slavery is opinion, and less certain.   No conclusion can be more certain that the premises on which it is based; to claim certainty for conclusions based on uncertain premises is fallacious.

3 To misuse words is a third common source of fallacious reasoning.   Some abuses of words are obvious: What the facts certify to be violent military conquest cannot honestly be termed "peaceful extension of trade."   Other abuses are less obvious: "Socialist art" and "democratic free enterprise" compound words with totally disparate meanings, and the result is fog.   Simple inexactness can wreak havoc with rational discussion; if we say "race" and mean "culture," or "reform" and mean "improvement," we destroy unwittingly distinctions of great importance.   Using the same word in different senses within the same argument (*equivocation*) is also destructive: If in the same essay the word "progress" is made to mean variously "change," "moral improvement," "biological adaption," "increased economic productivity," and "increased comfort," the cause of rational discourse can hardly be served.   Clarity in thought and discourse depends on agreement about the meaning of terms and on stability in their use; many arguments properly turn, therefore, on problems of terminology.

4 To make mistaken inferences from the evidence is a fourth way to miscarry into fallacy.   Mistakes in inference may rise from a failure to understand the meaning of the evidence or from a failure to grasp or to use properly the logical process itself.   Illogical inferences can be classified in many ways, and most of the illustrations that follow could be classified under more than one head.
   a Expanding a conclusion beyond the warrant of the premises.   (Fallacy of *Non Sequitur*—"it does not follow.")   The simpler forms of *Non Sequitur* enjoy a perennial popularity: "The premier of Gouda works

hard at his job and is absolutely honest; therefore, we should support his government." "The Gross National Product rises steadily year after year; nothing, therefore, can be fundamentally wrong with our civilization." The facts may be correct; the conclusion overreaches their warrant.

b *Mistaking the accidental for the essential.* (Fallacy of Accident.) "He loves dogs and horses; therefore, he must be nice." "She never loses her temper; therefore, she must be emotionally stable." "It moves; therefore, it must be alive." And in politics: "Gouda has a parliament; therefore, it is a representative democracy."

c *Mistaking one cause of a particular result for its sole cause.* (Fallacy of the Consequent.) "The settlement of America was the consequence of religious persecution in the Old World." "He got an A in 'expressive trampoline' because he studied hard." "Herbert Wampum was elected simply because he was rich."

d *Applying a general rule to a specific case, without regard for exceptional circumstances.* (Fallacy of *Secundum Quid*—"from which it follows.") "Policemen should not carry guns, from which it follows that prison guards should not carry guns." "The Aga Khan lives in France, from which it follows that the Aga Khan is French." "The fact that you broke your neck just before the final exam is irrelevant to your grade, which is F."

e *Deriving a general rule from an insufficient or unrepresentative number of specific cases.* (The reverse form of the previous fallacy.) "Irving Berlin was Jewish, and Berlin is a place-name, from which it follows that when a man's surname is also a place-name, he is Jewish." "Muldoon is opposed to the draft because he is cowardly, from which it follows that all opposition to the draft springs from cowardice."

f *Assuming among the premises of an argument an assertion that itself requires proof,* and so avoiding the real issue. (Fallacy of Begging the Question.) "I should not be punished because I acted according to my conscience," conceals the premise that "no person who acts according to his conscience should be punished," and so begs the real question.

g *Offering as premises statements that in fact presuppose the conclusion and so make the conclusion stand as evidence for itself.* (Fallacy of Arguing in a Circle.) The fallacy is often obvious: "The Interfaith Breakfast Club is a worthwhile organization because it believes in rational discussion of religious matters. It believes in rational discussion of religious matters because it is a worthwhile organization." "He thinks so clearly because he is a very rational person." But circular arguments can be more specious: "A program so unsound can never attract the support of reasonable men" appears to offer as criticism of the program the fact that it cannot attract the support of reasonable men, and as definition of "reasonable men" the fact that they are critical of the program. Similarly, to say that a specific idea is unacceptable because it is un-American is to fall into circular logic: We Americans cannot accept it because it is un-American, and it is un-American because we Americans cannot accept it.

h Confusing simple time sequence with causal sequence. (Fallacy of *Post Hoc Ergo Propter Hoc*—"after that, therefore because of that.") "The Great Depression happened because Hoover was elected President." At times, the causal link is merely implied: "Hoover was elected, and we had a depression."

i Raising several questions as if there were but one, under conditions that require a single reply. (Fallacy of Many Questions.) The classic one is, "When did you stop beating your wife?" But even in college the fallacy is not unknown: "Why didn't you read the assignment carefully?"

j Appealing to general ignorance of a true conclusion, in support of one's own. "It has never been proved that King David existed; therefore he is a literary fabrication." "It has never been proved that King David did not exist; therefore he did exist." To use ignorance in the support of belief is perhaps the silliest of all logical fallacies.

5 *To argue beside the point,* ignoring the real issue of debate, is perhaps the most obvious and popular of all kinds of fallacious reasoning. If the point at issue is the morality of a given act, then its political utility, its ease, its probable profits or losses, its precedents, the difficulty of escaping it, and even the personal character and motives of those implicated in it are all irrelevant. Most often, arguments that ignore the issue seek to convince by emotional rather than by rational appeal. In *Ad Hominem* (addressed to the man himself) argument, an attack on or a eulogy of personal character is substituted for discussion of the real issue: "Richard Quid has a beautiful wife, three short-haired children, and one long-haired sheep dog—how can you convict him of embezzlement?" Similarly irrelevant appeals can be made to pity, to personal interest or greed, to fear, to popular sentiment or prejudice, to traditional authority or symbol, to personal helplessness, and so on, in an effort to substitute emotional for rational conviction. Perhaps the most irrelevant and vicious of all such arguments is the appeal to force.

Figures of speech   A *figure of speech* is a brief passage deliberately breaking from the normal patterns of language in order to figure, or illustrate, as if in a visual image or a pattern of sound, the meaning aimed at. In *metaphor,* often identified as the basic figure of speech, an idea is represented by means of an image not normally within its range of meaning, and the idea and the image are equated: "He is a thistle blown on the wind." In *simile,* the identity of idea and image is weakened to mere comparison: 'He is like a thistle blown on the wind." A metaphor or simile extended into parts —into analysis, so to speak—becomes an *analogy.* In *personification,* an idea, inanimate object, or beast is presented as if a person: 'The empire, stiff with the accumulated diseases of extreme age. . . ." *Alliteration* and *assonance* are figures that address the ear, not the eye; they are discussed above.   An *apostrophe* is a deliberate invoking of or address to an entity not present or at least not visible: Adams's "The Court of the Queen of Heaven" relies heavily on extended apostrophe.   *Hyperbole* is deliberate exaggeration: "Any line you stand in around here ends up costing you money."

Many more figures of speech could be listed; those listed here are common in prose.   Figurative language is risky: a figurative turn that fails can distract the reader badly.   But its potential rewards are accordingly high: used with care and imagination, figures of speech can enhance greatly the sharpness and color of images, the resonance and solidity of ideas.

See the introduction to Part V of this text and notes here under *Alliteration and Assonance; Analogy; Diction; Emphasis; Image;* and *Sound.*

Focus   A writer's *focus* is that specific area within his subject matter on which he concentrates his attention.   Any subject proves, on examination, to have far too many facets to be dealt with as a whole in a single composition: Some facts must be relegated to the background, some to the wings; some angles of approach must be entirely ignored, and a single approach made dominant.   A steady point of view is crucial to clarity of focus: see Jarrell, Wilson, Synge, Dos Passos.   Frequently, focus is held by the use of a symbolic center (see Greene, Henderson, Nabokov, Huxley, Adams), by predominant use of a single method of exposition (see Haldane, Ellis, Morison) or of refutation (see Peirce, Ciardi, Swift), or by the restriction of discourse to a single part of the issue (see Wald, Muller).   Clarity of focus is essential to unity of effect.

See notes here under *Coherence, Linkage, and Transition* and *Unity.*

Form, matter, and subject   These three terms are indefinite in meaning, but name distinctions nonetheless real.   The *matter* of a discourse is its raw body of fact and customary interpretation—the largest boundary that can be drawn profitably around it.   Henry Adams writes about medieval culture. The *subject* of a discourse is the particular matter isolated so as to pose a question for direct or indirect examination: What force held medieval culture together?   The *form* of the discourse is its actual shape as a composition.   Discourse can be generally classified as falling into descriptive, narrative, expository, or argumentative form; description and narration can be further classified as essentially mimetic forms, and exposition and argument can be further classified as essentially logical forms.   But each successful composition has its own form, not to be fully caught within any set of general terms.

See also notes here under *Climax and Anticlimax; Focus;* and *Unity.*

Forms of discourse   See references under *Description, Narration, Exposition,* and *Argument,* and notes here under *Form, Matter, and Subject.*

Generalization   A *generalization* is a statement purporting to apply, in the absence of exceptional circumstances, to all members of a class.   Generalization is necessary but can be treacherous, for a generalization may be true ordinarily but false in a specific case.   To resolve or to explain thorny particular problems by resort to generalization is a tempting but sometimes bad strategy: "Of course I want to make money—everybody wants to make money."   The generalization is untrue.   See notes here under *Abstract and Concrete, General and Specific* and *Fallacies and Fallacious Reasoning.*

Illustration   An *illustration* clarifies and emphasizes the meaning of something, either by rendering it in more nearly specific or concrete terms (*example*) or by juxtaposing it to something whose similarities and differences can make its own features more striking and visible (see *comparison and contrast, analogy*).   Illustration is discussed in the introduction to Part III.   See also notes here under *Abstract and Concrete, General and Specific; Analogy; Anecdote;* and *Symbol.*

Image and mimesis   Linguistically, an *image* is an effort to create through words the mental version of a sensory, especially a visual, impression: "The pallid, streaming bark of birches shone in the rain."   By extension, any figure of speech that expresses or implies analogy (simile, metaphor, personification) can be called an image.

Any attempt to represent, as if in time and space, something not actually present and perceptible by the senses is *mimetic*—it imitates, by means of a medium of communication, something taken as real.   A portrait of Lincoln, a story or a dance about racial tensions, a narrative of the rebellion in heaven—all are mimetic.   Mimetic order is order as if in time and space. In composition, description imitates appearances in space, and narration imitates appearances in time; but actually the one form of imitation is dependent on and implies the other.   See the introduction to Part I of this text and note here under *Figures of Speech.*

Inductive reasoning   See *Deductive and Inductive Reasoning.*

Introduction and background   The *background* of any prose piece is its objective frame of idea or experience: Styron and Baldwin both write against a background of racial conflict within the society at large, and that background is itself composed of historical, ideological, economic, and other elements of life and thought in the United States.   The *introduction* of a prose piece is that section of it (always the first paragraphs) that presents the background in such a way as to locate the subject, define the point of view and focus, and anticipate the style of the total composition. In narration and description, this brief sketch of the necessary background is usually called the *exposition*. Logically organized discourse also establishes its background in the first paragraphs—sometimes by anecdote (see Tomlinson, Huxley, Morison), sometimes by definition (see Letwin), sometimes by expository narrative (see Wald), sometimes by other methods. The essential purpose of an introduction is to give the reader his bearings. The title is the first element of every introduction.

In an entirely different, nonrhetorical sense, any piece has a subjective background in the life of its author. A sketch of this subjective background often is part of the introduction, especially when the writer intends to use the personal voice throughout.

See notes here under *Anecdote; Context; Focus; Objectivity and Subjectivity; Point of View; Style;* and *Unity.*

Irony   In a general sense, any extreme contrast that emphasizes the discrepancy between appearance and reality, belief and truth, intention and result, etc., can be called *ironical*. In *verbal* irony, what is actually said is the exact reverse of what should be said. When, in Shakespeare's *Julius Caesar,* Antony calls Brutus an honorable man, he employs *conscious* irony: He means to suggest that Brutus is dishonorable. But Brutus is indeed an honorable man: There is *unconscious* irony in the fact that Antony is telling the truth without realizing it, and *dramatic* irony in that we, the audience, recognize the truth that Antony and the Romans do not.

Acts can be as ironical as words, and in parallel ways. It is ironical that the Agrarian party should have tried to preserve a democratic government in Gouda and succeeded in creating a dictatorship instead; it is doubly ironical that their successors in power should have tried to camouflage that dictatorship with the trappings of a democracy, only to see the camouflage become the fact.

Irony is a staple tonal device of good writers and takes many forms. There is irony in Synge's closing contrast between the noisy well-lighted inn and the wet, deserted coffin, and in Huxley's closing contrast between the smell of Jerusalem's sewage and the sudden sound of Bach. Letwin, too, heightens the emphasis of his conclusion by resort to irony. There is subtle irony in Wald's remark that a man attempting to put a new idea forward can ask for nothing better than a noisy and stubborn opponent, and less subtle irony in Milne's comment that a few "trifling" things stood between him and immortal fame. Ruskin's essay on war is heavily ironical, in several ways—not least, in the main point. The too common contrast between professed and actual public morality has never found a more savage or devastating expression than it does in Swift's "A Modest Proposal"—perhaps the greatest piece of sustained irony ever written.

Levels of usage   The social or formal character of a particular language style, largely the result of its diction and syntax, is its *level of usage*. *Formal English* is the level of usage commonly found in such settings as reference works, scholarly journals, commencement exercises; it is conservative, in that it employs a diction and syntax already current for some time in the work of esteemed writers, and it is ordinarily marked by extreme impersonality of voice.   *Informal English* is more likely to display the writer's personality directly; it is closer in diction and syntax to the current spoken language.   Most modern educated prose is written in informal English.

Occasionally, a writer will make use of a diction or syntax customarily barred from the written language.   *Colloquial English* is simply the speech of educated people, who, like all people, often speak in formally ungrammatical or incomplete sentences and often use words seldom met with in writing.   "Too bad!" is colloquial.   The dialogue of good narration generally tries to catch the colloquial turn, for obvious reasons.

Slang is spoken English of a special sort, recognized as new, local, and ephemeral.   In the 1940s, "That's tough!" meant "That's too bad!" (Colloq.), or "That is indeed unfortunate" (Formal); for a later generation, "tough" means "great," or "beautiful."   Slang seldom becomes standard English.

Illiterate English is by definition not the language of educated persons.   It is perhaps unnecessary to point out that this standard of correctness, however socially important, is quite arbitrary, and that illiterate speech can have much color and meaning.   *Huckleberry Finn*, a great American novel, is deliberately written in illiterate English; its illiteracy is a sign of its highly personal point of view.   In impersonal discourse, deliberate illiteracy is an unnecessary distraction.

In this text, Gibbon, Green, Collingwood, Ruskin, and Malthus write largely formal English.   Huxley, Milne, and Mencken write largely informal English.   Thurber, Synge, and Styron use illiterate speech for special purposes.   But any careful craftsman with words feels free to move from one level of usage to another, as his purposes suggest, using the social connotations of variant forms of speech to extend and reinforce his point.

Logic   Logic is the study of the conditions of valid inference.   Formal logic—the systems of rules by which valid inferences can be analyzed and formal fallacies detected—is not discussed in this text.   For an informal discussion of logical inquiry, see the introduction to Part II.

Contemporary logic is highly specialized and often highly abstract; symbolic logic presents its systems of valid inference merely by letters, numbers, and other nonverbal signs.   The logic of ordinary discourse is that derived, after many removes, from the ancient Greeks, and especially from Aristotle.

Aristotelian logic is based on the *syllogism.* The perennial illustration is:

All men are mortal.	(Major or general premise, of the pattern all A belongs to the class of B.)
Socrates is a man.	(Minor or particular premise, of the pattern C belongs to the class of A.)
Socrates is mortal.	(Conclusion—the application of the general premise to the particular case—of the pattern C belongs to the class of B.)

of logic is deductive. Behind the major premise, however, is inductive logic—a study of men's fates sufficient to support the general statement that all men are mortal. A and B are categories, or classes of things; the premises, therefore, are *categorical statements.* The relations among categories are strictly those of inclusion and exclusion, and the premises must be agreed to if the conclusion is to follow.

Most logically ordered discussions actually take the form of a chain of statements, in which the obvious premises are leaped (that is, assumed) and the conclusion of one series becomes a premise of the next series. In this text, Collingwood, Peirce, Hobbes, Darwin, and Malthus illustrate with unusual bareness the use of logical chains; few of their arguments would gain in power by being rephrased in syllogistic form, however, and it is very doubtful that any of those arguments were originally so developed. The study of logic is a valuable aid but not a prerequisite to rational thought: The system of analysis is not the thing analyzed.

See further the introduction to Part II of this text and notes here under *Abstract and Concrete, General and Specific; Common Ground, Assumptions, and Premises; Deductive and Inductive Reasoning; Evidence and Proof; Fallacies and Fallacious Reasoning; and Refutation.*

Meaning In composition, the sum total of what is communicated by a given linguistic sign or sequence is its *meaning.* There is no convenient way of distinguishing the meaning intended from the meaning expressed, and no virtue in excluding the emotional content of a passage from its total meaning. Most common words have both denotative and connotative meaning: sentences are vehicles for highly complex meanings; even punctuational signs have meanings (?).

Motive and purpose These terms are often used as if synonymous, but a distinction between them has value. The *purpose* of a writer is what he sets out to accomplish within his work—the exploring of a certain subject, to a certain conclusion, with a certain consequence. His *motive* is what prompts him to work in the first place. *Purpose,* then, is objective and capable of being inferred; *motive* is subjective and usually knowable only in part—if at all. Gibbon's purpose in writing *The Decline and Fall of the Roman*

Empire was to render, to account for, and to offer the lessons from that shattering historical episode; his motives were what pushed him to do so. The purpose of a writer is properly part of his composition and dominates its form and focus. The motives of a writer are properly part of his personality; they are irrelevant to the worth of what he writes, though revelant to its background. Arguments sometimes attempt to determine the truth or value of statements or acts by addressing their motives; such arguments are fallacious.

Narration To narrate is to tell about a pattern of event: The structural principle of narration is order in time. Where description imitates scene as organized and given natural sequence by the eye, in an artificially arrested moment, narration imitates scene as organized and given natural sequence by memory. Narration encloses description. All the essays in Part I of this text are narrative in form. Distinctiness in point of view is crucial in narration.

See further the introductions to Parts I and IV of this text, and notes here under *Climax and Anticlimax; Coherence, Linkage, and Transition; Description; Expository Narrative; Image and Minesis; Introduction and Background; Rendering; Scale;* and *Unity.*

Objectivity and subjectivity To be *objective* is to view experience as if it were detached from the personal point of view: An objective fact is one that can be vouched for by all experienced persons, no matter how mentally or emotionally constituted; an objective attitude is one that focuses on objective facts; and an objective judgment is one that is based on an objective attitude. To be *subjective* is to view experience as if it were contained within the personal point of view: A subjective fact is one that can only be vouched for by a specific person as part of his mental or emotional state and as consequence of his special perception; a subjective attitude is one that focuses on subjective facts; and a subjective judgment is one that is based on a subjective attitude. The objective world lies outside us; the subjective world lies within. Ordinarily, objective and subjective writing differ in the directness of their appeal to the emotions: In the former, the emotional dimension of experience is implicit, as it were, uninterpreted, and the reader is left to respond on his own; in the latter, that emotional dimension is interpreted and projected directly, by the writer's voice. Such distinctions are relative, however: There is no way of detaching completely the observer from the thing observed, and no way of enclosing the thing observed entirely within the observer. But the distinctions are real: Contrast the severely objective style of Berelson, Collingwood, and Letwin to the luxuriantly subjective style of Henderson, Ciardi, Tomlinson, and Sitwell. The handling of point of view in the dialogue form makes possible a particularly rich and interesting compound of the objective and the subjective:

see Thucydides.   Much narrative art reaches a similar balance by similar means: see Synge, Nabokov, Leighton, Thurber.

Organization and structure   The *organization,* or unique *structure,* of a composition is largely a function of its subject, purpose, audience, point of view, focus, and dominant form of discourse.   Every composition has an introduction, a main body, and a conclusion.   An essay often will echo deliberately in its conclusion the structure and even the language of its introduction, in order to "close the circle" and so reinforce unity of effect; a mechanically repetitious return to the beginning, however, is anticlimactic— it suggests that nothing new has been found, no further importance discovered, in the main body of the essay.

The introduction to Parts I to IV of this text are largely concerned with problems of organization and structure.   See also notes here under *Climax and Anticlimax; Coherence, Linkage, and Transition; Emphasis; Introduction and Background; Focus;* and *Unity.*

Point of view and voice   A writer's point of view can be (1) his general attitude, (2) his role as writer, and (3) the set of eyes from whose vantage point he asks us to see and to order the material within the composition. His voice can speak to us either personally or impersonally.   Point of view as general attitude is not discussed in this text.   Other aspects of point of view are discussed in the introduction to Part IV.

Refutation   An argument is composed of general and particular statements linked by chains of inference and confirmed by evidence.   It may be shown to be fallacious (i.e., refuted) by reason of (1) mistake in fact, (2) misuse of terms, (3) mistake in inference from fact, (4) irrelevant or insufficient evidence, and (5) conclusion contrary to truth.   The *basis* for refutation always lies in the analysis of the argument to be refuted, within its larger frame of fact and idea.   The following *strategies* of refutation are common:

1 Ignoring the original argument entirely, while offering an opposed one

2 Accepting the original argument in whole or in part, but showing that what is accepted actually supports a position different from that originally proposed

3 Placing the original argument beside a logically analogous argument whose absurdity is obvious

4 Showing that the original argument is self-contradictory, or is contradicted by premises of greater certainty

5 Showing that the original argument has consequences unacceptable even to its maker

6 Showing that the original argument results in absurdity if logically extended

7 Showing that the conclusion of the original argument poses an unpleasant dilemma, with no happy issue possible

It is common for several of these strategies to be combined in the same essay, with emphasis falling on the strategy that most brings out the weakness of the opposing view. Refutation plays a large part in the essays here by Peirce, Collingwood, Haldane, Ciardi, Letwin, and Muller. In a sense, Huxley refutes cosmic pessimism by embracing it (see item 2, above), and Swift refutes a utilitarian ethic by extending it into absurdity (see item 6, above).

See the introduction to Part II of this text and also notes here under *Common Ground, Assumptions, and Premises; Evidence and Proof; Fallacies and Fallacious Reasoning;* and *Logic.*

Rendering A scene is vividly rendered when it is full of image, movement, color—when it seems alive. The term is borrowed from painting. A vividly rendered surface is especially important in narration and description. As a rule, concrete details enhance vividness of surface, and abstractions diminish it. Because the emotional effect of a carefully rendered surface can be very great, it is important that the details actually rendered contribute to the overall tonal structure: Vivid rendering is not an end in itself, nor is it always valuable.

See the introductions to Parts I, III and V of this text and notes here under *Abstract and Concrete, General and Specific; Denotation and Connotation; Image and Mimesis; Scale; Sound; Style* and *Symbol.*

Satire A *satire* is an attack, ordinarily designed to provoke laughter and to suggest reform, on a common social or human failing or vice. Satire may be either direct or ironical, gentle or savage, universal or particular. Swift, Beerbohm, Milne, Mencken, Orwell, and Dos Passos illustrate different satirical structures and aims. Satire is less structurally important but nonetheless frequent in Muller, Thoreau, Ruskin, and Huxley.

Scale The *scale* of a figure is its proportionate size in its environment. The natural world suggests a relatively fixed sense of scale: A cow 10 feet high would seem out of proportion. To the perceiver, however, a charging bull might well seem 10 feet high—an "accurate" scale drawing would represent inadequately the beast's importance. Scale is one measure of emphasis; what is important simply takes up more space—must be drawn, as it were, on a larger scale.   The finding of a proper, expressive scale for every image, every idea, is an essential part of good writing.   See Green's treatment of Duke William at the battle of Hastings, Berelson's treatment of the classical voter, Wilson's treatment of Babeuf's words in court, Styron's treatment of Dan Seward, Wald's treatment of probability, Woolf's treatment of Camalodunum.   See also notes here under *Focus* and *Unity*.

Sequence   The *sequence* of a composition is the order in which its ideas and facts are made to succeed one another.   This text distinguishes two basic kinds of sequence, the mimetic and the logical.   *Mimetic sequence* is essentially an imitation of the order of time and space: *descriptive sequence* imitates the movement of the eye through space; *narrative sequence* imitates the movement of the memory through event.   *Logical* sequence is essentially an exploration of relations among categories, abstractions, and particulars: *Expository sequence* explains those relations that are generally accepted, and *argumentative sequence* revises and extends what has been accepted.   In actual writing, the forms of sequence are interdependent.

See the introductions to Parts I and II of this text and notes here under *Abstract and Concrete, General and Specific; Climax and Anticlimax; Coherence, Linkage, and Transition; Deductive and Inductive Reasoning; Expository Narrative; Image and Mimesis;* and *Logic*.

Sound   Although nearly all compositions now are read silently, latent sound remains an important element in tone—a fact for which the reader of poetry needs no proof.   The music of language seems able to survive the medium of print.   I know no useful way to prescribe a linguistic music, and no valid way to analyze its emotional effects.   Reading aloud seems still the best way to find out if a passage sounds as it should, and trial and error seems still the only way to capture the right music.   Every linguistic element contributes—even some nonlinguistic elements contribute.   Near-synonyms, such as "fall," "tumble," "topple," "crash," differ in emotional current partly because they sound different.   Different word orders create different effects, even when exactly the same words are used.   A long sentence broken into short sentences may show virtually no significant changes in wording; the emotional effect, however, will change.   Reiteration, parallelism, alliteration, and assonance—even punctuation, contribute significantly to latent sound and to its emotional effects.   Many long sentences in succession tend to slow the tempo of ideas; many short sentences tend to speed that tempo up.   The aural patterns of an essay can become also part of its dramatic development: Changes from one form of discourse to another are like changes in musical style; section-breaks marked off by white space or by Roman numerals seem to require an extended pause and to denote a shift in style.   The analogy between musical and verbal composition is close and important.   See the introduction to Part V and also notes here under

Alliteration and Assonance; Climax and Anticlimax; Denotation and Connotation; Diction; and *Emphasis.*

Specific   See *Abstract and Concrete, General and Specific.*

Style   A writer's total rhetorical manner is his *style.* Style *is* far more than a mere trick of expression, however, for it derives from and reflects the quality of the writer's engagement with his world.   It is his morality (Whitehead); it is the man himself (Flaubert).   A good style is a personal triumph. Its elements may be discussed, but it can be neither prescribed nor imposed.

Subjectivity   See *Objectivity and Subjectivity.*

Symbol   A symbol is an animate or inanimate object taken as embodying or as representing a cluster of ideas impossible to separate without loss. When the intended meaning of such an object can be readily paraphrased, the category it stands for readily defined, the object is a representation or illustration rather than a symbol.   The American flag is a symbol; a naval pennant meaning "stand by for orders" is a sign; both may be taken of course, as illustrations of the category "flag."   A given battleship can represent all battleships, illustrate a concept of naval power, and symbolize a civilization. In composition, symbols are valuable ways to unify and embody ideas otherwise too complex to phrase easily or completely.   See especially Forster, Huxley, Adams, Muller, Styron.

See also the introductions to Parts III and V of this text.

Tone   A composition's emotional currents comprise its *tone.*   A given tone can be identified, perhaps defined, to some degree analyzed, but seldom if ever fully described; for feelings generally elude full description.   Tone may be heightened either directly, by exploitation of the emotional currents generated in diction, allusion, figure, latent sound, dramatic structure, etc., or indirectly, by ironical contrast between matter and style: compare Swift and Ruskin.   Tone also may be kept deliberately flat, in order to prevent an emotional response where it is not wished for or required.   Because tone is the chief vehicle by which the writer transfers to his audience his own sense of concern, the careful evaluation of that audience is an essential part of his craft.

See the introduction to Part V and also notes here under *Alliteration and Assonance; Allusion and Reference; Analogy; Climax and Anticlimax; Denotation and Connotation; Diction; Emphasis; Figures of Speech; Irony; Rendering* and *Sound.*

Transition   See *Coherence, Linkage, and Transition.*

Usage   See *Levels of Usage.*

Unity   A composition is unified when all its elements seem to fuse in a single whole in which structure, purpose, and style complement and support one another.   In general, the writer who chooses (1) a steady point of view and voice, (2) a single dominant order of discourse, (3) a clear focus in a single argument, image, analogy, illustration, and (4) a dramatic contour and style capable of conveying his own sense of concern will find within those choices the larger congruence of ideas that is essential to unity. Composition is not only the expression but also the discovery of meaning.

INDEX

This index is a guide only to essays and their authors, and to major topics discussed in the part introductions, the main introduction, and the glossary. Glossary references are given on separate lines preceded by an asterisk. Page numbers of glossary entries that correspond exactly or partially to index entries are *italicized*. I have made no attempt to list every use of every significant term, nor to index the apparatus following each essay. Essays are indexed both by title and by author; glossary references to individual essays are listed under author's name. The essays are also grouped under the following thematic heads in bold face type. Some essays are indexed under more than one thematic head.

1 Personal vectors

2 Society and the individual

3 Politics and government

4 Conflict and conscience

5 Culture, technology, and progress

6 History: shape and meaning

7 Nature and the natural

8 Art and the artist

9 God, saints, and men

Audience:
in definition, 106
in description, 6
as determinant of angle of
approach, 395
in illustration, 264–265
in narrative, 11
*642, 659, 663
"Autumn Night in the Hills, An,"
John Millington Synge, 30
Average cases, as illustrations, 267

Background, *645, 655–656
Baldwin, James, "Notes of a Native
Son," 489
*645, 647
Beerbohm, Max, "Some Words on
Royalty," 601
*648, 661
Begging the Question, Fallacy of,
*648
Berelson, Bernard, "Voting Behaviour," 146
illustrative excerpt and discussion,
109ff.
*659, 661

Case studies, as illustrations, 271–
273
"Case Study of Innovation, A,"
Elting E. Morison, 317
Categories and categorical statements, *639, 645, 649, 658,
662–663
Cause and effect:
in essays organized both mimetically and logically, 11–12
in expository narrative, 112
in narrative, 10, 11, 403
Ciardi, John, "The Resonance of the
Civilizing Tongue," 163
*654, 659, 660

Circular Argument, Fallacy of,
*652
Classification:
as basis for illustration, 263–264
characteristics of, as logical mode,
106–109
as organizational principle in this
text, xi
as related to argument, 113
*642–643
Climax (see Anticlimax)
Coherence, *643–644
Collingwood, George, "Progress as
Created by Historical Thinking,"
219
*647, 648, 657–660
Colloquial English, *653
Comedy, as created by incongruity,
522–523
Common ground, 116, 121
*642, 644–645
Comparison and contrast:
as clue to analysis, 270
in narrative, illustrative excerpt,
8–9
as technique of illustration, 266,
269–270
*645, 650, 655
Completeness:
in argument, 118–119
in classification, 108
in definition, 105
"Concept of God, The," C. S. Peirce,
156
Conclusions:
in argument, 113, 115, 121
tonal function of, 522
*650, 651, 658
Concrete, details, in description and
narrative, 4
*639–640, 648, 661
Conflict and conscience:
James Baldwin, "Notes of a Native
Son," 489

Society and the individual:
Edward Gibbon, "The Slavery of the Romans," 346
Thomas Hobbes, "Of the Natural Condition of Mankind," 235
Randall Jarrell, "A Sad Heart at the Supermarket," 414
Henry David Thoreau, "On the Duty of Civil Disobedience," 242
Virginia Woolf, "Two Parsons," 587
"Some Words on Royalty," Max Beerbohm, 601
Sound, as element in tone, 520–521 *662, 663
Space, as dimension in description, 2–3
Structure, *659–660, 663
Style, *662, 663
Styron, William, "This Quiet Dust," 464 *645, 647, 657, 661, 663
Subject, *654–655, 656, 659
Subjectivity:
as related to impersonal voice, 397
as related to personal voice, 399–402
as related to secondary voice, 403–404 *659
Swift, Jonathan, "A Modest Proposal," 568 *645, 648, 654, 657, 660, 661
Syllogism, *645, 658
Symbol:
in description, 6
illustration as, 272–273 *654, 662–663
Synge, J. M., "An Autumn Night in the Hills," 30
illustrative excerpt and discussion, 1–6 *648, 654, 656, 657, 659

Theme:
as element in description, 4–5
as structural principle in this text, ix–x
"This Quiet Dust," William Styron, 464
Thucydides, "The Melian Debate," 446 *645, 659
Thurber, James, "Doc Marlowe," 338 *657, 669
Time, as dimension in narrative, 6–7, 9
Tomlinson, H. M., "A Lost Wood," 306 *656, 659
Tone:
characteristics of as element in discourse, xviii, 513–523
comedy and sentimentality, 522–523
as created by allusion and metaphor, 517–519
as created by denotation and connotation, 516–517
as created by illustration, 519–520
as created by latent sound, 520–521
as created by sequence and structure, 522
as related to point of view and focus, 515–516
in organization of this text, xi–xii *647, 661, 662, 663
Transition, as related to tone, 522 *649
Truth:
as function of tonal unity, 522
in logical statements, 113–114
"Two Parsons," Virginia Woolf, 587